The Quest for the Origins of Vedic Culture

The Quest for the Origins of Vedic Culture

The Indo-Aryan Migration Debate

EDWIN BRYANT

OXFORD
UNIVERSITY PRESS
2001

OXFORD
UNIVERSITY PRESS

Oxford New York
Athens Auckland Bangkok Bogotá Bombay Buenos Aires Cape Town
Chennai Dar es Salaam Delhi Florence Hong Kong Istanbul Karachi
Kolkata Kuala Lumpur Madrid Melbourne Mexico City Mumbai
Nairobi Paris São Paulo Shanghai Singapore Taipei Tokyo Toronto Warsaw

and associated companies in
Berlin Ibadan

Published by Oxford University Press, Inc.
198 Madison Avenue, New York, New York 10016

Library of Congress Cataloging-in-Publication Data
Bryant, Edwin
The quest for the origins of Vedic culture :
the Indo-Aryan migration debate / Edwin Bryant.
p. cm.
Includes bibliographical reference and index.
ISBN 0-19-513777-9
1. Indo-Aryans—Origin. 2. India—History—To 324 B.C.
3. Indus civilization I. Title.
DS425.B79 2000
934'.02—dc21 99-086274

1 3 5 7 9 8 6 4 2

Printed in the United States of America
on acid-free paper

To my father and sister
for all their support.
And to Fran, Ted, and Jack
for making this possible.

Acknowledgments

To Fran Pritchet, for taking me under her wing right from the start; Ted Riccardi, for always encouraging me to pursue my intellectual interests; and Jack Hawley, for making sure that I came up to standard. To Gary Tubb, for his comments, meticulous as always, and to Michael Witzel, for being so generous with his time and vast learning. To James Mallory, for extensive comments, and to Kim Plofker, for valuable criticisms. To Richard Meadow, Hans H. Hock, Hermut Scharfe, Peter Rahul Das, Jay Jasanoff, and Thomas Trautmann for providing feedback on various chapters or sections of this work. To Fred Smith, Carl Lamberg-Karlovsky, and Vasudha Narayanan for their help. To the many scholars whom I had the good fortune to meet in India, and who were so generous with their time and hospitality. Needless to say, the views represented herein are my own and not necessarily of those who have been kind enough to point out the most egregious errors in previous drafts of this work. Special thanks to Matthew Ekstrand-Abueg for doing a great job with the maps and diagrams despite the last-minute time constraints, and to Martin von Wyss from the Harvard map room; to Fritz Staal for his assistance in obtaining the photograph for the cover; to Pia Bryant for her extensive editing; to the American Institute of Indian Studies for providing me with a research and travel grant, and to the Charlotte Newcombe Foundation for offering me a Ph.D write-up grant.

Contents

Introduction, 3

1. Myths of Origin: Europe and the Aryan Homeland Quest, 13
    - Biblical Origins, 14
    - India, the Cradle of Civilization, 18
    - The Aryans and Colonial and Missionary Discourse, 21
    - German Aryanism, 30
    - Two Centuries of Homeland Theories, 35
    - Present-Day Homeland Hypotheses, 38
    - Conclusion, 43

2. Early Indian Responses, 46
    - Hindu Nationalist Responses, 47
    - The First Reactions: Hindu Religious Leaders, 51
    - Conclusion, 56

3. Vedic Philology, 57
    - The Racial Evidence, 59
    - The West-to-East Geographic Shift in Sanskrit Texts, 63
    - Conclusion, 67

4. Indo-European Comparative Linguistics: The Dethronement of Sanskrit, 68
    - The Law of Palatals and the Discovery of Hittite, 69
    - Objections from India, 72
    - Conclusion, 73

5. Linguistic Substrata in Sanskrit Texts, 76
    - Linguistic Innovations in Sanskrit, 78
    - Evidence of the Loanwords, 84
    - Terms for Flora in Indic Languages, 90
    - Place-Names and River Names, 98
    - Indo-Aryan, or Dravidian and Munda Migrations?, 102
    - Conclusion, 105

6. Linguistic Paleontology, 108
    - Flora and Fauna, 109
    - The Horse, 115

Criticisms of the Method, 120
Conclusion, 123

7. Linguistic Evidence from outside of India, 124
Semitic Loans in Indo-European: Nichols's Model, 124
Finno-Ugric Loans, 126
Other Traces of Indo-Aryan, 129
The Avestan Evidence, 130
The Mitanni Treaties, 135
Conclusion, 138

8. The Viability of a South Asian Homeland, 140
Center of Origin Method, 142
Dialectical Subgroupings: Gamkrelidze and Ivanov's Model, 145
Nichols's Sogdiana Model, 151
Conclusion, 154

9. The Indus Valley Civilization, 157
Indra Stands Accused, 157
The Religion of the Indus Valley, 160
The Sarasvatī, 165
The Horse, 169
The Chariot, 175
The Indus Script, 177
Urbanity and the Ṛgveda, 184
Conclusion, 192

10. Aryans in the Archaeological Record: The Evidence outside the Subcontinent, 197
Identifying Aryans, 198
The Northern Route, 202
The Southern Route, 208
Two Wave Theories, 217
Conclusion, 220

11. Aryans in the Archaeological Record: The Evidence inside the Subcontinent, 224
Gandhara Grave Culture, 225
Jhukar Culture, 226
Cemetery H Culture, 229
Painted Gray Ware Culture, 229
Aryans in the Skeletal Record, 230
Continuity and Innovation, 231
Conclusion, 236

12. The Date of the Veda, 238
Dating Proto-Indo-European, 239
Dating the Veda, 243
Astronomy and Vedic Chronology, 251
The Mathematics of the Śulvasaūtras, 262
Conclusion, 264

13. Aryan Origins and Modern Nationalist Discourse, 267
Nationalism and Historiography: General Comments, 268
The Aryans in *Hindutva* Ideology, 270
Stereotypes and Counterstereotypes, 275
Discourses of Suspicion, 286
Conclusion, 295

Conclusion, 298

Notes, 311

Works Cited, 349

Index, 381

The Quest for the Origins of Vedic Culture

Introduction

The solution to the Indo-European problem has been one of the most consuming intellectual projects of the last two centuries. It has captivated the imagination and dedication of generations of archaeologists, linguists, philologists, anthropologists, historians, and all manner of scholarly, and not so scholarly, dilettantes. Predicated on the deduction that cognate languages necessitate an original protoform spoken by a group of people inhabiting a reasonably delineated geographic area, the problem has resulted in a massive amount of scholarship attempting to reconstruct this protolanguage, locate the original homeland where it was spoken, and conjecture on the social and cultural life of the protospeakers. Although the endeavor has very much been a preoccupation of European scholars, the belief in and pursuit of the origins of European civilization have required scholars to attempt to reconstruct and reconfigure the prehistory and protohistories of other civilizations whose languages happen to belong to the Indo-European language family.

The publicization, in Europe, of the Sanskrit language and of its connection with the classical languages of Europe was the catalyst for the whole post-Enlightenment quest for the Indo-Europeans that continues, unresolved, to this day. This "discovery" of Sanskrit resulted in the earliest history of the Indian subcontinent also being subsumed by the problem of European origins. Although India was initially entertained as the homeland of all the Indo-Europeans, various arguments were raised against this proposal, and Indian civilization was construed as the joint product of an invading Indo-European people—the Indo-Aryan branch of the family—and indigenous non-Indo-European peoples. Yet although taking it upon themselves to determine the history of the Indian subcontinent in accordance with the currents of scholarship that have ebbed and flowed in academic circles in Europe over the decades, Western scholars have generally been unaware, or dismissive, of voices from India itself that have been critical over the years of this European reconstruction of their country's history. In the words of one of the scholars who will be featured here, "However well-meaning such [scholars] . . . and their publications are, they have taken it upon themselves the task of interpreting the past heritage of a very large number of people who belong to various nation states and may like to formulate their own ideas of the past" (Chakrabarti 1997, 207).

This book is primarily a historiographical study of how various Indian scholars, over the course of a century or more, have rejected this idea of an external origin of the Indo-Aryans by questioning much of the logic, assumptions, and methods upon which the theory is based. The aim of the book is threefold. A primary aim is to excavate marginalized points of view reacting against what is perceived as a flawed and biased historical construct. As a corollary of this aim, this work will further complicate the Indo-European homeland quest by exposing the whole endeavor to a critique from scholars outside mainstream European academic circles who do not share the same intellectual history as their Western peers. A further aim of this book is to present a comprehensive exposition and analysis of views from within mainstream academic circles addressing the issue of Indo-Aryan origins.

With regard to the primary aim, I have used the term *Indigenous Aryanism* to denote a theme that is common to many of the scholars I examine in this book. This runs the risk of essentializing a quite variegated cast of characters, and I merely use the term to encompass a position on Indian protohistory that I view as common to most of the arguments that I examine. The scholars referred to by this term all share a conviction that the theory of an external origin of the Indo-Aryan speaking people on the Indian subcontinent has been constructed on flimsy or false assumptions and conjectures. As far as such scholars are concerned, no compelling evidence has yet been produced to posit an external origin of the Indo-Aryans.

The various scholars whose work I have examined here are a disparate group. They range from brilliant intellectuals like Aurobindo, to professional scholars like B. B. Lal, to what most academics would consider "crackpots," like P. N. Oak.[1] The primary feature they share is that they have taken it upon themselves to oppose the theory of Aryan invasions and migrations—hence the label *Indigenous Aryanism*. Although I am not fully satisfied with my descriptive label, I could find no better term with which to conveniently refer to my target group. Initially I toyed with the idea of contextualizing these arguments into a "traditionalist" framework, with the corollary that such material was an encounter or response to modernity, but not all the scholars in my target group are traditionally oriented at all; nor do they all by any means have problems with modernity. "Indian responses to the Aryan migration theory" is an obviously inadequate label, since many Indian scholars support this hypothesis, and a number of Western scholars have begun to contest it. "Dissident voices from India" failed for similar reasons (the work of several scholars not resident in India is discussed herein), as did any thoughts of casting the debate in terms of "Hindu" responses to Western scholarship. Indigenous Aryanism is a convenient (if somewhat generalized) label, and no more.

A further qualification is in order at this point. The descriptive label *Indigenous Aryanism* should, in strict linguistic terms, be *Indigenous Indo-Aryanism*, since it specifically refers to the speakers of the Indic languages. The term *Aryan* was used to denote the undivided Indo-Europeans during most of the nineteenth century; for our purposes, the Indo-Aryans are primarily the Vedic- and pre-Vedic-speaking members of the family. However, *Aryan* is often used by the Indian scholars in my survey to denote the Vedic-speaking peoples. Since the term is, after all, Sanskrit (and Iranian), I have adopted this denotation, in the context of my descriptive label *Indigenous Aryanism*. Elsewhere, I use *Aryan* to refer to all the Indo-European speakers only in those contexts where the term was used in this general way (particularly when quoting nineteenth-century scholars), and the more precise term *Indo-Aryans* to refer to the speakers of Vedic (and related dialects).

My topic, then, is a debate. It is a debate about which most scholars in the West were unaware until very recently, which in itself says something about the balance of intellectual power in the academic field of Indology. In order to contextualize the responses of what I will call the Indigenous Aryan school—to summarize exactly what it has been reacting to—the first chapter lays out some of the more prominent features of the two-hundred-year history of the Indo-European homeland quest in Europe, particularly as it related to India. The various religious and political exigencies that influenced much of the scholarship during this period are touched upon, as are the many viewpoints regarding the Indo-European homeland. This should set the scene for the responses of my target group—the Indigenous Aryanists—who were observing this intellectual melee from outside mainstream Western academic circles.

Chapter 2 touches briefly on a variety of discourses that appropriated the Aryan theme in India in the hope of exploiting it for political or other mileage. The reaction to the theory by religious intellectuals is also addressed in this chapter, thus providing a brief Indian parallel to the nineteenth-century political and religious concerns of Europe in the first chapter. Chapter 3 initiates the analysis of the actual data concerning Indo-Aryan origins. By the mid-nineteenth century, one of the few things regarding the homeland that western Indo-European scholars did agree on was that it could not have been India; wherever the original homeland might have been the Indo-Aryans at least must have come to the subcontinent from outside. While not the slightest bit concerned with the homeland obsession of European scholars in general, Indigenous Aryanists soon reacted to the corollary of the problem when it impinged on the origins of their own culture. It seemed unacceptable to consider that such an enormously speculative gigantean and seemingly inconclusive European undertaking should be entitled to make authoritative pronouncements on the early history of the Indian subcontinent. The first voices of opposition that attempted to utilize critical scholarship to counter the claim that the forefathers of the Vedic Indians hailed from outside the subcontinent are introduced in this chapter. The initial objections raised concerned the philological evidence that had been brought forward as decisive by Western philologist. Since philology was a discipline that resonated with their own traditional *Śruti*-epistemologies, and since it focused on texts in their own ancient language, Vedic Sanskrit, the philological evidence was the most easily accessible to Indigenous Aryan scrutiny. Moreover, these texts that were suddenly of such interest to Western scholars happened to be their sacred ones, and this fueled their concern.

Chapter 4 traces the dethronement of Sanskrit from its initial position as the original protolanguage of all the Indo-Europeans in the opinion of the early linguists, to its ongoing diminishing status as a secondary language containing a number of linguistic features that are considered to be more recent than other Indo-European cognate languages. Chapter 5 analyzes the evidence for a non-Indo-Aryan linguistic substratum in Sanskrit texts, which has remained perhaps the principal and, to my mind, most persuasive reason brought forward in support of the Aryan invasions and migrations. The issue here is: Do the Vedic texts preserve linguistic evidence of languages preceding the Indo-Aryan presence on the Indian subcontinent? This is an essential aspect of this debate but one that has been mostly ignored by Indigenous Aryanists. Chapter 6 examines various points of view based on the method of linguistic paleontology—one of the most exploited disciplines used in the homeland quest, and one also fundamental in insisting that the Indo-Aryans had an origin external to the Indian subcontinent. Here we will find Indian scholars reconfiguring the same logic and method to arrive at very different conclusions from those of their Western counterparts. Chapter 7 deals with the linguistic evidence from outside of India, particularly loan words from the Finno-Ugric languages, as well as the Mitanni and Avestan evidence, all of which have a direct bearing on the problem. Here, too, Indigenists have their own way of accounting for this evidence. Chapter 8 deals with other linguistic issues often utilized in the homeland quest and Indo-Aryan origins, such as dialect geography and the implications of the subgroupings of the various cognate languages. It must be stated immediately that there is an unavoidable corollary of an Indigenist position. If the Indo-Aryan languages did not come from outside South Asia, this necessarily entails that India was the original homeland of all the other Indo-European languages. Indo-Aryan was preceded by Indo-Iranian, which was preceded, in turn, by Indo-European; so if Indo-Aryan was indigenous to India, its predecessors must have been also. Hence, if proto-Indo-European was indigenous to India, all the other cognate languages must have emigrated from there. Chapters six to eight discuss the possibility and problems of a South Asian homeland.

Chapter 9 deals with the relationship between the Indus Valley Civilization and the Indo-Aryans—a topic that has received a tremendous amount of attention from Indian archaeologists and historians. The issue to be discussed in this chapter is whether the Indo-Aryans preceded, succeeded, or coexisted with the inhabitants of the Indus Valley cities. Chapter 10 outlines some of the scholarship that has attempted to trace the trans-Asiatic exodus of the Indo-Aryans on their proposed route to India, across central Asia and chapter 11 examines the problems associated with identifying them in the archaeological record within the subcontinent. Chapter 12 examines the various attempts made to date Sanskrit texts upon which, as I shall argue, a tremendous amount hinges. How far back can we go with an Indo-Aryan presence on the subcontinent? The final chapter discusses some of the more modern ideological underpinnings of this debate in India as different forces compete over the construction of national identity. Other concerns motivating some of the participants on both sides of the Indigenous Aryan debate will also be considered in this chapter.

I have left this chapter on ideology until last, in order to present the intervening chapters on the evidence primarily in the terms, and through the logic and perspectives, of the various points of view. However, historical data do not tell their own story: they are interpreted. And interpretation emanates from human cognition that is structured by each individual's cultural, religious, political, economic and social circumstances and choices. People have a reason to contest or reinterpret history. The present volatile situation in India has made Western, and many Indian, scholars particularly concerned about the repercussions of communal interpretations of history. However, although the promotion of Indigenous Aryanism is undoubtedly extremely important to notions of identity and to the politics of legitimacy among certain Hindu nationalists, such concerns are not representative of all the scholars who have supported this point of view. Unfortunately, the whole Indigenous Aryan position is often simplistically stereotyped, and conveniently demonized, both in India and in the West, as a discourse exclusively determined by such agendas. This bypasses other concerns also motivating such reconsideration of history: the desire of many Indian scholars to reclaim control over the reconstruction of the religious and cultural history of their country from the legacy of imperial and colonial scholarship. In chapter 13 I discuss the manifold concerns that I perceive as motivating Indigenous Aryanists to undertake a reconsideration of this issue. I argue that although there are doubtlessly nationalistic and, in some quarters, communal agendas lurking behind some of this scholarship, a principal feature is anticolonial/imperial.

On a personal note, I am accordingly sympathetic to the Indigenous Aryan "school" (if, simply for ease of reference, I might be permitted to reify my motley group as a school) when I view it as a manifestation of a postcolonial rejection of European intellectual hegemony (since most of the voices are from India), especially since my analysis has led me to realize exactly how malleable much of the evidence involved actually is. This does not mean that the Indigenous Aryan position is historically probable. The available evidence by no means denies the normative view—that of external Aryan origins and, if anything, favors it. But this view has had more than its fair share of airing over the last two centuries, and the Indigenous Aryan position has been generally ignored or marginalized. What it does mean, in my view, is that Indigenous Aryanism must be allowed a legitimate and even valuable place in discussions of Indo-Aryan origins.

I am emphatically not sympathetic to the elements of the Indigenous Aryan school that I perceive as utilizing this debate to construct illusory notions of an indigenous Aryan pedigree so as to thereby promote the supposed Hindu descendants of these Indo-Aryans as the original and rightful "sons of the soil" in a modern Hindu nation-state. As an aside, this is illusory not only from a historico-philological perspective but also from the perspective of almost the entirety of the philosophical systems associated with what is known as Hinduism. Vedantic discourse, for one, would consider nationalism (whether Hindu, American, English, or anything else) to be simply another *upādhi*, or false designation, imposed on the *ātman* out of ignorance ("Hindu nationalism" from this perspective, is something of an oxymoron). Needless to say, any prioritization of the Hindus can only be at the expense of the "Other," namely, the non-Hindu communities—specifically Muslims and Christians. Since my task is to be receptive to all rational points of view, including the more cogent interpretations of the Indigenous Aryan school, there have been many moments when I have regretted undertaking this research for fear that it might be misconstrued and adapted to suit ideological agendas. This concern very much remains as a dark cloud hovering over what has otherwise been an intriguing and intellectually very fulfilling research project.

On the other hand, and again on a personal note, I am also concerned at what I perceive to be a type of Indological McCarthyism creeping into areas of Western, as well as certain Indian, academic circles, whereby, as will be discussed in chapter 13, *anyone* reconsidering the status quo of Indo-Aryan origins is instantly and a priori dubbed a nationalist, a communalist, or, even worse, a Nazi. Since I have observed that many scholars, when confronted with "Indigenous" voices of dissension, immediately assume that it must be just another manifestation of Hindu nationalist discourse (even without being aware of the linguistic and archaeological issues at stake), a few words on this issue might be in order at this point.

There is a major difference in focus between nationalism and anti-imperialism although they overlap in a number of ways. Nationalism involves attempts to concoct notions of shared identity in order to unify a variety of individuals and social groups into a cohesive political and territorial body in contradistinction to other such bodies—Anderson's "imagined" communities. Communalism, as understood in the context of academic discourse about India, also involves attempts to construct political unity between individuals and groups, but it is predicated on notions of shared religious affiliation that is distinct from that of other groups who are perceived as identifying with different religious communities. Anti-imperialism and anticolonialism, on the other hand, are the opposition, by a group of people, to alien power—often advantaged because of superior technology—to which it has been subjected against its will. It is a struggle against an oppressive, and generally stifling, force.

The alien power opposed by the anti-imperialist voices of the Indigenous Aryan school is intellectual: it consists of the construction of early Indian history by Western scholars using their "superior technology" in the form of linguistics, archaeology, anthropology, philology, and so forth. The version of historical events arrived at by these means was then imposed on the native population in hegemonic fashion. Indigenous Aryanism, from this perspective, is an attempt to adopt this same technology to challenge the colonial power (or the heritage it has left behind), to test its foundation, to see how accurate the Aryan migration hypothesis actually is by examining it with the same equipment, the same disciplines of archaeology, and so on, that were used to construct it in the first place. Obviously, in so doing it has been co-opted into a Western critical paradigm and has adopted the vocabulary and conceptual structures of the discourse (indeed, all of the arguments considered here are from English medium publications).[2] It is nonetheless an attempt to reclaim control over indigenous affairs—in this case the writing of Indian history—from the power of scholars who are perceived as being motivated and untrustworthy in their scholarship due to their status as imperialists, colonizers and rulers (and from the heirs of such scholars). In Gramscian terms, colonial intellectuals are seen as the "functionaries," the "deputies," of the coercive dominant power.

Naturally, perceiving a power to be alien necessitates defining oneself, and others like oneself, as native, and so anti-imperialism and nationalism often go hand in hand. Therefore, rejection of the Aryan migration—Indigenous Aryanism—has been co-opted into both anti-imperial and nationalist discourses. But there is a difference in focus between these two agendas, and it is this that I wish to emphasize. The focus of those who promote Indigenous Aryanism for nationalist purposes is to try to show that the Hindus are an integral, indigenous people who have always had the ingredients required for a nation-state in the form of a shared cultural past with clear links to the present: the "Vedic" culture. New nations paradoxically claim to be the opposite of novel, namely, rooted in the remotest antiquity; nationalists co-opt archaeology, philology, and linguistics in efforts to "prove" that the imagined nation has always existed. In the postcolonial climate of South Asia, this discourse shares many permeable borders with, and can clearly spill over into, communal discourse. The focus, in this latter case, is to set up a juxtaposition between those linked religiously (in however generalized ways) with the Vedic rubric in opposition to those not affiliated with any notion of Vedic identity—specifically the Muslim and Christian minorities. (Here, too, a paradox can arise when disciplines that are empirical in nature are adopted in attempts to prove scriptural authenticity, which is transcendental in nature, to legitimize notions of identity that are based upon them.)

The anti-imperialist concern, in contrast, is the rejection of the Aryan invasion hypothesis on the grounds that it is an alien intellectual import, assembled by Europeans as a result of exigencies, initially religious and then imperial, that were prevalent in nineteenth-century Europe. The theory was exported to the colonies, where it was introduced by an imperial, colonial power in order to serve imperial, colonial interests. Some Indigenous Aryanists construe this process as being a conscious one: planned and conspiratorial; others regard it as unconscious and the result of the inevitable bias and self-centered modes of interpretation that are inherent in the human psyche. The point I stress in chapter 13 is that not all Indigenous Aryanists are necessarily interested in the construction of notions of Hindu Aryan greatness or, with some exceptions, in the promotion of communal agendas. In much of the literature I have read, and in countless hours of interviews, an overwhelming concern of Indigenous Aryanists is to reexamine what is suspected of being a false account of Indian history concocted by European imperialists—an account that does not correspond to the "facts" even when analyzed by the modern processes of critical scholarship. In short, the Aryan invasion hypothesis is seen by many Indian historians as an Orientalist production. As a result, Indigenous Aryanism can be partly situated within the parameters of postcolonial studies.

Having said all this, I do not intend to suggest that the Indigenous Aryan school is somehow angelically engaged in the disinterested quest for pure knowledge. There is no disinterested quest for knowledge. Many Indigenous Aryanists are, indeed, engaged in the search for self-definition in the modern context. Some are Hindu nationalists, and some do engage in communal polemics. But much has been written on Hindu "revisionism" from this perspective; rather than a priori pigeonholing the Indigenous Aryan school into simplistic and conveniently demonized "communal," "revisionist," or "nationalist" molds that can then be justifiably ignored, this study is an attempt to analyze and articulate some of the actual empirical objections being raised to the colonial construction of Indian pre- and protohistory. This book, accordingly, is primarily an examination of the empirical, historical evidence—philological, archaeological, linguistic, and so on—and how this has been interpreted both to support the theory of Aryan migrations and to contest it. However, since interpretations take place only in a specific context, a secondary aim is to touch upon (and no more) some aspects of the religious and political forces, in both Europe and India, that influenced and continue to influence, the prioritization of certain interpretive possibilities and the exclusion of others.

A note on method. My intention herein has been not so much to take sides in the actual debate but to present the interpretations of the evidence from all rational perspectives and point out the various assumptions underlying them—this book is intended to be a reasonably thorough exposition of the entire problem of Indo-Aryan origins. Each chapter outlines some of the main features of the history of the data covered in that particular chapter. Since the relevant matieral is usually so voluminous, however, I have limited my selection to data that have either attracted responses from the Indigenous Aryan school or that are indispensable to a discussion on the origins of the Indo-Aryans. This book is not a comprehensive history of the greater Indo-European problem, but of the Indo-Aryan side of the family.

I have not hesitated to state my own opinion on the value of some of the arguments being contested, and my organization and presentation of the material will reveal much about my own estimation of the merit of some of these points of view. Nonetheless, my primary project has been to present the debate in its own terms, hence my decision to quote as much as possible so that the primary voices involved can be heard in their own right rather than paraphrased. I hold it important that marginalized points of view that have made a valuable contribution to this issue be brought into a more mainstream academic context, and it is often edifying to confront as much of the primary tone of the debate as possible. From the Indigenous Aryan side, the tone of these responses reveals much about how a historical construct that is taken very much for granted by most of us—the Aryan invasion/migration theory—is viewed when seen through very different cultural, religious, and political perspectives.

I have taken material from a wide variety of contexts if I feel that it can contribute to the debate. I have found that someone, Western or Indian, who can make an astonishingly infantile argument or reveal an alarming lack of critical awareness in one place can make a penetrating and even brilliant comment in another. Not all the scholars referred to herein are necessarily schooled in the same intellectual environments, versed in state-of-the-art academic rhetoric and vocabulary, or familiar with the latest conceptual structures current in Western academia. Nor do all scholars in India have anywhere near as much access to the latest cutting-edge scholarship or even, sometimes, basic seminal material as their Western colleagues. I have not rejected any worthwhile argument even if it is situated in a greater context that many would consider unworthy of serious academic attention; not all the arguments quoted here are from professional scholars, but I have allotted space to anyone whom I believe has anything valuable to contribute to the issue. I have taken it upon myself to wade through a good deal of, to put it mildly, substandard material in search of nuggets—but nuggets are to be found.

I have also separated my discussion of the evidence from discussion of the religio-political context of its interpretation: chapters 3 to 12 focus on the former, and chapters 1, 2, and 13 discuss the latter. Talageri the linguist has been critiqued in the chapters on linguistics, and Talageri the nationalist has been dealt with in the chapter on nationalism. The validity of a particular interpretation of some aspect of the data has not been minimized because of the author's overt religious or political bias, however distasteful they might be to the sensitivities of those of us who do not share those values. Ignoring a serious attempt to analyze data because of the author's ideological orientations does not invalidate the arguments being offered, or make them disappear. On the contrary, they resurface, often more aggressively because of having been ignored. I have attempted to analyze, as objectively as possible, any serious interpretation of the data that might further the task of accurately reconstructing proto-history, while also, in separate chapters, drawing attention to any ideological agendas that might favor the promotion of a particular point of view.

I would lie to note that while I have had training in historical Indo-European linguistics and in South Asia as a linguistic region, I am not an Indo-Europeanist—although I hold the contributions of this field indispensable to our knowledge of South Asian pre- and proto-history. I approach this material from the perspective of a historian of ancient Indian religions and cultures. I beg the indulgence of the specialists and request that I be forgiven for any errors in technical linguistic detail that they might encounter in these chapters, and that I be judged, rather, on my more general analysis of the data and of the conclusions that they can generate in matters pertaining to the origins of the

Indo-Aryans. I should also note that while I would like to think that this work might be of some interest to Indo-Europeanists, if only from a historiographical point of view, or from the perspective of the history of ideas, it is primarily intended for those involved in and interested in South Asian studies. With this audience in mind, I have eliminated all techincal linguistic detail that is not essential to illuminating the general linguistic principles and theories relevant to the quest for the Indo-Aryans.

In my fieldwork in South Asia, as well as in my research thereafter, I have had adequate opportunity to discuss the South Asian archaeological evidence with specialists in the field, although, here again, specialists will likely recognize that I am not an archaeologist. Nor am I a historian of science, despite my lengthy treatment of the astronomical evidence. Ultimately, in the hyper-specialized academic culture of our day, it is not possible for a single individual to have expertise in all of the disciplines and subdisciplines demanded by a topic such as this. I request my critics to consider that no one can be a specialist in nineteenth-century historiography in Europe, nineteenth-century historiography in India, Vedic philology, Avestan Studies, historical Indo-European linguistics, South Asian linguistics, Central Asia as a linguistic area, the archaeology of Central Asian, the archaeology of the Indian subcontinent, astronomy, and modern Hindu nationalism, to name only some of the areas covered here. Anyone attempting a multidisciplinary overview of such a vast amount of material will necessarily need corrections from the specialists in any of these fields. I hope that my efforts have at least been successful in gathering most of the materials relevant to the origins fo the Indo-Aryans, shedding some light on why these materials might be contested, and perhaps invoking further discussions by scholars more qualified then myself in these respective areas.

Perhaps this is an opportune moment to reveal my own present position on the Indo-European problem. I am one of a long list of people who do not believe that the available data are sufficient to establish anything very conclusive about an Indo-European homeland, culture, or people. I am comfortable with the assumptions that cognate languages evolve from a reasonably standardized protoform (provided this is allowed considerable dialectal variation) that was spoken during a certain period of human history and culture in a somewhat condensed geographic area that is probably somewhere in the historically known Indo-European-speaking area (although I know of no solid grounds for excluding the possibility that this protolanguage could have originated outside of this area).

However, regarding homelands, I differ from most Western scholars in that I find myself hard pressed to absolutely eliminate the possibility that the eastern part of this region could be one possible candidate among several, albeit not a particularly convincing one, provided this area is delimited by Southeast Central Asia, Afghanistan, present-day Pakistan, and the northwest of the subcontinent (rather than the Indian subcontinent proper). I hasten to stress that it is not that the evidence favors this area as a possible homeland—on the contrary, there has been almost no convincing evidence brought forward in support of a homeland this far east. As we shall see, the issue is that problems arise when one tries to prove that the Indo-Aryans were intrusive into this area from an outside homeland. In other words, one has almost no grounds to argue for a South Asian Indo-European homeland from where the other speakers of the Indo-European language departed, but one can argue that much of the evidence brought forward to document their entrance into the subcontinent is problematic. These are two separate, but obviously overlapping, issues.

Coupled with the problems that have been raised against all homeland candidates, these issues have caused me conclude that, in the absence of radically new evidence or approaches to the presently available evidence, theories on the homeland of the Indo-European speaking peoples will never be convincingly proven to the satisfaction of even a majority of scholars. This skepticism especially applies to the theories of some Indian scholars who have attempted to promote India as a Homeland. I know of no unproblematic means of re-creating a convincing history of the Indo-Aryan speakers prior to the earliest proto-historic period, at which time they were very much situated in the Northwest of the subcontinent (as, of course, were other Indo-European speakers elsewhere). I do not feel compelled to venture any opinions beyond this: how the cognate languages got to be where they were in prehistory is as unresolved today, in my mind, as it was two hundred years ago when William Jones announced the Sanskrit language connection to a surprised Europe. The Indigenous Aryan critique has certainly been one of the formative influences on my own point of view. In my opinion, this critique not only merits attention in its own right but, also, perhaps more important, must be addressed by western scholars, since it is rapidly rising in prominence in the country whose history is most directly at stake.

1

Myths of Origin

Europe and the Aryan Homeland Quest

The Indigenous Aryan debate can only be understood in the context of the history of the greater Indo-European homeland quest in Europe. The purpose of this chapter is to outline the most prominent features of this history that are most directly connected with the problems of Indo-Aryan origins. Indigenous Aryanists are almost universally suspicious of the motives surrounding the manner in which evidence was interpreted and construed by British and European scholars in the colonial period. It is important to clearly excavate the various biases that influenced the epistemes of the time before attempting to consider the evidence itself. This chapter will address some of the more blatant ideological and religious attitudes of the eighteenth and nineteenth centuries in the West that co-opted Aryan discourse in some form or fashion. Since there have been a number of studies focused on the general history of Indo-European Studies, I will focus only on the aspects of this history that are of particular relevance to the Indian side of the family.

One common characteristic of Indigenous Aryan discourse is the tendency to dwell on, and reiterate, the blatant excesses of nineteenth-century scholarship. This is perfectly understandable, and even justified, provided that one proceeds from such analyses to engage and address the more state-of-the-art views current in our present-day academic milieus. The function of this chapter is not just to tar and feather all eighteenth- and nineteenth-century scholars as racists and bigots in order to reject all and any conclusions formulated in that period as a priori tainted, but to thoroughly acknowledge the extremities within Western intellectual circles of the time. Only once all that is openly on the table can one attempt to extrapolate the data from the interpretational constraints of the time and move on to reexamine it all anew, albeit from within the contextual constraints of our own. Accordingly, although massive advances were made in the nineteenth century in the study of ancient India by many dedicated and sincere scholars, this chapter will focus on the more biased and ideological appropriations of Aryan discourse in Europe. After these elements have been adequately processed and acknowledged, we can move forward, hopefully somewhat free from the ghosts of the past, to reexamine the actual evidence from the perspectives of our own present-day postcolonial academic culture.

Biblical Origins

Scholars and thinkers of the late eighteenth century, enthusiastically pushing forward the scientific and intellectual frontiers that had become accessible in post-Enlightenment Europe, found themselves grappling with the historicity of Old Testament chronology. The discovery, through expanding European colonies, of other cultures claiming pedigrees of vast antiquity; developments in linguistics; and the proliferation of "hard" archaeological evidence provoked a drastic reevaluation of biblical narrative in matters of human origins. Features such as the monogenic descent from Adam, the evolution of all human language from the monolingual descendants of Noah, and the brief period that seemed to be allotted to the dispersion of the human race after the Flood became the subjects of intense debates. As the first pioneering British scholars in India began to discover Sanskrit texts, the promise of hitherto unknown historical information becoming revealed to Europeans became the cause of both great anticipation and epistemological anxiety.

Sir William Jones, the first Indologist to attempt a serious synchronization of biblical and Puranic chronology, exemplifies the tensions of his time. His predecessors, British scholars John Holwell, Nathaniel Halhed, and Alexander Dow—all associated in various capacities with the British East India Trading Company—had relayed back to an eager Europe gleanings from Puranic sources that described an immense antiquity for the human race.[1] These provided the ranks of disaffected Christians, such as the vociferous Voltaire, with valuable materials with which to attempt to shake off the constraints of Judeo-Christian chronology and to refute Jewish or Christian claims to exclusive mediation between man and Providence. Holwell, for one, believed that the Hindu texts contained a higher revelation than the Christian ones, that they predated the Flood, and that "the mythology, as well as the cosmogony of the Egyptians, Greeks and Romans, were borrowed from the doctrines of the Brahmins" (Marshall 1970, 46). Halhed, too, seemed to take the vast periods of time assigned to the four yugas quite seriously, since "human reason . . . can no more reconcile to itself the idea of Patriarchal . . . longevity" of a few thousand years for the entire span of the human race (Marshall, 1931, 159). Dow was instrumental in presenting Europe with a deistic image of India whose primitive truths owed nothing to either Jews or Christians. Such challenges stirred up considerable controversy in Europe, fueled by intellectuals such as Voltaire adopting such material in endeavors to undermine biblical historicity.

Naturally, such drastic innovations were bitterly opposed by other segments of the intelligentsia. For well over a millennium, much of Europe had accepted the Old Testament as an infallible testament documenting the history of the human race. Thomas Maurice, for example, complained bitterly in 1812 about "the daring assumptions of certain skeptical French philosophers with respect to the Age of the World . . . arguments principally founded on the high assumptions of the Brahmins . . . [which] have a direct tendency to overturn the Mosaic system, and, with it, Christianity." Such scholars were greatly relieved by "the fortunate arrival of . . . the various dissertations, on the subject, of Sir William Jones" (22–23). Jones was just as concerned about the fact that "some intelligent and virtuous persons are inclined to doubt the authenticity of the accounts delivered by Moses." In his estimation, too, "either the first eleven chapters of Genesis . . . are true, or the whole fabrick of our national religion is false, a conclusion which none of us, I trust, would wish to be drawn" (Jones 1788, 225).

Eager to settle the matter, Jones undertook the responsibility of unraveling Indian chronology for the benefit and appeasement of his disconcerted colleagues: "I propose to lay before you a concise history of Indian chronology extracted from Sanskrit books, attached to no system, and as much disposed to reject Mosaick history, if it be proved erroneous, as to believe it, if it be confirmed by sound reason from indubitable evidence" (Jones 1790a, 111). Despite such assurances, Jones's own predispositions on this matter were revealed in several earlier written statements: "I . . . am obliged of course to believe the sanctity of the venerable books [of Genesis]" (1788, 225); Jones (1790) concluded his researches by claiming to have "traced the foundation of the Indian empire above three thousand eight hundred years from now" (145), that is to say, safely within the confines of Bishop Usher's creation date of 4004 B.C.E. and, more important, within the parameters of the Great Flood, which Jones considered to have occurred in 2350 B.C.E.

Such undertakings afford us a glimpse of some of the tensions that many European scholars were facing in their encounter with India at the end of the eighteenth century; the influence of the times clearly weighed heavily. However, Jones's compromise with the biblical narrative did make the new Orientalism safe for Anglicans: "Jones in effect showed that Sanskrit literature was not an enemy but an ally of the Bible, supplying independent corroboration of the Bible's version of history" (Trautmann, 1997, 74). Jones's chronological researches did manage to calm the waters somewhat and "effectively guaranteed that the new admiration for Hinduism would reinforce Christianity and would not work for its overthrow" (74). Trautmann notes that, for the most part, up until the early part of the nineteenth century, British Indomania was excited about the discovery of Hinduism for several reasons: it provided independent confirmation of the Bible; its religion contained the primitive truth of natural religion still in practice, a unitary truth from which the forms of paganism of Rome and Greece were perverted offshoots; and its arts and cultures were connected to Egypt's (64).

Jones's much more lasting contribution, and one generally recognized by linguists as the birth of historical linguistics, was his landmark address to the Royal Asiatic Society of Bengal in 1786. This, by constant quotation, has by now become the *maṅgalācāra* of comparative philology:

> The Sanskrit language, whatever may be its antiquity, is of a wonderful structure; more perfect than the Greek, more copious than the Latin, and more exquisitely refined than either, yet bearing to both of them a stronger affinity, both in the roots of verbs and in the forms of grammar, than could possibly have been produced by accident; so strong, indeed, that no philologer could examine them all three, without believing them to have sprung from some common source which, perhaps, no longer exists: there is a similar

> reason, though not quite so forcible, for supposing that both the Gothick and the Celtick, though blended with a very different idiom, had the same origin with the Sanskrit; and the old Persian might be added to the same family. (Jones 1788, 415–431)

Significantly, this statement was almost a paraphrase of a not so well known declaration made over a century previously (in 1668) by one Andreas Jager in Wittenberg, before the discovery of the Sanskrit language:

> An ancient language, once spoken in the distant past in the area of the Caucasus mountains and spreading by waves of migration throughout Europe and Asia, had itself ceased to be spoken and had left no linguistic monuments behind, but had as a "mother" generated a host of "daughter languages". . . . [D]escendants of the ancestral language include Persian, Greek, Italic, . . . the Slavonic languages, Celtic, and finally Gothic. (Quoted in Metcalf 1974, 233)

Attempts to demonstrate that the disparate languages of the world stemmed from a common source long predated the discovery of Sanskrit. As early as 1610, J. J. Scaliger was able to distinguish eleven European language groups, such as Germanic, Slavic, and Romance, and was noteworthy for his time in challenging the idea that these languages derived from Hebrew—the opinion prevalent in his day.[2]

The idea of a common source—initially considered to be Hebrew—for all languages, which, it is important to note, was always associated with a common people, was taken for granted by most scholars in Europe until well after the Enlightenment. The idea was inbedded in the biblical version of history, in which Noah's three sons, Japheth, Shem, and Ham, were generally accepted as being the progenitors of the whole of humanity.[3] Prior to the construction of the city of Babel, there was one human race speaking one language. These linguistically unified and racially integral people were subsequently dispersed and scattered over the face of the earth. This theme, even when stripped of its biblical trappings, was to remain thoroughly imprinted in European consciousness until well into the twentieth century.

In 1768, even before the affinities of Sanskrit with the Indo-European languages had been officially broadcast by Jones, Père Coeurdoux foreshadowed much present-day opinion regarding the point of origin of this language by stating that "the Samskroutam language is that of the ancient Brahmes; they came to India . . . from Caucasia. Of the sons of Japhet, some spoke Saṁskroutam" (quoted in Trautmann 1997, 54). Once Sanskrit had become accessible to British scholars, its connection with the classical languages of Europe was suspected even before Jones's proclamation. Halhed had noted the possibility a few years earlier. James Parsons, too, physician and fellow of the Royal Society and of the Society of Antiquities, had also associated Indic with the European languages in 1776. In fact, almost two centuries earlier still, the Italian Jesuit Filippo Sassetti, who lived in Goa in the 1580s, had noted that in the language "there are many of our terms, particularly the numbers 6, 7, 8 and 9, God, snakes and a number of other things" (Marcucci 1855, 445). Jones's status and reputation, however, ensured that news of this language connection reverberated through the academic halls of Europe.

Once the discovery of Sanskrit as a language related to the European languages had been made public, it precipitated post-Enlightenment trends toward disaffiliation from Genesis. It was a traumatic time for Europe. As Max Müller , who "look[ed] upon the account of Creation as given in Genesis as simply historical" (1902, 481), later reminisced: "All one's ideas of Adam and Eve, and the Paradise, and the tower of Babel, and Shem, Ham, and Japhet, with Homer and Aeneas and Virgil too, seemed to be whirling round and round, till at last one picked up the fragments and tried to build a new world, and to live with a new historical consciousness" (Müller 1883, 29). This "new world," however, retained much of the old, and the biblical framework of one language, one race was transmitted completely intact. Even after developments in linguistics had irremediably established the existence of numerous completely distinct language families, and the times no longer required scholars to orient their positions around a refutation or defense of Old Testament narrative, the biblical heritage continued to survive in a modified form: the idea of one language family for the superior civilizations of Europe, Persia, and India—the Aryan, or Indo-European, language family—continued to be associated with the fountainhead of a distinct people that had originated in a specific geographical homeland.

The correlation of race and language, an assumption that still occasionally continues to haunt discussions on the Indo-Europeans, was reinforced by the very vocabulary adopted by the fledgling science of linguistics: Jager, as we have noted, referred to "mother" languages generating "daughters." This genealogically derived vocabulary later became established as standard linguistic parlance by Schleicher, whose basic paradigm of the family tree of languages is still in use, albeit usually in modified form. As Trautmann notes: "This tree paradigm remains very much the foundation of historical linguistics to this day, although a kind of willful collective amnesia has tended to suppress its biblical origins. . . . In the self-conception of linguistics there came to be a strong tendency to imagine that its central conceptual structure comes from comparative anatomy and to forget that it comes from the Bible" (1997, 57). The influence of the Bible, initially overtly and subsequently in a more inadvertent or subconscious fashion, pervaded the entire field of Indo-European studies in its formative stages throughout the nineteenth century:

> The authors of the nineteenth century were hostages, as we are no doubt too, to the questions they set themselves. Though they cast aside the old theological questions, they remained attached to the notion of a providential history. Although they borrowed the techniques of positivist scholarship, took inspiration from methods perfected by natural scientists, and adopted the new perspective of comparative studies, they continued to be influenced by the biblical presuppositions that defined the ultimate meaning of their work. Despite differences in outlook, Renan, Max Müller, Pictet and many others joined romanticism with positivism in an effort to preserve a common allegiance to the doctrines of Providence. (Olinder 1992, 20)

Another instant by-product of the discovery of Sanskrit was that a dramatic new ingredient had been added to Europe's quest for linguistic and racial origins. Up to this point, many European scholars, such as James Parsons in 1767, tended to be "persuaded that these mountains of Ararat, upon which the ark rested, [were] in Armenia; and that the plains in their neighborhood were the places where Noah and his family dwelt, immediately after they left the ark" (10). Even after Sanskrit had been "discovered," many scholars would not stray too far from this location. Jones himself was emphatic that the "primeval events" of the construction of the Tower of Babel and the subsequent scattering of the original monolanguage into different tongues "are described as having happened between the Oxus and Euphrates, the mountains of the Caucus and the borders of India, that is within the limits of Iran." There was no doubt about this, since "the Hebrew narrative [is] more than human in its origin and consequently true in every substantial part of it." Therefore, "it is no longer probable only, but absolutely certain, that the whole race of man proceeded from Iran, whence they migrated at first in three great colonies [those of Shem, Japhet, and Ham]; and that those three branches grew from a common stock" (Jones 1792, 486–487).

India, the Cradle of Civilization

Other scholars, however, upon learning of these linguistic (and therefore racial) connections of the distant Indic languages, felt that radical alternatives to the Armenian point of origin had now gained legitimacy. India, in particular, was a popular candidate, especially among segments of the intelligentsia in the late eighteenth century and first half of the nineteenth century, and especially (but not exclusively) on the Continent. As it had done in classical times, India again captured the imagination of Romantic Europe. The astronomer Bailly, the first mayor of Paris, was very influential in popularizing Indian wisdom. In 1777, after some deliberation, he situated the earliest humans on the banks of the Ganges. Even before Jones's announcement, Bailly stated that "the Brahmans are the teachers of Pythagoras, the instructors of Greece and through her of the whole of Europe" (51). Voltaire voiced his agreement: "In short, Sir, I am convinced that everything—astronomy, astrology, metempsychosis, etc.—comes to us from the banks of the Ganges" (Bailly 1777, 4).

The French naturalist and traveler Pierre de Sonnerat (1782) also believed all knowledge came from India, which he considered the cradle of the human race. In 1807, the well-known metaphysician Schelling could wonder "what is Europe really but a sterile trunk which owes everything to Oriental grafts?" (Poliakov 1971, 11). A year later, the influential Friedrich von Schlegel argued that "the Northwest of India must be considered the central point from which all of these nations had their origin" (505). In 1845, Eichhoff was adamant that "all Europeans come from the Orient. This truth, which is confirmed by the evidence of physiology and linguistics, no longer needs special proof" (12). Even as late as 1855, Lord A. Curzon, the governor-general of India and eventual chancellor of Oxford, was still convinced that "the race of India branched out and multiplied into that of the great Indo-European family. . . . The Aryans, at a period as yet undetermined, advanced towards and invaded the countries to the west and northwest of India, [and] conquered the various tribes who occupied the land." European civilization, in his view, was initiated by the Indian Aryans: "They must have imposed their religion, institutions, and language, which later obliterated nearly all the traces of the former non-Aryan language, or languages, of the conquered tribes" (172–173). Michelet held that the Vedas "were undoubtedly the first monument of the world" (1864, 26) and that from India emanated "a torrent of light and the flow of reason and Right" (485). He proclaimed that "the migrations of mankind follow the route of the sun from East to West along the sun's course. . . . At its starting point, man arose in India, the birthplace of races and of religions, *the womb of the world*" (Febvre 1946, 95–96).

According to Poliakov, it was Johann-Gottfried Herder, a Lutheran pastor, who (along with Kant) placed the homeland in Tibet, who was influential in introducing the passion for India into Germanic lands and prompting the imagination of the Romantics to seek affiliation with Mother India. Herder (1803) objected that "the pains that have been taken, to make of all the people of the earth, according to this genealogy, descendants of the Hebrew, and half-brothers of the Jews, are contrary not only to chronology and universal history but to the true point of view of the narrative itself." As far as he was concerned, "the central point of the largest quarter of the Globe, the primitive mountains of Asia, prepared the first abode of the human race" (517–18).

Although it was suspected, in some circles, that the enthusiastic acceptance of India as the cradle of the human race was a reaction against biblical chronological hegemony, the position did not initially appear to be without foundation: the new science of historical linguistics originally seemed to lend some support to this possibility because early linguists tended to treat Vedic Sanskrit as identical or almost identical to the original Indo-European mother tongue due to the antiquity of its textual sources. (Jones was actually exceptionally "modern" in considering Sanskrit, along with the other Indo-European languages, to be co-descendants of an earlier ancestor language, rather than the original language.) Linguists of the time believed that Sanskrit showed more structural regularity than its cognate languages, which, in keeping with the Romantic worldview, indicated that it was more "original" than Greek and the other cognate languages. Lord Monboddo, (1774), for example, felt that he would "be able clearly to prove that Greek is derived from the Shanscrit" (322). Halhed stated: "I do not ascertain as a fact, that either Greek or Latin are derived from this language; but I give a few reasons wherein such a conjecture might be found: and I am sure that it has a better claim to the honour of a parent than Phoenician or Hebrew (Letter to G. Costard, quoted in Marshall 1970, 10). Schlegel, (1977 [1808]), who played a leading role in stimulating interest in Sanskrit, especially in Germany, developed the concept of comparative grammar wherein "the Indian language is older, the others younger and derived from it" (429). Vans Kennedy (1828) felt the evidence demonstrated that "Sanscrit itself is the primitive language from which Greek, Latin, and the mother of the Teutonic dialects were originally derived" (196). These ideas were picked up by intellectuals outside the halls of academia: Blavatsky (1975), the theosophist, claimed that "Old Sanskrit is the origin of all the less ancient Indo-European languages, as well as of the modern European tongues and dialects" (115).

Although other languages also provided valuable material, the reconstruction of the original Indo-European was, in truth, completely dependent on Sanskrit, to which linguists invariably turned for ultimate confirmation of any historical linguistic formulation. It seemed logical, at the time, to situate the original homeland in the location that spawned what was then considered to be the original or, at least, the oldest, language. As Sayce (1883) noted in retrospect, "the old theory rested partly on the assumption that man's primeval birthplace was in the East—and that, consequently, the movement of population must have been from east to west—partly on the belief that Sanskrit preserved more faithfully than any of its sisters the features of the Aryan parent speech" (385).

In time, however, the linguist F. Bopp (n.d.) stated: "I do not believe that the Greek, Latin, and other European languages are to be considered as derived from the Sanskrit. . . . I feel rather inclined to consider them altogether as subsequent variations of one original tongue, which, however, the Sanskrit has preserved more perfect than its kindred dialects" (3). Once the news of this connection seeped out from the ivory towers, there were clamorous objections raised against the whole linguistic concept of Sanskrit even being a cognate language (not to speak of the "original" mother language), as will be discussed later, since the corollary was the outrageous proposal that the people of Athens and Rome should be considered to have a community of origin with the "niggers" of India. (The kinship of Europeans with Indians was of course, implied by Jones long before.) But Bopp's sound scholarship eventually prevailed, the "original tongue" eventually became known as Proto-Indo-European, and Sanskrit was demoted to the rank of a daughter language, albeit "the eldest sister of them all" (Müller 1883, 22).

The term *Indo-European* was coined in 1816 by the linguist Thomas Young. Rask toyed with various names such as European, Sarmatic, and Japhetic. Soon, however, zealous German scholars showed preference for the term *Indo-German*, popularized by Julius Klaproth in 1823 (but first used by Conrad Malte-Brun in 1810), on the grounds that these two languages encapsulated the entire Indo-European-speaking area—the farthest language to the east being Indic, and to the west, Germanic (Celtic had not yet been recognized as a distinct language group). This term unsettled the sensitivities of French and British scholars, who exerted their influence to reestablish the more politically neutral *Indo-European*. Bopp preferred to follow their example, since "I do not see why one should take the Germans as representatives for all the people of our continent" (quoted in Olinder 1972, 13). The term *Aryan* was also used extensively during the nineteenth century and the first part of the twentieth century. This is not to be confused with *Indo-Aryan*, which refers exclusively to the Indic-speaking side of the family. Nowadays *Indo-European* is the standard term for the whole language family, although some German scholars still prefer *Indo-Germanic* despite a history of complaints against it.

As a side note, obviously, there must have been a time prior to any hypothetical reconstructions of particular protolanguages and protocultures. Accordingly, Proto-Indo-European is generally defined by most linguists as a language that can be reconstructed at least theoretically, at a stage prior to its transformation into distinct languages, and which reveals a certain cultural environment at an approximate period in human development, in a potentially definable geographic location; linguists acknowledge that this location can only be identified for that particular (hypothetical) stage of language and culture. While such generalities are generally accepted, we shall see that anything much more specific is usually contested (and even these generalities have been challenged). In any event, in the opinion of most scholars (in the West at least), India soon lost its privileged position as the point of origin of the Indo-European languages.

A variety of reasons were brought forward to reject the proposal that India might have been the original homeland. In 1842, A. W. von Schlegel, in contrast to his brother Frederik, claimed that "it is completely unlikely that the migrations which had peopled such a large part of the globe would have begun at its southern extremity and would have continually directed themselves from there towards the northeast. On the contrary, everything compels us to believe that the colonies set out in diverging directions from a central region" (515). He felt that the Caspian Sea area possessed such required centrality. Lassen noted in 1867 that from the countries where the large Indo-Germanic family resided in ancient times, "India was the most peculiar, . . . and it would be very inexplicable that no traces of these Indian peculiarities should have been preserved by any Celtic race in later times, if they had all originally lived in India. . . . Among the names of plants and animals which are common to all these nations there is none which is native to India" (614). Benfey pointed out that South India was peopled by various non-Aryan tribes who could hardly have pushed their way through the superior civilization of the Sanskrit-speaking people had the latter been indigenous to the North. These tribes, therefore, must have been the original natives of India who were subjugated by the invading Aryans (Muir [1860] 1874, 311–312). Muir, summarizing the issues in 1874, fortified all these arguments by arguing that the Sanskrit texts themselves showed a geographic progression "of the gradual advance of the Āryas from the north-west of India to the east and south" (xx).

Such arguments were by no means uncontested. In 1841, Mountstuart Elphinstone objected that "it is opposed to their foreign origin that neither in the code [of Manu] nor, I believe, in the Védas, nor in any book . . . is there any allusion to a prior residence or to a knowledge of more than the name of any country out of India." Responding to some of the arguments that had been brought forward, he argued that "to say that [the original language] spread from a central point is a gratuitous assumption, and even contrary to language; for emigration and civilization have not spread in a circle." As far as he was concerned, "the question, therefore, is still open. There is no reason whatever for thinking that the Hindus ever inhabited any country but their present one, and as little for denying that they may have done so before the earliest trace of their records or tradition" (97–98).

But, as time went by, such objections soon became far too out of tune with the academic consensus, as well as with developing colonial exigencies. Soon after the mid-nineteenth century, few scholars were still open to considering either India as the homeland of the Indo-Europeans, or protestations regarding the indigenousness of the Indo-Aryans in the subcontinent. According to Chakrabarti (1976), "it is around the middle of the nineteenth century that this romantic view of India as sending out roving bands of ascetics died out. With the Raj firmly established it was the time to begin to visualize the history and cultural process of India as a series of invasions and foreign rules" (1967).

The Aryans and Colonial and Missionary Discourse

By the end of the nineteenth century, India was no longer referred to at all as a candidate for the original homeland, and most scholars had situated themselves somewhere within the parameters of Max Müller's ([1887]1985) accommodating opinion that "if an answer must be given as to the place where our Aryan ancestors dwelt before their separation, . . . I should still say, as I said forty years ago, 'Somewhere in Asia,' and no more" (127).[5] A few peripheral intellectuals noted the change with nostalgia, still hoping that there would be a reversal in India's fortunes as a homeland contender. In 1881, Olcott, a Theosophist, in a lecture given to native audiences in various parts of India, stated:

> The theory that Aryavarta was the cradle of European civilization, the Aryans the progenitors of western peoples, and their literature the source and spring of all western religions and philosophies, is comparatively a thing of yesterday. Professor Max Müller and a few other Sanskritists of our generation have been bringing about this change in western ideas.

> Let us hope that before many years roll by, we may have out the whole truth about Aryan civilization, and that your ancestors (and ours) will be honoured according to their deserts. . . . the Brahmins have their own chronology and no one has the means of proving that their calculations are exaggerated. . . . We Europeans . . . have a right to more than suspect that India 8,000 years ago sent out a colony of emigrants. (124)

In sharp contrast, the racial scientists, who will be discussed later, recorded the change of affairs with a note of indignant relief: "In our school days most of us were brought up to regard Asia as the mother of European people. We were told that an ideal race of men swarmed forth from the Himalayan highlands disseminating culture right and left as they spread through the barbarous West." As far as Ripley was concerned, such philological ideas represented the dark age of Indo-European studies: "In the days when . . . there was no science of physical anthropology [and] prehistoric archaeology was not yet . . . a new science of philology dazzled the intelligent world . . . and its words were law. Since 1860 these early inductions have completely broken down in the light of modern research" (Ripley 1899, 453).

Even during the earlier phase of the homeland quest, when India was still a popular candidate, many scholars were uncomfortable about moving the Indo-Europeans too far from their biblical origins somewhere in the Near East. There were those among the British, in particular, whose colonial sensibilities made them reluctant to acknowledge any potential cultural indebtedness to the forefathers of the rickshaw pullers of Calcutta, and who preferred to hang on to the biblical Adam for longer than their European contemporaries. Even well after Adam was no longer in the picture, there was a very cool reception in some circles to the "late Prof. Max Müller [who had] blurted forth to a not over-grateful world the news that we and our revolted sepoys were of the same human family" (Legge 1902, 710). Again, let us not forget the influence of the times: many scholars, quite apart from any consideration of India as a possible homeland, could not even tolerate the newfound language relationship. Müller (1883) again noted the mood of the day:

> They would not have it, they would not believe that there could be any community of origin between the people of Athens and Rome, and the so-called Niggers of India. The classical scholars scouted the idea, and I still remember the time, when I was a student at Leipzig and begun to study Sanskrit, with what contempt any remarks on Sanskrit or comparative grammar were treated by my teachers. . . . No one ever was for a time so completely laughed down as Professor Bopp, when he first published his Comparative Grammar of Sanskrit, Zend, Greek, Latin and Gothic. All hands were against him. (28)

Unlike some of his contemporaries, Müller was effusive in his admiration for things Indian (although he never subscribed to an Indian homeland). In his course of lectures "India: What Can It Teach Us?" (1883), he declared that she was "the country most richly endowed with all the wealth, power and beauty that nature can bestow," indeed, "a very paradise on earth," a place where "the human mind has most fully developed some of its choicest gifts, [and] has most deeply pondered on the greatest problems of life" (6). Such lavish praise was far too extreme for those who, as Müller himself noted, would be "horror struck at the idea that the humanity they meet with [in India] . . . should be able to teach *us* any lesson" (7).

Müller's concerns about the reactions that enthusiastic portrayals of India's superiority might provoke were not unwarranted. The Indomania of the early British Orientalists "did not die of natural causes; it was killed off" and replaced by an Indophobia initiated by Evangelicalism and Utilitarianism, epitomized by Charles Grant and James Mill, respectively (Trautmann 1997, 99). Well before Müller's glorifications of India, Grant, who was very influential in East India Company circles, promoted an aggressive Anglicizing and Christianizing relationship with India, which he provoked by completely disparaging Indian laws, religion, and character. In contrast to the Orientalists, Grant ([1790] 1970) stressed the absolute difference, in all respects, between the British and the despicable natives of the subcontinent: "In the worst parts of Europe, there are no doubt great numbers of men who are sincere, upright, and conscientious. In Bengal, a man of real veracity and integrity is a great phenomenon" (21). Most significantly, he made absolutely no reference to the kinship of Sanskrit and the European languages except, possibly, to note that "the discoveries of science invalidate none of the truths of revelation" (71). Nor did Grant have any regard for enthusiastic depictions of India. Grant was quick to criticize scholars who had never even visited India, thereby undermining the relevance of their scholarship to the real world: "Europeans who, not having *resided* in Asia, are acquainted only with a few detached features of the Indian character" (24).

Grant was by no means the first or sole Christian leader to engage in extreme diatribes against Hinduism—these continued throughout the colonial period. In 1840, the Reverend Alexander Duff briefly referred to the Aryan commonality by stating that the Hindus "can point to little that indicates their high original." But for the most part he also simply ranted that they "have no will, no liberty, no conscience of their own. They are passive instruments, moulded into shape by external influences—mere machines, blindly stimulated, at the bidding of another, to pursuits the most unworthy of immortal creatures. In them, reason is in fact laid prostrate. They launch into all the depravities of idol worship. They look like the sports and derision of the Prince of darkness" (107). In 1882, William Hastie, principal of the General Assembly of the Church of Scotland's institution in Calcutta, in letters he addressed to "educated Hindus" about their religion, considered that "no pen has yet adequately depicted all the hideousness and grossness of the monstrous system." Hastie was well aware that Hindu idolatry originated from the same Aryan stem as that of the Greeks. But the latter had been "recalled from their idolatrous errors," while India remained "the most stupendous fortress and citadel of ancient error and idolatry, . . . paralleled only by the spirits of Pandemonium," a country whose religion consisted of "senseless mummeries, loathsome impurities and bloody barbarous sacrifices." It has "consecrated and encouraged every conceivable form of licentiousness, falsehood, injustice, cruelty, robbery, murder," and "its sublimest spiritual states have been but the reflex of physiological conditions in disease" (24–33).

Müller, fully aware of the resentment generated by his Indophilic laudations, took pains to specify "at once" to the civil servants, officers, missionaries, and merchants who were actually in the "bazaars" and "courts of justice" of the real-life India that there were "two very different Indias." Müller was not unaware of the scathing and disparaging opinions that his contemporaries in the colonies held regarding the present state of civilization in India. The India he was referring to "was a thousand, two thousand, it may be, three thousand years ago" (1883, 7); it was "not on the surface but lay many centuries beneath it" (1899, 4). The golden age represented a thing very much in the past. Nonetheless, he did not hesitate in insisting that these ancient Indians "represented . . . a collateral branch of that family to which we belong by language, that is, by thought, and [that] their historical records . . . have been preserved to us in such perfect . . . documents . . . that we can learn from them lessons we can learn nowhere else" (*1899*, 21).

Such a claim would have been intolerable for the likes of Mill ([1820] 1975), who had previously censured Jones for indulging in "panegyrics," finding it "unfortunate that a mind so . . . devoted to Oriental learning . . . should have adopted the hypothesis of a high state of civilization in the principal countries of Asia" (109). Mill, too, had ignored the relationships between the Indian and Western languages, and, like Grant, insisted on emphasizing the tremendous difference, as opposed to the Orientalist sense of kinship, between the British and the Indians. These latter, for Mill, were ignorant and barbaric and despicable: "No people, how rude and ignorant soever, . . . have ever drawn a more gross and disgusting picture of the universe" (157). His was a far cry from the venerable status accorded to the ancient Hindus by Müller and the Orientalists. The extreme Indophobic discomfort with the connection of Sanskrit with Greek and Latin was exemplified by the conviction of the Scottish philosopher Dugald Stewart, who, without knowing a word of the language, proposed that Sanskrit was not a cognate of Greek, it *was* Greek. It had been borrowed by the wily Brahmans during Alexander's conquest and adopted to keep their conversations inaccessible to the masses (124). Max Müller (1875), commenting on Stewart's attempt, again reveals the mood of the time:

> This . . . shows, better than anything else, how violent a shock was given by the discovery of Sanskrit to prejudices most deeply engrained in the mind of every educated man. The most absurd arguments found favor for a time, if they could only furnish a loophole by which to escape the unpleasant conclusion that Greek and Latin were of the same kith and kin as the language of the black inhabitants of India. (164)

Clearly, the developing pressure to justify the colonial and missionary presence in India prompted the denigration of Indian civilization, and the shunning of embarrassing cultural and linguistic ties. Trautmann suggests that such considerations also explain why the British, despite having primary access to Sanskrit source material, did not pursue the study of comparative philology. This was to become a predominantly German domain.

The Indo-European language connection, however, was not about to disappear, and Trautmann masterfully traces the emergence of race science as the resolution of inescapable philological reality with the colonial need for cultural superiority over the natives of India. It should be noted that up until the middle of the twentieth century, the term *race* was used to designate what we would today call an ethnic group (rather than referring to the divisions of Caucasian, Negroid, Mongoloid, and so on, as per present usage). During the nineteenth century, race and nation were more or less interchangeable terms, but drifted apart in the course of the century as race became more biologized, and nation politicized. One of the catalysts for the development of race science was that some of the Orientalists, like Müller, in contrast to the Utilitarians, not only recognized and appreciated European linguistic and cultural brotherhood with the Hindu Aryans but also articulated these bonds in terms of racial equality:

> No authority could have been strong enough to persuade the Grecian army that their gods and their hero-ancestors were the same as those of king Porus, or to convince the English soldier that *the same blood was running in his veins as in the veins of the dark Bengalese.*

> And yet there is not an English jury now-a-days, which, after examining the hoary documents of language, would reject the claim of a *common descent* and a legitimate relationship between Hindu, Greek and Teuton. We challenge the seeming stranger, and whether he answer with the lips of a Greek, a German, or an Indian, we recognize him as one of ourselves. Though the . . . physiologist may doubt, . . . all must yield before the facts furnished by language. (Müller 1854a, 29–30; my italics)

The recognition of such racial kinship was repugnant to the ethnologists, who reacted by jettisoning the importance of language and scorning the Orientalist philologists. For them, fairness of skin paralleled highness of civilization, and the Indians were a beggarly lot who could not possibly be allowed to claim a common racial pedigree, not to speak of being recognized as "one of" the British. Isaac Taylor ([1892] 1988) scathingly exemplifies the antiphilological reaction of the race scientists: "It cannot be insisted upon too strongly that identity of speech does not imply identity of race, any more than diversity of speech implies diversity of race" (5–6). Anthropologists such as himself had scant regard for the Orientalists: "Max Müller, owing to the charm of his style, his unrivaled power of popular exposition, and to his high authority as a Sanskrit scholar, has done more than any other writer to popularise this erroneous notion." Despite the racist overtones, there was actually a good measure of truth to some of these criticisms: "Instead of speaking only of a primitive Aryan language, he speaks of an 'Aryan race' and 'Aryan family.' . . . more mischievous words have seldom been uttered by a great scholar" (3–4). As for Müller's English jury, "the evidence derived from the documents of language . . . which might be put before an English jury as to a 'common descent' and a 'legitimate relationship' between the negro and the Yankee, would be more intelligible to the twelve English tradesmen in the box than the obscure evidence which applies to the case of the Teuton and the Hindu" (6). Taylor attempted to point out that just as the African American and the European American spoke the same language but were not considered members of the same race, so there were no grounds to consider the Hindu and the European as being the same race on the basis of the Indo-European language connection.

Race science was precipitated by the discovery, by the Madras school of Orientalists, that the South Indian languages were not derivable from Sanskrit. This fact was combined with certain forced readings of the Vedic texts (which will be discussed in chapter 3) to produce images of the Aryans as white-skinned and dolichocephalic, in contrast to the dark-skinned, snub-nosed *dāsas*. Despite Taylor's comments, the one-language-one-race model inherited from Babel was retained—at least for the white Aryans—and India was reconstructed as the product of two original races: a fair invading race speaking an Aryan tongue, and a dark- skinned aboriginal one speaking Dravidian.

For our purposes, both Orientalist philologers and ethnologists agreed on one thing: Trautmann's "big bang" of Indian civilization consisted of the impact of Aryan invaders with the indigenes of India. What the racial theorists succeeded in doing, in their opposition to the philologists, was to uncouple the common language bond from the need to identify with the Hindus on any other level whatsoever. The Europeans, as a race, were now not required to acknowledge any common racial or even cultural bond with the Hindus: "To speak of 'our Indian bretheren' is as absurd and false as to claim relationship with the Negroes of the United States because they now use an Aryan language" (Sayce 1883, 385). Even the common Indo-European language was presented as being a gift to India from the West, just as it had been to the "negroes of the United States." The racial theorists paved the way for the postulate that the Aryans were an autonomous white race who brought civilization and the Sanskrit language to the different races of India—a development Trautmann holds as pivotal to the political construction of Aryan identity developing in Germany. The biblical model of the identity of language and race still held good for the original white Aryans, but not for the Hindus. These invading Aryans taught the racially and linguistically distinct natives the Indo-European language and the arts of civilization. But in so doing, they, in time, lost their superior status and became racially subsumed by the native population.

There were those in the colonial power who were much more comfortable with these new developments. The British presence in the subcontinent could now be cast as a rerun several millennia later of a similar script, but a script that hoped to have a different ending. The British could now present themselves as a second wave of Aryans, again bringing a superior language and civilization to the racial descendants of the same natives their forefathers had attempted to elevate so many centuries earlier. Some, drawing on the findings of racial science, believed that a lesson was to be learned from the earlier wave of Aryans who had allowed themselves to become degenerate due to their new environment. Bolstered with the new racial theories, such scholars could now exonerate themselves for, and indeed insist on, the need for remaining aloof and superior to their subjects. Thus in *Annals of Rural Bengal* (1897), W. W. Hunter describes the retardation of Aryan India, which had become "effeminated by long sloth" because of miscegenation, "but which could again be regenerated by British Rule" (193).[6] On the Continent, Gobineau saw India as a warning to Europe of the horrors resulting from the bastardization of Aryan culture. The trajectory that Aryanism took toward Nazism in Germany is beyond the scope of the present work, but it has been amply traced in numerous works, among which Poliakov (1971) is especially noteworthy.

The protestations of the race theoreticians notwithstanding, the equation of language with race remained entrenched. It certainly did not prevent some British representatives from exploiting this Aryan commonality in a variety of ways. Henry Sumner Maine made no bones about the fact "that the government of India by the English has been rendered appreciably easier by the discoveries which have brought home to the educated of both races the common Aryan parentage of Englishman and Hindoo" (18–19). The headmaster of Marlborough wrote in 1870 that "in coming to Hindostan with our advanced civilization, we were returning home with splendid gifts, to visit a member of one common family" (quoted in Maw 1950, 14–15). A few years earlier, one J. Wilson insisted that "what has taken place since the commencement of the British Government in India is only a reunion . . . of the members of the same great family." (14–15). Müller himself (1847) had earlier expressed that "it is curious to see how the descendants of the same race, to which the first conquerors and masters of India belonged, return . . . to accomplish the glorious work of civilization, which had been left unfinished by their Arian bretheren" (349).

This reunion, of course, was hardly on equal terms; as Maw (1990) notes, such scholars "refused to follow the notion to its logical conclusion: that consanguinity entitled contemporary India to a moral parity with Great Britain, and ultimately, to national independence" (36). Far from it. As H. S. Newman (n.d.) was quick to point out: "Once in the end of aeons they meet, and the Aryan of the west rules the Aryan of the east" (110). Farrer (1870), referring to the "common ancestors from whose loins we both alike are sprung," compared the reunion of offspring to that of Esau and Jacob. According to this association, "from the womb it had been prophesied respecting them that '*the elder should serve the younger*'" (50; italics in original). Havell (1918) took it upon himself to speak on behalf of the Indians, who, in his perception, accepted British rule because "they recognize that the present rulers of India . . . are generally animated by that same love of justice and fair play, the same high principles of conduct and respect for humanitarian laws which guided the ancient Aryan statesmen and law givers in their relations with the Indian masses" (vi). Clearly, the Aryan connection could turn out to be a politically shrewd card to play because "in thus honouring our Aryan forerunners in India we shall both honour ourselves and make the most direct and effective appeal to Indian loyalty" (ix).

The Aryan connection proved useful on a variety of occasions and in a variety of sometimes conflicting ways. Devendraswarup a historian of the colonial period (1993, 36) argues that after the British were shaken by the Great Revolt of 1857, certain individuals suddenly found reason to stress their common Aryan bond with the Brahmanas where others had previously shunned it. Since the Brahmanas were preponderant in the Bengal Native Infantry, which had taken part in the revolt, there were those among the British who conveniently began to propagate discourses of Aryan kinship in the hope of cultivating a sense of identification and allegiance with them (36). Chakrabarti (1997, 127) notes that the same Risley quoted previously who had voiced such relief that the new science of racial anthropology exempted the need for Europeans to affiliate themselves with the Hindu side of the family, did not hesitate in his 1881 Bengal survey on the races, religions and languages of India, to allot common Aryan descent liberally to the Indian groups predominant in the British army such as the Rajputs, Jats, and Brahmins. The Aryan connection was simply manipulated at will.

Such Aryan commonalty was not only adapted to suit colonial exigencies. Maw (1990) has thoroughly outlined how certain Christian evangelists also found advantages in discourses of Aryan kinship. As far as G. Smith was concerned, "the English-speaking Aryans had been providentially trained to become the rulers of India and evangelizers of India" since "the youngest civilization in the world was to instruct and correct the oldest" (quoted in Maw 1950, 35). He noted that "it is not the least of the claims of India on England that our language is theirs, our civilisation theirs, our aspirations theirs, that in a very true and special sense they are our brothers" (35). Samuel Laing held that the "two races so long separated meet once more. . . . the younger brother has become the stronger, and takes his place as the head and protector of the family. . . . we are here . . . on a sacred mission, to stretch out the right hand of aid to our weaker brother, who once far outstripped us, but has now fallen behind in the race" (quoted in Maw 1950, 37).

Along these same lines, a general history of the subcontinent, written by W. C. Pearce in 1876, compared the ancient pre-Christian Aryan invasion of the subcontinent to the modern Christian Aryan one. In his view, the ancient Aryans had descended from the highlands of Central Asia, bringing with them their language, civilization, and religion, which far surpassed those of the natives: "[The Aryan] religion was, in its poetic fancies, as far exalted above [the native's] crude systems of worship as the sublime teachings of Christianity soar above the doctrines of the code of Menu [*sic*]" (37). Hastie (1882) appealed to the "twin branches on the same original Aryan stem"—in this case the ancient Greek and modern Indic cultures—in order to suggest that the Church could extinguish the "tenacious survival of the old Aryan world" in modern India just as Paul had extinguished "the brighter and fairer Hellenism" in the ancient West (25–26).

In contrast to all this, Devendraswarup, (1993), touches on very different Christian appropriations of the work of the philologists and the discourse of Aryanism: "It seems that missionary scholars in India had already perceived the potential of the science of comparative philology in uprooting the hold of the Brahmins" (32). Unlike some of the discourses noted earlier, other missionaries found it preferable to target the non-Aryan identity of segments of the Indian populace rather than play up the Aryan commonalty. The missionaries were having little or no success in converting the Brahmans and upper classes. Devendraswarup finds the scholarly work of missionary intellectuals such as the Reverend John James Muir and the Reverend John Stevenson readily presenting the Brahmanas as foreigners who had foisted their Vedic language and texts onto the aboriginals of India. The idea in this case was to create a sense of alienation from Brahmanical religion among the lower castes, thereby preparing them for exposure and conversion to Christianity. Thus Wilson, in a letter to his parents, noted that "the Aryan tribes in conquering India, urged by the Brāhmanas, made war against the Turanian demon worship. . . . It is among the Turanian races, . . . which have no organized priesthood and bewitching literature, that the converts to Christianity are most numerous" (quoted in Devendraswarup 1993, 35). The Aryan invasion theory proved to be adaptable to a curious mismash of contradictory (but not necessarily competing) interests.

Like some of their administratorial counterparts, still other evangelicals also felt the need to be very clear about the distinction between the eastern and western branches of the Aryan family. In 1910, the missionary Slater was quite specific that Christianity had transcended its Aryan matrix, developing a higher spiritual expression as a result of influences from the Semitic encounter. India, in contrast, had decayed and remained "sunk in the grossest superstition." Slater could not countenace attempts to couple this sorry state of affairs with western religiosity under a common rubric of Aryan spirituality. (Maw 1950, 63). There was no shortage of voices who rejected an Aryanism that bonded British rulers with their ungrateful subjects (Day 1994, 19).

No one knew what to do about the corollaries of comparative philology. Depending on their agendas and strategies, British individuals glorified, stressed, minimized, shunned, or otherwise negotiated in some form or fashion with the Aryan connection. Scholars went backward and forward, attempting to balance colonial and missionary exigencies with the academic opinions of the day. For our purposes, whereas India had been viewed as the homeland of the Aryans and the cradle of civilization at the beginning of the nineteenth century, by that century's end, in the opinion of people like Enrico de Michaelis, it was considered its grave. It seems tempting to suggest that the concern of many British colonialists during this period was not so much where the Aryans had come from (there was, after all, no question that England could have been the homeland), provided they had not come from India, and provided the British did not need to acknowledge any embarrassing kinship with their Indian subjects. Despite having primary access to the Sanskrit source material upon which the rest of Europe was dependent, it was Germany, and to some extent France, but not Britain, that came to dominate the field of historical linguistics. Sayce was to lament as late as the end of the nineteenth century that "little is known about it [comparative philology] in England, for English scholars have but recently awakened to the value and meaning of the work done by Bopp and Schleicher and Curtius, and have not yet learned that this already belongs to a past stage in the history of linguistic science" (1883, 385). Although England did eventually become a principal center of Sanskrit study for all of Europe (and had been a pioneer in the early days with people like Jones, Maesden, Leyden, and Ellis), the British became wary of this new comparative philology. Colonial interests seem to have superseded this particular pursuit of knowledge.

The dilemma facing the rulers was how to avoid according cultural equality, not to speak of indebtedness, to the Hindu subjects they intended to govern. The Germans did not have the same colonial exigencies; on the contrary, philology offered certain German scholars an opportunity to compensate for their poor showing on the colonial scene. The British, as expert politicians, were able to turn previously awkward philological realities to their political advantage, but it would be well worth exploring the extent to which they remained wary, in the nascent stages of Indological studies, of the possibly embarrassing repercussions that might be inherent in exploring the field of philology. Doubtless other factors were also involved, but philology was nonetheless very much a German prerogative.[7] There were those among the British who were relieved to hand the Germans the philological baton of a white Sanskrit-speaking race that had come into India from somewhere else—anywhere else. And there were those among the Germans who were happy to take it and run.

Before turning to German Aryanism, it would be unfair to conclude this section without noting that not all British intellectuals can be generically categorized as arrogant elitists. While it is important to highlight the more extreme versions of Aryan discourse in order to best understand Indian reactions and responses, there were also voices of moderation and soberness. One cannot tar and feather all nineteenth-century scholars as racists and bigots. In 1870, Farrer, albeit still convinced of the modern West's advancement in civilization, was at least shamed by the excesses of some of his contemporaries in their reactions to the Aryan connection:

> Oh! if, instead of calling them and treating them as "niggers"; if, instead of absorbing with such fatal facility the preposterous notion that they were with few exceptions, an abject nation of cringing liars, to be despised and kicked, . . . if our missionaries had been tempered sometimes with their religious fanaticism of hatred against idolatry with a deeper historical knowledge of the religions of the world, . . . then, indeed, the Hindoos no less than ourselves would have recognized the bond of unity between us because of the common ancestors from whose loins we both alike are sprung. (48)

Other voices, too, had not hesitated to express disgust at their compatriots:

> Is it not something, also, that you all—our Arian friends—should be told, intensely as it may disgust you, that this Arian Bengali—whom, uncivilly and un-ethnologically, you have been in the habit of calling a "Nigger,"—is, stubbornly as you may kick against the conviction, *your Elder Brother*:—one who, much as you may glory in being descended from certain pig-herding Thegns or piratical Norse Vikings, is, in very truth . . . the representative of the pure Arian stock, of which you are a mere offshoot . . . whom it is your duty to treat with mercy, justice, and forbearance;—as you will have to answer for your dealing with him to the God and Father of us all. (Blackwell 1856, 548)

German Aryanism

Devendraswarup (1993) traces the beginning of Anglo-Germanic collaboration on intellectual and political planes to the arrival in England of the German scholar Chevalier Bunsen as ambassador of Prussia in 1841. The two countries shared an animosity toward France, which "provided an emotional bond between the rising German nationalism and British imperialism" (32). Bunsen, who was instrumental in bringing Max Müller to England, made a presentation to the British Association for the Advancement of Science, promoting the usefulness and importance of the sciences of philology and ethnology. The Philological Society was established in Britain the very next year, and the Ethnological Society the year after that. If the British needed prompting from the Continent, the Germans, in contrast, were very keen to pioneer the new science of philology. By 1906, the University of Strasbourg could boast a library holding some six thousand volumes on the Aryans, general ethnology, and related disciplines (Maw 1990, 113). Figueira (1994), in her analysis of Indian thought and the formation of Aryan ideology, identifies two connected reasons for the initial interest in Vedic scholarship in Germany: the search for the oldest forms of religion and language, and the inquiry into the origin and past of the German people through information drawn from ancient Sanskrit sources. These offered a cultural means to restore the ancient greatness of the Germanic tradition (145–146).

There were very good reasons that some Germans, in particular, took to the rapidly developing field of philology with such enthusiasm and became the principal promoters of what Raymond Schwab (1984) has called "the Oriental Renaissance." The southern Europeans, all things considered, could point to the grandeur of their ancient Greek and Latin heritage, and the British could afford to overlook their own potentially embarrassing pedigree problems and bask in the superiority of their colonial and technological advances in the modern, real world. It was German national pride that was most in need of some dramatic infusion from the past. Schwab outlines how, just as the arrival of Greek manuscripts in Europe after the fall of Constantinople had triggered the first Renaissance in the fifteenth century, the arrival of Sanskrit texts from India in the eighteenth and nineteenth centuries produced a "second Renaissance," with Germans scholars determined to capitalize on the unique opportunity. After all, if the Germans could somehow appropriate the mantle of the original Indo-Europeans (which they soon began to call Indo-Germans), they could then lay claim to being the progenitors of all subsequent derivative cultures, be they Greek, Latin, or colonial.

Much of Europe, from the eighteenth to the twentieth century, was intensely preoccupied with racial origins. England, for example, was beset with national identification problems due to its mixed pedigree of Norman, Anglo-Saxon, and Celtic. Likewise, French racial theorists had to decide whether a Frankish, Latin, or Gaelic association furthered their interests, and their affiliation varied according to time and place. In contrast to such ethnic hybridity, certain members of the German intelligentsia believed they could lay significant claim to an exclusively indigenous ancestry—claims, they argued, that were verified by passages in Latin sources as early as Tacitus's *Germania* (2.1, 4.1), which suggested that they were an unmixed and autochthonous people. While some British historians viewed the multiple invasions and ethnic intermixture that produced British culture as promoting a "hybrid vigour" that accounted for British preeminence in world affairs, German historians attributed their greatness to the alleged lack of physical or cultural influences from the inferior people that surrounded them (Trigger 1981, 145). This latter belief was soon to reappear in various scholarly guises during a phase of Indo-Germanic studies.

Not only did such individuals believe they were relieved of having to defer to external invaders for their sources of culture or potency, they could actually lay claims to being the exporters of the most powerful dynasties in Europe: the Swabians of Spain, Anglo-Saxons of England, Lombards of Italy, Franks of France, and Bavarians of Austria were all Germanic tribes. With such credentials, it was a short step for scholars like Leibniz to claim unabashedly as early as 1690 that "it is certain at any rate that most inquiries into European origins, customs and antiquities have to do with the Teutonic language and antiquities" (Leibniz [1690] 1981, 286). Not only this, but since writers of this period made no distinction between language and race, the Teutonic language, unadulterated by the alien influences that pervaded the other languages of Europe, was, if not the primeval language of mankind,[8] nonetheless "more natural, . . . more Adamic" than even Hebrew itself (281). The racial zealousness prominent among this group of scholars was to have dramatic repercussions in all areas of Indo-European studies, particularly in linguistics and anthropology. The groundwork for postulating a Germanic homeland for the Indo-Europeans had been laid well before the European discovery of Sanskrit:

> The myth of indigenous barbarian origins developed in Middle Europe, especially in Germany, which regarded barbarian Europe as the original source of uncorrupted freedom, maintaining individualism and freedom, as opposed to the despotism of Classical empires. With the aid of historical linguistics . . . and archaeology . . . a national-historical framework was constructed to legitimate the expanding German nation. Direct ethnic links were postulated between the prehistoric past and the present on the basis of ethnic explanations of archaeological cultures. . . . It later served as a platform for racist constructions of a Germanic "Urvolk" to serve the Nazi regime. . . . As a consequence, . . . emphasis on the myth of European oriental origins was toned down. (Kristiansen 1996, 141)

An oriental origin for the Indo-Europeans was no more compatible with German agendas and aspirations than with British ones.

Before a Germanic homeland could be postulated, however, the consensus regarding an Asian homeland had to be challenged. Although India had been eliminated as a potential homeland by the second half of the nineteenth century, scholars still almost unanimously limited their Aryan debates to other parts of Asia, particularly favoring Bactria, in present-day Afghanistan, or adjacent areas. Indeed, right up until the end of the nineteenth century (by which time other homeland contenders were gaining ground), scholars such as Monier Williams (1891) still held that "it is probable that one of the earliest homes (if not the first seat) of the members of the great Āryan family was in the high land surrounding the sources of the Oxus, to the north of the point connecting the Hindū Kūsh with the Himalayas . . . the Pamīr Plateau" (4). The first well-known step toward challenging an Asian homeland in favor of a European one is generally credited to an Englishman, the ethnologist Robert G. Latham, in 1862.[9]

For Latham (1862), "when philologues make the Veda 3000 years old, and deduce the Latin and its congeners from Asia, they are wrong to, at least, a thousand miles in space, and as many years in time" (620). Latham's rationale, which survives to the present day, was that "if historical evidence be wanting, the *a priori* presumptions must be considered. . . . the presumptions are in favour of the smaller class having been deduced from the larger rather than *vice versa*" (611). As a natural scientist, he illustrated this thesis by comparing language groups to distinct species of reptiles:

> *Where we have two branches of the same division of speech separated from each other, one of which is the larger in area and the more diversified by varieties, and the other smaller and comparatively homogeneous, the presumption is in favour of the latter being derived from the former, rather than the former from the latter.* To deduce the Indo-Europeans of Europe from the Indo-Europeans of Asia, in ethnology, is like deriving the reptiles of Great Britain from those of Ireland in herpetology. (Latham 1851, cxlii; italics in original)

Whatever the value of such reasoning, which will be discussed in chapter 8, Latham offered a new concept to his fellow scholars—a European homeland for the Aryans.

It was a very small step from zoology and ethnology to physical anthropology, which was soon pressed into service to identify these original Indo-Europeans in Europe. In 1878, the German philologist L. Geiger was the first to suggest that the Indo-Europeans were blond, blue-eyed people, and that these traits had become diluted and darkened in those places where there had been a foreign admixture of genes: "The Indo-Germanic people remain unadulterated wherever pure blonde traits are best preserved." His logic, which he bolstered by the same quotes from Tacitus, was that the then available data showed no evidence of a pre-Indo-European linguistic substratum in north Europe, unlike other European countries.[10] By the same rationale that India had been eliminated, such substrata in other areas of Europe suggested that the Indo-Europeans were not native to these areas but intruders who imposed themselves on preexisting peoples. Continuing this line of argument, the inhabitants of northern Europe, in contrast to their neighbors, must have been an indigenous Indo-European race. Since there was no indication that the Aryans had entered this area from anywhere else, the residents there must have been the pure descendants of the original Aryans. Their physical traits, by extension, since they had not been mixed with elements from any other people, must be those of the original Aryans. The original Indo-Europeans, then, were blond, fair, and blue-eyed.

Dubious interpretations of certain passages in the Vedic texts, which will be examined in the next chapters, were then introduced to produce readings of fair, invading Aryans clashing with snub-nosed indigenous dāsas. Armed with such data, another German, Theodor Poesche (1878), attempted to further the blond cause with an even more simplistic logic in the same year. He accepted without question that the original Aryans spoke Indo-European and were blond. Greeks, Italians, and French had the correct linguistic credentials but were disqualified due to being dark, while some of the Scandinavians had the right physical qualities but spoke the wrong language (41).[11] The Germans won by default.

Many in the German nation soon became captivated by the implications of such possibilities. In 1886, the anatomist and craniologist Rudolf Virchow published a lengthy report, "The Skin, Hair, and Eye Color of German Schoolchildren" (275–477), based on a massive investigation involving fifteen million schoolchildren. Questionnaires were sent out to schools in Germany, Austria, Switzerland, and Belgium to solicit information on the hair and eye color of the students. The statistics showed that a predominance of fair traits occurred in northern Germany and the Scandinavian countries. As far as German chauvinists were concerned, here was hard scientific proof correlating the Germans with the pure blond Aryans.

This discussion is circumscribed by focusing primarily on Aryan discourse among the British and the Germans, since, historically, these have exerted the most influence on the responses from South Asia, and fuller treatments of the concept of the Aryan race in Europe during the nineteenth century has been treated in detail elsewhere (Poliakov 1971; Day 1994). But I should at least note in passing that "France has been called 'the homeland of racial' theory" (Day 1994, 15). Indeed, Gobineau, whose belief in the blue-eyed, blond Aryan did not go down at all well with his contemporaries in his native France, was soon to have societies named after him spring up all over Germany. In any event, as scholars from other European countries began to voice their objections to this reconstructed, blond, Germanic Aryan superman, elements in European anthropology departments allowed their scholarship to degenerate into a puerile, but fatal, we're-more-Aryan-than-you level of discourse. Isaac Taylor ([1892] 1988), while on the one hand rejoicing that "the whilom tyranny of the Sanskritists is happily overpast" (332) and that, consequently, philology was no longer the determining method in Aryan studies, could nonetheless hardly avoid referring to the madness his own discipline had unleashed:

> The question has been debated with needless acrimony. German scholars . . . have contended that the physical type of the primitive Aryans was that of the North Germans—a tall, fair, blue-eyed dolicocephalic race. French writers, on the other hand, have maintained that the primitive Aryans were brachycephalic, and that the true Aryan type is represented by the Gauls. The Germans claim the primitive Aryans as typical Germans who Aryanised the French, while the French claim them as typical Frenchmen who Aryanised the Germans. Both parties maintain that their own ancestors were the pure noble race of Aryan conquerors, and that their hereditary foes belonged to a conquered and enslaved race of aboriginal savages, who received the germs of civilisation from their hereditary superiors. Each party accuses the other of subordinating the results of science to Chauvinistic sentiment. (226–227)

In 1887, Max Müller ([1887] 1985) joined in the remonstrations against the racial frenzy enveloping Europe and "declared again and again that if I say Aryas, I mean neither blood nor bones, nor hair nor skull. . . . How many misunderstandings and how many controversies are due to what is deduced by arguing from language to blood-relationship or from blood-relationship to language" (120). Müller may have well felt the need to stress that "an ethnologist who speaks of an Aryan race, Aryan eyes and hair, and Aryan blood is as great a sinner as a linguist who speaks of a dolicocephalic dictionary or a brachycephalic grammar"; after all, it was he who had been a principal cause in such misconceptions through his earlier remarks on the common blood that the "English soldier" shared with the "dark Bengali" (1854a, 29–30). Needless to say, his retraction went largely unnoticed, and the history books recorded the earlier Max Müller who, for a quarter of a century, had contributed to the idea of a common racial Aryan ancestry based on a common Aryan tongue. One has only to pick up any book on the subject from the period to see how effortlessly discourses of language slid into discourses of race from one sentence to the next: "From a common Proto-Aryan *speech* we infer also a common Proto-Aryan homeland. . . . Where was this primitive home from which the Aryan *blood* went out in so many streams over the earth?" (Widney 1907, 10; my italics).

Physical anthropology was not the only science invoked to reject the idea of an Asian homeland. Taylor's "tyrannical Sanskritists" inspired by the comparative grammars of pioneering linguists such as Schlegel, Bopp, Grimm, Schleicher, Grassman, Verner, Brugmann, and Saussure, developed comparative philology, which, in turn, led to linguistic paleontology. This methodology was first utilized in a serious way by Adolphe Pictet in 1859 as one "which utilizes words to culminate in things and ideas" (19). Linguistic paleontology, which will be discussed in chapter 6, in its basic form, proposes that cognate words denoting items of material or social culture found in all branches of a language family, such as 'wheel' or 'horse', can be used as linguistic evidence to prove that such items existed in the protoculture of that family. Pictet himself believed his method pointed to an original homeland in Bactria, present-day Afghanistan. His contemporaries, however, quickly co-opted the new discipline to support the German homeland. One of the items that was to be the most amenable in this regard was the common beech. Since the beech was well represented in the European side of the family, it was assumed to have existed in the protolanguage before the various linguistic branches separated.[12] Since this protolanguage necessitated a protohomeland, scholars such as Geiger then used this information to draw up maps of the geographic boundaries within which the beech tree grows—specifically, German-centered Europe—and the Aryan homeland was set within this area.

Although linguistics inaugurated the field of Indo-European studies, it did not take long for archaeology to be summoned to the witness stand to help solve the mystery of origins (or, in many cases, to provide further "proof" of predetermined concepts of the homeland). From abstract philological deductions, the Indo-Europeans had become reified into a very specific anthropological type living in a very identifiable homeland that archaeology, it was hoped, would now physically materialize through the archaeological record. In 1883, Karl Penka was one of the first scholars to use this method in conjunction with linguistics to claim that "the archaeological evidence argues convincingly for a Scandinavian homeland" based on the Mesolithic culture discovered there (68). More influential, however, was Gustav Kossina's defense of a German homeland, in 1902, which was based on linking the movement of peoples with ceramic changes in the archaeological record. Kossina believed the spread of the Corded Ware and Linear Ware archaeological cultures was indicative of Aryan dispersals. The assumptions upon which his methodology was based can be summed up as follows: (1) distinctive artifact types can be equated with "cultures"; (2) the distribution of such types represents "cultural provinces"; (3) such provinces can be equated with tribal or ethnic groups; and (4) these ethnic groups can be identified with historical peoples (provided there has been no major discontinuity in the archaeological record). Kossina's assumptions were formative to Childes's later work and underpin, to some extent, Gimbutas's well-known theories.

Once wedded, linguistics and archaeology have not proven to be very comfortable partners, since their relationship has been marred by acute handicaps in communication. Archaeology, in the absence of datable inscriptions that are readable, can give no indication of the linguistic identity of the members of a particular material culture. Linguistics, in turn, albeit providing some tantalizing glimpses of material culture through linguistic paleontology, cannot be easily connected to one specific archaeological entity to the exclusion of others. Moreover, even when an archaeological culture has been convincingly argued to be Indo-European, it has never been accepted uncontroversially as being *the* original protoculture.

Archaeology and linguistics have not been the only disciplines involved in the homeland quest, and neither, of course, have the Germans been the sole contributors. The variety of methods used, and the massive differences of opinion expressed over the years, are truly dizzying. Mallory (1973) has provided an excellent synopsis of some of the principal homeland hypotheses that have surfaced over the last century and a half. Before turning to the Indian responses to all of this, it would be useful to glance at a summary of Mallory's (1973) outline of some of the other more prominent homeland theories (prior to the 1970s) that have been articulated by Western scholars. This will give a clearer picture of the confusion that Indian scholars have had to confront over the decades and will further help set the stage for their responses.

Two Centuries of Homeland Theories

After the discovery of Sanskrit and the birth of comparative philology, many scholars of the eighteenth century and the early nineteenth century, as noted previously, maintained that India was the original homeland. Rask, however, preferred Asia Minor. Alexander Murray held Asia to be original, as did Renan, on the basis of the Indo-Iranian literary material in conjunction with the Bible. John Baldwin opted for Bactria solely on the basis of the Iranian material. Hehn reconstructed an Indo-European Stone Age pastoralist and also situated him in Asia, in contradistinction to Benfey, who felt geological evidence favored Europe as the most ancient abode. Pike, the forerunner of the astronomical approach that will be discussed in chapter 9, believed the Ṛgveda preserved a record of a vernal equinox that occurred in 5000 B.C.E. in Sogdiana.

Penka elaborated on Poesche's racial theories, mentioned previously, and bolstered them with linguistic and archaeological arguments to propose Scandinavia. Charles Morris, also using racial arguments, envisioned a Proto-Indo-European Mongoloid pastoralist from the steppe. Isaac Taylor was the first to use the evidence of both archaeology and loanwords, which he believed was indicative of Indo-European origins in Finland. D'Arbois de Jubainville felt cognate Indo-European words such as *house* and *door* indicated a sedentary life (as opposed to the usually depicted Indo-European pastoral-nomadic one) that flourished near the Oxus River adjacent to the great Asian civilizations. The anthropologist Brinton felt the Indo-European languages were the result of the coalescence of a variety of languages situated in western Europe, T. H. Huxley considered the Indo-European speakers to be blond dolicocephalics living between the North Sea and the Ural Mountains, while Otto Schrader, rejecting the racial input, situated the homeland in south Russia which could accommodate both agriculture and pastoralism. Schmidt foreshadowed some recent scholars by suggesting that the Indo-Europeans must have been adjacent to Babylon based on a shared duodecimal numbering system. This idea was opposed by Hirt, who preferred the Baltic area on the basis of linguistic paleontology.

Ripley's work, at the turn of the twentieth century, characterized the increasing use and promotion of archaeological evidence in homeland proposals; he was followed by Paape, who typified the rising vigor of the German *Urheimat* (original homeland) school.

Whitney disagreed with the latter, arguing that Germany was too cold and forested, preferring south Russia. This was also the area of choice for Sigmund Feist on the grounds of linguistic paleontology. Harold Bender differed somewhat and considered Lithuania more suitable, since Lithuanian was the most conservative Indo-European language, while P. Giles, who also believed that the Proto-Indo-European were agriculturists and not nomads, felt that they were more likely to have come from Hungary. Gordon Childe, however, felt that agriculture was a European innovation and located the homeland in southwest Russia on archaeological grounds. A. H. Sayce, who was to change his mind repeatedly, situated the homeland in Asia Minor based on the Hittite evidence in contrast to T. Sulimirski, another forerunner of Gimbutas, who saw the Indo-Europeans as Russian nomads who buried their dead in burrows called *kurgans*, and who invaded Europe—a theory supported by Georges Poisson.

I have discussed the partiality of German scholars to a German homeland in opposition to an eastern or steppe one, and such views were further propagated by Walter Schulz, on the grounds of central European archaeological continuity; by Gustav Neckel, on the basis of the proto-Indo-European steed being the European horse; by Hans Heger, on archaeological evidence; and by Fritz Flor, also on theories of horse-riding origins. Wilhelm Koppers disrupted the Germanic tendencies somewhat by advocating West Turkestan as a homeland on the basis of the Indo-European connections with the Altaic peoples, only to be succeeded by Julius Pokorny, who defended a Central Europe homeland on the old grounds that Germany showed no evidence of non-Indo-European substratum influence and on other evidence.

C. Uhlenbeck located the homeland in the Aral-Caspian steppes on grammatical grounds, while N. S. Trubetzkoy rejected the whole concept of a protolanguage, preferring to speculate that the originally different Indo-European languages had developed similarities through geographic proximity. Anything approaching a homeland, he believed, would be found in an area nearer the Finno-Ugrics, due to the structural analogues of Indo-European with the Uralic and Caucasian families. Stuart Mann predicated a north or northeast European homeland on the grounds of comparative folklore, not far from where Ernst Meyer decided to situate his nonnomadic, pig-keeping, sedentary Indo-Europeans. Anton Scherer tried to satisfy everybody by proposing a large area that stretched west from the Urals, right across central and south Russia, and up to the Baltic, since this was an area that could accommodate both nomadic and sedentary cultures. Wilhelm Schmidt narrowed this area back down to central Asia on the grounds of the domesticated horse; Georg Solta, like Trubetzkoy, also rejected the whole concept of a protolanguage; and Thieme resurrected the German *Urheimat* position, again on the basis of linguistic paleontology.

Alfons Nehring analyzed the non-Indo-European influences that he thought supported an Indo-European origin somewhere between the Altaic people and the Caucasus; Hugh Hencken, like Scherer, proposed a large compromise zone in southeast Europe and southwest Russia, while Weriand Merlingen supported Schrader's thesis, and Gustav Schwantes returned to the German *Urheimat* theme. Bosch-Gimpera and G. Devoto advocated the Danubian cultures of central Europe as the most likely homeland candidates, to which Wolfgang Schmid concurred, proposing a Baltic Homeland on the grounds of Hans Krahe's work on river hydronomy (which suggested that the rivers in Europe had old Indo-European names).

The original Aryans have been reconstructed as being nomadic pastoralists, sedentary agriculturists, dolichocephalic, brachycephalic, blond and fair, and brown-haired and dark. The Indo-European homeland has been located and relocated everywhere from the North Pole to the South Pole, to China. It has been placed in South India, central India, North India, Tibet, Bactria, Iran, the Aral Sea, the Caspian Sea, the Black Sea, Lithuania, the Caucasus, the Urals, the Volga Mountains, south Russia, the steppes of central Asia, Asia Minor, Anatolia, Scandinavia, Finland, Sweden, the Baltic, western Europe, northern Europe, central Europe, and eastern Europe.

Quite apart from the massive divergence of opinion among different scholars, on occasion even individual scholars cannot make up their own minds. In 1875, A. H. Sayce could "assume it has been proved that their original home was in Asia, and more particularly in the high plateau of the Hindu Kush" (389). In 1883, he was "much attracted by the hypothesis of Poesche which makes the Rokytno marshes the scene" (385). According to Sayce, "the evidence now shows that the districts in the neighbourhood of the Baltic were those from which the Aryan languages first radiated . . . though Penka rejects it with disdain" (385). Four years later Sayce (1887) had changed his mind to "conceive Dr. Penka to have been . . . right in identifying 'the Aryans' with the dolicocephalic inhabitants of central and North-western Europe . . . and thus remove the necessity of our falling back on Dr. Poesche's theory, which traces . . . the white race to the Rokytno marshes of Russia" (52–53). The same man ended up convinced, in 1927, that the facts revealed that Asia Minor was the actual homeland (Mallory 1989, 143).

Not everyone has been lured by the quest for the Indo-Europeans; there has been a long history in the West of scholars repeatedly voicing criticisms over the years: "The 'problem' is primarily in the head of Indo-Europeanists: It is a problem of interpretative logic and ideology. We have seen that one primarily places the IE's in the north if one is German, . . . in the east if one is Russian, and in the middle if, being Italian or Spanish, one has no chance of competing for the privilege" (Demoule 1980, 120). Earlier still, in 1948, Hankins articulated the level of disillusionment in his time:

> Skepticism in scholarly circles grew rapidly after 1880. The obvious impossibility of actually locating the Aryan homeland; the increasing complexity of the problem with every addition to our knowledge of prehistoric cultures; the even more remote possibility of ever learning anything conclusive regarding the traits of the mythical "original Aryans"; the increasing realization that all the historical peoples were much mixed in blood and that the role of a particular race in a great mélange of races, though easy to exaggerate, is impossible to determine, the ridiculous and humiliating spectacle of eminent scholars subordinating their interests in truth to the inflation of racial and national pride—all these and many other reasons led scholars to declare either that the Aryan doctrine was a figment of the professional imagination or that it was incapable of clarification because the crucial evidence was lost, apparently forever. (265)

Even Mallory (1989), who has been the most prolific scholar in quest of the Indo-Europeans, is moved to quip: "One does not ask 'where is the Indo-European homeland?' but rather 'where do they put it now?'" (143). He concludes his summary of the various Indo-European homeland theories by noting that "the cynical have been tempted to describe it as the phlogiston of prehistoric research" (1973, 60).

Present-Day Homeland Hypotheses

Gimbutas and the Kurgan Theory

Interest in the Indo-European homeland problem seemed to wane during the decades after the war. Sherratt (1988) wonders whether perhaps many prehistorians avoided this issue in reaction to the political abuses of archaeology under the Nazis and the explicit racism that was the ultimate outcome of the Romantic search for ethnic origins in Germany (459). The last two decades or so, on the other hand, have seen an explosion of renewed interest. However, even after two hundred years of intense speculation, there is still no significant consensus regarding "where they put it now"; the situation has hardly changed. Referring to the panoply of present-day opinions, Mallory's (1997) most recent conclusion is: "We have different sub-regions of an early IE world, scattered in space from the Baltic to Anatolia and east across the European steppe. . . . To unify these disparate geographical elements together into a single 'unified theory' seems to be as distant to those seeking such a goal in Indo-European studies as it is for physicists" (117).

Two or three current theories will illustrate the extent to which methods and conclusions vary. The Caucasus area has received considerable attention as a likely homeland, although this proposal is receiving increasing criticism of late. Marijas Gimbutas, for well over half a century, has proposed an Uralic/Volgan steppe homeland. This is based on an archaeological culture labeled the Kurgan culture, which is distinguished by a specific type of burial mound found in that region (*kurgan* is the Slavic and Turkic term for 'barrow'). Gimbutas argues that this culture can be adequately correlated with Indo-European culture as revealed by comparative philology.[13] Crucial to Gimbutas's theory is the thesis that these Indo-Europeans were mounted warriors with male-associated

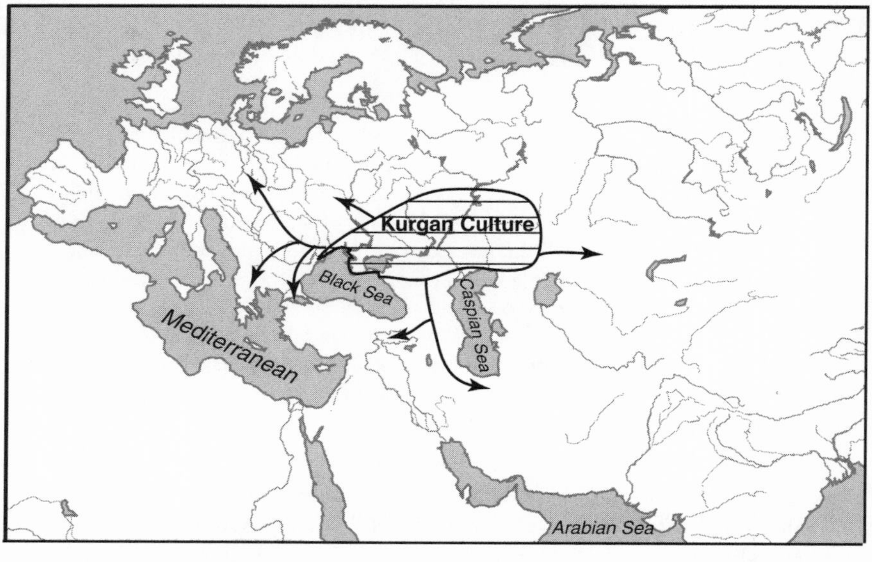

Gimbutas's Indo-European homeland.

thrusting weapons who, being the first people to domesticate the horse, used their martial advantages to impose their culture on their neighbors in Old Europe. Gimbutas's reading of the archaeological record reveals a dramatic upheaval in the life of the peaceful, egalitarian, agrarian, matriarchal and artistic Europeans of the fifth and fourth millennium B.C.E. as a result of these violent Kurgan intrusions.

As Mallory (1989) points out, however, scholars have argued that "almost all of the arguments for invasion and cultural transformations are far better explained without reference to Kurgan expansions, and most of the evidence presented so far is either totally contradicted by other evidence or is the result of gross misinterpretation of the cultural history of . . . Europe" (185). Refreshingly undogmatic about the whole homeland enterprise, he nonetheless holds that her homeland is the least problematic of the various options.[14] Anthony (1995b) Although also accepting the steppe as the Indo-European Homeland, claims that Gimbutas's Old-Europe theories would have passed unnoticed had they not caught the attention of ecofeminists. He points out that many Copper Age settlements in Old Europe, Gimbutas's "gynocentric utopias," were actually heavily fortified, and some of the weapons in the Kurgan graves were probably imports from "peaceful" Europe. He accuses Gimbutas of taking archaeological items out of their proper context and finds deforestation and environmental degradation a more likely culprit for the transformation of Old Europe. Schmitt (1974), too, has pointed out objections to Gimbutas's methods: "Here is the radical error: With the methods of linguistic paleontology anything may be proved as Proto-Indo-European, but it can *not* be proved as *typically* Proto-Indo-European. Such reconstructions do not exclude the possibility that this thing, institution or whatever it may be, may have existed also in other language families" (283).

Renfrew (1987) is also completely dismissive of the validity of linguistic paleontology, as many scholars have been, since he feels that this method could accommodate "almost any homeland theory" (86). Through this perspective, since the south Russian homeland was originally established on the grounds of linguistic paleontology, any attempt to examine the archaeological evidence in an area defined by a suspect method is itself a priori suspect. Moreover, he notes (1999) that the earliest evidence of mounted warriors is not until 1000 B.C.E., far too late for Gimbutas's theory and hence "without such military possibilities, the whole explanatory basis for the supposed 'kurgan' invasion at the beginning of the Bronze Age disappears" (268). Zimmer (1990b) points out that while the Proto-Indo-Europeans knew the horse, there is no proof that they necessarily knew the domesticated horse, and there is no linguistic evidence that they fought on horseback (316–317). Renfrew (1998) pursues this line of argument by arguing that anyway the horse was not of military significance in Europe until around 1000 B.C.E.; during the Iron Age, which "undermine[s] the principal rationale sustaining the 'Kurgan Migration' theory for the origin of the Indo-European languages" (207).

From a completely different angle, Dolgopolsky (1990–93) states that the "loan connections between IE and Semitic prove that speakers of proto-IE and proto-Semitic lived in territorial vicinity, which would have been impossible had we accepted Gimbutas's (and Mallory's) hypothesis of the Proto-Caspian steppes as the homeland of proto-IE" (244). Moreover, he notes that there are no loans from Proto-Indo-European into the Finno-Ugric languages or vice versa (although there are many from the later Indo-Iranian languages), which he believes should have been the case had the Proto-Indo-European been neighbors with these languages in the Pontic-Caspian steppes (245). Renfrew can find no convincing evidence for the motive behind such a Kurgan spread: he notes that central and western Europe are not really suited to nomad pastoralism.[15] He also rejects what he considers to be a migrationist view—a view, as we have seen, going back to Kossina, that treats any innovation in the archaeological record, such as a new pottery form or decorative style, as indicative of a migration of people and a displacement of language. Finally, in a response to his own critics, he points out that while the language of the Kurgan people may well have been Indo-European, "there is no logic in the inference that the belief system of the previous 'Old Europe' phase need be non-Indo-European simply because its iconography is different from what follows" (Renfrew 1990, 23).

The most recent critique of Gimbutas at the time of this writing argues that her homeland theory is completely incompatible with the linguistic evidence: "Although the hypothesis claims to have answered the question of the origins of Proto-Indo-European (PIE), an inherently *linguistic* construct, there are serious problems with this hypothesis from a linguist's point of view" (Krell 1998, 267). Krell compiles lists of items of flora, fauna, economy, and technology that archaeology has accounted for in the Kurgan culture and compares it with lists of the same categories as reconstructed by traditional historical-Indo-European linguistics (a method which will be discussed in detail in chapter 6). She finds major discrepancies between the two.[16] She also underlines the fact, which will be dealt with at length in later chapters, that we cannot presume that the reconstructed term for 'horse', for example, referred to the *domesticated* equid in the protoperiod just because it did in later times. It could originally have referred to a wild equid, a possibility that would undermine the mainstay of Gimbutas's arguments that the Kurgan culture first domesticated the horse and used this new technology to spread surrounding areas, thus spreading the Indo-European languages.

Krell (1998) further points out that the Proto-Indo-European had an agricultural terminology and not merely a pastoral one; "thus, one can hardly argue, based on the linguistic data, that Gimbutas' Kurgan economy is unmistakenly reflected in PIE" (274). As for technology, "there are also equally plausible reconstructions such as **nāu* . . . which suggest knowledge of navigation, a technology quite untypical of Gimbutas' Kurgan society" (274). Krell concludes that

> Gimbutas seems to first establish a Kurgan hypothesis, based on purely archaeological observations, and then proceeds to create a picture of the PIE homeland and subsequent dispersal which fits neatly over her archaeological findings. The problem is that in order to do this, she has had to be rather selective in her use of linguistic data, as well as in her interpretation of that data. This is putting the cart before the horse. Such an unsystematic approach should have given her linguistic proponents real cause for questioning the relevance of her theory, especially if one considers that, by virtue of its nature, the study of PIE is first and foremost a matter for linguistic, not archaeological investigation. (279–280)

Renfrew and the West Anatolian Homeland

Rather than an aggressive, mounted seminomad from the steppes, Renfrew (1987) constructs a peaceful, sedentary agriculturist from Anatolia as his Indo-European par excellence. No two accounts could be more at odds than Gimbutas's and Renfrew's. For the

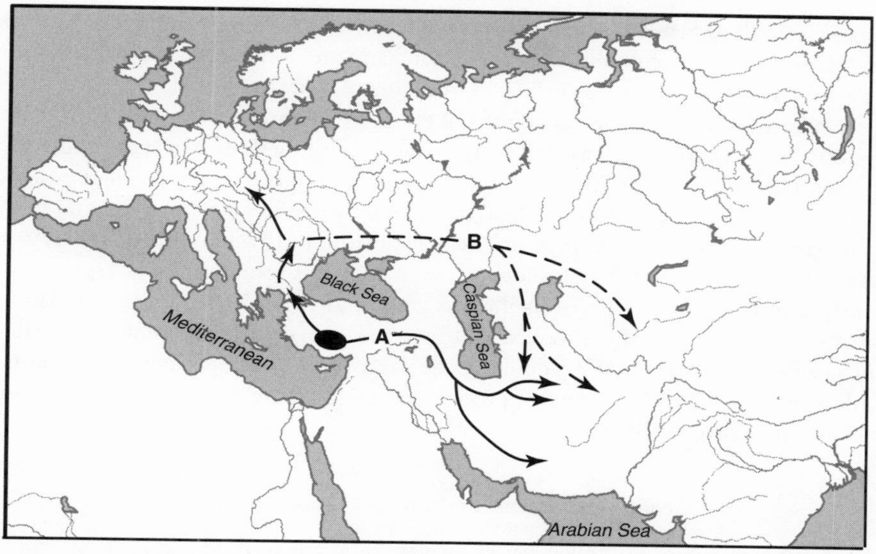

Renfrew's Indo-European homeland with two hypotheses (A & B) for the trajectory of Indo-Iranian.

latter, the spread of the Indo-European languages was achieved not by Gimbutas's horse-riding warriors but by the gradual spread of farming techniques. Moreover, faulting the circular reasoning that he feels is employed in support of the fifth millennium B.C.E. date commonly assigned to the united Proto-Indo-Europeans, Renfrew proposes a date around 7000 B.C.E., based on paleoethnobotanical dates for the introduction of farming into Europe from Anatolia. Quite apart from his assignment of a much earlier date than his peers are comfortable with, his theory has been particularly criticized on linguistic grounds. Place-names, for example, are the most conservative and durable part of a language and are generally retained even by other intruding linguistic groups that might superimpose themselves on an area, yet place-names in Anatolia are unanalyzable as Indo-European. Crossland (1988) wonders why, if Anatolia were the original homeland, the Indo-European language discovered there, Hittite, had so little impact on neighboring languages and was itself a minority language heavily influenced by the non-Indo-European languages in the environs such as Hurrian and Hattic. Renfrew has also been criticized for not accounting for the language connections between Finno-Ugric and Indo-European, which, if correct, would suggest the neighboring relationships of these languages in the Volga Valley.

Zimmer (1990a, 319) notes that there are no words reconstructable in Proto-Indo-European for wheat and barley, Renfrew's basic agricultural crops. This objection was elaborated upon by Haarmann (1994), who notes that Proto-Indo-European would have had a full-fledged agricultural vocabulary in the protolanguage were Renfrew's theory to hold good. This is not the case, since the European languages and the Indo-Iranian ones seem to have developed separate sets of agricultural terms after the dispersal. Haarman also notes that were Renfrew correct any such hypothetical Proto-Indo-European agricultural terms would have been borrowed by language families adjacent to

Anatolia, such as Semitic, which is not the case. Also, such terms would have surfaced in Greek, but the agricultural terms in this language are non-Indo-European. Archaeology, too, does not support an intrusion into Greece from Anatolia.[17]

Lamberg-Karlovsky (1988, 2) points out that if agriculture was invented by Indo-Europeans, then people in a broad area from the Sinai to the Iranian Plateau must have spoken Indo-European at 7000 B.C.E. at the very latest. Moreover, the earliest domestication of cereals began at least by 9000 B.C.E., not in Renfrew's 7000 B.C.E. and in the Natufian culture best known from archaeological work in Israel not in Anatolia. As far as he is concerned, "the complex interaction of *numerous* communities . . . spread over a *large* area of the Near East forms the background to an understanding of agricultural origins, . . . a process which took *several* thousand years, involved numerous distinct archaeological cultures that no doubt spoke a variety of different languages." He has little sympathy for such a complex process being "simplified by Professor Renfrew to the ludicrous formula 7000 B.C.E. Anatolia = farming = Indo-Europeans" (2).

Gamkrelidze and Ivanov and the East Anatolian Homeland

An Anatolian homeland, albeit based on very different methods and located farther east and much later than Renfrew's homeland has received the support of the linguists Thomas V. Gamkrelidze and V. V. Ivanov over the years (1983a, b, 1985, 1990,a b, 1995). They utilize the evidence of loanwords, particularly Semitic ones, to situate their homeland adjacent to the Middle East—not far from where, well over two hundred years ago, James Parsons had put the descendants of Noah. Using linguistic paleontology, these linguists have reconstructed a mountainous landscape for the Indo-European homeland, based on the many cognate words for high mountains, mountain lakes, and

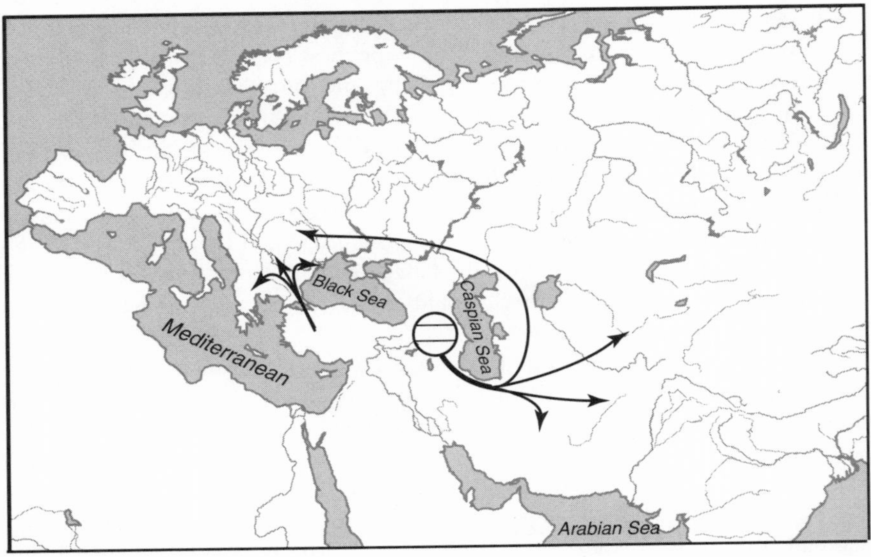

Gamkrelidze and Ivanov's Indo-European homeland.

rapid rivers flowing from mountain sources. They argue that this is incompatible with the plains of central Europe but quite suitable for the area around eastern Anatolia backed by the Caucasus. In addition, Gamkrelidze and Ivanov present a much warmer, and exotic, southern landscape and climate—replete with monkeys and elephants—than Gimbutas's cold, austere, northern scenario.

However, many of the Semitic loanwords that are fundamental to Gamkrelidze and Ivanov's situating of the homeland next to the Near East have been challenged by D'iakonov, who defends a Balkan-Carpathian homeland and finds particular problems with the details of the tribe migrations in their model. Manczak (1990) points out that the Indo-European language Armenian, which is spoken more or less in Gamkrelidze and Ivanov's putative homeland, shows signs of massive substratum influence, indicating that it was not indigenous to the area. Moreover, the archaeologists—such as Gimbutas and Mallory—feel archaeological evidence has not been sufficiently accounted for in Gamkrelidze and Ivanov's model, which is primarily linguistic, and that there is insufficient archaeological evidence accompanying the postulated spread of Indo-European languages from this area. Where Gimbutas relies almost exclusively on archaeology and demonstrates a panoramic mastery over a mass of archaeological minutiae in her series of articles, Gamkrelidze and Ivanov awe their readers with an encyclopedic exhibition of comparative linguistic detail in a thousand-page tome that requires a separate volume just to incorporate the bibliography and index. Yet these two scholars have reconstructed dramatically different locations and cultures for the homeland. Still another recent and innovative theory situating the homeland in Bactria, that of Nichols, will be discussed at length in later chapters.

Conclusion

Scholars hardly agree on even the most basic details of the Indo-European—any more in the present than they did in the past. Such lack of scholarly consensus on even basic points perhaps epitomizes the history and culture of the Indo-European homeland quest more than most other comparable undertakings. Typically, a convincing and detailed proposal offered in one field (e.g., archaeology) is undermined by evidence from another (i.e., linguistics) and vice versa. Any attempt to isolate or highlight one aspect of the data as paramount is inevitably countered by contradictory conclusions produced by other factors. A convincing picture has yet to emerge from the totality of evidence despite significant advances in the relevant disciplines.[18]

Even within disciplines, archaeologists such as Renfrew, Gimbutas, and Mallory, just like their predecessors in the last century or so, significantly disagree with each other despite their sharing a common field. As for dialogue across disciplines, that is, between archaeologists and linguists, even when a common language can be agreed upon, basic points of reconstructed Indo-European culture are often not. Gimbutas's (1985) reconstructed Proto-Indo-European, as noted, is a seminomadic pastoralist: "Neither archaeology nor linguistic evidence supports the hypothesis that the proto-Indo-European culture was in the stage of developed agriculture" (186). In the same journal, the linguist D'iakonov (1985) states: "The Proto-Indo-Europeans were not nomads: their well-developed agriculture and social terminology testifies against this; and so does history" (148).

Both linguists and archaeologists sometimes claim primacy for their discipline over locating the Indo-Europeans. The linguist Rüdiger Schmitt (1974) notes that several prehistorians have assigned a variety of quite different homelands to the Indo-Europeans that all seem to fit the presently available linguistic data reasonably well. Since the Indo-Europeans are a linguistic concept, he argues that it is ultimately meaningless to search for archaeological evidence of their existence until linguistics and philology can narrow down their whereabouts much more precisely. Only then should archaeology be called in to identify them materially. Otherwise, "prehistorians have no difficulty in finding evidence in many locations which will fit the existing linguistic data" (285). Gimbutas (1974), despite giving some token recognition to the "gold mine" of two centuries' worth of linguistic research, launches her response (which deals almost exclusively with archaeological material, as do all her publications) with an aggressive claim: "It is quite obvious that the solution of the PIE origins—on a spatial and temporal basis—is in the hands of archaeologists" (289). Responding to this remark, in turn, another linguist, Dolgopolsky, who also locates the homeland in Anatolia on linguistic grounds, retorts: "I completely disagree with Gimbutas' statement. . . . It is, on the contrary, far from self-evident how archaeologists utilizing the non-linguistic means at their disposal can determine *what language* the bearers of some Pit-Grave culture or Battle-Axe culture *spoke*" (1987, 7). He continues to give rein to his impatience: "It is here maintained that the linguists are ultimately responsible for determining the geographical and cultural parameters of the PIE community, and that any attempt on the part of the archaeologists to reach a conclusion without due consideration of all the relevant linguistic data is liable to lead them into serious error" (7). Linguistics must first do the groundwork: "Once the spatial and temporal parameters of the putative homeland have been identified on the basis of *linguistic* evidence, the archaeologist can set about the task of deciding which civilisation . . . can be plausibly associated with PIE" (7; *italics in original)*.

In addition to this divide within disciplines that is evident from the disagreements between archaeologists and archaeologists, and between linguists and linguists, and to the cross-disciplinary divide between archaeologists and linguists, there is also a massive East-West divide of which few in the West seem even aware. Until very recently, Western scholars have paid little or no attention to, or are completely unaware of, the reaction of scholars outside Western intellectual circles to the Indo-European debate. Western scholars, whose primary emphasis and concern, at least historically, have been the origins of Western civilization, have renegotiated and reconfigured the pre- and protohistory of other nations such as India as by-products of their investigations. Yet, for the most part, they have not been exposed to the concerns over, and responses to, their formulations expressed by the native scholars from those very countries. India, in particular, initiated the whole field of Indo-European studies when it's language and rich culture were "discovered" by Western scholars. Yet opinions from that country, especially if in disagreement with the more forceful voices in the West, are poorly understood or cursorily dismissed. This has deprived Western scholars of alternative views that might force them to question their own inherited assumptions—assumptions that have not always been shared by those outside mainstream Western academic spheres of influence who have filtered the Indo-European problem through different historical, religio-cultural, social, and political mind-sets. It has likewise deprived these Indian scholars of valuable feedback from their Western peers. The following chapters will attempt to help bridge this divide by articulating some of the more coherent, sober, and rational responses to the Indo-European homeland problem that have been expressed by intellectuals from the Indian subcontinent over the years.[19]

As we turn to some of the reactions to this massive European intellectual enterprise, it should not be surprising when some Indian scholars, trying to make sense of all this, complain:

> Instead of letting us know definitely and precisely where the so-called original home of the Aryans lay, they drag us into a maze of conjectures clouded by the haze of presumptions. The whole subject of the Aryan problem is a farrago of linguistic speculations or archaeological imaginations complicated by racial prejudices and chauvinistic xenophobia. It is high time we extricate ourselves from this chaos of bias and belief. (Prakash, 1966, xliv)

Given the history of the Indo-European problem, it seems hardly surprising that many Indian scholars have found themselves incapable of being co-opted by the prolific array of theories produced by their Western colleagues. In a remarkably penetrating and well-informed critique of the whole field written in the 1930s, when German Aryanism was in full swing, B. N. Dutta (1936) states: "'Germanism' arose amidst the peculiar political condition of nineteenth century Germany. . . . it has become the political shibboleth of the occidental nations. . . . we cannot see any reason why, in India, we should pin our anthropological faith in [it]" (238). Criticizing the "slave psychology of the Indian mind," Dutta continues:

> We find that pan-Germanic bias is in possession of the field of enquiry of the ancient Indian civilization and Indian scholars are imbibing it through the medium of the English language. In the field of anthropology, "Germanism" reigns supreme in India, the Indians, . . . seeing the outside world only through the English language, have accepted the views of the "Master" people as the only truth. . . . And we glory in it because it is the gift of the "Master" people. (247)

Such comments do not necessarily reveal some antischolarly quirk of a traditional Hindu mind-set. On the contrary, I have referred to a history of cynicism in Western intellectual circles over this issue. I hope, this chapter has suggested why, historically at least, there might be some very good reasons for Indian scholars to be suspicious of the whole enterprise, and of the ability of those engaged in it to make authoritative pronouncements on the early history of the Indian subcontinent and the Indo-Aryans. I can perhaps set the stage and the tone for the next chapters by concluding this brief survey of the history of the Indo-European homeland problem with some sympathy for another disillusioned response voiced from somewhere in South India—one that is quite representative of the Indigenous Aryan opinion of the whole Indo-European homeland enterprise:

> For nearly two centuries the investigations went on, and voluminous works were written on the subject. The net result of their investigations ended in failure, and nothing definite was settled either in the sphere of language or race. What they finally left behind is the fiction of Ursprache [original language] with a false Urvolk [original people], who are found located in an equally nebulous Urheimat [homeland]. (C. Pillai 1940, 2)

2

Early Indian Responses

It took considerable time for Indian literati to come to grips with the implications of the Indo-European debates raging in Europe. Kopf (1969) has outlined the various avenues through which European learning first became accessible to the Indian public.[1] There was, of course, the nationalist response, which has been the element of most interest to scholars studying Indian reactions to the colonial construction of ancient Indian history. The nationalists were quick to incorporate Orientalist portrayals of ancient India into their political agenda. As we have seen, the Orientalists, despite renegotiating certain historical and temporal details, had shown genuine appreciation for the achievements of the Aryan past, were quite happy to defer to the ancient Hindu Aryans as more civilized and advanced than their ancient European Aryan contemporaries, and generally contributed to a depiction of a previous golden age in which Hindus could take vicarious pride.

As was the case in the West, there were all sorts of reactions to, and appropriations of, the discovery of a shared Aryan pedigree from the Indian subcontinent in popular, political, and religious discourse. The first section of this chapter will briefly touch upon nineteenth- and early twentieth-century nationalistic co-options of the Aryan theory in terms of its applicability for Indian relations with the colonial power and for internal power dynamics among competing sets of interests among Indians themselves. This section could of course be the subject of a full treatment in its own right, so at the risk of not doing sufficient justice to an important topic, I will extract a brief selection of these reactions to provide something of a parallel to the Aryan discourse in Europe during the nineteenth and early twentieth centuries. The socio-political context of the modern period in India will be discussed in more depth in chapter 13. The second section of this chapter will describe the first stirrings of opposition to the theory itself, which were inaugurated by prominent religious leaders.

Hindu Nationalist Responses

To many Hindus, the concept of Arya served primarily as a patriotic rallying cry. Raychaudhuri (1988) outlines this immediate, and more euphoric, level of reflexive popular response:

> The Hindu self-image had received a moral boost from . . . the writings of Professor Max Mueller. His linguistic studies stressed the common origin of Indo-European languages and the Aryan races. These theories, translated into popular idiom, were taken to mean that the master race and the subject population were descended from the same Aryan ancestors. The result was a spate of Aryanism. Books, journals, societies rejoiced in the Aryan identity. . . . Educated young men, in large numbers, affected a demonstrative reversion to the ways of their forefathers—with fasts, pigtails, well-displayed sacred threads, and other stigmata of Hindu orthodoxy. The name "Aryan" appeared in every possible and impossible context—in the titles of books as much as in the names of drug stores. (34–35)

As outlined in the first chapter, Max Müller (1884) had been very influential in introducing the theme of shared ancestry in India: "We recognize in Ram Mohan Roy's visit to England the meeting again of the two great branches of the Aryan race, after they had been separated so long that they had lost all recollection of their common origin, common language, and common faith" (11). Understandably, not all Hindus were about to be taken in by this type of rhetoric; Müller himself quotes a "native writer" from the *Calcutta Indian Mirror* (September 20, 1874) who exclaimed: "We were niggers at one time. We now become brethren" (quoted in Chakrabarti, 1997, 99). Some had grown wary of Aryan discourses. But many Hindus, such as Tukaram Tatya, took the opportunity to point out that "the difference between the European and the Asiatic will be held to be of little moment" when consideration was directed to the common Aryan bond. After all, since "the Hindus represent the older branch of the great Aryan stock, . . . our European brethren should look upon us as filled with the same blood" (93).

There have been a number of studies outlining the various nuances in the relationship between the Orientalist construction of the Aryan past and the Indian nationalist movement (e.g., Leopold 1970). Scholars have long pointed out how early Orientalist and Romantic themes such as "India was the cradle of the arts and sciences," "Egypt, Greece, and Rome were her pupils and recipients," and "The Hindus were among the first civilized nations when the nations of Europe had hardly risen above the hunting or nomad state" were readily appropriated by Indian intellectuals, since they offered some level of consolation to a subjected people (McCully 1966, 245–248). Moreover, Hindu Aryanism could not just be vaunted as evidence of equality with the colonial rulers but as proof of the Hindus' moral superiority: British despotism and materialism were portrayed as deviations from Aryan principles (Leopold 1970, 278). Hindu reformers such as Vivekananda (1970–73) felt that it was the western Aryans that were being given the opportunity to learn from their Hindu Aryan brethren (i.e., more specifically, from himself): "Which of us ever dreamt that a descendant of the old Indian Aryans, by dint of Tapas, would prove to the learned people of England and America the superiority of the ancient Indian religion over other creeds?" (3:350). Nor was this exchange just to take place on Indian soil as a result of Western initiative; if the Western Aryans had overpowered India materially, the Indian Aryans were destined to conquer the West spiritually:

> Two curious nations there have been—sprung of the same race . . . the ancient Hindu and the Greek. The Indian Aryan . . . became introspective. The analysis of his own mind was the great theme of the Indo-Aryan. With the Greek, on the other hand, . . . his mind naturally went outside. It wanted to analyze the external world. . . . Today the ancient Greek is meeting the ancient Hindu on the soil of India. . . . We must be always ready to sit at the feet of all. . . . At the same time we must not forget that we have also to teach a great lesson to the world. . . . the gift of India is the gift of religion and philosophy, and wisdom and spirituality. . . . we must go out, must conquer the world through our spirituality and philosophy. (Vivekananda 1970–73, 3:269–273)[2]

Such sentiments were typical of the time. The Theosophists like Olcott also contributed to notions of Hindu Aryan superiority in their addresses to groups such as the Arya Samaj: "Recognizing as we do the Aryan source of our race and of its knowledge of things terrestrial and celestial, we, Theosophists will *feel proud to be permitted to call ourselves your disciples*" (Sarda 1946, 529; italics in original). Keshub Chandra Sen ([1901–4] 1954) later echoed similar themes when recognizing that "in the advent of the English nation in India, we see a reunion of parted cousins, the descendants of two different families of the Aryan race." Each had a valid role to play: "India in her present fallen condition seems destined to sit at the feet of England for many long years, to learn Western art and science. And, on the other hand, behold England sits at the feet of hoary-headed India to study the ancient literature of this country" (325). Unlike some of his other religious contemporaries, Sen did not hesitate to stress the duties Aryan kinship involved that were incumbent on the materialistic side of the family: "May England . . . [give] us as much of the light of the West as lies in her power! That is her mission in India. May she fulfill it nobly and honourably. Let England give us her industry and arts, her exact sciences and her practical philosophy" (325–326). His brother was equally idealistic: "The Hindu and the Englishman are brothers! . . . every brother man is learning to recognize in the face of his fellow-creatures the image of his first forefathers. . . . Let that unity be the groundwork of future peace and brotherhood" (Leopold, 273).

Not all were prepared to acknowledge the material advantages that might be gained from the English Aryan brethren, however. Although K. C. Sen (1954) had waxed eloquent about the benefits derivable from gallant Aryan England—"Fallen [Aryan] India cried for help, and lo! at Heaven's bidding England hastened to her rescue" (126)—others saw things differently. The very first line of Lajpat Rai's book *England's Debt to India* (1917) is "India once was rich." In contrast to Sen's rhapsody, despite appropriating Orientalist tropes of previous golden ages "when Greece and Italy, those cradles of European civilization, nursed only the tenants of a wilderness [and] India was the seat of wealth and grandeur" (4), Rai was adamant that the British conquest of India had been "the most insidious, most prolonged and most devastating to the conquered" (319). In this narrative, England had plundered her Aryan sibling, not "hastened to her rescue."

The more moderate Gokhale (1920), who was prepared to allow that other members of the Aryan family "brought their own treasure into the common stock" (1023), also appropriated Orientalist discourse: "The people of India are an ancient race who had attained a high degree of civilization long before the ancestors of European nations understood what civilization was. India has long been the birthplace of great religions. She was also the cradle and long home of literature and philosophy, of science and arts" (925). Dayananda Saraswati refused to recognize any Hindu Aryan debt to Europe even on a material level—everything came from India: "The people of Egypt, Greece or the continent of Europe were without a trace of learning before the spread of Knowledge from India" (238).

The construction of a golden past is hardly unique to India. The development of nationalisms almost invariably involves the creation of a sense of continuity between the past and the present. This past is mined for material with which to construe a sense of historic identity, unity, glory, and continuity to inspire political action in the present—Hobsbawn's "invention of tradition." Obviously, these themes offer hope for a future return to an idyllic state once real-life political obstacles are surmounted by adoption of a nationalist agenda. Bipan Chandra (1984) has argued that, on the one side, the nationalist leaders needed a theme with instant psychological appeal that could inculcate the idea of nationalism in the masses without alarming the imperialist powers; on the other, the British encouraged this sense of identification with an idyllic spiritual Hindu past so that the de facto material British present would not be jeopardized.

Just as the Aryan connection was configured to support a wide variety of domestic and colonial agendas by Europeans, it surfaced in a variety of ways among Indians in their internal negotiations with each other, in addition to their dealings with the external imperial power. The Aryan-Dravidian dichotomy was put to political use both by Brahman elitists in the North and by Tamilian separatist voices in the South who were quick to capitalize on the idea of Aryan invasions. From the former camp, for example, Ranade approved of the derogatory descriptions made by Western scholars like Abbe Dubois of the abominable practices extant in the South. In his view this situation occurred because Aryan Brahman influence had "hardly penetrated below the upper classes." The Aryan Brahmanical settlers were "too few in numbers and too weak in power to make any lasting impression beyond their own limited circle upon the multitudes who constituted the aboriginal races in the Southern Peninsula" (Ranade [1915] 1992, 205). The Orientalist view that Hinduism consisted of the morally and culturally superior Aryans who were detrimentally influenced by their merger with the backward and primitive aboriginals was happily regurgitated by many Brahmanas for whom Brahmanical Aryanism corresponded to civilization.

Although not all Hindu nationalists participated in the denigration of Dravidian culture, most did share a strong conviction that India could be saved by returning to the purity of a reconstituted Sanskritic Aryanism. Ramaswamy (1997) and Irschick (1971) outline the reaction to such attitudes that took firm root in the South in the form of neo-Saivism. According to spokesmen from southern castes like the Chetti and Vellala, who were particularly dismayed by the prospect of Brahmanical culture highjacking the emerging nation, "it was not the Dravidians who corrupted a pristine Hinduism. . . . on the contrary, it was Brahmanism and Aryanism that had debased the original Tamil religion and diverted it from its hallowed path of monotheism, rationalism, and egalitarianism into the 'gutters' of polytheism, irrational rituals, and unjust social hierarchies" (Ramaswamy 1997, 29–30). For them the Dravidian religion far predated that of the Aryans, not just in the South, but all over the subcontinent. Śiva was a pre-Aryan Tamilian deity whom the later Aryan intruders had pressed into service in their own pantheon. By the time neo-Śaivism was in full swing in the 1920s, it was not Sanskrit but Tamil that was the world's original, divine language. Others went further: "Most of what is ignorantly called Aryan Philosophy, Aryan Civilization is literally Dravidian or Tamilian at bottom" (Sundaram Pillai, quoted in Irschick, 1971, 152).

Phule, at the end of the nineteenth century, was one of the earliest proponents of such ideas:

> The aboriginals like the *Gonds* and the *Bhils* were the masters (rulers) of this land India, and the Iranians (Aryans) came to India at a later date (as invaders and interlopers). . . . The Aryan invaders (Brahmins) desecrated the sacred sacrifices here, robbed and oppressed the original inhabitants and stigmatised them as "*Dasyus*. . . . The (Indian) Civil Service has been (unjustly) monopolized by the Aryan Brahmans (here) and I beg to submit that it portends a great danger to the whole nation." (Patil 1991, 132)

Others went further. Perhaps the best known detractor of Aryan culture was Periyar E. V. Ramaswami, the leader of the Dravidian movement in South India. Ramaswami despised almost everything that has come to be known as "Hinduism," portraying it as an Aryan imposition on an indigenous Dravidian populace. He exhorted that "the Tamil . . . may liberate himself from the Aryan yoke." In his version of things, "the Aryans, when they invaded the ancient land of the Dravidas, maltreated and dishonoured the latter and had written a false and coloured history wholly fallacious. It is this they call Ramayana wherein Rama and his accomplishes are styled as Aryas, Ravana as Rakshasa." Ramaswami's book is dedicated "to mirror to the Tamils what ascendancy is given to the Aryan and how disgracefully the other communities are deprecated" (Ramaswami, 1981, 2–3). It is Ravana, in Ramaswami's reading of the plot, who is the true Dravidian hero who attempted, unsuccessfully, to save his people from the exploitation and tyranny of the invading Aryans. Ramaswami's mission was dedicated to detaching, both culturally and politically, the life of his fellow Tamils from Brahman-dominated Aryan influence.[3]

Ambedkar also attempted to uplift those who had suffered the most at the hands of Brahmanical Aryan culture: the Sudras. But, unlike Ramaswami, his method was not to attempt to uncouple this social class from an alien Aryan culture. On the contrary, according to Ambedkar (1946), "the *Shudras* were one of the Aryan communities of the Solar race. . . . The *Shudras* did not form a separate *Varna*. They ranked as part of the Kshatriya *Varna* in the Indo-Aryan society" (v). On the basis of a variety of passages, particularly Mahabharata, śanti parvan 38–40 (which describes a Sudra by the name of Paijavana performing a major sacrifice conducted by Brahamanas), Ambedkar argued that the Sudras were once wealthy, glorified and respected by *ṛṣis*, composers of Vedic hymns, and performers of sacrifice. Due to continuous feuding with the Brahmana class, the Sudras inflicted many tyrannies on the Brahmanas, who, in retaliation, denied them the *upanayana* initiation ceremony, causing them to eventually become socially degraded.

Ambedkar, in his book *Who Were the Śudras?* (1946) offers a critique of the philological basis of the Aryan invasion theory, that in places is well-informed and well-argued. He adamantly rejected this theory, which he saw as partly responsible for propagating the erroneous idea that the Sudras were a non-Aryan, indigenous ethnic group. Nonetheless, he does resonate with Periyar Ramaswami on one issue:

> The Aryan race theory is so absurd that it ought to have been dead long ago. But far from being dead, the theory has a considerable hold upon the people. . . . The first explanation is to be found in the support which the theory receives from Brahmin scholars. This is a very strange phenomenon. As Hindus, they should ordinarily show a dislike for the Aryan theory with its express avowal of the superiority of the European races over the Asiatic races. But the Brahmin scholar has not only no such aversion but most willingly hails it. The reasons are obvious. The Brahmin believes in the two nation theory. He claims to be the representative of the Aryan race, and he regards the rest of the Hindus as descendants of the non-Aryans. The theory helps him establish his kinship with the European races and share their arrogance and their superiority. . . . it helps him maintain and justify his overlordship over the non-Brahmins. (76)

Other spokesmen for the most disadvantaged castes had different ideas about how to redress injustices. In their estimation, better gains might be had by accepting the Aryan invasion theory, with all its implications, rather than rejecting it: "Even the present Swarajists [those demanding independence]—the Aryans—were themselves invaders like the Muhammadans and the Europeans. If this country has to be governed by aborigines, all the offices must necessarily be filled by the original inhabitants—the Chamars, the Kurumbas, the Bhils, the Panchamas, etc." (quoted in Irschick, 1971, 154). As far as some in the South were concerned, it was a "misrepresentation to say that the Brahmins belong to the same Indian nation as the non-Brahmins while the English are aliens. . . . Indian Brahmins are more alien to us than Englishmen" (Raghavan, quoted in Irschick, 1971, 158).

In short, although the excesses of Aryan ideology in Europe would be hard to surpass, the Indians themselves were not averse to attempting to extract political mileage from the Aryan theme to support their own agendas. Indeed, in about 1920, one Visnu Sakharam Pandit filed an immigration court case in America, claiming to be a European. Since immigration was closed to Asiatics at that time, the ingenious fellow said he could prove that he was a Brahman and therefore a fellow Aryan. The argument was even entertained for a while, until a California court ruled that the Aryan invasion theory was precisely that: just a theory, and therefore not citable as credible proof for immigration purposes.

The First Reactions: Hindu Religious Leaders

Before moving on to an examination of the historical evidence, I would like to touch on another dimension to the Aryan invasion problem here, in the context of early Indian responses, before addressing it in a more general way in chapter 13. This involves issues of epistemology. After all, the Aryan invasion theory had significant implications for traditional Hindu concepts of history. In traditional Sanskrit sources, the Aryans are portrayed as the enlightened and cultured members of a spiritually advanced civilization, and the Vedas, sacred to millions of Hindus, have traditionally been accepted by the orthodox as spiritual revelations, transmitted by generations of sages through the ages since time immemorial. They contain no reference to a primitive, nomadic origin outside of the subcontinent.

British scholars, particularly the utilitarians, enthusiastically expanding the scientific frontiers of post-Enlightenment, colonial Europe, were in no mind to seriously consider such propositions, especially after science and reason had forced them to relinquish the earliest historical claims of their own biblical tradition: "The Brahmens are the most audacious, and perhaps the most unskillful fabricators, with whom the annals of fable have yet made us acquainted" (Mill [1820] 1975, 34). The remote forefathers of the Indians, these scholars informed their South Asian subjects, were, as Emeneau (1954) was to put it later, "nomadic, barbarous looters and cattle-raiders" (287), not gentle sages teaching spiritual truths. Those very Vedas, they claimed, had been composed by fierce, nomadic tribesmen from Europe or central Asia—the Indo-Europeans, Indo-Germans, or Aryans—who had usurped the Indian subcontinent some time in the second millennium B.C.E. by force of arms, enslaving and exterminating those they encountered in their way. Viewed from within the framework of the rational, nineteenth- and twentieth century European mind-set, these Vedas were hymns of war and booty, and lusty invocations to anthropomorphic gods, not esoteric, divine revelations transmitted by enlightened beings from some imaginary golden age.

Fully committed to this rational and empirical worldview, and fortified by disciplines such as linguistics, epigraphy, numismatics, archaeology, anthropology, philology, and a host of other 'ologies', European scholars presented a historical account of ancient India that was radically different from the narratives that orthodox Hindus had preserved for many centuries. Moreover, these new disciplines were entirely incongruous with traditional epistemology, which was predominantly exegetical. All of a sudden, foreigners such as the Greeks, despite their traditional role as *mlecchās* (foreigners) and barbarians, became one of the only reliable sources for determining Indian chronology. Just as unexpectedly, the dates of heterodox figures such as the Buddha became the cornerstones of any attempt at historical reconstruction. A comparison of the sacred, Vedic language with rude, *mleccha* tongues from outside the sacred *Bhārata varṣa* resulted in the eternal Veda being demoted to a historical evolute from an even earlier language, Proto-Indo-European—a language spoken by coarse, violent horsemen from the barbarian lands far to the northwest of what was recognized by the *śāstras* as the sacred *Āryavarta*. A terminus a quo was established for the eternal Veda, corresponding to the supposed arrival of the Indo-Aryan branch of these Indo-Europeans into India around 1200 B.C.E. These interpretations of India's historical data by Europeans were made public through such institutions as the Royal Asiatic Society of Bengal and quickly became the standard version of ancient history taught in the schools and colleges that soon began to proliferate in British India. Understandably, such reductionistic, philologically derived depictions bruised religious sensitivities. According to Aurobindo (1956):

> In ancient times the Veda was revered as a sacred book of wisdom, a great mass of inspired poetry, the work of Rishis, seers and sages. . . . Truth . . . not of an ordinary but of a divine inspiration and source. Is this all legend and moonshine, or a groundless and even nonsensical tradition? . . . The European scholars . . . went on to make their own etymological explanation of the words, or build up their own conjectural meanings of the Vedic verses and gave a new presentation often arbitrary and imaginative. What they sought for in the Veda was the early history of India, its society, institutions, customs, a civilisation-picture of the times. They invented the theory based on the difference of languages of an Aryan invasion from the north. . . . The Vedic religion was in this account only a worship of Nature-Gods full of solar myths and consecrated by sacrifices and a sacrificial

> liturgy primitive enough in its ideas and contents, and it is these barbaric prayers that are the much vaunted, haloed and apotheosized Veda. (i–iii)

Such Indological depictions of the Vedic times continue to aggravate religious Hindus to this day. As described by Agrawal (1996):

> For thousands of years Hindu society has looked upon the *Vedas* as the fountainhead of all knowledge . . . and the mainstay of Hindu culture. . . . Never have our historical or religious records questioned this fact. And now, suddenly, in the last century or so, it has been propagated that the *Vedas* do not belong to the Hindus, they were the creation of a barbaric horde of nomadic tribes who descended upon North India and destroyed an advanced indigenous civilization. (3)

The first generations of Indians who undertook the challenge of mastering these unfamiliar methods of scholarship did so under the patronage and auspices of the British themselves; thus they were hardly in a position to challenge any of the conclusions being produced. Most of those who did submit to such authority were completely co-opted by the power of European intellectual prowess or dependent on the patronage of European institutions, and so accepted the new version of things unquestioningly. For those who were disposed to critique the colonial version, however, but who were outside the pale of mainstream facilities, the new unfamiliar disciplines such as archaeology and linguistics seemed formidable. This must have created a deep sense of frustration—especially for religious Hindu intellectuals. After all, if the Vedas were being shown as not even accurate with regards to mundane, verifiable, historical, and temporal matters such as the chronology and homeland of the Aryans, why should they be trusted as repositories of ontological knowledge? We can recall Jones's and Maurice's parallel concerns regarding Old Testament historicity when they encountered Indian sources of knowledge (with, in this earlier period, Europe on the defensive): "Either the first chapters of Genesis . . . are true, or the whole Fabrick of our national religion is wrong" (Jones 1788, 255), and "arguments principally founded on the high assumptions of the Brahmins . . . could their extravagant claims be substantiated, have a direct tendency to overturn the Mosaic system, and, with it, Christianity" (Maurice [1812] 1984, 22–23).

Similar concerns are evident whenever any traditional society encounters modernity. In nineteenth-century Bengal, one can sense the tension involved in maintaining both faith in scriptural validity and intellectual integrity in the *Śrī Kṛṣṇa Saṁhitā*. This book was written in 1879 by Bhaktivinode Thakur, a High Court judge in Jagganath Puri and father of Bhaktisiddhanta Sarasvati Thakur, the founder of the Gaudiya Math of the Chaitanya *sampradāya* that was to become an influential sect in eastern India and Vrindavan. Bhaktivinode's reaction to the Aryan invasion theory, as outlined by Shukavak Das (1996–97), is the earliest orthodox Hindu perspective on Shastric historicism that I have uncovered.[4] Unable to refute the historical formulations of European scholarship, Bhaktivinode adopted the tools of modern critical scholarship and, citing Western authorities such as Wilford, Pratt, Playfair, and Davis, at least nominally accepted the proposition that the Aryans had indeed entered India from the Northwest (although he negotiated with reason and argument his own date of 4463 B.C.E. for their arrival). However, Bhaktivinode did not allow this historicization to undermine the transcendence of the Vedic (and, more specifically, the Vaiṣṇava Bhāgavata) dharma.

In the introduction to the *Kṛṣṇa Saṁhitā*, Bhaktivinode states that scripture is of two types: *arthaprada*, knowledge which deals with phenomenal matters such as history, philology, linguistics, anthropology and archaeology, and so on; and *paramārthaprada*, knowledge that deals with transcendence. According to Bhaktivinode, *arthaprada*, even though derived from the sacred scripture, is answerable to human scrutiny and analysis and therefore can be adjusted and corrected according to time and place. Historical details are negotiable. *Paramārthaprada*, in contrast, is inaccessible to human reason. It is transcendent and beyond the purview of human interpretation and speculation (although realizable by the direct perception of the soul).

Bhaktivinode, in line with many other Hindu reformists of his day, concluded that much in the *śāstras* is aimed at attracting the neophyte religious consciousness by means of superhuman stories and fantastic time calculations. In nineteenth-century British Bengal, however, such accounts, alienated many of the more intellectual and westernized urban Bengalis from their religious traditions. The result was the creation of a spiritually disenfranchised Hindu intelligentsia whose intellectual needs made them vulnerable to modern, Western ideas and who were likely to be dismissive of traditional religious perspectives. This was Bhaktivinode's target group. To attract the minds of this educated but disoriented class to the *paramārthaprada* essence of the *śastra*, he was quite willing to utilize critical analysis to negotiate the *arthaprada* portions, such as the question of Aryan origins, in accordance with the intellectually authoritative sources in his day that were at his disposal. If the times were dominated by European methodologies such as linguistics and archaeology, then Bhakivinode had no difficulty adopting these methods and the conclusions they produced in order not to alienate those influenced by this type of rationalism. As a spiritual leader, his concern was to retain his contemporaries within the Vedic fold—specifically the Kṛṣṇa-centered realm of the Chaitanya tradition—while simultaneously encouraging them to engage intellectually with Western critical thought.

As for his more traditional-minded colleagues, Bhaktivinode could only appeal to them to try and understand the spirit of his historical formulations:

> With folded hands I humbly submit to my respected readers, who hold traditional views, that where my analysis opposes their long held beliefs, they should understand that . . . what I have said about dharma applies to everyone, but with regard to matters which are secondary to dharma, my conclusions are meant to produce benefits in the form of intellectual clarification only for qualified specialists. All the subjects which I have outlined in the Introduction concerning time and history are based on the logical analysis of *śastra*, and whether one accepts them or not does not affect the spiritual conclusions. History and time are phenomenal subject matters and when they are analyzed according to sound reasoning much good can be done for India. (Quoted in Shukavak Das, 1996–97, 139)

In this way, Bhaktivinode salvaged what he considered to be the essential aspects of the Vedic and Bhāgavata tradition from the firing line of any potentially embarrassing discoveries and conclusions of modern historical research. His absolute transcendence (the *saguṇa* aspect of Srī Kṛṣṇa) could then reside securely out of harm's way, safe from issues of historicity. Bhaktivinode did, however, invite future scholars to reexamine and improve the external, historical part of his formulations, such as the Aryan invasion, when developments in the appropriate fields permitted.

It took time for Indian scholars to adopt and learn the methods of Western critical scholarship to the point where they felt comfortable enough to actually challenge the status quo. The first outright voices of opposition against the Aryan invasion theory were not raised until the end of the nineteenth century. They were inaugurated by prominent religious figures, whose discourses were in direct political and religious response to the hegemony of British intellectual power, which was portrayed as untrustworthy in the face of Vedic *śabda pramāṇa* 'scriptural evidence'. In 1882, Dayananda Saraswati, founder of the Arya Samaj, protested:

> In the face of these Vedic authorities how can sensible people believe in the imaginary tales of the foreigners . . . no *Sanskrit* book or history records that the Aryas came here from Iran, and defeating the inhabitants of the country in battles, drove them away and proclaimed themselves the rulers of the country. How can then the writings of foreigners be worth believing in the teeth of this testimony? (266)

Elsewhere Dayananda drew on a literal reading of the Mahābhārata to claim that "the *Aryas* were the sovereign rulers of the whole earth" (329). But he did make some efforts to familiarize himself with European scholarship and, in the 1860s, employed a Bengali to read him Müller's translation of the Ṛgveda. His choice of Tibet as the homeland of the Aryans reflected the preference of Europeans such as Kant and Herder. Influenced by the Orientalist critique in ways that partially paralleled (from an Aryan perspective) the neo-Saivism of the South, his Samaj was dedicated to reestablishing the pristine monotheistic purity of the early Aryan Vedic literature, and jettisoning the later polytheistic accretions, superstitions, and corruptions that had accrued during the Puranic period.

The Theosophists, who established their principal ashram in South India, retained their belief in an Indian homeland well after such a position had long been considered passé in Europe. Olcott, (1881), as noted earlier, considered that "the Brahmins have their own chronology and no one has the means of proving that their calculations are exaggerated. . . . We Europeans . . . have a right to more than suspect that India 8,000 years ago sent out a colony of emigrants" (124). Blavatsky ([1892] 1975) likewise stated that "it has now become very clear to me that the Scandinavian, Egyptian, Greek, Central Asiatic, German and Slavonic gods were nearly all . . . born in prehistoric India" (608). She also attempted to make a case for the antiquity of the Vedas. Juxtaposing "the least age we can accord to the human race," namely, 240,000 years, with Max Müller's statements that the Veda represents "the very infancy of humanity, and when hardly out of its cradle," she quips that "it really seems the duty of the eminent Sanskritist and Lecturer on Comparative Theology to get out of this dilemma. Either the Rig-Veda hymns were composed but 3,000 years ago, and, therefore, cannot be expressed in the 'language of childhood' . . . or we have to ascribe to them an immense antiquity in order to carry them back to the days of human mental antiquity" (Blavatsky n.d., 47).

Aurobindo (1971), who also kept abreast of European knowledge, expressed his misgivings some years later: "The indications in the Veda on which this theory of a recent Aryan invasion is built are very scanty in quantity and uncertain in significance. There is no actual mention of any such invasion. The distinction between Aryan and un-Aryan on which so much has been built seems on the mass of evidence to indicate a cultural rather than a racial difference" (24). This absence of any mention in the Vedas of an external origin for the Aryans is the single most repeated objection raised by Indian scholars—an issue to which I will return shortly. Vivekananda, (1970–73), the first prominent Indian religious figure in the modern period to ignore the prohibition of the *śāstra* against crossing the seas, and the first to address an audience in the West, not only rejected the Aryan invasion theory but also issued a rallying cry to scholars among his countrymen to oppose it:

> And what your European pundits say about the Aryans swooping down from some foreign land, snatching away the lands of the aborigines and settling in India by exterminating them, is all pure nonsense, foolish talk! In what Veda, in what Sukta do you find that the Aryans came into India from a foreign country? Where do you get the idea that they slaughtered the wild aborigines? What do you gain by talking such nonsense? Strange that our Indian scholars, too, say amen to them; and all these monstrous lies are being taught to our boys! . . . Whenever the Europeans find an opportunity, they exterminate the aborigines and settle down in ease and comfort on their lands; and therefore they think the Aryans must have done the same! . . . But where is your proof? Guess work? Then keep your fanciful ideas to yourself. I strongly protested against these ideas at the Paris Congress. I have been talking with the Indian and European savants on the subject, and hope to raise many objections to this theory in detail, when time permits. And this I say to you—to our pundits—also, "You are learned men, hunt up your old books and scriptures, please, and draw your own conclusions." (5:534–535)

After Vivekananda's death, some notes were found among his papers containing forty-two points jotted down for a book he intended to write, ten of which dealt with issues connected to the Aryan invasion theory. However, it remained for others to take up Vivekananda's stirring call to arms.

Conclusion

We have seen how Aryanism was co-opted in all sorts of contradictory, but not necessary conflicting, ways by missionaries, colonialists, Orientalists, anthropologists, nationalists, and all manner of other ideologues in Europe throughout the nineteenth and twentieth centuries. The Aryan connection was configured in support of just about any agenda. A parallel situation holds true for India. Politically, in terms of its European connections, Aryanism was welcomed by some as evidence of equality between the colonizers and the colonized—and could even be invoked to elicit assistance from the English Aryan brethren. In other discourses, it was heralded as proof of the spiritual superiority of the Hindu Aryans in comparison to the materialistic Western Aryans. In terms of its ramifications in the Indian political scene, it was deferred to as proof of Brahmanical Aryan superiority over the rest of the subcontinent or, contrarily, as proof of Brahmanical Aryan exploitation of the same.

From religious perspectives, however, the theory was more fundamentally troubling at least from Brahmanical viewpoints. It completely undermined traditional concepts of history and portrayed the wise Aryans of yore as little better than marauding barbarians. It was on the basis of the scriptural evidence that the first voices challenging the basis of the theory—as opposed to coopting it for ideological purposes—were raised. Suspicion of the theory based on scriptural testimony—or lack thereof—remains an explicit or implicit factor in much Indigenous Aryan discourse. The science known as philology in the West, was to provide the terrain for the first forays by Indian Sanskritists against the conclusions of their Western peers. It is to this that I turn next.

3

Vedic Philology

Traditional Indian scholars immediately became suspicious of Western philology once it began to conflict with traditional conceptions of the Veda and its origins. It was primarily through philology that the Indian homeland proposed by the earlier romantic school was rejected by most scholars.[1] In 1909, the *Imperial Gazeteer of India* noted that "the uniformity of the Indo-Aryan type can be accounted for only by one of two hypotheses—that its members were indigenous to the Punjab, or that they entered India. . . . the opinion of European scholars . . . is unanimous in favour of the foreign origin of the Indo-Aryans. The arguments appealed to are mainly philological" (300).

Unlike comparative linguistics and archaeology, which were European innovations and alien to Brahmanical thought, Vedic philology was an area much closer to traditional Indian epistemological modes, since it required an expertise in Sanskrit and involved the study of familiar traditional texts; Indian scholars were much better equipped, in this discipline, to scrutinize the scholarship of Western savants. Although himself a latecomer to Sanskrit studies, Aurobindo (1971) considered many of the conclusions of the comparative philology of his day, despite containing "much that is useful," to be ultimately "an interesting diversion for an imaginative mind," the fruits more of "an ingenious play of the poetic imagination" (26). Aurobindo is reservedly appreciative but not co-opted or intimidated:

> Modern Philology is an immense advance on anything we have had before the nineteenth century. It has introduced a spirit of order and method in place of mere phantasy; it has given us more correct ideas of the morphology of language and of what is or is not possible in etymology. It has established a few rules which govern the detrition of language and guide us in the identification of the same word or of related words as they appear in the changes of different but kindred tongues. Here, however, its achievements cease. The

> high hopes which attended its birth have not been fulfilled by its maturity. There is, in fact, no real certainty as yet in the obtained results of Philology. . . . Yesterday we were all convinced that Varuna was identical with Ouranos, the Greek heaven; today this identity is denounced to us as a philological error; tomorrow it may be rehabilitated. . . . We have to recognize in fact that European scholarship in its dealings with the Veda has derived an excessive prestige from its association in the popular mind with the march of European science. The truth is that there is an enormous gulf between the patient, scrupulous and exact physical sciences and these other brilliant, but immature branches of learning upon which Vedic scholarship relies. (27–28)

Once the seemingly infallible facade of Oriental scholarship had been challenged by the opposition of prominent religious figures, one of the first attempts to refute the Aryan invasion theory by engaging the actual evidence at stake with reason and argument was published in 1884 in the *Theosophist*. The contributor, Ramchandra Rao (1880), voices his incredulity at the opinions of his day:

> We are told that the Aryan family, which lived in Central Asia, were a civilized people; and that their religion was that of the Vedas. They had chariots, horses, ships, boats, towns and fortified places before the separation took place. They were therefore not nomads. Max Müller adds that the younger branch left first and emigrated into Europe. . . . the oldest quitted its ancestral abode last of all, for a new home in India. The inference to be drawn, then, is that the old home was abandoned by every soul, and left to become a dreary and a desolate place as we now find it. . . . the efforts of philology . . . can hardly succeed in metamorphosing a vague theory into real Simon Pure, but must remain as they are—a hollow farce. (306–307)

In his opinion, the whole Aryan invasion theory was "nothing but a varnished tale, utterly undeserving of the name of traditional history" (305).

Similar misgivings were voiced in 1901 by one Aghorechandra Chattopadhyaya in Calcutta. In this book, one can sense the author seriously struggling to make sense of the conclusions of Western scholarship, yet unable to conceal his own bewilderment at the theories that he was encountering: "Whatever might be the credibility the scholars are blessed with, we can hardly reconcile ourselves with such an easy faith on a matter like this." Commenting on the spectacular achievements of the subbranches of the Indo-European family, such as the Vedic Indians, Greeks, Romans, and Persians, he wondered, with remarkable acumen for his time and sources, how the main trunk of the Indo-European tree could have produced such conspicuous fruits that survived for millennia, and yet leave no trace of itself:

> While the major branches of the main trunk gathered strength, looked healthy, and spread far and wide, the latter, at the same time, withered, shriveled, and failed to show any indication of life and vitality and disappeared from sight and was lost for ever without leaving any trace or mark that might lead to its identification, nor could any fossil remains of it be detected or found out, so that it could be inferred that such a society in such a stage of development existed at one time, on the surface of the earth. . . . A story so imperfect in every important respect is put forward seriously for people to believe in and accept as an authentic account of the ancient history of the Indo-European race. (59)

Chattopadhyaya also struggles to make sense of what appeared to him to be the contradictory proposals that the Indo-Europeans were wandering nomads and yet were held to have originated from a specific abode, and that they were primitive tribesmen and yet were able to formulate and utilize a language as intricate and complex as Indo-European. Albeit on a rudimentary level, some Indian scholars were beginning to pay closer attention to the specifics underlying the philological theories and speculations of Western scholars. There were two specific philological areas that were fundamental in asserting an Aryan invasion of India: the racial evidence, involving the distinctions between the Āryas and their enemies the Dāsas, and the geographic parameters of the texts themselves.

The Racial Evidence

The first prominent note of discord between traditional exegesis and Western scholarship was sounded because of the lack of explicit mention, in the Vedic texts, of a foreign homeland of the Aryan people. As mentioned previously, this conspicuous silence had been noted even by nineteenth-century Western scholars (e.g., Elphinstone 1841). The absence of any mention of external Aryan origins in traditional Sanskrit sources is, to this day, perhaps the single most prominent objection raised by much of the scholarship claiming indigenous origins for the Aryan culture. This consideration was summed up succinctly by Srinivas Iyengar in 1914:

> The Aryas do not refer to any foreign country as their original home, do not refer to themselves as coming from beyond India, do not name any place in India after the names of places in their original land as conquerors and colonizers always do, but speak of themselves exactly as sons of the soil would do. If they had been foreign invaders, it would have been humanly impossible for all memory of such invasion to have been utterly obliterated from memory in such a short time as represents the differences between the Vedic and Avestan dialects. (79–80)

A few Western scholars had tried to find some oblique references or reminiscences of the pre-Vedic people during their trajectory over central Asia. In 1913, Hillebrandt found reason to suppose that the Hariyūpiyā in RV 6.27.8 "is the Ariōb or Haliāb, a source river of the Kurum" (49). Other attempts to find traces of the Indo-Aryans in Iran and other places outside of India will be discussed in chapter 7. One should also note that several other Indo-European cultures, such as those of the Greeks and Scandinavians, also preserve no mention of their migrations into their historical territories, yet we know they were immigrants there at some point. That a historical event is lost from the collective consciousness of a people due to the passage of time, does not indicate that the event never took place. For the present purposes, the fact that the Vedas themselves make no mention of any Aryan invasion or immigration reveals a major epistemological concern in this debate. Scriptural testimony, *śabda pramāṇa*, in varying degrees, still holds a preeminent status as an authoritative source of historical information in the view of many Indian scholars.

Once the warning alarm had been raised regarding the lack of explicit mention of Aryan invasions, scholars began to look more carefully at the implicit evidence Western scholars had brought forward in this regard. It was the racial interpretations imposed on various Vedic passages, particularly those that referred to the battles between the Aryans and their foes, the Dāsas or Dasyus, that aroused the indignation of Indian scholars. Aurobindo (1971), again, was an outspoken, witty, and penetrating forerunner in this regard:

> It is urged that the Dasyus are described as black of skin and noseless in opposition to the fair and high-nosed Aryans. But the former distinction is certainly applied to the Aryan Gods and the Dasa Powers in the sense of light and darkness, and the word *anāsaḥ* does not mean noseless. Even if it did, it would be wholly inapplicable to the Dravidian races; for the Southern nose can give as good an account of itself as any "Aryan" proboscis in the North. (24)

The racial interpretations of the Vedic passages were inaugurated by Max Müller, who is both the hero and the archfiend of the Indigenous Aryan school. Factually: "The first effort to find direct evidence of the physical features of the Indian aborigines in the Sanskrit texts dating from the time of the Big Bang that brought Indian civilization into existence . . . boiled down to a matter of noses" (Trautmann, 1997, 197).

Müller (1854b), searching for clues in the Rgveda that might provide evidence of this "big bang," decided: "The only expression that might be interpreted in this way is that of 'suśipra,' as applied to Aryan gods. It means 'with a beautiful nose' . . . The Dāsa or barbarian is also called vrṣaśipra in the Veda, which seems to mean goat or bull-nosed, and the 'Anāsas' enemies whom Indra killed with his weapon (RV V,29,10) are probably meant for noseless . . . people". (346). Müller later recanted his interpretation of the word *śipra*, so the evidence was reduced to a solitary word, *anāsa*, in a single passage. This sole possible description of the Dāsa nose, however, like Pinocchio's nasal organ, was to have an expanded life of its own. By 1891, H. H. Risley, who was compiling his ethnological material on Indian tribes and castes, was able to say that "no one can have glanced at the Vedic accounts of the Aryan advance without being struck by the *frequent* references to the noses of the people whom the Aryans found in possession of the plains of India [whom] they spoke of as 'the noseless ones'" (249–250; my italics). The solitary nasal reference had suddenly become a frequent one.

McDonnell and Keith (1967), while at least acknowledging that both the *pada* text and Sāyaṇa, the oldest existing commentator on the Rgveda, had interpreted the word *anāsa* as meaning the equally valid alternative translation 'without face' (which is how Geldner and Grassman had accepted it) as opposed to 'without nose', nonetheless further cemented Müller's identification with their approval. As far as they were concerned, it "would accord well with the flat-nosed aborigines of the Dravidian type, whose language still persists among the Brahuis, who are found in the North-West" (348). Müller had construed the word as *a-nāsa*, 'without nose', as opposed to *an-ās* 'without mouth or face', as Sāyaṇa had construed it. The word occurs in a passage where the Dasyus are also described as *mṛdhavacaḥ*, which is glossed by Sāyaṇa with *hiṃsitavāgindriyān* 'having defective organs of speech'. This could reasonably simply refer to people considered rude or uncultivated barbarians by their Aryan detractors rather than to any racial term. However, the quest for textual evidence of the Aryan invasion caused the racial interpretation to be favored, and it is this interpretation that has continued to surface up to the present day: "The *Vedas* recognize a dichotomy between the Indo-Aryans and their dark-skinned enemies, the *Dāsa*, who are on one occasion described as 'nose-less,' which has generally been interpreted as a pejorative reference to Dravidian physical features" (Mallory 1989, 45).

Srinivas Iyengar, in 1914, was not convinced by this type of "great scientific hardihood":

> One solitary word *anāsa* applied to the Dasyu has been quoted by . . . Max Müller . . . among numerous writers, to prove that the Dasyus were a flat nosed people, and that, therefore, by contrast, the Aryas were straight-nosed. Indian commentators have explained this word to mean *an-āsa*, mouthless, devoid of fair speech. . . . to hang such a weight of inference as the invasion and conquest of India by the straight nosed Aryans on the solitary word *anāsa* does certainly seem not a very reasonable procedure. (6)

Iyengar is equally unimpressed by the racial interpretations of other passages in the Veda that had been given by Western scholars:

> The only other trace of racial reference in the Vedic hymns is the occurrence of two words, one *krishna* in seven passages and the other *asikini* in two passages. One of the meanings of these two words is "black," but in all the passages, the words have been interpreted as referring to black demons, black clouds, a demon whose name was Krishna, or the powers of darkness. Hence to take this as evidence to prove that the invading Aryans were fair-complexioned as they referred to their demon foes or perhaps human enemies as black is again to stretch many points in behalf of a preconceived theory. (6–7)

Iyengar is well worth quoting at length, because his arguments are well researched and penetrating:

> The word . . . *Arya* occurs about 33 times [in the Rgveda]. . . . the word *Dāsa* occurs about 50 times and *Dasyu* about 70 times. . . . The word *Arya* occurs 22 times in hymns to Indra and six times in hymns to Agni, and *Dāsa* 50 times in hymns to Indra and twice in hymns to Agni, and *Dasyu* 50 times in hymns to Indra and 9 times in hymns to Agni. The constant association of these words with Indra clearly proves that *Arya* meant a worshipper of Indra (and Agni). . . . The Aryas offered oblations to Indra. . . . The Dasyus or Dasas were those who were opposed to the Indra Agni cult and are explicitly described thus in those passages where human Dasyus are clearly meant. They are *avrata* without (the Arya) rites, *anyavrata* of different rites, *ayajavāna*, non-sacrificers, *abrahma* without prayers, also not having Brāhmana priests, *anrichah* without Riks, *brahmadvisha*, haters of prayers to Brāhmanas, and *anindra* without Indra, despisers of Indra. They pour no milky draughts, they heat no cauldron. They give no gifts to the Brāhmana. . . . Their worship was but enchantment, sorcery, unlike the sacred law of fire-worship, wiles and magic. In all this we hear but the echo of a war of rite with rite, cult with cult and not one of race with race. (5–6)[2]

Others have voiced just as penetrating critiques:

> In the attempt to ransack the latter-day Sanskrit texts for proofs of Nordic characteristics, . . . we forget that if in latter day Sanskrit texts sentences such as "Gaura [white, yellowish], . . . pingala [reddish brown, tawny, golden], kapilkesa [brown or tawny hair]" are to be found in Patanjali's Mahabhasya (V. 1. 115) and if Manu has said that a Brāhmaṇa should not marry a girl with *pingala* hair (38) there are other sentences in previous ages which contradict the strength of these characteristics. But with the help of these two sentences attempt is being made to prove the existence of Nordic characteristics amongst the Indian people. . . . The God Rudra is described to have possessed golden hair . . . yet we cannot make a Nordic viking out of him, as he had brown-hued skin-colour and golden-coloured arm. . . . Surely we cannot take the god Rudra as a specimen of race-

miscegenation. . . . we beg to state that these allegories should be accepted as poetic fancies. They cannot be used as scientific data, for anthropological purpose. (Dutta 1936, 248–252)

Interestingly, almost a full century after Indian scholars started objecting to the racial interpretations imposed on the Ārya-Dāsa dichotomy, Western scholars have recently also started drawing attention to nineteenth-century philological excesses. Levitt (1989), in his analysis of the word *anāsa*, points out that even if it does mean 'noseless', an equivalent term in the language of the Bhil tribe is used in an ethical as opposed to a racial sense to indicate someone who is untrustworthy. Schetelich (1990), in turn, has analyzed the three occurrences of the phrase *kṛṣṇā* (or *asiknī*) *tvac* used in conjunction with the dasyu, which has generally been translated as 'dark skin' (247). Her conclusion is that the word is a symbolic expression for darkness. Witzel comments on the same term that "while it would be easy to assume reference to skin colour, this would go against the spirit of the hymns: for Vedic poets, black always signifies evil, and any other meaning would be secondary in these contexts". (1995b, 325, fn). These realizations can be found in any number of Indigenous Aryan publications stretching back for at least a century. Trautmann (1997), in his analysis of the development of, and interaction between, ethnology and philology in the nineteenth century, finds his own experiment of subjecting the evidence for the racial interpretation of Indian civilization to a minimizing reading revealed just how soft that evidence is and the amount of overreading upon which it is based (213). He points out that the racial theory of Indian civilization is the product of the late nineteenth century, when the relations between whites and other ethnic groups in the Anglo-Saxon world were being reconfigured with ideological support from a spate of racial essentialism (208). Trautmann concludes: "That the racial theory of Indian civilization still lingers is a miracle of faith. Is it not time we did away with it?" (215).

Hock (1999b) suggests that the reluctance to review this racial material is due to the failure to live up to the scholarly ideals of constantly reexamining the evidence. He, too, undertook a similar exercise by extracting all the passages that Geldner had construed in a racial sense in his translation of the Rgveda and found them all to be either mistranslated or, at least, open to alternative nonracial interpretation. The reason racial readings were preferred was due to the "quasi-scientific attempts to provide a justification for 'racially' based European imperialism. . . . Moreover, the British take-over of India seemed to provide a perfect parallel to the assumed take-over of pre-historic India by the invading Indo-Aryans" (1999b, 168).

It seems fair to note, however, that for over a century many Indian scholars have been aware of, and objected to, such biased readings all along: "Thus 'Arya' moved from the Vedic literature to the European political arena. . . . They thought that as the Vedic people were the most cultured people of antiquity, they cannot but be 'white men,' no matter whether blonde or brunette, who conquered the noseless dark people of the Indus Valley" (Chandra 1980, 123).[3] B. R. Ambedkar (1946) delivered a particularly scathing critique of the whole enterprise of attempting to establish invasions on the basis of racial evidence in the Rgveda and concludes:

Why has the theory failed? . . . The theory of an invasion is an invention. This invention is necessary because of a gratuitous assumption which underlies the Western theory. The

> . . . assumption is that the Aryans were a superior race. This theory has its origin in the belief that the Aryans are a European race and as a European race it is presumed to be superior to the Asiatic ones. . . . Knowing that nothing can prove the superiority of the Aryan race better than invasion and conquest of the native races, the Western writers have proceeded to invent the story of the invasion of India by the Aryans, and the conquest by them of the Dasas and Dasyus. . . . The originators of the Aryan race theory are so eager to establish their case that they have no patience to see what absurdities they land themselves in. They start on a mission to prove what they want to prove and do not hesitate to pick such evidence from the Vedas as they think is good for them. (72–75)

Of course, despite offering elaborate and, in places, well-argued and legitimate refutations of the racial evidence along some of the lines outlined here, Ambedkar's research was not without a clear, and philologically questionable, agenda of its own, as was noted in chapter 2. But his point here holds good.

Philologists are not alone in being unable to identify any compelling racial traits in the Rgveda.[4] Present-day archaeologists also concur that there are no innovations in the skeletal remains of humans found in the subcontinent that necessarily correspond to an incoming group of people that are in any way distinct from a separate indigenous group of people. This evidence will be discussed in chapter 11. In terms of the literary material, in addition to the so-called racial references, another body of philological evidence has been very influential in supporting the position that the Aryans were immigrants into the subcontinent. This is based on the geographic boundaries alluded to in the texts themselves.

The West-to-East Geographic Shift in Sanskrit Texts

In 1860, Muir, in his arguments raised against the consideration of the Aryans being indigenous to India that was still lingering in his time, was the first scholar to attempt to argue extensively that the Sanskrit texts themselves could be used to demonstrate an Aryan invasion of India. Although beginning his thesis with a "candid admission" that "none of the Sanskrit books, not even the most ancient, contain any distinct reference or allusion to the foreign origin of the Indians" (Muir [1860] 1874, 322), he developed his case by documenting how the geographic horizons referred to in progressively later Sanskrit texts expand from the northwest part of the subcontinent to the eastern and, eventually, the southern parts. From this perspective, this textual awareness of increasing portions of India corresponded to the actual physical expansion of the Indo-Aryans themselves into India from the Northwest and then across the subcontinent.

Muir's arguments began with the Ṛgveda, which refers to the Kubhā river in Afghanistan and is firmly situated in the Punjab between the Indus and the Sarasvatī: "The oldest hymns of the Veda show us the Arian people still dwelling . . . between the Cabul river and the Indus" (339).[5] However, "the Gangā and the Yamunā are only mentioned once in the tenth book," and the southern Vindhya mountain range is not mentioned at all (347). This suggested to him that the Aryans had just begun to move east by the time they were compiling the later books of the Ṛgveda (such as the tenth). Muir fortified his case by interpreting the conflict between the Āryas and the Dāsyus in the racial manner discussed above, and then quoted a passage from the Śatapatha

Brāhmaṇa wherein "the gradual advance of the Aryas with their Brahmanical worship, from the banks of the Sarasvati eastward to those of the Sadānirā, and afterwards beyond that stream, is . . . distinctly indicated" (403).[6] Finally, the Rāmāyaṇa, with the conquest of Lanka, completed the Aryan expansion across the Vindhyas and on to the South. The fabulous creatures and beings described in this Epic are representations of the Aryan encounter with the aborigines—a proposal Muir bolstered with Ellis and Campbell's discovery that the Dravidian languages belonged to a different family from those of the North. Other geographic references have been brought forward since Muir to solidify this basic line of argument.

Muir's logic, then, is that certain parts of India are not mentioned in the oldest part of the Ṛgveda because the Aryans had not yet been to those parts. This argument can be used both ways, however. If it is to be deduced that because the Ṛgveda does not explicitly mention the East and the South of India, then the Aryans had not yet been or gone to these regions, then the same parallel logic cannot be denied for the absence of any explicit mention of the Caspian Sea or its environs in the Ṛgveda: one would be hard-pressed to use these particular grounds to disallow the oft-cited claim that the Aryans had equally not been, or come from, those regions either, since they too are not explicitly mentioned in any texts. If Vedic geography is silent regarding eastern and southern Indian landscapes and peoples, it is arguably also ignorant of distant, external northwestern landscapes and peoples. From this perspective, the two lacunae, both merely *argumenti ex silentio*, seem to negate each other in terms of providing solid evidence of the migrations of these people.

One line of argument attempts to brush off these geographic parameters by stating that all that the evidence indicates, without making assumptions, is that the composers of the hymns, who were certainly not cartographers, happened to make some peripheral references to the immediate areas where they lived and happened to make no mention of other places that were irrelevant to their hymns. Some scholars do not feel obliged to conclude from this that the Indo-Aryans were ignorant of other places because they had not yet arrived farther east or south in the subcontinent. The composers of later Vedic texts, and of the Epics and Puranas, happened to live elsewhere and therefore described different locations connected with the themes and events they were concerned with:

> What does it prove at best? It only proves that the people who sang the hymns lived in the land of the "Five (or Seven) Rivers"; nothing beyond that. It does not, for instance, prove that the land beyond the "Five Rivers" was *not* inhabited. . . . [In the] *Yājurvedic* tradition . . . Yajñavalkya [was] an inhabitant of *Mithilā*, which is very far removed from the "Five Rivers". . . . If then, at least one of the *Vedic Seers* inhabited the Eastern land of Mithila, and some inhabited the land of the Five Rivers—what *definite* conclusion can that lead to? (Jha 1940, 2)

This type of dismissal, however, needs to address the detailed philological work of Witzel (1989) who not only has excavated the geographic horizons known to each separate stratum of the Vedic texts but also has attempted to identify the different waves of tribal units that inaugurated the expansions and even the dialectal variants and archaeological cultures that accompanied the spread. He, too, notes that the Ṛgveda is limited to the Punjab and it surroundings, while the Atharvaveda knows all of the North Indian plains of the Ganges-Yamuna doab of Uttar Pradesh. The late Brāhmaṇa texts, in contrast, "suddenly have a geographical horizon reaching from Gandhara (and beyond) to Aṅga, from the Himālaya in the North to Vidarbha, Andhra in the South, and including the South-Eastern tribes" (Witzel 1989, 244). There does seem to be significant evidence to accept a movement across the subcontinent from the Punjab that cannot simply be brushed aside.

Curzon (1855), however, who, as I have noted, believed that the Indo-European homeland was in India, was not prepared to allow anything more than just this:

> Is it legitimate . . . to infer that because the Aryans early spread to the South . . . and extended themselves over the peninsula, they also originally invaded, from some unknown region and conquered India itself? If so, the same argument might be applied to the origin and spread of the Romans, who might be presumed to have invaded Italy from some external unknown region, because they early spread their conquests to the south. . . . But we know from authentic history that the Romans arose from one city and region in Italy: that . . . they gradually extended themselves over and subjugated those territories which subsequently formed one vast empire. (189)

Despite such objections, Muir's interpretation prevailed and is still a prominent support of the Aryan migration position: "The known historical expansion of Indic from north to both the east and the south, gives us every reason to deny the Indo-Aryans a prior home in those regions" (Mallory 1989, 44, my italics).[7] Needless to say, Indigenous Aryanists see things in the same vein as Curzon: "We may notice a greater acquaintance with Central and Eastern India in the latter [texts], showing perhaps the shift of the seat of Vedic Civilization more inland. But such a shift would be a matter of internal history and could have no bearing on the question of the Rigvedics hailing in 1500 B.C. from beyond the Afghānistān-Punjāb complex" (Sethna 1992, 14).

Just as this book is going to press, a new publication (Talageri, 2000) attempts to undermine these notions of a west-to-east spread of the Indo-Aryans in the subcontinent based on the geographical parameters of the texts. Restricting his focus to the ten *maṇḍalas* 'books' of the Rgveda, Talgeri establishes an internal chronology of this text consisting of four periods: Early (*maṇḍala* 6, 3, and 7, in that order); Middle (*maṇḍala* 4 and 2, in that order); Late (*maṇḍala* 5, 8, and 9, in that order), and Very Late (*maṇḍala* 10). He considers *Maṇḍala* 1 to cover a period from pre-Middle (but post-Early) to the Very Late period. Talageri's method involves establishing a relative chronology of the various composers of the hymns. If, for example, *maṇḍala* A is composed by someone who is an ancestor of the composer of *maṇḍala* B, or if the composer of *maṇḍala* A is considered, in *maṇḍala* B, to be a figure in the past, then Talageri assumes *maṇḍala* A is older. He also considers the lineages of kings and *ṛṣis* such that if *maṇḍala* C refers to a contemporary king or *ṛṣī* and *maṇḍala* D refers to this same *ṛṣi* or king as a figure in the past, he assumes *maṇḍala* D to be older.

He feels his ordering (*maṇḍala* 6, 3, 7, 4, 2, 5, 8, 9, and 10) is confirmed by the fact that the oldest *maṇḍala* demonstrate the most rigid family structure—every verse in *maṇḍala* 6 is composed by members of one branch of one family of composers—while at the other end of the spectrum, the hymns, *maṇḍala* 10, being composed by *ṛṣis* from almost every family, have the loosest family structure and contain a large number of hymns of unknown composition. He also notes that the hymns in the older *maṇḍalas* of his schema which are composed by the descendants of an important or eponymous composer, are generally attributed to that ancestral composer, while in later *maṇḍalas*, the hymns are attributed to the actual composer himself. He takes this development as further confirmation of his ordering.

The final step of this method is to examine the geographical horizons expressed in this chronological sequence. In *maṇḍala* 6, the Aryans were settled in the region to the east of the Sarasvatī, viz, in present-day Haryana and Uttar Pradesh. Toward the end of the Early Period, *maṇḍalas* 3 and 7, they had expanded westward into the Punjab, and by the Middle and Late Periods, the geographical horizons had spread westward as far as the southeastern parts of Afghanistan. In short, "the evidence of the Rigveda is so clear that it brooks no other conclusion except that the Vedic Aryans expanded from the interior of India to the west and northwest" (123–24).[8]

While this version of things awaits a response from Witzel, we should outline the picture produced from the latter's reading of the same texts. In terms of the internal ordering of the texts, Witzel (1995b) follows Oldenberg who as early as the nineteenth century had noted that the oldest *maṇḍalas*, 2–7, are the collections of the clans of poets. Within this core, the *maṇḍalas* are arranged according to the increasing number of hymns per book. Within each *maṇḍala*, in turn, the hymns are ordered according to deity, with Agni placed first, followed by Indra, followed by the other gods. Then, within the sections for each deity, the hymns are arranged according to *decreasing* number of stanzas per hymn. In case the number of stanzas in particular hymns are equal, the hymn with more syllables is placed first. In this way, a hymn can be immediately found by its family, deity, and meter.

Of course, this internal ordering need not correspond to chronology of composition (although it can be used to identify late additions if they disrupt this pattern). Witzel notes that "all we can say with confidence is that book 10, as such, is late but judgment must be exercised for each individual hymns. Some in book 8, sometimes even in book 1 and 10, can be as early as the 'family books'" (1995b, 310). In order to fine-tune the chronology of the hymns within the Rgveda, Witzel also accepts the internal relationship between the poets and kings to be decisive, and couples these individuals and the tribes with which they are connected with the geographical horizons of the texts that feature them; however, he produces a rather different picture from Talageri's.

Witzel (1995b) focuses his attention on the *pañca jana*, the five tribes of the Ṛgveda. He finds that four of them, the Yadu-Turvaśa and the Anu-Druhya, are regarded as already settled in the Punjab at the time of the composition of the Vedic hymns with "only the dimmest recollection of their move into South Asia" (339). The Pūrus are the next to arrive on the scene, "although their movement into the subcontinent had also become a done deed by the time most of the Vedic hymns were composed" (339). They dominate the remainder of the "five people." Meanwhile, Witzel sees a subsection of the Pūrus, the Bhāratas, situated in Afghanistan, on the grounds that their leader, Divodāsa, is fighting his enemy Sambara, who "was probably an aboriginal tribal chief in the mountainous Borderline zone" and is said to possess hill fortresses (332).

After the defeat of Sambara, Witzel finds the Bhāratas intruding into the subcontinent where they defeat the Pūrus in the famous battle between the Bhārata chief Sūdas, a descendant of Divodāsa, and the ten kings: "The entire book seven is a snapshot of history: the incursion of the Bhārata into the Panjab from across the Sindhu, and their battle with the "Five Peoples' and the Pūru" (1995b, 337). He sees the geographical referents of this battle hymn shift from west to east, beginning with the Bhārata priest

Vasiṣṭha's crossing of the Sindhu river, followed by the actual battle of the ten kings on the Paruṣṇi river (modern-day Ravi), and culminating with the Bhāratas eventual arrival on the Yamunā river (335). Emerging victorious, the Bhāratas then settle on the Sarasvatī (which would appear to be a movement back to the west), and this area becomes "the heartland of South Asia," considered in Ṛgveda 3.53.11 to be the center of the world (339). In short, where Indigenists would simply see strategic maneuverings backward and forward in battles between rival clans native to the North of the subcontinent itself, Witzel finds "successive waves of migrations," resulting in frequent warfare and shifting alliances (337).

Conclusion

The Ṛgvedic texts were read in the political context of nineteenth-century philology, which has been outlined in chapter 1. This certainly influenced the choice of possible interpretations placed on such words as *anāsa* and on the battles of the Āryas and the Dāsas. The racial interpretations extrapolated from the texts to support an Aryan migration have been justly challenged by both Indian and, albeit after the lag of a century, Western scholars. Their place in serious discussions of the Indo-Aryan problem is highly questionnable.

Geographically, however, the textual evidence for immigration is more persuasive. The sequence of texts does seem to suggest a movement of the Brahmanic geographical horizons from the Northwest to other parts of India. Nonetheless, the Indigenous response needs to be considered: the texts give no obvious indication of a movement into India itself. Indigenous Aryanists, on the whole, are prepared to accept a shift of population from the Sarasvatī region eastward toward the Gangetic plain (with increasing contacts with the South) in the historical period. (As we shall see in chapter 7, this is sometimes correlated with the drying up of the Sarasvatī and the eastern drift of the Indus Valley sites from the Mature to the Late and post-Harappan period.) But they do not feel compelled to then project this into preconceived hypothetical movements into the subcontinent itself in the pre- and protohistoric period.

It seems reasonable to accept that the Indo-Aryans spread into the east and south of the subcontinent from the Northwest. But to what extent can it be legitimately argued that they might have been indigenous to the Northwest itself? At this point, other disciplines must be introduced into the debate, and so it is to these that I turn in the ensuing chapters. But first, it is important to outline the history of Sanskrit in the field of Indo-European studies over the last two centuries. As we have seen, the demotion of India as the favored Indo-European homeland in the early nineteenth century had a lot to do with the demotion of Sanskrit from its status as *the* original tongue of the Indo-Europeans to a more secondary and reduced role as a daughter language that might be even younger than some of its siblings.

4

Indo-European Comparative Linguistics

The Dethronement of Sanskrit

Since no remnant of the original Proto-Indo-European language has been discovered, Indo-European historical reconstruction consists of comparing cognate words and grammatical forms in the various historical Indo-European languages and deducing the original forms, or protoforms therefrom. Obviously, such an endeavor is deductive, since, by definition, there are no written documents in a protolanguage so it can never be fully verified. Let us take a moment to note, along with Pulgram, that this protolanguage does not correspond to any de facto reality but to "something of a fiction," or, in Zimmer's terms, (1990a), not to "one of the languages spoken in an unknown antiquity by unidentified people but as a reference tool in discussing the history and development of the different Indo-European languages" (313). Pulgram (1959) further warns that "we must not make the mistake of confusing our methods, and the results flowing from them, with the facts; we must not delude ourselves into believing that our retrogressive method of reconstruction matches, step by step, the real progression of linguistic history." He continues: "We now find ourselves in possession of two entirely different items, both of which we call Proto-Indo-European: one, a set of reconstructed formulae not representative of any reality; the other, an undiscovered (possibly undiscoverable) language of whose reality we may be certain." The difference between the two should always be kept in mind: "Arguing about 'Proto-Indo-European' can be meaningful and fruitful . . . if we always explain whether we are talking about the one or the other—which, as we well know, we do not do" (424). In short, we know there was a Proto-Indo-European language; we do not know to what extent our reconstructions approximate it.

The Indo-Europeans are purely a linguistic entity: it was comparative Indo-European linguistics that necessitated the existence of a group of people whose language evolved into the classical and modern languages of Europe, Iran and India, and that co-opted archaeology, anthropology, and other disciplines into a quest for empirical evidence of their physical presence. Historical Indo-European linguistics got its start only when the Paninian analysis of an Indo-European language, Sanskrit, became known in Europe; the field was completely dependent on a mastery of Sanskrit grammar which still plays an indispensable role in Indo-European studies. Despite being naturally advantaged candidates for such studies, Indian scholars have made a negligible contribution to this field. While there have been a few outstanding Indian historical linguists—trained, for the most part, in either Europe, Calcutta or Poona—their number has been insignificant; with the exception of a history of Indo-European studies in Japan, the field of Indo-European historical linguistics has been almost exclusively a Western (and, most particularly, at least in its earlier phases, a German) domain.

One explanation for this regrettable dearth of Indian participation was made by the linguist D. D. Mahulkar (1992) in an attempt to promote the case for the study of historical linguistics in India:

> It was a matter of great pride for us to know that the European scholar's search for the "origin of language" had found its first springs on the Indian soil in the classical language of India, Sanskrit. Sanskrit since then began to play a role altogether undreamt of by its traditional grammarians. . . . [It became] the most authentic tool in the hands of European scholars for exploration into the origin of their languages. . . . but doubts started creeping into the science after the law of palatals (1870) came to be formulated . . . [which was] to dethrone Sanskrit from its pedestal of being the dialect nearest to the original language. . . . it appears that Indian linguists of the time gave up the study of linguistics out of the disillusionment over the see-saw position of Sanskrit in what Whitney named as "European Sanskrit Science." There was an overtone of emotionalism in their action. (4–6)

As discussed previously, Sanskrit was initially considered by early scholars such as Schlegel and Eichhoff to be the original mother language or, at least, as suggested by scholars such as Bopp and Pott, almost identical to it despite containing some innovations. Initially, the homeland was to a great extent situated in India because it seemed logical to locate it where the original, or oldest, languages were spoken. The complete dethronement of Sanskrit to the point where it was no longer deferred to as being the preserver of the most archaic linguistic forms in most circumstances took the best part of a century of comparative philological research.[1]

The Law of Palatals and the Discovery of Hittite

The law of palatals was the primary linguistic formula arrived at by the comparative method that dramatically shattered Sanskrit's preeminent status as the most venerable elder in this reconstructed family. It was preceded, in this regard, by an influential article by Grassman published in 1863. According to what came to be known as Grimm's law, certain regular changes had taken place in the Germanic languages when compared to other Indo-European languages such as Sanskrit. These included the observation that voiced stops had become voiceless stops (e.g. *b* had become *p*) in Germanic.[2] However, an irregularity to this sound change was evident. Sanskrit *bandh-* corresponded to Gothic *bindan*, where Grimm's law would have predicted *p* instead of *b* in the Gothic. Assuming Sanskrit to be the more pristine language, scholars intially thought the irregularities in correspondences between Germanic and Sanskrit were due to aberrations in Germanic. However, Grassman determined that this "irregularity" was due to Sanskrit, not Germanic, and was the result of a separate sound change. His observations resulted in a law which states that an aspirated sound looses its aspiration when followed by another aspirated sound. So an original Proto-Indo-European form **bhendh-* had become *bandh-* in Sanskrit. The *b* in *bandh-*, then, was due to innovations in Sanskrit, which up till then was generally assumed to have preserved the oldest forms, and not due to innovations in German as had originally been assumed. Sanskrit's deviation in this regard resulted in the reconstructed (i.e., unattested in any language) Indo-European forms being denoted with a preceding asterisk–as in **bhendh*. Previously, the Sanskrit forms had generally been accepted as representative of the proto-language.

The law of palatals solidified this demotion more conspicuously and sealed Sanskrit's fate as a sister language to Greek, Latin, Germanic, and the other Indo-European languages, rather than the more-or-less exact preserver of the original mother tongue. The final formulation of the law of palatals was the result of a series of discoveries by a number of European scholars.[3] Put briefly, Sanskrit has three primary vowels: *a*, *i*, and *u*. Up until the 1870s, scholars believed that this vowel triad represented the original Indo-European vowel system. However, while the occurrences of the *i* and *u* vowels in words cognate to Sanskrit and the other Indo-European languages was unproblematic (i.e., where a Sanskrit word contained an *i* or *u*, its cognates did likewise), the *a* vowel proved to be unpredictable. In words where Sanskrit had preserved an *a*, other Indo-European languages revealed cognate forms with either *a*, *e*, or *o* with no apparent consistency.[4] The method of historical linguistics is based on the tenet that all sound changes are rule-governed, but there did not seem to be any discernible rules governing these particular vowel correspondences. Although linguists found this multiplicity of Indo-European vowels in cognate forms bewildering and seemingly erratic, they assumed that Sanskrit had best preserved the original IE phonological system and that therefore Sanskrit *a* was the protosound that the other languages somehow had corrupted into *a*, *e*, and *o*. But they could not determine the phonemic laws governing such changes.

The law of palatals reversed all this by postulating that it was the other languages such as Greek and Latin that, in addition to *i* and *u*, had also faithfully preserved the original vowels *a*, *e*, and *o* from an original Indo-European pentad *i*, *u*, *a*, *e*, and *o*: Sanskrit had been the innovator by merging the latter three vowels into a single *a* to form its vowel triad.[5] Specifically, the law postulated that velars are replaced by palatals in the environments where Sanskrit *a* corresponds to *e* in other dialects, and that therefore Sanskrit once also contained an *e* in those environments The law was perceived most clearly in the reduplicated perfective form *cakāra* 'he/she did'. The basic characteristic of this preterit tense, termed *liṭ* by Pāniṇian grammarians, is that the first syllable of the root reduplicates. However, guttural (velar) stops are irregular in this regard, being replaced by palatals in the reduplicated form. Thus, *kṛ* yields *cakāra*, and *gam-* yields *jagāma*. Within Sanskrit, there is no explanation for this phenomenon–the reduplication should logically have resulted in *kakāra* and *gagāma*. Greek, however, showed that the reduplicated syllable has an *e* vowel. This was the clue that alerted the philologists.

Scholars argued that according to the law of palatals, the reduplicated form of *kṛ* was originally *kekora*, the first *k* being a reduplication of the root syllable in accordance with the regular laws of reduplication. However, it was proposed that due to the influence of the postulated vowel *e* following the reduplicated *k*, this latter transformed into *c*. The law of palatalization claimed that the vowel following the reduplicated syllable could not have been an *a*; otherwise, there would have been no stimulus for the palatalization of the guttural to have occurred in the first place. The change seems natural, in contrast, if the reduplicated vowel was an *e*. The reason is simply one of euphonic ease of articulation. Front vowels, such as *e*, cause palatalization, whereas back vowels, such as *a*, have no such effect. As Pedersen (1931) puts it: "This Indian law could not be seen unless one dared assume that the vowel system in Sanskrit is quite the reverse of primitive, and that the Latin *e* in *que* 'and' (Greek *te*) is older than the *a* in Sanskrit *ca* 'and'" (280). The thought was revolutionary. In one stroke, there was no more mystery concerning the vowel correspondences: method had finally been brought to the madness. The hitherto perceived conservatism of Sanskrit, however, was the casualty of this advancement in linguistics; it had now officially lost its exclusive claim of being the most archaic member of the family in all respects.

A later hypothesis that further significantly demoted Sanskrit from its venerable position in the eyes of many linguists as the most intact member of the Indo-European language family, was the discovery of the laryngeals in Hittite. Saussure initially postulated the existence of certain unknown resonant sounds in the Proto-Indo-European language.[6] These resonants, which Saussure called *coefficients sonantiques* (and represented as A and O) but were later called laryngeals, disappeared in the daughter Indo-European languages, but their original existence was deduced by Saussure from the effects they had left behind on neighboring vowels before becoming extinct.[7]

Over half a century later, in 1927, Kuryłowicz examined the Hittite documents that had been discovered in Anatolia during the First World War in the light of Saussure's contentions. He found that they actually contained a *h* phoneme in the exact linguistic locations that Saussure had predicted that his A resonant should have once existed. This *h* phoneme was termed a *laryngeal* by analogy with Semitic laryngeals, which were also lost after they had affected the vowel in a fashion similar to Saussure's proposed *coefficients*. What had been postulated by the inferential process of comparative linguistics had now been demonstrated as factual by empirical, inscriptional data.[8] While the discovery of the laryngeal greatly validated the efficacy and validity of the process of historical reconstruction, the discovery of Hittite and, to a much lesser extent, Tocharian (which will be discussed later) has significantly altered the appearance of the reconstructed protolanguage not only in phonology but also in morphology and lexicology. As an aside, as has been pointed out, these discoveries underscore the tentative nature of Proto-Indo-European reconstruction: any further future uncovering of presently unknown languages may cause linguists to alter their present reconstructions and produce a significantly altered reconstructed language that is different from the one linguists have reconstructed today. As Pulgram (1959) points out, "when a new dialect is discovered, the inventory of Proto-Indo-European phonemes may have to be revised, as indeed it was after we learned about Tocharish and Hittite. Needless to say, the inventory of real Proto-Indo-European is not subject to revision on the evidence of modern discoveries" (424).

Be that as it may, for our purposes, the discovery of the laryngeals, although still the subject of debate among linguists, reveals a written Indo-European language that had preserved linguistic features that were more archaic than Vedic. This "demotion" of Sanskrit has been ongoing ever since; although Indo-European studies is still heavily dependent on Sanskrit for any attempt at reconstruction (indeed, there is no way of determining if there even would have been a discipline of Indo-European studies without Sanskrit), it has been claimed that every commonly accepted adjustment to the reconstruction of Proto-Indo-European in the last century and a half has involved a further de-Sanskritisation of the protolanguage. As in any discipline, however, there are still "conservative" linguists who remain unconvinced about some of the new proposals concerning the protolanguage and who still accept Sanskrit as the most faithful preserver of most of the protoforms.

Objections from India

One of the very few Indian linguists who has contested some aspects of this de-sanskritization of Proto-Indo-European is Satya Swarup Misra (1977, 1994), who has particularly opposed the laryngeal theory for three decades.[9] His opposition, it should be noted, has nothing to do with the Aryan invasion debate or with issues connected with Vedic antiquity, since at the time he first published his thesis, he accepted the theory of Aryan invasions and the commonly accepted date of 1200 B.C.E. for the Ṛgveda.[10] Misra has repeatedly argued that the theory rests on limited evidence provided by only one member of the Indo-European language family—the Anatolian group.[11] He prefers to consider that the Hittite *h* symbol either had merely graphic status with no phonemic value or was a phoneme borrowed from another language family, perhaps Semitic, in a manner analogous to the supposed borrowing of retroflexes into Indo-Aryan from Dravidian (which are phonemes unattested in other Indo-European languages and therefore not ascribed to Proto-European).[12]

Nonetheless, apart from the laryngeals, Hittite is considered to have preserved other archaic Indo-European linguistic features that Sanskrit and other Indo-European languages have lost. Some linguists, for example, believe that it has retained the original common Indo-European gender where Vedic, and other languages, innovated the masculine-feminine gender distinction.[13] Although other linguists reject this idea, the gap between Sanskrit and Proto-Indo-European has progressively widened in the eyes of some linguists. Several scholars such as Polomé have argued that some features in Indic and Greek that have always been considered archaic, such as the reduplicated perfect, are actually late Indo-European innovations: "We must consider Greek and Indo-Aryan as reflecting the *most recent* developments in the Indo-European speech community at the time of its disintegration" (Polomé 1985, 682). Lehmann (1993) acknowledges that "many Indo-Europeanists still assume that the subgroup including Sanskrit and Greek is closest to the proto-language" but feels this position "requires extraordinary effort to account for the morphological structure of Hittite, especially because of its similarity with that of Germanic. It also overlooks innovations in Greek and Sanskrit that have not been extended throughout all categories in the early stages of these languages, such as the augment" (261). Indeed, Lehmann goes so far as to say that "the history of reconstructing Proto-Indo-European might be characterized as a continuing effort to liberate it from the heavy hand of Sanskrit" (261). Of course, the last word has yet to be said on such matters, and Polomé (1985) makes a point of adding that "all of this does not imply . . . that Indic does not show archaic features" (682). But Proto-Indo-European appears far less Sanskritic nowadays than it was in the fable Schleicher attempted to reconstruct in Proto-Indo-European in 1871, which was almost pure Sanskrit.[14]

More recently, since Misra (1992) has begun to reject the Aryan invasion theory on linguistic grounds, he has become more and more suspicious of the reconstructed proto-language. He has even reexamined the primacy of Greek and Latin *a*, *e*, and *o* over Sanskrit *a*. He suggests that the Gypsy languages provide evidence that an original Sanskrit *a* vowel does demonstrably evolve into *a*, *e*, and *o* in later languages.[15] The Gypsies are generally accepted as having migrated from India some time in the common era and speak languages that are Indo-Aryan in character. The logic here is that if, in the historic period, Indo-Aryan speaking tribes have left India and migrated to Europe, where they are found speaking dialects that have transformed an original Sanskrit *a* vowel into *a*, *e* and *o*, then the same could be postulated for the protohistoric period: Indo-European tribes could have left a homeland in India carrying a Proto-Indo-European *a* that evolved into the *a*, *e*, and *o* of the later Greek and Latin languages.[16] However, Misra's proposal, apart from anything else, gives only a passing reference to the law of palatalization which, as has been outlined, initially caused linguists to postulate a Proto-Indo-European *a*, *e*, and *o* triad, as opposed to a proto *a* form, in the first place.

It should go without saying that no serious linguist is about to reverse a century and a half of linguistic research to contemplate the proposal that proto-Indo-European was identical with Vedic, as some members of the Indigenous Aryan school might hope.[17] Of course, even allowing the more complete preservation of the Indo-European vowels in, say, Greek or other European languages, and of the laryngeals in Hittite, or of the archaic features in Lithuanian, Indian scholars can still argue that Vedic is, overall, the language that has most completely retained the Proto-Indo-European character despite the present trend among many linguists to consider the distinctive Vedic features to have been later innovations. But language is never static. Linguists cannot be expected to accept Vedic as an immutable linguistic entity that somehow transcends the transformations visible in every language known to man (transformations that are, indeed, perceivable in the Vedic texts themselves). The discourse of an eternal, unchanging Veda is a legitimate one for the ashram, not the academy.[18]

Conclusion

Whatever might have been the real nature of Proto-Indo-European, for the purposes of this study, the existence of various linguistic stages of Indo-European more archaic than Vedic is irrelevant (or, at least, peripheral) to the problem of the origin of the Indo-Aryans. In the absence of compelling counterarguments, there are no grounds to question that Proto-Indo-European resembles, more or less, the reconstructed entity diligently assembled to the satisfaction of most historical linguistics with its *e* and *o* vowels, its laryngeals, and the rest of its carefully formulated components. Unless this linguistic evidence is deconstructed in a thoroughly comprehensive methodological way, there are no a priori reasons to reject the basics of the Proto-Indo-European language as accepted by most linguists.[19] The real problem ultimately facing Indigenous Aryanists boils down to whether, or more specifically how, this Indo-European language could have originated in some area of India. If this proposal cannot be argued convincingly, then it at least must be demonstrated whether and how India can avoid being excluded as one potential homeland among others.

It is all well and good to insist that there is no evidence supporting the theory of an external origin of the Indo-Aryan language, but how are the connections between Vedic Sanskrit and the other members of the Indo-European language family to be explained? That cognate languages must, by definition, have a common linguistic and geographic origin is an assumption that few have challenged.[20] The history of the Indo-Aryan group of languages must always be reconstructed from within the context of its membership in the greater Indo-European language family of which it is an unassailable member. Any theories pertaining to one member of the family must be in harmony with the data connected with the other members of the family. If Indo-Aryan is to be considered indigenous to the subcontinent, then how is its relationship to the other Indo-European languages to be explained? Either the Indo-Aryan languages entered the subcontinent from an external geographic origin or, if it is to be argued that this group is indigenous, at least to the Northwest, the unavoidable corollary is that northwest India *is* the geographic origin of *all* the other Indo-European languages, which must have *emigrated* to the West from there. Indigenous Aryanists have to confront and address this language connection, with its inescapable requirement of a common language origin.

However, many scholars tend to avoid pursuing their claims of Aryan autochthony to this inevitable conclusion. Indeed, with a very few exceptions, most Indigenous Aryanists tend to completely ignore the linguistic evidence altogether. Others are almost cavalier in their dismissal of it: "All the comparative philological speculations, . . . according to some of us, provide the greatest stumbling-block to the appreciation of a multi-linear archaeological development of culture and civilisation in different parts of India" (Chakrabarti 1995, 429); "Ancient Indian history is ripe for a thorough revision. . . . one can begin by clearing away the cobwebs cast by questionable linguistic theories, . . . using every available modern tool from archaeology to computer science" (Rajaram 1995, 230).

There seem to be two very basic reasons for this neglect. Seeing the morass of opposing opinions supposedly based on the same linguistic evidence, some scholars have rejected the whole Indo-European enterprise as hopelessly speculative and inconclusive. To put it another way, they are not interested—this is primarily a European preoccupation.[21] Alternatively, for those interested in Indo-European historical linguistics, they soon find that the field is inaccessible to the dilettante and requires organized study that is not easy to come by in India. Current scholarly publications in Indo-European presuppose acquaintance with almost two centuries of linguistic discoveries (much of it in German and French and, more recently, Russian), as well as with at least a number of principle Indo-European languages (including, at least, Sanskrit, Greek, Latin, Hittite, and Germanic).[22] As mentioned earlier, although there have been, and still are, some exceptional historical linguists in India, their numbers are few. This is not a subject that is fruitfully pursued, and it has always remained predominantly a Western field of scholarship. It should be noted that there is very little facility in India for the study of historical linguistics. When I conducted my research (1994–95), only two universites in the subcontinent were actively offering adequate courses in this field.[23]

Perhaps the dethronement of Sanskrit as the most archaic Indo-European language did initially contribute to a loss of interest in this field as suggested by Mahulkar, but one suspects that present-day concerns are more pragmatic, at least in terms of the academic powers that be. As is increasingly apparent even in areas of the Western academy, sociolinguistics or modern language study produce more tangible fruits for dwindling government funding. Indian scholars, for the most part, simply do not have the training to embark on a scholarly critique or evaluation of the vast specialized field of Indo-European studies. For the most part, with some exceptions, Indigenists wishing to tackle the Indo-Aryan issue are left with the option of either ignoring the linguistic dimension of the problem or attempting to tackle it with sometimes hopelessly inadequate qualifications. Typically, the formulations of the Indo-Europeanists, being inaccessible, are dismissed in frustration as highly speculative and irrelevant. This attitude and neglect significantly minimizes the value of most Indigenist publications.[24]

In any event, as we shall see, a few scholars have argued that the linguistic evidence could just as well be reconfigured to postulate that even India might have been the Indo-European homeland. This challenge, when made by the more sober members of the Indigenous Aryan school, does not so much aim to prove that India factually was the original homeland as to assert that the linguistic evidence is not sufficiently conclusive to fully determine where the homeland was. In view of this challenge, we must, as a purely theoretical exercise, consider whether the linguistic evidence can exclude the possibility of a South Asian homeland as one candidate among others.

5

Linguistic Substrata in Sanskrit Texts

Another principal reason that South Asia had been excluded relatively early as a potential Indo-European homeland was that it showed evidence of a pre-Indo-European linguistic substratum—considered to have been of Dravidian, Munda, or other unknown languages. I use the term *substratum* in the sense of an indigenous language being subsumed and displaced by an alien incoming language. In this process, the indigenous language affects the dominant language by depositing into it its own linguistic features, such as vocabulary or morphology. These features form a substratum in the dominant language that can be discerned by diligent linguists. Such evidence is solid reason to exclude India and must detain us at length. Southern Europe had also been eliminated for the same reasons—northern Spain and southwestern France had a pre-Indo-European substratum in the form of Basque, and Italy had Etruscan. This method, which has sometimes been called the *exclusion principle*, initially serves to at least delimit the range of candidates for the Proto-Indo-European homeland from within the massive area where the cognate languages were and are spoken. Dravidian, Munda, Basque, and Etruscan are not Indo-European languages, suggesting that Indo-European was not the original language family in those areas and therefore must have intruded from elsewhere. The evidence of such a substratum remains one of the most cited and compelling reasons for accepting the verdict that the Indo-Aryan language must have had an origin external to the Indian subcontinent. As Emeneau (1954) puts it: "This is our linguistic doctrine which has been held now for more than a century and a half. There seems to be no reason to distrust the arguments for it despite the traditional Hindu ignorance of any such invasion, their doctrine that Sanskrit is the 'language of the Gods,' and the somewhat chauvinistic clinging to the old tradition even today by some Indian scholars" (282).

The best-known study of the Dravidian languages was made by the Reverend Robert Caldwell in his pioneering *Comparative Grammar of the Dravidian Languages* in 1856 (although, in actuality, the first publication on the Dravidian language family was by Francis Whyte Ellis, as far back as 1816—the year of Bopp's famous comparative grammar).[1] Until the founding of the Madras Orientalist school, scholars, who had assumed that all the languages of the subcontinent had a common origin, had been almost exclusively concerned with the Indo-Aryan languages because of the relationship these languages had with the classical languages of Europe and the exciting implications this connection suggested for the origins of Western civilization. In 1849, Alexander Campbell continued the work of Ellis and was able to demonstrate that "it has been very generally asserted, and indeed believed, that the Teloogoo has its origin in the language of the Vedums. . . . my inquiries have led me to the opposite conclusion. . . . Teloogoo abounds with Sanskrit words. . . . nevertheless, there is reason to believe that the origin of the two languages is altogether distinct" (xv–xvi). The breakthrough for these scholars was originally triggered by the extensive analyses of the traditional grammarians of India, who had noted the distinction between the Sanskrit words and the non-Sanskritic *deśya* ones. This alerted these linguists to the possibility of non-Indo-Aryan languages in the subcontinent.

The discovery of non-Sanskritic languages in the South provided important material that seemed to militate against the idea of the Indo-Aryans as indigenous to India—or at least to any of it except the Northwest. In a series of articles in the early 1840s, Stevenson (1844) laid out the implications of this non-Sanskritic, indigenous language base, which he perceived even in the northern vernaculars:

> If we can trace a language wholly different from the Sanscrit in all the modern dialects, . . . it will seem to follow, that the whole region previous to the arrival of the Brahmans was peopled by the members of one great family of a different origin. . . . I call the Brahmans a foreign tribe in accordance with indications derivable from the cast of their features, and the colour of their skin, as well as their possessing a language which none of the natives of India but themselves can even so much as pronounce; and the constant current of their own traditions making them foreign to the whole of India, except perhaps a small district to the north-west upon the Ganges. (104)

In another article, Stevenson (1851) elaborated more fully on his theory, which, is more or less an account that can still be found in texts on Indian prehistory. He envisioned tribes entering the main part of India, defeating the aborigines by force of arms, expelling them from the northern regions, and enslaving those that remained (73). By the middle of the nineteenth century, most Western scholars had accepted the existence of the Dravidian languages as conclusive proof that the Aryans could not have been indigenous to the subcontinent: "That the Arian population of India descended into it about 3000 years ago from the north-west, as conquerors, and that they completely subdued all the open and cultivated parts of Hindustan, Bengal and the most adjacent tracts of the Deccan but failed to extend their effective sway and colonization further south, are quasi historical deductions confirmed daily more and more" (Hodgson 1848, 551).

To this day, a few linguistic islands of Dravidian languages, of which Brahui occupies the largest area, exist in the North of India surrounded by an ocean of Indo-Aryan languages. They are generally explained as being isolated remnants that had somehow avoided being engulfed by the incoming tides of Indo-Aryan speakers encroaching on what had originally been a Dravidian language area spread throughout much of India. Moreover, a few words in the Ṛgveda, progressively more words in later Vedic texts, and a much larger number of words in later Epic texts were identified as being loanwords principally from Dravidian but with some forms traceable to Munda. The borrowings were held to have ceased shortly after the Epic period. This seemed to fit neatly into the hypothesis that when the Vedas were composed, the Indo-Aryans had only recently arrived into Dravidian-speaking India and had absorbed only a few words from the local Dravidian substratum.[2] As time went by and the Aryan speakers merged completely with the native population, more and more Dravidian words were absorbed, which emerged increasingly in the later texts. Sometime before the common era, when the Dravidian languages in the North had been completely subsumed by Aryan dialects, the borrowings ceased. This whole process is usually understood as being the result of the Aryans themselves adopting new items of the local lexicon and/or of bilingual Dravidian speakers increasingly adopting the new Aryan languages until they eventually became completely co-opted into speaking Indo-Aryan, but not without preserving a significant number of words and other linguistic features from their own languages. I will deal first with these other, nonlexical items. Here, as in the remaining chapters on Linguistics, I will try to keep technical details to a minimum.

Linguistic Innovations in Sanskrit

Vocabulary was not the only Dravidian element that seemed to have surfaced in Indo-Aryan: a number of syntactical and morphological features common to Dravidian, but alien to other Indo-European languages, had been identified since Caldwell's work in 1856. None of these features were explicitly present in other Indo-European languages, but they did occur in Sanskrit, Dravidian, and other South Asian languages. Such shared syntactical and morphological features reinforced the hypothesis that the Indo-Aryans were intruders to the subcontinent and that bilingual Dravidian speakers who preceded them in the North of India had welded some of their own local syntactical features onto the encroaching Aryan languages they were adopting. This idea of syntactical convergence has developed into the established paradigm of South Asia as a linguistic area.[3] In the case of Sanskrit, these syntactical innovations were generally held by most scholars to be due to a local substratum of Dravidian, which triggered this linguistic subversion (most recently Emeneau 1980; Kuiper 1991). Munda is another candidate (Witzel 1999, forthcoming b). Some scholars see a combination of both. Southworth, for example, on the basis of geographic dialect variations in the Aśokan inscriptions as well as in New Indo-Aryan languages, proposed that "while the population in the western areas . . . was probably mainly Dravidian speaking, in the Gangetic plain . . . the IA language was taken up by a predominantly Tibeto-Burmese population" (1974, 222).[4] An unknown primordial language, which was pre-Indo-Aryan, Dravidian, or Munda, called "language x" by Masica (1979) has also been identified in the texts.

As noted, bilingualism is held to be one of the mechanism of the innovations, with most linguists painting a picture of non-Aryan natives from the lower strata adopting the intruding elite language of Indo-Aryan (although Southworth 1979 sees social equals), but adapting it somewhat to accommodate certain lexical, phonemic, morphological,

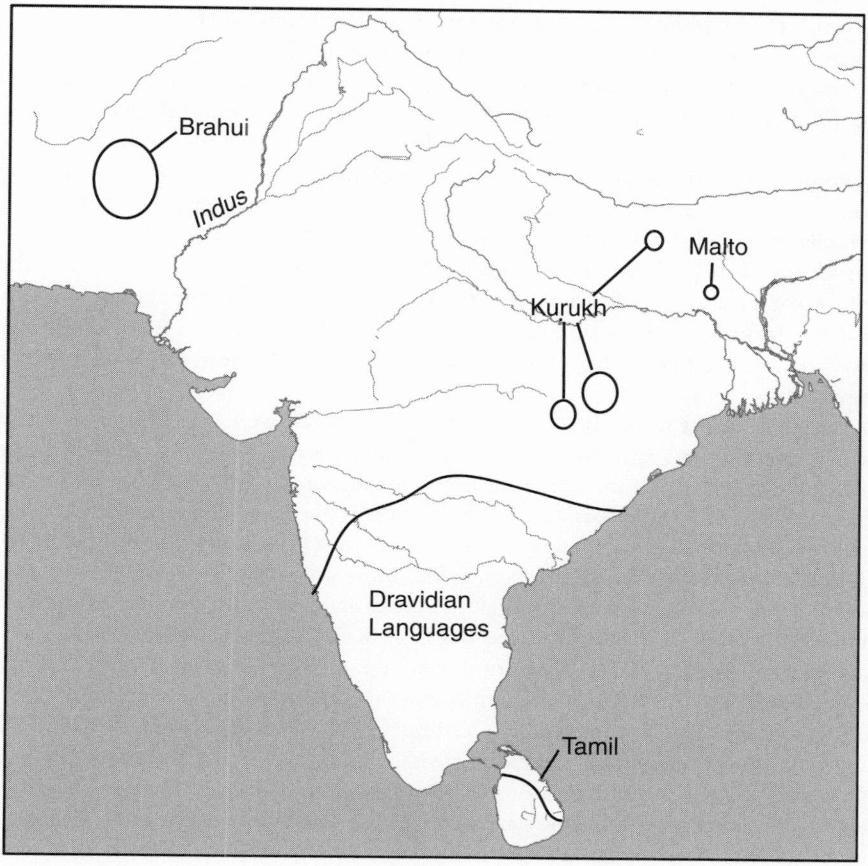

Dravidian languages in the Indian subcontinent.

and syntactic features of their own languages (e.g., Kuiper 1991, 96). Although this substratum language subsequently disappeared in North India, its original existence there could be inferred from the linguistic clues it had left behind in Sanskrit and later Indo-Aryan languages in the form of non-Indo-European syntax, vocabulary and root structure.

There are, in particular, three linguistic features that are innovative in the Ṛgveda and that have been the subject of the most discussion. Phonologically, there is the introduction of retroflexes, which alternate with dentals in Indo-Aryan; morphologically there are the gerunds, absolutives or verbal participles (e.g., *hatvā* instead of *jaghanvān*); and syntactically there is the use of *iti*, a postposed quotative marker. Other features have also been noted by linguists,[5] but since my focus is primarily on the Ṛgveda these items are among those particularly relevant here and serve as suitable exemplars for the purpose of this analysis.

Caldwell ([1856] 1875) who was the first to thoroughly examine such innovations, noticed instances where the North Indian vernacular languages shared certain particulars with the Dravidian languages that were not shared with other Indo-European languages (59).[6] Although accepting the hypothesis that the derivation of the North Indian languages from Sanskrit had transpired not so much because of natural processes as from the "overmastering, overmolding power of the non-Sanskritic element contained in them," Caldwell rejected the possibility that these non-Sanskritic elements—the substratum, in modern parlance—could have been Dravidian:[7] "Whatever the ethnological evidence of their identity may be supposed to exist,—when we view the question philologically, and with reference to the evidence furnished by their languages alone, the hypothesis of their identity [as Dravidian] does not appear to me to have been established" (58). Caldwell pointed out that the structural similarities common to Dravidian and the Indo-Aryan languages were also shared with other non-Aryan languages; Dravidian was not the only candidate that might have influenced the development of Sanskrit.

Such arguments would be of merely historical interest were they not to keep resurfacing. In 1924 and again in 1929, Jules Bloch reiterated some of Caldwell's objections, insisting that "in the present state of our knowledge, it is impossible to affirm that the form taken by the Aryan language in India is due to its adoption by a Dravidian-speaking population. If there is a substratum at all, this substratum could just as equally be looked for in other families, especially the Munda family" (1924–30, 20; my translation).[8] Bloch also remarked that Brahui quite easily could have migrated from central India to the North in the same way as the Dravidian-speaking Oraon and Maler tribes had migrated north to Chota Nagpur (2). Likewise, the Dravidian-speaking Kurukh and Malto tribes live in territory with Munda place-names and still maintain traditions referring to their migration into Munda territory (Bloch 1946; see also Hock 1996). Like Caldwell, Bloch rejected the idea that Dravidian could have been the origin of certain phonemic and syntactic innovations in Indo-Aryan, and stressed that Dravidian was not the only language sharing the syntactical features that distinguished Indo-Aryan from other Indo-European languages, some of which, he argued, could have been internal developments rather than borrowing.[8]

Over the last two decades, H. H. Hock (1975, 1984, 1996) has strongly challenged the notion that the linguistic convergences in the Indian languages could only have been due to a Dravidian substratum. For the most part, he argues that many of the innovative features Indo-Aryan shares with Dravidian actually have parallels in other Indo-European languages and are therefore more likely to have been internal developments and not borrowings from any other language at all. Citing examples of retroflexion occurring in other Indo-European languages, Hock proposed that this trait could have been an indigenous development (a possibility Burrow also felt was perfectly valid). Likewise, he listed occurrences of gerunds and participles (absolutives) in other Indo-European languages, as well as usages of the quotative marker *iti*. Hock (1984a) argues that the subject-object-verb (SOV) syntactical positioning Indo-Aryan shares with Dravidian may have existed in Indo-European itself in its eastern area (97). He also claimed that all the uses of *api*—'also', 'and', 'even', 'totality', and '-(so)ever'—have parallels in Indo-Iranian and Indo-European (103–104).

If Hock is corect that all these features could have developed in the other Indo-European languages that had no contact whatsoever with Dravidian, then their occurrence in Indo-Aryan must also be possible without requiring Dravidian influence (see Kuiper

1991, 10, for criticism). Like several linguists, Hock argues that retroflexion can be explained by purely internal developments; he notes that other Indo-European languages, albeit the more recent ones of Swedish and Norwegian, have developed the feature completely independent of any substratum. He reiterates and expands on Bloch's (1924) comments that the positioning and phonology of various retroflexes differ in Dravidian and Indo-Aryan. This fact alone problematizes the candidacy of Dravidian as a substratum for Indo-Aryan and caused Tikkanen (1987, 295) to postulate that both Dravidian and Indo-Aryan had received the feature from two separate substrata.

Hock's model (1993) is one of language "convergence" rather than "subversion" a process of mutual directionality or exchange between languages as the result of long-standing bilingual contact, as opposed to unidirectional transfers under conditions of social inequality—a process "similar to what we find in modern South Asia" (76). He notes a very important point: many of the early phonological differences between Indo-Aryan and Dravidian disappear toward the modern period, but this has nothing to do with subversion. It was caused by convergence. In other words, adstratum can account for this convergence, not substratum. In *ad*stratum situation, languages are geographically adjacent to each other, as opposed to one intrusive language being superimposed on a preexisting language.

The other type of stratum relationship, that of superstratum, entails linguistic intrusions into a preexisting dominant language area by other languages that were eventually subsumed (or that eventually proceeded on), but not before affecting the dominant language in some fashion. English, for example, intruded into India in the Colonial Period. It did not displace the local languages, but did pass many loan words into them. Hock also argues (1993) that the whole phenomenon of shared retroflexion (which, as noted earlier, could have been an internal development) also could have been caused by convergence between the two languages or by mediation by a third entity (96). Hock (1984a) concludes by encouraging scholars to look for alternative explanations to the Dravidian substratum hypotheses, since "the claim that Dravidian influence on Sanskrit began in pre-Rig-Vedic times must be considered not supported by sufficient evidence" (104). As we shall see, the vocabulary evidence does not favor direct contact with either Dravidian or Munda, thus causing scholars to postulate an even earlier unknown language. Hock (1996b) is open to the possibility that there may have been other languages, no longer extant, that could have preceded Sanskrit. He notes, however, that such a claim is "methodologically problematic, since it can be neither verified nor falsified" (57).

Reluctance to accept substratum influences, and particularly Dravidian substratum, as the cause of specific linguistic developments in Indo-Aryan has remained consistent. The possibility of the retroflexes in Sanskrit being a spontaneous phenomenon has been current since Bühler's work in 1864. As Kuiper ([1967] 1974) remarks, "No agreement has yet been reached after a discussion extending over more than a century" (138). Deshpande (1979), in accordance with other scholars such as Emeneau, does believe that Dravidian was the origin for this feature but argues that retroflexion did not exist in the original Ṛgveda. He believes that its origin "lies in Dravidian speakers adapting Aryan speech to their native phonology" (297). Kuiper (1991), in contrast, is quite adamant that they "must have penetrated into Indo-Aryan in a prehistoric ('pre-Vedic') period" (14). Hamp (1996), while prepared to allow that "Dravidian articulation habits may have contributed to these allophonic variations," demonstrates that the conditions "were laid and can be traced in the Indo-European patrimony of Sanskrit." He laid out the series of sound changes from purely inherited Indo-European material that arrive "by perfectly orderly *Lautgesetze*" to the distinctive feature of retroflexion (721; see also Vine 1987). In other words, retroflexion can be explained purely as the result of spontaneous linguistic sound processes inherent in Indo-Aryan itself: it need not be seen as the result of a linguistic imposition from a foreign language.

Similar disagreement revolve around other such innovations in Indo-Aryan. Like Hock, Tikkanen, for example, in his book on the Sanskrit gerund, finds that adstratum influences could just as easily account for the commonalty of this feature between Indo-Aryan and Dravidian.[9] Jamison, (1989) in her review of Tikkanen's book, dismisses any talk of substratum at all in this regard, "since one less committed to the substrate explanation can easily see mechanisms whereby the gerund could have independently acquired the value it has when it enters history" (461). (For criticisms, see Kuiper 1991, 10). Tikkanen's comment about adstratum, as opposed to substratum, influence, which parallel's Hock's notion of 'Convergence,' provides an alternative model for the linguistic history of South Asia that will be further discussed later.

The Indigenous Aryan school, for the most part, seems to be either completely oblivious to the whole linguistic substratum dimension of this issue or dismissive of it: "It now appears that the underlying linguistic theories may be enjoying a . . . charmed life. *All theories should be validated by data independent of the theory, and not by hypothetical constructions derived from the theory itself.* Until that happens, the safest course is to regard these theories as unproven conjectures and refrain from basing any key conclusions on their claims" (Rajaram 1995, 219: italics in original). This is a conspicuous and curious neglect. It is conspicuous because the whole theory of the external origin of the Indo-Aryans was greatly accelerated by the "discovery" of the Dravidian languages and of the non-Indo-European elements in Sanskrit, and this evidence needs to be addressed by those contesting the theory. It is curious because if we ignore, for the moment, all other types of data connected with the problem of Aryan origins, it would seem that there might actually be some scope in all this to challenge the assumption that there had to be a pre-Aryan linguistic substratum at all—at least in the matter of phonology, morphology, and syntax. Several linguists, all of whom accept the external origin of the Aryan languages on other grounds, are quite open to considering that the various syntactical developments in Indo-Aryan could have been internal developments rather than the result of substrate influences, or have been the result of adstratum. Dravidian in particular, the most popular candidate, has been consistently challenged as a possible linguistic substratum for Indo-Aryan.

Before proceeding any further, it is very important to note that there is a serious methodological drawback in these types of comparisons, since we cannot compare the syntax of the Ṛgveda with actual contemporaneous Dravidian texts, but only with a reconstructed proto-Dravidian. The oldest Dravidian literary evidence that we know of comes from epigraphs of old Tamil written in a form of Brāhmī script sometime between the third and the first centuries B.C.E. The first completely intelligible, datable, and sufficiently long and complete epigraphs that might be of some use in linguistic comparison are the Tamil inscriptions of the Pallava dynasty of about 550 C.E. (Zvelebil 1990), two entire millennia after the commonly accepted date for the Ṛgveda. Postulating syntactical influence on Vedic from Dravidian material attested after such a vast amount of time has obvious methodological limitations.

The Munda languages have left no significant literary tradition at all, so the interval in their case at least is a staggering thirty-five hundred years. Moreover, there is much less material available on comparative Munda, and much of the proto-language has been reconstructed from material drawn from members of the family outside the subcontinent—there are no etymological dictionaries of proto-Munda, nor of its daughter languages. Establishing connections with Munda is made more problematic, since, as Burrow (1968) noted (to the approval of Masica [1979] and Southworth [1979]), "the evidence as it is so far established would suggest that these languages in ancient times as well as now were situated only in eastern India" (328). However, this idea, as will be discussed later, has recently been challenged by Witzel (forthcoming).

The possibility of Indo-Aryan spontaneously evolving the syntactical innovations and then influencing Dravidian or Munda, as opposed to being influenced by them, needs to be excluded as a possibility. Hock (1993) complains that "implicit in the subversionist view of early Indo-Aryan/Dravidian contact is the assumption of unilateral influence of Dravidian on Indo-Aryan. . . . No mention is ever made of prehistoric Indo-Aryan influence on Dravidian " (85). Even Emeneau (1980), a committed proponent of Dravidian bilingualism, is remarkably cautious in his proposals and is forced to acknowledge that it could have been Indo-Aryan that influenced Dravidian as opposed to being influenced by it: "Is the whole IA [Indo-Aryan] history one of self-development, and the complex Dr. [Dravidian] development something triggered by IA, perhaps even NIA [new IA], influence, or, in the case of Kurukh, borrowed from NIA?. . . This . . . solution is less attractive than [Dr. influencing IA]. But no easy solution is yet at hand" (174).

As for Brahui, according to Dyen's lexicostatistical study (1956), "there is a choice whether Brahui was separated from the other languages by the Indo-Aryan invasion or whether it represents a migration [from the South]. Since a negative migration cannot be ruled out, the two inferences are equally probable" (625). It is, of course, a perfectly common linguistic phenomenon for intruding dominant languages to displace preceding languages, relegating them to small pockets in marginal areas. But it is just as common for small groups of language speakers to migrate and survive in small pockets outside the domain of their own language family; Brahui need not be considered a remnant of a pre-Aryan, Dravidian substratum, a possibility recognized even by Emeneau (1962b, 70). Like Bloch, Hock (1975, 88) finds the suggestion that Brahui could have emigrated from the South to the North to be perfectly possible. The Brahui, like the Kurukh and Malto, actually maintain traditions referring to their external origin.[10] This immigrant position of Brahui has again recently been asserted by Elfenbein (1987), who finds it impossible that it could have survived for five thousand years (the Dravidians as will be discussed below, are supposed to have migrated into India around 3000 B.C.E.) as a small, isolated linguistic group completely surrounded by alien languages.

All of the linguists who have puzzled over the linguistic innovations in Indo-Aryan have assumed that the Indo-Aryan speakers were newcomers into India and have, therefore, taken it for granted that "there must have been, from the earliest times, contacts between the Indo-Aryan invaders and the autochthonous population" (Kuiper [1967] 1974, 141). Other linguistic groups are therefore presumed to have preceded them in the North of the subcontinent. As Emeneau (1954) puts it, "These invaders did not penetrate into a linguistic vacuum (282)." Approaching the issue on purely linguistic grounds, those opposing this assumption would have to argue that the areal features of South Asian languages are independent, spontaneous developments in the languages concerned and/or that these features have developed as a result of mutual contact *other* than that of a substratum nature. This latter possibility would seem to be a perfectly valid one if only because the South Asian languages are *continuing to undergo the process of convergence*. Indeed, some linguists go so far as to suggest that "if the direction of their development does not change in the future, the now observed tendency to develop the formal similarity may gain strength and result in the formation of new relationship ties and of a new language family, which will be neither Indo-European, nor Dravidian" (Andronov 1968, 13; see also Dasgupta, 1982, 126).

This point, in my opinion, is crucial to this whole issue. If, in the modern and historical period that can be verified, linguistic convergence is an ongoing process that is obviously not the result of any bilingual substratum (although adstrata or other types of bilingualism may certainly be principal factors), then this certainly also could have been the case in the less-verifiable pre- and protohistoric period. In short, convergence, or any type of borrowing or similarities between languages, does not necessitate a situation of a linguistic substratum.[11]

Evidence of the Loanwords

Just as the syntactical innovations of Indo-Aryan have been interpreted as evidence of a pre-Aryan linguistic presence, so have the existence of loanwords, ascribed to either Dravidian, Munda, and/or unknown origins, been considered proof that the Aryans imposed themselves on a native populace. Bishop Caldwell presented the first list of words "probably" borrowed by Sanskrit from Dravidian that he identified according to certain criteria, most of which hold good today,[12] and which were further refined by Burrow in 1946.[13]

Having applied his criteria, Caldwell found that the Dravidian loanwords he came up with did not consist of the essential aspects of a vocabulary—the primary words such as verb roots denoting basic actions, pronouns, body parts, and so on. Such basic terms are the most durable aspect of a language, even when exposed to major influences from an alien language family. Caldwel! argued that had the pre-Aryan population of North India been Dravidian, it would have preserved at least some of its own primary Dravidian terms, which would have resurfaced in at least one or two of the northern vernaculars. This would especially have been the case in the hypothetical scenario involving a relatively tiny intrusion of Indo-Aryan speakers superimposed upon a massive population of Dravidian speakers. If these Dravidian speakers then adopted the language of the intruders, adjusting it with some of their own structural traits, then surely a few primary Dravidian words, particularly pronoun forms, also would have survived in some Indo-Aryan tongue. This was not what Caldwell found: the vocabulary borrowed consisted of words "remote from ordinary use."

Soon other lists of Dravidian loanwords in Sanskrit were compiled by scholars such as Gundert (1869) and Kittel (1894). In 1929, Bloch set the precedent for a practice that continues to the present day: he questioned the Dravidian etymologies for many of the Sanskrit words that had been proposed by these scholars, fearing that much etymologizing was not "self-evident" but "a matter of probability and to a certain extent, of faith" (743). He also made another interesting observation. Many of the Sanskrit words that were clearly loans had their equivalents in *southern* Dravidian languages. Whether or not the Aryans superimposed themselves on a Dravidian substratum in the North is one issue, but how could the Aryans in the North have been in contact with Dravidians from the South of the subcontinent? Bloch suggested that either the Dravidian languages themselves could have been intruders into India, in which case it could have been the Aryans who borrowed words from the Dravidian speakers who were en route to the subcontinent, rather than vice versa, or the words were increasingly borrowed into the written language from the vernaculars where they were in circulation (743). Since the Dravidian speakers are also generally considered immigrants into the subcontinent, this suggestion that loanwords could have been borrowed by Indo-Aryans from invading Dravidians, as opposed to by Dravidians from invading Indo-Aryans, is another possibility that has yet to receive scholarly attention[14] (although Witzel [forthcoming] is now also arguing for a similar possibility).

An indigenous Aryan position might well take interest in Bloch's suggestion that the lexical and other features shared by Indo-Aryan and Dravidian (or other languages) could well have been the result of Dravidian (or Munda) speakers migrating into an Indo-Aryan speaking area. This possibility will depend on chronology and other issues and will be discussed further later. Of some relevance, in this regard, is Southworth's contention, (1979), based on a comparison of the lists of loans from Dravidian into Indo-Aryan and vice versa, that "these two lists both seem to suggest a rather wide range of cultural contacts, and that they do *not* show the typical (or perhaps stereotypical) one-sided borrowing relationship expected in a 'colonial' situation, with words for technology and high culture mostly going in one direction and words for local flora and fauna mostly in the other (cf. English and Hindi, for example)" (196). In his opinion, "No picture of technological, cultural, or military dominance by either side emerges from an examination of these words" (204). This could support the consideration of adstratum influence between the languages.

Another explanation Bloch considers, which P. Thieme was to find intriguing, was that individual literary men from the Deccan could have imported Dravidian terms into classical Sanskrit (in which case, many of the terms would be provincialisms rather than real borrowings). The massive amount of Sanskrit vocabulary borrowed from the North by the Dravidian languages, after all, would have been imported by individual Brahmanas from the North rather than as the result of any major movement of population. This is a very significant point. These individual Sanskrit-speaking Brahmans who went south were the cause of extensive lexical adoptions by the Dravidians, but this has nothing to do with linguistic substrata. The reverse possibility, of individual southerners going north and importing Dravidian lexica into Sanskrit, seemed to be substantiated for Bloch (1928–30, 744) by the fact that many of the Dravidian loans did not survive to be inherited by the later Indo-Aryan vernaculars.[15] The fact that later Pali and Hindi often maintained the Sanskrit forms rather than the Dravidian ones suggested to Bloch that the Sanskrit forms had always been the actual words in currency; the non-Aryan foreign synonyms, although appearing in Sanskrit texts, were artificial and temporary innovations. His remarks seem to be underscored in a more recent study by Masica, who also noticed that many Dravidian words in Sanskrit had left no living descendants in Hindi.[16]

Thieme, in a critique of Burrow, also questioned the assumption that the foreign words in Sanskrit must have been borrowed from a Dravidian substratum. Burrow, in a series of articles (1945, 1946, 1983), as well as in an appendix to his book *The Sanskrit Language*, had compiled a list of approximately five hundred foreign words in the Ṛgveda that he considered to be loans predominantly from Dravidian. Thieme (1955) like Bloch, is much more inclined to ascribe most of them to borrowings from the vernaculars that increasingly crept into the more elite Brahmanical circles eventually becoming Sanskritized. He remarks:

> The bearers of the sacred language are obviously and professedly eager to keep their speech pure and unadulterated. . . . We have no evidence for speech contact with Dravidian-speaking people in the North of India in olden times: no Patanjali, Yaska gives us . . . any such indication. . . . all the Dravidian languages known to us fairly bristle with loans from Sanskrit and the Aryan vernaculars. Dravidian literature in South India came into existence under the impulse and influence of Sanskrit literature and speech. Wherever there is a correspondence in the vocabularies of Sanskrit and Dravidian, there is a presumption, to be removed only by specific argument, that Sanskrit has been the lender, Dravidian the borrower. . . . I should consider it likely that . . . loans had first been given a homestead in a vernacular and penetrated thence into Sanskrit. If Patanjali (Mahabh. I.2.7–9) looks on a Magadhi word as a 'barbarian' (*mleccha*) how much more would he have despised a word of a completely different language? (438–439)

That no native grammarians have recorded any awareness of a non-Sanskritic indigenous population (although they do draw attention to *deśya* words) is significant. Thieme's point is further bolstered by the fact that, to my knowledge, none of the earliest foreigners in India who left written records—the Greeks or the Chinese—made any reference to a subjugated population speaking a different language from the ruling elite, whether in domestic situations or in marginal geographic areas. Thieme is proposing that whatever words were undeniably loans could have infiltrated into the northern vernaculars somehow or other, perhaps as a result of individuals bringing them from the South, from where they surfaced into Sanskrit, just as loans circulate in any language. He then proceeds to give alternative etymological explanations for some of the words Burrow had listed, preferring to derive them from vernaculars or from Indo-European word forms rather than from Dravidian.[17] In 1994, he again challenged many supposed Dravidian etymologies, this time from Mayrhofer's *Etymologisches Wörterbuch*, stating that "it is . . . quite legitimate to consider the possibility of Sanskrit borrowing from any non-Aryan Indian language. Yet, if a word can be explained easily from material extant in Sanskrit itself, there is little chance for such a hypothesis" (327). His doubts about many of the alleged Dravidian etymologies have been supported by scholars such as H. H. Hock (1975, 1984d) and R. P. Das (1995).

The controversies between the "Dravidianists" and "Indo-Europeanists" on the origin of unusual Vedic and Sanskrit etymologies, with a subsequent rise of an "Austro-Asiatic" contingent, has been a strongly contested issue. Thieme characterizes the activities of some of his colleagues as a "zeal for hunting up Dravidian loans in Sanskrit" (1994, 327). From the other side, the advocates of a major Dravidian (and Munda) component in Sanskrit lexemes are not impressed by the "resort to tortuous reconstructions in order to find, by hook or by crook, Indo-European explanations for Sanskrit words" (Burrow 1956, 321).[18] Kuiper (1991, 91) feels such "dogged resistance" needs to be understood through the "psychological background," which he traces back to the days when Sanskrit was the undisputed model language for comparative Indo-European studies. As far as he is concerned, the very fact that satisfactory etymologies have not been found after a century and a half of etymologizing is sufficient evidence in itself to suspect the Indo-European pedigree of a word.

The fiercest controversy has naturally revolved around the oldest text, namely, the Ṛgveda since this preserves the earliest "real" linguistic evidence. Kuiper (1991) has laid claim to 380 foreign words, or 4 percent of the Ṛgvedic vocabulary (95).[19] This is dramatically ambitious in comparison to any other previous claim. Of special interest in his lists are at least thirty-five non-Aryan names for individuals, families, and tribes—including several, such as the *dāsa* Balbūtha Tarukṣa, who were patrons of priests and therefore participated in Vedic culture (6–8).[20] Witzel (1999a) reckons that almost half of the fifty-odd tribal and clan names in the Ṛgveda have no Indo-Aryan or Indo-European etymology.[21] Kuiper (1991) finds "clear traces of an influx of non-Aryan beliefs" that are "not so much a case of borrowing . . . as rather an echo of a foreign religion being incidentally audible in the circles of the Rigvedic *ṛṣis*" (16). In contrast to Southworth and Hock, he interprets the linguistic evidence as indicating that the social interaction took place at the lower end of the social echelon, not the highest.[22] He holds that these words have been borrowed from Old Dravidian, Old Munda, and several other languages. It is also important to note that most of the foreign words in the Ṛgveda and Atharvaveda are rare or *hapax legomena*. In addition to lexical and cultural influence, he elaborately documents traces of *patterns* of foreign influences in phonology, morphology, and syntax, as well as the adaptation of foreign phonemes. Kuiper's innovative and meticulous work is the result of perhaps half a century of research in this area.

Emeneau (1980) in contrast, would seem to be relieved if scholars would agree on even one single loan: "If any such words can be found, even one or two, they will provide secondary evidence [of a Dravidian substratum]. . . . I can only hope that the evidence for *mayuura*—as a RV borrowing from Dr. is convincing to scholars in general" (179–183). Hock (1996b) is reluctant to allow even this, noting that the Dravidian cognate *mayil* occurs in southern Dravidian languages, far from the northwestern lands of the Ṛgveda (38). Since Dravidian has a similar root denoting both 'cat' and 'peacock', and Sanskrit *mārjāraka* means both 'cat' and 'peacock', Hock prefers to consider the word onomatopoeic.[23] In any event, linguists are quick to warn that "evidence for substratum cannot rest on an isolated lexical item, but must be based on a coherent pattern" (Salmons 1992, 267). In this regard, it might be worth noting Hamp's comments (1990b) regarding substratum identification: "We cannot fasten upon single facts. This means that we cannot seize upon a single isolated personal name. . . . we must have homomorphous distributions of multiple sets of equivalencies. It is the same formal requirement, of course, that we insist on for demonstration of genetic *Lautgesetze*." The foreign features attributed to a substratum must be consistently perceptible over a range of data: "For acceptable substrata, when we finish stating these equivalencies we must make a cohesive statement of structural features which are to be assigned to those summaries of homomorphous equivalent sets. Only then can we say we have a substratum worth talking about. Until those requirements have been fulfilled you may have an interesting breakfast observation, but you do not have an argument" (293). Establishing such consistent features is exactly what Kuiper has attempted to do.

Kuiper's work, in addition to compiling a list of loanwords, has attempted to identify systematic patterns of non-Indo-Aryan linguistic features in the Ṛgveda, particularly in phonology and morphology, that can contribute to identifying features typical of the underlying foreign language(s) that influenced Sanskrit. This aspect of his work is more problematic to the Indigenous Aryan position than his list of foreign lexica. Many of these features, such as some of the prefixes, point to Munda. These "are unknown in Dravidian but were common in Austro-Asiatic. . . . According to some scholars Munda was never spoken west of Orissa, Bihar, Madhya Pradesh and eastern Maharashtra. . . . The obvious occurrence of Old Munda names in the Rigveda points to the conclusion that either this statement should be revised or that some parts of the Rigveda . . . stem from eastern parts of North India" (Kuiper 1991, 39–40). Michael Witzel has predicated more far-reaching conclusions on Kuiper's observations, which will be discussed later.

Nonetheless, Kuiper's etymologizing has been sharply criticized by Rahul Peter Das, who, in keeping with his predecessors, challenged the "foreignness" of many of Kuiper's non-Indo-Aryan words. Das (1995) warns that one should not assume that "problematic words are foreign—they might be, but they need not be, for not being able to find a clear Indo-European etymology does not automatically imply that an Indo-European origin is impossible." As far as he is concerned, there is "*not a single case* in which a *communis opinio* has been found confirming the foreign origin of a Rgvedic (and probably Vedic in general) word." The considerable differences of opinion "may be due to the fact that many of the arguments for (or against) such foreign origin are often not the results of impartial and *thorough* research, but rather of (often wistful) statements of faith" (208; italics in original). Das is here echoing the acknowledgment of Emeneau (1980) that vocabulary loans from Dravidian into Indo-Aryan are "in fact all merely 'suggestions.' Unfortunately, all areal etymologies are in the last analysis unprovable, are 'acts of faith'. . . . It is always possible, e.g., to counter a suggestion of borrowing from one of the indigenous language families by suggesting that there has been borrowing in the other direction" (177). Das (1995), who accepts the external origin of Indo-Aryan on grounds other than the substratum hypothesis, points out that there is "not a single bit of *uncontroversial* evidence on the actual spread of Dravidian and Austro-Asiatic speakers in pre-historic times, so that any statement on Dravidian and Austro-Asiatic in Ṛgvedic times is nothing but speculation" (218). He reiterates the caution that the material being compared is separated by vast amounts of time and distance, often with scant regard being paid to the need for extensive philological investigation in establishing the exact semantics of dubious words, particularly in the case of Dravidian and Austro-Asiatic.

One study conducted in 1971 gives an indication of the extent to which scholars can disagree. In his doctoral thesis at Poona University, A. S. Acharya took all the Sanskrit words that had been assigned a Dravidian etymology over the years, resulting in a list of over twelve hundred words said to be borrowings from Dravidian.[24] He then searched for these words in Mayrhofer's etymological dictionary and found that Mayrhofer had accepted only 25 percent of the words as being Dravidian with any degree of certainty

(Acharya 1971, 15–74). Along the same lines, he extracted all the Sanskrit words that had been assigned a Munda derivation by scholars and arrived at over one thousand different words.[25] Here, too, he found that Mayrhofer had accepted only 21 percent of these words as borrowings from Munda that had any degree of certainty. When we bear in mind that scholars such as Thieme and Hock consider even Mayrhofer's Dravidian etymologies to have been awarded far too liberally, the differences of opinion are considerable. Such problems are not unique to South Asia: Salmons (1992, 266) refers to scholars who have attempted to deny the role of substratum on Germanic on the grounds that patient etymological work could eventually reveal Indo-European forms for most of the items in question.

On a different note, there are also methodological problems with the often quoted idea—outlined, for example, by Burrow (1968c, 326)—that there seems to have been a small number of foreign words in the Ṛgveda, which increased marginally in the other Vedas, grew considerably in the later Vedic literature, and peaked in the Epics and Puranas, before dwindling in the Prakrits and new Indo-Aryan languages. These data fit neatly with the generally accepted scenario of pre-Vedic-speaking Indo-Aryans intruding into an area inhabited by speakers of other languages. It suggests that by the time the Aryans had composed the Vedic hymns only a few indigenous words had permeated the texts. As the process of bilingualism developed (involving both the indigenes in the north of the subcontinent preserving some of their native lexicon as they adopted the Aryan languages, and post–first generation Aryans themselves utilizing non-Indo-European words as they merged with the local people), the loanwords increased, namely, during the Epic period. Finally, there were no more bilingual speakers left—everyone had adopted a form of later Indo-Aryan—at which time the appearance of foreign lexemes appears to cease as evidenced by the decrease of loans in the later Indo-Aryan texts.

This idea of the number of loanwords in Sanskrit increasing and then decreasing seems to be methodologically untenable. First of all, whose lists do we go by—Kuiper's (380 loans in the Ṛgveda) or Thieme's (no loans at all)? Second, even if we allow that the number of loanwords in Sanskrit did increase in progressively later texts, it is misleading to conclude that this was the result of more loans filtering through. The number of loans has to be calculated as a ratio of the total number of words in the text, and the *percentage* of foreign words in earlier texts has to be compared with the *percentage* of foreign words in later texts to determine whether the number of loans was increasing, decreasing, or, as is quite likely, more or less constant. To my knowledge, no such study has been attempted. Moreover, Emeneau (1980, 184) recognized that the claim that New Indo-Aryan had ceased to borrow was erroneous, a conclusion he formed simply by looking at the number of New Indo-Aryan entries in Turner's *Comparative Dictionary of Indo-Aryan Languages* that had been assigned a Dravidian origin. Masica (1979) found that the "non-Dravidian, non-Munda element in the Indo-Aryan lexicon persists, and even grows" (138). There are large numbers of such foreign words in the modern Indic languages. As I stressed previously, the syntactical and lexical convergence of the South Asian languages is continuing and increasing to this very day to such a degree that some scholars have suggested that a new language family is developing in South Asia, distinct from both Indo-European and Dravidian. This continual process of accepting foreign words and syntactical features (possibly even at an increasing rate) in New Indo-Aryan is not the result of any foreign linguistic substratum, so it is perfectly legitimate to ask why this had to be the case in the protohistoric past. If adstratum can account for such interactions in the present, one would need to produce a convincing explanation for why this could not have been the case in the protohistorical period.

Moreover, even if for argument's sake it could be established that the percentage of foreign words in the Ṛgveda was considerably less than that of later texts, the explanation could well be a sociolinguistic (i.e., cultural) one. Many scholars such as Thieme have drawn attention to the linguistic puritanism of the Vedic texts. These are sacerdotal hymns describing ritualistic techniques that were preserved by a culturally distinct group of specialists who, like any elite, took pains to isolate their speech from common vulgarisms. The Epics and Purāṇas deal with the real world—tribes, geography, history, intrigue, war, and the religion of the people. Naturally, the vocabulary in these latter texts will be far less conservative and more representative of the language of the street, so to speak. One is not compelled to interpret any possible disparate proportion of non-Aryan words in different genres of texts as proof of a linguistic substratum.

Terms for Flora in Indic Languages

Nonetheless, even when the most generous allowance is made in favor of the Indo-Europeanists, few would deny that there are many words borrowed from non-Aryan languages in Sanskrit texts. Dravidian and Munda are not the only languages that have been considered as possible sources: the difficulty in tracing the etymologies of many of these words has caused most linguists who specialize in this area to propose that many of the features and loans in Sanskrit must have come from languages that have disappeared without a trace.[26] Burrow (1956) goes so far as to suggest that "it may very well turn out that the number of such words which cannot be explained will outnumber those which can be. This is the impression one gets, for instance, from the field of plant names, since so far only a minority of this section of the non-Aryan words has been explained from these two linguistic families" (327).

This point is significant, particularly if these are local plants native to the Northwest. If the Aryans were indigenous to India, why would they have borrowed names of native plants from other language families instead of possessing their own terms composed from Indo-Aryan roots or derivatives?[27] This discrepancy would be natural if the Aryans were newcomers to the subcontinent, in which case they would readily adopt the names of unfamiliar local fauna and animals current among the native population. Kuiper (1991) finds that the words from his list—which contain about a dozen words that can be directly connected with agriculture—"testify to a strong foreign impact in almost every aspect of life of an agrarian population. . . . an (originally) non-Aryan agrarian population was more or less integrated into a society of a predominantly different character" (15).

The "different character" referred to by Kuiper reflects the common opinion among scholars that the economy of the Indo-Aryans is one of predominantly nomadic pastoralism. This, to a great extent, is predicated on the fact that the Indo-Iranian terms for agriculture were different from the set of corresponding terms shared in the western Indo-European languages. Scholars since at least the time of Schrader (1890) have concluded from this that "it becomes impossible to doubt that the Indo-Europeans, when they made their first appearance in history, were still possessed with nomadic tendencies" (282). From such a nomadic genesis, the western branches and eastern branches subsequently encountered agriculture after they had gone their separate ways to the west and east, respectively, and borrowed or coined their respective sets of different terms independently. The Indo-Aryans, from this perspective, were still nomadic when they arrived in South Asia, although they practiced nonsedentary agriculture (i.e., they engaged in agriculture for periods of the year, according to seasonal and other factors, before moving on). Most Vedic philologists believe that this hypothesis is supported by the economic culture reflected in the Vedic texts. Nowadays, this lexical difference between the eastern and western indo-European languages is explained by the polycentric origin of agriculture from two or three food-producing centers (Makkay 1988; Masica 1979). Moreover, Indo-Europeanists (Diebold, 1992; Mallory, 1997) do argue that the proto-Indo-Europeanists were agriculturists.

Southworth (1988) determines that the agriculture of the Vedic Aryans was apparently limited to barley and beans in the earliest texts. Rice and sesame appear in later texts, and wheat later still: "These facts support the view that the earliest Vedic texts were associated with a mountain-dwelling, primarily herding people who were unacquainted with the type of floodplain agriculture practiced by the Harappans." The fact that some of the products cultivated in the Indus Valley—wheat, cotton, sesame, dates, and rice—are absent from the earliest Vedic texts "is evidence for a lack of substantial contact between these people and the Harappans" (663). The assumption here, which must be kept in mind, is that the fact that the Ṛgveda happens not to mention rice, wheat, and so on, indicates that these items were unknown to the earliest Indo-Aryans. Southworth's conclusions should be considered, provided one keeps in mind that the text is not a compendium of agricultural terms; one must be wary of drawing too far-reaching conclusions based on *argumenti ex silentio.*[28]

As I will discuss more fully later, the borrowing and coining words for flora and fauna peculiar to India, as opposed to possessing 'primitive' terms for them (i.e., their possessing an Indo-European root) generally indicates to linguists that the item in question is new and unfamiliar to the speakers of the Indo-Aryan languages. In his research, Masica found 80 percent of the agricultural terms in Hindi to be non-Aryan—55 percent of which were of unknown origin (some inherited from Sanskrit). What is especially important to note here is that out of the total number of items in the survey, only 4.5 percent were Austro-Asiatic—some of which Masica acknowledges could have been borrowings from Indian contacts with the Mon-Kmer peoples in Southeast Asia rather than from the Kolarians of India proper (Masica 1991, 129–139).

This insignificant number caused him to concur with Burrow's opinion that the Munda languages could not have been present in the Northwest of India in prehistoric times. Had they been a principal component in any pre-Aryan linguistic substratum, the number should have been far greater. The same would apply to Dravidian's poor showing. Masica's study (1991) presents a further obstacle to theories proposing a Dravidian linguistic substratum in North India—only 7.6 percent of agricultural terms in Hindi have Dravidian etymologies. Moreover, "a significant portion of the suggested Dravidian and Austroasiatic etymologies is uncertain" (134). Thus, 4.5 and 7.6 percent are generous. This lacuna forces him to wonder whether the Indus Valley might not have been multilingual and, in concordance with numerous linguists since the time of Caldwell, to postulate the existence of another unknown language (or languages) existing as linguistic substrata in Indo-Aryan times (138). He labels this tongue "language x."

Southworth (1979) is also specific in noting that the terms for flora did not come from Dravidian. Scouring the work of Burrow and Emeneau, he extracted fifty-four words for botanical terms, including trees, cereals, edible gourds, spices, and beans, that have been considered loans common to both Indo-Aryan and Dravidian. So Dravidian was not the lender for these botanical terms. Nor was Munda: out of these loans, Southworth (1979) finds only five that are shared with Munda, causing him to suggest that "the presence of other ethnic groups, speaking other languages, must be assumed for the period in question" (205), with hardly "the slightest hints" as to what these languages might have been.

Curiously, in contrast to Masica's results showing that 80 percent of the agricultural vocabulary in Hindi was non-Indo-Aryan, a study conducted by Wojtilla (1986) using the material offered by a few special vocabularies of agricultural terms in the Hindi belt, coupled with his own collection of terms from the vicinity of Varanasi, seemed to produce conflicting results. Wojtilla found that "the agricultural vocabulary so collected mostly consists of *tatsama* and *tadbhava* words already known in Sanskrit and Prakrits" (28). The article does not discuss why this finding contradicts Masica's (which Wojtilla uses as a model), but this suggests that further extensive analysis of this issue is in order. Wojtilla does concur with Masica on another point, however, which is that "Dravidian influence is less than has been expected by specialists" (34).

The matter of loanwords is another area almost completely overlooked by Indigenous Aryanists. S. G. Talageri is the only scholar I have encountered who attempts to address some of the issues connected with linguistic substrata, but he seems unaware of most of the work that has been done in this area. His sole source seems to be Chatterji's *Origin and Development of the Bengali Language*, wherein there is a short list of about forty words of "probable Dravidian origin" (Talageri 1993, 42). Talageri searches for each item in Buck's dictionary of synonyms and finds about 20 percent of them have been assigned Indo-European derivatives.[29] He then proceeds to try his hand at establishing a few Sanskrit etymologies for some of the remaining words,[30] finally concluding that "the overwhelming majority of Sanskrit names for Indian plants and animals are derived from Sanskrit and Indo-European roots" (205). This is a rather sweeping conclusion that does not seem to be based on an awareness of most of the basic material in this area—over a century of research in the area of Sanskrit loanwords deserves a less cursory dismissal.

Talageri (1993) does accept the existence of some loanwords from Austro-Asiatic and Dravidian and accounts for their existence by contending that "the Dravidian languages were always spoken in South India, . . . the Indo-European languages were always and originally spoken in North India, and the Austro-Asiatic languages were always spoken in north-eastern and east-central India" (206). He remarks that many of the plants and animals must have had geographically specific areas of cultivation and natural habitats so that "if the common name for any Indian plant is proved to be of Austric or Dravidian origin, it will help in locating the part of India in which the plant had its origin" (206). Although no language can have existed anywhere in the world since all eternity, the point is an interesting one: Masica (1979) remarks that "there is really no Indian agriculture as such, but a group of related regional complexes differing in important details, including inventories of cultivated plants. Sanskrit, being a supraregional language, incorporates terms relating to various regional features" (58). Since Talageri seems largely unaware of the significant number, or etymological nature, of the non-Aryan words for plants and animals found in Sanskrit texts, he offers only a single example in support of his premise (*elā* 'cardamom' from the Tamil, a spice thought to have originated in Kerala).

Nonetheless, this method, pursued with methodological rigor as Southworth (forthcoming) has done, will be an important contribution in this area. Agricultural terms are an essential part of the data concerning Aryan origins that Indigenous Aryanists have to address. As it stands, many of the words in Sanskrit for domestic animals and their products are generally accepted as Indo-European derivatives, but few agricultural or botanical terms are. Masica's study found a significant percentage of Hindi words connected with animal husbandry were Indo-European or derivatives thereof, but fewer cereals, pulses, roots, fruits, and vegetables could be accounted for in this way. Most scholars have quite reasonably inferred from such data that pastoral nomads entered into the subcontinent with their culture of livestock herding and encountered strange local flora whose names they had to borrow from the indigenous people. Such evidence is an important ingredient in the Aryan Invasion hypothesis. To my mind, the non-Indo-Aryan nature of the words for the flora of North India is one of the few truly compelling aspects of the entire substratum theory.

However, even in this regard, the existence of a pre-Indo-Aryan linguistic substratum does not have to be the only explanation for the many botanical terms in Sanskrit that do not have Indo-European etymologies. Scanning the gamut of Sanskrit texts from different chronological periods, Southworth (forthcoming) finds that from a total 121 terms for plants, only a little over a third have Indo-European etymologies, and an additional third have unknown etymologies. First of all, there is much more work to be done in scrutinizing the etymologies and compositions of problematic words—we have seen how dramatically scholars have disagreed with each other. The task is a daunting one, however, and a large proportion of words are likely to remain untraceable. With regard to such recalcitrant terms, because foreign botanical items (millet, sorghum, etc.) have been continually imported into the subcontinent since time immemorial, it is more than probable that some have maintained their original foreign names. In many cases, these non-Indo-Aryan designations could be traceable to other language families, and the linguistic history of such words could tell us much about the origin of their referents. In this category of words, then, *it is the plant, not the Aryans*, that would be the intruders to the subcontinent.[31] In addition, the same basic possibilities outlined earlier for Dravidian and Munda linguistic relationships need to be considered: to what extent can these unknown items ascribed to "language x" be the result of loans, or adstratum relationship between Indo-Aryan tribes and other unknown ones, rather than the result of substratum?

Even within the subcontinent itself, plants and vegetables need to be correlated with their areas of origin to see whether their names can be connected with the linguistic groups known to have resided there. Paleobotany has a potentially significant role to play in this type of "linguistic archaeology." The problems involved, however, are daunting—as Polomé (1990b) notes, "one is rather reluctant to extrapolate from relatively recent data to archaic ecology" (276). Southworth has taken some significant steps in this regard. His forthcoming book *Linguistic Archaeology of the South Asian Subcontinent*,[32] combines paleobotany with etymological analysis in an attempt to illuminate the historical relationship between plants and human societies in South Asia. He provides extensive lists of plants known in Sanskrit texts, determines their etymologies where possible, and identifies their probable places of origin.

Southworth lists six plants that are believed to have come from different parts of the African subcontinent (finger millet, sesame, bulrush millet, sorghum, cowpea, and okra). He finds that another six names with Dravidian etymologies refer to plants whose origins lie to the east of India, suggesting that they may have been transported by sea to peninsular India by Dravidian speakers (Mahdi's study [1998] on the transmission of Southeast Asian cultigens also finds that, with some exceptions, "the plants and crops from Southeast Asia acquired new names in the process of transmission to India" [411]). Southworth further identifies seven items (*karpāsa* 'cotton'; *kaṅgunī* 'foxtail millet'; *kadala* 'banana'; *tāmbūla* 'betel'; *nimbu* 'lemon'; *marīca*, 'pepper'; and *śarkarā* 'sugarcane') that are believed to have originated in Austroasiatic languages. Most of these too, predictably, have their domestic origin in the east of India. In short, we have a long history of plants being imported into the subcontinent.

More important, Southworth introduces the category of plants that may have originated in India. From these he identifies nine plant terms shared by Old Indo-Aryan and Dravidian where the direction of borrowing is not clear. These suggest to him that the terms may have been borrowings into Indo-Aryan and Dravidian, both of which he considers to be intrusive, from one or more previous, indigenous languages. However, the actual point of origin of most of these plants either is uncertain or occurred in the South (cardamom) or the Northeast (mango), in areas where the historical existence of non-Indo-Aryan languages is not under dispute. It is plants that are native to the Northwest that are critical for this discussion.

Apart from these, Southworth's work clearly reveals a history of plant importation into the Indian subcontinent. However, the importation of foreign plants need not denote the foreignness of Indo-Aryan speakers. Indo-Aryan speakers in India still to this day import and cultivate new crops and retain their foreign names, as they have done throughout history. One need only go to one's local supermarket to experience this principle: exotic fruits from exotic countries are imported into our societies (and sometimes even transplanted and grown locally) while nonetheless retaining their original foreign names, which soon become part of our own vocabularies. Therefore, although the foreign names for flora may very well be indicative of a pre-Indo-Aryan substratum, this need not be the only explanation; these terms could simply be loans denoting items imported into a preexisting Indo-Aryan-speaking area. Only the etymologies of terms for plants indigenous to the Northwest of the subcontinent have the potential to be conclusive. If the Indo-Aryans were native to the Northwest, one would expect Indo-Aryan terms for plants native to the Northwest. If such plants could be demonstrated as having non-Indo-Aryan etymologies, then the case for substratum becomes compelling. However, Southworth's lists show no instance of plants native to the Northwest that have non-Indo-Aryan etymologies.

This is the essential point. If the Aryans were indigenous to at least the Northwest of the subcontinent, one would expect that there should be a higher percentage of, if not Indo-European (since, as will be discussed in the next chapter, items unique to India would not be expected to have cognates elsewhere), at least Indo-Aryan-derived names for plants known to be common in the area inhabited by the compilers of the Ṛgveda (provided these terms exhibit permitted Indo-European forms). As a side note, it is also important to repeat that if the etymological obscurity of plant names in Sanskrit texts is to be considered detrimental to the case of the Indigenous Aryanists, it is equally detrimental to the case of anyone promoting Dravidian (or Munda) as the *indigenous* pre-Aryan language of the Northwest. Most of the plant names are not traceable to Munda or Dravidian either (although, of course, Dravidian or Munda could have preexisted Indo-Aryan and passed into Sanskrit terms that they had borrowed from the "language x" that preceded them, in turn).

Also of particular relevance are the etymologies in Sanskrit texts for the terms for plants that have been found in the archaeological record of the Northwest in strata that date prior to when the Indo-Aryans are supposed to have entered the subcontinent, namely, before the second millennium B.C.E. Southworth's study lists six plants from the pre-Harappan and Early Harappan period: *yava* 'barley'; *tūla* 'cotton'; *kharjūra* 'date'; *drākṣā* 'grape'; *badara* 'jujube'; and *godhūma* 'wheat'. All of these plant products were found in Mehrgarh, Baluchistan, around the sixth millennium B.C.E. except grape (Kashmir, late third millennium B.C.E.) and jujube (Mundigak in Baluchistan, fourth millennium B.C.E.). From these, only barley has a clear Indo-European etymology. *Godhūma* (lit. 'cowsmoke', *godum* in Dravidian) seems to be a folk etymology, which Witzel considers a Sanskritization (and Dravidianization) of a Near Eastern loanword (Proto-Semitic **ḥant*, Old Egyptian *xnd*). Four of the terms seem etymologically unaccountable from Indo-European or Indo-Aryan roots.

This evidence is problematic for the Indigenous point of view. If the Indo-Europeans had come from the Northwest of the subcontinent, one would expect that the plants cultivated there since the sixth millennium B.C.E. would have Indo-European etymologies, which would then have evolved into Indo-Aryan forms. The only way to otherwise account for the four items with foreign etymologies might be to argue that since all of these plants (with the exception, perhaps, of dates) might have been imports into South Asia (i.e., they have been found in earlier archaeological contexts outside the subcontinent), the original foreign names from their places of origin could have been retained throughout prehistory. After having been transmitted down through the centuries, such names eventually surfaced in the Vedic texts as foreign words, or were assigned folk etymologies.

Words consist of roots, suffixes, and endings (the word *singers* has a root *sing*, a suffix *-er*, and an ending *-s*). A new formation or coinage refers to a word that is Sanskrit in form (i.e., with known Indo-Aryan morphological units such as suffixs or prefixes) but that either does not contain as Indo-European root or contains morphological units that are Post Indo-European. Such later developments do not necessarily reveal an ancient Indo-European etymology but might suggest recent coinage and therefore immigration into a new area (although new formations do not always denote substratum, since there is nothing preventing indigenous people from continually coining new words that reflect the linguistic developments extant at different chronological periods). The safest way of determining whether a word is a loan is from the root. Briefly, Indo-European roots are of the forms (s)(C)CeC(C/s), where C is a consonant, ( ) is an optional consonant -C- is a standard Indo-European vowel (in the ablaut series e/o/Ø/ē/ō outlined in chapter 3), and s is a sibilant. There are, however, certain limitations in the consonant combinations of the roots. The following combinations, for example, are generally not tolerated in an Indo-European root: two voiced consonants (*deg*), unvoiced and aspirated consonants (*tegh* or *dhek*) and two identical consonants (*pep*), Also, the *b* consonant is very rare. A word not fitting the basic Indo-European root pattern is an immediate and obvious candidate for being a non-Indo-European loan. Thus, the name *Balbūtha* is a clear non-Indo-European, non-Indo-Aryan term. A few points should be borne in mind before insisting that unfamiliar botanical words in Sanskrit are, of necessity, proof of a non-Aryan linguistic substratum. As Masica (1979) points out from his study of agricultural terms in Hindi: "It is not a requirement that the word be connected with a root, of course: there are many native words in Sanskrit as in all languages that cannot be analyzed" (61). This inscrutability of certain terms is especially prominent in terms for flora. C. D. Buck (1949), who compiled a dictionary of synonyms in the principal Indo-European languages, remarks that for most Indo-European trees, "the root connections are mostly obscure" (528). Likewise, the same applies to the inherited names of animals (135). Friedrich (1970), in his study on Indo-European trees, found only three roots that could be "cogently connected with a verbal root. . . . the great majority of PIE tree names were . . . unanalyzable nominal roots, and . . . for their reconstruction the most relevant branches of linguistics are phonology and semantics" (155).

The general inscrutability of terms in Indo-European is an important point: Sanskrit words for plants and animals do not automatically have to be considered foreign and rejected as possibly being Indo-Aryan due to dubious derivation because obscure etymological pedigrees would appear to be the norm for most plant and animal terms in Proto-Indo-European in general (this could, of course, be explained by postulating that the Proto-Indo-Europeans were themselves intrusive into whatever area was their homeland prior to their dispersal and borrowed terms for fauna and flora from the preexisting substratum in that area).[33] Talageri (1993) comments in this regard that "unless one is to presume that the Proto-Indo-Europeans were not acquainted with *any* animals or plants *at all*, one has to accept that etymologically obscure names may be 'what were at first colloquial or even slang words,' and that etymological obscurity need not necessarily indicate a non-Indo-European source unless such a source . . . can be specifically . . . demonstrated" (206). One must be cautious of too-hastily branding a word as non-Indo-European simply because one has not been successful in establishing an Indo-European etymology. Talageri also makes the caveat, in the undeniable instances in which a term for an item is demonstrably a loanword, that such borrowing does not necessarily indicate a lack of prior acquaintance with that item; there may be cultural or other reasons for the adoption. Masica (1979) illustrates this point by remarking that the foreign name for an item may replace an older indigenous name—French 'pigeon' has replaced the older Germanic 'dove' (61) in English, for example, but this has nothing to do with linguistic substrata or with prior ignorance of the object. Folk etymologies can also replace older terms—Vedic *íbha*, for example, has been replaced by the popular folk etymology of *hastin*—'the one with a hand'. On the other hand, foreign words can be made to appear indigenous by Sanskritizing them or assigning a new Sanskritic name to their referent—a practice Sanskrit grammarians were expert at. In such an instance, a word derived from Indo-Aryan may be a later gloss over an original non-Aryan term.

As an aside, one wonders whether, if all branches of the Indo-European language family (Balto-Slavic, Italic, Germanic, etc.) had preserved ancient corpora of texts dating back to at least the early second millennium B.C.E., one might not have found that they all preserved evidences of foreign floral, faunal and other typical indicators of substrata. Where would one have placed the homeland if the areas where all the Indo-European languages are spoken were to be eliminated by the logic used to eliminate the Northwest of the subcontinent? While this may well be an unwarranted flight of fancy, it seems fair to point out that the homeland candidacy of the Volga Valley steppes, for one, is actually advantaged by the absence of ancient textual sources in the Indo-European languages spoken in that area (such as Balto-Slavic) that might well have proved detrimental to their case were they to have been preserved and discovered. The same holds true for other postulated homelands.

Returning to the Ṛgveda, Bloch's and Thieme's proposals also deserve to be kept in mind—many peculiar words are quite likely to have had their origin in the Prakrits or other "low" culture vernaculars. This is especially pertinent in the case of plants and other agricultural terms, since such words would have been the daily subject matter of the tribes and "lower" social groups who tilled the soil, gathered the flora and herbs, and dealt with animals. These tribes may have picked up foreign plants and their terms from their wanderings and trade interactions with other language groups. Kuiper (1955), who has classified the foreign words according to the various spheres of human life in order to estimate their general character, found that "the vast majority of the Rigvedic loan words belong to the spheres of domestic and agricultural life. They belong not only to the popular speech . . . but to the specific language of an agrarian population" (185). Although Kuiper sees this population as one preceding the Indo-Aryan-speaking one, the issue at stake is how to preclude the possibility that these people might always have been speakers of Indo-Aryan dialects, albeit saturated with a '*deshi*' folk lexicon, much of it etymologically unexplainable with our present resources. Sociolinguistics is likely to have a role to play here. These may not be the types of people likely to be overconcerned about preserving pristine speech forms (which could well explain why plant and animal forms in general are etymologically indeterminate). Nomadic tribes, perhaps trading animal and faunal products between different regions and language groups, easily could have been the bearers of loanwords connected to the merchandise they bartered. As discussed earlier, flora and fauna are precisely the types of items that are continually imported into new environments to this very day, often retaining their foreign names. Of course, certain things are more likely to be imported than others: edible items or flowering blossoms would likely be more amenable to trade than trees, for example, but this possibility has not recieved adequate attention.

There is ample evidence of foreign personages and tribes in the Vedic period. Kuiper lists some twenty-six names of Vedic individuals who have non-Indo-Aryan names, with which Mayrhofer concurs (Kuiper 1991, 6–7). Witzel (forthcoming a) points out that twenty-two out of fifty Ṛgvedic tribal names are not Indo-Aryan, with a majority of them occurring in later books. He sees these as direct takeovers of local names of tribes or individuals inhabiting the subcontinent before the arrival of the Indo-Aryans. While this may well be the most economical explanation, one nonetheless needs to eliminate the possibility, parallel to the one outlined throughout this section, that such tribes and individuals may have been itinerant individuals or groups intruding upon a preexisting Indo-Aryan community, as opposed to intruding Indo-Aryan-speaking groups intruding upon non-Indo-Aryan ones. It seems relevant, in this regard, that Witzel (forthcoming a) notes that many of these names have not survived even in the Atharvaveda and Yajurveda mantras, which could be taken to underscore their transience.

Place-Names and River Names

The non-Indo-Aryan nature of the terms and names noted earlier also has to be juxtaposed with the fact that the place-names and river names in northern India are almost all Indo-Aryan. These names are, to my mind, the single most important element in considering the existence of a non-Indo-Aryan substratum position. Unlike people, tribes, material items, flora, and fauna, they cannot relocate or be introduced by trade (although their names can be transferred by immigrants). In other words, it is difficult to exclude the possibility that the foreign personal and material names in the Ṛgveda were intrusive into a preexisting Indo-Aryan area as opposed to vice versa. This argument of lexical transiency can much less readily be used in the matter of foreign place-names. Place-names tend to be among the most conservative elements in a language. Moreover, it is a widely attested fact that intruders into a geographic region often adopt the names of rivers and places that are current among the peoples that preceded them. Even if some such names are changed by the immigrants, some of the previous names are invariably retained (e.g., the Mississippi river compared with the Hudson, Missouri state compared with New England).

In the 1950s Hans Krahe analyzed the river names in central Europe and found them to be Indo-European.[34] This evidence has been used to argue that the homeland must have been in central Europe, since had the Indo-Europeans intruded into this area from elsewhere, they would have borrowed names from the local non-Indo-European groups that preceded them. More recently, Theo Vennemann (1994) has argued that these river names are actually not Indo-European at all, thereby suggesting that the Indo-Europeans were intruders into the area after all, who adopted the local hydronymic and toponymic forms, since "toponyms are rarely changed, they are merely adapted" (264). In both cases, the assumption is that place names are conservative.

With this in mind, it is significant that there are very few non-Indo-Aryan names for rivers and places in the North of the Indian subcontinent, which is very unusual for migrants intruding into an alien language-speaking area. Of course, it could be legitimately argued that this is due to the Aryans' Sanskritizing the names of places and rivers in the Northwest (although this raises the issue of why the local flora and other names were was not likewise Sanskritized). In the hydronomy of England, Celtic names are fewer in the east, but they are preserved in major rivers (Hainsworth 1972, 45). On the other hand, they become more frequent in the center, and more numerous in the west, a pattern that can be correlated with the historical data on Saxon settlement, which would have been densest in the east, thereby explaining the fewer Celtic names in that area. Witzel finds the same holds true in Nepal: "The whole west of the country has been Indo-Aryanized thoroughly and early enough . . . as to eliminate most traces of earlier Tibeto-Burmese" (218). Such non-Indo-Aryan names become more visible in other parts of the country. All this is of comparative use to support the idea of Indo-Aryan migrations.

In terms of the oldest attested Indo-Aryan period, Witzel (1999) has done extensive work on river names and place-names in the Ṛgveda, from which I will focus on the Northwest. Witzel finds almost all the place-names in the Ṛgveda, which are few in number, are Indo-Aryan, or at least Sanskritized. In his estimation, "most of the forms are easily analysable new formations, so typical of settlement in a new territory" (368). While this is a significant point, the lack of non-Indo-Aryan terms for toponomy and hydronomy in this area immediately deprives us of essential data that have been fundamental in establishing the existence of substrata in other languages. As a point of contrast, classical Greek maintains only 40 names (from 140 toponyms in Homer) that are Greek from the point of view of the classical language (but not necessarily Indo-European, that is, they are new formations adopted after the break up of Proto-Indo-European): barely one-third of the total. The remaining two-thirds are etymologically obscure (Hainsworth 1972, 40). Such obscurity gives clear indication of a pre-Greek, non-Indo-European substratum. The lack of foreign place-names in the oldest Indo-Aryan texts, in contrast, is remarkable when compared with the durability of place designations elsewhere. The same applies to rivers. Witzel again notes that "such names tend to be very archaic in many parts of the world and they often reflect the languages spoken before the influx of later populations" (368–369). Yet here again, "by and large, only Sanskritic river names seem to survive" in the Northwest (370). In the Kurukṣetra area, "all names are unique and new formations, mostly of IA coinage" (377).

None of the river terms are Dravidian. The Ganges, which is the easternmost river mentioned in the Ṛgveda, has an unusual etymology containing a reduplicated form of *gam* 'to go', which Witzel believes is an old, non-Indo-Aryan loan, despite its Sanskritic look. Later texts, however, mention rivers farther east and south from the Ṛgvedic homeland that show signs of Munda and Tibeto-Burmese influence in the northeast, and Dravidian influence toward central India. For my purposes, paralleling the logic outlined previously concerning the local fauna and flora, if the Indo-European had come from the Northwest of India, one would also expect the terms for hydronomy and topography of this area to preserve acceptable Indo-European etymologies. In fact, the hydronomic and topographic evidence is much more decisive than that of the flora and fauna: river names and place-names cannot be loanwords or be the result of adstratum, unlike the rest of the material overviewed in this chapter. If it can be convincingly demonstrated that the majority of Indo-Aryan hydronomic and topographic terms could not have evolved from Proto-Indo-European, then the Indigenous case would lose cogency. Of course, this procedure would be off to a rather tricky start by the very fact that we can only guess at what any hypothetical Indo-European terms for places or rivers might look like in the first place, but there is agreement about what is acceptable in terms of Indo-European roots.

However, in "the 'homeland' of the Ṛgvedic Indians, the Northwest "we find "most Ṛgvedic river names . . . are Indo-Aryan, with the possible exception of the Kubhā, Śatrudrī, and perhaps the Sindhu" (373). These latter, according to Witzel (1999), "prove a local non-IA substrate. In view of the fact that Witzel has provided a list of thirty-seven different Vedic river names, these two or three possible exceptions do not make as strong a case as one might have hoped. All the rest can indeed be derived from Indo-European roots. Morever, other scholars have even assigned Indo-Aryan etymologies to two of these three possible exceptions.[35]

Witzel's reading (1999) of the evidence of hydronomy is as follows:

> During the Vedic period, there has been an almost complete Indo-Aryanization of the North Indian hydronomy. . . . Indo-Aryan influence, whether due to actual settlement, cultural expansion, or. . . . the substitution of indigenous names by Sanskrit ones, was from early on powerful enough to replace the local names, in spite of the well-known conservatism of river names. The development is especially surprising in the area of the Indus civilization. One would expect, just as in the Near East or in Europe, a survival of older river names and adoption of them by the IA newcomers upon entering the territories of the people(s) of the Indus civilization and its successor cultures. (388–389).

Such conservatism is, indeed, extremely surprising, especially since the Indo-Aryans did not enter in sufficient numbers to be perceivable in the skeletal record of the subcontinent, as we shall see in the next chapters. One also wonders how such small numbers of immigrants could have eradicated the names of rivers and places in the Northwest of the subcontinent in the few hundred years that separated their arrival from the time the texts were compiled—Witzel allows about seven hundred years from 1900 to 1200 B.C.E. (74)—and yet not succeed in doing the same when they Aryanized the eastern and south-central areas in the two or three millennia that followed (as I have noted, places in these areas show signs of pre-Aryan indigenous Dravidan and Munda etymologies to this day). Witzel agreees with Kuiper and others that the preexisting groups "must have had a fairly low social position as they were not even able to maintain their local place and river names, almost all of which were supplanted by new Sanskrit ones" (77). This position needs to accommodate the fact that preceding the arrival of Indo-Aryans in the Ṛgvedic homeland up to 1900 B.C.E. was the highly sophisticated urban culture of the Indus Valley (which, as will be discussed in the next chapters, did not just evaporate after the "decline" of the Indus Valley Civilization).

Place-names are not much more decisive in this matter either, although much more work needs to be done in the area of present-day place-names in the subcontinent, which have not received the attention they deserve. Growse (1883) was the first and one of the only scholars to devote attention to this area, and his work is still a useful place to start. From his perspective, "Neither from the intrinsic evidence of indigenous literature, nor from the facts of recorded history, is it permissible to infer the simultaneous existence in the country of an alien-speaking race at any period" (320). He has scant regard for the etymologizing endeavors of those who attempted to identify a pre-Sanskritic-speaking people on the basis of the place-names of North India: "The existence of such a race is simply assumed by those who find it convenient to represent as non-aryan any formation which their acquaintance with unwritten Aryan speech in its growth and decay is too superficial to enable them at once to identify" (320). He further complained that "a derivation from Sanskrit by the application of well-established but less popularly known phonetic and grammatical laws, is stigmatized as pedantic" (320).

Growse found that place-names in the North consisted of those compounded with an affix denoting place; those compounded with an affix denoting possession; and those without an affix, being an epithet of the founder or of some descriptive feature of the place. He found the most numerous were those in the first category compounded with the affix *pur* 'city, urban center' (discussed more fully in the next chapter)' which transformed into a number of forms such as *-oli,-uri,-uru*. He quotes a verse from Vararuchi's Prakrit grammar to show how inital *p-*, among other initials, can be elided.[36] He continued to use Prakrit rules to determine a number of other affixes and concluded his study with a statement with which many would still agree: "So many names that at a hasty glance appear utterly unmeaning can be traced back to original Sanskrit forms as to raise a presumption that the remainder, though more effectively disguised, will ultimately be found capable of similar treatment: a strong argument being thus afforded against those scholars who hold that the modern vernacular is impregnated with a very large non-Aryan element" (Growse 1883, 353).

In contrast, the only other recent study of place-names in the North of which I am aware,[37] which claims to be comprehensive, is dedicated to demonstrating that "before the Aryan invasion India was inhabited by the ancestors of the Dravidians, who migrated from the mediterranean region" (Das and Das 1987, 2). Even with such a starting premise, the book scarcely produces half a dozen possible Dravidian names from the Northwest of the subcontinent: the vast majority are from the east—Bengal and Uttar Pradesh—which few would dispute were originally settled by non-Aryans.[38] Southworth (1995) has argued for the existence of Dravidian place-names in Maharashtra, Gujarat, and Sindh. My concern is with the Northwest of the subcontinent. In this regard, Southworth has made some tentative identifications of a few place-names in Sindh ending in *-wārī, wari*, and the Punjab *-walī*.[39] As I have noted earlier, Growse (who was examining names in the Uttar-Pradesh area) considered similar forms to be Prakritizations of *pur* and therefore Indo-Aryan. Mehendale considers the 2,045 *wāḍi* settlements in the Retnagiri area that he surveyed to have come from the Sanskrit form *vāṭika* (a possible Prakritization of Sanskrit *vṛt*). In short, there is much to be done on the subject of place-names in the Northwest.

Apart from these observations, Witzel (forthcoming, 12) notes three place-names in Kashmir ending in *-muṣa* and a river called *Ledarī* that he considers non-Indo-Aryan. In any event, he concludes: "In light of the present discussion about the arrival of the Aryans in India and in some circles of Anglophone archaeology, that is the growing denial of any immigration or even trickling in of people speaking Indo-Iranian or Indo-Aryan dialects, it is important to note that not only the Vedic language, but the *whole* complex material and spiritual culture has somehow been taken over and absorbed in the northwest of the subcontinent" (72).

Of substantial importance is Witzel's discovery (forthcoming b) that there was no Dravidian influence in the early Ṛgveda. He divides the Ṛgveda corpus into three distinct chronological layers on linguistic grounds and finds that Dravidian loans surface only in layer II and III, and not in the earliest level at all: "*Consequently, all linguistic and cultural deliberations based on the early presence of the Drav. in the area of speakers of IA, are void*" (17; italics in original). Instead, "we find more than one hundred words from an *unknown* prefixing language" that is neither Dravidian, Burushaski, nor Tibeto-Burmese (6). On the basis of certain linguistic evidences, such as Munda-type prefixes (*ka-, ki-, kī-, ku-, ke-*, and "double prefixes"), he prefers to consider the pre-Aryan language an early form of Munda.[40] He finds the same prefixes in later texts whose geographic boundaries are farther east. These deductions, combined with the known position of Munda in the east, cause Witzel to postulate a Munda substratum in the oldest

Ṛgvedic period. He considers that an essential corollary of his findings is "*that the language of the Indus people*, at least those in the Punjab, must have been (*Para-*) *Munda or a western form of Austro-Asiatic* (12). He proposed that this language, in turn, was an overlay over an unknown, lost language (Masica's "language x").

As a side note, Witzel draws attention to another interesting point. Since the Indus Valley was a trading civilization, why did non-Indo-Aryan terms for trade not surface in the Ṛgveda? Why are all the loans identified primarily terms for fauna, flora, and agriculture (mostly from "language x")? Since most migrationists would accept that the Indo-Aryans interacted with the tail end of the Indus Valley Civilization, one would have grounds to expect that incoming Indo-Aryans would have borrowed trading terms from this civilization, which is not the case.

Dravidian, in Witzel's scenario (forthcoming b, 30), was a later intruder that, interestingly, he is prepared to consider as having arrived at about the same time as the Indo-Aryan languages, (30), explaining the subsequent influences of Dravidian on later Vedic [strata] (Dravidian, in the process, also absorbed retroflexes and lexical items for flora, and so on, from the unknown, preexisting language).[41] This causes me to again raise the previous consideration—perhaps an inescapable one from the perspective of Indigenous Aryanism—and one that has yet to receive scholarly attention. What is the possibility of all the various innovations noted here being the result of alien languages, whether Dravidian, Munda, or anything else, intruding on an Indigenous Indo-Aryan language as opposed to vice versa? Or of adstratum or superstratum relationships as opposed to substratum? Witzel has provided data to argue that this certainly must have been the case with Dravidian, since Dravidian influence is not visible in the earliest layers of the Ṛg but only in subsequent layers: "Such words could have been taken over any time between the RV . . . and the earliest attestation of Tamil at the beginning of our era" (31). He notes that most of the eight hundred words assigned a Dravidian etymology by the Dravidian Etymological Dictionnary are attested only in the later Epics or classical Sanskrit texts: "The Indo-Aryans *did not at once* get into contact with speakers of Drav. but only much later, when the tribes speaking IA were already living in the Panjab and on the Sarasvatī and Yamunā" (19). If Dravidian has influenced Indo-Aryan through adstratum or superstratum interactions, and *not* through a substratum relationship, then why could Munda (or other languages) not likewise have done so?

Indo-Aryan, or Dravidian and Munda Migrations?

I wish to further explore this possibility, first raised by Bloch, namely, that it was Dravidian that intruded into an Indo-Aryan speaking area and not vice versa. It seems to me that an Indigenous Aryan position would be forced to consider this possibility in one way or another. Linguistically, at least, there does not seem to be any reason that this could not have been the case. Brahui, in this scenario, could have been a language pocket of Dravidian that remained stranded in the North after the rest of the Dravidian speakers had continued down south. This would fit with the claim that Brahui is better connected to the southern language group of Dravidian rather than the northern one. While I will concentrate on Dravidian, here, since this has been the focus of most research in this area, the logic being outlined is just as applicable to Munda (which, until the work of Kuiper and Witzel, has received less scholarly attention in terms of its influence on Vedic than Dravidian), and even "language x".

There is also another very significant reason that Indigenous Aryanists would have to argue for a post-Indo-Aryan arrival of Dravidian (Witzel, personal communication). If the innovative features Indo-Aryan shared with Dravidian and/or Munda and/or other unknown languages, such as the retroflexes, were the result of adstratum influences between these languages in the proto-historic period, as has been presented as a possibility earlier, one would expect that some of these linguistic features would have rippled out into other adjacent Indo-European areas, or at least into neighboring Iranian. After all, from the perspective of a South Asian homeland, the Iranians could not have left the subcontinent much before the composition of the Ṛgveda due to the similarity of the languages. Therefore, from the perspective of a language continuum homeland with the Northwest of the subcontinent as its nucleus, Iranian would have been the closest to this nucleus. Why, then, did Iranian not share these innovations? Why do most of these South Asian areal features seem to stop at the Khyber Pass, so to speak?

In this regard, Hock (1993) notes that some of the innovations are actually shared by eastern Iranian, specifically retroflection: "The core area of the change must have been in South Asia proper, from which the change spread only incompletely to the Nuristani and East Iranian languages on the northwestern periphery, before coming to a complete halt in geographically even more remote Iranian territory" (96). He has also argued that a second of the three main features discussed in this chapter, namely, the postposed quotative marker *iti*, could have been paralleled by Avestan *ūitī* (although Kuiper [1991] feels this lacks any foundation). There have also been claims of loans from Dravidian into Avestan as well as Vedic, which have been construed as coming from the Indo-Iranian period (see Southworth 1990 for examples). Nonetheless, from the Indigenous Aryan perspective, it would be easier to argue that Dravidian and/or Munda, and/or "language x" speakers, intruded into an Indo-Aryan-speaking area after Iranian had already left, and that consequently the innovations were the result of a superstratum of these language speakers settling in Indo-Aryan-speaking areas in the Northwest.

Alternatively, these languages could have skirted the Indo-Aryan languages in the Northwest and influenced them as adstratum. The first issue to be dealt with in this case, of course, is chronological. Either it would have to be argued that the Dravidian/Munda/"language x" speakers entered the subcontinent after about 1900 B.C.E. and interacted with the Indo-Aryans as adstratum or superstratum during the period prior to the commonly accepted composition of the hymns. If this is too late for proto-Dravidian, it would have to be argued that the Indus Valley was Indo-Aryan and that the Vedic texts are far older than philologers have so far dated them. Both these latter issues will be discussed at length in the following chapters.

In terms of the possibility of a later Dravidian intrusion into the subcontinent, I will briefly review some of the theories pertaining to the chronology and origins of Dravidian. There is no consensus regarding the origin of Dravidian. McAlpin's attempt (1974) to connect Dravidian with Elamite is the most often quoted endeavor, although often without much critical analysis of the claims involved (perhaps because so few linguists are competent enough in the two languages involved to evaluate his work). The Dravidian linguist Krishnamurti (1985) appears unconvinced by this idea and wonders if "McAlpin was carried away by the flight of his imagination." As far as he is concerned,"many of the rules formulated by McAlpin lack intrinsic phonetic/phonological motivation and appear *ad hoc*, invented to fit the proposed correspondences," and "McAlpin's foray into comparative morphology is even more disastrous" (225–226). Other reactions to McAlpin's proposal, by Emeneau, Jacobsen, Kuiper, Rainer, Stopa, Vallat, and Wescott, have also been very reserved (although Paper and Zvebevil were more enthusiastic). (These responses were published in *Current Antropology* volume 16 [1975].)

Vacek (1987) gives an overview of scholarship attempting to connect Dravidian with the Altaic languages. While he is partial to this position, he is forced to acknowledge that "conclusions concerning the type of their relations are premature because the available data can often be interpreted in various ways" (12). Sjoberg (1971) also undertakes such an overview but is more partial to the attempts at finding connections with the Uralic languages, although admiting that this is at odds with genetic data pointing to links with southwestern Asia (16). Uralic was also favored by Tyler (1968). Another attempt at establishing genetic relationships has been with Japanese.[42] A further group of scholars see the typological or other features illustrated by all these efforts as evidence of a superfamily, Nostratic. *Nostratic* is a term coined by the Russian linguist Illich-Svitych to refer to a superlanguage family, or a protofamily of protofamilies. Depending on the linguist, this might include Afro-Asiatic, Elamite, Kartvelian, Uralic, Altaic, and Dravidian in addition to Indo-European, although many linguists believe this language is completely beyond the ability of current techniques in linguistics to demonstrate.

In any event, clearly, the origins of Dravidian are yet to be established; as Sjoberg (1971) concludes, "we can only speculate as to the time and place of the initial formation of a distinctive Dravidian people and culture" (17). Less work has been focused on the origins of Munda on the subcontinent, but here, too, any dating attempt can only be highly speculative. D'iakonov (1997) tentatively explores the possibility of its connection with Sumerian. Acknowledging that there are no "amazing similarities," he nonetheless hopes that "some suggestive material may perhaps emerge" (58). As for "language x," since it is primarily a hypothetical language, there are no grounds whatsoever for determining its chronology or point of origin (unless Kuiper's linguistic patterns can be correlated with other language families).

Chronologically, scholars have little of substance upon which to base their dates for the incursion of Dravidian into the subcontinent (all do seem to agree that Dravidian was not an indigenous language). Zvelebil (1972) considers them "a highlander folk,[43] sitting, sometime round 4000 B.C., in the rugged mountainous areas of Northeastern Iran. . . whence, round 3500 B.C., they began a Southeastern movement into the Indian subcontinent which went on for about two and a half millennia" (58). Needless to say, since the Elamite connection has not been widely accepted, there are no obvious traces of Dravidian outside the subcontinent that can determine either its point of origin, its chronology, or the overland route of its speakers, although attempts have been made to find traces of them in central Asia (e.g., Lahovary 1963). Pejros and Shnirelman (1989) volunteer a date of 3000 B.C.E. for proto-Dravidian without stating their grounds and hold that the language must have entered the subcontinent from the Northwest due to its Nostratic connection.

In reality, any attempt to establish a date for proto-Dravidian is ultimately, as Zvebevil (1972) acknowledges, "in the nature of guesswork," since glottochronology, as I will discuss in chapter 13, has been almost unanimously discredited. As far as I can determine, there is very little that is decisive that can be brought forward to deny the possibility that Dravidian or Munda speakers intruded upon an Indo-Aryan speaking area and not vice versa. This possibility would be reinforced if the claims of a greater antiquity for the Indo-Aryan language could be established. We might also bear in mind Bloch's suggestion that such intrusions could have been the result of individuals as opposed to major population movements, just as individual Sanskrit speakers coming from North India massively affected the southern languages (which became heavily Sanskritized) without migrating down in vast numbers.

Conclusion

There might be scope, in all this, for considering alternative models to that of invading Aryans borrowing a specialized lexicon from Dravidian, Munda, or linguistically unknown indigenous people. Indigenist suspicions are initially aroused due to the considerable differences in the opinions of the foremost authorities in this area. Some scholars are quite prepared to acknowledge the inconclusiveness of the linguistic evidence. Other linguists have concluded, both because of the syntactical reasons discussed earlier and because Dravidian and Munda can account for only a small minority of the unaccountable words, that unknown, extinct languages must have existed in the protoperiod. This is by no means an unreasonable proposal. There are a number of languages on the subcontinent apart from Dravidian and Munda. Tibeto-Burmese is the most widespread, but there are also the language isolates such as Kusunda, Nahali, and Burushaski that have been examined by Witzel (1999) as possible substratum candidates. Burushaski is of particular relevance, since it is situated in the Northwest. However, neither this nor any other known language has been recognized by specialists as a possible candidate for the innovations in the Ṛgveda.[44] Hence the need for "language x."

The problem is that the existence of such possible extinct languages is very hard to verify; Kuiper's attempt at pinpointing consistent alien structural patterns in Indo-Aryan might be the nearest one can hope for in terms of "proof." Emeneau (1980), a proponent of a Dravidian substratum, seems to recognize that resorting to such opaque explanations as extinct languages is hardly likely to satisfy empirically minded historians: "It hardly seems useful to take into account the possibility of another language, or language family, totally lost to the record, as the source [of the foreign words]" (169). Resorting to such explanations is seen as rather desperate pleading by the frustrated Talageri (1993), who "cannot proceed with these scholars into the twilight zone of *purely hypothetical* non-existent languages" (200; italics in original).[45] Mallory (1975) opines that "the reliance on simple a posteriori appeals to unknown (and perhaps non-existent) substrates to explain linguistic change should be dismissed from any solution to the IE homeland problem" (160). As has been noted, such a hypothesis can be neither verified nor falsified and thus is incapable of resolving this debate. Moreover, even if it could be verified—and, in deference to Kuiper's work, unknown languages can be "proved" if consistent phonemic or morphological patterns can be identified in textual sources—how can one discount the possibility that such linguistic influences could still be explainable along the same lines suggested previously: as resulting from adstratum, as opposed to substratum, relationships?

In summary, all these linguists are operating on the assumption, based primarily on *other* criteria, that the Aryans "must have" invaded India, where there could not have been a "linguistic vacuum." All alien linguistic features identified in Sanskrit texts have accordingly been explained as belonging to pre-Indo-Aryan substrata. Since Dravidian and Munda inadequately explain these changes visible in Sanskrit, many are forced to consider theories of extinct languages. How the data could be convincingly reinterpreted if this assumption were to be reconsidered remains to be seen, since a comprehensive and objective case has yet to be made by the "Indigenous Aryanists" despite their possessing the rudiments of a variety of alternative explanations already advanced by Western linguists. As I have attempted to outline, loanwords can enter a language in many ways without the need for postulating a substratum (or even an adstratum). Many of the foreign terms for flora and fauna could simply indicate that these items have continually been imported into the subcontinent over the centuries, as continues to be the case today. The exception to this is place-names and river names, but the absence of foreign terms for the topography and hydronomy of the Northwest deprives us of significant evidence that has been used to establish substrata elsewhere. Most important, the possibility of spontaneous development for many of the syntactical features common to Sanskrit and Dravidian and Munda, coupled with the possibility of an adstratum relationship for features that are undoubtedly borrowings between the languages, are the most obvious alternative possibilities that need to be fully explored.

Thomason and Kaufman (1988) have outlined a typology of change typically caused by the cultural pressure of a language on another—the more overpowering the influence, the more the language will transform. Casual pressure results in lexical borrowings only; less casual influence produces lexicon and minor structural borrowing; more intense contact increases the amount of structural borrowings; and strong and very strong cultural pressure result in moderate and extensive structural transformation. I am not aware of any technique available to present linguistic knowledge that, in a protohistoric setting, can determine whether such influences between languages—whether they be lexical or syntactical—are the result of adstratum, substratum, or even superstratum relationships.

Salmons (1992) notes the same concerns in his search for substratum influence in Northwest Indo-European vocabulary: "Adstratal borrowing or even internal innovations, not just substratal borrowings, might show these previously prohibited forms. Again, simple alternative explanations to the substrate hypothesis seem to present themselves" (274). He goes on to state that "as a result of the proclivity to speculate, substrate explanations carry a bad reputation among historical linguists. . . . all other avenues must be exhausted before we reach for a substrate explanation" (266). Caution must be exercised that substratum explanations are not resorted to as a kind of convenient linguistic dumping ground where anything that does not fit into the dominant recorded culture is heaped by default.

In conclusion, the theory of Aryan migrations into the Indian subcontinent would better be established without doubt *on other grounds*, for research into pre-Aryan linguistic substrata to become fully conclusive. That Indo-Aryan intruded onto a non-Indo-Aryan substratum still has much to recommend itself. Perhaps it is the least complicated way of accounting for the available evidence, but it is not without limitations. To reiterate, the main alternative possibilities that Migrationists need to eliminate are: (1) that Indo-Aryan could have spontaneously originated some of the non-Indo-European innovations visible in it and then shared these with Dravidian and/or Munda (or vice versa); (2) that the non-Indo-European words in Sanskrit texts from Dravidian, Munda and/or "language x" are simply loans resulting from trade or other nonsubstratum interactions between language groups; and (3) that any alien linguistic features in Sanskrit texts that cannot be accounted for by possibilities 1 or 2, whether phonemic or morphological, could be the result of adstratum (or superstratum) rather than substratum contacts. The other possibility that needs to be eliminated is that the Indo-Aryan names of places and rivers could not have evolved from Proto-Indo-European by inherent and natural internal linguistic developments. As for Indigenists, they must accept that any discussion of Indo-Aryan origins that neglects the substratum data, simply cannot be taken seriously.

All this resonates with Polomé's conclusion (1990b) to his researches on Germanic substratum: "In many cases the evidence remains inconclusive, and only when extralinguistic evidence can be coordinated with the lexical data can we posit a 'substrate' origin of the terms" (285). In short, while certainly suggestive, it is difficult to see how the "evidence" of a linguistic substratum in Indo-Aryan, in and of itself, can be used as a final arbitrator in the debate over Indo-Aryan origins.

6

Linguistic Paleontology

As mentioned previously, linguistic paleontology was inaugurated by Adolphe Pictet in 1859 in three volumes that covered every imaginable set of Indo-European cognates.[1] This method was fundamental in relocating the Indo-European homeland away from the East, where the early scholars had preferred to situate it. Just as paleontology involves attempting to understand the plant and animal life of previous geological ages from fossils found in the archaeological record, linguistic paleontology involves hypothesizing about the social, religious, political, economic, ecological, cultural, and geographic environment of protohistoric cultures from linguistic fossils, or cognate terms, preserved in the various members of a language family. As Otto Schrader (1890) put it, "As the archaeologist . . . descends into the depths of the earth . . . to trace the past in bone and stone remains, so the student of language might . . . employ the flotsam and jetsam of language . . . to reconstruct the picture of the primal world" (iii). Once a picture embellished with details such as flora, fauna, landscape, and economy has been formed by this method, the idea is to attempt to situate it in an appropriate geographic setting in the real world and then connect it with a corresponding archaeological culture. Nietzsche was to compare the philologist to an artist touching up an old canvas. In this case, however, the canvas was well over five thousand years old. Could philology bring this completely faded picture back to life, or would it paint right over it and create a completely different landscape?

This section will outline some of the features of this method that have been relevant to the history of the quest for the Indo-Aryans, or that have attracted responses from the Indigenous school. Since I am not an Indo-Europeanist myself and my audience is primarily scholars of South Asia who are interested in the protohistory of the Indian subcontinent, I will not attempt to represent most of the discussion and debate amongst linguists concerning technical details such as the protoforms of words that are relevant to this section, but will address the more general conclusions drawn from them. I should also note that most present-day Indo-Europeanists are fully aware of the limitations of this method, and of its checkered history. However, much that will be considered passé to specialists in the field still surfaces in books on Indian proto-history and therefore remains relevant to the purposes of this work.

Flora and Fauna

One set of cognates, which became extremely influential in supporting a German homeland, involved the term for the common beech tree. As Friedrich (1970) notes, "The botanical beech line, partly because it has been so often misused, has guaranteed this tree a sure place in all discussions of the Proto-Indo-European homeland" (106). Pictet triggered the popularity of this tree among homeland-seekers by presenting an array of cognates for this term from all the Indo-European languages accessible in his time. Since this tree had cognates in both the Indo-Iranian and the European side of the family, it was assumed to have existed in the proto-language before the various linguistic branches separated. Words with cognates in only the western (or only the eastern) branches retain the possibility that their referents might have been encountered after the common Proto-Indo-European period in a secondary, western (or eastern) location, and therefore not indicative of the original homeland. As mentioned previously, scholars such as Geiger used this information to draw up maps of the geographic boundaries within which the beech tree grows—specifically, German-centered Europe (thus excluding the Asian hypothesis that was still almost universally accepted in Pictet's time)—and the Aryan homeland was set within this area. The beech evidence was particularly used by Thieme (1964, 597) who argued for a homeland between the Black Sea and the Baltic with an eastern border fixed by the boundaries of the beech habitat.

There are various problems with this approach. It has been noted that the beech is linguistically unattested in Anatolian, but this language was spoken in the very area where scholars believe the beech was native. In other languages spoken in the heartland of beech territory, the word was transferred to refer to the 'oak' so that "the concatenation of assumptions required to press the 'beech line' into argument would appear to be exceedingly dubious" (Mallory and Adams 1997, 60). Friedrich (1970) points out further limitations of the birch evidence based on its shifting habitat and concludes that "none of Thieme's well-known criteria support his homeland hypothesis" (30). The area where the beech, or any tree, grows now may not be the same as where they might have grown many millennia ago. Paleobotony might help locate prehistoric trees to some extent, but Friedrich explicitly encourages the philologist to "retain a due skepticism of 'hard science'" (14)[2]

But such methods have other limitations when it comes to locating homelands. Friedrich (1970), in his taxonomy of Indo-European trees, proposes that linguistic paleontology reveals eighteen categories of trees that were known to the ancient Indo-Europeans.[3] His findings reveal that all three divisions of the Slavic languages have at least one of the reflexes for each of these eighteen terms, indicating that the Slavs were familiar with all eighteen Indo-European trees; the correspondence, in this case, is 100 percent. This suggests, to him, that the speakers of the common Slavic period lived in an ecological, that is, arboreal, zone similar or identical to that of the Proto-Indo-European's (167).[4] In sharp contradistinction, the paucity of these eighteen stocks attested in Indic, Anatolian, and Tocharian suggests to Friedrich "substratum influence" or "movement into a radically different environment" (169). This evidence is taken as significant evidence that the Indo-Europeans must have come into India from elsewhere (e.g., Possehl 1996, 65). Friedrich himself seems aware of the possible objections that drawing too far-reaching conclusions from his results might provoke and is hasty to add that he "would be the first to insist that the arboreal evidence cannot be used in *isolation* to construe a conclusive argument for a Proto-Indo-European homeland in the Ukraine or the Cossack steppe" (168).

The immediate objection from the perspective of the Indigenous Aryan school was first articulated by Dhar, head of the Sanskrit department at Delhi University in 1930, when confronted with similar arguments. Dhar's (1930) is the first serious attempt that I can trace to challenge the prevailing ideas regarding the Aryan invasions on linguistic, as opposed to philological, grounds:[5]

> Central Asia might be the secondary home of the Aryas [Indo-European's] . . . but their primary home might be situated outside central Asia, in the Himalayas. . . . Of late, the beech argument is much advertised by the promoters of the Indo-European theory of the home of the Aryas. But the term for the "beech" might have been coined by the Aryan settlers in Europe only where the tree grew. (26)

The logic here is that if the Indo-European tribes had, hypothetically, journeyed forth from an Indian homeland, they would obviously have encountered strange trees, animals, and fauna that did not exist on the subcontinent and for which they would have coined new terms or borrowed names from the indigenous people resident in those areas. Subsequent Indo-European tribes would have adopted the same terms from their predecessor Indo-Europeans resident in the places where the unfamiliar items were encountered.[6] Such new lexical terms would obviously not surface in the Indo-Aryan languages that remained behind in the subcontinent, since the objects they denoted did not exist in India. Nor would they surface in other Indo-European languages such as Tocharian and Anatolian, which were geographically removed from the well-trodden northwestern path taken by most of the Indo-European tribes that eventually resurfaced in the west. The result would be a large number of common terms in the western Indo-European languages (since they are numerically greater) and a smaller number in Indo-Iranian.[7]

Friedrich's results, then, indicating a paucity of his reconstructed tree stocks in Indic, Anatolian, and Tocharian, would not be incongruous to the Indigenous Aryan position. On the contrary, anyone postulating a South Asian homeland would anticipate such findings. Dhar's basic premise can be used to challenge conclusions drawn from any other cognate terms of material culture extant in the western Indo-European branches but absent in the Indo-Iranian or Indo-Aryan ones. As Polomé (1990b, 274) notes, there are two equally logical ways of accounting for the lacuna of some linguistic feature in one particular language that is shared by its cognates in other languages: either it was never there to start with or it has been lost somewhere along the way. Indeed, other linguists use exactly the same arguments as Dhar has used to account for items reconstructed in Proto-Indo-European that happen to be absent in their proposed homeland: "Part of these terms cannot be reconstructed for the period of proto-Indo-European unity, but only for later dialect groupings. . . . hence the picture of the ancient Indo-Europeans' plant and animal world is to be thought of as . . . one which changed as speakers of the dialects moved to their later territories" (Gamkrelidze and Ivanov, 1995, 573); "What is especially interesting about these words is that most of them denote natural objects . . . typical of Europe and less typical of SW Asia. My impression is that these words were borrowed when the W [west] Indo-European ethnic community migrated from some region of SW Asia . . . to Europe . . . and got acquainted with objects of nature which had been unfamiliar or less familiar earlier" (Dolgopolsky 1989, 18).[8]

Along very similar lines, another group of cognate terms was prominent in attempts to locate the homeland in Europe or southern Russia. Thieme in particular held that the term for 'salmon' is "especially characteristic" of the Indo-Europeans. According to him, this fish is found only in the rivers that go into the Baltic and German Seas (1964, 597).[9] The salmon evidence is still in circulation, especially among those promoting a northern German homeland (e.g., Diebold 1991, 13).[10] However, the salmon case is slightly more complicated for the Indigenous Aryan school, since, in this case, Sanskrit might have a cognate term (*lākṣā*, 'lac') with the same etymology that has been assigned to the Proto-Indo-European form for the salmon (**lóḱs*). If the Sanskrit form is, indeed, a cognate, then how did the word come to mean 'lac' in Sanskrit, and 'salmon', or 'fish', in other languages?

Since Sanskrit also has a term *lakṣa*, which means a very large number, Elst (1996), who argues for a South Asian homeland, has proposed that Indo-European tribes, upon leaving the subcontinent, came across unfamiliar fish in large shoals to which they gave the term 'numerous; hundreds of thousands'.[11] The interchange of number terms with the nomenclatures of species that cluster together in multitudes is not uncommon. Elst compares the *lākṣā*/lakṣa case with the Chinese use of an insect character, *wan*, to denote ten thousand. This general term for fish, which was preserved in Tocharian, then eventually entered into some Indo-European languages to refer to more specific types of fish. The word was applied to 'salmon' (Old High German *lahs*, Russian *losos'*, etc.) when the speakers of these languages encountered this specific reddish species of fish (perhaps prompted by the almost identical Indo-European word for red) and, in other languages, such as in Iranian Ossetic, to trout (*läsäg*).[12] In any event, some linguists claim that the Indic forms (particularly *lākṣā*) are not actual cognates, in which case it could be argued that the word for 'salmon' could have been coined by tribes after they had left the subcontinent along the lines outlined earlier. Using similar arguments, Gamkrelidze and Ivanov (1983b) state that "in the specific meaning of 'salmon' . . . the word is common to the 'Ancient European' dialects and Eastern Iranian. . . . Of course the word would have acquired this meaning in those areas where salmon was found, in regions near the Aral or Caspian Seas" (77).[13]

These are the types of arguments that have to be made to account for any terms either not preserved in Indo-Aryan but present in other Indo-European languages or preserved in Indo-Aryan but with a different meaning from cognates in other Indo-European languages.[14] What must be noted is that scholars, such as Thieme, have used exactly the same series of deductions, but in reverse. Indeed, as with so much of this debate, Elst has basically redirected Thieme's exact arguments. In Thieme's scenarios, (1953, 552), a protoword for 'salmon' in a salmon-breeding homeland gets transferred onto other fish by tribes moving out of the salmon area and becomes a number, or adjective meaning red, in India. Both ways of presenting the series of semantic transferal are, arguably, possibilities.[15] Clearly, in all homeland explanations, a certain amount of juggling has to be done to account for all the available data, but we find other linguists such as Gamkrelidze and Ivanov utilizing similar arguments to Dhar and Elst in defense of their Near Eastern homeland.[16] This brings us back to the focus of this inquiry. Can India be convincingly denied the status of an *urheimat* contender by the method of linguistic paleontology?

India has repeatedly been excluded as a potential homeland based either on the logic outlined here, that is, that it does not have cognate forms for items of material culture attested in other languages, or, by the inverse logic, that exotic items unique to India are unattested elsewhere. This latter process of elimination has been consistently used to exclude South Asia. Thus Thieme (1964) notes: "We can eliminate [as homeland candidates] those [languages] for whose characteristic plants and animals no reconstructable designations are available, that is India: (no Proto-Indo-European words for elephant, tiger, monkey, fig, tree, etc.), [and] Iran (no proto-Indo-European words for camel, donkey, lion, etc.)" (596; see also Bender, 1922, 21). More recently, Witzel (1995a) has remarked along the same lines that "turning to Sanskrit, it is interesting . . . that 'tropical' [Indo-European] words are . . . absent in it, which indicates that it was an immigrant into South Asia. Words for *lion, tiger, elephant* are either loanwords from local languages, or are new formations, such as *hastin* 'elephant; the one with a hand'" (101). This argument basically holds that since the terms for exotica typical of India have no cognates elsewhere, these terms could not have been in Proto-Indo-European, and therefore Proto-Indo-European could not have been spoken in the areas, such as India, where such exotica are to be found.

Similar arguments were actually countered over a century ago by Western scholars themselves. Lassen ([1851] 1867), as mentioned in chapter 1, was the first to attempt to deny India the possibility of being the homeland on these very grounds that the other Indo-European languages lacked terms for the exotica present in India. His reasoning was immediately dismissed by his colleagues: "The want of animals specifically Asiatic . . . can be explained simply by the fact of these animals not existing in Europe, which occasioned their names to be forgotten" (Weber 1857, 10). Max Müller ([1857] 1985) also rejected this line of argument: "And suppose that the elephant and the camel had really been known . . . by the united Aryans, when living in Asia, would it not have been natural that, when transplanted to the northern regions, their children who had never seen a camel or elephant should have lost the name of them?" (101). Keith (1933) likewise complained:

> Nothing is more unsatisfactory than to attempt to define Indo-European society on the assumption that the Indo-Europeans knew only what can be ascribed to them on conclusive evidence. *Ex hypothesi*, there were great dispersals of peoples from the original home, and those who wondered away were unquestionably constantly intermingling with other peoples . . . and it is not to be wondered at that in new surroundings new words were employed; still less can it be a matter of surprise that peoples which ceased to be in contact with natural features soon dropped the names which had become useless. (189–190)

Lassen's reasoning occurs in the *Cambridge History of India*, wherein Giles (1922) had stated that "the primitive habitat from which the speakers of these languages derived their origin . . . is not likely to be India, as some of the earlier investigators assumed, for neither the flora nor fauna, as determined by their language, is characteristic of this area" (68). Dhar (1930) again rose to the challenge:

> The absence of common names in the Indo-European languages for such Asiatic animals as the lion and the tiger and the camel, cannot prove the European origin of the Aryas [Indo-Europeans], for the names of such animals as are peculiar to the East might easily be forgotten by the people [after they had left India] in the West where those animals were not found. Or it is very probable that there may be several synonyms for the same object in the Aryan mother tongue—the one tribe of the Aryas in Asia or India having taken the fancy for one name while the other for another. . . . Professor Giles is an advocate of the European home of the Aryas. He ought to realize that his argument cuts both ways, for the names of European flora and fauna do not exist in the Asiatic Aryan languages either. Really it should not be difficult to understand that the names for trees and animals disappear as the trees and animals themselves disappear. (30)

Dhar's reasoning is simple but logical, and it returns to the same basic point. If the Indo-European's had migrated from India, it would, indeed, be possible that the words for uniquely Indian objects would disappear from use and would not surface in the western cognate languages. This exactly mirrors the logic outlined in the previous section in reverse: the newly coined words in the western languages to describe exotic items not extant in India would obviously not be evidenced in the Indo-Aryan languages remaining in India.

Here, again, we find present-day Western scholars reiterating exactly the same arguments: the importance of terms in the protolanguage designating plants, animals, and other geographically bound concepts

> should not be overestimated. If a given proto-language was spoken in an area outside that of its daughter languages, specific words designating features of the ancient habitat are not usually preserved in the attested languages. Therefore, if a language ancestral to a group of European languages originated in Africa, we would not be able to find in the extant lexical stock ancient words for "giraffe" and "elephant" which could suggest its African origin. (Dolgopolsky 1987, 8)

Regarding the possibility of synonyms, Polomé, (1990b) along the same lines as Dhar, also objects to speculations that "fail to take into account such basic facts as the possibility that several designations . . . [for words in Indo-European] may have coexisted, differentiated by the context in which they appeared and the people who used them" (270). Furthermore, as Dhar notes, the argument cuts both ways: why should the Indic languages be held accountable for containing the names of exotica not evidenced in the western languages, and the western languages not have to account for their unique terms with no Indic cognates?

Moreover, proto-Indo-European might even have retained protoforms for exotica such as the monkey and elephant, at least according to Gramkrelidze and Ivanov (1995), which, if we are to accept the evidence of such reasoning *ex silentio*, further problematizes the European and Russian homeland theories and could even be used in support of the case of the Indian homeland if we are to follow the same logic that has been levied against it. Gamkrelidze and Ivanov (1995) reconstruct Indo-European animal words for wolf, bear, leopard, lion, lynx, jackal, wild boar, deer, wild bull, hare, squirrel, monkey and elephant.[17] Contrary to Thieme's objection mentioned earlier, we find that, according to Gamkrelidze and Ivanov, items unique to India actually might have cognates elsewhere. They claim that the monkey (Skt. *kapí* < **qhe/oph*) has widely distributed cognates (442).[18] Sanskrit 'elephant' also shares a cognate form with Latin 'ivory' (Skt. *íbha*, Latin *ebur* < **yebh-* or **Hebh-*). Hittite-Luwian, and Greek, point to another protoform (**lebh-onth-* or * *leHbho-*), which suggests to Gamkrelidze and Ivanov that the two words are related to a single Proto-Indo-European form for this animal.[19] Likewise, although there are a variety of terms for lion, Dolgopolsky (1987, 10) considers the form **singh* as one of the few Proto-Indo-European animal terms that appear to be fairly reliable on the basis of Indic (*siṁha*) and Armenian (*inj* 'panther').

Clearly, there are problems with some of the arguments outlined here; Gamkrelidze and Ivanov's reconstructions are by no means universally accepted—the terms for elephant and monkey may have been loans into later languages. Moreover, few Indo-Europeanists still champion the beech or salmon evidence. But the point is that if beeches or salmon or any other item can be promoted as proof of an European or Russian homeland, there is little to prevent disenchanted Indian scholars from coopting Gamkrelidze and Ivanov elephants and monkeys in support of a South Asian one in order to demonstrate the maleability of this method. However, even allowing all of the arguments by Dhar and others noted here, unless a few unambiguous inherited cognates among the Indo-European languages for items unique to South Asian can be found, it is unlikely that claims for a South Asian homeland will attract any serious attention from Indo-Europeanists. Some cognates of tribal names from the Ṛgveda, at least, would be expected to surface in the West if Indo-European tribes had emigrated there from India (and if the Ṛgveda is as old as Indigenists would have it). Of course, as Gamkrelidze and Ivanov's reconstruction has shown, surprises are always possible (although not always accepted), particularly when the data are approached with different perspectives; but, with the exception of Elst and Dhar, linguistic paleontology remains another aspect of this issue almost completely ignored by the Indigenous School.

Witzel, in the earlier remark about the elephant (*hastin* 'possessing a hand'), articulates a further, often encountered observation regarding the names of some animals in India: they are coined terms, newly formed from Sanskritic elements, as opposed to terms formed from a primitive Indo-European verbal root. Masica (1991) elaborates:

> Although spokesmen for the traditional Indian view try to fight back with selective modern arguments, the philological evidence alone does not allow an Indian origin of the Aryans. . . . the names of things peculiar to India . . . are for the most part either borrowed or coined (rather than "primitive"), either of which may be taken as an indication that the thing in question is new to the speakers of a language. (38)

Again, Elst takes (1996) objection to this: "Far from being an indication of more recent and 'artificial' coinage, these descriptive nouns are the typical PIE procedure for creating names for animal species" (380). He notes that Proto-Indo-European **bheros* 'brown' has yielded the name bear; **kasnos* 'the gray one', hare; **ekwos* (which linguistis would nowadays reconstruct as *h_1éḱwo-) 'the fast one', horse; he argues that these are all creatures with accepted Proto-Indo-European pedigree, yet their nomenclatures consist of 'coined' rather than 'primitive' terms. Of course, as was pointed out in chapter five, one has to see which words fit the appropriate Indo-European phonemic pattern, but, as we will encounter repeatedly with Indigenous Aryan arguments, Elst simply reverses the logic of those supporting the Aryan invasions to conclude that "the argument from the colourful descriptive terms in the Indo-Aryan languages will, if anything, rather plead in favour of the IUT [Indian Urheimat Theory] than against it" (382). As for Dhar (1930), he seems bewildered by such logic: "One fails to understand what has the admission of Aryas into India got to do with the appellative name *Hasti*. Why could not the Aryas be natives of India and at the same time give the elephant a name . . . 'animal with a hand' . . . having been struck naturally by the animal's unique and prominent trunk?" (44).

Dhar has a point; even though *-in* suffixes are late derivations, Sanskrit does have an old term for elephant, *ibha*, which it shared with a Latin cognate and might even have been, at least according to Gamkrelidze and Ivanov, Proto-Indo-European: so the Indo-Aryans had no need to invent a new term. It is quite likely that the word *hasti* is arguably a secondary, later, popular, folk term that gained currency. As Mallory (1975) remarks, "Would we lay the blame to a non-Germanic substrate should Dobbin or Rover replace 'horse' and 'dog'?" (142). This comment is also relevant to the previous chapter on substratum; language is never static, old terms get dropped, and new terms are coined to replace them, but this need have nothing to do with immigration into a new, unfamiliar landscape.

The Horse

Gamkrelidze and Ivanov's book, (1995), although not without its critics, is the most comprehensive recent work on linguistic paleontology. Actually, there is not much in their reconstructed PIE environment that would compel Indigenous Aryanists to change their views. Northwest South Asia contains many of the features that these scholars have assigned to the homeland: it is certainly mountainous and forested, possesses mountain lakes and fast-rushing streams, can be characterized by cloudy skies with frequent thunderstorms, is subject to heat and cold,[20] knew herding and agriculture from the seventh millennium B.C.E., contains most of the animals listed by Gamkrelidze and Ivanov, produces honey, and certainly had a developed water transportation system by the third millennium B.C.E.

The most pressing item from Gamkrelidze and Ivanov's reconstructions that is likely to be raised as an objection against an Indian homeland is the much later appearance of the horse in the South Asian archaeological record as opposed to its much earlier use in the steppes, where it was domesticated six thousand years ago (Anthony, Telegin, and Brown 1991, 94). Apart from one or two reports of early horse bones, which will be discussed in chapter 9, the earliest evidence of horses in the Indian subcontinent is generally dated to around the first half of the second millennium B.C.E. In the opinion of many scholars, this paucity of horse bones in India indicates that the Indo-Aryans entered this region well after dispersing from their original homeland. The horse evidence has long favored the Russian steppe homeland hypothesis and is the mainstay of Gimbutas's homeland theory. The horse has been the primary animal for which scholars have tried to account in the homeland quest, since it is culturally central to the various Indo-European traditions and was clearly known to the undivided Indo-Europeans. Beekes (1995) finds the horse an "essential clue" providing "concrete evidence" from the "facts" provided by linguistic paleontology that otherwise "don't give us very much to hold onto" (50). The horse is an essential part of the Indo-European world.

Accordingly, Mallory (1989, 163) immediately eliminates the Balkans and all other areas where the horse was a late arrival from serious consideration as possible homelands. Indian detractors of the Indigenous Aryan school, such as R. S. Sharma (1995) and Shireen Ratnagar (1996b), also lean heavily on this late arrival of horse bones on the subcontinent in support of their views. This lacuna in the Indian archaeological record tends to haunt any attempt to argue for an Indian *urheimat*, and even (as will be discussed in chapter 9), any efforts to correlate the Indus Valley Civilization with the Vedic culture, which is a horse-using one. Since this animal has become almost synonymous with the Vedic Aryans and, by extension, the whole Indo-Aryan migration debate, the horse evidence has to detain us at length, both here, in terms of linguistic paleontology, and in the chapter on the Indus Valley, in terms of the archaeological record.

When all is said and done, however, even the Proto-Indo-European status of this animal is not without problems. There seems to be a recurring opinion among linguists, going back at least to Fraser (1926), that considering **ekwos* to have been a domesticated horse involves accepting some assumptions that can be called into question: "The significance attached to the fact that the Indogermans were acquainted with the horse . . . may have been exaggerated. We do not know the precise meaning of the Indogermanic words in question; we do not know whether they mean the domesticated or the wild animals." For these types of reasons, "it is difficult to see how these names can be safely used for determining the original home of the Indogermans" (266–267). D'iakonov (1985) has reiterated this point more recently: "The Proto-Indo-European term for 'horse' shows only that horses were known (nobody doubts this); it does not mean that horses were already domesticated" (113). Dolgopolsky (1990–93), noting the denotative vagueness of the term, argues that in horse-breeding cultures there are words for 'mare' and 'foal'. The fact that these terms cannot be reconstructed in Proto-Indo-European suggests to him that the referent of **ekwos* must have been a wild horse (240–241); (however, some linguists do reconstruct a term for mare, or, at least, that a word for 'mare' would have been expressed by a word for 'horse', coupled with an indicator of feminine gender as in classical Greek.[21] Zimmer (1990a) points out that the inference that the horse was known to the Indo-Europeans is primarily based on such poetic formulas as 'swift horse', 'horses of the sun', 'characterized by good horses', and so on. He feels that "the formulas tell us nothing specific about the use of horses, but archaeology and history supply the necessary information" (316). This observation is significant. Diebold (1987) has elaborated on these points:

> IE linguistics can agree on the reconstructed Proto-Indo-European etyma **ekwos* 'horse'. . . . But let us note [that] the animal terms tell us, in and of themselves, nothing about the cultural uses of those animals or even whether they were domesticated; but only that Proto-Indo-European speakers knew of some kind of horse . . . although not which equid. . . . The fact that the equid **ekwos* was the domesticated *Equus caballus* spp. Linnaeus . . . come[s] not from etymology but rather from archaeology and paleontology. The most we can do with these prehistoric etyma and their reconstructed proto-meanings, without archaeological and paleontological evidence (which does indeed implicate domestication), is to aver a Proto-Indo-European familiarity with these beasts. (53–54)

There is an element of circularity with the horse evidence. Linguistics cannot tell us whether Proto-Indo-European **ekwos* known to the Proto-Indo-Europeans was the domesticated *Equus caballus* Linn, or whether it referred to some other species of wild equid: the archaeology of the homeland does. But the archaeology of the homeland is primarily located in the Kurgan area *because* that is where *Equus caballus* Linn was first domesticated (an occurrence supposedly confirmed by linguistics)! Understandably, such logic will hardly assist in convincing those already suspicious of the steppe homeland. Since northwestern South Asia is the home of *Equus hemonius khur*, an equid subspecies called onager, I have even encountered the argument, using the logic outlined earlier, that Proto-Indo-European **ekwos* might just as well have originally referred to a northwestern, South Asian *hemonius khur*, which was then transferred onto other types of equids by outgoing Indo-European tribes leaving an Afghanistan/South Asian homeland—although this is unlikely, since the word seems to have been generally applied to denote the horse and not to donkeys or other equids (with the exception of Armenian where the cognate *ēš* does mean donkey).[22] Again, such possibilities are relevant not as serious proposals suggesting that such an occurrence actually happened but as illustrations of how the assumptions involved in linguistic paleontology can be challenged and reversed.

It is also important to note that, according to Dogra (1973–74), "only once do we hear of actual horse riding in the *Ṛgveda* (V. 61–62)" (54). McDonnell and Keith ([1912] 1967) note one or two other probable references to horse riding involving terms for whips and reins (while remarking on some difference of opinion among scholars in this regard), but they stress that there is no mention of riding horses in battle, which is the image that has always been promoted by advocates of the classical Aryan invasion/migration theory. Also of relevance is the fact that no words for typical riding equipment such as cheek pieces or bridles can be reconstructed for Proto-Indo-European, nor is there a Proto-Indo-European etymon for horse riding (Zimmer 1990a, 321). Ivanov (1999) notes that "if horseback riding really did began at the turn of the IV mil. B.C. before the dispersal of Proto-Indo-European, it did not leave traces in the vocabulary of the later dialects. . . . Thus it cannot be proven that this type of ancient . . . horseback riding had originally been connected with Indo-Europeans" (233).[23]

Coleman (1988, 450) notes that five different roots are attested for the animal in various Indo-European languages. This suggests to him that either the protolexicon contained several words for horse depending on its function or that the animal was known only in some areas of Proto-Indo-European speech, with the principal reconstructed original word **ekwos* being a dialectal one, and the other words innovatory after the dispersal. Along similar lines, Lehmann (1993, 272) argues that the fact that there is only one solidly reconstructable word (**ekwos*) for an item that was of such centrality to a culture further underscores the lateness of the borrowing into Proto-Indo-European. He notes that modern terms of equivalent centrality, such as automobile, are known by a myriad of terms. The generic term is initially adopted and then various languages innovate their own names for the item. But only one term is reconstructable for horse in Proto-Indo-European underscoring the fact that it had not been in the protolexicon for very long before the dialects dispersed.

Alternatively, Lehmann also argues that **ekwos* could have been a later loanword that circulated throughout the various dialectics after their dispersal, perhaps being phonemically restructured in some areas. This generic loan was maintained along with other terms that arose in time in individual languages. Lehmann (1993, 271) refers to the many phonological problems, as well as desperate solutions, incurred by linguists in attempting to reconstruct the protoform for this term and suggests that the word may have been a borrowing that was adjusted to fit the phonemic pattern typical of individual dialects or dialect groups.[24] He illustrates this possibility by means of the example of *batata* 'potato' that was introduced into Europe in the sixteenth century. This word was restructured as *patata, pataka, patalo, tapin, katin, patal*, and so forth, simply in the Romance languages alone. He notes that even these cognates within Romance show far less diversity than the variants for *equus* in Indo-European. This is a relevant observation. In the earlier phases of the expanding linguistic continuum of the Indo-European languages out of the homeland, wherever that might have been, the dialectal differentiation within the continuum (which will be discussed in chapter 8) would not have been as pronounced as in later periods. So the horse or wheel, for example, could have been new items that were encountered at some point on the continuum, which were then shared, along with their names, with the other Indo-European speakers elsewhere on the continuum. These terms, although loans, would appear to be inherited since the dialectal differentiation between the languages that adopted the terms might not be sufficient to detect them as loans. Lehmann's comments could support such a possibility, especially since he holds that the dialectal differentiation is indeed sufficient to identify this word as a loan, which might mean that the loan circulated at a later time when the dialects had differentiated more.

If these linguists are corrent that the word for horse could have circulated *after* the dispersal of the Indo-Europeans, and then been restructured according to individual dialects, then stating that the Indo-Europeans knew the horse *before* their dispersal and therefore must have inhabited an area wherein the horse is native (and eliminating other areas where the evidence for the horse is a later phenomenon) becomes less convincing. Indeed, the corollary of all these arguments suggesting that **ekwos* is either a late Proto-Indo-European word or a loanword that circulated after the dispersal of the Indo-European languages is that the homeland could not have been in the steppes where the horse is native. Had the homeland been there, the Proto-Indo-Europeans would have always been around horses and would have had an ancient word for the animal in their lexicon, and not a more recent or a restructured one.

However, not all linguists would agree that the word is either late or borrowed. If we accept that the word is inherited from the proto-period, and accept that the Indo-Europeans were an undivided entity until somewhere between 4500 and 2500 B.C.E., as most scholars would hold, then we have anything from about a one to three millennia gap between when the horse was known to the Indo-Europeans and when it is unambiguously evidenced in the South Asian archaeological record. This is irrespective of whether the horse was domesticated or wild. How can a South Asian homeland account for this?

Allowing that **ekwos* does refer to a domesticated *caballus* Linn, the most convincing argument used by the Indigenous Aryan school to account for its absence in the subcontinent is that horse domestication may well have occurred in the steppes, since this is the natural habitat of the animal, but it is an unwarranted assumption to then conclude that the Indo-European homeland also must have been in the same area. As D'iakonov remarks: "The Proto-Indo-European term for 'horse' shows only that horses were known" (113). Indeed Ivanov (1999), who has undertaken by far the most comprehensive study of the cognate terms for horse in Indo-European as well as the adjacent languages of Northern Caucasian and Hurrian, points out that "the Indo-European homeland need not be identical to the area of horse domestication, but should be connected to it. The ways in which names and technical knowledge . . . spread should be explored" (1971). Thus Talageri (1993), argues that "the horse could have been very well known to the proto-Indo-Europeans in their original homeland before their dispersal from it (which is really the only thing indicated by the facts), without the horse necessarily being a native of that homeland, or they themselves being its domesticators" (158). The horse, according to this line of argument, was an import into India—a highly prized, elite item. The paucity of horse bones in the early archaeological record is due precisely to the fact that the animal, although highly valued, was a rare commodity used in elite priestly or military circles. According to the horse specialist Bokonyi (1997):

> It is well known that wild horses did not exist in India in post-Pleistocene times, in the time of horse domestication. Horse domestication could therefore not be carried out there, and horses reached the Indian subcontinent in an already domesticated form coming from the Inner Asiatic horse domestication centres via the Transcaspian steppes, Northeast Iran, South Afghanistan and North Pakistan. The northwestern part of this route is already more or less known; the Afghan and Pakistani part has to be checked in the future. (300)

In fact, the horse has always been highly valued in India. From the Vedic, through the Epic, and up to the Sultanate period, it has always been an elite item, and it has always been an import. According to Trautmann (1982), "the supply of horses . . . has been a preoccupation of the rulers of India, from, nearly, one end of its recorded history to the other. . . . It has yet to be determined why exactly India has never been self-sufficient in horses. Climate? A relative scarcity of pasture?" For our purposes, the fact remains that "whatever the reason, the stock has always had to be replenished by imports, and the imports came from westward in the ancient period. . . . It is a structure of its history, then, that India has always been dependent upon western and central Asia for horses" (261).

Elst (1996) ruminates on what a prehistoric scenario might look like from an Indigenous Aryan point of view:

> The first wave of Indo-European emigrants . . . may have reached the Caspian and Black Sea coasts and domesticated the horse there, or learnt from the natives how to domesticate the horse. They communicated the new knowledge along with a few specimens of the animal to their homeland . . . along with the appropriate terminology, so that it became part of the cultural scene depicted in Vedic literature. Meanwhile, the Indo-European pioneers on the Black Sea made good use of the horse to speed up their expansion into Europe. (40)

The logic here is that the horse is highly prized in all the literary records throughout Indian history, but it has never been indigenous (although foreign breeds have been imported and bred on the subcontinent with varying degrees of success in the Northwest—later Vedic texts speak about the fine horses of Kandahar and other places).[25] That it was central to the Vedic texts, despite not being indigenous, is therefore no indication of the indigenousness of the Indo-Aryans themselves—it was the horse that was imported, not the Indo-Aryans. Elst is extending this same logic to argue that all the Indo-Europeans could have been situated in India, where the horse was a highly prized but imported and rare luxury item in the collective Indo-European consciousness. The animal was encountered in the steppe area by the northwesternmost border of the Indo-European language continuum that was expanding out of India. The creature, and its name, were then relayed back to other areas of the language continuum, including India. Lehmann observed that the term could have been restructured according to the various dialectics that were germinating in this continuum, making the term appear inherited rather then a loan. Since the horse was such a useful creature, but also a rare one, it became a much prized item in the Vedic sense.

While all this may be possible from a linguistic point of view, from an archaeological perspective the burden of proof will still remain with anyone who proposes that a particular animal or item existed in the proto-historic period. As will be discussed in the chapter on the archaeology of the Indus Valley, the horse remains a problem for the Indigenous position even if, as Renfrew (1999) and others hold, "the significance of the horse for the understanding of the distribution of early Indo-European has been much exaggerated" (281).

Other scholars have tried to compensate for the lack of horse bones in India by countering that the Russian steppes also lack faunal remains that are clearly Indo-European. Such negative evidence was used by patriotic European-homeland promoters in the nineteenth century to reject an Asian steppe homeland because of the absence there of another important IE creature with very well attested cognates—the bee (and its honey). Dhar rejected the steppes of southern Russia because they were unsuitable for agriculture. Gamkrelidze and Ivanov have used the presence of exotic items such as the monkey and elephants in Indo-European as evidence also opposing a Russian homeland. Most recently, as discussed in chapter 1, Krell (1998) has produced lists to argue that the Kurgan area is significantly incompatible with the evidence of linguistic paleontology. Using such negative evidence, by the same logic used to eliminate India as a candidate, ultimately any potential homeland can be disqualified due to lacking some fundamental Proto-Indo-European item or another. In addition, it has long been pointed out that this use of negative evidence is suspect, since we have many examples of other flora and fauna that must have been known to the earliest Indo-European-speaking communities but show minimal or no evidence of cognates across Indo-European stocks (Mallory 1997).

Criticisms of the Method

Linguists have long been aware of the speculative nature of linguistic paleontology: "All prehistoric reconstruction is of course purely hypothetical, that is, based on conjectural assumptions. Strictly speaking any conjectural assumption is a guess. . . . A prehistorian depends on . . . his imagination . . . trained by experience" (Thieme 1964, 585); "The apparent existence of a common term in the language, which is attained through reconstruction on the basis of the attestations in the daughter languages, does not prove that the item it denotes actually existed in the relevant original society" (Polomé 1992, 370).[26] Other scholars have been much more radically dismissive of the whole premise of reconstructing a hypothetical language and culture on the basis of cognate words present in textual or spoken languages existing thousands of years later. The linguist J. Fraser (1926), for example, presented a well-known (but faulty) caricature of the whole enterprise by reconstructing a proto-Romance scenario from the paleolinguistic evidence of the historic Romance languages: "By th[is] same method of investigation we shall discover that the Romans had emperors, and a republic; that they had priests, called by a name represented by the French *prêtre*, and bishops; that they drank beer, probably, but certainly coffee, and that they smoked tobacco" (269). Unfortunately, *bière*, *tabac*, and *café* are all loanwords, minimizing the persuasiveness of Fraser's caricature (which was more accurately a reconstruction of the Vulgar Latin of much later times), but linguists disillusioned with this whole method nonetheless supported the spirit of his critique:[27]

> Now the more sophisticated among us could easily object here that it would take a great deal of naiveté on the part of linguistic palaeontologists to propound such views, . . . yet such naiveté seems to enjoy the status of high acumen, as anyone can see who reads some of the numerous volumes that deal with the "Indo-Europeans," their lives and their mores. But if the authorship of such works is not astonishing enough, the uncritical and admiring credulity bestowed upon them by a vast number of scholars certainly is. (Pulgram 1958, 147)[28]

Latinists in particular, like Lazzeroni, supported Pulgram's *punto fundamentale* and rejected the capability of linguistics to ever be able to determine where a protolanguage was spoken, even if it could reconstruct portions of what was spoken.

Fraser (1926) also pointed out that words in language A, associated with particular geographic locations, travel freely and are borrowed by speakers of language B outside those locations. Such words, if found by the linguistic paleontologist, could be erroneously interpreted as indicating that the speakers of language B originated in the territory of language A. These criticisms are well worth quoting, bearing the horse evidence in mind:

> The English language has laid under contribution almost every language on the face of the earth. We speak freely of the fauna and flora of other countries, not merely [of] England. . . . Names like 'lion', 'tiger', 'wine', 'cotton' . . . and hundreds of other things which are not indigenous in England but are perfectly familiar to every speaker of the English language all over the world. . . . I do not see how scholars placed in the same relation to English as we are to Indo-Germanic could tell that the Englishman knew cotton, wine, and the like only through literature or as articles of commerce, and not because he lived in a region which produced them all. That the palaeontologist of the future . . . should describe the Englishman as tending his vines in the neighborhood of tiger-infested jungles, would not, perhaps, be very astonishing. (272)

There are, of course, ways that a linguist can, in some cases at least, determine whether a word is a later loan or an item inherited from the protolanguage. In the latter case, the phonemic or morphological properties of the word and its root structure would be expected to be consistent with the rest of the language in which it occurs. As noted in chapter 5, the basic axiom is that if a word is inherited from the protolanguage, it must show all of the sound shifts that its phonemes should have undergone over the relevant period of time (i.e., that other words in the language with similar phonemes and in similar linguistic contexts would have undergone) according to the rules of evolutionary sound and change. If any phonemes in the word fail to demonstrate a required sound shift, or if the word shows a non-I.E. root structure, then it is a good candidate for consideration as a loanword. Nonetheless, Fraser's objections are still echoed by scholars such as Renfrew (1987, 1988) in his scathing (and criticized in turn) critique of linguistic paleontolgy, to the approval of Coleman (1988), and should be kept in mind when building up a theory overly dependent on cognate words. As Lehmann (1993) and others have argued, Proto-Indo-European **ekwos* could have been a new innovation or loanword that, along with knowledge of horse use, spread throughout the dispersed Indo-European- language-speaking area after the breakup of Proto-Indo-European (although not later than the stage of Old Indo-Iranian).[29]

Such inherent imprecision of linguistic paleontology has provoked consistent criticisms of the method by linguists. Keith (1933) had long pointed out that:

> The determination of the Indo-Euopean civilization is precisely the point which affords least hope of any satisfactory result. It rests on linguistic evidence pure and simple, and it is open to the gravest doubt whether such evidence is capable of giving the results which are claimed for it by those who seek to determine the Indo-European home. . . . It should suffice to remember that on the basis usually adopted we would have to conclude that the Indo-Europeans knew snow and feet, but were ignorant of rain and hands. The difficulty, of course, is in theory recognized by all who deal with the issue; the trouble is that in practice they tend more or less completely to ignore it, and to create for us a picture of the Indo-Europeans which is probably a mere delusive shadow of the actual civilization of the people. Yet it should be a warning when we find that linguistically we may assert that the Indo-Europeans knew butter but were unacquainted with milk. (189–190)

Pulgram (1958) was even more dismissive:

> It is an elementary mistake to equate common Indo-European words with Proto-Indo-European words and to base thereon conclusions concerning the Proto-European *Urvolk* or *Urheimat*. Yet this is precisely what has often been done. . . . impassioned linguistic palaeontologists have gone even further. From the existence of certain items of vocabulary in all or a majority of the extant Indo-European languages, and blandly ignoring all the pitfalls just noted, they even fabricated conclusions concerning the social organization, the religion, the mores, the race of the Proto-Indo-European. (Pulgram 1958, 145–146)

More recently, Coleman (1988) while noting that some progress had been made, and more could be expected from the method, nonetheless confers that "the arbitrary and unrigorous methods that have characterized much of this linguistic paleontology certainly deserve Renfrew's scepticism. . . . Most of the lexemes that can be confidently assigned on the basis of widespread attestation . . . do not tell us much" (450). McNairn, commenting on Kossina's and Gimbutas's employment of the method, remarks that "the clues afforded by linguistic paleontology were either so general that they accommodated both centres without much difficulty, or they were so hypothetical that they could be easily ignored if unsuitable" (quoted in Anthony 1995b, 96).

Most recently, Krell (1998) argued that "the old, pliable crutch of linguistic paleontology should certainly be abandoned, at least until the theoretical uses and limitations of the Proto-Indo-European lexicon have been more precisely defined" (280). She points out that the reconstructed lexicon does not provide a linguistic picture of a group of Proto-Indo-European speakers at one point in time, or even in one location in space; it may well represent a linguistic continuum of several millennia into which different lexical items were introduced at different stages. Most important, she reiterates the common objection that it is virtually impossible to identify the exact or even approximate referent of a reconstructed lexical item: "It is imperative, in working with the problem of Indo-European origins, that the contents of the PIE lexicon not be treated too literally. Historical linguistics has shown numerous examples of how dramatically the meaning of a given word can shift in the course of a few centuries, let alone several millennia" (279). She concludes that "the use of so-called 'linguistic paleontology' . . . has always been a popular method in the construction of Proto-Indo-European *urheimat* theories. It rests entirely on the supposition that the *meaning* of a proto-form can be reconstructed beyond a reasonable doubt, a supposition which I argue is false" (279).

Conclusion

Despite such inherent problems, theories about the Indo-European homeland are still sometimes predicated on linguistic paleontology for their geographic identification.[30] Thus Mallory (1989) first uses the method to delineate a broad area and then concludes: "We have pushed the linguistic evidence about as far as we may; now it is the turn of the archaeologists" (165). Clearly, however, anyone disenchanted by the initial linguistic method is not likely to give much credence to the secondary auxiliary archaeological evidence that might be called in for support. And archaeology by itself, as Talageri (1993) notes, echoing objections outlined in chapter 1 that have been repeatedly made, tells us nothing about the language spoken by the members of a material culture.[31] One material culture does not indicate one linguistic entity, nor does the spread of a particular material culture necessarily equate the spread of a particular language group, any more than the spread of a language group corresponds to the distribution of a specific material culture (135).

One has only to glance through any of the various homeland hypotheses to see how the same linguistic evidence is utilized very differently by different scholars. Depending on one's own perception of things, one will find alternative theories far too complicated. Any claimant for the homeland has to engage in special pleading, or at least feels that other contestants are more extreme pleaders, which underscores the limitations of the method of linguistic paleontology. The judgment on Occam's razor is very likely to be perceived quite differently in India than in the West.

Ultimately, the dramatically different scenarios still arrived at by different scholars using linguistic paleontology are, in themselves, sufficient proof of its unreliability, if not inadequacy, at least in its present state. If Gimbutas is satisfied that linguistic paleontology can support the reconstructed Proto-Indo-European par excellence as an aggressive, mounted, nomad warrior where Renfrew (albeit dismissive of the whole method) believes it cannot exclude his gentle, sedentary agriculturist, or if the method can be used to promote the environment of the proto-*urvolk* as the harsh, cold, and austere northern one of the steppes but yet be adopted by Gamkrelidze and Ivanov to suggest a warmer and more exotic southern one with tropical animals, then obviously something is inadequate with the present state of the method. If the method is so problematic or limited in reliability, and treated sceptically or rejected even by most present-day Western linguists, one is forced to question how it can be used as conclusive or even persuasive evidence to compel disenchanted Indian scholars to believe in the theory of Aryan invasions or migrations into the Indian subcontinent predicated on this type of data.

7

Linguistic Evidence from outside of India

Potentially devastating evidence against the case of the Indigenous Aryanists is the existence of loanwords between Indo-European, Indo-Iranian, and Indo-Aryan, and non-Indo-European language families. These suggest the geographic proximity of the Indo-Europeans and/or the Indo-Aryans with other language groups far from the horizens of the Vedic Indo-Aryans. Loanwords are often taken to be an essential ingredient in geographically tracing the prehistories of language families, since, if they occur in sufficient numbers, they suggest that the families in question were once situated adjacent to each other. Accordingly, if Proto-Indo-European contains loanwords from language families far from South Asia, then these loans provide compelling evidence that Proto-Indo-European could not have originated in South Asia. The same method applies to Indo-Iranian and Indo-Aryan. Loans between these and other languages provide relevant data for attempting to chart respective points of origin, migrations and trajectories of these languages.

Semitic Loans in Indo-European: Nichols's Model

The detection of such loanwords is the primary method used by a number of linguists who locate the homeland in the Near East. Gamkrelidze and Ivanov, for example, to a great extent base their homeland thesis on the number of loanwords, particularly from Semitic and South Caucasian (Kartvelian), that they trace to Proto-Indo-European.[1] This evidence suggests to them that the Proto-Indo-Europeans must have been situated adjacent to the Semitic and Caucasian language families, somewhere in the vicinity of Armenia. Etymologizing rarely produces consensus, as we have already seen, and most of Gamkrelidze and Ivanov's etymologies have been challenged in one way or another by D'iakonov, an advocate of a Balkan homeland, but supported by Dolgopolsky, who also accepts a Near East homeland, albeit more in central Anatolia (and with different dialectal maneuverings therefrom). Shevoroshkin likewise supported a homeland in the eastern part of Asia Minor but differed from Gamkrelidze and Ivanov about whether there were significant loans between the north and south Caucasian languages and Proto-Indo-European and whether these language groups were therefore immediately adjacent to each other.[2]

With regards to such Semitic and Caucasian loanwords in Proto-Indo-European, Nichols, who translated Gamkrelidze and Ivanov's magnum opus from Russian into English, offers a theory that is particularly relevant to our line of inquiry. Her methodology involves tracing the linguistic history of Semitic cultural loanwords from urban and cosmopolitan Mesopotamia into the surrounding areas (which might be considered to have had "lower" culture and therefore to have been more prone to borrow). Loanwords often emanate out from a central area—especially if this area is perceived as a "higher" or more prestigious urban culture—and are borrowed by adjacent languages, which can rephonemicize the words according to their own phonetic system. Nichols notes that these loanwords may then be passed on in turn to the other neighbors of these languages (which are thereby not immediately adjacent to Mesopotamia but twice removed). These further rephonemicize the words according to their own sound systems. An expert linguist could, at least theoretically, trace those words' history, which could be indicative of the relative geographic situation of all these languages, and in particular of Proto-Indo-European. The assumptions here (which can obviously be called into question, since loans can travel vast distances through trade or other means) are that significant loanwords between language groups indicate geographic proximity of these groups, and lack of loanwords indicates that the languages in question were not immediately adjacent to each other.[3]

In terms of linguistic geography, Nichols translates these findings into the following conclusions: Proto-Indo-European could not have been situated between Mesopotamia

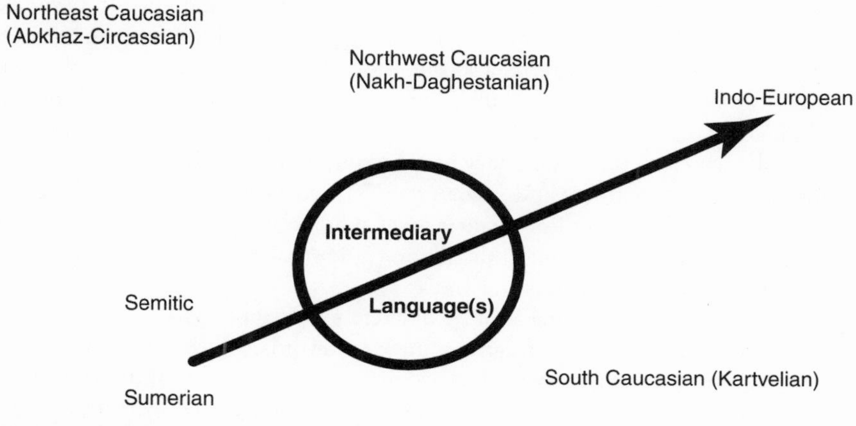

Nichols's schematic rendition of Indo-European in relation to other languages (after Nichols, 1997).

and the Black Sea coast, since culturally laden vocabulary emanating from Mesopotamia did not surface in the language spoken in this coastal area, West Caucasian (Abkhaz-Circassian), via Proto-Indo-European.[4] Proto-Indo-European was not situated between Mesopotamia and the eastern Caucasian foothills and Caspian coastal plain for similar reasons: the language spoken there, East Caucasian (Nakh-Daghestanian), also shows no sign of Proto-Indo-European loanwords. As an aside, and irrespective of any possible Semitic loans from Mesopotamia, we can note that if Proto-Indo-European did not impart any of its own native words either into the languages spoken on the Black Sea Coast or into those spoken in the eastern Caucasian foothills, then the claim of geographic distance between Proto-Indo-European and these languages is reinforced, at least from the perspective of this method. These data are further obstacles for those proposing a steppe homeland.[5]

Be that as it may, at this point Nichols deduces that Proto-Indo-European did not lie to the northwest or northeast of Mesopotamia. It did lie in a direct trajectory of Semitic and Sumerian loanwords but not one immediately adjacent to Mesopotamia, since, according to Nichols, the Semitic loans in the protolanguage show signs not of direct borrowing but of filtration through an intermediary.[6] Nichols accordingly situates Proto-Indo-European still farther to the northeast, in Bactria-Sogdiana, since that is where it could spread across the steppe.[7] She reinforces this with an innovative model of language spread and dialect geography which will be discussed in chapter 8. This location, needless to say, would be welcomed by the Indigenous Aryanists since it overlaps the area under consideration here, namely, an Afghanistan/Pakistan/Northwest Indian locus of origin.[8] I will return to Nichols later.

Finno-Ugric Loans

Of more pressing significance to the Indo-Iranian languages are the loanwords that have been transmitted from them into the Finno-Ugric language family, which was probably spread throughout northern Europe and northwestern Asia in the prehistoric period.[9] Finno-Ugric contains numerous loanwords that, depending on the linguist, have been identified as either Indo-Iranian, Iranian, or Indo-Aryan, indicating that these languages must have been adjacent to each other in prehistoric times. Since there is absolutely no evidence suggesting the presence of Finno-Ugric speakers near the Indian subcontinent, it is reasonable to conclude that Indo-Iranian speakers must have been present in northwest central Asia. How, then, could they have been indigenous to India or, even, the far Northwest of the subcontinent and Afghanistan? The conventional explanation for this is that the Indo-Iranians, after leaving their original homeland wherever that might have been, sojourned in areas adjacent to the Finno-Ugric speakers before proceeding on to their historic destinations in Iran and India.

S. S. Misra (1992) has offered a rather different explanation. Misra draws attention to one rather significant feature regarding these loanwords, which he believes is decisive in determining the direction of language flow corresponding to Indo-Aryan movements: *the loans are from Indo-Iranian into Finno-Ugric*. There are no loans from Finno-Ugric into Indo-Iranian. This is a crucial point. Misra argues that had the Indo-Iranians been neighbors with the Finno-Ugrians in the regions to the north of the Caspian Sea

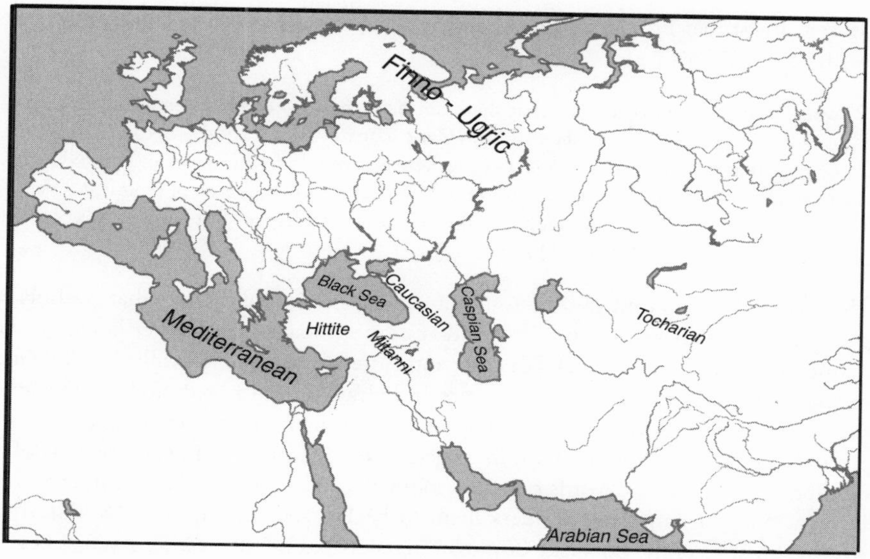

The Finno-Ugric language family.

for so many centuries, then both languages would have borrowed from each other. If the Indo-Iranians, as per the standard view of things, had, then, journeyed on toward their historic destinations in the East, they should have brought some Finno-Ugric loans with them in their lexicons, at least a few of which should reasonably be expected to have surfaced in the earliest textual sources of India and Iran. But, as Burrow noted some time ago, it is usually quite clear that these words have been borrowed by Finno-Ugric from Indo-Iranian and not vice versa (1973b, 26).[10] There do not seem to be any Finno-Ugric loans evidenced in the Veda or the Avesta. This, for Misra, indicates that the Indo-Iranians never went from the area neighboring the Finno-Ugrics down to Iran and India; they went from India to the Caspian Sea area, where they encountered Finno-Ugrians. The Finno-Ugrians, in this version of events, could therefore freely borrow from the Indo-Iranians, but since those emigrating Indo-Iranians never returned to Iran and India (at least in large enough numbers to affect the lexicon back home), no Finno-Ugric loans ever surfaced in the Indo-Iranian literary sources. This version of events accounts for the one-way borrowing. The argument is ingenious. However, as with everything else, counter arguments can be brought forth, such as the power dynamics of sociolinguistics (whereby a lower status group may borrow terms from a higher one without the latter, in turn, borrowing terms from it). Moreover, Rédei (1983) finds it "possible" that the Uralic languages did not just borrow from the Aryan ones but also loaned them words as well (15). Joki (1973), while criticizing the work of earlier linguists who had attempted to find Uralic loans on the Indo-European side, nonetheless states that "in his view, it is not impossible" that a dozen or so such cases can be argued in the Aryan languages (373).

Since these loans are specifically from Indo-Iranian (and not Proto-Indo-European) Dolgopolsky (1990–93) has employed a parallel logic (in support of his Balkan homeland) to insist that Proto-Indo-European could never have been spoken in the steppes north of the Caspian Sea:

> What really matters is the fact that there are *no proto-Indo-European loanwords* in Uralic (or Finno-Ugric) and no Uralic or Finno-Ugric loans in Proto-Indo-European. It strongly suggests that there was *no* territorial vicinity between Proto-Indo-European and proto-Uralic or proto-Finno-Ugric, that is that Proto-Indo-European *was not spoken in or near the Volga or Ural region*, including the steppes to the North of the Caspian Sea (Gimbutas's "Indo-European homeland"). (242–243)

This, too, is a significant observation, particularly in view of the fact that Nichols has pointed out that there were no Proto-Indo-European loans in the other languages bordering the steppes on the Black Sea coast and eastern Caucasian foothills.[11] While most linguists seem to agree that the loans are Indo-Iranian and not Proto-Indo-European, there is disagreement over whether they are specifically Indo-Iranian, Iranian, or Indo-Aryan.[12] Misra (1992), in addition to reversing the direction of language flow, is of the opinion that most of the words can be accounted for as Old Indo-Aryan forms and not Iranian. Shevoroskin also considers them to be Indo-Aryan (and even Middle Indo-Aryan). Most recently, Lubotsky (forthcoming) concurs that the oldest layer of borrowings are often of Sankrit and not of Iranian (6). D'iakonov (1985) and Dolgopolsky (1993) consider them Indo-Iranian. Gamkrelidze and Ivanov (1983b) in contrast, are quite specific that they should be interpreted as early Iranian and not as Indo-Iranian, "or even less as Old Indic" (67). Joki (1973, 364–365) also considers them to be mostly Iranian or Middle Iranian. As Mallory (1997) quips: "Will the 'real' linguist please stand up? It should be obvious that linguists have as much difficulty in establishing the chronological relationships between loanwords as any other 'historical science'" (98).

The identification of the words as Indo-Aryan is crucial to Misra's attempt to date the Ṛgveda. His line of reasoning is predicated on the work of the Hungarian linguist Harmatta, who analyzed these loanwords into eleven consecutive chronological periods based on different stages of phonemic development. In Harmatta's schema, the earliest loans are Indo-Iranian, and later loans contain a variety of Iranian forms (recognizable as Proto-Iranian, Old Iranian, and Middle Iranian),[13] stretching over a very long period from the first half of the fifth millennium B.C.E.[14] to the Hun invasion of Europe in the fourth century A.D.

In Misra's analysis (1992), only the last (and chronologically latest) of the eleven stages of Harmatta's list contains forms clearly Iranian; all the earlier stages contain Indo-Aryan forms.[15] Since Misra considers Old Iranian to have had a similar linguistic and temporal relationship with Old Indo-Aryan as Middle Indo-Aryan had—namely, that it was later—he concludes that the earliest loans were from the period before the Iranians had split from the Indo-Aryans. Since Misra clearly considers proto-Indo-Iranian to be very similar to Old Indo-Aryan, and since Harmatta had speculated that the oldest Indo-Iranian loanwords occurred in the fifth millennium B.C.E., Misra concludes that, if this date is correct, Indo-Aryan must also be assigned to this period and therefore be very much older than the commonly assigned date of 1200 B.C.E. One must note at this point, that the value of Misra's work is dependent on the value of that of Harmatta's. In any event, the dating of the Veda will be discussed in chapter 12 and is peripheral to Misra's essential point; for the purposes of the present discussion, Misra's main argument is that since the loanwords are only from Indo-Iranian into Finno-Ugric and not vice versa, is just as likely, or even more likely, that the Indo-Iranians came from South Asia or Afghanistan to the Caspian Sea area and not vice versa.

It must, be noted however, that a possible objection to both Nichols's and Misra's east-to-west direction of language flow has been raised by some linguists (Shevoroskin 1987; Dolgopolsky 1989). These scholars hold that "the *linguistic evidence*, indeed, fully *corroborates the eastward direction of the migration of Indo-Iranians*," which they argue are evidenced by the chronological spread of loanwords from west to east (Shevoroskin 1987, 229; italics in original). The argument is that loanwords in the East Caucasian language are the oldest and bear witness to Old Indo-Iranian, while the Finno-Ugrian family of the lower Volga Valley has somewhat later loanwords from Middle Indo-Iranian. According to Shevoroskin, loans from the Late Indo-Iranian linguistic period can be found in languages emanating further eastward across the steppe.[16] These findings fit comfortably with their proposed Near Eastern homeland: "The historical implications of this linguistic evidence are obvious: the proto-Aryans appear to move eastwards across the Ponto-Caspian steppes, from the region north of the Caucasus, where they were in contact with proto-Nakh-Daghestanian, into the Lower Volga area, where they contacted proto-Finno-Ugrians" (Dolgopolsky 1989, 29).

As we have seen with the Finno-Ugric borrowings, however, there is unlikely to be agreement among linguists regarding the exact linguistic (and therefore chronological) identification of such loans as Indo-Iranian, Indo-Aryan, or Iranian—what to speak of more subtle distinctions such as whether they are Old, Middle, or Late Indo-Iranian. Clearly, tracing chronological trajectories of loanwords from east to west or west to east will entail levels of linguistic sophistication and an adequate degree of agreement among linguists that is something we have yet to look forward to. And such research would have to account for *all* the Indo-Iranian loanwords in the Caucasian and Ugric languages, not just a select few.[17] Moreover, even if it could be determined that Nakh-Dagestanian (East Caucasian) has older loanwords than Finno-Ugric from an unified Indo-Iranian period, these data are not incompatible with a position similar to Nichols's model (1998) which will be considered in the next chapter. In her model, Older loanwords could have belonged to an earlier wave of Indo-Iranian from an eastern locus of origin which impacted Finno-Ugric, and this could have been followed by a later wave of Middle Indo-Iranian, which influenced the more southerly Caucasian area. Ultimately, there is little in the history of loanwords that can eliminate a variety of historical possibilities.

Other Traces of Indo-Aryan

The Finno-Ugrics were not the only other language family to borrow from the Indo-Iranians, who seem to have left linguistic traces across large areas of Asia over a wide time span. Where Nichols seems to have found Proto-Indo-European loans, Harmatta finds evidence of a number of proto-Iranian or proto-Indo-Aryan loans in the Caucasian and Ketic languages. The Iranians seemed to have gone as far as the borders of China and Korea, since here, too, he finds Iranian loanwords; again Misra considers them to be Indo-Aryan (on the grounds that they show *s* in places where Iranian shows *h*). Russian linguists have also pointed out Indo-Iranian, or possibly Indo-Aryan, tribal names and hydronyms in the Kuban region north of the Black Sea, as well as around the Caspian Sea.[18] Telegin (1990) draws attention to thirty Iranian hydronyms in the Dnieper basin. There are also Indo-Aryan and Iranian terms in European hydronomy (Schmid 1987, 331). The Russian linguist Karamshoyev (1981) finds Iranian words (to which Misra agrees) in the Pamir languages of Afghanistan—the much favored homeland of the nineteenth century.

Burrow (1973a) found evidence of Indo-Aryans in western Iran, south of the Caspian Sea. The Avesta, which is geographically centered in eastern Iran, makes mention of the Māzanian *daevas*, who are worshipers of the Indo-Aryan gods. According to Burrow, Māzana is known in Iranian sources as the territory between the southern shore of the Caspian Sea and the Alburz Mountains. These *daeva* worshipers, although still in existence at the time of the inscriptions of Xerxes, were condemned by the reformer Zarathustra, persecuted, and eventually subsumed by the Iranians from the East. Parpola (1988, 127) notes that in Latin sources, Strabo (11.9.2) refers to a people called Párnoi who belonged to the Da(h)as, who were said to have lived in Margiana, from where they founded the Arsacid empire of Parthia. Actually, in this instance, we have a clear indication of a movement from east to west, since the Dahae came to live on the east coast of the Caspian Sea, north of the Hyrcania (Gurgun), where there is still a district called Dahistān. Parpola notes that the Párnoi corresponds to the Sanskrit term Paṇi (if this is accepted as a Prakrit development <*Pṛni). The Dahas/*Dahae* correspond to the Dāsa and the Paṇis to another tribe that fought the Aryan Divodāsa on the banks of the Sarasvatī.

When the unambiguous Indo-Aryan names found in documents in the Middle East (to be discussed later), are also taken into account, the picture that emerges through linguistic and philological sources is of Indo-Iranian, Indo-Aryan or Iranian tribes spread out over an extended period and across a vast area stretching from India to the Middle East and across to the Great Hungarian Plain, up to the north of the Caspian Sea, and over as far as the Ordos in northern China (Harmatta 1992, 359). These have invariably been taken by Western scholars to be reminiscences or preserved traces of the Indo-Aryans and Iranians on their way to India and Iran from a western point of origin.

Misra's contention is that, since none of these tribes brought Finno-Ugric Caucasian (or even Chinese or Korean) loanwords from these areas into the Avesta or Veda, they could not have been coming from these areas to Iran or India. If, on the other hand, the reverse were to be considered—that they were traveling from India and eastern Iran/Afghanistan to these other areas—then the lacunae would be much better accounted for. In such a scenario, these other language families could have logically borrowed from these emigrating Indo-Aryans and Iranians before subsuming them. Other Indian scholars have responded to such evidence in similar ways. Let us see if the Avesta can discount these claims or throw any light on the Indo-Iranian homeland.

The Avestan Evidence

The oldest parts of the Avesta, which is the body of texts preserving the ancient canon of the Iranian Zarathustran tradition, is linguistically and culturally very close to the material preserved in the Ṛgveda. Zarathustra preserved some of the cultural Indo-Iranian features common to the Ṛgveda and developed, reformed, or rejected others

(Humbach 1991, 2).[19] Operating within the same social and religious milieu that is reflected in the Ṛgveda, Zarathustra's teachings are to some extent defined vis-à-vis this milieu. Both cultures, for example, place enormous economic importance on cattle. However, unlike in the Vedic ethos, where cattle raiding is glorified as a heroic undertaking, Zarathustra condemns such exploits as wicked and selfish. Likewise, he opposes the worship of *devas* (who are the chief benefactors in the later Vedic tradition), demonizes them, and supplants them in terms of righteousness with the benevolent *Ahuras* (Vedic *asuras*, who are in turn depicted as malevolent entities in most of the Vedic tradition).[20] There seems to be economic and religious interaction and perhaps rivalry operating here, which justifies scholars in placing the Vedic and Avestan worlds in close chronological, geographic, and cultural proximity to each other not far removed from a joint Indo-Iranian period. If the evidence preserved in the Iranian tradition, the Avesta, contradicts the hypothesis of an Indo-Aryan linguistic community indigenous to India, then one need waste no further time speculating on how the other members of the Indo-European family might be accounted for in the Indigenous Aryan scenario.

Linguistically, the oldest sections of the Avesta are almost identical to the language of the Ṛgveda. This oldest part is called the Yasna (Vedic *yajña*), which is the principal liturgical work of the sacred canon and accounts for about a third of its bulk. The nucleus of the Yasna consists of the five Gathas (Vedic *gātha* 'song'), a collection of seventeen hymns (each Gatha containing from one to seven hymns), which are the only authentic literary heritage left to posterity by Zarathustra himself (Humbach 1991, 3). Along with a few other texts in the corpus, these Gathas contain the most archaic language of the Avesta. The language displays the same richness as Vedic in its verbal inflection, contains almost identical morphology, exhibits the same processes of word formation, and consists, for the most part, of words that have cognate forms in Vedic that are distinguished by minor phonetic changes (Kanga and Sontakke 1962, xx).[21] The proximity of this language to Vedic is so remarkable that whole Avestan passages can be transformed into Vedic simply by making these minor phonetic correspondances (e.g., Sanskrit *s* = Arestan *h*).[22] With such close economic, religious, and linguistic overlap, the two texts are considered to be very similar literary offshoots of a not-too-distant, proto-Indo-Iranian period. This is significant because if Zarathustra's date can be determined with any degree of accuracy, it might serve as an anchor to secure the date of the compilation of the Veda in close chronological proximity, since, as noted earlier, the oldest part of the Avesta is attributed to Zarathustra.

Zarathustra's date, unfortunately, is far from certain. Previously, a sixth century B.C.E. date based on Greek sources was accepted by many scholars, but this has now been completely discarded by present-day specialists in the field. Two dates for the prophet were current in Greek sources: 5000 years before the Trojan War, that is, 6000 B.C.E., and 258 years before Alexander—the sixth century B.C.E. date. This more modest date has been shown to be completely fictitious, but it initially gained wide acceptance because it seems to have been adopted by the later Zarathustran scholastics themselves in the Pahlavi books (Boyce 1992, 20). Since there is no specific historical information in the tradition itself, once this chronological anchor had been unfastened, dating the Avesta can only be based on the same conjectural suppositions that characterize attempts to date the Veda.

The lower date for the Avesta, as with the Veda, is comparatively easy to establish.

Although there is much that is very arbitrary in the assignment of figures to genealogies, Boyce (1992, 29) claims a lower date of no later than 1100 B.C.E. for the Gathas on the basis of the lineages, and so on, recorded in the texts.[23] As for the higher date, Boyce has less to work with. Since, like the Ṛgveda, the *Avesta* is well acquainted with chariots, and since the earliest remains of a spoked-wheel chariot dated to before 1600 B.C.E. have been found in the Sintashta Cemetery in the Inner Asian steppes (from where Boyce is assuming the Iranians entered Iran), she tentatively proposes an upper limit of 1500 B.C.E. for the Gathas (44). Gnoli (1980, 159), who is also supportive of an earlier date (end of the second, beginning of the first millennium B.C.E.) along many of the same lines as Boyce, points out that the oldest Avestan texts reflect a milieu that is certainly much different than that of the Medes and the Achaemenians. Significantly, the texts make no mention of urban centers, or even of geographic regions in the west of Iran. Such features all indicate a decidedly prehistoric period. When we consider that these tentative dates are bolstered by coordination with the generally accepted date for the composition of the Vedic hymns (Boyce 1992, 29) and the movements of the Indo-Aryans (Boyce 1992, 41)—both of which, from the perspective of this study, are under reconsideration—it becomes clear that the Avestan evidence, rather than helping to secure the Vedas temporally, simply becomes an extension of the same chronological problem.

Geographically, the Avesta has little to offer the quest for the homeland of the Indo-Aryans speakers—with one very important exception. In sharp contradistinction to the lack of any clear reference in the Vedic tradition to an outside origin, the Avesta does preserve explicit mention of an *airiianəm vaējō*, the legendary homeland of the Aryans and of Zarathustra himself.[24] The descriptions of this place, despite the fact that "it is revealed that Ohrmazd made [it] to be better than the other places and regions," speak of severe climatic conditions (Humbach 1991, 35).[25] Gnoli (1980, 130) situates the *airiianəm vaējō* in the Hindu Kush because all the identifiable geographic references in the Avesta are of eastern Iran, south central Asia and, Afghanistan, with an eastern boundary formed by the Indus. There is no mention of any place north of the Sir Darya (the ancient Jaxartes),[26] nor of any western Iranian place (Boyce 1992, 3).

Skjaervo (1995) finds the identity of the *airiianəm vaējō* to be insoluble, but finds it possible that it might have changed as the tribes moved around. He reiterates the notorious difficulties involved in using the Avesta as a source for the early history of the Iranians and cautions against circularity, since, if "we use archaeology and history to date the Avesta, we cannot turn around and use the Avesta to date the same archaeological and historical events, and vice versa" (158). While skeptical of attempts to pinpoint the exact locus of their composition, he concurs that the internal evidence of the Avestan texts makes it impossible to avoid the conclusion that they were composed in northeastern Iran and traveled from there to the south and southwest (165–166). Witzel (forthcoming, b) undertakes a thorough analysis of all the philological, linguistic, environmental, and climactic pointers in the texts and feels the Avestan homeland points to the central Afghan highlands including, perhaps, areas north and south of the Hindukush.

So the geographical boundaries of the Avesta are approximately coterminus with the western part of the area under consideration by Indigenous Aryanists (and the favored homeland of nineteenth-century scholars). Of course, all this could be a reference to a secondary Indo-Iranian homeland, and not the primary Indo-European one, but, like the Veda, the Avesta preserves no clear memory of an overland trek from the Caspian Sea. However, the Hapta Hendu (Vedic Sapta Sindhu or Panjab) is known, as is the Harahvaiti (Vedic Sarasvatī),[27] which denotes an Iranian river. Boyce, in harmony with most Indo-Europeanists, believes that the oblique geographic indicators in the Avesta refer to the Inner Asian steppes, but, regrettably, there is little that is of real help in locating the homeland of the joint Indo-Iranian speakers unless one is prepared to apply the data to a homeland already prefigured on other grounds.[28] Nor is there any reason for Indigenous Aryanists to disagree that the Avestan *airiianəm vaējō* could have been Afghanistan and the Hindu Kush, as these scholars suggest.

There are also identical names of rivers common to both Iran and India, such as the Iranian Harahvaiti and Harōyū, which correspond to the Indian Sarasvatī and Sarayū (Sanskrit *s* = Iranian *h).* In and of themselves, all that can be said of this data is that these names could have been either transferred by incoming Indo-Aryan tribes from Iranian rivers to Indian ones, as is generally assumed, or by outgoing Indo-Iranian tribes from Indian rivers (although any transfer from Iran to India must have occurred before Iranian developed the *h* phoneme, since *s* can become *h* but never vice versa). Scholars have conventionally interpreted these transferals as evidence of the movement of the Indo-Aryans toward India from the Caspian Sea area via Iran. Burrow, (1973a) for example, considers that the Vedic name Sarasvatī belonged originally to the river in Iran that it refers to in the Avesta and was later imported into India by the incoming Indo-Aryans. Another set of Indo-Iranian river terms river—Sanskrit 'rasā', Avestan 'Raŋhā'—has been identified with cognates in Russia, where 'Rosa' is a frequent river name, which to some is an indication of the steppe origins of the Indo-Aryans. A number of Baltic river names have the form 'Indus', 'Indura', 'Indra', and so on, which are explainable by comparison with Sanskrit *indu* 'drop' (Mallory 1975, 169). These hydromic etymologies have been accepted as signs of Indo-Aryans (or Indo-Iranians or Iranians) moving across Asia toward their historic seats in India and/or Iran.

Indigenous Aryanists maintain that they could all just as easily be signs of tribes emigrating from the Indian subcontinent and its environs toward Iran and the Northwest. Even Max Müller (1875) considered that the "Zoroastrians were a colony from Northern India. . . . A schism took place and [they] migrated westward to Arachosia and Persia. . . . They gave to the new cities and to the rivers along which they settled, the names of cities and rivers familiar to them, and reminding them of the localities which they had left" (248). More recently, Erdosy (1989) has also noted that "it would be just as plausible to assume that Saraswati was a Sanskrit term indigenous to India and was later imported by the speakers of Avestan into Iran. The fact that the Zend Avesta is aware of areas outside the Iranian plateau while the Rigveda is ignorant of anything west of the Indus basin would certainly support such an assertion" (42). Certainly, the Indus Valley, which Indigenous Aryans, as we shall see in the next chapter, consider to have been Indo-Aryan, formed a trading and cultural zone with central Asia, Afghanistan, and Baluchistan in the third millennium B.C.E. The Avesta, then, simply deepens the mystery of Indo-Aryan origins.

Lubotsky (forthcoming) has identified a number of words shared between the Indo-Aryan and Iranian branches that are not evidenced in any of the other Indo-European languages. Some of these are inherited from Indo-European, but others exhibit phonological or morphological features that make them conspicuous as loans. Lubotsky finds that the structure of these loans in Indo-Iranian is similar to the structure of the loans in the Ṛgveda found by Kuiper, suggesting that they were borrowed from the same language (or, at any rate, two dialects of the same language). In Lubotsky's view, "in order to account for this fact, we are bound to assume that the language of the original population of the towns of Central Asia, where Indo-Iranians must have arrived in the second millennium BCE, on the one hand, and the language spoken in the Punjab, the homeland of the Indo-Aryans, on the other, were intimately related" (4). Since there are some irregularities in the Iranian correspondances, Lubotsky further infers that the Indo-Aryans formed the vanguard of the Indo-Iranian collective heading southeast and were thus the first to come into contact with the tribes who spoke foreign languages. After adopting the loan words from these tribes, they passed them on to the Iranians, who adjusted the phonemes somewhat, thus producing these irregularities.

As a side note, if the subtratum language of Central Asia and that of the Punjab were the same, then the question arises as to why Iranian was not affected by at least some of the same non-Indo-European phonological and morphological features unique to Vedic and Sanskrit that have generally been assigned to the Punjab substratum, as was discussed in chapter 5. Also of interest is the fact that Lubotsky is surprised to find that many of the loans into Finno-Ugric are only attested in Sanskrit, and not Iranian—an observation that would doubtlessly be of use to Misra's thesis as outlined here. Lubotsky holds that this could be because the Indo-Aryans were the vanguard of the Indo-Iranians, but one might wonder why the Iranians in the rearguard did not likewise impart loans.

Lubotsky (forthcoming) notes that the landscape of Indo-Iranians must have been quite similar to their original homeland since there are no new terms for plants or other items of the environment. There are loans for new animals such as the camel, as well as for irrigation, elaborate architecture (including permanent houses), clothing, and hair styles. There are few terms for agriculture, reinforcing the idea of their nomadic lifestyle, and there is a paucity of terms for military technology, which underscores Aryan military supremecy. All of this "is a strong confirmation of the traditional theory that the Indo-Iranians came from the North. . . . The Indo-Aryans formed the vanguard of the Indo-Iranian movement and first came in contact with the original inhabitants of the Central Asian towns. Then, presumably under pressure of the Iranians, who were pushing from behind, the Indo-Aryans moved further south-east and south-west, whereas the Iranians remained in Central Asia and later spread to the Iranian plateau" (5).

While this is a perfectly satisfactory interpretation of the data, these foreign terms in Indo-Iranian are subject to the same possibilities as the substratum elements discussed in chapter 5: How can one dismiss the possibility that it was the foreign terms that were entering into an Indo-Iranian speaking language group already situated in East Iran, Afghanistan, and the Punjab, rather than the opposite—the Indo-Iranian speakers immigrating into the territory of a preexisting indigenous language group situated in the same area? A good number of the terms—'bad,' 'smell,' 'head hair,' 'milk,' 'belly,' 'spit,' 'tail,' 'heap,' 'penis,' etc.—are surely items that exist in any language. If the Indo-Iranians borrowed such terms, it is not because they did not already possess equivalents in their own dialects. Terms often get replaced and new synonyms are added to a vocabulary as tribes interact with each other. As for the terms denoting new or unfamiliar items such as garments, the camel, or bricks, how can we eliminate the possibility that these were not simply exotic, desireable, or useful foreign items that entered a language area through trade or other means and that retained their foreign names?

Moreover, as has already been discussed, what mechanisms can linguistics provide to determine whether such loans are due to substratum, superstratum, or adstratum? Lubotsky (forthcoming) himself notes that "I use the term substratum to refer to any donor language, without implying sociological differences in its status, so that 'substratum' may refer to an adstratum or even superstratum" (1). These are all issues that need to be resolved before determing that such terms reflect preexisting substratum languages that can be used to chart the movements of the Indo-Aryans.

The Mitanni Treaties

Another set of data crucial to the Indo-Aryan saga, and one of the few happy occasions when archaeology and linguistics coincide unambiguously, is the inscriptional evidence demonstrating the presence of Indo-Aryans throughout the Near East in the fourteenth century B.C.E. By the turn of the twentieth century, Indologists in the West had long ceased to contest the picture of an overland trek of the Indo-Aryans from a European or Caspian Sea homeland across the Asian steppes into India. It came as a great surprise to learn about these Indo-Aryans that had suddenly come to light as a result of Hugo Winckler's excavations in Boğazköy, Asia Minor, during the summer of 1907. These Indo-Aryans were not just misplaced wondering nomads who had happened to take a premature turn at the wrong steppe, but rulers of the Mitanni kingdom in north Mesopotamia and rulers of neighboring principalities as far as Syria and Palestine. How did they get to be there?

The principal texts that have generated the most interest among scholars interested in this topic are the treaty between a Hittite king and a Mitanni king wherein the Vedic gods *Indara* (Skt. *Indra*), *Mitras*(*il*) (Skt. *Mitra*), *Nasatia*(*nna*) (Skt. *Nāsatya*), and *Uruvanass*(*il*), (Skt. *Varuṇa*) are mentioned, and a treatise on horse training and upkeep

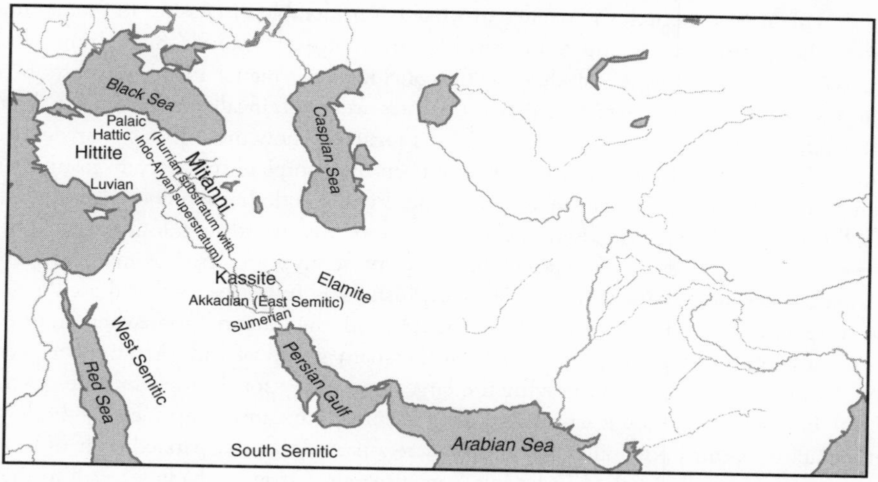

The Mitanni kingdom.

by a Mitannian called Kikkuli wherein technical terms related to horsemanship are in Indo-Aryan. (For a comprehensive discussion of the Boğazköy texts, see Starke 1995.) The text suggests Indo-Aryan prominence in this field. Aryan traces also appear in Kassite documents from the Babylon dynasty, such as *Surias* (Skt. *Surya*) and the war god *Maruttas* (Skt. *Marut*, although this latter always occurs in the plural). In addition, over a hundred such names of local personalities have been produced by scholars. (See, for example, Dumont 1948, 56–63 and appendix.) The Indo-Aryan character of these is accepted by most scholars. Moreover, they referred to kings and ruling elite spread out over an area that included Syria and Palestine.[29] Although these rulers were Indo-Aryan, the population was not, being mostly Hurrian. This suggests elite dominance of the Mitanni state and a large area of neighboring territories by an intruding, martial, Indo-Aryan class.

Jacobi, more concerned with the temporal as opposed to the geographic significance of the findings, was delighted at the news. He and Tilak, as will be discussed in chapter 12, had utilized Vedic astronomical references to argue for a much older date for the Ṛgveda than Western scholars had ever considered before, but both attempts had been criticized by some of their peers. Urging restraint on the belligerent Tilak (who was unbowed by the negative responses to his astronomical theories, and "who wished to enter upon a campaign against all opponents"), Jacobi told him that "the discussion would have no definite result unless excavations in ancient sites in India should bring forth unmistakable evidence of the enormous antiquity of Indian civilization" (Jacobi 1909, 722). Learning of the findings at Boğazköy, Jacobi felt somewhat vindicated that at least the late date his colleagues were proposing for the Ṛgveda was now discredited, since the Mitannians, whom Jacobi assumed had come from India, were already worshiping the Vedic gods in "full perfection" in the fourteenth century B.C.E. Obviously, their worship must have been even earlier in India itself, so that he might consequently "perhaps think that [his] chronological argument will yet survive" (726). It has been suggested that some of the names go back to the seventeenth century B.C.E. (Dumont 1948, 63) or earlier still (Akhtar 1978–79, 66).

As might be expected, the treaties provoked considerable discussion for some time over whether the names and terms recorded in them were Indo-Iranian, Iranian, or Indo-Aryan. Paul Thieme's study of 1960 concluded the matter to the satisfaction of most scholars by demonstrating that the names were specifically Indo-Aryan.[30] Four possibilities have been considered by scholars regarding how these Indo-Aryans ended up in the Near East. First, they might have been the complete Indo-Aryan group that, after its split with the Iranian members of the original Indo-Iranian collective, initially took over the Mitanni kingdom and then proceeded eastward to colonize the Northwest of the subcontinent. This possibility is not presently considered by most scholars. Another alternative, to which most Western historians subscribe, is that these Aryans were a segment of the Indo-Aryans (after the split with the Iranians) somewhere in north Iran or central Asia who peeled off from the main group of Indo-Aryans who were migrating east toward India. Leaving the larger body, they sought their fortunes in the Near East, where, although successful, they eventually became subsumed by the local population. A third possibility is that they were a part of the unseparated body of Indo-Aryans who initially reached India but, sometime after arriving, bade farewell to their kinsmen, retraced their steps, and headed back east.[31] Sten Konow (1921, 37), who agreed with Jacobi's proposal that the Vedic culture in India must have had a much higher antiquity than most scholars were willing to allow, argued for a version of this third possibility. He proposed that although the Indo-Aryans were immigrants to India, once they had established the Vedic culture on the subcontinent, some of them traveled back out of India and into Mesopotamia. This chain of events would require assigning the Ṛgveda a date considerably older than that of the Mitanni treaties.

The fourth possibility, supported by Jacobi and Pargiter in the West, and often viewed as the least complicated one by Indigenous Aryanists, is that these Indo-Aryans could have been Vedic-speaking tribes from the Indian subcontinent who left their homeland in the Punjab for the Near East, bringing their favorite gods with them: "[The Mitanni evidence] can either mean that the Aryans were on their trek to India from some upland in the north or the Indo-Aryan culture had already expanded from India as far as Asia Minor" (Vidyarthi 1970, 33); "Did the worshippers of Indra go from an earlier home in the Indus valley to Asia Minor, or was the process just the reverse of this?" (Majumdar 1951, 25). There is nothing in the Near Eastern documents themselves that militates against either the third or the fourth possibility. On the contrary, as will be discussed more thoroughly in chapter 10, archaeologists point out that there is not a single cultural element of central Asian, eastern European, or Caucasian origin in the archaeological culture of the Mitannian area (Brentjes 1981, 146). This is a significant obstacle to those proposing versions of the first or second possibilities.

In contrast to this lacuna, Brentjes draws attention to the peacock element that recurs in Mitannian culture and art in various forms (to be eventually inherited by the Iranians), a motif that could well have come from India, the habitat of the peacock. Since this motif is definitely evidenced in the Near East from before 1600 B.C.E., and quite likely from before 2100 B.C.E., Brentjes (1981) argues that the Indo-Aryans must have been settled in the Near East and in contact with India from well before 1600 B.C.E.[32] The corollary of this is that the Indo-Aryans "could not be part of the Andronovo culture [a culture dated around 1650–1600 B.C.E. with which they are usually associated], but should have come to Iran centuries before, at the time when the Hittites came to Anatolia" (147).

Satya Swarup Misra (1992) again presents some linguistic comments in support of this greater chronology.[33] He argues that many of the linguistic features in the Anatolian documents are much later than Vedic but identical to the forms found in Middle Indo-Aryan.[34] These were also noticed by Kenneth Norman (1985, 280).[35] Hodge (1981) also draws attention to *satta* 'seven', which is the Prakrit form of Sanskrit *sata*, and remarks that the inscriptions show a Prakritic form of Sanskrit a thousand years before such forms are known in India itself on inscriptions. These observations fit comfortably with the proposal that the Near Eastern kings could have left the Indian subcontinent after the early Vedic period, bringing post-Vedic, Indo-Aryan linguistic forms with them. The most drastic corollary of such a claim, as Jacobi noted, would be a major reevaluation of the dating of the Ṛgveda, which must have considerably predated the appearance of the Near Eastern texts in 1600 B.C.E. if these do, indeed, represent a diachronically later, as opposed to a synchronically contemporaneous, or dialectal, form of Indo-Aryan.

There has been some controversy over the numeral *aika* 'one', which some linguists hold could be from Indo-Iranian which has the form *aika* (e.g. D'iakonov 1985, 158), rather than from Indo-Aryan. However, (the Iranian term for 'one' is *aiva*, but it is quite possible that Indo-Iranian could have had two terms for 'one' since *eva* survived in Sanskrit as 'alone') suggesting that this term could indeed be Indo-Aryan.[36] Misra (1992), and others we can recall, hold that the loanwords in Finno-Ugric were Indo-Aryan, which if correct would indicate that the Indo-Iranians had split into Iranians and Indo-Aryans long before the Mitanni treatise. However, Norman (1985, 280), in contrast to Misra, accommodates the possible Middle Indo-Aryan linguistic features in the treatise with the commonly held opinion regarding Indo-Aryan origins by proposing that Middle Indo-Aryan dialectal variations were already in existence within the Indo-Aryan community as they were en route to India. Of relevance here is that scholars (e.g. Elizarenkova 1989) have noted certain Middle Indo-Aryan forms present in Vedic but absent in Sanskrit, which lends support to this possibility of Middle Indo-Aryan forms being extant as optional or dialectal forms during the Vedic period itself. Accordingly, since Misra's observations can be interpreted as indicating that these MIA forms were already extant in the Indo-Aryan language on its way to India, they do not prove a greater antiquity of the Veda. But Misra's claim remains a possibility nonetheless. In fact, all of the various arguments presented by Indigenous Aryanists so far reject the 1200 B.C.E. date commonly assigned to the Ṛgveda. This is a most crucial issue, and one to which I will turn in chapter 12.

Conclusion

In conclusion, then, the recurrent theme of this work has been to show how different perspectives and assumptions result in different interpretations of the evidence and produce different conclusions. From post-Proto-Indo-European to the historical period (as known from Greek sources), we find traces of Indo-Iranian, Indo-Aryan, and/or Iranian speakers spread out over a vast area stretching from North India across the Middle East, central Asia, the Caucasus, and up to the Caspian Sea. Indigenous Aryanists believe nothing in any of this evidence can deny the possibility that the Indo-Aryan and Iranian tribes might have been emigrating from a northwest South Asian/Afghanistan homeland toward the Northwest as opposed to immigrating from the Northwest to the Southeast.

As a side note, one reference in particular is repeatedly produced from the Purāṇas as evidence of a large emigration from Gandhara, Afghanistan, to the northern regions. The narrative is situated in the time of Māndhātṛ, who drove the Druhyu king Aṅgāra out of the Punjab. Pargiter ([1922] 1979) notes that the next Druhya king, Gāndhāra, retired to the Northwest and gave his name to the Gāndhāra country (which survives to the present day in the name Kandahar in Afghanistan). The last king in the Druhyu lineage is Pracetas, whose hundred sons take shelter in the regions north of Afghanistan '*udīcīm diśam āśritaḥ*'and become *mlecchas*.[37] The Puranas make no further reference to the Druhyu dynasty after this.[38] The more enthusiastic see this as "evidence of the migration of Indo-Europeans from India to Europe via Central Asia" (Talageri 1993, 367).

Most scholars, of course, will respond to such a claim by pointing out that the Purāṇas are generally considered to have been written much later than the terminus post quem date for the Indo-European dispersal. This dispersal must have occurred before the earliest recordable evidence for distinct, already separated IE languages, such as the Hittite and Mitanni documents, which are datable to the first half of the second millennium B.C.E. Scholars do acknowledge that much material in the Purāṇas does go back to the Vedic age—indeed, Rocher, who posits an ur-Purāṇa, declines to even attempt to date them—and although the Druhyus are certainly mentioned in the Ṛgveda as one of the tribes fighting in the *dāśarājña* war, scholars are hardly likely to assign an earlier date to some of the contents of the Purāṇas than the date they have assigned to the Ṛgveda of 1500–1200 B.C.E. Not surprisingly, the Indigenous Aryan school disagrees completely. For them, the assignment of such dates is rather arbitrary, and most are open to the possibility of a Veda as old as the third, or even fourth, millennium B.C.E. coexisting with strands from the contents of the material recorded in the Purāṇas.

Be all that as it may, it certainly cannot be stated that all historical movements connected with the Northwest of the subcontinent have been from west to east, as some scholars imply when comparing the Indo-Aryan migrations with those known to history such as the Greeks, Kuśāṇas, Śakas, Moghuls, and others. Scholars of the nineteenth century protested against the opposite tendency of their time, which was considering people's movements to have always been from east to west—Michelet's ex Oriente lux. In addition to the earlier reference from the Purāṇas, Indian scholars have often pointed out that, in later times, the Gypsies emigrated from India to the West, as did Indian Buddhists to the Northwest, influencing significant areas of central Asia (and, of course, China and the East). Hock (1993, 82) draws attention to other Indo-Aryan groups from the subcontinent who have followed a northern trajectory: Gandhari or Niya Prakrit in early medieval Khotan and farther east; modern Dumaki in northwestern South Asia; and the Parya who came to modern Uzbekistan via Afghanistan. Earlier still, Indus seals found their way to Bahrain, Mesopotamia, and central Asia (although this is likely to have been through trade rather than emigration). Of course, the historic situation need have nothing to do with the protohistoric one, but the point sometimes made by Indigenous Aryanists, of course, is that South Asians have not been reluctant to emigrate to the Northwest in the modern, historic, and protohistoric periods (to which even the modern-day South Asian diaspora attests), so, by comparison, there is no a priori reason to suppose that this could not have happened in prehistory.

But such suppositions have little to do with serious arguments. The ultimate point, from the perspective of the present discussion, is not that the evidence in this chapter in any way suggests a South Asian homeland. The point is that it merely cannot exclude it as one possibility among a number of others: there is little in the matter of loanwords outside the Indian subcontinent that might convincingly persuade Indigenous Aryanists to change their view. Much of the evidence is malleable and has been reconfigured by scholars with different perspectives and presuppositions such as Misra. Here, too, compelling proof of Indo-Aryan origins eludes us.

8

The Viability of a South Asian Homeland

Since the principle that cognate languages stem from some kind of a protoform has yet to be refuted, as has the postulate that protolanguages must have been spoken in some kind of a reasonably delimited geographic area, there seem to be only three (or four) options that could account for the connection of the Indo-European languages as a family. Either the Indo-Aryan languages came into India from outside or, if it is to be claimed that the Indo-Aryan languages are indigenous to India, the corollary must be that the other Indo-European languages left from India to their historically known destinations. The third alternative is that there was a very large surface area stretching from the Northwest of the subcontinent to the Caspian Sea wherein related, but not necessarily homogeneous, Indo-European languages were spoken. Trubetzkoy (1939) offered a fourth proposal, that Indo-European was a language created by the creolization of several different languages in contact.[1]

The third proposal is attractive in a "politically correct" sort of way in that it bypasses the need for subscribing to either an immigration into or an emigration out from India; indeed, K. D. Sethna (1992, 75) has settled on this very solution, as has Kenoyer (1997). However, linguists are likely to object that such an area is too vast to account for the morphological, lexical, and other shared features of the Indo-European languages, which would require a much more compact and limited geographic origin. Such a vast geographic area of origin for a language family has never been attested in linguistics—the Romance languages, as a point of comparison, originated in a limited area around Rome, although they spread all over southern Europe. Unfortunately, the minute one tries to further narrow this vast Indo-European-speaking area, one enters the quagmire of speculation and disagreement that has been characteristic of the Indo-European homeland quest since its inception. What Western scholars have not been aware of until very recently is that some Indian scholars have utilized the same linguistic evidence used in debates in Western academic circles to argue that even India cannot be excluded a priori from being a possible homeland candidate.

This does not mean all Indigenous Aryanists believe that India was factually the homeland of all the Indo-Europeans. Of course there are certainly those who, perceiving the fallacies in many of the theories being promoted by their Western colleagues, nonetheless attempt to utilize similar methods and logic to promote India as a homeland. Perhaps this is understandable after being subjected to two centuries of unbridled European intellectual hegemony on the Indo-European homeland problem. But clearly an Indian homeland theory is as open to the same type of criticism that Indigenous Aryans have vented on other homeland theories. Most scholars simply reject the whole endeavor as irremediably inconclusive, at best, and "a farrago of linguistic speculations," at worst. The more careful members of the Indigenous Aryan school, at least, simply recognize that all that can be factually determined with the evidence available at present is that "the Indo-Europeans were located in the Indus-Sarasvati valleys, Northern Iran, and Southern Russia" (Kak 1994, 192).[2] From this perspective, if the shared morphological and other similarities mandate that the Indo-Europeans had to come from a more compact area, that is, from one side of this large Indo-European-speaking expanse, most Indigenous Aryanists see no reason that it has to be the western side: "We can as well carry on with the findings of linguistics on the basis that India was the original home" (Pusalker 1950, 115). In other words, by arguing that India *could* be the Indo-European homeland, the more cautious scholars among the Indigenous Aryanists are demonstrating the inadequacy of the linguistic method in pinpointing any homeland at all, rather than seriously promoting India as such.

Factually, however, the fact that so few scholars have really taken it upon themselves to engage the linguistic issues is the Achilles' heel of the Indigenous Aryan school. The Indo-Aryan invasion theory was originally constructed on linguistic grounds, and it can be effectively and convincingly dismantled only by confronting its linguistic infrastructure. Even Indian archaeologists who have been the most stalwart supporters of Aryan invasions or migrations defer to the linguistic evidence:

> It has been repeatedly denied that there was any Aryan movement into India. . . . [A]rchaeology has not "proved" the intrusion of the Indo-Aryan languages into South Asia . . . [but] equally . . . absence of such "proof" is not tantamount to refutation *of the theory of linguistics*. . . . [I]t appears as if archaeological data and methods are not appropriate tools with which we may study the problem. *From historical linguistics* we learn that speakers of the earliest/ancestral Indo-European languages originally lived in a common homeland in Eurasia and subsequently . . . dispersed . . . eastward into Iran and India. (Ratnagar 1996a, 1; my italics)

As we shall see in the following chapters, South Asian archaeologists have indeed repeatedly insisted that the archaeological record shows no sign of Indo-Aryan incursions and that, therefore, the Aryan invasion theory is at best a linguistic issue; and, at worst, it is simply a figment of nineteenth-century European imagination. As a point of comparison, similar arguments were made in 1992 in a series of essays by a Western archaeologist, Alexander Häusler (Lehmann 1993). Häusler found that the archaeological evidence in central Europe showed continuous linear development, with no marked external influences. This caused him to reject Gimbutas's three-stage invasion hypothesis from the Russian steppes, as well as the whole notion of an Ursprache "proto-language." However, as Lehmann curtly points out, "He has no proposal for the source of the Indo-European language or languages. . . .For Häusler. . .the notion of an Ursprache is obsolete. Yet on the basis of linguistic study we must assume that societies maintained common languages that, like languages today, were open to change. . . .Accordingly we posit proto-languages" (285–286). Archaeologists, whether Western or Indian, cannot simply dismiss, or ignore, linguistic reality.

Center of Origin Method

As noted previously, the first serious attempt I have found that challenges the prevailing ideas regarding the Aryan invasions by utilizing linguistic, as opposed to philological, data was by Lachhmi Dhar in 1930. The then commonly accepted status quo, as mentioned in chapter 1, had been established by Robert Latham, an ethnologist, who was the first to challenge the idea of an Asian homeland. Latham had proposed that languages are analogous to biological species: the geographic center of origin of a species exhibits the greatest variety of features. The homeland of the Indo-Europeans therefore must be found wherever the greater variety of language forms were evidenced, that is, in or near Europe. The Indo-Iranian languages, in contrast, being more homogeneous, were more peripheral to the area of greatest variety and therefore must have been peripheral to the homeland. More recently, Dyen (1965) has articulated this principle on similar grounds:

> The strongest hypothesis regarding the homeland of peoples speaking languages belonging to the same language is one that assigns this homeland to the area in which the genetically most diverse members of the family are to be found. It is reasonable that the whole of a large number of groups of people is not likely to migrate as a collection of distinct groups. If then we find the most diverse collection of languages belonging to the same family in a particular area, there is a prima facie argument that the languages grew different in that area rather then elsewhere. (15)

In other words, it is more probable that one or two groups moved out from a geographic maitrix that had become linguistically heterogeneous, than that many linguistically distinct groups moved out from a linguistically homogeneous area.

Although this line of reasoning is certainly more sophisticated than the proposals to simply situate the homeland in the exact geographic center of the whole Indo-European-language-speaking zone, various objections were raised, most notably that the existence of the Tocharian language in the eastern group disrupted its homogeneity somewhat. At the time of writing, there is still no consensus on proto-Bangani, which Zoller has claimed to be an Indo-European language in India itself that contains very archaic Proto-Indo-European features that would significantly demarcate it from Indo-Aryan. In addition, the center of gravity argument, which is no longer accepted by most linguists, ignores possibly more important factors that will be discussed later.[3]

In 1930, in response to Latham's hypothesis, Lachhmi Dhar provided a different explanation for this greater linguistic diversification in the western Indo-European languages of Europe. Dhar argued that the European side of the family, upon leaving its original homeland, which he situates in the Himalayas, had to impose itself on the indigenous, pre-Indo-European languages known to have existed in Europe (such as Basque, Etruscan, Iberian, and Pictish) and thereby absorbed more foreign linguistic elements.[4] This resulted in the greater linguistic variety perceivable in Europe. The Indo-Iranian languages, in contrast, developing organically from Proto-Indo-European, which was native to India, absorbed no such alien influences and thereby remained relatively homogeneous and conservative. Dhar's position invokes a linguistic principle based on the conservation principle. This holds that the area of least linguistic change is indicative of a language's point of origin, since that area has been the least affected by substrate interference. The very characteristics used by Western scholars to postulate a European homeland were used, by Dhar, as evidence that this homeland could certainly not have been in Europe, and the disqualification assigned to Indo-Iranian, he reconstrued as its qualification. Actually, Dhar's line of argument has a history in Western debates in the Indo-European homeland. (e.g., Feist, 1932; Pissani, 1974).

Dhar (1930) went on to argue that "ancient Sanskrit possesses the greatest number of roots and words and the greatest variety of grammatical forms, belonging to the Aryan mother tongue, when compared with all the other Aryan languages in the world" (59). Here, Dhar is referring to the long-established position of his time: "The Sanscrit is the language which has retained the most primeval form and has adhered the most tenaciously to that parent ground. . . . [It] has preserved a great number of roots which have been lost in the other languages (Weber 1857, 6). Most particularly, Dhar singled out the accent as the specific feature of the Vedic language that is homogeneous with Proto-Indo-European, since "every student of comparative philology knows that the Vedic Sanskrit preserves most faithfully the accent of the Aryan mother-tongue, although, quite naturally, traces of the original Aryan accent are also noticeable in some other Aryan languages such as the Greek and Pre-Germanic languages etc." (45). Dhar wonders:

> How is it that as the speakers of the language traveled all their way from Europe to Asia and then finally settled in India, they were able to retain in India alone of all countries—their final destination which they must have reached after a course of several centuries—almost exactly the same accent on words which their European forefathers used to possess centuries before in their forest-home in Europe or their Asiatic fathers on the table-land of Asia away from India, but which their bretheren in different countries . . . could not preserve. . . . Nor can the Aryans be supposed to have traveled through an ethnic vacuum as they started their journey from Europe or outer-Asia and traveled across thousands of miles of land before they could reach India, and escaped the influence of alien speech habits on their language. . . . [on the contrary, it was] the Aryas in their journeyings in Europe and Asia outside India [who] could not avoid . . . [being] overwhelmingly swamped by foreign people. . . . thus the ethnic disturbances have disturbed the original Aryan [Indo-European] accent in Outer-Asia or Europe. . . . the continuity of the original Aryan accent in ancient India implies the unbroken geographical and ethnic continuity of the Aryan race from the most primitive times in India. . . . Thus the home of the primitive Aryan language can be located round the home of the Vedic speakers who possessed almost exactly the same word or sentence-accent as their Aryan [Indo-European] fathers did. (47–51)[5]

It is true that the Vedic accent "reflects most faithfully the original Indo-European accentual system" (Halle 1977, 210; see also Kiparsky, 1977), but, of course, Dhar's reasoning can be countered by arguing that Vedic retained the Indo-European accent because it was a sacerdotal language, which artificially preserved forms that would otherwise have evolved in a normal spoken language; there may be other factors involved in the conservation of archaic features apart from absence of substratum. Nonetheless, Dhar made a serious effort to address the full range of linguistic data available to him, and some of his arguments were as well-reasoned as anything that was on offer by some of his Western colleagues of the day.

Other Indian scholars have repeatedly raised the same objections with regard to other archaic features in Indo-Aryan:

> The Vedic Sanskrit has the largest number of vocables found in the Aryan languages. . . . if the pre-Vedic Aryan language was spoken in different parts of Europe and Asia where the Aryans had settled, . . . how is it that only a few vocables are left in the . . . speech of those parts, while the largest number of them is found in the distant places of ultimate settlement and racial admixture in India? On the contrary, this disparity can easily be explained if the pre-Vedic was the language of the homeland of the Aryans and the other Aryan languages came into existence as a result of the contact between migrating Aryans and non-Aryan elements outside India and Persia. (Majumdar 1977, 216)

The same arguments recur almost verbatim in numerous publications (Luniya 1978, 71; Pillai 1988, 78) and must have been widely circulating in India—perhaps because some nineteenth-century Western scholars who were partial to a Bactrian homeland had made the same case: "The nearer a language is to its primary centre, the less alteration we are likely to find in it. Now of all the Aryan dialects, Sanskrit and Zend may, on the whole, be considered to have changed the least" (Sayce 1880, 122).

Although questionable, such arguments are interesting if only because the same logic has been used repeatedly regarding Lithuanian as well as, more recently, Anatolian. Both of these languages have also preserved very archaic Indo-European features, causing them to be promoted as being situated in, or adjacent to, a postulated homeland. The archaisms in Lithuanian were first accounted for by Latham as being due to this language's being spoken in the vicinity of the original homeland north of the Black Sea, where it was not subject to alien substratum influence.[6] More recently, Kortlandt (1990), while promoting the eastern Ukraine as the best candidate for the original Indo-European homeland, holds that the language of the Indo-Europeans who remained in this area after the migrations eventually evolved into Balto-Slavic. Accordingly, "the deceptively archaic character of the Lithuanian language may be compared to the calm eye of a cyclone" (136–137). Along the same lines, as additional support for their Anatolian homeland, Gamkrelidze and Ivanov state that "proto-Anatolian moved a relatively small distance from the proto-Indo-European homeland. This explains the extreme archaism of the Anatolian languages" (1995, 790). Dhar, then, adopted a line of reasoning that is well used in such debates.

It seems clear that linguists have presented many factors as being involved in the mechanics of language change, which vary according to time, place, and individual cases. Few, nowadays, will accept overly simplistic explanations such as that either variegation and innovation or homogeneity and archaicness automatically indicate autochthony. Conservatism has indeed been demonstrated as corresponding with indigenousness in a number of case studies (e.g., Ross 1991), and foreign substrata influences are certainly principal causes of language change in nonindigenous languages on the periphery (e.g., Blust 1991). But it has also been well established that indigenous languages tend to innovate, while emigrating ones peripheral to the homeland are often conservative. One must conclude, then, that standard formulas cannot be applied generically: linguistics has provided two acceptable models here that appear to conflict with each other.

Whichever model one adopts, one is still left with the fact that the extent of conservatism or the degree of lexical and structural innovation evidenced in the various Indo-European languages will depend on the reconstruction of the original lexicon and morphology of the Proto-Indo-European language. Linguists disagree considerably in their reconstructions, and few would posit *an* original, monolithic Proto-Indo-European at all, since the so-called proto-language is a conventional term for a certain dialectal continuum (D'iakonov, 1988). Accordingly, the model from which to compare later Indo-European languages so as to determine their degree of transformation is not universally accepted. This leaves room for debate regarding whether Sanskrit is more or less conservative or archaic vis-à-vis other Indo-European languages.[7] It has already been noted in chapter 4 that historically Sanskrit has always been considered the most conservative Indo-European language and that some linguists would still agree with this. However, there is a growing body of linguists, including Gamkrelidze and Ivanov themselves, who consider some of the features long held to be archaic in Sanskrit and Greek to be later innovations while the more simple morphology of German and Hittite more closely represents that of the original language.

If one bears in mind the time in which he was writing, Dhar's arguments are intriguing because they challenge established assumptions and reconfigure the same data to reverse the direction of the Indo-European movements. More significantly, he shows considerable awareness of the linguistic theories of his day and argues in a manner just as reasonable, logical, and coherent as that articulated by many of his Western counterparts sixty years ago.[8] This intensifies the crucial issue: To what extent can the direction of Indo-European speech movements be reversed to support the possibility of linguistic emigrations from India as opposed to immigrations into it? Can the linguistic data accommodate the possibility that the Indo-European language might actually have originated in India and broken up into daughter dialects that, with the exception of Indo-Aryan, emigrated from the subcontinent in much the same fashion and order as linguists would have them leave from the Volga Valley, Anatolia, Central Europe, or any other proposed homeland? Can the position of the Indigenous Aryan school be supported by simply reversing the generally accepted direction of linguistic flow out of the subcontinent rather than into it, at least in theory?

Dialectal Subgroupings: Gamkrelidze and Ivanov's Model

Hock (1999a) notes that "the 'PIE-in-India' hypothesis is not as easily refuted [as arguments claiming that Proto-Indo-European is Vedic]. . . . Its cogency can be assessed only in terms of circumstantial arguments, especially arguments based on plausibility and simplicity" (12). There is, in other words, the issue of Occam's razor. In Hock's estimation (forthcoming), the consideration that Proto-Indo-European could have developed dialectal diversity within India, "while . . . not in itself improbable . . . has consequences which, to put it mildly, border on the improbable and certainly would violate basic principles of simplicity" There are corollaries to such a theoretical move. According to Hock. (1999a):

> What would have to be assumed is that the various Indo-European languages moved out of India in such a manner that they maintained their relative position to each other during and after the migration. However, given the bottle-neck nature of the route(s) out of India, it would be immensely difficult to do so. Rather, one would expect either sequential movement of different groups, with loss of dialectal alignment, or merger and amalgamation of groups with loss of dialectal distinctiveness. (16–17)

Misra's response (forthcoming) to this is that "simplicity is no argument. Migration is not supposed to occur in a planned manner. . . . On this basis India can not be excluded." In other words, Occam's razor may have no resemblance to reality. From this perspective, it is impossible to demonstrate why the trajectories of protohistoric languages need correspond to present-day notions of ease or simplicity, or why a scenario deemed less complicated on a theoretical diagrammatic linguistic map need represent historical reality any better than a more complicated one. Diebold (1987), in response to Dyen's principle noted earlier, articulated similar feelings: "Some languages . . . simply will not stay put, and the migratory routes they pursue may be little affected by such principles" (46). Occam's razor is, however, the only tool that historians have at their disposal when faced with a body of data, irrespective of how accurate their interpretations factually are. Hock's point is that Proto-Indo-European must have contained dialectal variations prior to splitting up. He finds it very unlikely that the languages which shared dialectal isoglosses in a hypothetical Proto-Indo-European homeland in India would all emigrate and then resettle themselves with the same dialectal relationships they had previously, leaving only Indo-Aryan behind. It seems simpler to posit one migration into India.

Koenraad Elst (1996) tries his hand in actually offering a falsifiable model of how migrations from a South Asian homeland might have occurred from within the parameters of the relevant dialectal relationships:

> We propose that there is no necessary link between the fact that Sanskrit is not the oldest form of IE and the hypothesis that India is not the oldest habitat of IE. It is perfectly possible that a Kentum language which we now label as PIE was spoken in India, that some of its speakers emigrated and developed Kentum languages like Germanic and Tokharic, and that subsequently the PIE language in its Indian homeland developed and satemized into Sanskrit. (227)[9]

Elst raises the possibility of Proto-Indo-European evolving into Vedic in India itself, an evolution which involved, over time, the loss of certain archaic Proto-Indo-European traits. Meanwhile, other Indo-European languages left India at various stages, some of them preserving particular Proto-Indo-European linguistic features that were not preserved in Vedic (such as the maintenance of velars where Vedic had developed palatals in Elst's *kentum-satem* (nowadays denoted as *centum/satəm*) example, which will be discussed later).

Let us consider the Proto-Indo-European-in-India hypothesis as a purely theoretical linguistic exercise. I wish to stress again that this exercise becomes relevant to the field of Indo-European studies not as a presentation of theories claiming India to be the actual

Indo-European homeland, but as an experiment to determine whether India can definitively be excluded as a possible homeland. If it cannot, then this further problematizes the possibility of a homeland ever being established anywhere on linguistic grounds. If the linguistic evidence cannot even eliminate India as a candidate, then any attempt at archaeologically identifying the Indo-Europeans in an area supposedly preconfigured by linguistics becomes even further complicated.

The Indo-European languages were initially divided on the basis of the velar-palatal distribution of cognate terms into a Western branch, called the *centum* group (Latin *centum* < PIE **kṃtom* 'hundred'),[10] which had preserved the Proto-Indo-European velar phoneme *-k* and a *satem* (Avestan *satəm*/Sanskrit *śatam* < PIE **kṃtom* 'hundred') branch, which had developed a palatal phoneme *-s* for the same term. The *centum* group included Celtic, Greek, Italic, Germanic, and Anatolian, and the *satem* group, Balto-Slavic, Indo-Iranian, Albanian and Armenian. This neat east-west division, however, was short-lived. A *centum* Indo-European language called Tocharian was found as far east as Chinese Turkestan (Xinjiang).[11] Moreover, Melchert (1987) has argued that the Anatolian language Luvian is neither *satəm* nor *centum*, thus questioning the heuristic value of the entire divide. In any event, Elst's proposal that earlier tribes could have emigrated from India bearing the *centum* characteristics and, after the velars had evolved into palatals in the Indian *Urheimat*, later tribes could have followed them bearing the new *satem* forms (while the Indo-Aryans remained in the homeland), cannot actually be discounted as a possibility on these particular grounds. This scenario would receive some support if the recent report by Zoller of a *centum* language spoken in the North of India proves well-founded.[12] This language, called proto-Bangani, although largely assimilated by the surrounding dialects, has supposedly preserved some *centum* vocabulary, especially, and significantly, in the context of old stories.

However, there are other more significant isoglosses that need to be addressed by an Indian or any other *Urheimat*, some of which cut across the *centum-satem* divide. Isoglosses are bundles of common linguistic features that crisscross over language areas. If a significant number of isoglosses coincide, the area they demarcate can be considered a specific dialect or, if the number is sufficiently high, a language.[13] Gamkrelidze and Ivanov (1995) have presented a temporal and spatial model for the segmentation of Proto-Indo-European into the historically attested Indo-European dialects, which we can apply to the Indian *Urheimat* to see if it fits.[14] The model (which combines the Stammbaum model and the wave theory model)[15] is based on isoglosses that bind, or separate, various Indo-European languages into groups that require geographical proximity, or segregation, at various stages of linear time.[16] Initially, in the Proto-Indo-European stage, all the languages are united temporally and geographically, that is, they exist at the same time and in more or less the same place, whenever and wherever they might be.[17]

According to the Gamkrelidze and Ivanov model, this protolanguage initially contains two major dialect groupings, which they call A and B.[18] Group A consists of Anatolian, Tocharian, and Italic-Celtic, group B, of Indo-Aryan, Greek, Armenian, Balto-Slavic, and Germanic.[19] Anatolian, which is held to have uniquely preserved some very archaic language features as I have discussed, is the first to break away from the homeland, leaving the rest of group A and group B together for a period during which they develop some common isoglosses not visible in Anatolian.[20] Many scholars hold that Tocharian was the next to break off (Ringe et al. 1998). After the initial departure of

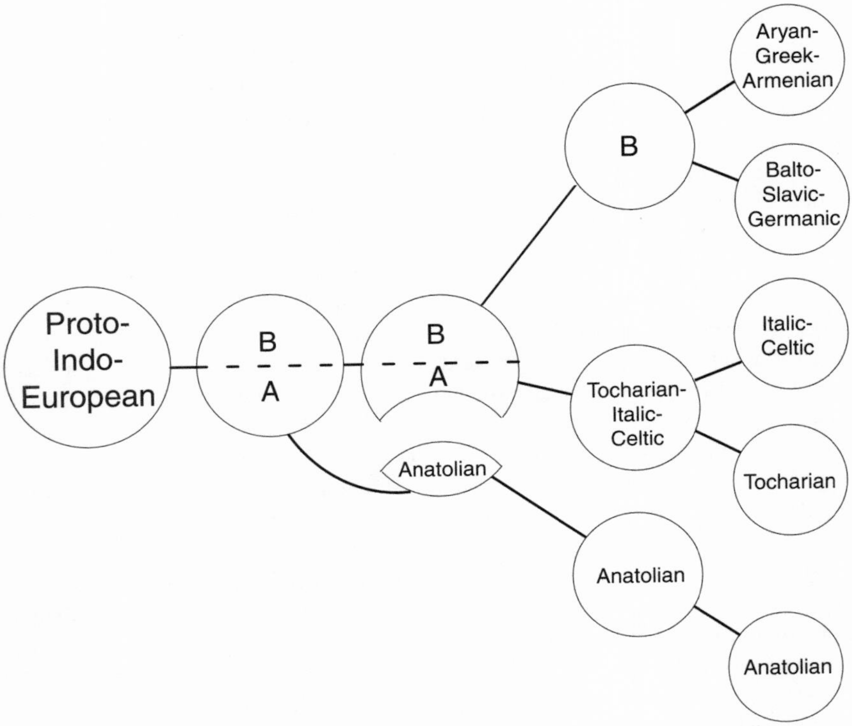

Gamkrelidze and Ivanov's model for the segmentation of Proto-Indo-European (after Gamkrelidze and Ivanov, 1994).

Anatolian, and Tocharian group A my parts company with group B and eventually subdivides into the Celtic and Italic language groups that enter into protohistory.

After being separated from group A, several isoglosses in group B require that Indo-Iranian, Greek, Germanic, and Balto-Slavic all coexisted in some degree of proximity.[21] Subsequently this group also subdivides into Balto-Slavic-Germanic and Indo-Iranian-Greek-Armenian,[22] but in such a way that Indo-Iranian maintains a central position for a period. This centrality allows it to share isoglosses with Slavic, on the one hand,[23] and Germanic, on the other,[24] even while remaining more closely affiliated with Greek and Armenian. Balto-Slavic-Germanic also goes its separate way in time, and the remainder of group B, having developed some common features among its members, also eventually breaks down into the individual Indo-Iranian, Greek, and Armenian groups that ultimately manifest in the historical record. These morphological isoglosses separating the various groups are further reinforced by phonemic and lexical isoglosses, which are "unambiguous evidence for the historical reality of the dialect areas of Indo-European" (Gamkrelidze and Ivanov 1995, 364).[25]

While several Indo-Europeanists have found a variety of features in Ivanov and Gamkrelidze's account that they disagree with to a greater or lesser extent (particularly in their location of the homeland, the migrational routes they propose therefrom, and their identification of specific loanwords), their basic outline of the isoglosses and groupings joining the Indo-European dialects is more than adequate for the present purposes, which is to consider to what extent dialectal geography can delimit the homeland. There seems little in Gamkrelidze and Ivanov's model, in and of itself, that rules out a priori, an Indian homeland (or a variety of homelands, for that matter). Scholars such as Elst have argued that Proto-Indo-European could have developed the dialectal distinctions outlined earlier in South Asia itself. Anatolian could have peeled off and made its way to its historic location from the subcontinent. The rest of group A, Celtic, Tocharian, and Italic, could, in time, have also headed out for greener pastures. The remaining dialects could have continued to evolve their defining characteristics in India. The Indo-Iranian tribes, or speakers, could have been neighbors with the proto-Greek and Armenian speakers, on one side, and the proto-Balto-Slavic and Germanic speakers, on the other, resulting in whatever shared isoglosses need to be accounted for with these various groups. Satemization, for example, could have been an isogloss that partially spread throughout this area but without reaching Germanic on one side, or Greek on the other.

In time, the Balto-Slavic-Germanic speakers moved on, in turn, leaving the remaining three dialects—Greek, Armenian, and Indo-Iranian—to continue to interact linguistically, explaining the close similarities between them. Eventually, even Greek and Armenian departed for the Northwest, leaving Indo-Iranian behind. The Iranians had the least distance and were the last to move: any hypothetical eastern homeland could, perhaps, have included parts of northeastern Iran.[26] The out-of-India model as outlined by Elst is really just a co-option of Gamkrelidze and Ivanov's model but with an even more southeasterly point of origin. This scenario basically differs from the more common Caspian Sea homeland model by postulating a linear and sequential initial point of origin rather than one radiating out in a more circular fashion. Ultimately, there is no internal mechanism in the direction of language spread that can a priori discount such a model, even if it disregards Dyen's principle that language family homelands are more likely to be located in the area where there is maximum contiguity between the cognate languages of the family (or, to put it differently, the area from where the minimum number of migrations are required to connect the distributions of these cognate languages).

Or course, many other issues remain to be dealt with. Migration routes need to be postulated whereby loanwords into the Indo-European languages from other language families can be accounted for; Gamkrelidze and Ivanov's whole case is heavily dependent on Semitic and Caucasian loans which they have identified in Indo-European. Their etymologizing and interpretations of the implications of these loans are, in turn, contested by their detractors who propose different homelands. Ultimately, since it is clear that our study group is interested only in the indigenousness of the Indo-Aryans, and not in the saga of the other Indo-European speakers, Indigenous Aryanists are not likely to contest any migration details proposed for the other languages unless they militate against a South Asian homeland. Thus, Elst is quite happy to note that, in Gamkrelidze and Ivanov's model (1996),

> all the migrations required are the same as in the IUT [Indian *Urheimat* theory], which would equally bring the IE tribes to the East of the Caspian sea first, then let them move on from there. . . . From an IUT viewpoint, all this falls neatly into place. . . . [Italic,

> Celtic, Germanic, Baltic, and Slavic] entered Europe through Ukraine, north of the Black Sea, while Greek and Palaeo-Balkanic parted company with Armenian on the South coast of the Caspian Sea. (237–239)

In fact, Gamkrelidze and Ivanov's migration routes have received criticism from scholars on linguistic grounds (e.g., D'iakonov 1985). Every homeland theorist runs into problems with Occam's razor at some point or another. But the point holds good: the phonemic, morphological, and lexical relationships between the various Indo-European languages, in and of themselves, are not sufficient as data to pinpoint the original homeland; the diachronic and synchronic relationship between the various dialects can be accounted for in a variety of ways and from a variety of homelands.

Ultimately, apart from non-IE influences, such as loanwords, there is nothing in the languages themselves that can give any indication of how far the languages might have traveled to reach their historic destination. In the words of Latham (1862), who, in the mid–nineteenth century was attempting to challenge the then very entrenched idea that Asia was the homeland of the Aryans (the exact reverse of what the Indigenous Aryan school is doing today): "A mile is a mile and a league is a league from which ever end it is measured, and it is no further from the Danube to the Indus than it is from the Indus to the Danube" (612). Of course, it can be pointed out that Elst's model appears clumsy, since "it is easier to accept that remotely related languages developed separately within the same region rather than that several unconnected waves of migration to that same region brought remotely related languages with them" (Pejros 1997, 152). Be that as it may, none of these arguments can be used convincingly to insist on an external origin for the Indo-Aryan languages.

In my opinion, the most serious objection against a South Asian homeland from the perspective of the evidence being considered in this chapter is not the dialectal alignment of the languages but the homogeneity of Indo-Aryan in the subcontinent. If Proto-Indo-European had developed dialectal isoglosses in India in the manner outlined by Elst why would all the different dialects have emigrated to eventually become distinct languages, leaving only one solitary language behind? Why did some of the dialectal variants germinating in our hypothetical Proto-Indo-European in South Asian not remain to develop into other non-Indo-Aryan, Indo-European languages on the subcontinent itself? After all, Sanskrit developed into a variety of mutually incomprehensible, distinct languages in the historic period, such as Braj, Bengali, Punjabi, Gujarati, Marathi, and so on. So why would PIE not likewise have developed into other distinct Indo-European languages in addition to Sanskrit in the subcontinent itself in the protohistoric period? Why did they all emigrate?

Of course, one could argue that there may have been other ancient South Asian Indo-European languages that suffered 'language death' because Old Indo-Aryan (Vedic) became a culturally elite language that subsumed them, but unless proto-Bangani becomes accepted as a genuine non-Indo-Aryan, Indo-European language, there would need to be compelling evidence to consider such pleading (although Old Indo-Aryan did contain dialectal variants; see, for example, Emeneau 1966). Another argument is that there may have been less language variety on the western side of the Indo-European family in the second millennium B.C.E. at a time contemporaneous with Vedic and that therefore Indo-Aryan might have been less conspicuously homogeneous in the

Southeast. Part of this western heterogeneity, after all, is established on the basis of languages most of which are first attested well after Vedic at a time when the Indo-European South Asian languages had also developed some degree of heterogeneity; we have no texts or sources from Europe informing us of the degree of differentiation of the European Indo-European languages in 1500 B.C.E. Our oldest actual empirical evidence for the major families in Gamkrelidze and Ivanov's group A is the Italic group in the form of inscriptions that may date to the seventh century B.C.E. well after the most conservative date assigned to the Ṛgveda. The Germanic group is not attested until the Runic inscriptions of the third century C.E.; Insular Celtic (in the form of Irish Ogam), in the fourth century C.E. (although there are Continental Celtic languages which are earlier, as well as some Gaulish names and inscriptions from prior to the common era; Slavic (in the form of Old Church Slavonic) from the ninth century C.E.; and Baltic (in the form of Old Prussian) from the fourteenth century C.E. In 1200 B.C.E. we only have solid evidence for the existence of Greek, Anatolian, Iranian, and Indic. However, despite the comparative lateness of evidence for most of the European languages, there are reconstructable linguistic grounds (e.g., Ringe et al., 1998) to suggest that Anatolian was the first to separate from the Indo-European collective, followed by Tocharian and then Italo-Celtic, which does indicate differentiation in the family before Indo-Iranian took its distinctive form.

Nonetheless, it is relevant to note, in this regard, that although the Veda and older sections of the Avesta are so close linguistically, had these old texts not been preserved for posterity and linguists had only the modern Iranian and Indo-Aryan languages as data with which to plot language relationships, there is no certainty that a grouping of these modern languages into an Indo-Iranian subfamily would have been evident. Dyen et al.'s (1992) lexicostatistical analyses, which are based on an analysis of modern languages only, show a failure to distinguish an Indo-Iranian group; the New Indo-Aryan languages in particular, demonstrate the same affinity with the European languages (Italic, Celtic, Germanic, and, especially Balto-Slavic) as with the Iranian ones. In other words, in the modern situation, there is no obvious homogeneity among the eastern languages—we just happen to have Vedic and Avestan texts informing us that there was such homogeneity in the ancient period.

Nichols's Sogdiana Model

In any event, a less hypothetical explanation for this eastern homogeneity, and one that may partly address Hock's concern, noted above, has recently surfaced. Johanna Nichols presents an alternative model for the epicenter of the Indo-European linguistic spread that could possibly be reformatted to accommodate a South Asian homeland (with perhaps less effort than that involved in the co-option of Gamkrelidze and Ivanov's model and more in accordance with Dyen's principle). The model also addresses the issues raised earlier concerning center and periphery. Nichols (1997) argues for a homeland "well to the east of the Caspian Sea . . . somewhere in the vicinity of ancient Bactria-Sogdiana" (123–137). Since this area overlaps the territory being considered here for the purpose of argument, namely, a Northwest Indian/Pakistan/Afghanistan homeland, it merits particular attention. Nichols's theory is partly predicated on loanwords between Indo-European and other language families that were discussed in the previous chapter.

Nichols holds that the principle that the area of greatest genetic diversity of a language family is indicative of its locus of origin is demonstrably false for the languages of central Asia. She cites Iranian, which spread over enormous stretches of Asia in ancient times, and Turkic, which likewise spread over major portions of Asia, as examples of languages whose greatest diversity occurred in refuge areas on the western periphery of their point of origin. Nichols then draws attention to Dyen's definitions of a homeland as a continuous area, a migration as a linguistic movement out of this area that causes it to become noncontinuous (in other words, which separates itself from this area), and an expansion as a movement that enlarges this area. As noted previously, Dyen's homeland-locating formula discourages migration and prioritizes contiguity.

In Nichols's Bactrian homeland, Proto-Indo-European *expands* out of its locus, eventually forming two basic trajectories, appearing, on a language map, like two amoebic protuberances bulging out from a protoplasmic origin. The language range initially radiates westward, engulfing the whole area around the Aral Sea from the northern steppe to the Iranian plateau. Upon reaching the Caspian, one trajectory expands around the sea to the north and over the steppes of central Asia to the Black Sea, while the other flows around the southern perimeter and into Anatolia.[27] Here we have a model of a continuous distribution of Proto-Indo-European—which has been defined as being, in reality, a dialectal continuum—covering a massive range from where the later historic languages can emerge, without postulating any migrations whatsoever. By the third or second millennium B.C.E. we have the protoforms of Italic, Celtic, and perhaps Germanic in the environs of central Europe (and presumably Balto-Slavic as well), and the protoforms of Greek, Illyrian, Anatolian, and Armenian stretching from northwest

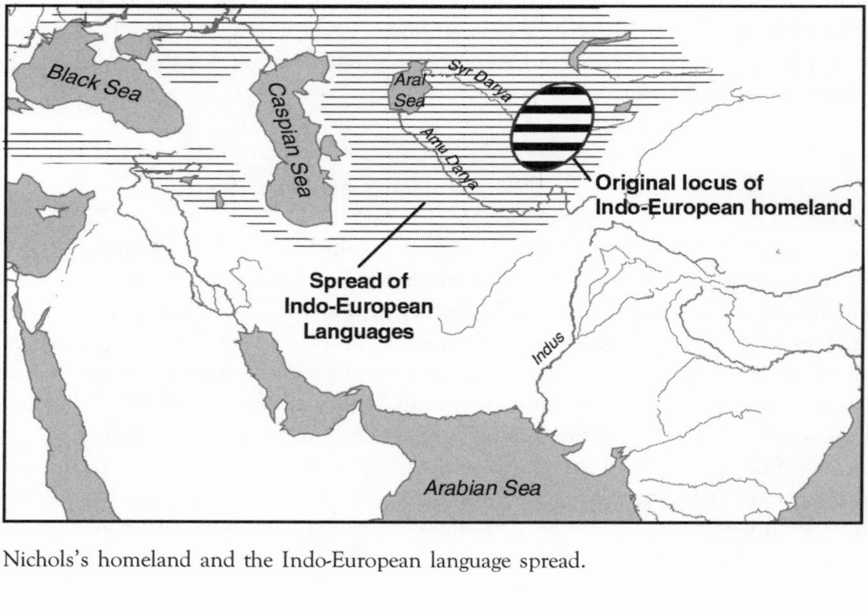

Nichols's homeland and the Indo-European language spread.

Mesopotamia to the southern Balkans (Nichols 1997, 134). Proto-Indo-Aryan was spreading into the subcontinent proper, while proto-Tocharian remained close to the original homeland in the Northeast.

As this expansion was progressing into Europe, a new later wave of Indo-European language, Iranian, was moving behind the first language spread (Nichols does not indicate an exact time frame except to note that this spread was posterior to the first expansion, presumably some time in the second millennium B.C.E.).[28] Nichols also does not indicate the exact point of origin of Iranian, but one might assume that it was the evolute of Proto-Indo-European that emerged from more or less the same locus, since it follows the same trajectories taken by the preceding waves of Indo-European.[29] However, sweeping across the steppes of central Asia, the Caucasus, and the deserts of north Iran, the Iranian dialects separated the two preceding trajectories—which until that time had formed a continuum—into two noncontiguous areas (one in central Europe to the north of the Caspian Sea, the other in Anatolia to its south). Along the same lines, Iranian also separates Tocharian from the other languages (which would eventually become completely severed from other Indo-European languages by the incursion of Turkic into this area). In time, the two original trajectories coincided in the Balkans. The southern trajectory had formed a continuous chain of Dacian, Thracian, Illyrian, Greek, and Phrygian spreading from West Anatolia to the Danube plain (Nichols 1997, 136).[30] From the northern trajectory, Italic spread to Italy from central Europe, and Celtic to its historic destination, followed in time by Germanic, which was followed in turn by Balto-Slavic. All of these languages spread by expansion—there are no migrations throughout this whole immense chronological and geographic sequence.[31]

The corollary of Nichols's model is that it portrays the homogeneity of Indo-Iranian and the heterogeneity of the western languages in a new light. The assumed variegation of the western languages is only due to the fact that the later Iranian language had spread and severed the contiguity of the northern and southern Indo-European trajectories (which had previously formed an unbroken continuity around the east coast of the Caspian), thereby making them appear noncontinuous while leaving behind Indo-Iranian and a stranded Tocharian to the east. The variegation of western languages is actually due to their situation on the western periphery of the original locus, or homeland. This model might also address the issue of why Proto-Indo-European did not evolve into more dialects in the putative homeland: the later westward spread of Iranian obliterated all of the eastern parts of the protocontinuum except for Indo-Aryan to its east and the isolated Tocharian to the northeast.[32]

From the perspective of dialect geography, the question arises whether Nichols's homeland model, if enlarged somewhat, or relocated a little toward the southeast, could be applied to the hypothetical Bactrian/Pakistan/Northwest Indian homeland. From this perspective, one would have to postulate a scenario along lines similar to the following: Proto-Indo-European could have evolved in west South Asia into a continuum of dialects that radiated westward in the protohistoric period, covering an unbroken area from the desert of Iran to the steppes of central Asia. In this continuum, Indo-Iranian held a central position. More specifically, the evolving Proto-Indo-Aryan elements in Indo-Iranian held a central position, with the evolving Proto-Iranian dialectal elements manifesting on the western perimeters of the Indo-Aryan core as the part of the continuum nearest the locus of origin.[33]

This western periphery of Proto-Indo-Iranian was flanked on its northern side by Balto-Slavic, Germanic, Celtic, Italic, Tokharian, and Anatolian. Anatolian may have peeled off earliest to resurface in its destination in the Near East, while Tocharian expanded farther to the northeast and off the western path of subsequent language spread, becoming a language isolate (or separate, in Dyen's terms).[34] Italic and Celtic continued to expand as the vanguard of the northwest trajectory over the steppes. They formed a continuum and shared an isogloss with Germanic—*tt* > *tst* > *ts* > *ss* (Hock forthcoming)—which, in turn, was followed by, and shared isoglosses with, Balto-Slavic.[35] Balto-Slavic was immediately contiguous with the northwestern part of the Indo-Iranian dialects (which, as noted, were central to this whole Indo-European continuum), producing a further isogloss between these particular dialects (a merger of velars and labiovelars).

On the southwestern side of the core area, Armenian was immediately contiguous to Indo-Iranian and was in turn connected on its western periphery with Greek.[36] Satemization was an isogloss that spread through a core area of Indo-Iranian and its adjacent dialects on both sides—to the northwest and the southwest. On its southwesterly side, it affected Armenian and, in diminishing degrees, the transition areas of Thracian, Pelasgian, and Phrygian[37] but without reaching Greek, which was farther southwest. The change also rippled through a transition area of Balto-Slavic, to the northwest of Indo-Iranian, but without reaching Germanic, which was farther northwest again.[38] Another isogloss, that of the preterit augment, was shared by Indo-Iranian, Armenian, and Greek.[39] Dhar's comments about Indo-Aryan conservatism and the influence of substratum on the languages of the western expansion of Indo-European are not incompatible with this model. It seems that other significant isoglosses can also be accounted for in this system.[40]

This model seems less clumsy than Elst's co-option of the Gamkrelidze and Ivanov model, which involves a kind of staggered exodus of several distinct groups and is subject to Hock's criticism noted earlier. In D'iakonov's view (1990, 156), the Indo-European language speakers never left their homeland, wherever it may have lain; rather, there was the constant spread of an increasing population to neighboring, peripheral territories. I will leave it to linguists more qualified than myself to fine-tune the details of Nichols's model or point out its irreconcilable flaws, which can then be compared with the linguistic idiosyncracies that have been pointed out in all the other homeland models.[41] And, of course, there are Indo-Iranian loans in Finno-Ugric as well as in the Caucasian languages that need to be accounted for. Nichols does not directly address the issue of Indo-Iranian loans into Finno-Ugric, but one might assume that her model allows for these loans to have occurred when the Iranian languages swept over the steppes on the heels of the first wave of Indo-European languages.

Conclusion

The immediate objections to Dhar's, Elst's, and Nichols's linguistic theories are likely to come from archaeologists. Indeed, even prior to reading the formal publication of Nichols's arguments, Mallory was moved to outline an archaeological response to the very idea of an eastern homeland. He claims that there is little evidence of urban-steppe interaction, which Nichols's model would require, before about 2000 B.C.E., which is far too late for Indo-European dispersals. No obvious candidate in the archaeological record has been found that might correspond to a movement of peoples from Bactria (or the Northwest of the subcontinent) to the west in an appropriate time frame. Such objections, of course, are based on the assumption that language spread can be traced in the archaeological record. There has been a recent chorus of objections to this idea. Mallory himself notes in an earlier publication that "as the IE homeland problem involves a spatial definition of a prehistoric *linguistic* construct, the utility of any other discipline, such as archaeology, depends on whether a linguistic entity can be translated into something discernable in the archaeological record. In short, any solution not *purely* linguistic must involve some form of indirect inference whose own premises are usually, if not invariably, far from demonstrated" (Mallory 1997, 94).

Indeed, as will be discussed later, scholars have consistently pointed out that there are no archaeological traces of the movements and migrations of a number of ethnic groups, such as the Huns, or of the Helvetii, and one would never have known that such occurrences had ever taken place had they not been documented in historical records. Mallory (1989, 166) has also noted that there is no archaeological evidence that can be correlated with the introduction of Gaelic into Scotland; likewise with the movements of the Slavs into Greece and the Galatians into central Anatolia (Crossland 1992, 251).

The argument that there is no archaeological evidence to substantiate any hypothetical linguistic spread from the east to the west is especially unlikely to find much favor on the subcontinent. As we shall see in chapters 10 and 11, Indian archaeologists have long pointed out that there is no consistent archaeological culture that can be traced across central Asia to penetrate into the subcontinent that might be correlateable to the Indo-Aryans; they have long been informed by linguists that there need not be any archaeological evidence of such movements, since language can spread without any change in the material culture. They are hardly likely to now accept that such archaeological invisibility applies only to immigration into the subcontinent but not to emigration out of it. Actually, no South Asian archaeologists that I know of have ever attempted to argue for an emigration—as I noted earlier, it is the details of the Indo-Aryans that are of concern, not those of the other language family members. While this may be somewhat myopic and unsatisfactory from an Indo-Europeanist's point of view, Indigenous Aryanists have a right to expect that, at least in theory, whatever arguments are brought forward by Western scholars as holding good for immigration in the archaeological record should equally be expected to hold good for any emigration, however hypothetical. Let us not forget that Indian scholars have every reason to suspect a history of Western bias in the handling of the Indo-European problem. I will be turning to the archaeological record in the next chapters.

The point of all this is not to argue that Dhar's arguments, or Elsts's co-option of Gamkrelidze and Ivanov, or Nichols's enlarged model actually support or suggest a South Asian homeland. The point is merely to suggest that these types of linguistic data are unequipped to *exclude* such possibilities. The point is also to provide some sense of how those suspicious of the entire homeland-locating enterprise can approach the material with different presuppositions and perspectives, rearrange the same data, and assemble entirely different hypothetical version of proto-historic events. At this point, scholars will have to resort to Occam's razor to judge between the various homeland claims—which scenario requires the least amount of special pleading in accounting for the whole range of data. As the two-centuries-old history of the Indo-European problem demonstrates, however, there is not likely to be more consensus in this regard among scholars in the present than there has been in the past. Moreover, the judgment regarding which case requires more special pleading is likely to be viewed very differently by many Indian scholars than by some Western ones.

The basic thrust of the previous chapters has been to show some of the problems that have arisen in the attempt to pinpoint the origins of the Indo-European—and of their offshoots, the Indo-Aryans—through linguistic methods. At this point I should note that relatively few Indo-Europeanists nowadays have an active interest in the matter of the *urheimat*. For decades, scholars have realized that the difficulties with the linguistic evidence are considerable enough to make each and every conclusion based on it problematic; however, the issue remains of considerable concern to many scholars of South Asia. In the next three chapters, we will turn our attention to the archaeological evidence, bearing in mind that the Indo-Aryans are a linguistic and philological entity. Archaelolgists can only attempt to trace speakers of a language family when linguistics and philology have provided them with clear and unambiguous information about an identifiable material culture that can be associated with such speakers.

9

The Indus Valley Civilization

In the words of one of India's leading nationalist historians: "There is one curious fact in regard to the beginnings of Indian history. For the Indus Valley culture, we have abundant archaeological data, but no written evidence. For the early Vedic culture we have abundant written evidence but no archaeological data" (Majumdar 1959, 6). The Indus Valley Civilization covers about a million square miles, yet there is no consensus regarding who its inhabitants were. The archaeological sites of the Indus Valley occupy much of the same geographic horizons known to the composers of the Vedic hymns. It seems understandable that many scholars might be tempted to fit the two together. Numerous books and articles have attempted to fit Vedic descriptions of culture, society, and religion into the ruins of the Indus Valley. Such endeavors, for the most part, take great interpretative liberties, and I will only touch upon a few of them here to give a sense of some of the issues involved, since some general comments on the Indus Valley are unavoidable, in any discussion of Indo-Aryan origins. It is essential for the Indigenous Aryan case that the Indus Valley Civilization be an Indo-Aryan one for obvious reasons. The issue that needs to be addressed in this chapter, accordingly, is: Did the Indus civilization precede the Vedic one, did it follow the Vedic one, or were the two contemporaneous?

Indra Stands Accused

Up until the discovery of the Indus Valley Civilization in 1922, images of virile, blond, northern tribes swooping across the mountain passes on chariots and overpowering the primitive and ill-equipped natives they found on their way were presented as the stan-

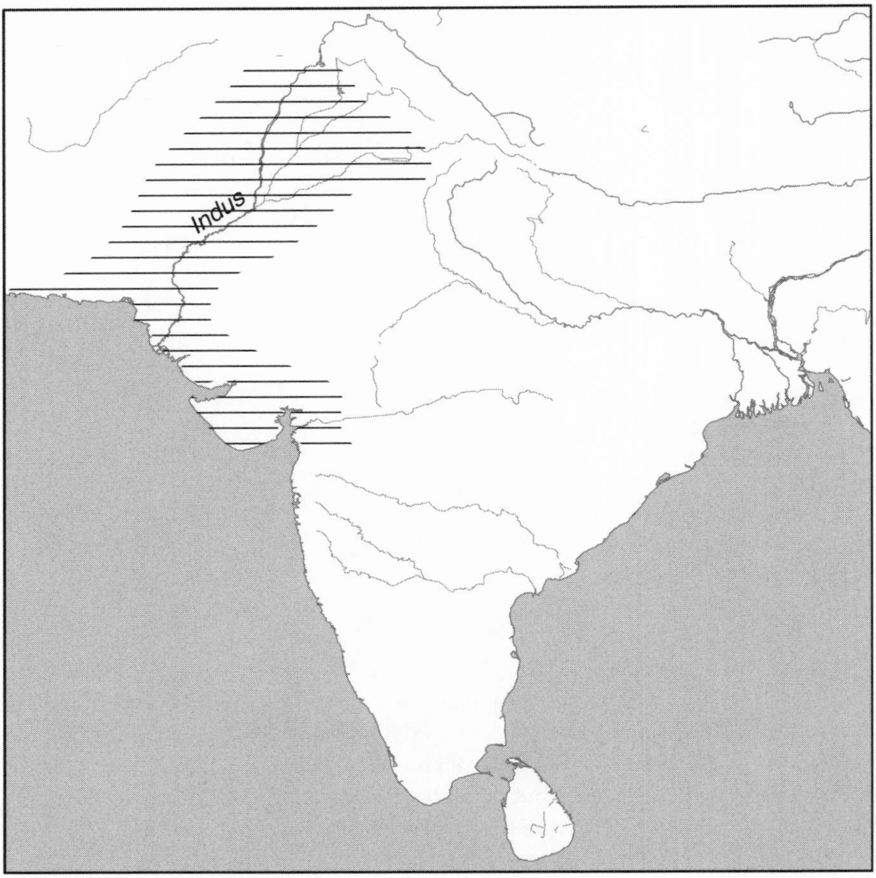

Area of the Indus Valley Civilization.

dard version of the early history of the subcontinent. The 1920 edition of *The Oxford Student's History of India* (reprinted 1933), for example, states that "as they advanced the Aryans [who were 'tall, fair, long-nosed and handsome'] subdued, more or less completely, the 'aborigines' ['short, dark, snub-nosed and ugly'], whom they called Dasyus, and by other names" (Smith 1933, 25–26). Likewise, the *Vedic India* volume of the popular Story of the Nations series informs its readers that "the natives . . . belonged to a black, or at least a very dark race, and everything about them, from their color and flat noses, to their barbarous customs, such as eating raw or barely cooked meat, and their Shamanistic goblin-worship, was intensely repulsive to the handsome, gentler mannered and, to a certain degree, religiously refined and lofty-minded Aryas" (Ragozin 1895, 113).

Then, in 1922, the Indus Valley Civilization was discovered.[1] Sir John Marshall (1931) describes the civilization of these pre-Aryan natives of India in his official account of the archaeological excavations at Mohenjo-Daro carried out between 1922 and 1927:

> Hitherto it has commonly been supposed that the pre-Āryan peoples of India were . . . black skinned, flat nosed barbarians. . . . Never for a moment was it imagined that five thousand years ago, before the Aryans were heard of, Panjāb and Sind . . . were enjoying an advanced and singularly uniform civilization of their own . . . even superior to that of contemporary Mesopotamia and Egypt. . . . there is nothing that we know of in prehistoric Egypt or Mesopotamia or anywhere else in western Asia to compare with the well-built baths and commodious houses of the citizens of Mohenjo-dara. . . . nothing that we know of in other countries at this period bears any resemblance, in point of style, to the miniature faience models . . . which . . . are distinguished by a breadth of treatment and a feeling for line and plastic form that has rarely been surpassed in glyptic art. (v–vii)

Edmund Leach (1990) comments wryly on the academic reaction to Marshall's disclosures:

> Common sense might suggest that here was a striking example of a refutable hypothesis that had in fact been refuted. Indo-European scholars should have scrapped all their historical reconstructions and started again from scratch. But that is not what happened. Vested interests and academic posts were involved. Almost without exception the scholars in question managed to persuade themselves that despite appearances, the theories of the philologists and the hard evidence of archaeology could be made to fit together. The trick was to think of the horse-riding Aryans as conquerors of the cities of the Indus civilization in the same way that the Spanish conquistadores were conquerors of the cities of Mexico and Peru. . . . The lowly Dasa of the Rig Veda, who had previously been thought of as primitive savages, were now reconstructed as members of a high civilization. (237)

Scholars like Stuart Piggott and Sir Mortimer Wheeler are especially targeted as the quintessential creators of such images of incoming Aryan aggressors destroying this newly found civilization of the erstwhile lowly Dāsa: "Tangible archaeological evidence of the Aryan conquest of India consists of nothing but the ruins of the cities they wrecked" (Piggott 1952, 285). Pivotal to such theories was the discovery of thirty-seven skeletons in various locations of Mohenjo-Daro—especially of a huddled group of half a dozen skeletons sprawled in one of the lanes in the city. Two of these skeletons had marks on their skulls suggestive of a blow from a sharp object. On the basis of these skeletons, Wheeler (1968) confidently stated that "the end of Mohenjo-daro . . . was marked by a massacre as [this] evidence quite unquestionably indicates" (83).[2] This evidence was then juxtaposed with so-called citadels found in several sites such as Mohenjo-Daro, Harappa, and Kalibangan, which Wheeler took to be fortified mounds—the *pur* of the Ṛgveda (78). With Indra, whose epithet in the Ṛgveda is *purandara* 'fort-destroyer', as his chief protagonist, Wheeler had a dramatic script that he could have marketed in Hollywood. "Indra stands accused" was his lighthearted, but later regretted, caricature of the principal culprit behind the demise of the great civilization (Wheeler 1953, 92).[3]

Scholars soon began to react against Wheeler's version of events. In time, most scholars judged that "Indra stands completely exonerated" (Dales 1964, 42; See also Srivastava 1984, 441). George Dales (1964) pointed out the obvious: "Where are the burned fortresses, the arrowheads, weapons, pieces of armor, the smashed bodies of the invaders and defenders? Despite the extensive excavations at the largest Harappan sites, there is not a single bit of evidence that can be brought forth as unconditional proof of an armed conquest and destruction on the scale of the Aryan invasion" (38). Not a single one of the thirty-seven skeletons was found within the area of the so-called citadel, which presumably would have been the locus of the heaviest fighting in the siege of a city. Besides this, the celebrated group of skeletons were found to belong to a period posterior to the abandonment of the latest stage of the city (38). Moreover, Kenneth Kennedy (1994, 248), who inspected thirty-four of the skeletons, found only one revealed a cranial lesion that might have been inflicted by a weapon; the marks on the remaining skulls, apart from one that had a healed wound mark unconnected with the cause of death, were cracks and warps caused by erosion, not violent aggression. Kenoyer (1991b) sums up the situation: "Any military conquest that would have been effective over such a large area should have left some clear evidence in the archaeological record. . . . evidence for periods of sustained conflict and coercive militaristic hegemony is not found" (57).

Few archaeologists today refer to Aryan aggression in connection with the demise of the Indus Valley, although occasionally the old paradigm stirs again; as recently as in Possehl's 1993 edition of *Harappan Civilization* F. R. Allchin (1993) still ponders, although more hesitantly than in 1968: "Would the attackers have been Aryan? . . . there is no inherent impossibility in such a thing" (389). For the most part, however, various alternative ecological or socioeconomic theories have been accepted regarding the gradual abandonment of the vast civilization.[4] Few scholars are ready to attempt a retrial of Indra and his Aryans. So what were our invading, or intruding, Aryans doing if they were not destroying the cities of the Indus Valley? A growing number of Indian archaeologists believe that the Indus Valley could have been an Indo-Aryan civilization or, at least, that the two cultures could have coexisted. A variety of evidence has been brought forward to support this possibility, some of which will be reviewed in the following pages.

The Religion of the Indus Valley

As a result of excavations at the site of Kalibangan on the banks of the dry Ghaggar River in North Rajasthan, a number of Indian archaeologists, including Migrationists such as as Parpola and Allchin, accepted that the findings there "are highly suggestive of an Indo-Iranian, if not more specifically Indo-Aryan, element in the culture of the period covered" (Allchin 1993, 388; see also Parpola 1988 149). Allchin proposes that intrusive Indo-Aryan groups had synthesized with indigenous Indus dwellers, resulting in these possible Indo-Aryan cultural traces that had been uncovered in this Indus site.

These findings, which have been termed "fire altars" or "ritual hearths," were found in both public and residential locations. In a nonresidential area of Kalibangan, a series of raised platforms was excavated, each of which was accessible by a flight of stairs. Atop one of these, a row of seven clay-lined pits was discovered, each one measuring seventy-five by fifty-five centimeters and containing traces of ash, charcoal, and the remains of a clay stele. The layout of the pits was such that the officiator would have been obligated to sit facing east (Lal 1984, 57). According to the excavators, this parallels the seven *dhiṣṇya* hearths of the Vedic soma sacrifice where the priests sit to the west of the hearths facing east. Most significantly, a short distance away from these altars in Kalibangan were found a well and the remains of a few bath pavements on the same platform, which "clearly suggest that ceremonial bathing constituted a part of the ritual" (57). On another nearby platform were the remains not only of a fire altar and well but also of a rectangular brick-lined pit containing bovine remains and antlers "evidently representing some kind of sacrifice" (57). The gates leading to the whole area where the platforms were situated were flanked by salients, and access could only be attained via steps, thus precluding the entrance of vehicular traffic. All this "may perhaps . . . appropriately be termed a 'Temple-complex'" (58).

In another part of the town was found another structure built of mud bricks. On top of this was an impressive wall that enclosed a room containing four or five more of the same types of fire altars. No other building existed on this mound, nor was any of the usual occupational debris found, suggesting that "the lonely structure with the altars was used for ritual purposes" (Thapar 1975, 28). Domestic fire altars were also found in numerous residential houses in the "Lower Town." In many of these houses a room seemed to have been set aside especially for the fire altar, which was renewed repeatedly as the working level went up (Lal 1984, 58). The chronology of this period was about 2300 to 1750 B.C.E. The official report of this excavation has yet to be published, and, unfortunately, Thapar has since passed away. I should note that Thapar did believe in Aryan migrations (pesonal communication).

The excavator of Lothal, S. R. Rao, found as many as six fire altars similar to the ones in Kalibangan in different blocks of the Lower Town. From their layout and construction, he denies that they could have been domestic ovens and that "it is obvious that they could not serve any other purpose than a ritualistic one" (Rao 1993, 175).[5] In one of these, a charred bovine mandible was found. Nearby another much larger altar, which Rao (1979) suggests was used for "community fire-worship," a terra-cotta "ladle" was found that "must have been used for pouring clarified butter into the sacrificial fire" (176). Rao precludes possible suggestions that the Indo-Aryan presence was in the final stages of occupation of the town by stating that "it is not only in the final stages of Kalibangan but also in the early stages of Harappa culture at Lothal and Kalibangan that altars for fire-worship and animal sacrifice were built and made use of" (173). In addition to Kalibangan and Lothal, H. D. Sankalia (1974, 350) refers to a fire altar noticed by Casal at Amri, and S. R. Rao (1993, 173) refers to similar reports from Bisht at the Banawali site. Allchin and Allchin (1982) are prepared to accept that, what they prefer to call "ritual hearths," occur in the beginning of the Harappan period, suggesting an Indo-Aryan presence in the "still flourishing Indus civilization" (303).

Not everyone accepts Rao's and Thapar's identifications. Dhavalikar (1995) wonders whether we are dealing with fire altars or with fire pits that could have been used for cooking or baking. He finds them very similar in size, plan, and shape to his excavations at Inamgaon in the Deccan. Indeed, he sees similarities between them and cooking pits used in Maharashtrian villages to this day. For Dhavalikar, the clay stele in the center of the pits, noted by the excavators, "bears a striking resemblance with the clay *tavā* . . . that is in use in Maharasthra . . . which was obviously for baking bread" (7). In this view, "since the Kalibangan 'fire altars' are identical in every respect with those in Inamgaon, their association with the religious beliefs of the people becomes doubtful" (7). One would also have to note that Lal's identification of these altars as Vedic seems to be primarily influenced by the fact that there were seven of them, thereby paralleling the number of hearths in various Vedic sacrifices. However, while this is correct, these sacrifices do not *just* consist of these seven hearths but include a variety of other hearths as well, none of which were unearthed in Kalibangan.

Much has been written on the religion of the Indus people; the implications of interpreting Indus artifacts as Vedic or non-Vedic are obvious. Rather than burden the reader with an overly detailed exposition of views on this matter, a brief glance at some of the creative interpretations inspired by the so-called Paśupati proto-Śiva seal will give some sense of the series of assumptions that are often made in assigning meaning to innate archaeological objects. The seal consists of what appears to be an ithyphallic figure on some kind of a seat in yogic posture with arms resting on knees and crowned with a horned headdress. The figure is surrounded by a number of animals, and there is an inscription above the figures.

Sir John Marshall (1931) was the first to volunteer an identification. Taking the figure to be "recognizable at once as a prototype of the historic Śiva," he assigned the name—Paśupati, 'king of the beasts'—to the seal in view of the animals surrounding the figure. The animals are a tiger, elephant, rhinoceros, buffalo, and two deer. He believed that the figure had three faces, which is a feature sometimes ascribed to certain forms of Śiva. Moreover the yogic posture suggested to Marshall the ascetic nature of this deity, while the horned headdress conjured up associations with Śiva's trident. Marshall was convinced that the Indus Civilization existed prior to the entry of the Indo-Aryans, and that Śiva was a pre-Aryan, Dravidian god who was later co-opted into the Vedic pantheon (54). Marshall's identification was to influence all subsequent interpretations.

The Indus 'Proto-Śiva' seal.

Other scholars who also posit a Dravidian affiliation for the Indus Valley have interpreted the seal differently. Hiltebeital (1978) developed a case for considering the horned figure to be Mahiṣa, the buffalo demon foe of the goddess. He located the goddess herself as represented in the form of a tigress—one of the animals surrounding the figure—an animal frequently depicted as the mount of the goddess. Sullivan (1964) also favored a goddess identification, albeit on different grounds, and argued that the so-called erect phallus was really a girdle such as is found only on female figurines. Fairservis (1992) was prepared to go further and tried his hand at a Dravidian translation of the inscription. He held that the seal referred to "a paramount chief named Aṇil . . . a primary chief of the four sodalities, each one represented by one of the animals" (200). Parpola (1994) feels that the "so-called 'yoga' posture may simply be an imitation of the Proto-Elamite way of representing seated bulls" (250). His Dravidian reading of the seal is "*mīn-ā āḷ* 'the man (or servant) of (the god represented by) *mīn*,'" which he considers in this case to mean fish (188). He finds the animal representations in the seal best resemble those associated with Varuṇa, an entity associated with the aquatic themes that he finds prominent in the Indus religion.

A number of other scholars have also taken this seal as a Vedic deity, but, unlike the authors, mentioned earlier, who understand Śiva, Varuṇa, and the goddess as being pre-Aryan deities who were later amalgamated into the Vedic pantheon, this group believes that their Vedic identifications point to the Indo-Aryan identity of the Indus Valley Civilization. S. R. Rao (1991) reads the inscription as *ra-ma-trida-ośā*, "conveying the sense of being 'pleasant and shining (or burning) in three ways'. The three-headed deity who is burning or shining in three ways is none other than Agni conceived in his three forms" (288). The animals, for him, represent different clans that have accepted the supremacy of the fire god. M. V. N. Krishna Rao (1982), in contrast, believes Indra is represented by the figure. In terms of method, he finds reason to bypass the tiger, on the grounds that it is somewhat larger and more prominent than the other animals, as well as the two deer, on the grounds that they are seated below the main figure. He then takes the first phoneme of the Sanskrit terms for the remaining three animals and the first phoneme of the word 'man' *nara* (which he somehow feels deserves to be represented twice) and construes the term *makhanāśana*, an epithet of Indra.

S. P. Singh (1988–89) also identifies the central figure as Rudra, who is the protoform of Śiva in the Ṛgveda. However, his method is based on identifying the animals surrounding the figure with the Maruts, who are referred to as the sons of Rudra in hymn 1.64. His grounds for this, in turn, are that this hymn describes the Maruts as bulls of heaven, eating up the forests like elephants, roaring like lions, beauteous as antelope, and angry as serpents. E. Richter-Ushanas (1997) considers the central figure to be the sage Ṛṣyaśṛṅga, 'the sage with horns', who officiated over the sacrifice of King Daśaratha in the Rāmāyaṇa. He connects the animals with the four seasons and finds similar motifs on the Gundestrup cauldron discovered in Denmark (Taylor 1992; as a side note, Talageri [1993] and Rajaram and Frawley [1995] see this cauldron as persuasive evidence pointing to India as the original home of the Indo-Europeans). Feuerstein, Kak, and Frawley are quite happy accepting Marshall's identification of the seal except with an understanding that Śiva is an Indo-Aryan deity. The list goes on, but I trust that the point has been made and will spare the reader further expositions on proto-Śiva, pre-Aryan 'earth goddesses', vedic 'soma filters', 'lingams', 'yonis', Vedic 'vrajras', and a host of other

Aryan, or non-Aryan, religious characteristics that have been reconstructed from other Indus artifacts.

The relevance of finding items of an unambiguous Indo-Aryan nature on the Indian subcontinent dating back prior to the second millenium B.C.E. is obvious. One report of such an item that might have had an immediate bearing on the ethnic identity of the Indus Valley Civilization, as well as massive repercussions for academic interpretations of Indian protohistory and, indeed, the entire Indo-European question were it to be accurate, somehow appeared in the pages of the *Journal of Indo-European Studies* (Hicks and Anderson 1990). The authors claimed to have dated a life-sized copper-based head, dubbed 'Vasiṣṭha's head', with tilak markings on the brow and handlebar mustache. The hair was styled in the manner described for the Vedic Vasiṣṭhas—coiled with a tuft to the right. MASCA-corrected $^{C}14$ testing produced a date centered around 3700 B.C.E. (give or take eight hundred years).

Hicks and Anderson state that the head had been tested by advanced technique in carbon dating in Zurich by the Laboratory for Nuclear Science at the Swiss Federal Institute of Technology, through the use of a cyclotron at the University of California, as well as by means of a Davis (Pixie) ion probe and Van de Graaf linear accelerator at Stanford University. The tests included spectographic analysis, X-ray dispersal analysis, and metallography. The authors stand firm by these results (personal communication). I should note that Hicks and Anderson are not involved in the polemics of the Indigenous Aryan school; they do not contest the migration of the Indo-Aryans into the subcontinent but feel that this find warrants backdating their arrival to about 4000 B.C.E.

However, the origins of the head, which was "rescued from being melted down in 1958" in Delhi, are dubious. The head has not generated much attention, even among the Indigenous Aryan school, primarily, perhaps, because it was not discovered in situ and therefore appeared outside of an archaeological context. Therefore, although the carbon 14 tests were determined from a small quantity of carbon deposits on the inside surface of the cast, one could argue that this particular image had been recast from an older copper item that had been melted down. This possibility is reinforced by the fact that the piece bore the inscription "Nārāyaṇa," which the authors believed had been incised at a later time. Had it been otherwise, such a discovery would have sent shock waves through departments of ancient Indian history worldwide (although even this probably would not have been decisive for some in terms of the Indo-Aryan identity of the Indus Valley, since it could always have been argued that the head represented a pre-Aryan figure whose markings and hairstyle were appropriated into Vedic and post-Vedic culture).

Before moving on to other issues, it seems relevant to note a provocative new hypothesis suggested by Lamberg-Karlovsky (forthcoming), who draws attention to the astounding degree of cultural homogeneity in the vast area of the Indus Valley Civilization, juxtaposed with the lack of any evidence for a centralized political structure. Not only is there a uniformity of culture, but the physical layout of the community is replicated irrespective of whether it is the 5-acre site of Allahdino or the 150 acre site of Mohenjo-Daro. Lamberg-Karlovsky believes this "enigma" can be adequately explained by supposing that only an exceptional social organization such as the caste system can account for this. He finds a variety of archaeological evidence to support this. The residential units at Indus sites, for example, were much larger than other contemporaneous sites, suggesting a stronger sense of kin identities or groupings. He notes that competition in a class-structured society results in a much wider variety of styles and methods of production, whereas in a caste system, much more uniformity is to be expected, as is evidenced by the artifacts unearthed in the Indus Valley sites. Caste organization would also explain the social stability of such a massive culture in the absence of a centralized state or chieftainship. Finally, the concern with purity in a caste system is amply evidenced in the archaeological record by the unparalleled attention and concern given to the control of and access to water and sanitation; at Mohenjo Daro, there is an average of one well for every three houses.

Lamberg-Karlovsky (forthcoming) notes that, "if valid, such a hypothesis would impose a radical rethinking of the current consensus of the allegedly Indo-European origins of the organizational patterns characteristic of traditional Indian society" (1). For those convinced that the Indus Valley Civilization was pre-Aryan, accepting Lamberg-Karlovsky's tentative hypothesis would indeed entail reconsidering the Indo-European origins of caste. For Indigenous Aryanists, needless to say, The discovery of an Indus Valley Civilization structured by caste would be yet another indication that this was an Indo-Aryan culture.

The Sarasvatī

The quintessential domain of the Ṛgveda is the land of the Sapta Sindhu, or 'Seven Rivers', a land which, as we have seen, goes by this name even in Avestan sources (*Hapta Hendu*). The heartland of this area more or less corresponds to the present-day Punjab in India and Pakistan and surrounding areas. Among these seven rivers, the Sarasvatī is praised as the best[6] and as distinct in majesty (R.V. vi.61. 13). Likened to a fortress of metal (R.V. vii. 95. 1), it presses forward like a chariot fighter going from the mountains all the way to the river (or ocean).[7] Its prestige is such that various rulers (R.V. viii.21.18) situated themselves on its banks, and it causes the five 'peoples' to prosper.[8] Over sixty hymns referring to Sarasvatī in the Ṛgveda, many of which are specifically dedicated to it,[9] attest to its importance in the world of the Vedic poets. An invocation in R.V. 10.75.5, which lists the rivers in geographically correct order from east to west, situates Sarasvatī between the Yamunā and the Śutudrī (Sutlej). However, although the other rivers in the list are all still presently extant in the north of the Indian subcontinent, nothing is to be found of the mighty Sarasvatī today except for an insignificant stream in the foothills of the Himalayas that preserves its name.

Scholars initially attempted to account for this lacuna by suggesting either that the Indus River is the actual referent of these hymns[10] or that the verses allude to the memory of a river outside of India, or, along with Max Müller, that the present-day Sarasvatī was once a much larger river. (See Keith and Macdonell [1912] 1967, ii, 434–436, for a summary of opinions in this regard.) Pious Hindus, anxious to reconcile the spiritual and physical importance accorded to the Sarasvatī in the Vedic and Epic texts with its inexplicable absence in reality, have either suggested that it was primarily a celestial river (Sharma 1949, 53–62) or resolved the problem by concluding that it must join the Gangā and Yamunā at the Triveṇī[11] by flowing there hidden underground as the *suptā nadī*, or 'Sleeping River'. (Murthy, (1980, 19.) Interestingly, their faith in the veracity of the traditional narrative has not been placed completely in vain. Archaeological researches in the Cholistan desert have uncovered the bed of a once-massive river—up to ten kilometers wide, (Misra 1989, 159)—situated between the Yamunā and the Sutlej, exactly where the Ṛgveda places the Sarasvatī. This river is presently known as the Hakra in Pakistan, and the Ghaggar in India. The drama of this discovery was captured in the title of an article in *Geographical Magazine*: "Fabled Saraswati Flows Again."

The first person who attempted to correlate the textual descriptions of Sarasvatī with empirical paleogeology was C. F. Oldham, in 1874. He surmised that "the waters of the Sarasvatī [are] continuous with the dry bed of a great river [Hakra], which, as local legends assert, once flowed through the desert to the sea" (Oldham 1893, 54). Oldham was convinced that the dry riverbed had once been fed by the Sutlej River, before the latter changed its course westward. However, the person most responsible for drawing public attention to the Sarasvatī River was Sir Aurel Stein.[12] At eighty years of age and almost blind, this archaeologist par excellence, adventurer, and veteran of some of the world's most inhospitable climes undertook an expedition in 1940–41 along the banks of the Sarasvatī/Ghaggar/Hakra River in the Bikaner area, Rajasthan, and the Bahawalpur area, present-day Pakistan.[13]

Sir Aurel was fascinated by the traditional belief that the Ghaggar or Hakra riverbed was none other than the Sarasvatī of Vedic and Epic lore and that, although long since abandoned for most of its course, the bed once corresponded to a mighty river that flowed down to the ocean. Since the Vedic world seemed to orient itself around the banks of the Sarasvatī, Stein felt that his expedition would be of relevance in the "still obscure question as to where those earliest records of Indian thought were composed" (Gupta 1989, 9). While he was successful in geographically locating this nucleus of the Vedic world, he was forced to conclude that in terms of chronological value "it would seem hazardous at present to use the archaeological observations concerning the ancient river course for any attempt to date the references made to the Sarasvatī in early Vedic Texts" (94). It is precisely such temporal possibilities of the riverbed that are of special relevance in the question of whether the inhabitants of the Indus Valley Civilization and the Vedic-speaking Aryans might have been one and the same.

In addition to locating and mapping a number of Harappan and post-Harappan sites along the banks of the Sarasvatī (some of which he excavated with a few exploratory trenches), Stein, like Oldham before him, also concluded that the main reason for the demise of the river was that the waters of its main tributary, the Sutlej, had been detoured, thus depriving it of the bulk of its water flow. Satellite imagery has confirmed his observation. The present Sutlej River, rising in the Himalayas, heads in a southeasterly direction directly toward the old bed of the Ghaggar. In the vicinity of modern-day Ropar, about a hundred kilometers from where it would have coincided with the Ghaggar bed had it continued in a straight line, it suddenly takes a sharp right-angle turn to flow away from the Ghaggar in a westerly direction, where, after about 150 kilometers, it is joined by the Beas. These two rivers then merge and proceed in a southwesterly course until they join the Indus and then on to the Rann of Kutch.

The satellite imagery revealed the following data: (1) The sudden westward turn of the Sutlej is suggestive of its diversion in the past for which no physical obstruction is evident.[14] (2) At the point where the Sutlej would have impacted the Ghaggar riverbed had it not deviated, the latter suddenly widens. Since the bed of the Ghaggar upstream from this point is considerably narrower, this can only be explained if a major tributary was joining the Ghaggar at this place. (3) A major paleochannel can be clearly seen to connect the Sutlej from the point where it takes its sharp westward turn to the point on the Ghaggar where the old bed suddenly broadens. (4) Paleochannels from the Yamunā River show that it also once flowed into the Ghaggar and then subsequently changed its direction three times before assuming its present course. This deviation of the Yamunā also would have deprived the Ghaggar of a substantial supply of water (Pal et al. 1984, 492–497). There is general agreement among scholars that all this demonstrates that "it can be stated with certainty that the present Ghaggar-Hakra is nothing but a remnant of the ṚgVedic Sarasvatī which was the lifeline of the Indus Civilization" (V. N. Misra 1994, 511).

In the course of a survey project limited to only a section of the Hakra/Ghaggar in the Cholistan desert in Bahawalpur state (representing three hundred miles of the Pakistan side of the Hakra part of the riverbed), Mughal (1993, 85) mapped out a total of 414 archaeological sites on the bed.[15] This dwarfs the number of sites so far recorded along the entire stretch of the Indus River which number only about three dozen (Gupta 1993b, 28). The centrality of the river, both archaeologically and culturally, has led a minority of Indian archaeologists to propose, and to begin to adopt, the term *Indus-Sarasvatī Civilization* in lieu of the labels *Harappan* or *Indus Valley Civilization*.[16]

The crucial issue in all this is the date when the Hakra/Ghaggar would have been a full-flowing river corresponding to its state in the Ṛgvedic hymns. This date is seen as powerful archaeological evidence that must be taken into consideration when dating the composition of the Ṛgveda. It also has a direct bearing on the relationship between the Indo-Aryan composers of the hymns and the Indus Valley Civilization. Mughal (1993) proposes the following outline:

> On the Pakistan side, archaeological evidence now overwhelmingly affirms that the Hakra was a perennial river through all its course in Bahawalpur during the fourth millennium . . . and early third millennium B.C. About the middle of the third millennium B.C., the water supply in the Northeastern portion of the Hakra [the Yamunā] was considerably diminished or cut off. But, abundant water in the lower (southwestern) part of this stream was still available, apparently through a channel from the Sutlej. . . . About the end of the second, or not later than the beginning of the first millennium B.C., the entire course of the Hakra seems to have dried up. (4)

Mughal's broad chronological periods are not specific enough to assist us in definitively situating the Vedic-speaking Aryans as inhabitants of the Indus Valley Civilization. It is significant, however, that about 80 percent of Mughal's 414 archaeological sites along a three-hundred-mile section of the Hakra were datable to the fourth or third millennium B.C.E, suggesting that the river was in its prime during this period.[17] The dating range proposed by Pal et al. (1984) is no more specific: "The Ghaggar continued to be a living river during the pre-Harappan (c. 2500–2200 B.C.E.) and the Harappan times (c. 2200–1700 B.C.E.)" (496). A third, even wider, dating range (8,000 B.C.E.–1800 B.C.E.) was proposed for the Sarasvatī's channels through which it discharged into the Rann of Kutch via the Luni River (see Ghose et al., 1979 for additional information on the Sarasvatī's previous drainage system and course shifting). Lal (1997, 9) considers the Sarasvatī to have been alive in Kalibangan in the third millennium B.C.E. and dried up at the turn of the millennium: "The Sarasvatī dried up around 2000 BC. This clearly establishes that the Rigveda, which speaks of the Sarasvatī as a mighty flowing river, has to be assigned to a period prior to 2000 BC. By how many centuries it cannot be said for certain" (Lal, forthcoming). The Sarasvatī as known to the Ṛgveda must have well predated the end of the second millennium B.C.E., when the entire course of the Hakra had already dried up. A further terminus ante quem can be postulated by the fact that Painted Gray Ware (PGW) sites dated to around 1000 B.C.E. were found on the bed of the river, as opposed to on its banks, indicating that the river had already become dry well before this time (Gaur 1983, 133).

Anything more than this—that is, whether the Sarasvatī known to the composers of the hymns was the river in its full glory of the fourth millennium, the more diminished version of the third millennium, or a dwindling body of water sometime in the first half of the second millennium B.C.E.—cannot be stated categorically. Advocates of the Aryan invasion/migration theory can still claim that the Indo-Aryans could have arrived during or toward the end of the Indus civilization and then settled down on the banks of the river. However, the Vedic hymns preserve no reference to of the river drying up (although this is explicitly described in the Mahābhārata; see 3.130.3; 6.7.47; 6.37.1–4; 9.34.81; 9.36.1–2). Even if the Aryans had come from outside the subcontinent, one would have to allow at least several centuries for them to settle down on the riverbank and completely forget their overland odyssey.

What seems apparent is that the composers of the Ṛgveda were living on the Sarasvatī's banks when it was a mighty river, with no clear recollection of their having come from anywhere else recorded in the texts they left to posterity. However, even this claim is not without problems. Witzel (1999) notes a verse from one of the older hymns in the Ṛgveda, 3.33, where mention is made of the confluence of the Sutlej and the Beās. According to the evidence outlined previously, the Sutlej was the main tributary of the Sarasvatī. Its deviation from the Sarasvatī and subsequent joining with the Beās was the principal factor that caused the Sarasvatī to be deprived of much of its water input and therefore go dry. This verse might suggest a memory of a hydronymic event that corresponds not with Sarasvatī as a mighty river but with it as a diminished stream deprived of its principal source of water. Granted, this is a solitary reference and is dwarfed, numerically, by the frequent references to Sarasvatī's grandeur, but it cannot be brushed aside. If the references to Sarasvatī as a mighty flowing river can be construed to suggest that the Indo-Aryans must have been coeval with the mature Harappan phase, then the same logic applied to this reference would suggest that the Indo-Aryans were coeval with a Late or Post-Harappan phase (which most "Migrationists" would be prepared to consider). According to Witzel this provides "a date *ad quem* for this part of the ṚV, once the relevant geological and geographical data have been confirmed, . . . and it speaks against the current revisionist fashion of assigning a pre-Harappan date to the *ṚV*" (37).

Francfort (1992) of the French expedition which had been specifically studying irrigation and the peopling of central Asia, has scant regard for the "mythico-religious tradition of Vedic origin, reinforced by the illusory existence of proto-historic settlements concentrated along the banks of an immense perennial river, the ancient Sarasvatī" (90–91). In striking contrast to other dating attempts, as far as Francfort is concerned, "when the proto–historic peoples settled in this area no large perennial river had flowed there for a long time" (91). The Hakra/Ghaggar River, according to these researches, predated the entire pre- and proto-Harappan period. The Harappan sites considered by the scholars noted earlier to have been sustained by the Hakra/Ghaggar/Sarasvatī, were, according to the team, not actually situated on the banks of the riverbed, but were outside of them, irrigated by small river channels. The team included a strong geoarchaeological element that concluded that the actual large paleocourses of the river have been dry since the early Holocene period or even earlier (Francfort 1985, 260). Ironically, the findings of the French team have served to reinforce the "mythico-religious tradition of Vedic origins." Rajaram's reaction (1995) to the team's much earlier date assigned to the perennial river is that "this can only mean that the great Sarasvatī that flowed 'from the mountain to the sea' must belong to a much earlier epoch, to a date well before 3000 BCE"(19).

To sum up, Sarasvatī's rediscovery, although arguably suggestive of considerable Vedic antiquity (which one would be hard-pressed to accommodate within the commonly accepted 1200 B.C.E. date for Vedic compilation), cannot be used to *prove* absolute synonymity of the Indus Valley residents and the Vedic Aryans. Nonetheless, the river's remanifestation, albeit in the form of a paleoincarnation, has been significant in other ways. Archaeologist S. P. Gupta (1989) voices the value that such archaeological undertakings can have: "At last, we found true what was recorded in oral traditions" (x). For the geologist S. R. N. Murthy (1980), such findings are essential because "some authors believe that it [Sarasvatī] is a 'myth'—an imaginary river. There can hardly be a damage equal to such interpretations due to sheer ignorance of scientific data specially which discredit the authenticity of the Veda" (191). For many, a primary significance of the exploration of an old, dry riverbed is that such undertakings have enhanced the epistemological value of the Veda. At least in this case, the validity of *śabda pramāṇa* 'verbal testimony' (recorded in written texts) has been somewhat verified by *pratyakṣa pramāṇa* 'empirical proof'.

The Horse

If the Aryans cannot be identified in the archaeological record, can they at least be excluded from it? More specifically, is the evidence from the principal archaeological culture in the subcontinent, the Indus Valley, incompatible with the literary evidence on the Vedic culture? As a result of the massive amount of attention the Aryan problem has been generating in Indian academic, political, religious, and popular discourse, a leading Indian publishing house issued a booklet written by one of the principal opponents of the Indigenous Aryan school. The author, R. S. Sharma (1995), concludes his arguments with the two most common objections against those attempting to correlate the Indus Valley with the Vedic culture: "It is claimed that the Aryans created the Harappan culture. However, such a claim is baseless. . . . It is significant that the *Ṛg Vedic* culture was pastoral and horse-centered, while the Harappan culture was neither horse-centered nor pastoral" (65). Likewise, Parpola (1994) states: "The view that an early form of Indo-Aryan was spoken by the Indus people continues to have its supporters. It is therefore necessary to emphasize in conclusion one important reason why the Harappan people are unlikely to have been Indo-European- or Aryan speakers. This is the complete absence of the horse (*Equus caballus*)" (155). Since the time of Sir John

Marshall, the absence of this creature has been the mainstay of the belief that the speakers of the Vedic language must have succeeded the Harappan civilization: "In the lives of the Vedic-Āryans the horse plays an important part. . . . To the people of Mohenjo-Daro and Harappā the horse seems to have been unknown" (Marshall 1931, 111).

As we have seen the term *aśva* 'horse' is a word with Indo-European credentials. In its various forms, it is mentioned 215 times in the Ṛgveda and is the subject of two complete hymns (Sharma 1995, 14). Macdonell and Keith ([1912] 1967) conclude from one Vedic verse (RV viii. 55, 3). which mentions a gift of four hundred mares, that the animal could not have been rare in the Vedic world (I, 42).[18] There are over fifty personalities with horse-connected names and thirty with chariot-connected names in the Vedic literature. The horse is clearly an animal highly valued in the Vedic world. It is perfectly reasonable to expect that if the Aryans were native to the Indus Valley their presence would be evidenced by remains of the horse there. Such evidence, or lack thereof, has become crucial to—and almost symbolic of—the whole Aryan controversy. The horse, as a result, is presently "the most sought after animal in Indian archaeology" (Sharma 1974, 75).

The report claiming the earliest date for the domesticated horse in India, ca. 4500 B.C.E., comes from a find from Bagor, Rajasthan, at the base of the Aravalli Hills (Ghosh 1989a, 4).[19] In Rana Ghundai, Baluchistan, excavated by E. J. Ross, equine teeth were reported from a pre-Harappan level (Guha and Chatterjee 1946, 315–316).[20] Interestingly, equine bones have been reported from Mahagara, near Allahabad, where six sample absolute carbon 14 tests have given dates ranging from 2265 B.C.E. to 1480 B.C.E. (Sharma et al. 1980, 220–221).[21] Even more significantly, horse bones from the Neolithic site Hallur in Karnataka (1500–1300 B.C.E.) have also been identified by the archaeozoologist K. R. Alur (1971, 123).[22] These findings of the domestic horse from Mahagara in the east, and Hallur in the south, are significant because they would seem inconsistent with the axiom that the Aryans introduced the domesticated horse into the Northwest of the subcontinent in the later part of the second millennium B.C.E. Due to the controversy generated by Alur's report, a reexcavation of Hallur was undertaken to collect fresh samples of animal bones. Alur (1992) again insisted that specimens of *Equus caballus* Linn were definitely present in the collection. His response is worth quoting at length to give a sense of the controversy and significance surrounding this animal:

> When I wrote this report, I least expected that it might spark off a controversy and land me in the witness box before the Indian historians' jury. . . . I was apprised of the gravity of the situation when I began to get letters asking me for clarification of the situation against the prevalent belief that the horse is a non-indigenous species and was introduced into India only by the (invading) Aryans. . . . To make my position clear, I wrote in my article . . . that whatever may be the opinion expressed by archaeologists, it cannot either deny or alter the find of a scientific fact that the horse was present at Hallur before the (presumed) period of Aryan invasion. . . . I have only declared the findings that horse bones were traced in the faunal collection from Hallur and *am responsible to that extent only*. (562, italics in original)

In the Indus Valley and its environs, Sewell and Guha, as early as 1931, had reported the existence of the true horse, *Equus caballus* Linn from Mohenjo-Daro itself,[23] and Bholanath (1963) reported the same from Harappa, Ropar, and Lothal. Even Mortimer Wheeler (1953) identified a horse figurine and accepted that "it is likely enough that camel, horse and ass were in fact all a familiar feature of the Indus caravan" (92). Another early evidence of the horse in the Indus Valley was reported by Mackay, in 1938, who identified a clay model of the animal at Mohenjo-Daro. Piggott (1952, 126, 130) reports a horse figurine from Periano Ghundai in the Indus Valley, dated somewhere between Early Dynastic and Akkadian times. Bones from Harappa, previously thought to have belonged to the domestic ass, have been reportedly critically reexamined and attributed to a small horse (Sharma 1992–93, 31).[24] Additional evidence of the horse in the form of bones, teeth, or figurines has been reported in other Indus sites such as Kalibangan (Sharma 1992–93, 31);[25] Lothal (Rao 1979),[26] Surkotada (Sharma 1974), and Malvan (Sharma 1992–93, 32).[27] Other later sites include the Swat Valley (Stacul 1969); Gumla (Sankalia 1974, 330); Pirak (Jarrige 1985);[28] Kuntasi (Sharma 1995, 24);[29] and Rangpur (Rao 1979, 219). A. K. Sharma (1992–93) comments on the academic reaction to these not inconsiderable reports:

> It is really strange that no notice was taken by archaeologists of these vital findings, and the oft-repeated theory that the true domesticated horse was not known to the Harappans continued to be harped upon, coolly ignoring these findings to help our so-called veteran historians and archaeologists of Wheeler's generation to formulate and propagate their theory of "Aryan invasion of India on horse-back." (31)

The exact species of the equid is the crucial issue in these identifications. The debate over horse bones has become acrimonious ever since Zeuner (1963) questioned the identification of Ross's pre-Harappan findings: "The earliest horse remains so far reported come from Rana Ghundai in Northern Baluchistan . . . the date of which is regarded as earlier than 3000 B.C. . . . this identification cannot be accepted as reliable unless it is carefully checked" (332). Since this challenge, detractors of the Indigenous Aryan school have been able to reject claims of horse bone findings as unreliable, since the bones might have appertained to the domestic ass, *Equus asinus*, or the hemione, *Equus hemionus khur*. Although the latter is indigenous to the Northwest of the subcontinent it is *Equus caballus* that is the sought-after Aryan steed. Until recently, these distinctions had hampered widespread acceptance of any existence of the horse at all in the Indus Valley because there are only minor differentiating features between the various species of *Equus* (See Meadow 1987, 909). These are either difficult for experts to identify or, unless the specific distinguishing parts of the skeleton are found (certain teeth and the phalanges—toe bones—are particularly important for differentiating equid subtypes), impossible to determine with certainty. Many of the remains could have belonged to either *Equus caballus* Linn or to some other member of the horse family and are thus rejected as incontestable evidence of the former. Thus Meadow (1987) writes:

> There are, as yet, no convincing reports of horse remains from archaeological sites in South Asia before the end of the second millennium BC. Many claims have been made (e.g., Sewell 1931; Nath 1962, 1968; Sharma 1974) but few have been documented with sufficient measurements, drawings, and photographs to permit other analysts to judge for themselves. An additional complication is that some specimens come from archaeological deposits which could be considerably younger than the main body of material at the site. (908)

The situation took a new turn, somewhat melodramatically, a few years ago. The material involved had been excavated in Surkotada in 1974 by J. P Joshi, and A. K.

Sharma subsequently reported the identification of horse bones from all levels of this site (circa 2100–1700 B.C.E.). In addition to bones from *Equus asinus* and *Equus hemionus khur*, Sharma reported the existence of incisor and molar teeth, various phalanges, and other bones from *Equus caballus* Linn (Sharma 1974, 76). Although some scholars accepted the report, doubts about the exact species of *Equus* represented by the bones prevented widespread recognition of Sharma's claim. Meadow (1987) has written: "It is on the basis of this phalanx that one can ascertain from the published photographs that the 'horse' of Surkotada, a Harappan period site in the little Rann of Kutch, . . . is likewise almost certainly a half-ass, albeit a large one" (909).

Twenty years later, at the podium during the inauguration of the Indian Archaeological Society's annual meeting, it was announced that Sandor Bökönyi, a Hungarian archaeologist and one of the world's leading horse specialists, who happened to be passing through Delhi after a conference, had verified that the bones were, indeed, of the domesticated *Equus caballus*: "The occurrence of true horse (*Equus caballus* L.) was evidenced by the enamel pattern of the upper and lower cheek and teeth and by the size and form of incisors and phalanges. Since no wild horses lived in India in post-pleistocene times, the domestic nature of the Surkotada horses is undoubtful (reproduced in Gupta 1993b, 162; and Lal 1997, 285). Sharma, vindicated, received two minutes of applause from the entire assembly (Sharma 1992–93, 30); there now seemed to be no doubt about the horse at Surkotada. Sharma comments on this validation:

> This was the saddest day for me as the thought flashed in my mind that my findings had to wait two decades for recognition, until a man from another continent came, examined the material and declared that "Sharma was right." When will we imbibe intellectual courage not to look across borders for approval? The historians are still worse, they feel it is an attempt on the part of the "rightists" to prove that the Aryans did not come to India from outside her boundaries. (30)

This poignant statement reveals two significant dimensions to the Aryan problem. Sharma's comments afford us a glimpse at the political tension underlying even as innocuous a piece of data as a horse's molar. Second, and (only) partly as a corollary of the emotionalism that the Aryan problem generates in India, many Indian scholars still value the opinion of a Western scholar more than that of their compatriots.[30]

Bökönyi's endorsement of the Surkotada findings have also been challenged, in turn however. Bökönyi had identified six tooth specimens that could "in all probability be considered remnants of true horses" (1997, 298–299). Meadow's subsequent investigations into these identifications caused him to conclude that "we agreed to disagree on all these matters and noted the need for further research. . . . we cannot accept without serious reservations Bökönyi's identifications of any of the Surkotada material as true horse, but in the end that may be a matter of emphasis and opinions" (1997, 315).[31] Unfortunately, Bökönyi was not able to write a reply before his death. Meadow's reservations refer to the problems outlined previously relating to the difficulty of distinguishing between the different equid species in an unambiguous fashion.

Although A. K. Sharma claims that the bones of *Equus caballus* have been discovered "from so many Harappan sites and that too right from the lowest levels [thus establishing] that the true domesticated horse was very much in use by the Harappans" (1992–93, 33), with the exception of the report from Rana Ghundai, which was questioned by Zimmer,[32] and Piggott's reported horse figurine from Periano Ghundai, it would appear that much, if not all, of even the contested evidence comes from strata associated with later Harappan sites or at least not from the Pre-Harappan or Early Harappan period. This, of course, as with the Sarasvatī, and the fire altars at Kalibangan, leaves scope for the proposal that, even if for argument's sake one is prepared to allow the claims regarding horse bones, it could still be argued that the Aryans could have introduced the "true" horse into the subcontinent during the Harappan period itself: "Indeed with the present state of evidence it would be unwise to conclude that there is any proof of the regular use of the horse in pre-Harappan or Harappan times" (Allchin and Allchin 1982, 191). Even B. B. Lal (1997), who is prepared to question the theory of Indo-Aryan migrations, has to acknowledge that "one would like to have much more evidence, to be able to say that the horse did play a significant role in the Harappan economy" (162).

A more significant horse lacuna, in the opinion of some, is that "several animals appear on Harappan seals . . . but the horse is absent" (Sharma 1995, 17).[33] In view of the fact that thousands of seals have been found, this absence is quite remarkable and potentially fatal to the Indigenous Aryanists, since, if the Aryan horse were indeed present in the Indus Valley, surely it would have attracted the artistic attention of, at least, the odd seal maker or two. Parpola, critiquing Sethna's rejection of the Aryan Invasion hypothesis, drew attention, among other things, to the horse lacuna on the seals. However, the Indigenous Aryanists are extremely resilient to what might appear to be fatal criticisms from their opponents. Sethna (1992) counters:

> As there are no depictions of the cow, in contrast to the pictures of the bull, which are abundant, should we conclude that Harappā and Mohenjo-dāro had only bulls? And what about that mythical animal, the unicorn, which is the most common pictorial motif on the seals? Was the unicorn a common animal of the proto-historic Indus Valley? Surely, the presence or absence of depictions cannot point unequivocally to the animals known and decide for or against Aryanism. (180)

Unless we are to suppose the existence of unique, monogenetic species of Harappan bull, it must be conceded that Sethna has a point; the cow is, indeed, also completely absent from seal depiction, although massive quantities of bovine bones have been found. Actually, such arguments were dismissed as early as Sir John Marshall's time: "The negative argument . . . is not altogether conclusive; for the camel, too, is unrepresented, though the discovery of a bone of this beast . . . leaves little doubt that it was known" (Marshall 1931, 28).[34] It seems safer to assume that certain animals appear on the seals at the exclusion of others as a result of culturally conditioned criteria, rather than because they document the complete zoological diversity of the Harappan landscape.

It is fair to note that even if some or all of the identifications of horse evidence is ambiguous, this should not then be translated into proclamations that the horse was not present in the Indus Valley; one would only have a right to say that the findings could belong either to *Equus caballus* or to another type of equid and that there has so far been no *unambiguous* evidence. The result of Bökönyi's endorsement of the horse bones at Surkotada was that "many other excavators of Harappan sites started searching for the bones of *Equus caballus*, with at least one further siting claimed at Dholavira" (Sharma 1992–93, 31). Obviously, the horse would never have been an issue had it not been linked with the Indo-Aryans. If Indigenous Aryanists seem keen to promote any reports of horses in the Harappan civilization as evidence of the Aryan presence, their detractors seem just as keen to find reason to challenge all such reports. Clearly, were it not for the politicization of the Aryan issue, the reports of horse evidence, albeit sparse, would hardly have raised any eyebrows.

There is a strong feeling among many of the archaeologists I interviewed that there are probably horse bones present in the many bags of bones that can be seen lying around in any Indian museum, but that they had never formerly been checked properly because the Indigenous Aryan position has only relatively recently climbed to ascendancy in India. In other words, scholars had previously just assumed that the Aryans were invaders and therefore were not so concerned about identifying horse bones. Hence, A. K. Sharma (1992–93) issues an appeal to young, up-and-coming archaeologists to be very attentive in their handling of animal bones and skeleton remains found in excavations, and not to attempt any personal weeding out of the material in order "to lessen the volume of finds, for fear of cost and labour involved in transporting them to headquarters" . . . [Once here,] they should not be . . . dumped . . . in some packing case for decades" (34).[35]

This is an important petition because unless horse bones are undeniably found in the Early, Pre-, and Mature Harappan strata, the Indo-Aryan speakers may be (and already are) allowed a degree of synthesis with the later Harappan civilization, but their status as intruders, albeit considerably earlier than previously held, will still not be considered convincingly undermined to the satisfaction of all. As two scholars who reviewed the horse evidence conclude, "considering that the presence of the horse during the Harappan period is a matter of popular controversy in Indian archaeology, the subject deserves more serious and systematic treatment than it has so far received" (Thomas and Joglekar 1994, 187).

It might be timely to again briefly refer to some of the Indigenous Aryan positions on this crucial issue, which were discussed in chapter 6. The horse has always been an elite animal in the subcontinent, but a nonnative and rare one, hence the paucity of evidence in the archaeological record. This, however, need have nothing to do with the indigenousness of the Indo-Aryans themselves, who simply imported this prized animal in the ancient period, as they have always done right up to the modern period. Bridget Allchin (1977) voices a similar position after the exchanges between Bökönyi and Meadow:

> From early historical times forward we know that horses have been regularly imported to South Asia. We also know the Indus had a long tradition of trade with centres to the west and north. Would it be surprising therefore if horses were occasionally acquired through trade, ultimately reaching the Indus world by land or sea? This would account for the occurrence of a small number of their bones in various contexts without the need to assume their presence must necessarily be associated with profound cultural change. (316)

The paucity of horse bones could simply denote the possibility that the animal was an elite and rare item. All this, of course, will be considered special pleading by the detractors of the Indgenous school.

Another observation that needs to be pointed out is that a number of scholars are prepared to consider that the Bactria Margiana Archaeological Complex (BMAC), which will be discussed in the next chapter, is an Indo-Aryan culture. The horse has been evidenced in this culture in the form of representations in grave goods. However, no horse bones have been found despite the availability of a large number of animal bones. This again underscores the point that lack of horse bones does not equal the absence of horse. Nor, at least in the opinion of those who subscribe to the Indo-Aryan identification of the BMAC, does this lack equal the absence of Indo-Aryans. Therefore, anyone prepared to associate the BMAC culture with the Indo-Aryans cannot then turn around and reject such an identification for the Indus Valley on the grounds of lack of horse bones in the latter.

As a final note, if the horse is to be promoted as the Achilles' heel of the Indigenous Aryan school, those advocating the Dravidian speakers as the inhabitants of the Indus Valley have their own lacuna to account for:

> It has been stated by the supporters of the Dravidian theory that the Aryan invaders chased away the Dravidian-speaking Harappans to the southern part of India. . . . Those who hold this view have squarely to answer: If the Aryans pushed the Harappans all the way down to South India, how come there are no Harappan sites at all in that region? The southernmost limit of the Harappan regime is the upper reaches of the Godavarī. There is no Harappan site south of that. (Lal 1997, 284)

This observation merits consideration. Even if the Dravidians had not been pushed down, but subsumed, one would have some grounds to expect seals, samples of the Indus script, or any item of material culture from any hypothetical Dravidian Harappans to have been shared with their fellow Dravidian speakers down South (and consequently surface in the archaeological record).[36] This is not the case. Even before the Harappan decline, one would have expected much greater trade and cultural exchange with the South had the two areas shared a common language and culture. The same can be said for any attempts to link the Harappans with the Munda speakers from the east. The Dravidian Harappanists, while very conscious of the horse evidence, tend to overlook this objection to their own position. On the other hand, there are plenty of examples of different types of socioeconomic cultures and civilizations that nonetheless share the same language: Lal himself, in a later chapter, argues that the nomadic Indo-Aryan composers of the Ṛgveda, could have coexisted with urban Indo-Aryans of the Indus Civilization.

The Chariot

The spoked-wheel chariot also is fundamental to Aryan identification. If the Aryans were a principal linguistic community within the Indus Valley Civilization, their existence there should be confirmed not only by the horse but also by the spoked-wheel chariot. This piece of technology, called *ratha* in Sanskrit (< PIE **rota*), is common to the Indo-European peoples, since, like the horse, its nomenclature has cognates in Indo-Iranian, Italic, Celtic, Baltic, and Germanic. Likewise, the terms for the parts of the chariot—the wagon pole, harness, yoke, and wheel nave—also have cognates generously distributed in various Indo-European languages. Either the Proto-Indo-Europeans knew the chariot or it was a later innovation that swept across the Indo-European-speaking area. In either event, the Indo-Aryans certainly utilized the technology after the dispersion of the various Indo-European tribes, an inference evidenced by the central role it plays in the Veda (which parallels its importance in other old Indo-European texts such as the Homeric hymns). The quest for the Indo-Aryans, then, as a result of a logic analogous to that impelling archaeologists to look for the horse, unavoidably involves searching for archaeological evidence of the chariot.

Although iconographic representations of solid-wheeled vehicles are attested as early as the fourth millennium B.C.E.,[37] the earliest evidence of the spoked-wheel chariot occurs in wheel imprints in the Sintashta cemetery dating to about 2000–1800 B.C.E., in representations from Syrian seals from the Anatolia, Uruk, and on eighteenth and seventeenth centuries B.C.E. Syrian seals (Mallory 1989, 69). Just as *Equus caballus* Linn. is the precise equid scholars have selected to demonstrate Aryan identity, the spoked-wheel chariot is the specific vehicle involved in the same task. Scholars have generally held that the horse-drawn, spoke-wheeled chariot was introduced into the Near East by Indo-Aryan-speaking peoples intruding from the north. The principal support for this hypothesis is the famous Hittite manual from Bogazköy, mentioned previously, wherein technical terms relating to the training of chariot horses are used. The text is written in Hittite, an Indo-European language, but, as I have discussed, the technical terms are in a dialect of Indo-Aryan very closely connected with Vedic Sanskrit. Although Piggott (1977, 1983) maintained that the arrival of these Indo-European groups did, indeed, inaugurate the new technology in Mesopotamia,[38] Littauer and Crouwel (1979, 68) prefered to consider the chariot a local, Mesopotamian development,[39] while Moorey (1986, 211) considered that a combination of local and external factors resulted in the innovation.

Evidence for chariot use prior to the common era is documented much less by actual archaeological finds of the vehicle itself than by iconographic and literary evidence of it. In India, however, the earliest evidence of the chariot seems to have been at Atranjīkherā in the Upper Gaṅgā Basin sometime between 350 and 50 B.C.E. (Gaur 1983, 373) and representations occurring in the late first millennium, on stupas, Ashokan pillars and Kushana art.[40] There is plenty of evidence of wheeled vehicles in the Indus Valley, particularly in the form of miniature models or toys (Mackay 1943, 162–166),[41] but nothing suggestive of spoked-wheels or chariots. Of course, this is negative evidence based on *argumentum ex silentio*, and one could argue that it is not practical to construct miniature spoked wheels from clay hardy enough to withstand the abuse of children, hence the lacuna of the spoked wheel. Moreover, many of the toys are missing their wheels, so spoked wheels could have coexisted with solid ones, as is the real-life case in the Sindh today. Piggott (1970, 202), at least, was not averse to considering that some of the wheels that are missing from the carts may have been spoked and correlatable with intruding Aryans. Nonetheless, the absence of definite evidence of the spoked wheel is a lacuna that is levied against the case of the Indigenous Aryanists.

This absence is mitigated to a certain degree in that, even if we accept the latest date assigned by scholars to the Ṛgveda, namely, 1200 B.C.E., the chariot as known to this text must have unquestionably been in existence on the subcontinent for approximately a millennium before becoming evidenced in iconographic form just before the common era. Witzel's date of 1700 B.C.E. increases that period to a millennium and a half. If we accept the opinion of those who hold that the "fire altars" in Kalibangan, the evidence of the horse in later Harappan sites, and the circumstantial evidence of the Sarasvatī suggest (even to scholars who insist on their ultimate external origins) that the Indo-Aryans had some presence at least in the later period of the Harappan civilization, the period increases further still. The archaeological *argumentum ex silentio* clearly shows its limitations in this period during which we know the chariot was extant from the literary evidence, despite the fact that it has not been verified archaeologically. Obviously, the farther back in time we go, the more the likelihood of finding such iconographic evidence decreases. Indeed early archaeological evidence for the oldest discovered spoked chariot wheel in the Sintashta Cemetery of the Andranovo culture, can only be inferred from soil discoloration from the decayed spokes, and slots in grave floors (Piggott 1983, 91).

Therefore, since archaeology has not unearthed any signs of spoked wheels or chariots in the period of one, or one and a half, millennium during which we know from Vedic texts that the chariot was very much present in the Northwest of the subcontinent, it seems legitimate to question the validity of this evidence as the final arbitrator of Aryan origins, especially since chariots leave little archaeolgical residue. In the event of a lucky find, archaeology can confirm, in such cases, but it cannot deny, in the absence of the same. Such limitations causes some scholars to lament the perceived overdependence on archaeological evidence: "Unfortunately some archaeologists seem to have no eyes to see anything but what the spade digs up from the bowels of the earth, and no ears to hear anything that is not echoed from excavated ruins" (Majumdar 1959, 11). Nonetheless, if the method of archaeology is to be allowed any value at all, then the burden of proof rests with those who wish to argue that chariots (and horses) were in use in the Indus Valley Civilization. While any archaeologist would agree that "absence of evidence is not evidence of absence," theories can only be established on the presence or absence of evidence until falsified by later discoveries. Otherwise, archaeologists would have to accept everything as possible and be unable to formulate any hypotheses at all concerning cultural evolution.

The Indus Script

While some of the evidence discussed here has caused many South Asian archaeologists to reconsider or modify their positions regarding Indo-Aryan intrusions into the subcontinent, one piece of evidence that has been in academic custody since even before the official discovery of Harappa could, if made to testify, immediately bear witness to the linguistic identity of the inhabitants of the Harappan civilization. This would have immediate repercussions for the entire Indo-Aryan debate and, indeed, to all intents and purpose could conclude the whole matter. The Indus seals (64), and a few other assorted items are imprinted with symbols of an unknown script. The decipherment of this script would determine in one decisive stroke whether the principal language spoken in the Indus Valley was Indo-Aryan, Dravidian, Munda, or some other linguistic entity. Despite dedicated efforts spanning almost seventy years (which have included the use of sophisticated computer techniques), the script remains tantalizingly resistant to being deciphered. Needless to say, if these endeavors ever bear fruit, the need for searching through old bags of bones in quest of *Equus caballus* molars will be eliminated in one decisive stroke. If the script can be shown to be some form of Indo-Aryan, there can be no further serious debate about the dominant linguistic identity of the Indus Valley. On the other hand, if it can be shown to be a non-Indo-Aryan language, then the entire case of the Indigenous Aryanists will lose most of its cogency.

Just as this book is going to press, the discovery of what appears to be proto-Indus writing on shards of pottery from the Ravi phase that are as early as 3500 B.C.E. has been announced.[42] If this script contains the same language as the later Indus script (there is always the possibility that the same script might contain different langauges at different chronological periods), then any Indo-Aryan decipherment would have major repercussions for the whole Indo-European problem, not just the identity of the Indus Valley. The Indo-Europeans could still have been an undivided entity at this time, as will be discussed in chapter 12. An Indo-Aryan language during this period will drastically affect the whole Indo-European homeland locating quest and provide unprecedented support for Indian homeland proponents. The script, for a number of reasons, is of great interest to Indigenists and Migrationists alike.

The fact that both the language and the script are unknown makes the task extremely difficult. Other decipherment attempts have involved known languages in an unknown script (when decipherment is virtually guaranteed)[43] and unknown languages in a known script—a much more difficult combination. Although Hittite is an example of an unknown language successfully extracted from a known script (cuneiform), this second category is by no means guaranteed to bring success. Etruscan continues to refuse to yield to complete translation attempts despite being written in a form of Roman script, with even some bilingual inscriptions available in Latin. All this should sober any would-be decipherer intent on attempting the third and most difficult type of decipherment project: an unknown language in an unknown script. Such is the Harappan case. The task is not impossible: cuneiform, Linear B, and the Egyptian hieroglyphics are successful examples of previously unknown languages being extracted from unknown scripts, but, without bilingual inscriptions, success in this category is extremely unlikely. Cuneiform and the Egyptian hieroglyphs were deciphered with the aid of lengthy bilingual and trilingual inscriptions containing known languages. Even then, Jean-François Champillon, who succeeded in deciphering the hieroglyphs, spent fifteen years compiling all the signs and variants before even attempting a reading, despite having access to the famous Rosetta stone, where the Egyptian pictographs were accompanied by a Greek translation. The decipherment of the Linear B script without any bilingual inscriptions by Michael Ventris in 1951 ranks as a great and rare achievement in the annals of decipherment.

Like Linear B, there are no bilingual inscriptions of the Indus script, but, unlike Linear B, the Indus seal decipherment is further hampered by the extreme brevity of the seals, each of which contains an average of only five symbols. The longest inscription is twenty-six symbols on three sides of an amulet, while the longest single-sided inscription is only seventeen symbols. To extrapolate a morphologically or syntactically consistent language from seals averaging a mere five signs is a nearly impossible task. The length of the seals parallels that of the Etruscan inscriptions, the brevity of which has also prevented their decipherment (apart from a few names). Yet, in the Etruscan case, some bilingual inscriptions are available, as is an extensive knowledge of the cultural setting of the people.

The brevity of the Indus inscriptions allows various sounds from the same, or different, languages to be assigned to the same symbols and, with a little fudging and coaxing, still result in meaningful words on some kind of a regular basis; hence the plethora of so-called decipherments. As Allan Keislar (n.d., 6) notes, however, spurred on by apparent success in assigning phonemes to some of the symbols and producing meanings that appear reasonable, at least to themselves, many would-be decipherers believe the reality of their system has been validated. If even a single lengthy text were to be found, then all the competing sound values could be put to the test to see if a semantically coherent and morphologically and syntactically consistent language emerged. Ventris applied his tentative sound correspondences to the Linear B script and was surprised to find Greek emerging from the texts (he was expecting a pre-Greek non-Indo-European language). Likewise, the Brahmī inscriptions were decipherable from a few Ashokan pillars, but the inscriptions were lengthy enough to allow a clearly identifiable Prakritic Sanskrit to emerge.

One of the few things on which most scholars do agree is the direction of the writing on the seals, which is obviously the first feature to be established before any attempts can be made to "read" the signs. Lal, in 1966, pointed out that on some inscriptions incised on pottery shards, certain symbols had been superimposed over the symbol to their right, which they partly effaced, thereby indicating that they had been inscribed after the right-hand symbol had been written; this would indicate writing from right to left. An inscription along three sides of another seal also shows that the writing could only have been from right to left. However, the situation is complicated somewhat by similar evidence indicating that the writing was sometimes incised in a boustrophedonic fashion ('as the ox plows,' i.e., left to right to left, etc.).

There is still no agreement among scholars regarding whether the script is logo-syllabic, or syllabic. Many scholars feel that it represents a logo-syllabic script, based on the fact that they identify approximately four hundred distinct principal signs (excluding hundreds of additional signs, which they construe either as variations of these or as conjunct signs). Logographic scripts, where a sign denotes a complete word, need a much larger number of signs—up to nine hundred—to represent the range of words required in communication. Syllabic scripts, where each sign represents a syllable, need fewer signs—typically fifty to one hundred—to denote the entire possible range of syllables utilized in a language.[44] Since the number of distinct Indus signs appears to fall between these two categories, the script has been designated as logosyllabic by some. In the opinion of other scholars, however, the script is considered to be primarily syllabic. Such scholars perceive a much smaller number of basic signs in the script and construe the remainder as being conjunct forms or voweled variants of these basic signs.

Sanskrit Decipherments

Several scholars have a priori ruled out the possibility of a Sanskrit language being uncovered in the seals. Zide (1979) feels that this is "completely inadmissible on the grounds of chronological incongruity . . . and so is immediately discredited" (257). In other words, since the Indo-Aryan language is assumed not to have entered the subcontinent until after the Indus Valley, it is not even a candidate. Along the same lines, Possehl (1996) states that "Indo-Aryan is dismissed since the Fairservis position is that representative languages of the family arrived in the subcontinent at ca. 1500 B.C." (153). Such a priori grounds will not be invoked in this analysis, which has suspended all presuppositions concerning the origins of the Indo-Aryans.

However, other scholars believe that the script cannot be Sanskrit for structural reasons. Computer analyses of the morphology of the script suggest to them that it did not have prefixes and inflectional endings. If this were to be proved true, then Indo-Aryan and any other early Indo-European language, which do contain such features, would have to be disqualified as likely candidates. This would result in the entire Indigenous Aryan position losing cogency. It is imperative for the entire Indigenous case that the script be Indo-Aryan. On the other hand, it has also been argued that it is unlikely that the script is Dravidian, since it uses a numbering system with a base ten. Dravidian uses base eight.

S. R. Rao's claim of decipherment, which he has presented in a variety of publications (1979, 1991), is the best known attempt from the Indigenous Aryan school because of this scholar's preeminent status in Indian archaeology. An official Indian government tourist publication on Dvārakā presents one of Rao's translations for a seal found off Dvārakā as factual (Keislar n.d., 19),[45] Since his efforts are often promoted by the Indigenous Aryan camp, Rao's work merits some attention.

Based on the strata in which certain seals were found, Rao (1991) proposes that the script underwent an evolution from logosyllabic, in the Early Harappan period, to phonetic, in the Mature and Late Harappan period. Rao identifies thirty-four basic cursive signs that occurred in the Mature Harappan period, but, since he considers some of these to be alternative signs, he reduces the number occurring in the Late Harappan period to twenty-four. Thus the script, in Rao's system, is essentially phonetic, although it developed from a logosyllabic progenitor. He sees all the remaining Indus signs that are not pictographic or basic as being either compound forms, diacritic markers, or vocalic indicators that qualify this basic group.

Having reduced the total number of signs to this essential core, Rao's method involves comparing this nucleus with similar signs from the Semitic script, specifically the Old North Semitic and South Semitic scripts of the Phoenicians, Hebrews, and South Arabs. The oldest inscriptions in these scripts date from 1600 to 1200 B.C.E., a period that overlaps with the Late Harappan period and the latest attested samples of the Indus script. Rao considers this method justifiable because there were substantial trading and cultural connections between the Indus Valley and Mesopotamia. He finds seventeen of his thirty-four signs common to the two scripts, with some minor alterations, and assigns the same phonetic value from these seventeen Semitic signs to their Indus counterparts. He also finds 16 of the basic Indus signs have a close similarity to the much later South Asian Brāhmī script, despite the chronological gap of circa one millennium between the two.[46] His readings, however, seem to be based mostly on the letters with Semitic similarities. Rao finds that the seals read by his method reveal an Old Indo-Aryan language.

While Rao's procedure, so far, is a reasonable one to consider, at least as a working hypothesis, his treatment of two other signs from his basic core, the 'man' sign and the 'fish' sign, which are among the most common of the Indus signs but do not have Semitic equivalents, seems much more arbitrary. Taking the Sanskrit word for 'man' *nṛ/nara* and for 'fish' *śakala*, Rao assigns the second letter *ṛ* from the former and the first letter *ś* from the latter to the man and fish signs, respectively. He follows a similar procedure in assigning sound values to various other common pictographic signs, except, in these instances, instead of extracting a single phoneme, he chooses to assign a full syllable from the Sanskrit word corresponding to the sign (i.e., *sak* for the 'bird' picture). Rao justifies such apparent arbitrariness, including the choice of the particular Sanskrit synonym he decides to select for the picture (i.e., *śakuna* 'a bird of omen' as opposed to the more common words for bird such as *pakṣī* or *vihaga*) simply because it works—words meaningful to his sensibilities are produced by the assignment of certain syllables as opposed to others.[47] The problem, of course, is that the script can also be made to "work," at least to the satisfaction of other would-be translators, by assigning a wide variety of syllables to the same symbols. Keisler produced a chart showing the wide assortment of phonemes or syllables assigned to the same Indus sign by the various principal decipherment contenders—all of whom seem satisfied that their particular versions are valid because they work.

Another interesting decipherment attempt by Subhash Kak, a professor in the electrical and computer engineering department of Louisiana State University, also connects the Indus script with Indo-Aryan and is noteworthy because of its innovative methodology. As Possehl (1996) notes, "Kak's work brings to it the serious mind of a scientist, and his ability to deal with the problem in a quantitative way is needed." As he points out, this is a welcome change: "Kak's great strength is that he brings mathematics into play on the study of the script. His is not the old-fashioned iconography analysis, tried again and again" (148). Kak sets out to determine whether the later Brāhmī script might be connected with the Indus signs, since it is the oldest known orthographic script for the Indic languages. Like Rao, Kak considers the script to be syllabic on the grounds that if the thirty-three consonants known to Brāhmī are conceived of as being modifiable in ten different ways by the addition of ten different vowel signs, the resulting number approaches the basic corpus of signs recognized by most scholars. Kak reduces the 300-odd Indus characters down to a set of 39 primary signs, most of which he feels are easily identifiable (either as primary signs or as combinations of primary signs). These 39 signs, singly or in combination, account for 80 percent of all the signs; in comparison, Brāhmī has 45 primary letters.

Kak's next observation is that although logosyllabic scripts have more signs, each individual sign occurs more consistently than in a syllabic system where some signs occur with high frequency and others rarely. Thus, from a random 13,000 letters in English, a syllabic script, for example, one would expect to see *E* about 1,700 times, *T* about 1,200 times, and *J*, *Q*, *X*, and *Z* only 17, 16, 20, and 10 times each, respectively. In parallel fashion, from a corpus of 13,000 Indus signs, two signs constitute 2,000 of the total, while more than 200 signs occur less than 10 times each (Kak 1987a, 54). Kak then takes ten different Sanskrit texts of one thousand words each (in order to represent a range of different genres), processes the combined ten thousand words through a computer, and draws up tables of the ten most commonly occurring Sanskrit phonemes. These are (in decreasing order): *t, r, v, n, m, y, s, d, p, and k*. He then assigns the Brāhmī characters for these letters and compares them with a table of the ten most commonly occurring Indus symbols. He finds there are convincing parallels between four of the two sets, Brāhmī *v*, *m*, *t*, and s, which even appear in the same order of frequency. Certain changes, he feels, have taken place (e.g., the fish sign had been flipped sideways), but he argues that such modifications can also be seen in the evolution of Brāhmī to Nāgarī. According to Kak's calculations (1988, 135), the probability of these resemblances occurring by chance is 0.1×10^{-12}. It should be noted, however, that the phonemes he assigns to the Indus script on the basis of their similarities differ from the phonemes Rao assigns to his Brahmī/Indus correlations.

Nonetheless, granting all of Kak's observations, all that can be inferred at this point is that perhaps the Brāhmī script was derived from the Indus script. This possibility does not deal with the language family represented by the script. Kak is wise enough not to proclaim that he has deciphered the script or to produce long lists of translations, but he does offer one tentative, but potentially very significant, morphological observation. He sees evidence in the Indus inscriptions for a Sanskrit genitive case marker: "The genitive case-ending in Sanskrit is often *-sya* or *-sa* and in Prākrit the ending is generally *-sa* or *-ssa* and this is what we frequently see in these inscriptions. This suggests that the Indus language is likely to have been Prakritic" (1992, 206).[48]

Kak's methodology in determining this case ending is to correlate the *s* phoneme in the Brāhmī script with the most frequently occurring Indus symbol, the jar sign. He argues that if the three types of Sanskrit *s* (dental, palatal, and retroflex) were counted as one (as occurred in Pali and later prakrits where they were merged into one sibilant), then this phoneme would occur first in the list of the ten most frequently occurring Sanskrit phonemes, thus corresponding in frequency to the most commonly occurring Indus sign, the 'jar'. Most significantly, he finds that the Brāhmī sign for *-s* does actually resemble this jar sign. Since this sign occurs very frequently at the end of inscriptions, and since the seals of the historic period, from Ashoka's time and after, almost all ended in the genitive case, Kak believes he has grounds to identify it as a genitive case marker. Seals ending in the genitive possessive marker—denoting ownership of goods—would quite likely be used for trading purposes. Most scholars do actually believe that the seals were connected with trade (they have been found in Bahrain and Mesopotamia). Interestingly, Parpola (1994) agrees that this sign does occur frequently at the end and also proposes that it could be a genitive marker (although not an Indo-Aryan one).[49] By simply trying to identify one element of Indo-Aryan morphology in the script, Kak can claim that the principal language of the Indus Valley Civilization was Indo-Aryan without claiming to have deciphered the script. This is a more discreet and effective statement, to my sensitivites, than one claiming to be able to read entire signs. Whether it is correct, of course, is another matter.

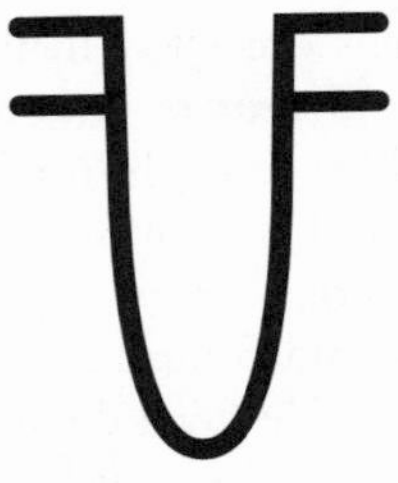

The Indus 'jar' sign.

Dravidian Decipherment Attempts

A brief glance at how the most common Indus sign, the 'fish,' has been deciphered by one or two principal scholars promoting a Dravidian language will suffice to parallel the I-A attempts. (For a complete overview of most decipherment attempts, see Possehl 1996.) The most popular candidate for the script, from the non-Indo-Aryan side, is Dravidian. Just as there are a priori objections against considering the script to be Indo-Aryan, there is an a priori objection against a Dravidian identification, paralleling Lal's comment, noted earlier, that there is no trace of the Indus culture in the areas where Dravidian speakers are known, and have been known, to reside. As Sjoberg (1992) puts it: "If we assume that some Dravidian speakers at least . . . formed part of the Harappan civilization, with its cities and its special script, the question arises: Why is there no record of a non-Aryan writing system in South India? Writing, so far as we know, was an Aryan introduction" (7). The same consideration applies to Munda. Moreover, as noted earlier, the numbering system of the script, which uses a base of ten, does not appear to correspond to that of Dravidian, which uses a base of eight.

Parpola's (1994) work is useful exposition of everything that has been done on the script by scholars so far with the aid of computers.[50] All these efforts are essential in order to gain some glimpses at the possible morphological and inflectional structure of the Indus language, but, as Parpola (1994) acknowledges, despite the significant input from computer analysis, "we must conclude by frankly admitting our present inability to identify morphological markers with any certainty" (97). The formal grammar of the script being prepared by such efforts "will be useful in limiting the range of guesswork when a breakthrough is achieved. But the breakthrough itself cannot be achieved by this method" (101).

Anyone attempting to crack the Indus script with the presently available resources must venture into the realm of speculation and guesswork. Parpola's presupposition (1994) is "that the Harappan language is most likely to have belonged to the Dravidian family" (174). He limits his attempts at decipherment to a small number of symbols, fully aware of the shortcomings of such endeavors. His principal decipherment involves the common Indus sign 'fish,' to which he assigns the syllable *mīn*. He considers this an appropriate identification because the word *mīn* means 'fish' in most Dravidian languages and is reconstructed as such in proto-Dravidian.

The Indus 'fish' sign.

However, since this extremely common sign could hardly refer to 'fish' everywhere it occurs, Parpola prefers to consider it a referent to 'star', since *mīn* is a homonym for both 'fish' and 'star' in the Dravidian languages. He himself notes, however, that some Harappan pottery bears symbols that specifically resemble stars, leaving one to wonder why the symbol for another word would need to be used for the star, which has a natural-looking symbol of its own. He then finds reason to believe that the star, by extension, is primarily a symbol for a god or astral divinity when it occurs in the seals. This is quite a series of assumptions and transferrals: Parpola's principal sign, the most common Indus fish sign, is the symbol for a god, by association with star, which is a Dravidian homonym for fish, which is the iconographic form that he sees in a common Indus symbol.

Fairservis, (1992) who is also operating on the assumption that the Harappan language must have been Dravidian, does not believe the symbol to be a 'fish' at all, for a variety of reasons, but prefers to consider it to be a loop. The Dravidian for 'loop' (*pir*) also denotes a 'chief' or leader, which is the meaning Fairservis assigns to the sign. Where Parpola translates 'star', then, Fairservis reads 'leader'.[51] Just as there are discrepancies between Rao's and Kak's Indus-to-Brāhmī correlations, so Fairservis differs from Parpola in his Indus-to-Dravidian assignments, and both differ from Mahadevan, who has also attempted to decipher the script as a Dravidian language.[52] His efforts, as well as the dedicated and important efforts of Russian scholars, are amply outlined in Possehl (1996) and need not detain us here. In conclusion, then, I will again refer to Parpola (1994): "It looks unlikely that the Indus script will ever be deciphered fully, unless radically different source material becomes available. That, however, must not deter us from trying" (278).[53]

Before concluding, we must pay heed to Witzel's discoveries, outlined earlier, that the linguistic influences detectable in the earliest hymns of the Ṛgveda are from Munda and decidedly *not* from Dravidian, which surfaces only in later strata of the *Ṛg* and in later texts. Since he holds that the Indo-Aryans entered the subcontinent at the tail end of the Indus civilization, he infers that the language immediately prior to their arrival was Munda—Dravidian entered later, thus influencing the later texts:

> As we can no longer reckon with Dravidian influence on the early RV, . . . this means that the language of the pre-Ṛgvedic Indus civilization, at least in the Panjab, was of Austro-Asiatic nature. This means that *all proposals for a decipherment of the Indus script must start with the c. 300 Austro-Asiatic loanwords in the RV* and by comparing other Munda and Austro-Asiatic words. . . . The decipherment has been tried for the past 35 years or so mainly on the basis of Dravidian. Yet, few Indus inscriptions have been "read" even after all these years of concerted, computer-aided attempts, and not in a fashion that can be verified independently. . . . Yet, Kuiper's '300 words' could become the Rosetta stone of the Indus script. (Witzel b, 13; italics in original)

Urbanity and the Ṛgveda

At this point, we should recall that the options for the Indigenous Aryan school are that the Vedic culture either preceded the Indus Valley culture, was contemporaneous with it, or succeeded it. There are two other significant and commonly encountered objections that would seem to controvert attempts to correlate the Vedic period with the Indus civilization. First, smelted iron artifacts have not been found in the cities of the Indus Valley to date, but iron is known in the Atharvaveda and the Śatapatha Brāhmaṇa, which would suggest that these texts, at least, were post-Harappan. As with the horse, the introduction of iron has long been associated with the incoming Indo-Aryans. More significantly, scholars from Marshall's time to the present day have repeatedly drawn attention to the claim that the economic landscape that can be glimpsed through the Vedic hymns appears to be a rural pastoralist one, with no indication of urban centers.

The introduction of iron into the subcontinent by the Indo-Aryans is another discarded intruding-Aryan tenet that is no longer accepted by archaeologists: "Archaeologically . . . the problem of the Aryans and their association with iron remains as confusing as ever, regardless of the earlier strongly expressed theories of their apparently tautological association" (Banerjee 1981, 320). Iron occurs in a number of locations that could not have been influenced by one particular source. Chakrabarti (1993–94) was one of the first to reject the idea that the Iron Age represents a "major social and economic transformation" (25). Questioning the idea of its external origin, he claims that iron appears in the archaeological record without causing any significant cultural break. Here, again, he complains about "the role of the Aryans in this context which seem[s] to have forced scholars into a position where their primary concern has been to correlate the early Indian data on iron to some diffusionary impulses through the northwest" (25).

Of greater implication is Shaffer's argument (1984a, 49) that during the late third millennium B.C.E. iron ore was recognized and utilized in southern Afghanistan and was manipulated to produce iron luxury items. The fact that there are early Harappan artifacts in the same stratigraphic proveniences as the iron artifacts suggests to him that "the 'Early Harappan' complexes had access to, or knowledge of, an iron technology." In actual fact, although there is no evidence for awareness of smelted iron technology, iron ore and iron items have been uncovered in eight bronze age Harappan sites, some going back to 2600 B.C.E. and earlier. (These will be described in chapter 12.) So there was as awareness of iron, which may have been encountered accidently during the smelting of copper, and a willingness to exploit it. The Harappan awareness of iron ore cannot be considered an "iron age," which is when smelted iron items became common items of household use and occurred around 1000 B.C.E. According to Possehl (1999b), "the iron age is more of a continuation of the past then a break with it" (165). Moreover, iron tools did not "lead to the subjugation of indigenous population by invading warriors" (164). In any event, Shaffer concludes with a complaint that has become standard for South Asian archaeologists: "Ideas of invasions, diffusions, and conquests have obscured and hindered investigation into the region's indigenous cultural processes. To fully understand and appreciate the various solutions to cultural problems recorded in the South Asian archaeological record, alternative explanatory frameworks must be considered" (59).

Regarding the connection between the Vedic landscape and the Harappan one, almost all Indigenous Aryanists feel that the Vedic poets either preceded and/or coexisted with the Harappan world. Scholars since the time of Marshall (1931) have long since discarded the former possibility, since "if the Vedic culture antedated the Indus, how comes it that iron and defensive armour and the horse, which are characteristic of the former, are unknown to the latter?" (111). Moreover, anyone open to considering whether the Vedic people coexisted with or authored the Indus Valley Civilization would be "wholly at a loss to explain how the Indo-Āryans came to relapse from the city to the village state, or how, having once evolved excellent houses of brick, they afterwards contented themselves with inferior structures of bamboo" (112).

From the Indigenous Aryan side, there have been dozens of books attempting to fit the hymns of the Ṛgveda into the ruins of the Indus (e.g., Prakash 1966; Sankarananda 1967; Chandra 1980; Deshmukh 1982; Singh 1995). This position has to contend with the conclusions of Wilhelm Rau, who combed the early strata of Vedic literature in search of literary evidence for permanent Vedic settlements. His main concern was to evaluate Wheeler's suggestion that the fortified citadels of the Harappans must have been those that the Vedic Aryans destroyed. Although hardly any scholars uphold Wheeler's position today, Rau's remarks are very pertinent to anyone attempting to correlate the Indus Valley Civilization with that of the Indo-Aryans, since he is evaluating whether the Indo-Aryans had any familiarity with urban centers. His method is primarily an analysis of the attributes of a *pur*, which means 'city' in later texts, (as noted earlier, in the Ṛgveda Indra is called *purandara* 'fort-destroyer').

Rau (1976, 41) believed his work permitted him to state the following conclusions "with confidence." A *pur* in the Ṛgvedic period consisted of one or several concentric ramparts on a round or oval groundplan; was built of mud or stone; was fortified with combustible defenses; had gates made of wattle or prickly shrubs; was furnished with wooden sheds as quarters for human occupants; was stocked with provisions for man and cattle; was not permanently occupied but served as a refuge in times of need; was erected in war as a base of operations; and probably needed repairs after the rainy season. Some of Rau's interpretations are based on inferences, which it might be useful to reproduce so that they can be compared with those of the scholars attempting to correlate the Indus cities with Vedic testimony.

That the *puraḥ* consisted of concentric ramparts seems to be based on the fact that Indra entered ninety-nine *puraḥs* in one day, on the adjective *śatábhujiḥ* (hundred-armed) which accompanies the word twice (it is also used with the river Sarasvatī), and on the prefix *pari* used when the sacrificer makes a *puraḥ* 'around' himself (Rau 1976, 24–25); that the *puraḥ* were made from mud is based on the word *dehī* in two verses and the emendation of *vipram* to *vapram* in a third (26); that they were combustible is based on the fact that Agni helped Indra break the *puraḥ* of the enemy (27); that they are made of wattle and palisades is based on the fact that the *puraḥ* are made to bow down, fall backward, lie on the ground, or be rent like a garment (28); that they were fortified by prickles is "likely" based on verses produced from the very much later Arthaśāstra of Kautilya (ca. fourth century B.C.E.); that the human occupants lived in sheds (*vímita*) is based on two verses in which a golden and mighty *vímita* is said to exist in the creator Brahma's world *brahmaloke*; that the *puraḥ* were not permanently occupied seems to be predicated on verses stating that the enemy were driven into their *puraḥ*, and that the demons enter into theirs (34); that they were erected in war, and so on, is based on verses suggesting that the gods, disadvantaged without *puraḥ*, decided to make some of their own; and, finally, that they needed repairs after each rainy season is inferred from the fact that the term *puraḥ* is juxtaposed with the word *śāradīḥ* 'autumnal' (37).

There seems to be a good deal in Rau's interpretations (1976) that is not explicit in the texts. Nonetheless, he reiterates an often cited observation: "Not a word is said in our texts of the characteristic features of the Indus cities, of brick walls, brick houses, brick-paved streets laid out on an orthogonal pattern, of granaries or public baths. . . . No statement in Vedic literature prompts us to assume a . . . formidable civilization" (52).

In terms of the habitations of the Indo-Aryans themselves, Rau (1977) concludes from the relevant terms that *grāma* denotes "a train of herdsmen roaming about with cattle, ox-carts and chariots in quest of fresh pastures and booty," as well as "a temporary camp of such a train, sometimes used for a few days only and sometimes for a few months at the most" (203). He reads another term, *sālā*, as referring to lodgings that "consisted of transportable sheds . . . made of bamboo-poles and reed mats, which could be assembled and dismantled in a minimum of time" (205). Although he notes that "there cannot be the slightest doubt that the Vedic Aryans practiced agriculture from the very beginning," he nonetheless maintains that this "cannot prove the existence of 'villages' in our sense of the term. . . . even a migrating population could do a little tilling of the soil on the side when resting for a while" (205). Rau, then, does not allow even villages as a feature of early Indo-Aryan society (except for some rare references), not to mention cities or an entire civilization such as that of the Indus Valley. He finds that the term *nagara*, which means 'town' from the time of the *Taittirīya Āraṇyaka*, occurs only once in an earlier text.[54]

In contrast to Burrow (1963), Rau considers *arma* or *armaka* to refer to rubbish heaps. Burrow accepted Wheeler's theory that the Aryans were responsible for the overthrow of the Indic civilization and interpreted the terms *arma/armaka* as the ruined sites of this encounter, since "during the early Aryan period, the ruins of many Indus cities must have formed a conspicuous feature of the countryside" (Burrow 1963, 160). Rau, in contrast, envisions herdsmen revisiting the same camping grounds by rotation and developing the habit of throwing rubbish over the years regularly in the same spots. This rubbish accumulated into heaps, from which only potsherds can remain in the long run (potsherds from *armas* are prescribed for making certain ritual vessels). Here, again, he concludes that the immigrating Vedic Indians by necessity must have been constantly on the move during the centuries they conquered the plains of the Punjab and the Gangā-Yamunā Doab. In this scenario, permanent settlements are not to be expected at all, since the migrating trains left behind only deserted resting places. Accordingly, "it is useless to look for structural remains dating from Vedic times, in northwestern India" (Rau 1997, 206). If this conclusion is correct, it is puzzling since, as Burrow noted, much of the area known to the composers of the Vedic hymns must have been littered with hundreds of Indus sites during the time frame normally allotted to Indo-Aryans intrusions. If the Vedic texts do not refer to such sites, it surely cannot be because the Indo-Aryans were not aware of them. This lacuna seems to be a peculiarity of the texts rather than a reflection of the Vedic landscape. The same, as I will argue later, holds true for any absence of references to urban centers.

Bhagavan Singh's (1995) is a recent and perhaps the most ambitious exposition of those holding contrary views to scholars such as Rau. Singh has compiled a glossary of all the technical terms and items relating to material culture from the Ṛgveda. The references are extracted from all contexts—poetic analogies, metaphors, similes, and so forth—on the grounds that the composers of the hymns could utilize such figures of speech only if their referents were a part of their everyday environment. Rau (1976) at least agrees with this basic point that "the world of the gods has always been fashioned in analogy to the human environment of their worshippers"(9).

Singh's lists are extensive.[55] I will select a few examples, which will suffice to illustrate his attempt to subvert the claim that the Indo-Aryans knew no urban centers and were simple nomad pastoralists. I should note that specialists in Vedic philology will doubtlessly find plenty of words that Singh has translated in ways they will object to, and even more that are fanciful to the extreme.[56] His efforts to connect the Vedic Aryans with the Indus Valley go to the extreme of suggesting that the Ṛbhus were seal makers (Singh 1995, 162)! As mentioned in the introduction, I have examined evidence from every context, since I have often found that a scholar who can make an almost comically uncritical argument in one place can sometimes make a very insightful contribution in another. If nothing else, Singh has compiled useful lists that can provide the basis for further careful scrutiny.

Of the seventy or so words Singh has extracted connected with cities and dwelling places, *bṛhantam mānam sahasradvāram gṛham* 'very large house with a thousand doors' and *sahasrasthūṇa gṛham* 'house with a thousand pillars' are of particular interest, since they suggest to him acquaintance with monumental structures.[57] Likewise, from another long list of words associated with navigation, *daśaritrā* 'ship with ten oars'; *śataritra* 'ship with hundred oars'; and Vasiṣṭha in a ship in midocean make his best case. Singh has compiled numerous words connected with government, thereby arguing the existence of quite a sophisticated system of organization involving *rāṣṭra* 'kingdoms'; a variety of types of rulers: *rājā*, *ekarāj*, *samrāj*, *janarāj*, *jyeṣṭharāj*, and so on; and various terms for assemblies, and similar gatherings: *saṁsad*, *sabhā*, *samiti*, and so on. Of course, all these concepts could have existed among nomadic people: one has no right to assume that these political terms had the same denotation in the protohistoric period as they did in later texts. And one could always explain any genuine references to cosmopolitan life by postulating that the Aryans must have been aware of, and interacted with, cities in central Asia or even the Near East. Thus Braarvig (1997), for example, explains the reference to the hundred-oared ship—which he believes is "a type of ship scarcely used in Vedic culture"—as an image "that had probably followed the Vedic Indo-European culture from other locations where such ships were in use . . . a symbol which had got its meaning elsewhere" (347). Nonetheless, whatever their own level of social attainment might have been, there are a variety of reasons to review the long-held assumption that the Indo-Aryans knew no urban centers. These will be touched upon in the following discussion and in the next chapters.

Some Western scholars have also been struck by discrepancies between the Vedic landscape and a nomadic one. Basham (1989) comments: "It is surprising that the Āryans, who at this time had never organized a settled kingdom or lived in a city, should have conceived of a god like Varuṇa, the heavenly emperor in his glorious palace, with innumerable messengers flying through the cosmos at his bidding" (12). As far as Singh is concerned, if one is looking for nomads in the Ṛgveda, one will find nomads. He, at least, does not read the texts with the same assumptions:

> There was nothing in the *Ṛgveda* to look for a primitive or primarily nomadic society [*sic*]. . . . Chariots and wagons and boats which occur so frequently in the *Ṛgveda* do not

agree well with nomadism. Movement of cars presupposes existence of roads and defined routes, which in turn presuppose settlements and regular traffic from point to point. Boats and ships are not floating logs. They presuppose ferry ghats and fixed destinations. . . . there was much in the *Ṛgveda* that defied explanation. . . . But instead of reconciling the discordant features, scholars either ignored them or distorted the facts and features. (Singh 1995, 8)

Bisht (forthcoming) has also tried his hand at establishing "points of convergence" between the Harappans and the Ṛgveda. Like Rau and Singh, Bisht also pulls out extensive references from the Vedic texts that he feels could correspond to urban architectural features. He also draws attention to Mitra and Varuṇa in their structures containing a thousand pillars, as well as to a settlement or house with a hundred doors, a house with a thousand doors, a mansion with a thousand columns, a huge column supporting the firmament, a construction of six pillars, columns of copper, and a house raised in the sea. A house compared to a pond particularly catches his attention: "Does not the comparison of a house to a pond indicate that such tanks were sometimes alongside or within a building, the kind of which we see in the elaborate structure containing the Great Bath at Mohenjo-Daro" (421), as do the pillared structures, which "remind one of the large columnal hall in the citadel of Mohenjo-Daro" (420).

Bisht finds evidence of a tripartite settlement in a variety of terms such as *tridhātu śarman* 'triply defended dwelling' and *tripura,* which he thinks are good candidates for three separate divisions of an intricately fortified multi-dimensional settlement the like of which may be seen in the Harappan city of Dholavira. . . . Harappa is also emerging as a multi-divisioned city. . . . Kalibangan too seems to be having three divisions" (413). This interpretation can be kept in mind when we encounter Parpola's interpretations of the word *tripura* in the next chapter. Moreover, Bisht's *purs* are far more sturdy and sophisticated than Rau's, being *dṛḍhā* 'solid'; *dṛṅhitā*, 'strengthened'; *adhṛṣṭā* 'impregnable'; *aśmanmayi* 'made of stone'; *pṛthvī* 'extensive'; *mahī* 'spacious'; *āyasī* 'made of metal, metal-strong'; and *iṣa* 'affluent'. The *śatabhuji* 'hundred-armed' forts that Rau took to indicate concentricity are taken by Bisht as "having a hundred . . . bastions." Bisht makes a point, perhaps also with Wheeler in mind, of noting that the Aryans also owned *purs*; indeed, out of twenty-seven adjectives describing *purs*, "there occur as many as fifteen terms that qualify the Āryan *purs* in contrast to only eleven or twelve in favour of the non-Āryan ones" (410). The Aryans did not just destroy the *purs* of the Dasyus, they owned their own as well.

Bisht is well aware of the plethora of opinions proffered in interpretations of the Vedic landscape: "Diametrically opposite views have been expressed and rejected due to intrinsic contradictions, lack of coherence or consistency inherent in the approaches, or due to the appearance of fresh evidence" (392). Like Singh, he believes previous interpretations were predisposed to anticipating the Indo-Aryans to be "barbarian equestrians who, before entering India, roamed about in Central Asia and the Iranian Plateau . . . [and] thrived on stock-breeding and primitive farming" (392). He, too, finds that "the information gleaned from the *Ṛgveda* projects a picture of considerably civilized Aryans." They had "a variety of permanent settlements and fortified towns as well as monumental structures. They were advanced in agriculture, stock-breeding, manufacture of goods and long distance trade and commerce via roads, rivers, and seas" (393).

B. B. Lal (1997) is a little more cautious in denying the nomadic character of the Indo-Aryans: "Just as there were cities, towns and villages in the Harappan ensemble (as there are even today in any society) there were both rural and urban components in the Vedic times. Where then is the 'glaring disparity' between the cultural levels of the Harappan and Vedic societies?" (285). S. P. Gupta (1996) elaborates on this perspective:

> Once it becomes reasonably clear that the Vedas do contain enough material which shows that the authors of the hymns were fully aware of the cities, city life, long-distance overseas and overland trade, etc. . . . it becomes easier for us to appreciate the theory that the Indus-Saraswati and Vedic civilizations may have been just the two complementary elements of one and the same civilization. And this, it is important to note, is not a presupposition against the cattle-keeping image of the Vedic Aryans. After all, ancient civilizations had both the components, the village and the city, and numerically villages were many times more than the cities. In India presently there are around 6.5 lakhs of villages but hardly 600 towns and cities put together. . . . Plainly, if the Vedic literature reflects primarily the village life and not the urban life, it does not at all surprise us." (147)

Allowing the primarily nomadic life of the Vedic poets, the possibility of nomadic cultures coexisting with urban societies merits consideration. Witzel (1989) notes that the possibility of urban centers being known to the Indo-Aryans "cannot simply be dismissed," since, although "there is no mention of towns in the Vedic texts . . . this may be due to the cultural tendency of the Brahmins who . . . could preserve their ritual purity better in a village than in a busy town" (245).

Potentially significant evidence against the claim that the Indo-Aryans knew no cities is that archaeology is revealing settlements and small urban centers in the Punjab even in the Post-Harappan period, precisely where and when few question that the Aryans were present:

> Sites such as Harappa continued to be inhabited and are still important cities today. . . . Late and post-Harappan settlements are known from surveys in the region of Cholistan, . . . the upper Ganga-Yamuna Doab, . . . and Gujarat. In the Indus Valley itself, post-Harappan settlement patterns are obscure, except for the important sites of Pirak. . . . This may be because the sites were along the newly-stabilized river systems and lie beneath modern villages and towns that flourish along the same rivers. (Kenoyer 1991b, 30)

As will be discussed in the next chapter, the excavator of Pirac, situated in the Indus Valley and dated between 1700 and 700 B.C.E. exactly where and when the Indo-Aryans were present in the subcontinent, considers the site a town of some size with elaborate architecture. Moreover, it revealed a more intense level of irrigation and cultivation than existed in the third millennium B.C.E. How does this evidence fit with the pastoral, nonurban horizens of the Indo-Aryans? The following is also noteworthy:

> Although the overall socio-economic organization changed, continuities in technology, subsistence practices, settlement organization and some regional symbols show that the indigenous population was not displaced by hordes of Indo-Aryan speaking people. . . . For many years, the "invasions" or "migrations" of these Indo-Aryan speaking Vedic/Aryan tribes explained the decline of the Indus civilization and the second rise of urbanization in the Ganga-Yamuna valley. . . . This was based on simplistic models of culture change and an uncritical reading of the Vedic texts. Current evidence does not support a pre- or proto-historic Indo-Aryan invasion of southern Asia. . . . Instead, there was an overlap between Late Harappan and post-Harappan communities . . . with no biological evidence for major new populations. (Kennoyer 1991b, 30)

So the hymns are not necessarily sparse in urban references because of ignorance or unfamiliarity with large settlements and urban centers. This evidence will be discussed further in chapter 11.

Regarding the pastoral nature of the Indo-Aryans, Chakrabarti (1986) adds a further observation that "the inconvenient references to agriculture in the Rigveda are treated as later additions. The scholars who do this forget that effective agriculture is very old in the subcontinent, and surely no text supposedly dating from 1500 B.C. could depict a predominantly pastoral society anywhere in the subcontinent. Something must be wrong with the general understanding of this text" (Chakrabarti 1986, 76). In other words, if the Indo-Aryans were pastoralists, they must have always coexisted with agriculturists in India since agriculture predates the assumed date for their arrival by millennia. There could never have been a purely pastoral economic culture.

In fact, the often held assumption that the undivided Indo-Europeans, at least, were pastoralists has been reconsidered by Indo-Europeanists. This assumption was stimulated both by the belief that the Indo-Europeans were nomadic hordes that alighted all over Eurasia, and the fact that agricultural terms seem to be somewhat confined to the European side of the family. Mallory (1997) points out the this belief meant that the Indo-Iranians lost their original Indo-European agricultural vocabulary but preserved a pastoralist one. Or it meant tht the Indo-Europeans themselves were pastoralists and that agriculture was a later development, or encounter, by the western Indo-Europeans after the Indo-Iranians, who preserved the old Indo-European pastoralist lifestyle, had departed from the common home. Or it meant that the homeland contained a mixed economy in its western parts and a primarily pastoral one in its eastern areas.

Diebold (1992), however, has reconstructed a system of settled agriculture for the original Indo-Europeans in what he terms "Indoeuropa." Mallory (1997) agrees that there is solid evidence in both European and Asiatic stocks for Proto-Indo-European cereals, as well as the agricultural terminology required to process them. He notes that "while the economic emphasis of the immediate ancestors of the Indo-Iranians may have been towards pastoralism there is good evidence that they too are derived from a mixed agricultural population" (236–237) There are a variety of reasons to reconsider the view that the character of the Indo-Aryans was purely pastoral.

While most South Asian archaeologists, in interviews and publications, seemed quite open to the possibility that the world of the Ṛgveda could have coexisted with and preceded that of Harappa, others object on archaeological grounds. In her critique of an Indigenous Aryan book, Ratnagar (1996b) does not attempt to refute the Vedic/Harappan correlation but does point out that the few pre-Harappan sites that have been excavated display signs of only rudimentary technology and humble material culture: "We ask how the fast horse-drawn chariot of the Rgveda could have been made at any of the 4th millennium B.C.E. sites, without the metal saws, adzes and chisels that make accurate carpentry" (75). Whereas the Ṛgveda is often considered too humble, materially, to be associated with the Harappan civilization, it is here considered too sophisticated for the Pre-Harappan culture.

This point warrants attention, although, in my opinion, one should be cautious in attempting to connect the material from the Vedic hymns with the archaeological record. As Elizarenkova (1992) notes, "either one comes to know things due to archaeological findings and in this case their names and purpose may remain unknown, or only the names of the things are known from the texts, but the things themselves, as well as their purpose, are unknown" (129). Even if an archaeology of the Veda must be attempted, there are limitations in drawing far-reaching conclusions from *argumentum ex silentio* in the archaeological record. Quite apart from not unearthing any saws, adzes, and chisels for the making of chariots, we should not forget that archaeology has not unearthed the actual chariot itself, either, until at least a full millennium after it was known to have existed on the subcontinent. Besides, archaeology has a tendency to suddenly unearth material that completely subverts previously held assumptions. Mehrgarh is the prime example. Prior to its discovery, scholars were inclined to believe that agriculture and urbanization were both diffused from West Asia. Mehrgarh, an agricultural settlement dating back to the seventh millennium B.C.E., dramatically demonstrated that "the theoretical models used to interpret the prehistory of Southern Asia must be completely reappraised" (Jarrige and Meadow 1980, 133).

Most dramatically, Mehrgarh threw the date for evidence of agriculture back *two entire millennia*. This clearly underscores the danger of establishing theories predicated on *argumentum ex silentio* in the archaeological record. Mehrgarh also undermined previous assumptions that urbanization and agriculture were diffused from the centers of civilization to the west of the subcontinent. The site also set the stage for the indigenous development of complex cultural patterns that culminated in the great cities of the Indus Valley: "The origins of the Indus urban society can be traced to the socio-economic interaction systems and settlement patterns of the indigenous village cultures of the alluvial plain and piedmont. More importantly, the factors leading to this transformation appear to be autochthonous and not derived from direct stimulus or diffusion from West or Central Asia" (Kenoyer 1991b, 11).

This continuum of the archaeological record stretches from the seventh millennium B.C.E. right down through the Early, Mature, Late, and Post-Harappan periods. Of course, as in any cultural area over the course of time, there are regional variations and transformations, but no sudden interruptions or abrupt innovations that might alert archaeologists to an intrusive ethnic group: "There were no invasions from central or western South Asia. Rather there were several internal cultural adjustments reflecting altered ecological, social and economic conditions affecting northwestern and north-central South Asia" (Shaffer 1986, 230). More than everything else, this lack of cultural discontinuity has caused an ever-increasing number of South Asian archaeologists to question: *Where are the supposedly invading Aryans in the archaeological record?* Since this invisibility is the single most significant factor that has caused the Indigenous Aryan position to jettison the commonly held theories of philologers and become so widespread in India in recent years, it to this that we must turn in the next chapters.

Conclusion

A primary reason that Indian archaeologists have become disillusioned with the whole enterprise of the Indo-Aryans is because they have been offered, and initially accepted, a progression of theories attempting to archaeologically locate the Indo-Aryans on the grounds of the philological axiom that their nature was intrusive. These theories have successively proved to be wrong or questionable. The course of scholarship in the last century has evolved from images of blond, soma-belching, Germanic supermen "riding their chariots, hooting and tooting their trumpets" as they trampled down the inferior aboriginal Dāsa (Singh 1995, 56),[58] through speakers of an Indo-Aryan language destroying the highly advanced civilization of the superior Dāsa; to discrete trickles of Indo-Aryan speakers possibly coexisting in a neighborly fashion in the cities of the Indus Valley with the hospitable Dāsa. As a result many archaeologists have become frustrated with the whole Aryan-locating enterprise and jettisoned the linguistic claims altogether. Failure to find any tangible evidence whatsoever of the Aryans has resulted in the present trend among many South Asian archaeologists, which is toward considering the indigenousness of both the Indo-Aryans and the Dāsa, period. As we saw in the greater Indo-European problem among Western scholars, in India, too, there is a chasm between many archaeologists and Western historical linguists, particularly since there are so few historical linguists in India itself and so little contact with linguistic theories originating in the West. Accordingly, the debate in India has been primarily conducted among archaeologists, with a growing number rejecting the whole idea of anything but indigenous origins for the various developments of the protohistoric archaeological record.

Vedic philology, however, being more readily at hand, cannot be jettisoned so easily and a good number of South Asian archaeologists are quite proficient in, if not Vedic, then at least classical Sanskrit (which may be a disqualification from the perspective of Vedicists since words in the classical period may not have the same meanings as in the Vedic period). Accordingly, the relationship between the Vedic Aryans and the ruins of the Indus Valley has been negotiated in a variety of ways. Both Wilhelm Rau and Bisht, for example, and especially Singh have taken certain liberties according to their particular viewpoints in extracting a picture of Vedic society from the hymns and attempting to correlate it with the archaeological record. There is little doubt that predispositions flavor the images that both have attempted to create. There is also a question of boundaries. Who is deemed authorized to make interpretations, and by whom? I will only note in this regard that Rau immediately introduces his research with a caveat that "as a philologist, I lack the archaeological knowledge to tackle the problem in all its aspects" and concludes that, since "Sir Mortimer's theory is sustained by no literary evidence, it must rest entirely on archaeological facts and their interpretations." He is speaking as a Vedicist. Bisht, although clearly proficient in Sanskrit, is trained as an archaeologist, not a philologist. He has taken it upon himself to visit the Vedic texts as an archaeologist who has excavated extensively in the Indus Valley, particularly in Dholavira, and is looking for descriptions of material culture that will add meaning to the bricks and pots of his excavations. Singh is a layman. These backgrounds are relevant to issues of authority and jurisdiction in the interpretation of evidence from differing disciplines. Must we accept all opinions as equally valid? To what extent should scholars not specialized in a particular field be given consideration when they critique or challenge the opinion of specialists in that area?

In conclusion, our options, then, are to locate the Indo-Aryans either before, during, or after the Indus Valley. The references to the full-flowing Sarasvatī make the strongest suggestion that the Indo-Aryans could have been present in the Mature Harappan period (although the reference to the confluence of the Sutlej and Beās must also be taken into account). Even allowing the Sarasvatī evidence, it does not, of course, prove that they were not immigrants, albeit earlier than has been assumed, nor that they were the dominant presence—only the script can determine that. The so-called fire altars are dubious as indicators of an Indo-Aryan presence, but as evidence they are as strong or as weak as anything that has been brought forward to identify them in their overland trek through central Asia. This should be borne in mind as the central Asian material is reviewed in the next chapter. The lack of urban references in the Vedic texts may be a peculiarity of these texts since settlements continued in the post-Harappan period and Pirak, at least, was a town of some size and sophistication.

The chariot is also a dubious indicator of Indo-Aryan origins since it seems too precarious to draw overly far-reaching conclusions about such a perishable item based on argumentum ex silentio in the archaeological record. The horse, by contrast, to my mind remains a serious obstacle to the Indigenous position, although it has always been a rare, imported item and also unlikely to provide much evidence in the archaeological record. Nonetheless, the burden of proof lies with those claiming that the horse (and chariot) were utilized in the Indus Valley, which would need to be the case if one is to argue for a Vedic presence there. Unlike chariots, which leave little archaeological residue unless decorated with metal parts (the earliest evidence of the spoked-wheel chariot in the Sintashta cemetery can only be inferred from soil discoloration), horse bones are no more degradable than other animal bones, which have been found in plenty.

Of course, there are social considerations: if horses weren't eaten, they are far less likely to show up in settlements; and if they weren't buried with the deceased, they would not show up in cemeteries. Nonetheless, the horse evidence will continue to haunt the Indigenous position. As an aside, given the insistence from the Migrationist side that evidence of this animal must accompany any identification of the Indo-Aryans in the archaeological record, one can be sure that if unambiguous evidence of the horse does surface in a reliable Mature Harappan context, there will be an uproar on the subcontinent. Until such evidence is produced, however, attempts to correlate the Vedic Aryans with the ruins of the Indus Valley will have to engage in a certain amount of special pleading.

Ultimately, the answer to the linguistic identity of the Indus Valley lies in our hands, but it has yet to yield its secret. If the Indus script turns out to represent an Indo-Aryan language, then I submit that most of the linguistic argument pertaining to the origins of the Indo-Aryans, and, indeed, the proto-Indo-Europeans over the last two centuries must be, if not completely jettisoned as some would have it, then throughly reevaluated. An Indo-Aryan script would also suggest that these speakers were the dominant linguistic entity in the subcontinent at this point in time and makes a far stronger case for the possibility of Dravidian/Munda and or "language x" (y or z) intruding on an ancient Indo-Aryan-speaking area rather than vice versa. I have attempted to thoroughly outline the assumptions underpinning the linguistic evidence in the previous chapters, and much of it will be instantly subverted if the script reveals an Indo-Aryan language dominating the Northwest of the subcontinent at such an early date.

Indeed, an Indo-Aryan language during this period would have implications and corollaries for the entire Indo-European homeland problem, if the script does indeed go back to 3500 B.C.E., since most Indo-Europeanists hold that the Indo-Europeans were still undivided until sometime between 4500–2500. In other words, an Indo-Aryan script on the subcontinent at a time frame when the Indo-Europeans were still more or less undivided would constitute a solid argument for anyone choosing to locate the Indo-

European homeland in India. And the assignment of a 1200 or 1500 B.C.E. date for the Ṛgveda, as will be discussed in chapter 12, will merit the skepticism that Indigenous Aryanists have generally directed to such efforts, as would the skepticism some scholars have directed toward attempts at dating Proto-Indo-European.

On the other hand, if the script turns out to be any language other than Indo-Aryan, then the Indigenous case no longer merits much further serious scholarly consideration (although there could still have been Indo-Aryan pastoralists interacting with these urban centers from very ancient times, even if the dominant language of the latter turned out to be non-Indo-Aryan). But the Indigenous case, at least to my mind, will be closed. No doubt, diehards on both sides will attempt to reconfigure things to salvage their respective points of view if the language revealed by the script confounds their expectations: if it turns out to be Indo-Aryan, Migrationists will likely suddenly find reason to suppose that the migration must have taken place two millennia earlier than had previously been thought. If it turns out to be other than Indo-Aryan, Indigenists will likely demote their Indo-Aryans to a dominated or colonized position in the Indus Valley (although I doubt that this is the type of secondary status for the Indo-Aryans that will be of interest to most Indigenists). At that point both positions become even more interesting subjects for historiographical and sociological analysis in my estimation. In particular, if the script turns out to be Indo-Aryan, and especially if the incisions on the shards from the Ravi phase of 3500 B.C.E. are proto-Indus writings that do incorporate the same language, the Indo-European homeland locating enterprise is likely to accrue even more scorn from the cynics than it has hitherto—Edmund Leach's comments at the beginning of this chapter will take on a new significance. Whatever language is contained in the script, in my opinion, it would be unwise for decipherers to eliminate either Sanskrit, Dravidian, or Munda as possible candidates.

In the meantime, for as long as the script remains resistant to decipherment, possibly the path of least resistance from a philological perspective would be to suggest that the Indo-Aryans who composed the Vedic hymns were primarily pastoralists. One has to work rather hard to fit the landscape of the Ṛgveda into the ruins of the Indus Valley civilization. This does not preclude the possibility that the Indo-Aryans might have interacted with the urban residents of the Indus Valley, whatever language they spoke. Of relevance here is Possehl's observation (1977) of the "extraordinary 'empty spaces' between the Harappan settlement clusters," as well as "the isolated context for a number of individual sites" (546). He proposes that "pastoral nomads, or other highly mobile (itinerant) occupational specialists filled in the interstices," since such spaces are unlikely to have been unoccupied. He goes so far as to suggest that "pastoralists formed the bulk of the population during Harappan times since there do not seem to be any settled village farming communities there" (547). Pastoralists and farmers coexisted "not . . . as isolated from one another, but as complementary subsystems: two aspects of an integrated whole. One relied on the intensive exploitation of plants and arable land, the other on the extensive exploitation of animals and pastures" (547). Moreover, "the presence of pastoralists makes very good sense if we see them as the mobile population which bridged the gap between settlements as the carriers of information, as the transporters of goods, as the population through which the Harappan Civilization achieved its remarkable degree of integration" (548). Bridget Allchin (1977) produces case studies to demonstrate how "nomadic herdsmen form an important element of rural life in India and Pakistan today, including the old province of Harappan culture." She adds that "there is every reason to suppose that they did so in Harappan times, and that they played an important part in the economy and organization of the Harappan world" (139).

As a final note, even if the composers of the Vedic hymns did not live primarily in the cities of the Indus Valley, this fact in and of itself does not mean that the Harappans could not have contained Indo-Aryan speakers: a language family can obviously encompass urban dwellers as well as village dwellers, just as we see in numerous places today. It is important to stress in this regard that *anyone promoting Dravidian or Munda as the language of the Indus Valley will anyway have to accept an identical situation*: urban Dravidian or Munda speakers coexisting with nonurban tribal Dravidian or Munda speakers (some of which have remained tribal to this day). The southern Dravidian culture and eastern Munda culture were radically different from that of the Indus Valley in the third millennium B.C.E., so if hypothetical urbanized Harappan Dravidians or Mundas could have coexisted on the subcontinent with their nonurbanized fellow language speakers to the south or east, then Indo-Aryan speakers could have done likewise. Therefore, even if the Ṛgveda does not elaborately describe the flourishing cities of the Indus, there is no way to discount the possibility that it could still have been the product of an Indo-Aryan pastoral society that coexisted with an Indo-Aryan urban one. Moreover the Indus Valley Civilization may very well have been multi-lingual.

As for the possibility of the Vedic landscape preceding the Indus one, here, again, if we are prepared to overlook the horse and chariot lacuna in the archaeological record, this is a chronological question that hinges on the date of the Veda. This will be thoroughly discussed in chapter 12. For the present purposes, for all of the reasons outlined here, it seems fair to conclude that the archaeological evidence in the Indus Valley Civilization, whatever might have been the language of its residents, has not been able to resolve this debate. What might accomplish this is clear archaeological evidence of the Indo-Aryan migration across central Asia and into India. So it is to this evidence that we must now turn.

10

Aryans in the Archaeological Record

The Evidence outside the Subcontinent

The previous chapters have outlined the assumptions underlying the linguistic evidence that is generally accepted as decisive in eliminating South Asia as a potential origin for the Indo-European languages and holding that the Indo-Aryan languages must have entered the subcontinent from the outside. The question has been raised regarding the extent to which the various linguistic methods are capable of determining whether the language flow of Indo-European immediately after the dissolution of the protolanguage was from north to south or south to north, or from west to east or vice versa. And the observation has been made that while the Vedic texts themselves can be used to demonstrate an escalating movement into the eastern and southern parts of India, they do not provide unambiguous evidence for a movement into the Northwest itself.

The other major discipline that has been an indispensable part of the quest for the Indo-Europeans is, of course, archaeology. While Nichols's linguistic model could be adopted or adapted somewhat to account for an Indo-European language spread from an eastern point of origin, there is no archaeological evidence that can be readily invoked to substantiate it. Archaeologists have not found any outgoing material culture correlatable with the Indo-Europeans that can be traced as flowing from the east to the west in a chronologically and geographically acceptable fashion. Accordingly, the discussion in this section must be restricted to examining the proposals of those scholars who have attempted to use the archaeological record to trace the incoming migrations of the Indo-Aryans. This limitation is not likely to escape the attention of the detractors of the Indigenous Aryan position: "The archaeological lack of evidence for inward migration often cited by proponents of the 'Out-of-India' hypothesis would have to be balanced with the lack of archaeological evidence for the presumably much more massive and prolonged outward migration required under this hypothesis" (Hock 1999a 16).

Although it is debatable whether an outward migration would need to be much more massive than an inward one, the point holds good. Indeed, as we have seen, Nichols's homeland was a priori subjected to this criticism before her thesis had even been published. A parallel archaeological lacuna has been one of the principal objections raised against the central Anatolian homeland. As Gamkrelidze and Ivanov (1983a) themselves hasten to point out in anticipation of their detractors' reactions: "It should be noted at the outset that the original area of distribution for the Proto-Indo-European language in the fourth–fifth millennia B.C. does not have an archaeological culture which might be identified in any explicit way with Proto-Indo-European" (35). As we have seen, Renfrew, (1987) an archaeologist defending more or less adjacent geographic contours as these linguists, does provide a material culture, but one in a significantly different temporal bracket. However, in so doing, he completely undermines the traditional criteria used in searching for the Indo-Europeans in the archaeological record. Since his Proto-Indo-European is a sedentary agriculturist to be traced paleobotanically via the spread of agriculture, he bypasses the traditionally almost exclusive focus on grave goods and pottery styles. This raises the first very obvious and rather crucial issue: What exactly is it that we are looking for in the archaeological record that might correspond to the speakers of an Indo-European language? This chapter will examine this issue from the perspective of the assumed overland routes of the Indo-Aryans on their way to the subcontinent.

Identifying Aryans

Nowadays all careful scholars begin their speculations regarding the linguistic identification of an archaeological culture with preambles stressing the need to be cautious about correlating material culture with linguistic groups. Lyonnet (1994), for example, notes that "it may be in vain to try and identify the Indo-Aryans," since "language, ethnic identity and culture are individual components that can be combined in many different ways, and nothing allows us to state that, knowing language x and culture x, we are dealing with ethnic group x" (425). At least on a theoretical level (if not always in practice), it is by now universally acknowledged that one material culture may incorporate more than one language group, and one language group may encompass more than one distinct material culture. The spread of a material culture, then, need not at all correspond to the spread of a language group, nor need a material innovation or development within a material culture reflect the intrusion of a new language group (although one can also certainly not categorically deny the possibility that it may in individual cases).

Moreover, postmodern theoretical considerations have not bypassed archaeology. Decisions regarding how to interpret the archaeological record are no longer seen as value-free and neutral: "It may be taken as a sign of the increasing theoretical maturity of the discipline of archaeology that it is beginning to see itself as a product of the forces of history. . . . there has been a shift from an internal understanding of archaeology as an objective and value-free practice towards a broader understanding that situates archaeology in its social and political context" (Kristiansen 1996, 139). Of particular relevance to this chapter, the adoption of migrationism as an acceptable model to account for innovations in the archaeological record has enjoyed such a checkered history among archaeologists that theoreticians in the discipline have explored social contexts and psychological paradigms to explain its rise and fall. From the times and profound influence of preeminent archaeologists such as Kossina and Childe, innovations in the archaeological record have typically been interpreted as evidence of some kind of a migration or intrusion of new peoples. Allowing some variations distinguishing Continental and American schools, this mode of interpretation remained in vogue until the 1960s, when an antimigrational mode of archaeological interpretation started to gain the upper hand. This inturn remained dominant until the late 1980s, when migrationism again began to make something of a comeback in some quarters with appeals to not throw out "the baby with the bath water" (Anthony 1990, 895).

The existence of such quasi-Foucaultian paradigm shifts prompted a recent publication on the subject containing articles focusing more on the interpreters of archaeological data rather than on the data itself (Chapman and Hamerow 1997). Concerns focused on "the intersection of the subjective, the inter-subjective and the objective insofar as it relates to the use and misuse of invasions and migrations to constitute explanatory models in 20th century prehistory" (Chapman 1997, 11). In his introduction to the volume, Chapman muses on the formative impression that the impact (or absence) of real-life modern migrations in the life experience of the archaeologist might have on his or her interpretations:

> There are several generations of archaeologists living in Europe whose life experiences bore the often devastating effects of invasions and migrations in two World Wars and their aftermaths. It is hard to resist the notion that these personal experiences did have an effect on the models of explanation which they proposed. . . . It is not a coincidence, I believe, that the "Retreat from Migrationism" arose precisely in countries not invaded in either world war—in Britain, America and parts of Scandinavia. . . . I suggest . . . that the personal impact of migrations and invasions on archaeologists has been a factor much underestimated in past "explanation" of the changing modes of archaeological explanation. I would like to suggest that there is a yet largely untapped reservoir of information and insight about the writing of archaeological texts relating to the subjective experiences of scholars." (18)

Along the same lines, critics such as Champion (1990) and Megaw and Megaw (1992) have also noted that the fortunes of migrationism can be correlated with the prevailing political or intellectual milieu of the time. Anthony (1997), supporting the return of migrational modes of interpretation back into "semi-respectability" in the late 1980s, acknowledges that "the rise, fall and recovery of migration models is partly embedded in paradigm shifts in archaeological theory, with all the socio-political factors of academic competition that are entailed." He notes that it is no accident that migrations and invasions as forms of cultural change are again in vogue after two decades of neglect: "The insistent clamour of the homeless, the migrant and the refugee is rarely still and we cannot but face its consequences on an academic as well as a human level" (21).

Nonetheless, with due precaution, it is the material culture of migrants that can provide the only chance of physically identifying the Indo-Aryans who would otherwise simply remain an abstract linguistic entity. Even in terms of material culture, the prospects are restricted: physical anthropology, a method upon which Aryan seekers once pinned high hopes, is currently no longer deferred to by specialists, since skeletal remains "do not sort into 'types' along biological, linguistic or cultural lines." Accordingly, "the quest for the elusive Aryans lies far outside the agenda of present-day skeletal biologists, who acknowledge the fall of the biological race concept in their discipline. Racial palaeontology went defunct in the middle part of this century." This forces us to confront the crucial issue: "How could one recognize an Aryan, living or dead, when the biological criteria for Aryanness are non-existent?" (Kennedy 1995, 61).[1] What exactly is it that we are looking for in our quest to identify Indo-Aryans in the archaeological record?

Our primary and only literary sources in this regard (in addition to the cultural traits assigned to the Indo-Europeans by comparative reconstructions) are the Veda and the Avesta. However, while Lyonnet (1994), for example, acknowledges that "both archaeologists and linguists have made attempts to find [the Indo-Aryans and Iranians] in Central Asia on the basis of both the precisions of the *Ṛgveda* and the *Avesta*, and archaeological data," she echoes the opinion of most archaeologists that none of these attempts "are entirely satisfactory either chronologically, linguistically or archaeologically" (425). Nonetheless, she provides a list of material characteristics corresponding to a fairly typical version of the reconstructed material culture of the Aryans. Since this list still seems representative of the primary features archaeologists and historians have in mind when looking for telltale signs of the Indo-Aryans (Mallory 1989; Parpola 1994), it seems useful to reproduce it here. According to Lyonnet (1994, 425), the literary sources in the Ṛgveda provide the following information that could potentially be translated into hard evidence retrievable from the archaeological record:

- The Aryans are intruders, pastoralists also practicing agriculture;
- The Aryans conquer the Dāsas, the local wealthy dark-skinned population who live in or near a mountainous area, in forts that might be circular with a triple surrounding wall; this conquest is violent, implying destructions by fire, and involving an elite of warriors on horse-drawn chariots;
- The Aryans practice the fire cult and the sacrifice of animals (among these is the horse sacrifice, very rare and highly prized) and even of human beings;
- They encourage cremation;
- They press soma."

From this list, the intrusiveness of the Aryans (which is *not* ostensibly evidenced in the texts, as I have noted) is the issue being debated and is not being accepted as a priori in this discussion. The rationale behind the skin color of the Dāsas has been outlined in chapter 3 and can be legitimately ignored. Their residence in circular forts with triple walls is an interesting interpretational proposal by Parpola, but one that will be problematized later and need not compel us at this point.

In terms of a picture that most scholars would accept, we are therefore left with an Indo-Aryan cultural group of pastoralists who practiced agriculture, contained an elite warrior group, used chariots, and knew the domesticated horse. Their religion was centered on fire sacrifices, and they practiced cremation (as well as other burial practices). Obviously, such identification does not mean that all people who were pastoralists, or practiced agriculture, or had a martial elite who used chariots, or even practiced fire sacrifices were Indo-Aryans, since such characteristics were widespread in many cultures of the ancient world at various points in history, but they are typically accepted as circumscribing the Indo-Aryan quest somewhat. And they are the best indicators to which we can lay reasonable claim.

Several other assumptions need to be laid out clearly before proceeding any further. The first is temporal and will be critiqued fully in chapter 12. For the present purposes, I will simply outline the logic underlying the assignment of dates commonly accepted as corresponding to the Indo-European language dispersals from the unified Proto-Indo-European stock. I know of no objections to the terminus ante quem of Indo-Aryan as a separate linguistic entity. The Mittani treaties have been dated to about 1500 B.C.E. (as has the Ṛgveda for reasons that will be examined later). Since almost all authorities agree that the language of the treatise is specifically Indo-Aryan, then this language was distinct from other Indo-European languages, including Iranian, by this time at the latest.

The terminus a quo for Proto-Indo-European as a unified entity is more problematic. For now, suffice it to say that many scholars have accepted the wheeled vehicle and related items as temporally most diagnostic (since the horse evidence has been subject to so many objections). The rationale here, briefly, is that the cognate terms for the wheeled vehicle indicate that this item was known to the undivided Indo-Europeans. Since the first evidence of wheeled vehicles in the archaeological record occurs at the turn of, and throughout, the fourth millennium B.C.E., the first assumption is that the wheel was therefore actually invented at around this time, and the second is that the dispersal of the various languages must have occurred after this point. The time frame involved in the development of the Indo-Aryans as a distinct entity, then, is generally accepted as being between 4000 and 1500 B.C.E. once other diagnostic items such as 'plows', 'yoke', 'wool', and 'silver' are factored in using the same logic outlined above.

Having established a time frame of two and a half millennia or so, the next step for most archaeologists interested in this problem is to commit to a particular geographic route. Again, and at the risk of repetition, all of this would make much less sense without the a priori methodological imperative that "*since Indo-Iranian languages are assumed (by linguists) to have been brought into South Asia by migrants*, we must begin by examining the archaeological record for evidence of migrations, and then justify the link between these and the spread of the Indo-Iranian languages" (Erdosy 1995a, 9; my italics). I hope the preceding chapters have given the reader a clearer idea of the various rationales underpinning these 'linguistic assumptions'. Clearly, those who find the linguistic premises of the migration theory questionable are unlikely to be swayed by the archaeological details that are predicated upon such foundational linguistic assumptions. At the very least, those unconvinced by the linguistic evidence are likely to expect some reasonably compelling degree of archaeological evidence.

We can immediately note that there is no more consensus regarding the identification of the Indo-Iranians in the archaeological record than regarding that of the Indo-Europeans in general. Moreover, until relatively recent work by primarily Russian archaeologists, the identification of the Indo-Iranians has received much less scholarly attention than that of the western Indo-Europeans for reasons that should be obvious from chapter 1; once it had been determined that the homeland of the Indo-Europeans could not have stretched too far east of the Caspian Sea, the trajectory of the Indo-Iranians was, if not superfluous, then of secondary importance to most western scholars. Nonetheless, since all scholars, whatever position they might hold on the ultimate homeland of the Indo-Europeans, accept that the Indo-Aryans, at least, entered India from the West, almost all who have attempted to trace the itinerary of the Indo-Aryans do so by tracing the latter's itinerary from the vicinity of some part of the Caspian Sea.

There are two obvious routes to the Indian subcontinent from the Caspian Sea area: a northern route from the northeast of the Caspian Sea through the steppes of central Asia and down through Afghanistan and into India; and a southern route from the southeast of the Caspian Sea through the deserts and plains of northern Iran and into Afghanistan. The two routes have diametrically differing archaeological cultures. Both have been identified with the Indo-Aryans in a variety of ways by different scholars, and both have received extensive criticisms from promoters of different routes. The principal material involved will be examined in the following sections. I request the nonarchaeologists to bear with the sometimes tedious details of relevant archaeological minutiae, which have been minimized and simplified as far as possible; even a minimally comprehensive study of the Indo-Aryans must unavoidably plow through at least the basic archaeological material at stake.

The Northern Route

Vedic Burial and Funerary Practices

The northern route is based primarily on the evidence of grave sites. These graves contain traces of material culture that are perceived as corresponding to items of Indo-Aryan culture as understood from Vedic texts. The first task, then, is to glean any information pertaining to burials that is available in these texts. Ṛgveda 7.89 speaks of going to the 'house of clay' *mṛnmáyam gṛhám* (which has been correlated with the kurgan burials); 10.18.10–13 also clearly speaks of burial in the earth. However, some scholars see signs of cremation a few hymns earlier (10.16.1–6) were Agni is requested not to fully consume the body but to send the deceased to the forefathers after he had been fully cooked.

The Śatapatha Brāhmāṇa (8.1.1 ff.) gives a variety of recomendations pertaining to the appropriate geographic location for burial (such as near waters flowing in a southeasterly direction). It prescribes the construction of tombs with four corners and the size of a man (leaving no room for another). For a Kshatriya, the sepulchral mound should be as high as a man with arms upstretched; for a Brahmana, it should reach up to the mouth; for a woman, up to the hips; for a Vaisya, up to the hips; and for a Shudra, up to the knee (having said all this, the text then states that one should rather make the tomb so that it reaches below the knee, underlining the previous injunction that this would thereby leave no room for another—multiple burials seem to be clearly discouraged in this text). The text continues to say that some bank up the site after covering the mound. It is then enclosed by means of stones. Datta (1936), who has compiled all the references to burial practices in the earliest Vedic texts, notes that, in contrast to this description, the later Asvālayana Gṛhya Sūtra describes how the body is burned, and the bones subsequently gathered and placed into lid-covered urns (with special markings for men but not for women), so cremation and urn burials seem to be practiced in this later period.

Since the Agni hymn just mentioned is generally considered to be a later hymn, it is possible that burial was the older practice, which continued in later times along with crematory practices (although one must be wary of basing far-reaching conclusions on *argumenti ex silentio*). One could therefore argue that burial practices characterized the Indo-Iranians and Indo-Aryans in the earlier part of their trajectory, and that the practice of cremation developed as they neared the subcontinent. However, as Erdosy notes, cremations are rare in central Asia (being evidenced only in the cemeteries of southern Tajikistan), and, "on present evidence, cremations appear to have originated in the Indo-Iranian borderlands and spread northwest (and southeast) thence, against the postulated movements of Indo-Aryan speakers" (11). In short, Vedic burial practices leave us with too many possible options—burials, cremation, and postcremation urn burials—to be of much real use in identifying specific Aryan graves in the archaeological record to the exclusion of others.

The Pit Grave (Jamna) Culture and Related Cultures

I have already outlined how the Kurgan culture is particularly favored by some scholars, since the horse has been domesticated there since at least the fourth millennium B.C.E. by people practicing a pastoral economy. Wheeled carts are also known there since the third millennium B.C.E. I have noted Talageri's (and the Russian linguists') calling into question the assumption that the place of domestication of the horse must correspond to the original homeland of the Proto-Indo-Europeans; from their perspective, the horse could have been known to the undivided Proto-Indo-Europeans without they themselves being inhabitants of the locus of domestication, or personally being the domesticators. There has been a litany of objections to the Kurgan homeland theory, which have been touched upon throughout the previous chapters, but, as will be obvious by now, *Indigenous Aryanists are primarily interested in the history of the Indo-Aryans*; from their side, there have been very few critiques of the various homeland proposals of the pre-Indo-Aryan, undivided Proto-Indo-Europeans.

Talageri, an exception in this regard, has examined Gimbutas's Kurgan theory and rejected it using arguments similar to those of some of the scholars noted in chapter 1. He finds Gimbutas's assignment of Indo-European attributes to archaeological artifacts—such as construing a figure with a mace in his hand as a male thunder god divinity—far too generalized and vague to be meaningful. He also objects that the items Gimbutas has promoted as reconstructable Proto-Indo-European—the use of copper, vehicles, boats, and so on—are actually shared by many Old World cultures that were not Indo-European-speaking. He argues that the same could be said of some of the social and religious features brought forward—male dominance, sun worship, and so forth. For the most part, however, Indigenous Aryanists are not particularly impressed or concerned with the homeland speculations of their Western colleagues or with the trajectories of the other Indo-European languages. It is the Indo-Aryans who are of concern to them, and it is with the evidence concerning this side of the language family that they are prepared to debate.

In somewhat parallel fashion, apart from relatively recent work by Russian archaeologists and one or two other notable exceptions (e.g., Parpola), Western scholars have traditionally paid very little attention to the archaeological traces of the Indo-Aryans, focusing primarily, and sometimes exclusively, on the origins of European civilization. In a recent edited collection of her articles, Gimbutas, who has otherwise written prolifically on the Indo-Europeans, makes barely a passing reference to the Indo-Aryans. Her only comment is that "the point of origin for the Old Indic people . . . [is most probably] migrations of the so-called Tazabag'jab Bronze Age culture, kin to the proto-

Scythian Andronovo and timber-grave culture of the Eurasian Steppes . . . around the 15–14th centuries BC, the date which agrees with the destruction of the walled cities of the pre-Aryan civilization" (Gimbutas 1997, 14). Mallory (1975) notes that "archaeological solutions to the IE problem. . .have involved considerable concern with the cultural development of central and eastern Europe, possibly at the expense of analyzing the problem in terms of also explaining the Indo-Iranian migrations where archaeological evidence is still quite scarce" (344). He does, however, dedicate an adequate section to this group in his 1989 book and in a recent article, which will be discussed later. Renfrew (1987), was torn between two hypotheses for India that are diametrically opposed both temporally and culturally (A: a Neolithic agricultural incursion, which would make the Indus Valley Indo-Aryan; and B: the traditional Post-Harappan, Steppe invasion model); this simply underscores the problematic nature of identifying this language group in the archaeological record. (Since 1988, Renfrew has been in favor of the first of these options.)

The northern route typically commences with the Kurgan culture. This culture was initially identified by Childe (1926), who believed that the south Russian steppes "correspond admirably to the character of the Aryan cradle as deduced by linguistic palaeontology. . . . The remains in question are derived almost exclusively from graves containing contracted skeletons . . . surmounted by a mound or *kurgan*" (183). More recently, Gimbutas has been the principal advocate of this position. This view has received plenty of criticisms, which were outlined in chapter 1 and can be encountered in the works of anyone promoting a different homeland. They need not detain us here, since our concern is specifically the Indo-Aryans. The Kurgan (Pit Grave) culture in the Pontic-Caspian steppe (3500–2800 B.C.E.) evolved into the Hut Grave culture (2800–

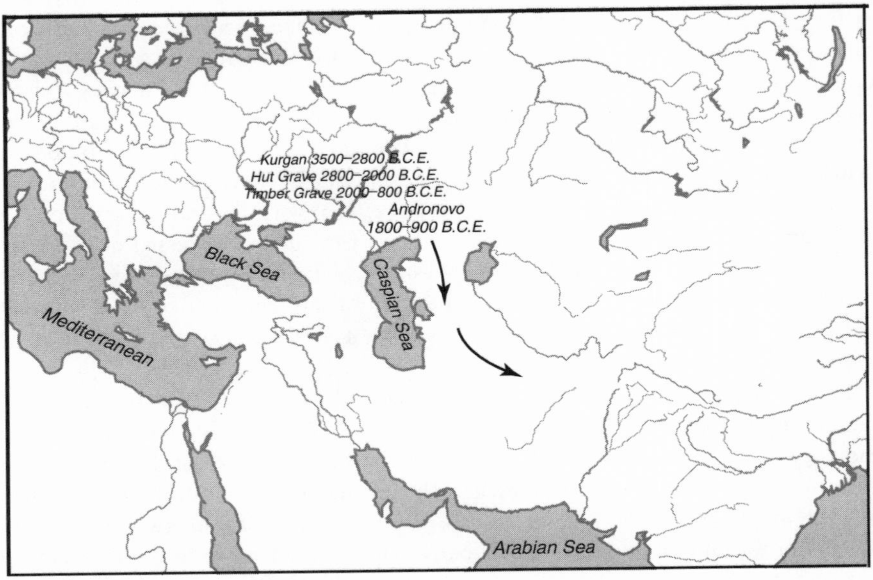

The northern route.

2000 B.C.E.), which in turn was succeeded by the Timber Grave (Srubnaya) culture (2000–800 B.C.E.) and the related Andronovo culture (1800–900 B.C.E.), which covered an enormous area from south of the Urals, across Kazakhstan, and into southern Siberia. (For a comprehensive classification and periodization of Androvo Cultural Sites see Kuzmina 1985.) The Andronovo culture is especially associated with the Iranians (or sometimes Indo-Iranians or Indo-Aryans) by Soviet archaeologists.[2] The identification is fortified by the fact that these cultures were the direct ancestors of the Iranian-speaking Scythians and Sakas in historical times and fit appropriately with Lyonnet's criteria.[3] As is evident from the names of these steppe cultures, graves are used to inter the dead, and the various cultures are to a great extent characterized by distinctive burial arrangements.[4] A variety of pottery types found in the graves is also of relevance.

Kuzmina (1994) narrows her criteria for identifying the Indo-Iranians down to one positive item (that of horse-drawn chariots) and two negative ones (they did not know temples, nor [following Rau 1974] the potter's wheel). This last criterion requires that "one has to look for a culture with hand-made pottery" when attempting to locate the original Indo-Iranians (404). As for chariots, Kuzmina argues that the grave goods from the cemeteries of the Sintashta-Petrovka culture in the southern Urals—of which the Sintashta cemetery is most notable—and in northern and central Kazakhstan show the earliest remains of this technology. As I have discussed, a chariot with spoked wheels dated to about 1700–1500 B.C.E. was found in the Sintashta cemetery, an early Andronovo burial in the Kazakh steppes of the southern Urals. This, coupled with a variety of weapons also found as grave goods, are associated with paraphernalia utilized by the Indo-Aryans (as evidenced by the Hurrian Mitanni texts on horsemanship and by the Ṛgveda).

Anthony (1995a) notes that horses were often sacrificed in the mortuary rites of the Sintashta culture, which he attempts to correlate with a hymn from the Ṛgveda wherein a horse is offered to the gods. He especially draws attention to one burial that contained the corpse of a decapitated victim whose head had been replaced by that of a horse. He finds reason to connect the fate of this individual with the Dadhyañc myth in the Ṛgveda (1.116). In brief, Dadhyañc was given a horse's head through which he could tell the Aśvins about Soma and the beheading of the sacrifice. This horse's head was then cut off by Indra and replaced with his own head. Although, the context of this myth has nothing to do with burials or funeral rites, the attempt to correlate this story with the contents of a solitary grave does gives some indication of the paucity of evidence available to archaeologists in the quest for the Indo-Aryans. In any event, Anthony (1998) suggests that the instance of this burial custom in the Andronov culture "might therefore be seen as something more significant than just the spread of a new burial custom. It might well represent the adoption of a larger Indo-Iranian identity, a necessary part of which was the Indo-Iranian language" (108).

One constantly finds archaeologists interpreting reliefs on seals or pottery, or even innocuous items of material culture, in terms of Vedic or Avestan religious narrative. Gening (1979), for example, also underscores the Indo-Iranian identification of the Sintashta graves, but, takes major liberties in assigning Vedic significance to the various features connected with the graves. As far as he is concerned, the fact that the horse skeletons found in the cemetery were always unharnessed reflects the unharnessed wanderings of the horse before the *aśvamedha*; the dog burials are related to motifs from the much later Mahābhārata and to the dog Saramā, which helps Indra find the cattle; the remains of straw and posts covering the grave conjure up the *barhis*, or sacred straw covering the sacrificial spot. Klejn argues against an Indo-Iranian or Indo-Aryan identification of the Andronov culture, but some of his correlations also display a questionable degree of interpretative liberty: the red-ocher powder covering the skeletons in the catacomb graves is connected with the red powder used in modern Indian weddings; the stone battle-ax found in many graves, with Indra's *vajra*; stone pestle grave goods, with soma-pressing implements; the concave walls of the graves, with the Vedic *vedi* sacrificial altar. Clearly, if one is so inclined, any innocuous grave detail can be connected with something from the gamut of Sanskrit literature and interpreted as proof of the Indo-Aryans.

According to Kuzmina, the fact that the essential equipment of the Indo-Aryan charioteers in the Mitanni kingdom and in India has no prototypes or analogies in either the Near East or Harappan India, but rather does show affinity with the items in the Sintashta-Petrovka burials mentioned earlier, "corroborates the hypothesis that locates the Indo-Iranian homeland on the Eurasian steppes between the Don and Kazakhstan in the 16th–17th centuries BC." She adds, appropriately, that "to dispel all doubts we have only to find warrior burials similar to those of the steppes in Mitanni and in the northern parts of the Indian subcontinent" (Kuzmina 1994, 410). These have yet to be found. Where Kuzmina finds Andronovo archaeological prototypes for the inferred Indo-Aryan cultural equipment known by the Mitanni Syria in the Near East and the Vedic speakers in India, Klejn points out that no actual trace of this Andronovo culture in the archaeology of either of these-Indo-Aryan cultures in the Near East or India has come to light. Klejn's critique of this Andronovo hypothesis raises important objections. While acknowledging the Iranian identification of the Andronovo culture, he finds it much too late for an Indo-Aryan identification, since the Andronovo culture "took shape in the 16th or 17th century B.C, whereas the Aryans already appeared in the Near East not later than the 15th to 16th century B.C." More important, "these [latter] regions contain nothing reminiscent of Timber-Frame Andronovo materials" (Klejn 1974, 58). This is an essential point, especially since, as we have seen, some scholars date the Indo-Aryan presence in the Near East to the 18th or 17th century B.C.E. How, then, could the Indo-Aryans have been represented in a completely different material culture in the steppes at more or less the same time? An Indo-Iranian affiliation of the graves is even more unrealistic, since the joint Indo-Iranian period would have been much earlier than the dates for the Andronovo period. Brentjes (1981), we can recall, pointed out the same objections with the Andronovo theory.

As for India, as Lyonnet (1993) notes: "To this day no traces of such stock breeders have been detected south of the Hindukush" (82). This is the most serious, and obvious, shortcoming of the Andronovo Indo-Aryan or Iranian identification. Francfort (1989) stresses this point: "Nothing allows us to dismiss the possibility that the Andronovians of Tazabagjab are the Indo-Iranians as much as the fact that they vanish on the fringes of sedentary Central Asia and do not appear as the ephemeral invaders of India at the feet of the Hindu Kush" (453). A later Iranian affiliation of the Andronovo culture is sometimes suggested, although, even here, Bosch-Gimpera (1973) objects that "there is nothing in Iran in the second millennium that is related to Andronovo, something which one would expect if the cradle of the Indo-Iranians were to be found in this territory"

(515). Such Archaeologists of the region are quite specific that "the notion of nomads from the north as the original Iranians is unsupported by the detailed archaeological sequence available" (Hiebert 1998, 153). As far as Sarianidi (1993b) is concerned, the Andronovo tribes "penetrated to a minimum extent . . . not exceeding the limits of normal contacts so natural for tribes with different economical structures, living in the borderlands of steppes and agricultural oases" (17).[5]

Beshkent and Vakhsh Culture

The Beshkent and Vakhsh culture, in southern Tajikistan, known so far only by its cemeteries, has also been related to the Indo-Iranians: "In the Beshkent cemeteries we have cremation rites; ritual hearths were built in the graves; and swastikas were used in marking the site. In the Vakhsh cemeteries funeral pyres were lit around the grave of a leader. A number of beliefs and cult practices that can be reconstructed from the materials found in the Vakhsh cemeteries recall common Indo-European rites and beliefs or specifically Indo-Iranian ones" (Litvinsky et al. 394). With these hearths we again find hasty correlations with later Vedic characteristics: "The sacred fires of India hold the key. . . . the existence of round and square hearths-altars in ancient India . . . is identical with the phenomenon we find at the sites in the West Pamirs" (Babayev 1989, 93). Yet the Indian hearths being referred to are the *gārhapatya* and *dakṣiṇa* fires, which are performed in sacrificial contexts that have nothing to do with burials.

The primary characteristics of the cemeteries is that they are of the kurgan type, typical of the steppe people. The pottery, on the other hand, is comparable with the ware produced by the sedentary agriculturists of northern Afghanistan. Litvinsky and P'yankova interpret these two influences as a fusion of cultures between southern sedentary agriculturists from Bactria and Indo-Iranian steppe pastoralists from an Andronovo prototype. They find reason to consider them to be proto-Iranians (following an earlier Indo-Aryan wave) sweeping eastward from sites like Namazga VI in southeastern Turkmenistan, who pushed up into the valleys of southern Tajikistan, where they adopted burial rites and certain economic systems from the more northern Andronovo steppe cultures. (See also Piankova 1982 for an analysis of the Tajikistan culture.) Other scholars, such as Vinogradova (1993), primarily stress the Andronovo proto–forms for the graves. The original excavator of the site, Mandel'shtam, and more recent scholars such as Klejn (1984), have considered these graves to be of Indo-Aryans but unconnected to the Andronovo culture.

Like all other archaeological cultures, there is no unanimity concerning the Indo-Iranian or Indo-Aryan ethnic identification of these burials either. Lyonnet wonders why, if they had been Indo-Aryans who had provoked or appeared at the time of the collapse of the Bactria and Margiana Archaeological Complex (BMAC), Namazga, and Harappan civilizations, they did not continue to foster the links between these regions, which had previously been connected for millennia. Rather, these connections collapse at this time (Lyonnet 1993, 83). She underscores the extreme paucity of metal objects found in the graves, which "is rather odd for a culture considered to come from the Andronovo people, famous for their metallurgy" (Lyonnet 1994a, 430). Moreover, "no trace of the horse is found, there is no evidence of any social differentiation, and, altogether, the material is rather poor" (430). As far as she is concerned, "if we are dealing with intruders, as some features suggest, and if it is certain that they are not Andronovians, we do not have enough evidence to identify them as Indo-Aryans. We can only compare their movement to the textually known much later migrations of two other groups, who, coming from 'the steppes,' went through Central Asia into India." These are the Kuṣāṇas around the beginning of our era, and the White Huns in the fifth century A.D.: "All these nomads, albeit at different periods, took exactly the same path, used exactly the same areas for their cemeteries consisting of kurgans that all look alike from the outside" (430).

Tribes that bury their dead in kurgans (which are so common over vast geographic and temporal expanses) have been migrating into India throughout its history, but these have not induced language shift across the entire north of the subcontinent. So one is hardly compelled to interpret the scanty evidence of the Bishkent and Vakhsh cultures as evidence of the arrival of a new language group on its way to Indo-Aryanize North India. Like the Andronovo culture, this culture does not enter the subcontinent either. Moreover, Piankova (1982) dates the graves to the last quarter of the second millennium, which is far too late for migrants who are supposed to already have completely settled down and written the hymns in the Indian subcontinent by this time, even allowing the lowest possible dates proposed by scholars for the Ṛgveda. Moreover, anyone prepared to gloss over the absence of horse bones in these sites cannot then deny the presence of the Indo-Aryans in the Indus Valley Civilization on these particular grounds.

The Southern Route

On the grounds of such objections, the correlation of the Indo-Aryans with the Andronovo culture has been rejected by a number of scholars who prefer to opt for a southern route. Bosch-Gimpera (1973) notes that "it would seem more likely that we should seek for the antecedents of the Indo-Iranians by tracing their subsequent migration into Iran by way of the Caucasus, not across the Oxus" (515).[6] He interprets various artifacts found in the Indus Valley (such as the copper weapons and other items that will be discussed later) as indicative of "an immigration of people into India with a culture related to northern Anatolia, the Caucasus and possibly even to Mesopotamia" (517).

This southern route, across the Gorgan Plain in southern Turkmenistan and northeastern Iran, is littered by the sites of sophisticated urban centers. It has long been recognized that many of these sites, such as Tepe Hissar III, seem to have been abandoned roughly at the same time after a period of urban florescence.[7] According to Kohl (1984), it is debatable "whether or not the collapses were due to the cessation of overland long-distance trade or, say, to the incursions of steppe nomads from the north or to some other unspecified cause" (226–227). The possibility of an invasion of these sites by Indo-Iranian steppe nomads from the northern steppe route was previously accepted by most scholars and is still entertained by some: "A widespread destruction of the north Iranian sites such as Tepe Hissar IIIB coupled with the equally widespread lack of archaeological evidence of the early second millennium B.C. . . . are often associated with peoples variously designated as the Indo-Iranians, Aryans or proto-Indic Peoples" (Thomas 1992, 20; see also Dyson 1968; Masson 364b 1992). However, this interpretation

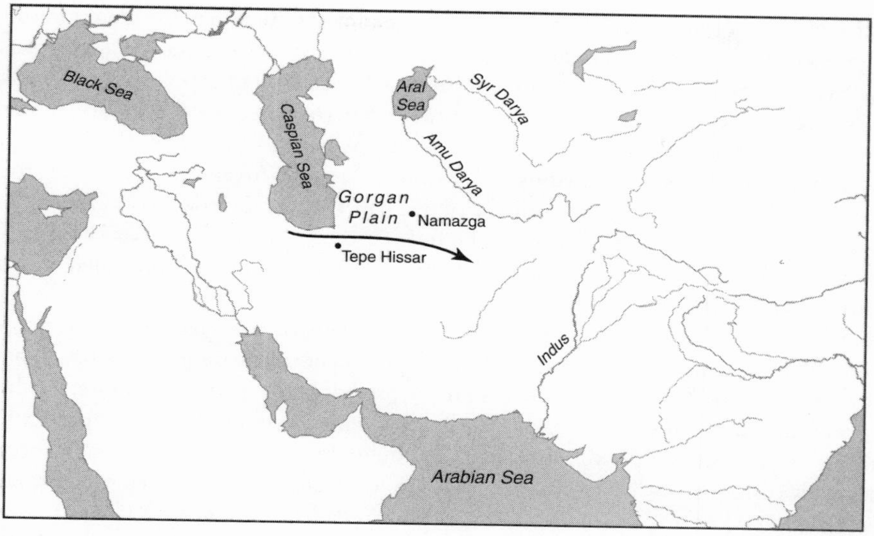

The southern route.

is falling into disfavor among a number of archaeologists of this area, since "there is no documentary evidence of steppe cultures invading agricultural oases. . . . Archaeological data was found but failed to convince. More or less intensive contacts were an established fact, but . . . archaeological diggings testify to the fact that various influences, including mass migrations, moved only from south-west to north-east" (Khlopin 1989, 75–76).[8] Hlopina (1972) noted that "the excavations of the Bronze Age sites show no trace of destruction," and that "it may well be that . . . we shall have to abandon the hypothesis that, at the end of the 2nd millennium before our era, the agricultural sites in these areas were subjected to the influence of the livestock-raising tribes of the steppes and their cultures, and that this is why these sites entered on a period of tangible decadence" (213).

A substantial body of scholars consider these urban cultures themselves to have been Indo-Iranian in some form or fashion, rather than being invaded by Indo-Iranian steppe nomads from the north. Roman Ghirshman (1977) has been a particularly influential proponent of the Indo-Aryan nature of the southern route. As far as he is concerned, the culture of the Andronovo tribes has no semblance whatsoever with that of the Indo-Aryans. In contrast, Ghirshman builds up a case on the Grayware found in sites such as Tepe Hissar III in the Gorgan Plain of northern Iran, which "is different from everything we know in Iran, Mesopotamia and Asia Minor" (12). But he does find connections between this and the innovative black ceramics of the Mitanni kingdom (8). The discovery of a seal in Tepe Hissar III containing a motif of a horse-drawn chariot and of possibly horse-controlling trumpets reinforces this region's connection with the horse-and-chariot-using Mitanni Indo-Aryans.[9] All this, for Ghirshman, points to the arrival of Indo-Aryans in the Iranian plain of Gorgan.

In this version of events, the Indo-Aryans of the Gorgan Valley, under pressure from nomadic invasions from the north (by the very people whom some other archaeologists consider to be the same Indo-Aryans!), fled their homes. Ghirshman's evidence for this assertion is the identification of houses burned by fire and the existence of arrowheads. One group headed south toward Syria to become the Mitanni of Syria. Another branch proceeded farther east; evidence of their journey is inferred from the appearance of black pottery along the Kopet Dagh chain in sites such as Namazga IV, where it appears in distinction to the pottery preceding it.[10] In time, the Indo-Aryans were expelled from Namazga IV, too, by the same nomadic steppe tribes, and proceeded east. Ghirshman (1977) tries to find further evidence of the Indo-Aryans in the Balkh region of Afghanistan but is forced to account for the different, clear-colored pottery found there as "indicating a change of taste" (40).

Scholars arguing for an Indo-Aryan element in southern sites take the same interpretative liberties as those interpreting grave goods in the northern steppes to support their case. Kurochkin, for example, sees an Aryan presence in a pestle and mortar with a spout found in the royal cemetery of Marlik in northern Iran, which he compares with a Śiva liṅga. It should go without saying that upholders of an Aryan migration theory generally consider the Śiva liṅgam to be a *pre*-Indo-Aryan icon from India, which would have no connection with any hypothetical Indo-Aryans in northern Iran.

As with the northern route, there is no dearth of criticisms that have been levied against such a southern route.[11] One objection points out that "the similarity is not very close" between the Mitanni pottery and that of the Gorgan plain (Parpola 1994, 148). Deshayes (1969) notes that "the grey ware did not at that date spread beyond the limits of the plain of Gorgan" (13). Others object that even within the spread of this ware, the Mitanni were not the only language group present; there were non-Indo-European language groups such as the Lullubu, Guti, and Hurrians (Kuzmina 1993, 403). Grantovsky (1981) complains that the grayware can be traced back to the fourth millennium B.C.E. and is therefore too early for the Indo-Iranians. He also notes that the Indo-Aryans are considered to be pastoralists and therefore cannot be connected with the southern urban sites, with their agricultural base. Kuzmina (1981) draws attention to the lack of horse bones in southern central Asia and Iran, which corresponds poorly with horse-using Indo-Aryans.

Cleuziou expresses frustration that the appearance of the grayware is typically accepted as heralding Indo-European invaders (with some scholars promoting an eastern movement, others a western movement, and still others a movement in both directions), and then its disappearance is also considered to be due to Indo-European invaders! He echoes objections to such reconstructions that are by now quite standard: "Migrationists consider that movement of people is responsible for the movement of pottery assemblages, and they think that it suffices to demonstrate that potteries have moved to demonstrate the migrations" (Cleziou 1986, 244). He notes that no one has yet come up with an archaeological origin for these hypothetical Grayware people. This "remains a challenge for the advocates of the migratory hypothesis" and prohibits confirmation of "the hypothetical reconstructions of philologists" (232–233). As far as he is concerned, "No migration from outside is necessary to explain its [the grayware's] development in the Southeast Caspian area, and since it is the *necessity* of such a migration which is the ultimate argument of its advocates, this can no more be regarded as conclusive" (236; italics in original).

Here, Cleuziou has articulated the main point that I am attempting to underscore in this chapter. It is the verdict of linguistics that is compelling archaeologists to interpret practically every innovation in the archaeological record between the Caspian Sea and India as possible evidence of Indo-Iranians. As far as Cleuziou is concerned, the spread of Indo-European "is a philological concept and we entrust the philologists to discuss about its relevance" (245). As far as the archaeology of the southeastern Caspian area is concerned, one could just as well argue that "local evolution led to a regression of urban centered settlements and of settled agriculture, probably with an extension of pastoral economy, and the early Iron Age represents a renewal of settled agriculture with re-occupation of some areas." There is no need to postulate the intrusion of foreign tribes: "Whoever were the people concerned is not of interest here, as archaeology will probably never tell it" (244). Moreover, and equally relevant, it is important to again stress that "interaction between nomads and sedentaries does not imply different people (nor different languages)" (247). I will return to this shortly.

Those who do find reason to connect the trajectories of pottery with that of the Indo-Aryans need to address one line of argument that will disqualify the Indo-Aryans from having any connection with wheel-made pottery at all. Wilhelm Rau has compiled the Vedic references to pottery from the oldest strands of the Black Yajurveda and found that although the potter's wheel was known, it was hand made pottery that was prescribed for the ritual sphere. This suggests to him that "the more primitive technique persisted in the ritual sphere while in secular life more advanced methods of potting had already been adopted." Should this assumption be correct, "we can pin down the transition from hand-made to wheel-thrown pottery, as far as the Aryans are concerned, (down) to the earlier phases of Vedic times" (Rau 1974, 141).[12] Of relevance to this line of argument is a verse from the Taittirīya Saṁhitā (4, 5, 4), stating that what is turned on the wheel is *Āsuric* and what is made without the wheel is godly (e.g., Kuzmina 1983, 21). According to Rau's philological investigations, the characteristic of this oldest pottery was that it was made of clay mixed with various materials, some of them organic, resulting in porous pots. These pots were poorly-fired and ranged in size from about 0.24 m to 1.0 m in diameter at the opening and from 0.24 m to 0.40 m in height. Furthermore, they showed a lack of plastic decoration and were unpainted (Rau 1974, 142). Of further relevance is the fact that firing was accomplished by the covered baking method between two layers of raw bricks in a simple open pit. In later times this was done with materials producing red color. Rau advises excavators to be "on the lookout for ceramics of this description among their finds" (142).

Kuzmina (1983), at least, has taken this advice seriously. As far as she is concerned, "all . . . evidence as to the character of the pottery produced in Asia Minor and Central Asia in the third and second millennium B.C. categorically rules out searching for the proto-home of the Vedic Aryans throughout [this] entire stretch" (23). According to her, then, the southern route is ruled out. In contrast, she holds that on many essential points Andronovo pottery techniques are absolutely similar to those practiced by the Vedic Aryans (as reconstructed by Rau): "Ceramic finds trace the gradual infiltration of the farming oases of Marghiana and Bactria by the late-Andronovo tribes and their emergence on the mountain passes leading into the Indian subcontinent, which may provide the clue to the problem of the origin of the Aryans" (24–27). Kuzmina is forced to concede, however, that "in the Andronovo culture it was mainly the womenfolk who engaged in the making of pottery. . . . in the case of the Vedic Aryans it was the male paterfamilias."[13] Moreover, "The second major distinction is the richness of the impressed decoration of the Andronovo pottery, whose geometrical designs include triangle, meander, swastika, lozenge and herringbone" (26). Vedic pottery is supposed to be plain. Neither southern nor northern routes, then, have fully fulfilled Rau's Vedic pottery criteria.

Sarianidi (1993c), another prominent adherent to a southern route, agrees with Ghirshman on the basic thesis that the Aryan tribes "should not be derived from the pastoral tribes of the Andronovo culture of the vast Asian steppes but—on the contrary—from the highly developed Near Eastern centres" (256). While disagreeing with Ghirshman about the grayware pottery/Indo-Aryan correlation, Sarianidi accepts the difference between Hissar III and previous levels at that site. He further notes the commonalties between Hissar III and the BMAC, which he considers evidence of the presence of Indo-Iranians migrating into northern Afghanistan from Iran. Sarianidi is sympathetic to an ultimate Near Eastern Proto-Indo-European homeland as argued by Gamkrelidze and Ivanov. As far as he (1997) is concerned, "it may be considered proved that the peopling of the Bactrian Plain was the result of the arrival of tribes from the West" (644).[14] However, this westerly origin for the BMAC, previously accepted by scholars (i.e., e.g. Kohl 1981), is presently under reconsideration by scholars such as Hiebert (1995, 200).

The Bactria and Margiana Archaeological Complex

The BMAC culture, which has been dated to the turn of the third to second millennium B.C.E.,[15] was excavated initially by Sarianidi and his colleagues and more recently by Fredrik Hiebert. Sarianidi (1993a) considers the whole BMAC complex to have been specifically Indo-Aryan partly due to the discovery there of seals bearing religious motifs similar to those found in northern Syria during the time of the Indo-Aryan Mitanni kingdom. This identification is reinforced by other objects common to the two areas—miniature stone piles and ritual vessels—and the discovery of axes with horse heads found in some of the BMAC graves.

More dramatically, perhaps, in the BMAC site called Dashly-3, Sarianidi (1977) found ash pits raised on brick platforms in a circular "temple." Also reported from Dashly-3 is "the occurrence of a shrine inside the fortress with an altar against the wall [which] validates a suggestion that this was a ceremonial centre, probably a temple with numerous services, repositories, granaries, dwelling-houses for priests and auxiliary personnel" (Tosi et al, Shahmirzadi and Joyenda 1992 220). In addition, in the southeastern Kara Kum desert, other sites on the western limits of the BMAC culture that have been labeled-"temple-forts" (Parpola 1995) or "ceremonial centres" (Jettmar 1981) have been found. Most striking of these are the sites of Togolok-21 and Gonur-1, where the excavator reported a variety of "altars," two of which showed signs of the hallucinogenic ephedra when subjected to microscopic analysis (Sarianidi 1990, 1993b, c). Poppy pollen was also identified on pestles and grinding stones of the site.

Opposite these "altars" were "fire altars," or, perhaps more accurately, rooms that showed the effects of fire. Summing up the archaeological evidence, Sarianidi (1930c) concludes, "It can be said with a high degree of certainty that Togolok-21 must have

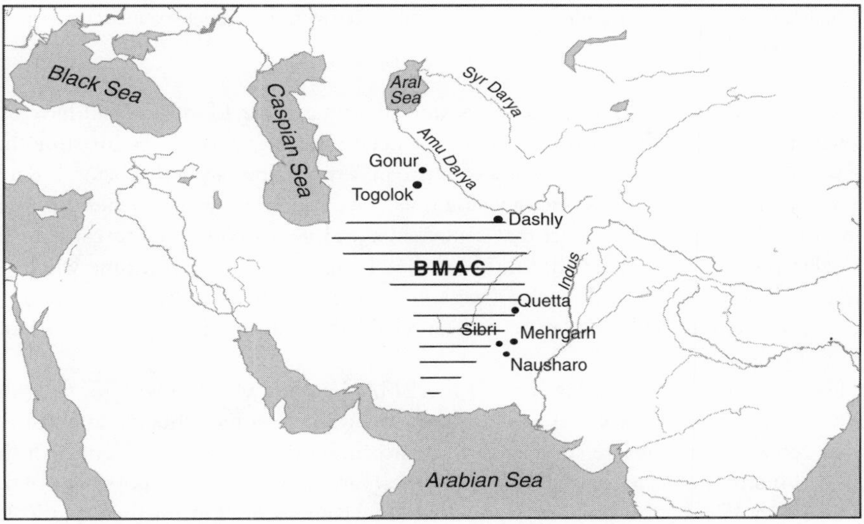

The BMAC (Bactria Margiana Archaeological Culture).

been a temple connected in some or other way with a religious cult during which venerations of the sacred fire and libations took place" (252). Chemical analysis performed upon vessels discovered in a similar site at Gonur determined that the vessels had contained cannabis, ephedra, and poppy. Also of relevance at this site was the discovery of ceramic stands and sieves "by means of which the juice was divided from the solid pressed-out mass" (252). If one is to follow, for example, Nyberg (1995), then ephedra is the most likely candidate for the *soma/hoama* cult of the Indo-Aryans and the Iranians. This is certainly the connection that Sarianidi makes. In short, he holds that "the Vedic Aryans were part of the BMAC tribes whose culture replaced the Harappan" (1993c, 263). Nyberg (1995), however, subjected the samples from these sites to pollen analysis at the University of Helsinki but could not find any trace of ephedra (although Sarianidi, 1999, has questioned this analysis).

While all this is well and good, attention must be drawn to the fact that the BMAC was a sophisticated civilization consisting of fortified towns. The temple structures just noted were "monumental"; the Gonur temple occupies an area of two hectares (from a total area of twenty-two hectares) and was surrounded by walls up to four meters thick (Sarianidi 1993b, 8). Indeed, according to later excavators of BMAC sites:

> The extensive distribution of the BMAC, together with the recognition of the considerable size of their cities . . . and the monumental nature of single architectural units, . . . combine to suggest that we are dealing here with a socio-political phenomenon of considerable magnitude . . . that involved a substantial region of Middle Asia. . . . It is our belief that the BMAC, if not itself a state, appears to mirror a facsimile of state-structured polity of power. The 15 km. distance from Gonur to Togolok in Margiana is no greater than the distance which separated Lagash from Girsu in Mesopotamia. Nor is there a great difference in the relative size of these respective cities. The latter are taken, without

qualification, to be important "city-states" within Mesopotamia. (Hiebert and Lamberg-Karlovsky 1992, 11)

As discussed in the last chapter, scholars since the time of Sir John Marshall have disallowed the possibility of an Indo-Aryan presence in the Indus Valley by insisting that the social horizon of the Ṛgveda knows no urban settings and is purely pastoral. Rau's depiction of the Vedic *pur* is one of wattle huts. I will question later whether this position is tenable based on the fact that settlements and towns continued to exist in the post-Harappan period, albeit shifting from the Harappan nucleus, at a time when no one can doubt that the Indo-Aryans were very much situated in the region. Lack of urban references in the Ṛgveda may not be a reliable indicator of the Indo-Aryan's ignorance of urban centers.

The same logic is applicable here. If the BMAC culture was Indo-Aryan, then the Indo-Aryans certainly knew and lived in (and, according to some scholars, established) urban centers in a state-like context. Anyone accepting the Indo-Aryan identity of the BMAC (or any of the sites on the southern routes) cannot then deny the possibility of the Indus Valley Civilization possibly being an Indo-Aryan civilization on these particular grounds, namely, the apparent lack of urban references in the Ṛgveda. Even if it is argued that the Indo-Aryans were not the founders of this civilization, but arrived toward the end of the Bactria and Margiana cultural complex (they were initially held to have destroyed it until it was realized that no traces of destruction have been found), they nonetheless must surely have passed through this whole area on their way to India and so must have been aware of, and interacted with, such towns. Accordingly, it becomes very hard to deny the possible residence of the Indo-Aryans in, or coexistence with, urban centers.

Also of relevance to the last chapter (where we found that the principal reason given for the non-Indo-Aryan identity of the Indus Valley is the absence of horse bones there) is the fact that although the horse was certainly utilized in the BMAC, as attested by its representation on grave goods, no horse bones have been discovered there (despite the fact that an unusually high number of animal bones have been found). So we have proof of horse, but no horse bones. Absence of horse bones, then, may not equal absence of horses, nor necessarily of Indo-Aryans. A final related point is that the Vedas make no mention of temples, or temple structures. What are we to make of "ceremonial centers" of the sites of Togolok-21 and Gonur-1 discovered in the same BMAC where we have fire worship and the ritual usage of hallucinogens in a templelike setting? Any acceptance that all this was the handiwork of Indo-Aryans will entail abandoning certain stereotypes such as that the Indo-Aryans knew no urban centers or temples and that the failure of archaeologists to uncover horse bones equals the real-life absence of horses in a society.

Hiebert and Lamberg-Karlovsky disagree with Sarianidi concerning the external origin (from southeastern Iran) of the BMAC, preferring to consider it "the development of a new type of social structure within an ongoing culture, rather than migration or invasion" (Hiebert 1995, 200). This position has been accepted by Tosi (1988), albeit in conjunction with a "massive immigration of external elements" (62). Hiebert and Lamberg-Karlovsky note that there is no site in southeastern Iran providing any evidence for such a claim, and that any BMAC material found on sites from that area is intrusive in nature. In other words, if there is a movement, it is from east to west. These scholars are prepared to consider, however, that the BMAC culture is Indo-Aryan. Of particular relevance is the intrusion of burial assemblages with artifacts typical of the BMAC culture into the Iranian plateau and the western borders of the Indus Valley in the sites of Mehrgarh VII and Sibri in Baluchistan, which "may be correlated with the introduction of the Indo-European language" (Hiebert and Lamberg-Karlovsky 1992, 1).

While acknowledging that "we must distinguish between the movement of peoples from the movement of objects and/or styles by exchange and/or stimulus diffusion," these scholars are of the opinion that the "evidence suggests that the people buried in the tombs, with an exclusively Central Asian [BMAC] material inventory, came from Central Asia" (Hiebert and Lamberg-Karlovsky 1992, 3). However, they also note that the tombs with such exclusive material are "rare." Nonetheless, here we do seem to have the first evidence of an archaeological intrusion into the subcontinent from Central Asia during the commonly accepted time frame for the arrival of the Indo-Aryans: "Since the BMAC is clearly *intrusive* on the Iranian Plateau and in the hill country of Baluchistan, we suggest that the BMAC provides the first archaeological evidence that meets both the chronological and historical requirements for the introduction of the Indo-Iranian language onto the Iranian Plateau" (10). Kohl (1984) likewise accepts "the possibility of a movement of peoples to the south, possibly displaced by steppe and mounted nomads from further north" (242). Other scholars have also correlated the apparent intrusiveness of these graves with the Indo-Aryans (Parpola 1994, 147; Allchin 1995, 47). Scholars also point to the similar pottery sherds found in nearby Nausharo, connecting this site with Mehrgarh VIII and Sibri, as further evidence of such incursions.

The Mehrgarh and Sibri cemeteries, excavated by Jean-François Jarrige, yielded "abundant material presenting obvious parallels with East Iran (Shahdad), Northwest Afghanistan (Dashly) southern Uzbekistan (Sappali) and the Murghab region" (Jarrige and Hassan, 1985, 150). Ceramic objects and an amulet also "indicate some degree of contemporaneity and interaction between the Mehrgarh VII/Sibri complex and the Indus civilization" (150). There is debate regarding the origin of these finds. Lamberg-Karlovsky (1993) points to two possibilities—"The movement of peoples from Central Asia . . . or, in the absence of such a migration, the presence of strong cultural influences uniting these two areas" (35)—but favors the former hypothesis. However, Jarrige (1989), the excavator of the site, is less inclined to see these finds as evidence of population movements: "The evidence of a formative period of the cultural complex of Mehrgarh VIII/Sibri at Nausharo . . . cannot be interpreted in term of invasions from the north-west to the south-east but within the framework of fruitful intercourse at a time when Mohenjo-daro is still an active city" (67). Moreover, there is no evidence of the horse at Sibri (Santoni 1985), which scholars have long insisted must accompany any proposed Indo-Aryan identification.

Along the same lines, the antiquities discovered at Quetta in 1985, which are also sometimes connected with intruding Indo-Aryans (i.e., e.g. Allchin 1995), can also simply be viewed as reflecting "the economic dynamism of the area extending from South Central Asia to the Indus Valley." The fact that similar objects are also found in graves and deposits in northern Iran, eastern Iran, northwestern Afghanistan, South Turkmenia, and Baluchistan might simply indicate "a wide distribution of common beliefs and ritual practices" (*Jarrige and Hassan (1985) 1989*, 162–163). Jarrige and Hassan reject the idea that these finds were associated with invaders related to the Hissar III C complex, since "there is nothing in the Gorgan Plain and at Hissar to prove that northern Iran has been a relay station for invading people. The . . . grey ware can very well be explained within its local context" (163–164). Nor are these scholars partial to the northern steppe Andronov alternatives, since:

> *We leave to the linguists* the problem of whether Indo-European languages were introduced into the Middle Asian regions from a still unknown part of the Eurasian steppes in the course of the third millennium or if Indo-Iranian languages have been associated with these regions for a much longer period. As far as archaeology is concerned, we do think that it is increasingly necessary for specialists in Indo-Iranian studies to pay attention to the . . . interrelated cultural entities of the late third and early second millennium in the regions between Mesopotamia and the Indus. It is a direction of research that is likely to be more fruitful than are traditional attempts to locate remains left by nomads from "the Steppes," attempts that were in fashion when the Indo-Iranian Borderlands were thought to be a cultural vacuum. (164; my italics)

Despite inviting linguists to reconsider the northern steppe hypothesis in favor of the southern route, it can be inferred from Jarrige and Hassan, as from the work of a number of archaeologists considering the problem of Indo-Aryan origins, that the Indo-Aryan-locating project exists solely due to linguistic exigencies:

> The development of original but closely interrelated cultural units at the end of the third and the beginning of the second millennium cannot be explained just by the wandering of a single group of invaders. The processes were obviously multidirectional in regions with strong and ancient cultural traditions. This does not preclude the fact that movement of population and military expeditions . . . may have played an important historical part but, as far as archaeology is concerned, there is nothing to substantiate a simplistic model of invasion to account for the complex economic and cultural phenomena manifest at the end of the third millennium in the regions between Mesopotamia and the Indus Valley. (164)

Nonetheless, those who do find the aforementioned linguistic exigencies compelling must find some way of getting the Indo-Aryans speakers into the subcontinent by some means or another. Mallory (1998) feels comfortable enough ascribing some form of Indo-Iranian identity to the Andronovo culture but admits that, "on the other hand, we find it extraordinarily difficult to make a case for expansions from this northern region to northern India . . . where we would presume Indo-Aryans had settled by the mid–second millennium BCE" (191). Referring to the attempts at connecting the Indo-Aryans to such sites as the Bishkent and Vakhsh cultures, he remarks that "this type of explanation only gets the Indo-Iranian *to* Central Asia, but not as far as the seats of the Medes, Persians or Indo-Aryans" (192). He points out that suggesting an Indo-Aryan identity for the BMAC requires a presumption that this culture was dominated by steppe tribes. However, "while there is no doubt that there was a steppe presence on BMAC sites, . . . this is very far from demonstrating the adoption of an Indo-Iranian language by the Central Asia urban population" (192).

Mallory (1998) offers a *Kulturkugel* (culture bullet) as a possible explanatory model for the Indo-Aryan incursions, although remarking that "German is employed here to enhance the respectability of an already shaky model" (192). This conceptual projectile is envisioned as an Indo-Iranian linguistic bullet propelled by the social organization of the steppes outlined previously and tipped with a nose of malleable Andronovo material culture. After impacting the BMAC culture, the projectile continues on its trajectory, but now as an Indo-Aryan linguistic bullet with a BMAC cultural tip. In other words, the steppe tribes entered the BMAC, shed the trappings of their Andronovo heritage, and then, reacculturated, continued on their way toward India after having adopted the cultural baggage of the BMAC and undergone the linguistic transformations separating the language of the Indo-Iranians from that of the Indo-Aryans. Mallory is too good of a scholar not to immediately include an addendum, stating that "the introduction of the *kulturkugel* emphasizes the tendentious nature of any arguements for the dispersals of the Indo-Iranians into their historic seats south of Central Asia" (193). He is also candid enough to point out that "it is . . . difficult to imagine how such a concept could be verified in the archaeological record or, to continue the metaphor, could be traced back to the original 'smoking gun'" (194). Mallory's *Kulturkugel* is the type of gymnastics incumbent on anyone atempting to find archaeological evidence of the Indo-Aryans all the way across Asia and into the subcontinent.

Two Wave Theories

The idea of a two-wave (or multiple-wave) incursion into India has been suggested several times by linguists for over a century and has entered the realm of archaeology more recently through the work of Asko Parpola. Hoernle (1880) laid the genesis of the idea in 1880 based primarily on the phonemic and morphological features that distinguished the New Indo-Aryan languages into two main groups, which he termed the "Ṣauraseni Prákrit tongue" (Ṣr. Pr.) and the "Mágadhi Prákrit tongue" (Mg. Pr.). From a historical perspective, he envisioned this situation coming about as follows: "The Mg. Pr. and the Pashtú and Káfirí were once in close connection, perhaps one language. . . . at some time in the remote past, they became separated by the Ṣr. Pr. tongue, like a wedge, cleaving them asunder and gradually pushing the Mg. farther and farther away towards the east" (Hoernle 1880, xxxiv).

Grierson (1903) took Hoernle's wedge concept and expanded it further. He envisioned the Aryan invasion taking place over centuries in multiple waves. Using the first and the last of such waves as reference points, he proposed that the earlier comers spoke a non-Sanskritic Indo-Aryan dialect,[16] and the newcomers a Sanskritic one: "The later invaders . . . reached the Punjab which they found already settled by Indo-Aryans from the West speaking a closely cognate tongue" (52) From there, they forced their way to the eastern Punjab, which they wrested from the first comers, pushing them to the surrounding areas: "It is reasonable to suppose that the tribes who composed this later invasion (wherever they came from) should have expanded as time went on, and should have thrust outwards in each direction the members of the earlier incomers" (53) Grierson observes that in medieval Sanskrit geography, Madhyadeśa is continually referred to as the true, pure home of the Indo-Aryan people. He further notes that the modern Sanskritic Indo-Aryan vernaculars fall into two main families, one of which is spoken in a compact tract of country almost exactly corresponding to this ancient Madhyadeśa and centered in modern-day Uttar Pradesh. The other surrounds it in three-quarters of a circle, commencing in Kashmir and running through the western Punjab, Sind, Maharashtra, central India, Orissa, Bihar, Bengal, and Assam (52–53). These two areas represent the offspring of the two waves of Aryan incursions.

Asko Parpola (1988, 1993, 1994, 1995, 1997) has offered the most elaborate attempt to identify a two-wave Indo-Aryan incursion in the archaeological record. Parpola attempts to harmonize the discrepancies of associating the Indo-Aryans with the Andronovo culture as well as with the BMAC one by proposing a twofold incursion of Indo-Aryans into the subcontinent. The first of these–the Dāsas of the Ṛgveda–were Andronovo-related tribes that took over the BMAC. The sudden upsurge of wealth of the BMAC around the twenty-first century is likely to have been due to the strong hierarchical influence of this ruling elite. Moreover, he points out that, the BMAC occupies precisely the area around the Oxus where Persian and Greek historical sources place the Da(h)as (< Dāsas). The Parna (< Paṇis), another Ṛgvedic tribe inimical to the Āryas, are also identified in these classical sources as coming from this area.

This first wave of Indo-Aryans was engulfed by later soma-pressing Indo-Aryan Andronov tribes that eventually became the composers of the Ṛgveda wherein they refer to themselves as Āryas. Their arrival in this area may well have been the cause for the sudden collapse of the BMAC around 1700 B.C.E. This date synchronizes neatly with the Gandhara Grave Ware culture (which will be discussed in the next chapter), the first unambiguous appearance of the horse in the subcontinent, as well as with the subsequent appearance of the Mitanni in Syria around 1500 B.C.E. By this time, the Āryas and Dāsas had merged as evidenced by the juxtaposition of the Aryan Indra, with Varuṇa of the Dāsas in the Mitanni treatises. Parpola's method, to some extent, involves determining the route the Aryans must have taken in order to reach India, examining the archaeological record along this route, and composing an elaborate historical scenario that he believes accords with Ṛgvedic narrative: : "The valley of Swat occupies a strategic position in the archaeological identification of the early Ṛgvedic Aryans, because they *must* have passed through this area. . . . Therefore we *must* briefly review its archaeological history to check the match" (Parpola 1994, 153; my italics).

Parpola (1988) extracts the Ṛgvedic verses where Indra, the *purandara* 'fort-destroyer' is active in the destruction of the ninety-nine or hundred *puras* 'forts' of his enemies, the Dāsas.[17] Based on a verse from the Śatapatha Brāhmaṇa (6.3.3.24–25), and drawing on the work of Wilhelm Rau discussed earlier, Parpola proposes that a significant feature of these forts is that they are *tripura*, or have a threefold structure. Parpola takes this to mean not only that the forts are surrounded by concentric circular walls but also that the forts themselves are circular in construction. Although only one such round fort from this period has been unearthed to date, Parpola believes that there must have been more, since circular forts with concentric walls survived there until Achaemenid times. He argues that both of these details preclude the possibility of the cities of the Indus Valley representing the Dāsa forts, since these are neither round nor fortified by three concentric walls. TheṚgveda, however, is firmly situated in more or less the same geographic area occupied by the Indus Valley, so if the Dāsa forts were not those of the Harappans, whose were they?

Parpola argues that even though the famous Sudās of the Ṛgveda is clearly associated with the Punjab,[18] his forefather, Divodāsa, need not be. Divodāsa's chief enemy,

Śambara, possessed a hundred (or ninety-nine) forts and was said to have resided in a mountainous domain. This, according to Parpola, could have been Bactria, northern Afghanistan. As has been discussed, there is a site in this area called Dashly-3, which is dated to about 2000 B.C.E. The site, although surrounded by square walls, consists of various buildings, among which stand three concentric walls. Although these urban structures are a far cry from the temporary mud and wattle *purs* reconstructed by Rau, these three walls correspond, for Parpola, to the *tripura* of the Dāsas. He believes he has found the evidence representing the Dāsa forts attacked by the Aryans on their way to the subcontinent.[19]

K. D. Sethna, who is questioning the very assumption that the Indo-Aryans need be considered intruders at all, has dedicated half of the second edition of his book *The Problem of Aryan Origins* (1992) to critiquing Parpola's 1988 article, which had been published in the interim between editions. Sethna's general objections concerning interpretative methodology echo those of many South Asian archaeologists: "The picture we derive from Parpola is of a traffic to and fro of cultural modes—continued from a fairly long past and across sufficiently wide areas—against a common religious background of various shades. It is a picture of contacts and exchanges. . . . none of them necessarily bespeak large-scale movements of population" (229). Since all the specific objections against each step of Parpola's reconstruction are quite voluminous and painstakingly argued, one example (central to Parpola's theme) of how Sethna sees the "evidence" being artificially construed to fit a series of assumptions will suffice for our purposes.

Sethna finds the passage from the Śatapatha Brāhmaṇa upon which Parpola bases his case of concentric walls actually describing the gods as fearful lest the *Rakṣasas*, the fiends, might slay their Agni.[20] The passage explains why the priest draws three concentric lines around the fire during a particular ritual. The practice, mentioned in two other places in the Brāhmaṇas, is enacted to ward off demons during the performance of the sacred rites. Sethna points out that, first of all, the three walls represent fire (*agnipurā*), not stone and mortar. Parpola has reified a magico-ritualistic ceremony into a real-life fortification. Second, it is the Aryan sacrificers who are drawing the sacred lines (or building the forts as per Parpola), not the Dāsas or Āsuras, as Parpola's version requires. Moreover, neither the word *tripura* nor any of its associations mentioned earlier occur anywhere in the Ṛgveda itself. As we have seen, in the Ṛgveda, the *puras* are described variously as wide and broad, made of stone, made of metal, hundred-curved, or with the strange epithet "'autumnal," but there is no mention whatsoever of three concentric walls.[21] One might add, too, that in this account Sudāsa and his father Divodāsa, as is obvious by their names, are themselves Dāsas, despite being unquestionably Āryans *par excellence*, which throws the whole Ārya-Dāsa dichotomy into even further confusion. Parpola sees the Dāsas as a first group of invading Indo-Aryans, displaced by a second group who called themselves Āryas and their foes, the first group, Dāsas. This raises the question of why Sudās and his father, who were leaders of the second, victorious group, would call themselves, or have been called, Dāsas (Parpola accounts for this by supposing that the Vedic group had adopted Dāsa traits from early on).

Sethna further points out that the three concentric walls of Dashly-3, even if we allow them to be the real-life protoforms of the protective fire lines drawn by the priest in the much later Vedic rituals, are a single archaeological occurrence. No other fortified village in Bactria has three concentric walls (we can recall that Śambara alone, whom

Parpola considers to be one of the leaders of the *Dāsas* in their concentric forts in Bactria, is described as having ninety-nine forts). Nor, as Parpola (1988, 138) himself notes, is there any evidence that any of these fortified villages were burned, unlike those described in the Ṛgveda. Moreover, the solitary site that does have three concentric walls does not stand out on its own, as Parpola's conjectured Dāsa forts should, but occurs inside the square walls surrounding the fort. It would have been these square walls that would have been visible to any invading Aryans, not the concentric ones of Parpola's account. Sethna (1992) continues at length in his criticisms and concludes: "I do not think we have any reason to visualize or locate Dāsa forts in the way Parpola does" (313).

Parpola's account has received criticisms from various other quarters. Sarianidi (1993b) notes:

> It should be indicated that the available direct archaeological data contradict the theory, suggested long ago, concerning the intensive penetration of the steppe Andronovo-type tribes into traditional agricultural areas. Direct archaeological data from Bactria and Margiana show without any shade of doubt that Andronovo tribes penetrated to a minimum extent into Bactria and Margianian oases, not exceeding the limits of normal contacts so natural for tribes with different economical structures, living in the borderlands of steppe and agricultural oases." (17)

Lyonnet (1993) also points out that "no traces of systematic destruction, at least in Bactriana and Margiana, have been observed and nothing else allows us to state that there was an intrusion of invaders. This intrusion of new objects could be considered the result of peaceful trade, and the new rites could be due just to local change" (428). Like Sethna, she also draws attention to the fact that Dashly-3 is the only circular fort with three surrounding walls that has been found, and to the fact that the proto-urban aspect of the site does not accord well with the generally accepted notion of the Ṛgvedic descriptions which are suppossed to know no urban centers. Moreover, Jettmar (1981) observes that the "circular walls had no value of defence," since houses lean on both sides of them directly and they "were rather thin" (222). Parpola himself is prepared to "admit that concrete evidence of an invasion of steppe nomads into Bactria and Margiana is missing" (1993, 55). While not sharing the same views as Parpola, I would like to agree with Sarianidi (1993b) that "you can only admire A. Parpola having taken on gigantic effort and his having made an attempt to logically unify archaeological and linguistic data. . . . no archaeologist has dared to undertake such a thankless and titanic work" (18).

Conclusion

From the perspective of archaeology, then, we have two basic options. We can either accept (or renegotiate) the temporal and geographic contours assigned to the trajectory of the Indo-Aryans from a non–South Asian origin and attempt to correlate their movements into the subcontinent with some of the innovations in the archaeological record, both in central Asia and into the subcontinent. Or we can challenge or (as with many Indigenous Aryanists) simply ignore all these assumptions and interpret the continuities and innovations in the archaeological record as nothing more than regular exchanges and interactions among various ethnic and socio-economic groups without feeling impelled to connect them with the physical movements of a new language group (this is not to suggest that most Migrationists do not also accept such exchanges and interactions). Of those following this latter course, some are simply unconcerned with the linguistic evidence and operate purely as archaeologists, while others hold that the Indo-Aryan languages have always been indigenous to the subcontinent. All these positions have corollaries.

If we adopt the first Migrationist position, we need to orient ourselves around either a northern course or a southern course (or some combination of both). The most serious, obvious, and oft-cited objection against the northern Andronovo course is that the steppe culture does not intrude into the South Asian borderlands (not to speak of the heartland). Why, then, should one accept it as representing Indo-Aryan speakers intruding into South Asia (although these steppe people may certainly have been speakers of Indo-Iranian dialects)? Such a position can only be predicated on an acceptance of the linguistic assumptions outlined in the previous chapters and not on the archaeological data per se.

In response to this, one can try one's hand at mixing and matching and propose that the Indo-Aryans adopted significantly different local cultures as they moved along or suggest that they arrived in separate waves. Or, since "in the northwest zone there is a striking absence of uniformity and common traits in any of the cultures identified as 'Aryan'" (Dikshit 1985, 57), one can choose to find traces of Indo-Aryans in every place where any innovations are to be found at all. Allchin finds Aryans at Hissar III, at Namazga, in the cemeteries of Tajikistan, in the BMAC, in Mehrgarh, Sibri, and Quetta, as destroyers of the Mature Harappan cities, as residents of the Mature Harappan cities, in Cemetery H, in Chanhu-daro, and in the Gandhara grave culture. This entails subscribing to a "model flexible enough to allow for several different types of movement, probably taking place on more than one occasion, and representing a number of stages in time and place" (Allchin 1995, 47). Mallory's "bullet" is a somewhat less ambitious version of this method. Such arguments, however, cannot be premised on the archaeological data. They can only be supported by philological predispositions imposed upon whatever archaeological evidence appears amenable or most readily at hand. As far as B. K. Thapar (1970) is concerned:

> The archaeological and the anthropological evidences, represented by the various culture-groups of the second millennium B.C., *are inconsistent with the philological evidence*. Even the archaeological and anthropological evidences have been found to vary from region to region—Anatolia, northern Iraq, northern Iran, Soviet Central Russia, Swat valley and Gandhara region or Pakistan and Ganga-Yamuna *doab*. . . . It is obvious, therefore, that there was no single culture associated with the Aryans in all these regions. . . . Are we to assume that the Aryans were migrants with no defined culture but with adherence to a linguistic equipment? (160)

Dilip Chakrabarti's comments (1986) are of relevance here: "Archaeology must take the entire basic framework of the Aryan model into consideration. It should not be a question of underlining a particular set of archaeological data and arguing that these data conform to a particular section of the Vedic literary corpus without at all trying to determine how this hypothesis will affect the other sets of the contemporary archaeological data and the other sections of the Vedic literary corpus" (74). As far as Thapar and Rahman (1996) are concerned, there is nothing "to show that the Indo-Aryan peoples possessed a specific material culture, special pottery, or particular figurines that would enable us to establish some kind of identification marks for their migration" (1996, 277). Edmund Leach (1990) rejects the whole method of using the Ṛgvedic literary corpus to try to extract clues that can be correlated with the archaeological record. He objects to the entire procedure whereby "an oral tradition has been treated as if it were a datable written record and myth has been confused with history as if it actually happened" (230).[22] Leach throws out an appeal to his colleagues: "If only . . . [scholars] would stop thinking of the Rig Veda as a garbled history book" (244). As far as he is concerned, "The Aryan invasions never happened at all", but, he adds, "of course no one is going to believe that" (245).

The immediate objection against the southern course is that the Indo-Aryans are primarily considered to have been pastoralists who supposedly knew no urban centers (and what to speak of states) or monumental places of worship, and were not agriculturists. I have already indicated my position that the Indo-Aryans must have interacted with urban centers whenever and wherever they were. Moreover, it has been pointed out that agriculture is very old on the subcontinent, and so no pastoral group could have existed there oblivious to farming cultures. Therefore, such objections need qualifications.

From Indigenist perspetives Pastoralists and farmers have always coexisted in the subcontinent. Both pastoralists and agriculturalists presently are, and have long been, Indo-Aryan speakers. But how far can we go back in India with an Indo-Aryan presence? Have the Indo-Aryans, whether agriculturists, pastoralists, or both, been in the subcontinent since all eternity? The immediate issue confronting an Indigenous position is that if the Indo-Aryan speakers are autochthonous to South Asia, then how are they related to the other Indo-European languages? The corollary can only be that the other Indo-Europeans left the subcontinent for their destinations to the west.

This raises the immediate objection that if archaeology cannot trace any consistent material culture identifiable as Indo-Aryan arriving into the subcontinent from outside, it most certainly cannot identify any such culture emanating out. Accordingly, as far as archaeology is concerned, we have reached a stalemate (although from a Migrationist perspective there is, arguably at least, some kind of chronological sequence of archaeological culture that at least heads toward the general direction of the subcontinent, even if it does not penetrate it). Ultimately, however, the Aryans cannot be satisfactorily identified in the archaeological record as either entering or exiting. The trajectory of the Indo-Aryans, indeed the necessity of their very existence, is a linguistic issue that archaeology, as most archaeologists are well aware, cannot locate in the archaeological record without engaging in what, to all intents and purposes, amounts to special and often complicated pleading. On the basis of the present evidence, linguistics cannot decisively determine with any significant degree of consensus where the original homeland actually was. And archaeology can only hope to be productive in identifying the material remains of a linguistic group if linguistics has already done the groundwork of pinpointing its geographic area of origin with a reasonable degree of precision.

Accordingly, archaeology cannot deny the possibility that Indo-Aryan and Iranian (which were preceded by Indo-Iranian) languages might have been spoken in the area of the Punjab, Pakistan/Afghanistan, southeast central Asia/northeast Iran since the second, third or even fourth millennium B.C.E. The problem is chronological. In fact, archaeologically at least, South Asian archaeologists often draw attention to a cultural continuum that can be traced as far back as Mehrgarh in the seventh millennium B.C.E. within which innovations and developments can be explained simply by internal developments and external trade. If there were no constraints stemming from the date commonly assigned to the Veda, this whole area could have included urbanites and agriculturists from the South, as well as nomads and pastoralists from the North, interacting together in the millennia B.C.E. as they always have been and still do in the present day. Both steppe dwellers and urban farmers could have been speakers of related Indo-Iranian dialects in protohistory just as they are today and have always been in recorded history. There could have been invasions, migrations, trade, cultural exchanges, all manner of interactions—cultural evolution and devolution (followed sometimes by renewed evolution)—as well as all manner of diversification in chronological time. And all within a large, heterogeneous ethnic and cultural area of people who nonetheless spoke related dialects—whether living in towns, mountains, or agricultural plains—just as has always been the history of the subcontinent. Sarianidi (1999), for one, is prepared to countenace something along these lines in the second millennium BCE (albeit from a Near Eastern homeland):

> The northern branch of the Indo-Iranian tribes had separated early on from its Indo-Iranian mother country and settled widely in the wood and steppe zone of Eurasia . . . We find this reformed culture in the Andronovo tribes in the middle of the second millennium BC in Central Asia where they contacted the Indo-Iranian population of the farming oasis of the BMAC . . . And maybe for this reason the Andronovo tribes found no confrontation in the territory of the BMAC (not to speak of a military invasion). On the contrary they peacefully co-existed with the ancient farmers of Margiana, south Turkmenistan and Bactria as they were all tribes of related origin. (323)

It is not archaeology that can discount the possibility of all this. As I have asserted elsewhere, everything depends on the date of the Ṛgveda. Before turning to the problems involved with the dating of this text, there is one last aspect of the archaeological record that must briefly detain us. This is the attempt to trace the trajectory of the Indo-Aryans from within the subcontinent.

11

Aryans in the Archaeological Record

The Evidence inside the Subcontinent

Once it had been determined and accepted by a majority of scholars that the Indus Valley Civilization was definitely not to be connected with the Vedic Aryans, and that the Vedas were to be dated sometime around 1200 B.C.E., the time span for the main entry of the Indo-Aryans into the subcontinent could be narrowed down to a post-Harappan period between approximately 1900 and 1200 B.C.E. I have discussed how the archaeological cultures from the Caspian Sea area to Afghanistan in the particular time frame deemed appropriate for the trans-Asiatic saga of the Indo-Aryans were scoured and how archaeologists interpreted a variety of material cultures as evidence of Indo-Aryans, either by attempting to correlate them with written sources or on the basis of their innovatory nature in the archaeological record. A parallel logic has prompted a series of interpretations from within the Indian subcontinent and within this later time frame.

The immediate and most obvious archaeological candidates were the archaeological cultures known variously as Late Harappan, Post-Harappan, or Post-Urban, during which period the Indo-Aryans are assumed to have entered the subcontinent. Allchin (1995, 29), opting for Possehl's term of Post-Urban, dates this phase from 2000 B.C.E. to the last quarter of the second millennium B.C.E. Allchin notes a variety of factors that contributed to the weakening of the urban Indus culture, which he suggests "presented an invitation to some of their predatory neighbours, and thus coincided with incursions of peoples from the hills to the west, who almost certainly established for themselves dominant roles in relation to the existing population of the Indus system" (38). A number of regional cultures flourished during this period, from which I will consider the ones that have been typically connected with intruding Indo-Aryan elements. These are the Gandhara Grave Culture; the Jhukar Cultures, the Cemetery H culture, and the

Painted Gray Ware culture. I will first discuss the ways in which these cultures have been related to the Indo-Aryans and then discuss interpretative options. Again, I will attempt to spare the reader excessive detail and simply touch upon the arguments likely to be most commonly encountered in this regard.

Gandhara Grave Culture

A variety of graves were found in the environs of the Swat Valley by A. Dani, who coined the name for this culture, and by members of the Italian Archaeological Mission.[1] Some of the graves are of fractional skeletons,[2] which, according to Dani (1992), are the only graves associated with iron "and must be understood as an intrusive phenomenon by a people who introduced iron" (405). In one graveyard, a burial of two horses was found at surface level (Antonini 1973, 241), which, as we know, will immediately capture the attention of Aryan-spotters. In addition to a red ware pottery, there is a plain grayware that belongs to a tradition "very different from those of the periods immediately preceding and immediately following, in shapes and decoration and in the production techniques of the vessels" (Stacul 1973, 197). Dani (1978) and Stacul (1969) connect this gray pottery with the plain ware, from northeast Iran, noted previously.[3] Various bowls, vases, and bronzes similar to objects from Hissar III fortify this association. Dani finds close relations between the material culture of the Northwest and that of the northeastern part of Iran in the second and first millennium B.C., but with little direct link with the areas in Soviet Central Asia or western Asia. According to him, this part of Iran, lying to the east of the Caspian Sea, should be regarded as a nucleus zone for the diffusion of cultures to different directions. The culture he sees diffused from this area is that of the Indo-Aryans: "The literary accounts have talked of the people who call themselves Aryans in the Vedic literature. . . . as far as we are concerned, we . . . have shown how in the three periods of the graves we should now understand the literary records which we have so long taken for historical truth" (Dani 1978, 53).

Stacul (1969) finds the excavations can be assigned to seven quite distinct periods, although "we are unable to define just how much such clear differences between period and period depend on the fragmentary nature of our data . . . and how much is the result of sudden changes and upheavals due to the instability of the dominant tribal groups" (86). Unlike Dani, he does connect such groups with the central Asian peoples he believes were involved in the decline of the urban centers in Afghanistan, northern Iran, and central Asia. But he notes that "the complexity of these phases and the generally scarce archaeological documentation hinder even a summary reconstruction of these events, which should presumably be linked to the spread of the Aryan tribes in the regions of the Indo-Pakistan sub-continent" (86–87).[4]

For those undertaking the mix-and-match project that is the inevitable lot of anyone attempting to identify the Indo-Aryans in the archaeological record, there is no consensus among archaeologists regarding any possible foreign affiliation of the graves. Thapar and Rahman (1996) find "their connection to central Asia and Iran are definite, though of what character is still not known" (268). Kuzmina (1976) is much more confident that the burial rites and pottery from both the Beshkent and the Gandharan cemetery provide "grounds for attributing an Indian origin [to the Beshkent group] and for supposing that it later shifted to Hindustan where the Swāt cemeteries are thought to have been its legacy" (131).

Antonini, in contrast, has rejected attempts to correlate the graves with the Beshkent and Vakhsh graves of Tadjikistan (for references to these attempts by scholars such as Kuzmina and Litvinskij, see Antonini 1973). Antonini (1973, 239–244) points out differences in tomb structures, metal objects, and pottery types between the two cultures, as well as the absence in the Swat graves of items that were typical of the Tadjikistan graves, such as male-female differentiation in inhumation, miniature hearths, stones arranged as swastikas, and animal remains. Although both Dani and Stacul accept some Iranian parallels with the grave material, Dani (1977) finds "very little" that provides a link with central Asia, while Stacul also notes that the Tadjikistan graves "do not seem to indicate affinities with the graves found in Northern Pakistan" (198). In terms of other connections, Parpola (1993), following Mallory, accepts that this culture is "by no means identical with the Bronze Age Culture of Bactria and Margiana" either (54).

Tusa (1977) believes that "the so-called 'grave culture' is not in fact due to a sudden interruption in the life of the valley but to an appreciable, substantial change perhaps due to new contributions that are nevertheless in line with the cultural traditions of the previous period." He echoes objections that have been raised so many times by South Asian archaeologists: "The existence of contributions from the outside, for too long used to justify cultural change in the sub-Himalayan area, has in my opinion been exaggerated even though it could conceivably have been a factor in cultural change without being the only one" (690). As far as he is concerned, "to attribute a historical value to . . . the slender links with northwestern Iran and northern Afghanistan . . . is a mistake "because . . ." it could well be the spread of particular objects and, as such, objects that could circulate more easily quite apart from any real contacts" (691–692).

Jhukar Culture

This culture is situated in the Indus Valley itself and named after Mughal's excavations at Jhukar. It includes the sites of Amri and Chanhu-daro. Chanhu-Daro, was excavated by Mackay, and a report was published in 1943. Allchin draws attention, on the one hand, to the complete absence of typically Harappan seals and other characteristically Harappan urban craft products at this site, and, on the other, to the presence of stamp seals with parallels in eastern Iran, Afghanistan, and central Asia, as well as to a range of copper tools and pins with analogues in those regions, but equally "foreign" to the Harappan world. Allchin (1995, 32) is aware that the "foreign" elements noticed at Chanhu-Daro have not been evidenced at other sites such as those in Saurashtra. He also acknowledges that "while it is possible to argue, as some have done, that the metal artifacts of 'foreign' type may be no more than the products of trade," he nonetheless holds that the presence of the stamp seals is unequivocal in implication: the absence of Harappan seals—the symbols of Harappan political and economic power—and their displacement by these foreign seal types "must indicate that a new power was dominant at Chanhu-daro and by inference in the middle and lower Indus region" (31).

Jarrige (1983), in contrast, had long since pointed out that there were chronological problems with correlating the seals and other artifacts with the Indo-Aryans: "The migration of these [seminomadic] groups [coming from central Asia] would sometimes be traced on maps based on the accidental discovery of certain types of artifacts[5]—principally metal objects and seals—which could be stylistically associated with the Hissar III C complex." He points out, however, that this complex is now dated to the end of the third millennium B.C. making it contemporary with the Mature Harappan and not later, as was previously thought: "Thus most of these finds must be interpreted in the context of international exchange covering the whole of the Middle East and cannot be interpreted as reflecting the invasion of pastoralists in the mid-2nd millennium BC" (42).

Jarrige (1973) complains of the tendency of lumping everything not typically Harappan under the rubric of the Jhukar culture, "a problem which is further complicated when, by attempting to harmonize the archaeological data with philological arguments, people have developed the habit of attributing to the Jhukar culture all discoveries amenable of offering some correlation with the Iranian world and Central Asia" (263). Jarrige goes on to consider whether there was a disruption of sedentary urban life in the Indus Valley and a sudden drop in agricultural productivity of that area accompanied by a shift to seminomadic pastoralism with evidence of warfare—in short, all of the features that would ideally accompany an intrusion of Indo-Aryan nomads. As the excavator of Pirak, the only well-preserved second millennium B.C.E. site from the area (which he dates from 1700 to 700 B.C.E.), Jarrige (1985) finds a "town" of some size with "elaborate architecture" and evidence of a more intense level of irrigation and cultivation than occurred in the third millennium B.C.E.: "Just the opposite of that which has been presumed on the basis of negative evidence" (46). In view of the fact that Pirak is widely accepted as heralding the Indo-Aryans due to the discovery of the horse there, my previous remarks about Indo-Aryans and urban centers are reinforced. Those wishing to consider Pirak as evidence of nomad Indo-Aryan pastoralists must address the fact that it was "a town of some size with elaborate architecture" that *increased* the agricultural productivity of the area.

Jarrige's study of continuity and change concludes that the people living in the Kachi plain during the second millennium B.C.E. undoubtedly experienced the major economic transformations of the time yet maintained significant elements of cultural continuity and conservatism from the early third millennium B.C.E. and earlier. He underscores the continuity aspect of the area by comparing the ancient ruins of residential buildings from the excavations at Pirak with the very recent ruins of a house deserted by Hindus at partition in the same district. The resemblance is striking, while the samples of cooking pots between the two periods seem almost identical. Regarding the transformations, he doubts whether every newly attested item in the Kachi archaeological record of the second millennium B.C.E. could be attributed to an influx of new peoples, "since the processes . . . are too complex to be attributed to the arrival of invaders who at the same time would have had to have introduced rice from the Ganges, sorghum from the Arabian Gulf, and camels and horses from Central Asia" (Jarrige 1983, 56).

The discovery of the horse in Pirak, however, must detain us. The evidence consists of figurines of horses and horsemen. By the end of Pirak II, the figurines are painted with trappings, and some are wheeled. This is the first evidence of *Equus caballus* Linn in South Asia that is accepted by Meadow (1997, 309) from the evidence he has been able to examine so far. While (Jarrige (1983) is skeptical that "the dream of several generations of scholars—to find a continuous line of sites from the Eurasian steppes to the Ganges valley all with 'typical' grey ware or 'steppe-style' pottery which could be used to map the movements of Indo-Aryan populations" will ever materialize (63), he does find this attested presence of the horse significant in this regard. It is only with the introduction of this animal (allowing that this is the earliest uncontested evidence for the horse) that Jarrige is prepared to consider "groups related to those from the Eurasian steppes and Central Asian highlands [beginning] to play an important role in the functioning of social and economic systems in the northwestern part of South Asia" (60).

In view of all that I have discussed regarding the horse in the previous chapter, I will simply note that Jarrige (1985) specifically mentions that the existence of the Indo-Aryans has "so far only been deduced on the basis of *linguistic* evidence" (62; my italics). Otherwise, "what we see is a dynamic system of multidirectional contacts and 'influences' extending throughout a vast area from southern Central Asia to the Ganges valley and continuing from the beginning of the 2nd millennium into the 1st millennium BC" (62). If the linguistic evidence to which archaeologists defer for the status of the Indo-Aryans as intruders into South Asia is brought into question, then the horse could simply become another innovatory item introduced into South Asia through trade. In the absence of irrefutable linguistic evidence, there is no reason to feel compelled to believe that the introduction of the horse into the subcontinent is indicative of the introduction of new peoples any more than the introduction of any other innovatory items of material culture (such as camels, sorghum, rice, lapis lazuli, or anything else) is representative of new human migratory influxes:

> There is evidence for the intensification of subsistence practice, multicropping and the adoption of new forms of transportation (camel and horse). These changes were made by the *indigenous* inhabitants, and were not the result of new people streaming into the region. The horse and camel would indicate connections with Central Asia. The cultivation of rice would connect with either the Late Harappan in the Gaṅgā-Yamunā region or Gujarat. (Kenoyer 1995, 227; my italics)

Moreover, if the arrival of a new people can be promoted on the basis of the introduction of an essential new item from central Asia, then why should using an inverse logic *denying* any such arrival because of the *non*introduction of an essential item from central Asia not also be given consideration? According to Kenoyer (1995):

> In earlier models, the northwestern regions were the source of the so-called movements of Indo-Aryan speaking peoples. Yet, if there were such movements, why were the migrants not supplying one of the most important raw materials for bronze production, i.e. tin? This cannot be answered simply by saying that iron was replacing copper and bronze, because the prominent use of iron does not occur until much later, in the NBP [Northern Black Polished Ware] period. (230)

The Vedas, after all, speak of and value bronze as well as the horse. The argument here is why did the bronze-using Indo-Aryan speakers not convey tin into the subcontinent from the northwest if they were arriving from those areas?

Cemetery H Culture

The Cemetery H excavations, a description of which appeared in a report published by Vats in 1940, contained pottery that the excavator considered indicated a "Rigvedic" pattern of belief. Wheeler (1947) noted:

> The intrusive culture, as represented by its pottery, has in origin nothing to do with the Harappā culture; its ceramic differs from that of the latter both in finish and in decoration, and its dwellings . . . are notably more roughly constructed than those of Harappā proper. Its analogues have not yet been identified, and it appears in fact as abruptly as did its Harappan predecessor. The suggestion has been made [by Childe] very hesitatingly, that the Cemetery H intruders "may belong to the Āryan invaders." (81)

He then proceeded to support this suggestion using the types of arguments I outlined in the previous chapter. This line of interpretation is still occasionally found in currency: "The evidence is admittedly slender, but there appears to be a good case for seeing in the Cemetery H culture the presence of an element of foreign intruders who have dominated the existing population and exploited their craft products, though modified to suit their own tastes" (Allchin 1995, 33).[6] Nowadays few South Asian archaeologists would concur with this opinion, and I shall simply note with Kenoyer (1991b) that Cemetery H "may reflect only a change in the focus of settlement organization from that which was the pattern of the earlier Harappan phase and not cultural discontinuity, urban decay, invading aliens, or site abandonment, all of which have been suggested in the past" (56).

Painted Gray Ware Culture

The Painted Gray Ware (PGW) type of pottery was especially promoted by B. B. Lal (1978) as best representing the Aryan presence. Outside of professional archaeological circles, it still surfaces to this day in discussions concerning evidence of Aryan intrusions. The PGW is found in quintessential Aryan locales such as Hastinapur, Mathura, and Kurukshetra, as well as in the Sarasvatī valley from where the Aryans are supposed to have arrived. It also coincides with the earliest discovery of iron in the archaeological record, and with findings of horse bones (e.g., Hastinapur). Lal's theory, if viewed from within the framework that the Aryans must have come into India in the mid–second millennium B.C.E., seemed persuasive at the time. Objections had already been raised, however. Chakrabarti (1968), for example, pointed out that sites like Hastinapur contain evidence of rice use and of the presence of domestic pig and buffalo alongside the PGW, which are all features that have been ascribed an eastern origin, as opposed to the traditional northwestern origin of the Aryans. Moreover, B. K. Thapar (1970, 156) remarked that had the PGW been symptomatic of the Aryans coming in from the Northwest, then the same pottery type would be expected to occur in Iran and Afghanistan. It does not, which threw serious doubts on Lal's thesis. As far as archaeologists like Shaffer are concerned, "there is no connection between the PGW and the 'Aryans'"; it is an indigenous culture. Accordingly, "If PGW has an indigenous South Asian origin it cannot, therefore, represent an intrusive culture with a western origin." Most important from the perspective of this chapter, "this conclusion . . . means that we have no archaeological culture which might represent the Aryan phenomenon" (Shaffer 1986, 232).

In any event, Lal (1997) himself has changed his views, and his recently published book contains an appendix called "It's Time to Rethink" (281–287). Pressed to address the Indo-Aryan issue because of his preeminent status in Indian archaeology, and due to the immense controversy in India surrounding the origins of the Indo-Aryans, he proceeds to analyze all the arguments that are commonly raised against the possibility that the Indo-Aryans could have been Harappans. He concludes:

> Is it not time to *rethink* about the entire issue? Could the chalcolithic people of Mehrgarh [seventh millennium B.C.E.], who in the course of time evolved into Bronze Age Harappans, themselves have been the Indo-Aryans? These chalcolithic people had relationship with areas now compromising northern Afghanistan, northeastern Iran and even southern part of central Asia—which area may have been the habitat of the Aryans prior to the composition of the Ṛgveda. (287)

Lal's proposal, of course, must address the chronological issues involved in dating the Vedic texts. But it does illustrate the tendency among South Asian archaeologists to emphasize continuity and trade, rather than innovation due to migrations. In conclusion, cultural evidence of the Indo-Aryans whether in central Asia or within the subcontinent, cannot be readily traced in the archaeological record. What about the Indo-Aryan speakers themselves? Can they be connected with a specific racial type in the archaeological record?

Aryans in the Skeletal Record

Initially, Guha, in 1935, had identified four racial elements at Mohenjo-Daro. Kumar, who examined the cranial remains from the Harappan material in 1973, suggested that the rugged proto-Nordic elements from these might be indicative of an influx of Indo-European or Indo-Iranian people, despite acknowledging the difficulty in identifying racially distinct Aryans (Kumar 1973, 74). His starting premise, however, was that "the Aryan invasion . . . is accepted on the basis of the evidence of the Vedas" (67), by which he was referring to the racial references outlined in chapter 3.

K. Kennedy (1984), however, who was able to examine all three hundred skeletons that had been retrieved from the Indus Valley Civilization, found that the ancient Harappans "are not markedly different in their skeletal biology from the present-day inhabitants of Northwestern India and Pakistan" (102). He considers any physical variations in the skeletal record to be perfectly normal for a metropolitan setting and consistent with any urban population past or present (103). As far as he is concerned, the polytypism in the South Asian record represents an "overlap of relatively homogeneous tribal and outcaste groups and their penetration into villages, then into urban environments of more heterogeneous people." There is no need to defer to intruding aliens for any of this: "This dynamic rather than mass migration and invasions of nomadic and warlike peoples better accounts for the biological constitutions of those earlier urban populations in the Indus valley." Here, again, we encounter the same objections raised repeatedly by South Asian archaeologists: "*Of the Aryans, we must defer to literary and linguistic scholars* in whose province lies the determination of the arrival and nature of the linguistic phenomenon we call the Aryans. . . . But archaeological evidence of Aryan-speaking peoples is questionable and the skeletal evidence is nil" (104; my italics).

Not only is the skeletal evidence nil, but "if invasions of exotic races had taken place by Aryan hordes, we should encounter obvious discontinuities in the prehistoric skeletal record that correspond with a period around 1500 BC." Whatever discontinuities do occur in the record are either far too late or far too early (Kennedy 1995, 58). These discontinuities were taken from a further study undertaken on the skeletal remains in the Harappan phase "Cemetery R37" (Hemphill et al. 1991). The results of this survey showed two periods of discontinuities: the first occurs during the period between 6000 and 4500 B.C.E. between the Neolithic and Chalcolithic inhabitants of Mehrgarh, and the second at some point before 200 B.C.E. (but after 800 B.C.E.), which is visible in the remains at Sarai Khola (200 B.C.E.). Clearly, neither of these biological discontinuities corresponds with the commonly accepted period for Indo-Aryan intrusions. The Aryans have not been located in the skeletal record. It is important to note, at the risk of repetition, that Kennedy, like almost all South Asian archaeologists, has deferred to the "literary and linguistic" evidence for the arrival of the Aryans, since archaeology has not uncovered any trace of them.

Continuity and Innovation

Archaeologists today speak of "integration," "decentralization," "localization," and "regionalization" to characterize the relationship of the various cultures of Northwest India/Pakistan with the Mature Harappan period (Shaffer 1992). In the Post-Harappan period, various regions, such as Jhukar and Cemetery H, are seen as "springing from the Mature Harappan but having distinct assemblages localized in their own areas" (Mughal 1988). Aryans are not a mandatory ingredient in this process:

> Although the overall socioeconomic organization changed, continuities in technology, subsistence practices, settlement organization, and some regional symbols show that the indigenous population was not displaced by hordes of Indo-Aryan speaking people. . . . For many years, the "invasions" or "migrations" of these Indo-Aryan-speaking Vedic/Aryan tribes explained the decline of the Indus civilization and the second rise of urbanization. . . . This was based on simplistic models of culture change and an uncritical reading of Vedic texts. Current evidence does not support a pre- or proto-historic Indo-Aryan invasion of southern Asia. . . . Instead, there was an overlap between Late Harappan and post-Harappan communities . . . with no biological evidence for major new populations. (Kenoyer 1991a, 371)

The vast majority of the professional archaeologists I interviewed in India insisted that there was no convincing archaeological evidence whatsoever to support any claims of external Indo-Aryan origins. This is part of a wider trend: archaeologists working outside of South Asia are voicing similar views. Lamberg-Karlovsky (1993) comments on the extraordinary complexity and considerable debate within the archaeological literature on the issue of external versus internal "causal premises" for the origin of the Bactrian

Bronze Age: "It must be admitted that within recent years there has been a penchant to emphasize the indigenous nature of social processes. While vaguely admitting to some degree of interaction archaeologists have emphasized the autochthonous nature of virtually every archaeological district" (34). R. Dyson (1993) remarks, in his discussion of changes taking place in the field, that the invasion thesis "becomes a paradigm of limited usefulness" (576). He proposes that "by freeing themselves from this hypothesis drawn from earlier linguistic studies, archaeologists may now focus their attention on the archaeological evidence in its own terms" (576). Commenting on the "continuing lack of agreement over the criteria by which the presence of the Indo-Aryans can be demonstrated," he outlines the alternative paradigm taking shape in the archaeology of the whole region I have been discussing: "The suggestion of an indigenous Indo-Aryan population going far back into pre-history in Northeastern Iran and nearby Turkmenia is now taken quite seriously." With this trend in mind, he finds it interesting that the discussion between contributors of Possehl's *Harappan Civilization* "indicated a parallel trend" (577).

Among Western archaeologists, Jim Shaffer has been the most outspoken critic of the Aryan invasion theory. According to Shaffer (1984b):

> Current archaeological data do not support the existence of an Indo-Aryan or European invasion into South Asia at any time in the pre- or protohistoric periods. Instead, it is possible to document archaeologically a series of cultural changes reflecting indigenous cultural development from prehistoric to historic periods. . . . The Indo-Aryan invasion(s) as an academic concept in 18th- and 19th-century Europe reflected the cultural milieu of that period. Linguistic data were used to validate the concept that in turn was used to interpret archaeological and anthropological data. What was theory became unquestioned fact that was used to interpret and organize all subsequent data. It is time to end the "linguistic tyranny" that has prescribed interpretative frameworks of pre- and proto-historic cultural development in South Asia. (88)

Shaffer complains that archaeological data can be artificially constrained to support commonly held beliefs and presents the case of urbanization in the Northwest of the subcontinent as an example. As has been noted, it is generally held that the Vedic texts represent a nonurban pastoral society, in sharp contrast to the cities and towns of the Indus Valley. Scholars have generally postulated a distinct break of over a millennium between the urban centers of the Indus Valley and the reemergence of urbanization in the Gangetic Plain. This hiatus is taken to correspond neatly to the period assigned to the arrival of the supposedly nonurban Aryan nomads sometime in the second millennium B.C.E.

Shaffer (1993) refers to one set of data that undermines this simplistic portrayal of an apparent devolution and re-evolution of urbanization, which "has nearly become a South Asian archaeological axiom" (55). Although there appears to have been a definite shift in settlements from the Indus Valley proper in late and Post-Harappan periods, there is a significant increase in the number of sites in Gujarat, and an "explosion" (300 percent increase) of new settlements in East Punjab to accommodate the transferal of the population. Shaffer (1995) is insistent that "*this shift by Harappan and, perhaps, other Indus Valley cultural mosaic groups is the only archaeologically documented west-to-east movement of human populations in South Asia before the first half of the first millennium* B.C." (139; italics in original).

Moreover, although there is a general decrease in the size of the settlements not all of these were small and insignificant in comparison with the large, complex structures of the Mature Harappan period. Data from Bahawalpur, the region in Pakistan most thoroughly surveyed, suggests an *increase* in size in the settlements of the Late Harappan period in comparison to the Harappan period (Shaffer 1993, 57). This is very significant: "More surveys have revealed large, post-Harappan settlements in the Indus region after the major Indus centres were abandoned. . . . Research . . . is beginning to demonstrate that there really is no Dark Age isolating the protohistoric from the historic period" (Kenoyer 1987, 26).[7]

As with the BMAC culture, these data also problematize the notion that the Vedas know no urban centers and therefore must be Post-Harappan. If the Vedas are, in fact, silent regarding large settlements, it is not because of a lack of such settlements at the approximate time and place the hymns are assumed to have been composed (viz., Punjab in the mid–second millennium B.C.E.) because, as Shaffer has noted, settlements did not disappear; they simply shifted east. This would have been caused by the hydrological, ecological, and other factors mentioned previously that had struck sites farther west. Thus, there was "reorganization and expansion" (Kenoyer 1995, 234), but not dissolution. And Pirac, we can recall, was a town of some size.

Once it had become established lore that the Indo-Aryans had intruded into the subcontinent around the middle of the second millennium B.C.E., archaeologists naturally began looking for innovations in the archaeological record that could be used as evidence of their arrival. D. K. Chakrabarti (1968) decades ago voiced the by now familiar complaint among South Asian archaeologists that such an a priori precommitment blinkered and actually hampered proper examination of the archaeological material in its own light: "To what extent has this Aryan hypothesis contributed to a better understanding of the relevant Indian archaeological data? In two cases at least . . . the Painted Grey ware and Ahar cultures this seems to have actually distracted attention from the basic task of a proper evaluation and analysis of the cultures themselves" (358).

The Aryans have not been pinpointed in the archaeological record with anything approaching general consensus among archaeologists. B. B. Lal, in his earlier work, demonstrated the inadequacy of other material cultures that had been identified as Aryan.[8] B. K. Thapar (1970) undertook a similar process of elimination. There is more or less unanimous agreement among present-day Indian archaeologists that there is no material culture that can be identified with any incoming Aryans. Clearly, any proposals made in the past could only have appeared attractive, that is to say, less defective than other alternatives, because their advocates had embarked on their investigations with the assumption that the Aryans must have entered the subcontinent in the Late or Post-Harappan period and must, therefore, sooner or later correspond to some innovative archaeological entity. In Chakrabarti's estimation, all claims of Aryan identification have been either much too general to be meaningful,[9] positively misleading, drawn from cultural assemblages sometimes separated by as much as several millennia, or connected to West Asia, from where not a single feature occurs in the supposedly corresponding Indian counterparts (Chakrabarti 1977b, 33–34).

Other artifacts, often solitary pieces, such as the shaft-hole ax from a late level of Mohenjo-Daro, the Rajanpur sword, and the trunnion ax, all of which are considered to be non-Indian but have wide currency in Afghanistan, eastern Iran, and the Oxus, are also sometimes heralded as proof of an alien Indo-Aryan presence. Heine-Geldern (1936), an early forerunner in this regard, while admitting that "we may not as yet say with certainty whether these . . . shapes have been brought to India by trading intercourse or by an ethnical migration" (104), nonetheless was inclined to consider that "they were from a later date than the Indus civilization and possibly belonging to the Vedic age" (23). Chakrabarti (1977b) finds that they "may more satisfactorily be explained as nothing more than what they apparently are: isolated objects finding their way in through trade or some other medium of contact, not necessarily any population movement of historic magnitude" (31). He notes that prior to the artificial boundaries demarcated by the British, the southern part of the Oxus, eastern Iran, Afghanistan, and the Northwest of the subcontinent all constituted an area with significant economic and political interaction throughout the ages—a sphere of activity distinct from the Iranian heartland to the west and Gangetic India to the east. In such an economic and geopolitical zone, "any new significant cultural innovation in any one area between the Oxus and the Indus is likely to spread rapidly to the rest of this total area" (31). As far as he is concerned, "the archaeological data from the Indus system and the area to its west. . . . which have been interpreted as different types of diffusion from a vague and undefined West Asia are no more than the indications of mutual contact between the geographical components of this interaction sphere" (35).

Chakrabarti also voices the by-now familiar complaint that Indian archaeology is overly dominated by diffusionism—a method of interpretation that views every innovation in the archaeological record as evidence of the movements of a particular people. B. Singh (1995) uses a modern example to better contextualize the potential interpretative excesses resulting from this method:

> If we count the gradual increase of china in Indian houses during the recent decades, and sit down to judge as future archaeologists with as mechanical an approach as is evident among those who equate pottery with people, we would find the entire country suffused by a new people. The same inference would be drawn from the sudden popularity of stainless steel followed by aluminum alloy and the like. (137)

Although such interpretations are no longer much in vogue elsewhere, the quest for elusive Indo-Aryan intruders ensured their survival for much longer in Indian archaeology. Chakrabarti (1997b) believes such constraints have severely crippled the visualization of "protohistoric growth in inner India in its own terms, without any reference to the supposed multiple waves of people pouring in from the West" (35). The same could be said for the archaeological cultures generally associated with the Aryans on their supposed route from the Caspian Sea to the subcontinent.

Erdosy (1995a), who is prepared to find "some support" for small-scale migrations associated with the intrusive BMAC elements noted earlier, nonetheless states: "Several cultural traits with good Vedic and Avestan parallels have been found widely distributed between the southern Urals, Central Asia and the Indo-Iranian borderlands. However, even allowing for the uncertain chronology of Central Asian sites, few of these traits show the northwest-southeast gradient in chronology predicted by our linguistic models." Rather, in the manner of other traits commonly associated with the "Aryans" within South Asia, "they originate in different places at different times and circulate widely, undoubtedly through the extensive interaction networks built up in the mid-3rd to early 2nd millennia B.C." The main point is that "it is impossible, thus, to regard the widespread distribution of certain beliefs and rituals, which came to be adopted by Indo-Iranian speakers, as evidence of population movements" (12).

Not surprisingly, this basic line of interpretation is favored by Indigenous Aryanists. Once the underlying equation that diachronic commonalties of the archaeological record in adjacent geographic areas equaling the physical movement of peoples has been brought into question, there is little to compel Indigenous Aryanists to accept the theory of the migrations of the Indo-Aryans from an archaeological perspective. S. P. Gupta's two-volume survey (1979) on the archaeology of central Asia and the Indian borderlands, for example, also concludes that although artifacts from central Asia do occur sporadically in the Indian borderlands and the Indus basin, this phenomenon can "best be interpreted in terms of exchanges" (318). He points out that none of the central Asian protohistoric cultures reached the Indus region in totality as would have been expected had large groups of Indo-Aryans been on the move. Along the same lines, a doctoral dissertation focused exclusively on ethnic movements in the second millennium B.C.E. between the Caspian Sea and the Indus basin concludes that "there is no case of the Aryan migration from West Asia to India in the first part of the second millennium B.C. If there is any case, the case is that of economic ties" (Kesarwani 1982, 312).

A few points need to be made from the perspective of Aryan migrations, however. The fact that no satisfactorily consistent archaeological culture can be found stretching across central Asia or the steppes does not necessarily dispel the possibility that large numbers of people could nonetheless have been on the move. Anthony (1986) draws attention to an example from the historic period: the Helvetii. The migration of these people which was recorded by Caesar in some detail, involved the movement of a population mass said to have numbered 360,000 initially and found to number 110,000 in Caesar's military census of the defeated remnant. According to Anthony (1986), "Even assuming a certain amount of exaggeration, this was a very substantial population movement and one that current Western archaeology theory would neither predict nor explain. Caesar's account makes it clear that this was not a unique event" (300). The same can be said for the horse-riding Huns: "There is yet no answer to the question of what happened to the mortal remains of these fearful conquerors and their strange mounts. Hun domination was short-lived and *if* the dead were cremated and the horses' bodies not put into the graves, the likelihood of finding their bones is necessarily limited" (Sinor 1990, 203). Mallory (1989, 166) underscores the same point by noting the absence of archaeological evidence to substantiate the introduction of Gaelic into Scotland in the fifth to sixth centuries A.D.

Elsewhere, Mallory (1997) complains that the "argument of archaeological continuity could probably be supported for every IE-speaking region of Eurasia where any archaeologist can effortlessly pen such statements as 'while there may be some evidence for the diffusion of ideas, there is no evidence for the diffusion of population movement'" (104). India is not the only Indo-European-speaking area that has not revealed any archaeological traces of immigration. But the Indo-Europeans must have come from somewhere. If archaeology cannot confirm the trail of the Indo-Aryans, it cannot deny it either:

> The critical point is that language and ethnic shift can take place without radical change in the material particulars of life and with an amount of change in the gene pool so small

> as to be for all practical purposes undetectable. We should not replace the fallacy of assigning all significant culture change to migration with the fallacy of thinking that language shift and the spread of new ethnic self-identification occur only with major or radical cultural transformations. (Ehret 1988, 565)

However, we must bear in mind that such arguments work both ways. They cannot be introduced to rebut the objections of those archaeologists working in South Asia who see no evidence of Indo-European immigrations into the subcontinent, and then be denied to anyone choosing to argue for an emmigration of Indo-Europeans from the same subcontinent despite the lack of archaeological evidence. We must grant, however, that there is at least a series of archaeological cultures that can be traced approaching the Indian subcontinent, even if discontinuous, which does not seem to be the case for any hypothetical east-to-west emigration.

Conclusion

Postmodernism has impacted archaeology under the rubric of post-processualism, which holds that every reading or decoding of a text, including an archaeological text, is another encoding, since all truth is subjective. As Trigger (1995) notes, some scholars maintain that all archaeological interpretations are subjective constructions that are constrained scarcely, if at all, by archaeological data:

> The claim by archaeologists to be able to falsify interpretations on the basis of new evidence or by means of new techniques of analysis is dismissed by extreme relativists as an untenable manifestation of elitism and intellectual hegemony, which must be resisted with counterclaims that all interpretations of the past are subjective and hence there is no way to demonstrate that the insights of a professional archaeologist are necessarily superior to those of anyone else. (276).

The same, of course, could be said about linguistics. Trigger rejects such relativity and believes that as disciplines such as archaeology develop, they acquire a larger database and new methodologies that act as constraints on the imagination and excesses of scholarly interpretation. In the South Asian case, there seems to be a growing disjunct between philology and linguistics, on one hand, and archaeology, on the other, and this dichotomy seems to only increase as the database grows larger.

There is little to conclude in this chapter that has not been stated or paralleled in the previous chapter. As with the central Asian material, innovative items in the archaeological record can be seen either as items exchanged by trade and other forms of interaction, perhaps between different economic groups such as pastoralists and agriculturalists, as has always been the case on the subcontinent to this day. This interpretation seems favored by a significant number of South Asian archaeologists. Or, such items can be read as possible remanants of a new language group—the Indo-Aryan speakers—as others hold. Or there may well have been a linguistic intrusion which did not leave any distinct cultural remnants that could ever surface in the archaeological record. Interpreting the archaeological evidence from within the subcontinent will, to a great extent, reflect the attitude one holds toward the linguistic evidence outlined in the previous chapters.

Those who find the conclusions drawn from the linguistic evidence compelling will consider it legitimate to identify some of the archaeological cultures outlined in this chapter as evidence of an intruding linguistic group. R. S. Sharma (1998), in a barely veiled reference to Hindu nationalism, finds that "the commitment to cultural continuity . . . reminds us of the eternal *sanatana dharma* [eternal religion] propagated in present-day India" (95). I will discuss the Indian social context of all this in chapter 13. Sergent finds antimigrationist positions "obscurantist" and points out that India was invaded nine times in one millennium by Achemenides, Macedonians, Bactrians, Greeks, Śakas, Kuśans, Sassanides, Yuezi, and Hephtalite Huns, just in antiquity. And then, of course came the Turks, Mongols, Afghans, Portugese, French, and British. How, then, he wonders, can one realistically deny invasions or migrations? What needs to be mentioned here, however, is that these migrations are not quite adequate comparisons with any migrations that might be postulated for the Indo-Aryans because *none* of these groups eradicated the preexisting languages on the subcontinent as the Indo-Aryans are assumed to have done. They did, however, act as adstrata and superstrata, and consequently might have added loanwords or other linguistic features. I discussed the possible parallels to this in chapter 5.

Those finding the linguistic evidence more inconclusive will, in the absence of compelling contrary proof from archaeology, likely be more inclined to at least consider the possibility of an indigenous Indo-Aryan language group in the Indian subcontinent with all that this entails. Those archaeologists who consider that much of the linguistic evidence supporting such migrations can be called into question are not likely to feel constrained to interpret the archaeological record under these parameters unless the archaeological evidence itself calls for such an interpretation in its own right. But this does not legitimate proclaiming that the theory of Aryan migrations has been disproved as some Indigenists feel entitled to do. Far from it: any and all of the archaeological cultures examined in this or the previous chapter could have corresponded to an intruding Indo-Aryan ethnic group. An Indigenous Aryan position can only hope to coexist with the Migrationist's position, not displace it, at least on the grounds of the presently available data.

But even this position has a corollary in addition to the fact that an Indigenist position requires that all the Indo-Europeans came from the Northwest of the subcontinent and its environs—for which no compelling evidence has yet been produced. If we allow, for arguments sake, that much of the linguistic and archaeological evidence is ambiguous, there is still a massive chronological obstacle to an Indigenous Aryan position. How far back could Indo-Aryan have existed on the subcontinent? Since all eternity? I conclude this chapter as I have several preceding ones: before we can explore any possibility of a hoary Indo-Aryan language any further, we need to first direct our attention to the dating of the Veda, which is the topic of the next chapter.

12

The Date of the Veda

Everything hinges on the date of the Vedas. Indispensable support for the Indigenous position would result if the possibility of a much greater antiquity for the Vedic corpus could be convincingly demonstrated. Indeed, as I have noted in previous chapters, the Indigenous case actually loses plausibility unless such antiquity can be demonstrated. On the other hand, if, as some Indigenous Aryanists would have it, the Ṛgveda is a thousand or more years older than the date of 1500 B.C.E. presently assigned to it by most Indologists, a variety of issues will be affected. Since the Vedic horizons are solidly situated in the Northwest of the subcontinent, a much stronger case could be made supporting an Indo-Aryan presence in, or coexistence with, the Indus Valley Civilization, which shares much of the same horizons in approximately 2500–1900 B.C.E. The whole horse argument becomes less compelling whilst those promoting the Sarasvatī evidence become vindicated. In addition, there would be very strong grounds for would-be decipherers to approach the script as containing an Indo-Aryan language.

If the Ṛgveda is at least a millennium older than its commonly accepted date, then the possibility of Dravidian and/or Munda and/or unknown linguistic influences on Vedic Sanskrit being the result of the speakers of these languages intruding on an Indo-Aryan-speaking area after the other languages had already left, as opposed to vice versa, becomes a much more serious consideration. Moreover, the relationship between Vedic and Proto-Indo-European would need to be reconsidered. Any proposal associating the overland trajectory of the Indo-Aryans with the Andronovo culture, a southern Iranian route, or any Post-Harappan culture in the subcontinent loses value. For these and other reasons, a much older date for the Veda is foundational to the Indigenous position and is promoted almost universally by those adhering to this point of view (whether aware of all these implications or not). If by contrast, the oldest strata of the Ṛgveda cannot be far removed from the conventionally accepted date of 1200 or 1500 B.C.E. (or, with Witzel, even 1900 B.C.E.), then the Indigenous case looses cogency. Not far before the oldest strata of these texts is the joint Indo-Iranian period, which, in an Indigenist scenario, would have to be correlated with the Indus Valley Civilization proper if the conventional dates for the Ṛgveda are accepted; prior to that is the late proto-Indo-European period, which would have to be contemporaneous with the pre- and early Harappan period. Neither of these propositions would attract the attention of serious scholars in the field for some of the reasons already outlined at length (apart from anything else, no one has attempted to reconstructed the Indo-Iranians or late Indo-Europeans as urban dwellers living in such a sophisticated civilization). Indigenists, then, *must* demonstrate that the Ṛgveda could be at least a thousand, fifteen hundred, or even two thousand years older than has been generally accepted.

Dating Proto-Indo-European

Obviously, any dating for Indo-Aryan must be posterior to the terminus post quo date established for the undivided Proto-Indo-European language prior to its disintegration into the various cognate languages. The terminus ante quem date can be stated with some security: Anatolian is attested in Akkadian trading documents of about 1900 B.C.E. and is subsequently followed by the emergence of Hittite, Palaic, and Luwian in written texts. Indo-Aryan is attested in the Mitanni kingdom by 1600–1500 B.C.E., while Linear B Greek can be dated to 1300 B.C.E. So it is safe to assume, and is universally accepted, that by about 2000 B.C.E., Proto-Indo-European was already differentiated, and that Indo-Aryan was already a linguistic entity distinct from the Iranian speakers by 1600 B.C.E. at the latest.

The terminus a quo is much more problematic. All commonly accepted dates have been based on archaeological finds—no linguistic means attempting to document the rate of language change has been proposed since the rejection of glottochronology as valid. Glottochronology was a method introduced by Swadesh, whereby a word list of one hundred common vocabulary items was drawn up (this was later increased to two hundred). The idea was that time periods could be assigned to the intervals between different stages of a language, or between cognate dialects and their mother tongue, depending on what percentage of these lexical items had been preserved in the stages or dialects under comparison and what percentage had been altered or changed. For example, by calculating the amount of change in these one or two hundred items between, say, the English of Chaucer and that of Shakespeare and correlating that percentage of change with the time known to have transpired between these two stages of English (and comparing this with similar calculations from other known stages of historical languages), an attempt can be made to establish a rough overall formula such as *y* percentage of language change approximately equals *x* period of time. This formula might then theoretically be applicable in calculating the rate of change evidenced between unknown reconstructed pre- or protohistoric languages and later known stages of these languages and hence provide approximate dates for a language such as Proto-Indo-European.

The idea is actually ingenious and seemed very promising until it was pointed out that languages do not change at standard rates. Lithuanian, for example, preserves very archaic Indo-European features to this very day. The method was accordingly discarded as unreliable by most linguists. Recently, however, Starostin (1999) has attempted to revive the method. He maintains that Swadesh's method should not be jettisoned but improved in a variety of ways (such as using roots, rather than words, as comparisons since roots tend to have better retention rates). Pejros (1999), too, sees value in fine-tuning the method of gluttochronology (with more carefully formulated word lists).

Because, in the absence of dateable inscriptions, there are no other ways accessible to linguistics that can be used to date languages, Indo-Europeanists defer to archaeology. However, the archaeological method of dating languages is predicated on the clues offered by linguistic paleontology, so the data invoked to date the protolanguage assume some validity to this method. Since at least the time of Otto Schrader (1890), scholars have pointed out that there are cognate words in various languages for copper (Sanskrit *ayas*), but none for bronze or iron. Proto-Indo-European is accordingly deduced to have preceded the Bronze Age and Iron Age, but to have corresponded to the Copper Age. This evidence entails accepting a date for the differentiation of the Indo-European languages earlier than the attestation of bronze—4500 B.C.E. for arsenic-copper alloys, and at least 3500 B.C.E. for copper tin bronzes (Mallory 1975, 32)—and later than the attestation of copper, which is known in Europe since 5500 B.C.E. (Mallory 1975, 31). Thus this method will lead us to a date between 5500 and 3500 B.C.E. for an undivided (and therefore pre-Indo-Aryan) Proto-Indo-European

Historically, the domestication of the horse has been another often-cited chronological indicator on the grounds outlined in chapter 6. Anthony, Telegin, and Brown (1991) have proposed a date as early as 4000 B.C.E. for domestication based on the discovery of bit wear on horse premolars discovered in the Sredni Stog site of Dereivka. However, since, as has been discussed, many linguists have challenged the assertion that the IE's necessarily knew a domesticated horse rather than some other type of equid, the reliability of this data can be questioned. In a more recent article, Anthony (1995a) relies more heavily on the evidence of the wheel to make his case. He argues that the PIE's were undoubtedly familiar with wheeled vehicles, since at least six different terms have been reconstructed: three for 'wheel', one for 'axle', one for 'thill', and a verbal root meaning to 'convey in a vehicle' (there is no shared root for 'spoke', which could suggest that this development was a later technology). Wheeled technology appears between 3300 and 3100 B.C.E. in four different media in Europe and the Near East.[1] Anthony (1994) accordingly concludes that this evidence "requires a dispersal no earlier than about 3300 B.C. (192). If this reasoning is valid, it sets some kind of a terminus a quo for Indo-Aryan as a differentiated speech community.

Some major assumptions are embedded here that one must accept before agreeing with this conclusion. First, one must be comfortable with the techniques and efficacy of archaeological dating. Next, one must allow some validity to the method of linguistic paleontology which, as we have discussed, has been severely criticized by linguists. Objections can be raised against almost any diagnostic piece of Indo-European culture that might be correlatable with the archaeological record. Coleman (1998), for example, who is sympathetic to Renfrew's critique of this method, notes that there are four different roots for the wheel in the Indo-European languages. This suggests to him that "it looks as if 'wheel' was not in the proto-lexicon and the various words for it were created independently after the dispersal, in some areas no doubt by loan-translation from adjacent Indo-European dialects/languages" (451). Along similar lines, D'iakonov (1985) states that "some processes in which rotating was required were known to mankind since Palaeolithic times, and we do not necessarily have to associate them with the wheel; and it has yet to be clarified if the terms for 'wheel, chariot' were not used in an earlier period for 'potter's wheel.'" (113) I have noted how Lehmann and other linguists have raised parallel arguments about the horse evidence.

A further assumption one must accept is that the first occurrence of an artifact in the archaeological record is indicative of its actual date and locus of invention.[2] Anyone viewing this as an act of faith is likely to remain unconvinced by dates based on the conjunction of archaeology with linguistic paleontology. I have discussed how in the Indian context, at least, the spoked wheel was undoubtedly present for a full millennium or so before surfacing archaeologically, and probably much longer. Be all this as it may, (and most Indo-Europeanists are not unaware of these problems) when other factors known to linguistic paleontology and archaeology such as 'plows', 'milk', 'wool', and 'silver' are factored in along the same lines—most scholars have resigned themselves to a bracket of about 4500–2500 B.C.E. for the period of the dispersal.

There have been a number of notable exceptions. As noted, Renfrew has scant regard for linguistic paleontology and proposed situating the beginning of the Indo-European dispersal at around 6000 B.C.E. (in order to coincide with the evidence for the spread of farming). Other scholars have objected. For example, Crossland (1988, 453) points out that such a time frame would require supposing that the first Greek and Hittite texts had been written four thousand years after the initial breakup of the Indo-European languages, and the first Lithuanian and Albanian texts nearly seventy-five hundred years thereafter. As far as he is concerned, on this time scale one would expect far greater linguistic diversity in Indo-European than is the case. He draws attention to the diversity among the Romance languages in somewhat less than two thousand years from their point of origin as a comparable parallel.

Whether or not the diversity among the Romance languages is at all comparable to the degree of diversity between Greek and Hittite is debatable, and Renfrew (1988) is unswayed by all such arguments and challenges his critics to "substantiate more securely their 'hunch' that the proposed time scale is too long". He notes that, after all, "all agree that the supposedly regular divergence rates proposed by the practitioners of glottochronology are to be rejected" (463). Renfrew (1990) has continued to defend this position adamantly: "Many linguists have commented that these proposed dates of separation are 'too early,' but how . . . do they know this, or judge this?" (19). As will be discussed later, there are no convincing criteria to determine the conditions in which conservatism might prevail in a language and over what time period. Earlier, Crossland (1972) himself had made the following comment:

> It is disappointing to have to say that at present there seems to be no hope of estimating objectively and with a useful degree of precision how long an originally homogeneous Indo-European language would have taken to develop into derivative groups or languages which diverged as much as Greek, Sanskrit and Hittite did when the earliest texts in them were composed. Some linguists seem to think that they can make intuitive judgements about the minimum time which a particular phonetic or other change in a language would have taken. But the results of intuition when applied to estimating the minimum time in which a group of cognate languages or dialects would have differentiated to

an observed extent vary so much that no useful deductions can be made from them. . . . I sympathize with archaeologists and other prehistorians who are not primarily linguists over this. Linguists are unable to provide the information which would be most useful. (46–47)

Other archaeologists have also argued that the whole reason scholars have failed to identify the Indo-Europeans or their homeland is because they are looking in a temporal bracket that is far too late: some archaeologists believe that the dispersal of the Proto-Indo-Europeans took place in the much earlier Mesolithic or even Paleolithic (Thomas 1982, 84). Linguists have also argued for a far greater antiquity. Dolgopolsky (1990–93), in contradistinction to Coleman, unambiguously rejects a post–4500 B.C.E. date, since "Mallory's dating, which presupposes that Proto-Anatolian, Proto-Indo-Iranian, Greek and other descendant languages could have diverged from each other for a mere 2000 years, is absolutely inconceivable" (239). While well aware of the inadequacy of the glottochronological method, Dolgopolsky nonetheless tries to illustrate his argument by pointing out that all the Germanic languages, over a comparable time depth of two thousand years, maintained cognates for the same Germanic word for the term 'hand' (German *hand*; Icelandic *hönd*, etc.). Likewise, all the Slavic languages maintain cognates for their word for hand, **roka*, as do the Romance languages for *manu*. In contrast, over the same time period of 2000 years, the Indo-European languages have not maintained cognates for one proot-Indo-European term for hand, but developed five distinct terms for this basic item of vocabulary. This is conspicuous since body parts are often the most change-resistant items in a vocabulary. In other words, "if the degree of closeness between proto-Germanic, proto-Balto-Slavic, proto-Indo-Iranian and other daughter languages of Indo-European were comparable to that of the modern Germanic languages, we should expect to find the same word for 'hand' in all descendent proto-languages of the Indo-European family, i.e., no cases of replacement. The reality is quite different: we find no less than five cases of replacement" (239). According to Dolgopolsky, a 4500 B.C.E. time frame is "utterly unrealistic."

Dolgopolsky, believes the terms for material culture commonly used to date Proto-Indo-European, such as copper, horse, and wheeled vehicles, cannot be reconstructed in the Anatolian languages and therefore belong to a later, post-Hittite Indo-European and not Proto-Indo-European. Proto-Indo-European, accordingly, did not know all these items, since it was much earlier. He reiterates the arguments outlined previously, suggesting that the horse known to the Proto-Indo-European's was not the domesticated but the wild variety, and claims that the word **ayes* did not originally refer to copper but to metal in general, and it may then later have been transferred to copper in some countries when this metal entered common usage: "Hence none of these words can serve as evidence for dating Proto-IE" (Dolgopolsky 1990–93, 241). As noted earlier, these same arguments have been raised by several linguistics (Coleman 1988; D'iakonov 1988). Dixon (1997) voices similar misgivings:

What has always filled me with wonder is the assurance with which many historical linguists assign a date to their reconstructed proto-language. . . . We are told that proto-Indo-European was spoken about 6,000 years ago. What is know with a fair degree of certainty is the time between proto-Indo-Aryan and the modern Indo-Aryan languages—something in the order of 3,000 years. But how can anyone tell that the development from proto-Indo-European to proto-Indo-Aryan took another 3,000 years? . . . Languages are known

> to change at different rates. There is no way of knowing how long it ook to go from the presumed homogeneity of proto-Indo-European to the linguistic diversity of proto-Indo-Iranian, proto-Celtic, proto-Germanic, etc. The changes could have been rapid or slow. We simply don't know. . . .Why couldn't proto-Indo-European have been spoken about 10,500 years ago? . . . The received opinion of a date of around 6000 BP for proto-Indo-European . . . is an ingrained one. I have found this a difficult matter to get specialists to even discuss. Yet it does seem to be a house of cards. (47–49)

Zimmer (1988), who prefers a relatively much later date, states: "It must be stressed, and cannot be said often enough, that whatever date is given for 'PIE,' it is necessarily no more than pure speculation" (372). Zimmer does not mince his words: "Every attempt, then, to give absolute dates for 'Proto-Indo-European' (or dates for alleged different stages of 'PIE') is either based on the speculative identification of an archaeological culture with the speakers of the 'language of the PIE's' (e.g. Gimbutas, Renfrew, Mallory) or on what may be called 'intelligent guesses,' deliberations of probability and feelings of appropriateness (e.g. Meid, Gamkrelidze-Ivanov)" (372). This results in problems all around: "The first type of proposal is usually contested by fellow archaeologists and doubted by linguists, the second, being purely subjective because objective arguments simply do not exist, is bound to remain noncommittal. As is easily to be seen, many dates of both types have found their way to an often far too skeptical public" (372). Accordingly, "It is therefore *historically irresponsible for the linguist* to speak of 'Proto-Indo-European' in the 4th millennium, and *linguistically meaningless for the archaeologist* to argue about 'Proto-Indo-Europeans' living somewhere before ca 2500 B.C." (374–375; italics in original). In short, these Indo-European dating conjectures serve as a backdrop to the chronology of the Indo-Aryans.

Dating the Veda

It is from within this framework that one must negotiate the date of the Ṛgveda, which is the oldest record of the Indo-Aryans apart from the few scanty words revealed in the Mitanni documents. An exceedingly prominent area of contention among almost all scholars who have argued for the autochthony of the Aryan speakers in India is the late, and perceived arbitrary, date that has been assigned to the Vedic texts by most Western scholars. Such consensus was not always the case. Almost a century ago, Winternitz ([1907] 1962) was refreshingly forthright about the lack of agreement regarding even the approximate date of the Veda: "It is a fact, and a fact which it is truly painful to admit, that the opinions of the best scholars differ, not to the extent of centuries, but to the extent of thousands of years, with regard to the age of the Ṛg Veda. Some lay down the year 1000 B.C. as the earliest limit for the Ṛg Vedic hymns, while others consider them to have originated between 3000 and 2500 B.C." (253). Despite such differences of opinion in this matter, eventually, communi consensu, the Indological community settled on 1200 B.C.E. as the probable date for the compilation of the Ṛgveda–a date that has remained standard to this day. As opponents never tire of pointing out, "it was Max Müller who put forth the hypothesis . . . that the Ṛgveda began to be composed in 1200 B.C." (Varma 1984, 2).

Müller based his calculations on information he gleaned partly from the Kathāsaritsāgara, a collection of stories written in the twelfth century C.E. by Somadeva. In one of these stories, we find a Kātyāyana Vararuchi, who was reported to have eventually become a minister in the court of King Nanda. Since, in the Purāṇas, Nanda is the predecessor of the Mauryas, Müller assigned him a date in the second half of the fourth century B.C.E., shortly before the accepted date for this dynasty.[3] In brief, Müller felt he now had a reasonably secure date for Kātyāyana Vararuci. His next step was to correlate this Kātyāyana with a Kātyāyana who was said to have authored a variety of sūtras.[4] Since other sūtras were both anterior and posterior to this latter Kātyāyana, to whom he had assigned a date in the fourth century B.C.E., Müller ([1859] 1968) decided that "as an experiment, therefore, though as no more than an experiment, we propose to fix the years 600 and 200 B.C. as the limits of that age during which the Brāhmanic literature was carried on in the strange style of Sūtras" (218).

Preceding the sūtras are the Brāhmaṇa portions of the Vedic texts (since the latter are presupposed by the former). Regarding these, Müller ([1859] 1968) considered that "it would seem impossible to bring the whole within a shorter space than 200 years. Of course this is merely conjectural" (395). Conjectural or not, the Brāhmaṇas, in Müller's schema, are consequently assigned a date from 800 to 600 B.C.E., "although it is more likely that hereafter these limits will have to be extended" (406). Older still than the Brāhmaṇas are the Mantras, which, in turn, are anterior to the Chandas so, since he seemed to be on a roll with these concise 200-year brackets, Müller felt that "if we assign but 200 years to the Mantra period, from 800 to 1000 B.C., and an equal number to the Chandas period, from 1000 to 1200 B.C., we can do so only under the supposition that during the early periods of history the growth of the human mind was more luxuriant than in later times" (525). As Winternitz ([1907] 1962) points out, "it is at the fixing on these purely arbitrary dates that the untenable part of Max Müller's calculations begins" (255).

Reaction to Müller's perfectly synchronized, two-hundred-year periods for the development of these different genres of literature was not slow in coming. Goldstücker ([1860] 1965) objected that "neither is there a single reason to account for his allotting 200 years to the first of his periods, nor for his doubling this amount of time in the case of the Sūtra period" (80). He points out that, ultimately, "the whole foundation of Müller's date rests on the authority of Somadeva . . . [who] narrated his tales in the twelfth century after Christ [and] would not be a little surprised to learn that 'a European point of view' raises a 'ghost story' of his to the dignity of an historical document" (91). Barthelemy Saint-Hilaire (1861) remonstrated that "Mr. Max Müller would have done well not to have fixed things so precisely, and not to have circumscribed things so neatly" (54; my translation). H. H. Wilson (1860) joined in the cacophony of objections to Müller's methodology:

> We must confess that we are disposed to look upon this limit [two hundred years for the Brāhmaṇas] as much too brief for the establishment of an elaborate ritual, for the appropriation of all the spiritual authority by the Brahmans, for the distinctions of races or the institutions of caste, and for the mysticism and speculation of the Aranyakas or Upanishads: a period of five centuries would not seem to be too protracted for such a complete remodelling of the primitive system and its wide dissemination through all those parts of India where the Brahmans have spread. (376)

Bühler (1894), utilizing evidence from ancient Jain and Buddhist sources, found it inconceivable that "the ancient Indians raced through the so-called Chandas, Mantra and

Brahmana periods at a furiously fast pace" (246). Jacobi (1884) constructs a scenario to give a better conceptual image of the mechanics and time span involved in oral transmission in the days long before computer technology and electronic media:

> It is easy to see that this estimate [i.e., two hundred years] is far below the minimum of the possible period, during which in India a department of literature could take its rise, reach perfection, become obsolete and die out, to give place finally to a thoroughly new departure. For a Brahmana, for example, could only be widely spread by being learned by heart by a gradually extending circle of Brahmanas, and with the size of the country this would certainly demand a long time. Every man, who learned such a work, became, so to say, a copy of it. . . . But several of such works must successively take the place of their predecessors, before the entire class of works in question becomes obsolete. I maintain that a minimum of a thousand years must rather be taken for such a process, which in the conditions that prevailed in ancient India was of necessity a very slow one, especially when we take into consideration that in historical times the literature of the classical period remained for more than a thousand years unaltered. (158)

Each of the periods between the different genres of literature would have required at least a millennium to develop, spread, and become obsolete for Jacobi, who, as we will see, had argued for a fourth millennium date for the Ṛgveda. (Of course, the assignment of one thousand years to these periods is as arbitrary as Müller's two hundred years.) Winternitz (1907), too, felt that since "all the external evidence fails, we are compelled to rely on the *evidence out of the history of Indian literature itself*, for the age of the Veda. . . . We cannot, however, explain the development of the whole of this great literature, if we assume as late a date as round about 1200 or 1500 B.C. as its starting point. We shall probably have to date the beginning of this development about 2000 or 2500 B.C." (310; italics in the original).

Max Müller (1892), who hastily acknowledged that he had only considered his date for the Veda a terminus ad quem, completely submitted to his detractors: "I need hardly say that I agree with almost every word of my critics. I have repeatedly dwelt on the hypothetical character of the dates. . . . All I have claimed for them has been that they are minimum dates . . . Like most Sanskrit scholars, I feel that 200 years . . . are scarcely sufficient to account for the growth of the poetry and religion ascribed to the Khandas period" (xiv–xv). A few years later, at the end of his long and productive life, he again acknowledged the complete arbitrariness of his previous calculations: "Whether the Vedic hymns were composed 1000, or 1500, or 2000, or 3000 years B.C., no power on earth will ever determine" (Müller 1891, 91). Elsewhere, Müller (1897, 87) was quite happy to consider a date of 3000 B.C.E. based on Sayce's discovery of two Babylonian ideographs—cloth + vegetable fiber (which Sayce believed was cotton)—that had to be pronounced '*sindhu*'. This suggested that the Babylonians knew of the river Sindhu and, by extension, since he considered this word to be Sanskrit, the Indo-Aryan-speaking people, in 3000 B.C.E.

However, despite Müller's willing retraction of his hasty attempt at chronology:

> It became a habit already censured by W. D. Whitney, to say that Max Müller had proved 1200–1000 B.C. as the date of the Rg Veda. It was only timidly that a few scholars, like L. von Schroeder ventured to go as far back as 1500 or even 2000 B.C. And when all at once, Ḥ. Jacobi attempted to date Vedic literature back to the third millenary B.C. on the grounds of astrological calculations, scholars raised a great outcry at such heretical proce-

dure. . . . Strange to say it has been quite forgotten on what a precarious footing stood the "opinion prevailing hitherto," which was so zealously defended. (Winternitz [1907] 1962 256)

Whitney ([1874] 1987) had made a point of mentioning that Müller himself had made no pretensions that his dates had "in any essential manner contributed to the final settlement of the question." But his concern is that Müller "is in danger of being misunderstood as doing so; we have already more than once seen it stated that 'Müller has ascertained the date of the Vedas to be 1200–1000 B.C.'" (78). Winternitz (1907), too, hastened to note that "Max Müller himself did not really wish to say more than that such an interval *at least* must be assumed. . . . He always considered his date of 1200–1000 B.C. only as a *terminus ad quem*" (293).

These exchanges have been presented in some detail not merely on account of their historical interest: Müller's initial calculation (albeit no longer for the same reasons) is still the cornerstone of Vedic dating. As Varma (1984) states, "it is amazing to note that all the supporters of the date 1200–1000 B.C. for the Veda *very conveniently* ignore the caution which Max Müller had initially observed" (6). Indeed, we find present-day scholars stating that "Max Müller's chronological estimate, though not devoid of weak points, has . . . often been more or less tacitly regarded as nearest the mark. . . . As far as the Ṛgveda is concerned [his] computation is not unreasonable" (Gonda 1975, 22).

To be fair, there are more substantial reasons that have been brought forward to support Müller's initial formulations. There are philological clues that can be connected with archaeology, although these, too, can be brought into question. A summary of some of the issues raised in the previous chapter is relevant at this point in connection with their usefulness for dating. The argument that the Ṛgveda knows no urban centers and therefore postdates the Indus Valley Civilization is problematic since archaeology has revealed large late and Post-Harappan urban settlements exactly where and when the Aryans are supposed to have been entering. Besides, the Aryans either would have passed through the BMAC if they entered via the northern route or were the authors of that urban culture (according to a number of scholars) and established urban centers along a southern route, if we are to follow Sarianidi. So the Ṛgveda is not silent about urban centers due to the Indo-Aryan's ignorance of them. Moreover, several scholars have proposed that nomadic and urban cultures must always have, by necessity, coexisted.

Along the same lines, it has been argued that the absence of horse bones and of the chariot does not have to be synonymous with absence of the Indo-Aryans themselves. Indeed, the chariot is not attested archaeologically until a full millennium after it was indisputably present in South Asia, so the archaeological record has its limitations. From the Indigenous Aryan side, the references to the Sarasvatī have been produced in support of a greater antiquity for the text through this philoarchaeological method as have the less convincing references to the fire altars (although these too can be challenged).

However, there is a more important datable item that is first mentioned in the Atharvaveda (11.3.7; 9.5.4) and again in the Śatapatha Brāhmaṇa: *kṛṣṇa ayas,* 'black metal/bronze' namely, iron.[5] Smelted iron first appears in the archaeological record in a variety of places by the thirteenth to tenth century B.C.E.—including the Deccan (Chakrabarti [1997a] notes that the iron in inner India is attested earlier than in the northwestern borderlands). The mention of iron in these texts is as solid a chronological indicator as one can expect in the reconstruction of protohistory and cannot be cursorily dismissed. Moreover, the dates for iron in India are in sync with the dates for this metal attested in central Asia and Iran: if anything, the Indian context is the earliest and most likely to have influenced the others (Koshelenko 1986, 73). Even if, with Dikshit (1985), we push this back to a highest possible terminus a quo bracket of 1500 B.C.E., we have a significant terminus post quo basis for arguing that these texts were written after the attestation of iron, by the same logic and method, discussed earlier, that has convinced most IE'ists to require that the Indo-Europeans were a united entity during the Copper Age but before the Bronze Age. One would have difficulty on philological grounds, accordingly, in placing the Rgveda, too much earlier than the Atharvaveda, since the language of this text, although later, is not sufficiently different to warrant an interval of too many centuries. The iron evidence supports the consensus that will place the date of the Rgveda somewhere within a 1900–1200 B.C.E. bracket.

This bracket seems to be justified, provided we can be assured that the *kṛṣṇa ayas* of the texts refers to smelted iron objects and not to iron ore. After all, *kṛṣṇa ayas* simply means 'black metal.' As has been discussed previously, while there is no evidence of smelted iron in Harappa, iron ore has been found in eight sites, and household items have been made from it. In Mundigak, five iron items dated between 2600 and 2100 B.C.E.[6] were found, including a copper/bronze bell with an iron clapper, two iron "buttons" on a copper/bronze rod, an iron button on a copper/bronze mirror, and two indistinct lumps of "carbonates of iron" (Possehl 1999b, 159). Some of these seem to be items of everyday use. Other sites have revealed: Said Qala Tepe, "ferrous lumps' (2700–2300 B.C.E.); Ahar two iron arrow heads (ca. 1275 B.C.E.); Chanhu-Daro, an "iron artifact" (context questionable); Mohenjo-Daro, some lollingite (an iron bearing mineral that may have been used in copper smelting); Lothal, a fragmentary piece of metal (2500–1800 B.C.E.); and Katelai Graveyard in the Swat Valley, a single piece of iron (1500–1800).

In actual fact, it has even yet to be discounted that some of these might have been even smelted: "None has been analyzed to determine their technical properties and we do not known which of them is meteroic and which (if any) were smelted" (Possehl, 1999b). Either way, items made of black metal go back to the Bronze Age in Harappa, whether or not they were smelted. This does somewhat minimize the persuasiveness of the 1100 B.C.E. date for the Atharvaveda on the ground that it refers to *kṛṣṇa ayas*. The black metal could have been accidentally encountered as a by-product of the smelting of copper, manipulated in some of the ways noted here, and referred to as the 'black' *ayas*. Moreover, since the Ṛgveda knows no iron, one should not be surprised if the listed items surface in Indigenous discourse as proof that the Ṛgvedic Aryans must have existed in the area before such awareness of iron since their texts do not mention this metal.

Moreover, I have encountered the argument that we must consider the possibility that the word *kṛṣṇa* 'black' was inserted in the texts at a later period to qualify the term for bronze. The rationale here is that the older versions of these texts may have originally contained simply the word *ayas*, meaning metal or bronze, and *kṛṣṇa* was added as a supplement to the original wording in later redactions of the text after *kṛṣṇa ayas* 'black bronze' had been discovered and was becoming a more commonly available metal. The original recension of the text, however, could have been handed down through the centuries from a period much older than this discovery in 1100 B.C.E., at which time the metal referred to by the text could have been bronze. Although this possibility might appear to be a case of special pleading, it must be kept in mind. After all, it has been argued (e.g., Dolgopolsky 1990–93) that **ayes* originally simply referred to metal in Proto-Indo-European times, and that the word was transferred to bronze at a later point when this metal became widely utilized by the Indo-Europeans. Such semantic transferrals are quite common. So it is possibile that the older texts knew only bronze, which was then modified to iron in the course of oral transmission. This would simply involve adding something rather than changing an existing word in a sacred text.

This explanation, however, which might work for the prose Śatapatha Brāhmaṇa, does not work so well for the Atharvaveda, which is in meter. Any inserted word would disrupt metered verse. Since I have noted in the conclusions to previous chapters that the Indigenous Aryan position can remain cogent only if the Indo-Aryan language can be argued to have had a great antiquity, if a date shortly prior to the discovery of smelted iron is proved to be indisputable, the Indigenous Aryan argument loses cogency. Therefore, the iron evidence must be questioned by those supporting this point of view.

Chakrabarti (who has written extensively on iron in both literary and archaeological contexts) argues (1986) that one should be wary of "underlining a particular set of archaeological data and arguing that these data conform to a particular section of the Vedic literary corpus without at all trying to determine how this hypothesis will affect the other sets of the contemporary archaeological data and other sections of the Vedic corpus" (74). If iron is to be extracted as a chronological indicator, it must be juxtaposed with other indicators. Chakrabarti produces another reference from the same text in an attempt to counter the implications of the iron evidence:

> Another instance which comes readily to mind is the reference in the Śatapatha Brāhmaṇa to the spread of agriculture in the Sadanira or Gandak river valley. . . . agriculture was well established in the Gandak valley as early as the third millennium B.C. The *SB* tradition apparently contains a dim protohistoric memory. To fix this text within the straightjacket of a late date (c. 700 B.C.) is surely not a logical exercise. (74)

Chakrabarti does not state his reference, but he presumably is referring to the same verse quoted in chapter 3, which describes the first arrival of *agni*, fire, on the other side of the Sadānīra River. Chakrabarti seems to be arguing that agriculture requires knowledge of fire to prepare the land: if agriculture was on the other side of this river in the third millennium B.C.E., then so must fire have been. Accordingly, the Śatapatha Brāhmaṇa must date back to at least the third millennium B.C.E.

In terms of *argumentum ex silentio*, Sethna (1981) has written a whole book predicated on the fact that since the Vedas do not mention cotton, and cotton is known from Harappan times onward, then the Vedas must be pre-Harappan.[7] Southworth (1988, 663) uses the same lacuna to draw the opposite conclusion, namely, that the fact that the earliest Vedic texts do not mention cotton—nor, for that matter, wheat, dates, sesamum, and rice, all of which are present from Harappan times onward—suggests that the early Indo-Aryans were unaware of such things and so must be post-Harappan. Philoarchaeology, then, like everything else, can be used to support different contentions depending on different presuppositions and cannot easily solve the problem of

Vedic chronology to everyone's satisfaction (especially since the texts are not catalogues of agricultural products).

Ultimately, all that can be authoritatively established about the chronology of the Vedic corpus (viz., Saṁhitas, Brāhmaṇas, Āraṇyakas, and the earliest Upaniṣads) is that it preceded the Buddhist literature that refers to it. Such a terminus ad quem seems reasonable. But one of the main rationales offered for establishing an initial date for the composition of the Ṛgveda is the entrance of the Indo-Aryans themselves into the subcontinent, since "the determination of the *terminus a quo* is closely connected with . . . the vexed problem of the time at which the Aryans arrived in India" (Gonda, 1975, 20). And this is clearly not accepted as an a priori fact by the subjects of this study. Since conventional scholarship has assigned the Aryan arrival in India to about 1500 B.C.E., Max Müller's date of 1200 B.C.E. for the composition of the Ṛgveda remains acceptable to most Indologists. This allows an interval of three hundred years for the Aryans to settle down in the Panjab and completely forget about their overland saga. Needless to say, since the whole Aryan arrival is questioned by the Indigenous Aryan school, any date for the Veda predicated on proposed dates for supposed Indo-Aryan movements is, by extension, considered unacceptable.

The Avesta, as we have seen, anchors its chronology on the same Indo-Aryan migrations, so it is in no position to offer any extraneous assistance. Moreover, as Gonda (1975) notes, "besides the uncertain date of the *Avesta*, the cases of cultural, stylistic and lexicographical parallelism between texts of this description do not necessarily point to simultaneity" (21). The same can be said for the Mitanni treaty, generally dated to the sixteenth century B.C.E. Here we do have archaeologically datable evidence for the Indo-Aryan language. The Mitanni treaty provides additional evidence that fits smoothly with a date of about 1500 B.C.E. for the Veda in India: some Indo-Aryans settled in the Near East shortly before, or while, others were settling in India. However, the same arguments could be raised here: the parallels between the Mitanni documents and that of the Veda also do not necessarily demonstrate simultaneity. The case of modern Lithuanian, which has preserved very archaic Indo-European features into the modern period despite being separated from the protolanguage by so many millennia, demonstrates that the Mitanni could, likewise, have preserved Vedic forms that may have been much more ancient than the second half of the second millennium B.C.E. And Misra, (1992) we may recall, holds that the language revealed in the treaty contains Middle Indo-Aryan forms and could therefore be much later than the Ṛgveda. Of course, this view is by no means a fait accompli, there are other ways of interpreting the evidence, but it cannot be rejected as a possibility. Unfortunately, we are dealing with a few words in these documents, which does not allow us to document the full degree of correspondence between the Indo-Aryan of the Mitanni and that of the Ṛgveda.[8] Those arguing for a greater antiquity for the Vedic texts will in all events have to argue that the Indo-Aryan language maintained unusual linguistic stability over a vast period.

Woolner (1986, 80) provides some parallels for this: he notes that in Egyptian records, the lapse of a thousand years made little difference to language and style, the language of King Sargon in the Assyrian records appears to be much the same as that of Nebuchadnezzar about two millennia later, and even Chinese has changed relatively slowly during the last two thousand years, apart from phonetic decay. He acknowledges however that this may be representative of the stability of the script rather than the underlying phonetic system, or it may indicate a fixed literary language, which could be expected to remain more stable than a folk one. Nonetheless, Woolner is clearly unconvinced by the assumptions underpinning the date commonly assigned to the Vedas and attempts to undermine this by means of analyzing the often-cited claim, first suggested by Geldner, that the difference between the Avestan and Vedic dialects is no more than that between any two Romance languages.[9]

While pointing out a variety of assumptions and pitfalls involved in his exercise, Woolner nonetheless proceeds to compare Spanish and Italian versions of the psalms on the grounds that such hymns provide some sort of parallel to the liturgico-poetic nature of the two Aryan texts, the Ṛgveda and the Avesta. In addition, these two languages are commonly held to be as approximately divergent as their Aryan counterparts.[10] He dates these psalms to a mean of about 1500 C.E.[11] Adopting Woolner's method, but adjusting the dates he assigns to the Veda, the Avesta and the joint Indo-Iranian period to reflect the more recent opinion of specialists (which will produce results that illustrate his point even more effectively than the dates he adopts), we will follow Boyce in dating the upper limits of the oldest parts of the Avesta to 1500 B.C.E., the acceptable date of 1500 B.C.E. for the Veda (Witzel's earlier date of 1700 BCE works just as well, as does a later one of 1200 B.C.E. for either text) and assign a (relatively) uncontroversial date of about 2000 BCE for the common Indo-Iranian period. This produces a period of about five hundred years that seems to represent, by communi consensu, the time taken for the two dialects to split from their common origin.

The point is that upon applying this five-hundred-year period to the supposedly parallel case of the Romance languages, one would arrive at a date for the common Latin period of 1000 C.E. (1500–500), which, as Woolner's notes, is "patently absurd," being about twelve centuries too late! If, Woolner argues, we calculate the period we *know* elapsed from the Latinization of Spain (we have the Roman colonization of this area as a definite historic starting point for the Latin origin of Spanish) until the period when Spanish and Italian had taken their distinctive forms as represented in the psalms, we arrive at a figure of seventeen centuries. Applying this *known* figure of seventeen centuries to the hypothetical period separating the joint Indo-Iranian from Vedic and Avestan in 1500 B.C.E. (which is supposed to parallel the Romance situation), one would arrive at a period of 3200 B.C.E. for this proto-Indo-Iranian period.[12]

Obviously, there is much that can be challenged in such an exercise, since there are so many variables that can be brought into question. Moreover, the method is predicated on the assumptions of glottochronology, which is no longer accepted by most linguists, since, as I have noted, languages cannot be demonstrated to evolve at predictable rates. But Woolner's point, I think, is to show how arbitrary the allotment of any kind of chronological assignment actually is. Woolner (1986) concludes: "Perhaps it may be asked–is there then no limit? Can we equally go back to 3000 or even 4000 BCE?" He concedes that it is doubtful whether anyone would propose so remote a date as 4000 B.C. for the *actual text* of any hymn, or for the Aryan settlement in the Punjab (which he accepts), but argues that "the highest possible date for the Vedic deities, and of many elements of Vedic culture, not to speak of possible reminiscences of older periods, is a very different matter" (83). Accepting such dates for the actual Vedic texts themselves would involve expecting philologers to allow a period of linguistic stability in a literary language that is far greater than anything recorded anywhere else in the world.

Most Indigenous Aryanists seem to feel that there is no convincing reason that this cannot be the case: after all, the oral recensions of the texts have been maintained with meticulous precision for at least three millennia, and this has no known parallel anywhere else in the world. But apart from this, for well over a century, many Indian scholars (and several Western ones) have been convinced that the Vedic texts do actually contain solid philological evidence that requires the texts to be dated in the third or even fourth millennium B.C.E. (or earlier). This evidence is astronomical.

Astronomy and Vedic Chronology

Europeans first became interested in Indian astronomy for the same reasons that they eagerly scrutinized ancient Indian texts in general: there was a sense of concern regarding whether Sanskrit sources would discredit or substantiate Old Testament narrative. As we have seen, Sir William Jones was very preoccupied with the traditional date for the Kali Yuga. If this could be established, he felt confident that he could assign an average reign period to the kings of the pre–Kali Yuga dynasties and thereby determine whether Indian history could be accommodated within the generally accepted date for the Flood.[13] In 1790, he was the first to attempt to use the astronomical method to calculate the age of Parāśara Muni, whom he supposed might have lived until the Kali Yuga. Taking statements from Varāha Mihira describing the position of the sun in the constellations at the equinoxes in Parāśara's time, and estimating the degree of difference in its equinoctial position in his own time due to the precession of the equinoxes, Jones calculated that the Muni must have lived about 1181 B.C.E. The traditional date for the Kali Yuga, by such reckoning, was a serious miscalculation by the Brāhmaṇas.[14]

H. T. Colebrooke (1803) also used this method to calculate the degree of difference between the constellation in which Spring, and hence the vernal equinox, began in the Veda and the constellation in which it began in his own time. He concluded that the Vedas "were not arranged in their present form earlier than the fourteenth century before the Christian era" (284). Like Jones, he too felt assured that this invalidated the traditional date for the Kali Yuga. In his opinion, this information provided a terminus a quo for the compilation of the Vedas. Not all scholars were so conservative, however. The astronomer and onetime mayor of Paris, Jean-Sylvain Bailly, in his *Histoire de l'astronomie ancienne et moderne* (1805), felt that "these tables of the Brāhmana are perhaps five or six thousand years old" (53; my translation).[15] Bailly approved of the traditional date of the Kali Yuga, and seemed to have convinced at least some of his colleagues such as Laplace and Playfair of the accuracy of the Indian astronomical claims (Kay, [1924] 1981, 2). This was bitterly opposed by another astronomer, John Bentley ([1825] 1981), with a concern that we have seen was typical for the times: "If we are to believe in the antiquity of Hindu books, as he would wish us, then the Mosaic account is all a fable, or a fiction" (xxvii). As was discussed in chapter 1, much was at stake in such differences over the antiquity of the Indian sources.

Almost a century later, in 1894, another remarkable controversy erupted briefly in the pages of *Indian Antiquary* and other Indological journals concerning sensational claims for determining the dates of Vedic texts. Bal Gangadhar (Lokamanya) Tilak and Herman Jacobi, completely independently of each other and initially oblivious of each other's research, claimed a great antiquity for Vedic culture on the basis of astronomical clues that were hidden in the Brāhmaṇas and other Vedic texts, and one far greater than anything that was under consideration in the academic circles of their day.[16] The two scholars submitted their results to Bühler for his consideration within six weeks of each other. After their findings had been made public, Bühler published an article of his own, which approved of their basic conclusions and contributed additional material in support of their arguments. These publications were followed in 1895 by three responses, from W. D. Whitney (published posthumously), G. Thibaut, and H. Oldenberg—all of which attempted to refute the arguments of Jacobi and Tilak.

After this sudden and quite dramatic interchange, and although Jacobi continued to defend his contentions, (see Jacobi 1895, 1909, 1910), the astrochronological method disappeared from the pages of Indological journals—at least in mainstream academic circles in the West. Tilak, unbowed, went on to use his findings in his book *The Arctic Home of the Aryans*. As is obvious from the title of this book, Tilak was not attempting to assert that India was the homeland of the Aryans—he accepted, at least at this point, that the Aryans had invaded India—but was arguing that the Vedic texts might be much older than had been generally acknowledged.[17] He had also begun to prepare another book on the subject before his demise, of which the introduction, the first chapter, the outlines of eight more chapters, and some incomplete appendixes were published posthumously under the title *Vedic Chronology and Vedanga Jyotisha*. Since then, numerous Indian scholars have continued to insist that the method and its conclusions are valid. In 1965, N. N. Law, founder-editor of the *Indian Historical Quarterly*, resurrected the whole debate in support of the positions of Jacobi and Tilak, and the "astronomical evidence" has kept surfacing ever since. As Pingree (1970) puts it, "speculations abound concerning alleged astronomical data in the *Vedas*, in the *Brāhmaṇas*, and in other early Sanskrit Texts" (534).

The astronomical data are not dismissed quite so lightly by most Indian specialists in this field.[18] The Indian National Science Academy of New Delhi, for example, published a *History of Astronomy in India* in 1985, wherein the Indus Valley and the Brāhmaṇa period are correlated, and dates in the seventh millennium B.C.E. for the Vedas are proposed. In 1994, a number of the papers at a conference at the B. M. Birla Science Center and Planetarium in Hyderabad on "Ancient Indian Chronology" were based on astronomical claims. Such assertions have a direct bearing on the age of the Ṛgveda and, hence, on the greater issue of Indo-Aryan origins. The Ṛgveda is located primarily in the Punjab. If these claims of enormous antiquity for the texts have any validity, then the case for the Indo-Aryans being placed in this area at a time early enough to supersede any attempt being made to trace them archaeologically or even to decipher the Indus script becomes much more feasible. Accordingly, since the astronomical debate is clearly not settled in the minds of many scholars, it seems useful and relevant to examine the more sober and carefully presented arguments connected with this method.

The main issues involved here are actually not astronomical; that is to say, the controversy is not one involving the actual astronomical computations, which are quite elementary and not under dispute. As Tilak remarks, the debate is primarily exegetical and to be judicated by Indologists who need not feel they must defer to astronomers.[19]

The controversy is over the interpretation of certain passages in Vedic texts. The only technical astronomical knowledge required to evaluate this method is that of the precession of the equinoxes. The rate of precession is best calculated on the basis of any of four conspicuous days that occur during the course of the sun around the heavens: the two solstices (summer and winter) and the two equinoxes (vernal and autumnal).[20] Because the earth wobbles on its axis like a slowly spinning top, solar events located upon the celestial equator,[21] such as the equinoxes and solstices, also slowly drift among the stars in the celestial sphere. This westward drift is called the precession of the equinoxes.

Since the Indic system is moon-based, the celestial sphere is divided into twenty-seven *nakṣatras* 'lunar mansions' or constellations in Indian astronomy (Western astronomers have divided the celestial sphere into the twelve constellations, since Western astronomy is based on the movements of the sun). It takes 27.3 days for the moon to make a complete revolution in the sky, so the celestial sphere was divided into twenty-seven portions such that the moon could appear in a different constellation each night. It takes approximately twenty-six thousand years for a point on the celestial equator to make a full circuit of the celestial sphere as the result of precession. Since the Indian *nakṣatras* are twenty-seven in number, points such as the equinoxes or solstices will be situated in a particular *nakṣatra* for about a thousand years before slowly moving into the adjacent *nakṣatra*. In a period overlapping about 3000 B.C.E., the sun would have been in the *nakṣatra* constellation of *Mṛgaśira* at the vernal equinox; around 2000 B.C.E., in *Kṛttikā*; in about 1000 B.C.E. in *Aśvinī*, and so on to the present day. Obviously, such a phenomenon can be an invaluable tool for dating ancient texts or inscriptions, provided they contain unambiguous information about the position of the sun or full moon in the zodiac at the equinoctial or solstitial points and provided these points have been calculated accurately.

Our knowledge of Vedic astronomy[22] is gleaned mostly from peripheral statements—usually connected with the times prescribed for performing sacrifice. Although there were professional *nakṣatra darśas* 'observers of the lunar mansions' at the time of the Brāhmaṇas (see Vājasaneyi Saṃhitā, xxx, 10; Taittirīya Brāhmaṇa, iii, 4, 4, 1), the oldest astronomical manual preserved for posterity is the Vedāṅgajyotiṣa, whose date will be discussed later. In terms of specific astronomical information enunciated in the Vedic texts that is relevant to this debate, there is a year of 360 days mentioned in the Ṛgveda, called *saṁvatsara*, which was divided into twelve months.[23] The months were divided into two *pakṣas*: *pūrvapakṣa*, between new moon and full moon, and *aparapakṣa*, between full moon and new moon. The year was divided into two *ayanas*: the *uttarāyaṇa*, the six months when the sun travels north from its course nearest the horizon—from winter solstice to summer solstice—and the *dakṣiṇāyana*, or *pitṛyāṇa*, when it travels back down to the south. There is no explicit mention of solstices or equinoxes, although knowledge of the solstices, at least, is implicit in any awareness of *ayanas*. There are twenty-seven or twenty-eight *nakṣatras*, which are always listed in the texts as beginning with *Kṛittikā* (several of which are mentioned in the Ṛgveda). The first explicit reference to the beginning of the year, which is the crucial issue in this method, occurs in the *Vedāṅgajyotiṣa*, which states that the new year begins at the winter solstice. In the historical period there were several year beginnings, and both Jacobi and Tilak argue that the same was also the case in the Vedic period.[24]

I would like to reassure the reader at the outset that this section does not involve technical astronomical calculations, although there is an unavoidable plethora of *nakṣatra* names occurring in close juxtaposition that can be difficult to keep track of. The confusion is exacerbated by the need to remember whether the sun, the moon, or the month is being referred to, whether these are in conjunction with one of the solstices or one of the equinoxes, and which epoch in time is being discussed; keeping track of this material can be frustrating. I have attempted to spell everything out as clearly as possible to minimize confusion, and have bypassed the technicalities of Jacobi's, Tilak's, and Thibaut's interpretations of the astronomical passages, along with N. N. Law's counterresponses for which the reader can best refer to the originals. I will give only a brief summary of some of these arguments in this section, focusing primarily on the different underlying assumptions involved in the debate. It will be helpful to refer to table 12.1 for the next section.

Beginning with the more speculative and controversial claims, Jacobi (1909) combining the interpretations of two separate hymns, found reason to suppose that at the time of the Ṛgveda, one of the dates for beginning the year was at the commencement of the rainy season—which corresponds with the summer solstice—with the sun in *Phalgunī*.[25] This would have occurred sometime between 4500 and 2500 B.C.E. (see table). He bolsters this claim by finding other statements from various sūtras which prescribe the commencement of the *upākaraṇa*, the period dedicated to study, for the rainy season (and, hence, the summer solstice) with the full moon in *Bhadrapadā*. As can be seen from the table, the full moon was in *Bhadrapadā* when the sun was in *Phalgunī* during this 4500–2500 B.C.E. period.

However, Jacobi found other sūtras that prescribed the full moon of *Śravaṇā* for the same event (which the table chart indicates occurred in the period 2500–600 B.C.E.). Jacobi explains this discrepancy by claiming that the former prescription occurred during an earlier period, but, in the course of a millennium or more, due to the precession of the equinoxes, the summer solstice no longer coincided with the full moon in *Bhadrapadā* but with that in *Śravaṇā* instead. Out of deference to the sanctity of the Veda, the outdated prescription was not removed from some of the texts. Bühler, in support of Jacobi's (and Tilak's) line of reasoning, found references in eighteen different sutras assigning either one or the other, or both, of these full moons as suitable for the event. He, too, felt that the older, outdated prescriptions were sometimes replaced, and sometimes kept or juxtaposed alongside the more current prescriptions, out of deference to the sanctity of the texts.

Table 12.1 The precessional chart of Nakṣatras.

	4500–2500 B.C.E.		2500–600 B.C.E.	
Time of year	Position of sun	Position of full moon	Position of sun	Position of full moon
Vernal equinox	Mṛgaśirā	Mūlā	Kṛttikā	Viśākhā
Summer solstice	Phalgunī	Bhadrapadā	Maghā	Śravanā
Autumn equinox	Mūlā	Mṛgaśirā	Viśākhā	Kṛttikā
Winter solstice	Bhadrapadā	Phalgunī	Śravanā	Maghā

Tilak arrived at identical conclusions, although mostly supported by different passages and, unaware of Jacobi's work at the time of his research. Coincidentally, both Jacobi and Tilak did note in harmony that the etymological meanings of the *nakṣatras* make perfect sense when connected with the various year beginnings that they have postulated for this 4500–2500 B.C.E. epoch (i.e., *Mūlā* 'root' and its older name *Vicṛtau* 'the dividers', both terms appropriate for the first month of the year, as is the term for the preceding month—the last month of the previous year—called *Jyeṣṭhā* 'the oldest'). Like Jacobi, Tilak, also finds support for a year beginning with the summer solstice in this ancient period. Among a variety of arguments, he notes that the *pitṛyāṇa*, the fortnight dedicated to the forefathers, is prescribed for the two weeks after the full moon in *Bhadrapada*. He wonders why this date was selected and argues that this makes perfect sense sometime during the 4500–2500 B.C.E. period. At this time, this two-week period would have occurred right after the summer solstice (with the sun in *Phalgunī*) and would then have been the first two weeks of the *pitṛyāṇa*, the six months of the year dedicated to the *pitṛs*, when the sun begins its journey (*ayaṇa*) southward. Situating the two-week ceremony to the *pitṛs* at the beginning of the *pitṛyāna* made logical and coherent sense to him. Nowadays, due to precession, the fortnight of the *pitṛs* no longer corresponds to the first two weeks of *pitṛyāṇa*. Tilak held that there is no other logical reason or explanation for its present occurrence and observation in the middle of the *pitṛyāṇa*.

Like Jacobi and Bühler, Tilak also argues that these ancient prescriptions were maintained in some texts out of deference to the sanctity of the sacred texts and juxtaposed with other dates that were inserted in later periods to correspond more accurately to later astronomical situations. Tilak produces a variety of passages that he believes support the later epoch with the year beginning with the sun in *Kṛttikā* (Pleiades) at the vernal equinox in around 2500 B.C.E.. For example, he notes that the earlier texts often refer to the *Kṛttikā* as the beginning, or *mukham* 'mouth' of the year. Tilak considers that this beginning must have once occurred at the vernal equinox, since the Vedāṅgajyotiṣa explicitly places the vernal equinox with the sun very close to *Kṛttikā* (due to being composed a little later, when the equinox had shifted a little due to precession). Moreover, *Kṛttikā* always heads up the lists of *nakṣatras* in the earliest texts, thereby paralleling *Aśvinī*, which headed up the later lists of *nakṣatras*, and corresponded to the vernal equinox in historical times. Tilak attempts to fortify this claim by referring to a wide variety of passages that describe *Kṛttikā* as the *mukham* 'mouth' of the year.

Thibaut (1895), critiquing Jacobi's and Tilak's more ambitious fourth millennium proposals at length, "would rather have recourse to any explanation than [these]" (90). Reluctant to allow that the texts record an observation of *Kṛttikā* at the vernal equinox in the later epoch starting in 2500 B.C.E., Thibaut believes that the vernal equinox is not explicitly referred to in the Brāhmaṇas and that "we must . . . disabuse our minds of the notion of the equinoxes . . . having been of any importance for the Hindus previous to the . . . influence of Greek astronomy" (90). He also points out that there is no proof that the boundaries between the *nakṣatras* as known by the Brāhmaṇas were the same as those known in the later period. In other words, even if the sun did rise in *Kṛttikā* at the vernal equinox, how can one be sure that this *nakṣatra* corresponded to the same portion of the celestial sphere in the ancient period as it did in later times? In fact, at the time of this controversy, there was considerable debate over whether the Indian *nakṣatra* system was indigenous or had been borrowed from China or Mesopotamia.[26]

Whitney (1895), with scant regard for the astronomical abilities of the ancient Indians, believes that *Kṛttikā* heads the list because the Indians borrowed the whole *nakṣatra* system from Mesopotamia and "would probably have retained it in that form [i.e., with *Kṛttikā* at the vernal equinox of 2300 B.C.E.] until the present day but for the revolution wrought in their science by Greek teaching" (365).

Whitney (1895) has little of significance to add to Thibaut's more specific and much more respectfully framed objections, except disparaging remarks that even the editor is moved to preface as being stated with his "characteristic vigor and disregard of the feelings of others" (361n). Whitney shows little regard for Tilak's various attempts to bolster his arguments with comparative mythology, which he considers "is only to be paralleled with the endeavor to extract sunbeams from cucumbers" (369). According to him, the alternative dates recognized for the *upākaraṇa* might have varied "according to the suggestions of locality and climate . . . or to the caprice of schools" (363). In fact, this does seem to be the case with the idiosyncratically varying calendric traditions in much of the ancient world (Kim Plafker, personal communuication). Whitney's main objection to the whole method of Jacobi and Tilak is that "nothing in the Ṛg-Veda nor in the Brāhmaṇas, and nothing in the later Sanskrit literature, tends in any degree to give us the impression that the ancient Hindus were observers, recorders, and interpreters of astronomical phenomena" (365). As far Whitney is concerned, the earliest astronomical manual, the Vedāṅgajyotiṣa, is "mostly filled with unintelligible rubbish," and the credit for any astronomical observations of value "belongs to the Greeks, and not to the Hindus" (365). Thibaut (1895) has voiced similar misgivings: "Anything like a fairly accurate fixation of the sun's place among the stars at the winter solstice, cannot be imagined to have been accomplished by the people who had no approximately correct notion of the length of the year" (99).[27]

In such remarks, Thibaut and Whitney vividly highlight the main difference dividing the two opposing camps on this whole issue: were the ancient Indo-Aryans able to chart and coordinate the precise motions of the sun and moon in the celestial sphere in an organized and accurate fashion, or did their needs simply require a basic and approximate observation of the heavens sufficient to synchronize certain human activities? Tilak (n.d.a) finds it unreasonable to hold that the ancients did not have some kind of an accurate calendar, since "no sacrificial system could be developed without the knowledge of months, seasons and the year" (11) Tilak's first assumption, which he shares with Jacobi, is that although certain basic astronomical observations, such as solstices and equinoxes, are not specifically mentioned in the early texts, this does not mean that they were unknown to the Indo-Aryans. They both attempt to demonstrate that the ancient Indo-Aryans, who were definitely aware of the *uttarāyaṇa* and *dakṣiṇāyana* movements of the sun, and hence the solstices, were also more specifically aware of the equinoxes. Moreover, they were capable of determining these with some degree of accuracy, even if such knowledge is not explicitly detailed in the oldest texts.

Immediately after Jacobi, Tilak, and Thibaut had published their opinions, another astronomer, Sankar B. Dikshit, published a short article in *Indian Antiquary*. He had come across a passage in the Śatapatha Brāhmaṇa (ii.1.2. 2–3) that added support to Jacobi's and Tilak's contention that *Kṛttikā* once corresponded to the vernal equinox. Intending originally to publish a detailed paper on the matter, after the astronomical debate suddenly erupted, he was inspired to immediately bring his findings to the attention of the Indological community. He translates the passage as follows: "[One] should, therefore, consecrate [the sacred fires] on Kṛittikâḥ. These, certainly, do not deviate from the Eastern direction. All other *nakṣatras* deviate from the Eastern direction" (S. B. Dikshit 1985, 245). Dikshit interpreted the passage as indicating that *Kṛttikā* was situated due east, as opposed to the other stars which were either to the left, or to the right of this point. This suggests that they were situated on the celestial equator during the vernal equinox, or that their declination was nil when the passage was composed.[28] Nowadays, *Kṛttikā* is to the north of the celestial equator, due to the precession of the equinoxes. Dikshit calculates that the brightest star of this *nakṣatra* would have been on the equator around 2990 B.C.E.

Keith (1909) remarks that a similar statement of the *Kṛttikā* not deviating from the East occurs in the Baudhāyana Śrauta Sūtra (xviii 5), coupled with another statement describing this equinoctial point as being between *Citrā* and *Svāti*. Since this later event would have occurred at a much later period, the former statement, in his view, was thereby deprived of any chronological value (427). A reply by Kamesvara Aiyar (1919), another astronomer supporting Dikshit's position, adopts the explantion fundamental to this astrochronological line of interpretation: the *Citrā* and *Svāti* references were added at a later time when, due to precession, *Kṛttikā* no longer corresponded to the east point, but the text preserved the record of both epochs. Winternitz ([1907] 1962) believes the passage: "should not be interpreted as meaning that they [*kṛttikās*] rose 'due east' (which would have been the case in the third millennium B.C., and would point to a knowledge of the vernal equinox): the correct interpretation is more likely that they remain visible in the eastern region for a considerable time—during several hours—every night, which was the case about 1100 B.C." (260). Commenting on these remarks, Aiyar objects that even if someone had no knowledge of the equinoxes, he could still be perfectly capable of recognizing the eastern point. The Brāhmaṇas, after all, speak of the four cardinal points as well as four intermediate points: "Could not then the Brāhmaṇas be held to have some idea of what they said, when they spoke of east or west or of the sun turning north or south or of an asterism not swerving from the east?" (183).

All that a simple observatory would require, Aiyar (1922) argues, is twenty-seven poles planted equidistant in a circle around a house or open space with the observer occupying the same central space every day:[29] "It would be unfair to suppose that such a feat was difficult of accomplishment by generations of Brahmavādins whose chief work in life appears to have been to regulate their rites by the seasons and the position of the sun and the moon in the Zodiac" (184). Likewise, he argues that the estimation of the equinoxes could be accomplished by the simple act of tracing and counting the different daily lengths of the shadow of a stick, that is, by the simple act of inferring that midway between a day that is shorter than the night, and a night that is shorter than the day, must be a time with equal day and night. One could, of course, counter this by arguing that it might not actually be so easy to determine the longest or shortest shadow measurements to the exact day, since the daily change of size would be very small. Moreover, Pingree (1989) points out that parts of the constellations *Hasta* and *Viśākhā* were also on the equator in 3000 B.C.E.

Aiyar (1922) produces another verse from the Maitrāyaṇa Brāhmaṇa Upaniṣad, which he translates as follows: "The manifest form of time is the year. . . . One half of this year is *Āgneya* (the warm half) and one half *Vāruṇa* (watery or cold). When the sun moves from the beginning of Maghā to half (the segment of) Śravishṭhā in the regular order . . . it is Āgneya [warm]. When the sun moves from the beginning of Śārpa (Āśleshā) to the end of Śravishṭhā half, in the inverse order, it is *Saumya* [cool]" (188). Aiyar interprets this as a direct reference to the *uttarāyaṇa* and the *dakṣiṇāyana* of the sun when it was situated in *Maghā* at the summer solstice. As can be seen from the chart, *Maghā* was at the summer solstice in the era when *Kṛttikā* was at the vernal equinox.[30] Dikshit and Aiyar have thus produced additional references in an endeavor to support Jacobi and Tilak's contention that the texts refer to *Kṛttikā* coinciding with the vernal equinox which would have been the case in about 2500 B.C.E.

The Polestar

A final chronological observation based on another side effect of the precession of the equinoxes was made by Jacobi (1909). As mentioned previously, the precession of the equinoxes is caused by the wobbling motion of the earth, which totters on its axis like a spinning top that is slowing down. As a result, the axis of the earth slowly revolves around the celestial sphere at the rate of approximately one revolution every twenty-six thousand years. The star that lies at the end of the celestial pole is called the polestar.[31] Although the earth revolves around its axis, from the perspective of an observer on earth, it is the stars that appear to be revolving—all except for the polestar, which, being situated on the end of the earth's axis appears to remain stationary. However, because of the precession, the pole does not always point to the same star. In different epochs, different stars that come close enough to the pole to appear motionless are considered the polestar. According to Jacobi, in the last seven thousand years, only two stars have come close enough to the celestial pole to be considered stationary. The remaining stars, at their minimum distance from the pole, spun around it in a circle with a diameter of at least nine degrees—a motion easily visible to an observer. One of the two fixed stars is the present one, '*a ursae minoris*',[32] the other, '*a draconis*', was exactly on the pole in about 2780 B.C.E.[33]

Jacobi points out that the Gṛhya Sūtras preserve a well-known custom according to which the husband points out the polestar (called *dhruva* 'fixed') to his newlywed wife and exhorts her never to forsake her home just as the polestar never changes its position. He concludes that these sūtras preserve a memory of the ancient time when the polestar appeared stationary. Bühler (1894) fortifies Jacobi's observation by precluding the possibility that perhaps the star, at a much later date, was not actually at the pole but was near enough to appear almost motionless. He notes, in this regard, that the Maitrāyaṇa Brāhmaṇa Upaniṣad illustrates the mutability of all material beings by commenting that even *dhruva*, the polestar, is subject to motion. This observation, he feels, represents a later time when the polestar was no longer stationary, and the ancient Indians were perfectly capable of noting this fact. Despite Bühler's endorsement, however, Whitney (1895) was not impressed, since "for such observers, and for such a trifling purpose, any star not too far from the pole would have satisfied both the newly wedded woman and the exhibitor" (365). Keith (1909, 1101–1102), also finds it incredible that a usage in the relatively late Gṛhya Sūtras could have been preserved from such a remote age and refuses to concede that the Hindus could have been such keen observers of the stars that they would have noticed the circular motion of some other, later star that was near, but not on, the North Pole. It is relevant to note, also, that Jacobi (and others) are assuming a single and consistent astronomical view in these varying texts (which was not evidenced in Western sources in antiquity).

Discussion of the Astronomical Evidence

Some scholars seem very unwilling to stray too far from the chronological security of the explicit statement in the Vedaṅgajyotiṣa that places the vernal equinox in 10 degrees of *Bharaṇī*, the winter solstice in the beginning of *Śraviṣṭhā*, the summer solstice in the middle of *Āśleṣā*, and the autumnal equinox in 3 degrees of *Viśakhā*. Astronomers have assigned this conjunction dates ranging from 1391 to 1181 B.C.E. (Keith [1912] 1967, 423) Even this text, since the time of Max Müller (1892, xxix) and despite containing such specific information regarding the position of all four equinoctial and solsticial points, has not been unanimously accepted as a reliable record of the second millennium B.C.E. Whitney, like Thibaut, also questions the correspondence of the *nakṣatras* mentioned in the Vedāṅgajyotiṣa to the equal 13½ degree divisions they denoted in later times.

Scholars like Tilak find it difficult to understand reluctance to allow the Indo-Aryans the simple ability of dividing the sky into twenty-seven equal segments so that the moon would appear to rise in a different part of the heavens, or *nakṣatra*, each night (we can recall Aiyar's simple astronomical observatory constructed with twenty-seven posts): "To use the words of Max Müller, we must, in such cases, 'keep our preconceived notions of what people call primitive humanity in abeyance for a time'" (Tilak n.d.a, 71).[34] On the other hand, as Kim Plofker has pointed out (personal communication), however simple this task might seem from our perspectives, we know that Babylonian observers, whose activities were recorded, were watching the night sky for a millennium or more before coming up with the idea of an equally divided zodiac, so this idea does not appear to have been immediately obvious to them.

Whitney (1895) also questioned the ability of the Indo-Aryans at the time of the Vedāṅgajyotiṣa to judge solstitial and equinoctial points to within several degrees of accuracy: "To look for an exact observation of the place of the colures in a treatise which adopts a year of 366 days, and assumes and teaches the equable increase and decrease of the length of the day from solstice to solstice, is obviously in vain" (331). He thinks a margin of an entire millennium would not be excessive to accommodate all the possible errors and uncertainties involved in such calculations: "A period of a thousand years is rather too little than too great to allow for all the enumerated sources of doubt and error. He who declares in favour of any one of the centuries between the eighth and the eighteenth before Christ, as the probable epoch of the Jyotisha observation, does so at his own peril" (327). Accordingly, Keith and Macdonell ([1912] 1967, 425) assign the Vedāṅgajyotiṣa a date in harmony with that commonly accepted for the Brāhmaṇas, namely, 800–600 B.C.E. The logic here seems to be that since there is a hypothetical possibility that there *could* have been several centuries' worth of miscalculation due to imprecise observational techniques, therefore there *was* such miscalculation, therefore the date of the Vedāṅgajyotiṣa actually *is* not earlier than the eighth to sixth centuries B.C.E.

Most Indian astronomers I interviewed find it difficult to accept this series of assumptions, and consider such conclusions to be unnecessarily biased. Even if it is conceded that one has to allot a millennium or so leeway to compensate for possible mistakes, then, (were there no other factors involved) the error margin must, in theory at least, be a thousand years spread out over *either side* of the 1391–1181 B.C.E. bracket, as Whitney himself notes in the earlier quote, since the Indo-Aryans may have erred on the posterior, as opposed to the anterior, side of things.[35] Of course, there are other factors (linguistic and philoarchaeological) that need to be taken into consideration at this point. Keith, Whitney, and Thibaut, in their date assignments, are operating within the chronological infrastructure of the Indo-Aryan literature as a whole, which was outlined at the beginning of this section. To a great extent their partiality for the arguments suggesting a later date is influenced by an acceptance of the date of the Ṛgveda itself in *c* 1200 B.C.E.; naturally the language of the Vedāṅgajyotiṣa would set it several centuries later than this. Anyone adhering to the commonly accepted date for the Ṛgveda is constrained to date the Vedāṅgajyotiṣa much later and therefore consider reasons for distrusting the explicit references in this text. And, of course, the reverse holds true: anyone questionning the dating of the Ṛgveda is more likely to consider the astronomical arguments, and/or anyone considering the astronomical arguments will be impelled to reconsider the date of the Ṛgveda as a corollary.

More recently, Jean Filliozat (1969) has also supported the *Kṛttikā* arguments of Dikshit and Tilak:

> It is certain, as S. B. Dikshit and B. G. Tilak have amply emphasized, that it is only thus that one can interpret the statement of ŚB. In spite of the systematic doubt from Thibaut, Whitney . . . and other authors, who have refused to accept a conclusion arrived at by Dikshit and Tilak, the ancient dates attributed to some Vedic texts, referring to the Pleiads [*Kṛttikā*], and not only the text of the ŚB, but also the Buddhist lists . . . point to a real determination of the vernal equinox and of the movement of the Sun through Pleiads. (125)

Filliozat points out that a variety of later Buddhist texts, which have borrowed the order of the *nakṣatras* in the Vedic lists more or less exactly, have divided the *nakṣatras* into four parts. Each part represents the stars protecting the four directions, with *Kṛttikā* heading up the list as protectors of the East. She notes that the references to this *nakṣatra* suggesting its placement at the vernal equinox are too frequent and dissimilar to have been a later interpolation. Like Aiyar, she also argues that knowledge of the equinoxes simply requires "the use of the eyes, of a vertical stick, and of a rope to determine the meridian by the shadows of the stick and . . . its perpendicular, pointing out on the horizon the true East and West" (126). This technique, called a *gnomon*, was known in later texts, (but is not mentioned in the Vedāṅgajyotiṣa). A gnomon is a stick placed in the ground to record the daily length of the shadow every noon. Moreover, she points out that since we do have these lists of *nakṣatras*, we can deduce that it was known that the *nakṣatra* directly opposite *Kṛttikā* was *Anuradhā* (which is fourteenth on the list after *Kṛttikā*). Therefore, "it sufficed to verify that a full moon occurred in Anuradha, in order to know that the sun was in the Kṛttikas" (126).

The rejection of such arguments has been upheld by Pingree who prefers a date of 400 B.C.E. for the Ṛgveda recension of the Vedāṅgajyotiṣa and as late as 500 C.E. for that of the Atharvaveda. Referring to the very specific testimony of the Vedāṅgajyotiṣa,

Pingree (1973) echoes Whitney: "Since a displacement of the beginning of the equal nakṣatra by some 10 degrees, or an error of ten days in computing the date of the winter solstice, or some combination of these two effects is all that is required to bring the date from the twelfth century to the fifth century B.C., we should not lend much weight to this chronological argument" (10). Pingree (1992), however, does introduce a variety of additional evidence in support of this later date. He argues that the Sanskrit omen texts, such as the Gargasaṁhitā of about A.D. 100, as well as the Buddhist Dīghanikāya of the approximately fourth century B.C.E. and later omen texts have borrowed much, albeit significantly modified in form, from the Mesopotamian texts in subject matter and sequence of material. The direction of borrowing is determined by the fact that the Mesopotamian texts are earlier. He also finds reason to believe that the Vedic liturgical calendar, as well as some aspects of its conceptions of the *nakṣatras*, can be traced back to MUL.APIN, a Mesopotamian astronomical text. As far as astronomy goes, he also finds a variety of reasons to conclude that it "has borrowed much from Mesopotamian astronomy of the seventh and sixth centuries B.C." and accordingly must postdate the Babylonian texts (Pingree 1973, 6).

One primary reason he presents for the direction of borrowing is based on the fact that the Ṛgveda recension of the Vedāṅgajyotiṣa uses a ratio of 3:2 for the longest to the shortest day of the year. This ratio is determined by a zigzag function common to the Babylonian texts and the Arthaśāstra to obtain the length of the shadow of a gnomon. The zigzag function is the method for calculating the incremental difference in length of this shadow between the equinox and solstice days, and is common to both traditions.[36] According to Pingree (1973), this is "a ratio inappropriate to all parts of India save the extreme north-west, but one that is well attested in cuneiform texts . . . [and] indicates a terrestrial latitude of about 35 degrees—that is, somewhat north of the latitude of Babylon" (4–5). Therefore, this formula must have been borrowed.

As Pingree himself notes, however, this ratio is, indeed, applicable to the Northwest of the subcontinent, which is adjacent to the geographic location of the Ṛgveda, the epicenter of the Indus Valley where Indigenous Aryanists place the Indo-Aryans in the ancient period. Accordingly, Kak (1994b) adjusts the latitude of thirty-five degrees to account for refraction, so that "after corrections are made this corresponds to a latitude of thirty-four degrees which is correct for northwest India to the North of the Sarasvati valleys" (101). Since this ratio is applicable to Northwest India, he considers it perfectly acceptable to propose that the Vedāṅgajyotiṣa could have been composed in this latitude.[37] This view has received support from Yukio Ohashi (1997), who believes that "it is clear that this formula is based on the observation in North India" and more specifically the "Kashmir area, and much north of the basin of the Ganga River which was the central area in post-Vedic period [*sic*]." According to yet another astronomer, Narahari Achar, "It does not follow that India borrowed from Mesopotamia, or, for that matter, Mesopotamia borrowed from India; nothing precluded the possibility of parallel development in both countries independent of each other."[38] More important, he notes that "a ratio of 2:1 for the duration of the longest day to the shortest day was used in the early days of Mesopotamia and was only modified to the value 3:2."[39] An independent origin of the astronomy of the Vedāṅgajyotiṣa, and of the validity of, at least, the *Kṛttikā* evidence was favored by all of the astronomers I interviewed in India during my research.[40]

The Mathematics of the Śulvasūtras

Another line of argument is sometimes encountered in Indigenous Aryan literature in discussions of Babylonian borrowings and of Vedic dating. This deals with mathematics. Seidenberg (1960; 1978; 1983) contends that the Śulvasūtras must be dated much earlier than presently acknowledged, and that Indians certainly did not borrow the mathematics of these texts from the Babylonians (although, even if his arguments are valid, this does not mean that they could not have borrowed the astronomical knowledge evidenced in other texts). Seidenberg proposed that there was either a common, unknown source of origin, or that it was the Babylonians who borrowed their mathematics from the Indians, but certainly not vice versa. And this, according to him, necessitates a date of at least 1700 B.C.E. (and most probably 2200 B.C.E.) for the mathematics of the Śulvasūtras. Seidenberg's arguments are deferred to by scholars such as Kak to question the assertion that, since the Babylonian texts were probably compiled in about 700 B.C.E., this date is necessarily a terminus post quo for the Sanskrit sources.

The Śulvasūtras are a class of works, preserved in various schools, such as those of Baudhāyana, Āpastamba, and Kātyāyana, which are often referred to as manuals of altar construction. (Others include those of Satyāṣāḍha, Mānava, Maitrāyaṇi, and Vārāha.) In these texts, the construction of a wide variety of altars is described—square, circular, or falcon-shaped—the form depending on the type of ritual to be performed. In certain of these sutras, the formula that came to be known in the West as the theory of Pythagoras is expressed.[41] Thibaut (1875), who was the first to translate the sūtras into English, felt that "the general impression we receive from a comparison of the methods employed by Greeks and Indians respectively seems to point to an entirely independent growth of this branch of Indian science" (228). Such a statement was quite significant in Thibaut's time, since the scientific achievements known to the Indo-Aryans were generally held to have been borrowed from the Greeks.

Seidenberg (1983), a historian of science,[42] described the reaction to Thibaut's claim: "Thibaut himself never belabored or elaborated these views, nor did he formulate the obvious conclusion, namely, that it was not the Greeks who invented plane geometry, it was the Indians. At least this was the message that the Greek scholars saw in Thibaut's paper. And they didn't like it" (103). Eventually, Thibaut was pressured into proposing a date for the sūtras that would disarm the Greek scholars, but he would not forgo the possibility that the two different peoples could at least have developed the same knowledge independently. The date he offered was the fourth or third century B.C.E. Seidenberg (1978) comments: "A terrible statement! I cannot help thinking that it shows battle-weariness rather than a considered opinion. . . . Anyway, the damage had been done and the Śulvasūtras have never taken the position in the history of mathematics that they deserve" (306).

Seidenberg (1983), "regard[s] it as certain that knowledge of Pythagoras' Theorem was known to the Śatapatha Brāhmaṇa, which mentions calculations connected with the *puruṣa* bird altar, and to the Taittirīya Saṃhitā, which showed similar geometrical awareness" (106). Since these texts are generally dated to around 1000–800 B.C.E., "Greek geometry did not somehow make its way into Vedic geometry, as Greek geometry is only supposed to have started about 600 B.C." (108). Scholars no longer consider Vedic geometry to have been borrowed from the Greeks, so Seidenberg's more controversial claim in the modern context is his rejection of the possibility that the algebra either of the Indians or the Greeks was derived from Babylonia, since the former were aware of aspects of the theorem to which the Babylonians make no reference. He also rejects the possibility that these aspects could have been discovered by the Indians after receiving the basic theorem from Babylonia and then transforming it, and concludes that either "Old Babylonia got the theorem of Pythagoras from India or that Old Babylonia and India got it from a third source" (Seidenberg 1983, 121).

Seidenberg's next steps involve a series of assumptions that need to be laid out. He first states that since the Babylonian sources are dated to 1700 B.C.E., the mathematical knowledge in the Śulvasūtras must predate that. His next statement is significant: "Now the Sanskrit scholars do not give a date for the geometric rituals in question as early as 1700 B.C. Therefore I postulate a pre-Babylonian (i.e., pre-1700 B.C.) source for the kind of geometric rituals we see preserved in the Śulvasūtras, or at least for the *mathematics* involved in these rituals" (1983, 121). Seidenberg assigns a date of 2200 B.C.E. for the common source, but upon being told by his Indological colleagues that the Aryans were not even in India in 1700 B.C.E. (1978, 324), let alone 2200 B.C.E., he is forced to postulate that the Aryans and Greeks inherited their mathematics from the joint Indo-European period, and the Indo-Aryans brought the knowledge into the subcontinent with them. Needless to say, for Indigenous Aryanists, such adjustments are unnecessary, since they hold that the Aryans were very much in India in 2200 B.C.E. From this perspective, Seidenberg's dating of the Śulvasūtras, or at least of the mathematics known in them, is often introduced as supplementary evidence to support a much older date for the Ṛgveda that must considerably precede the sutras and Brāhmaṇas containing these mathematical formula.

Boyer (1989) finds that all the triads involved in the Pythagorean theorem "are easily derived from the old Babylonian rule; hence, Mesopotamian influence in the *Śulvasūtras* is not unlikely," but he does acknowledge that Āpastamba does contain a formula that connot be derived from Babylonian sources (233). He is also prepared to consider that "references to arithmetic and geometric series in Vedic literature that purport to go back to 2000 B.C. may be more reliable" but adds that "there are no contemporary documents to confirm this." This, of course, as with the astronomical claims, is the crux of the matter; these possibilities are tantalizing, and certainly possible, but without explicit confirmation in the relevant textual sources, they remain unprovable.

Furthermore, as Plofker has pointed out (personal communication), Seidenberg's assertions are most immediately vulnerable in his claim that the Śulvasūtras must have predated the Babylonian texts from 1700 B.C.E. on the grounds that they contain mathematical information not known in Mesopotamia. There is always the possibility that any such material could have been a later Indian development from an earlier, Babylonian borrowing; even accepting an Indian origin for this material, it could still have been an independent development at a much later period. Also, even allowing an earlier date, it could be argued that the date assigned to the knowledge of a particular mathematical formula does not have to correspond to the date of the texts that encapsulate this knowledge, nor the geographic location wherein the texts were written (they could, after all, be primordial memories of the Indo-Aryans from somewhere east of the Caspian Sea as Seidenberg himself finds acceptable). As I have already suggested with the reference to iron in the texts, there are many pitfalls in the general method of dating texts on the basis of solitary pieces of information or references: these could be stray pieces of information that are much older, or much younger, than the texts that happened to preserve them at a particular point in time.

Conclusion

Such consistent refusal to consider a greater antiquity for the Vedic texts, and to suggest a foreign origin whenever the occasion presents itself, has been a source of puzzlement and resentment for many Indian scholars such as Tilak (n.d.a), who "cannot understand why scholars should hesitate to assign the Vedic works to the same period of antiquity which they allow to the Chinese and the Egyptians" (56). Other scholars conclude that there must be more sinister motives afoot and that "Indians cannot help feeling that it is all camouflage, an ingenious device to shut out a whole class of evidence" (Aiyer 1992, 176).[43] If some Indologists sometimes suspiciously wonder why some Indian scholars are so concerned about promoting the antiquity and indigenousness of the Vedic culture, these scholars, in turn, are at a loss to understand why some Western scholars take such pains in insisting on a more recent chronology and foreign origin whenever the possibility presents itself. Such sensitivities notwithstanding, the debate must be resolved by the best manner of accounting for the evidence.

The attempts to defend, or refute, the validity of this type of astronomical evidence are predicated on a series of assumptions. Depending on how one evaluates which set of assumptions is more or less reasonable, one will be inclined to approve, or disapprove, of the conclusions proposed. It will be helpful, in this regard, to summarize the issues on each side of the debate. Those advocating the astronomical method believe that the ancient Indo-Aryans must have had certain astronomical skills. Although these are not specifically delineated in the earliest texts that have come down to us, they can be inferred from statements made in these texts. These skills would include the ability to divide the celestial sphere into twenty-seven *nakṣatras* corresponding to the twenty-seven-day lunar sidereal month. The *nakṣatra* system corresponds to the same stars as it does in the historical period. Two principal days for beginning the year were the winter solstice and the vernal equinox. The Indo-Aryans were well aware of both these year beginnings and could calculate them with some degree of accuracy. They had a lunar and solar calendar, which they coordinated by a functioning intercalary system.[44] The information contained in the Vedāṅgajyotiṣ is to be understood in its own terms with regard to its date. finally, the Indo-Aryans were specific in the terms they used: when the texts say that *dhruva* is motionless, or that *Kṛttikā* does not move from the east, they mean exactly that (and not *per modo di dire*—nearly motionless or in the eastern direction in general). Their point of view, on the whole, is fairly and aptly represented by the astronomer Gorakh Prasad (1935), who investigated this whole debate and concluded: "If we exclude the possibility of every astronomical notice in Vedic literature being a record of ancient tradition, which is extremely unlikely, we can say that there is strong astronomical evidence that the Vedas are older than B.C. 2500. They might be as old as B.C. 4000. There is some support for this date, but it is not convincing (136).

The basic presuppositions of those opposed to such conclusions assume, in their turn, that nonmention of these specific astronomical abilities in the earliest texts indicates nonacquaintance with such skills and anything more than this is simply speculation. If the Indo-Aryans did have precise observational and computational astronomical abilities, why did they not record them, or why did any hypothetical record of these disappear? Even explicit astronomical specifications such as those found in the Vedāṅgajyotiṣa have to be regarded as unreliable for chronological purposes on the grounds that there is no guarantee that the earliest Indo-Aryans astronomers had exactly the same *nakṣatra* map, or the same degree of accuracy, in their earlier calculations as they developed in the later period (nor, perhaps, were these so important or relevant earlier in time): a few degrees of inexactitude can translate into centuries or a millennium or more of chronological difference. Likewise, the arguments advocating an early third millennium date for the polestar can be dismissed by suggesting that the Hindus were not as meticulous in their observation of the stars as they eventually learned to be, and not rigorous in their use of terms such as *dhruva*.

In my view, the references connected with the fourth millennium B.C.E. date, although intriguing, are too speculative to be used as substantial evidence. In the post–2500 B.C.E. period, however, the quality and quantity of references supporting the position of the sun in *Kṛttikā* at the vernal equinox are more substantive. They should be given due consideration as a serious possibility. They are as valid a chronological indicator as anything else that has been brought forward to date the Vedic texts. But they cannot win the day in and of themselves without additional, outside support. And they can be countered by the iron evidence provided we are prepared to take *kṛṣṇa ayas* to mean smelted iron as opposed to items made from iron ore. As has been noted, household items with iron parts have been found in a number of Harappan sites some of which date to 2600 B.C.E. or earlier. Also, if one is to impartially consider all possibilities, even if we allow that these references are valid astronomical observations, proponents of Aryan migrations can still argue that they refer to primordial memories that were retained by the Aryans during their overland trek to India, which they then inserted in later texts. In any event, it seems unadvisable and rather precarious to rest the whole dating of the Ṛgveda and other Vedic texts primarily on references to single items, whether this be the references to *Kṛttikā*, for an earlier date, or to the adjective *kṛṣṇa* supplementing the word *ayas*, for a later date.

All of the astronomical proposals outlined in this chapter have been challenged, or the passages where they occur reinterpreted. These reinterpretations, in turn, have been and can be critiqued. Therefore, the astronomical references in the texts can neither apodictically prove the antiquity of the Vedas nor be categorically disproved as preserving evidence of the same. Other chronological indicators are dependent on the quirks of the archaeological record for their dating value. By this process one would have to date the spoked wheel to after the fourth century B.C.E., when even a 1500 B.C.E. date for the Ṛgveda assures us that they were present a millennium or so earlier. Other archaeo-philological introduced by Indigenists, such as the Sarasvatī, are likewise problematic.

Other chronological anchors such as the Mitanni documents, while certainly supporting a 1500 B.C.E. date for the Ṛgveda, might also be open to alternative possiblities. Even if there are forms in these documents more archaic than the Ṛgvedic parallels (which is debated), which could suggest that the Vedas should be dated posterior to them, can we eliminate the possibility that these forms may have been preserved from a much older period than 1500 B.C.E.? One cannot predict which languages might preserve archaic Indo-European forms from millennia ago.

The same argument might apply to the Anatolian group. If Anatolian is considered an older language than Vedic, and was the first to peel off from the proto-language, and if Anatolian is attested in documents at circa 1900 B.C.E. how can the later Vedic language be older than this date? This, too, is a chronological anchor that reasonably secures the date of the Ṛgveda to after 1900 B.C.E. However, here we also need to eliminate the possibility that the Anatolian languages might have been much older than the date when they emerge in dateable records, and that they preserved certain archaic features from a hoarier antiquity (as Vedic preserved other archaic features).

I concluded several preceding chapters by deferring to chronology and stating that everything depended on the date of the Ṛgveda. My own view is that the philological arguments presented in this chapter are not sufficiently solid to convince even a majority of the parties in this debate of either an earlier or a later date. At the risk of being frustratingly agnostic I maintain that we must again defer to the evidence discussed in chapter 9 for solid, irrefutable evidence that will have massive implications on this whole issue: the Indus script. This is the only item that can *convincingly* settle this entire debate and will be discussed further in the conclusion. Another decisive factor, of course, would be if an item of irrefutable Indo-Aryan pedigree such as a (genuine) Vasiṣṭha's head were fortuitously to surface in a datable pre- or mature Harappan context somewhere on the subcontinent (rather than in a Delhi bazaar).

In the absence of such evidence, there remains one last dimension of this debate that needs to be discussed. In chapter 1, I analyzed some of the influences that might have affected the interpretations of Indo-Aryan history in Europe. I now need to conduct a parallel discussion on the subcontinent. Allowing that much of the evidence of Indo-Aryan migrations from an outside homeland can be brought into question, one must also acknowledge that there is certainly no compelling evidence to support a South Asian Indo-European homeland as the nucleus of an external emigration. Since most of the evidence is so malleable, what might cause scholars to argue so persistently for a position of Indigenous Aryanism?

13

Aryan Origins and Modern Nationalist Discourse

Chapter 1 summarized how the discourse of Aryanism affected religious and political identities in post-Enlightenment Europe. Chapter 2 touched upon parallel phenomena in pre-independence India. This chapter will consider how the same theme of Aryan origins has been utilized to support a variety of agendas on the Indian subcontinent in the modern period. Here, among the linguistic descendants of the Indian branch of the Indo-European language family, the Aryan invasion debate is intensely relevant to the constructions of several very different sets of competing identities: associations of colonizer and colonized, neo-colonial and Hindu fundamentalist, Vedic Hindu and biblical Christian, Hindu and Muslim, indigene and foreigner, Aryan and Dravidian, and Hindu communal and Marxist secularist are all permeated in one way or another with a variety of notions connected with Aryan origins. Contesting the foreign origin of the Indo-Aryans undoubtedly receives the support of certain Hindu nationalists and ideologues. But this mind-set cannot account for everyone prepared to reconsider this issue. Since there is a tendency to stereotype any local reconsiderations of ancient Indian history whatsoever as nationalist or communal, the purpose of this chapter is to suggest that a wide variety of motives inspire Indian scholars to revisit the topic of Indo-Aryan origins: it is erroneous to lump them all into a simplistic, hastily identified and easily demonized *Hindutva* category.

Most of the scholars I have quoted so far in the body of this book have been professional academics or have contributed arguments that I have considered valuable to this debate. In the footnotes to this chapter, in addition to these more critical scholars, I will also introduce some of the more peripheral members of the Indigenous Aryan school. To accomplish this, I will provide information about the publications produced by some of these people, to give some idea of the views of the authors themselves. The indigenous Aryan camp is not a homogeneous group, and just as it is simplistic to lump all its members into a *Hindutva* category, it is equally erroneous to judge everyone espousing similar views by the standards of scholarship (or lack thereof) of the more peripheral and outlandish publications that have surfaced over the years. Any analysis of the sociology and historiography of this point of view, if it is to be useful, needs to be aware of a wide spectrum of backgrounds, motives, and contexts of the various contributors to avoid convenient stereotypification or hasty generalizations. Such concerns will be the topic of this chapter.

Nationalism and Historiography: General Comments

A number of recent volumes have analyzed the influence of nationalism on archaeological and historical interpretations (Kohl and Fawcett 1995; Graves-Brown et al. 1996; Bond and Gilliam 1994; Hodder 1991; Gathercole and Lowenthal 1990). As Trigger (1995) notes, the main impact of nationalism has been to influence the questions about the past that archaeologists are prepared to ask (or not to ask) and the amount of evidence that is required to sustain a particular position. This has had positive and negative effects. On the positive side, nationalist archaeology has stimulated asking questions about local cultural and ethnic configurations that would not have occurred to colonially oriented archaeologists. It has brought different assumptions, perspectives, and concerns to the data, exposed colonial predispositions and imperial biases, forced a reevaluation of old dogmas, and provided resistance to racism and colonialism. Bond and Gilliam's *Social Construction of the Past* (1994) focuses on how historical reconstructions are crucial elements in the process of domination, subjugation, resistance, and collusion. This volume is sympathetic to the indigenous reclamation of subjugated views and demonstrates the ways in which power and economic domination establish one rendering of history and culture as objective and ethically neutral and brandish another as subjective and partisan: "Colonialism provides the immediate touchstone and background against which many post-colonial scholars and leaders have pursued strategies to reclaim their past and assert their individual and national identities" (3).

On the negative side, nationalism has encouraged the misinterpretation of archaeological data for political purposes and ignored important aspects of human history. As a result, much of the scholarship in such volumes as Kohl and Fawcett's *Nationalism, Politics and the Practice of Archaeology* is highly critical of perceived attempts to distort that past, limit the questions that are asked, or delimit the sum total of data that is brought into consideration. Clearly, archaeological interpretation can reinforce and articulate the centralizing policies of emerging nationalisms, as well as be used to legitimize ethnic cleansing or territorial expansion. Archaeology, and historical reconstruction in general, has always been deeply involved in nationalist enterprises. Silberman (1995) traces this tendency back to the early Renaissance and Italian reaction against High Gothicism. Kohl and Fawcett (1995a), note that the relationship between nationalism and archaeology seemed so natural and close at so many levels that it remained largely unexamined and subconscious throughout the nineteenth century.

Härke (1991) traces the history of German archaeology from the days of Kossina and draws attention to the importance that the Nazis attached to archaeology as demonstrated by the speed with which they attempted to take control of archaeological institutions. The number of archaeology chairs at German universities increased from one to eight in the first three years of the Third Reich, and by four years later had exploded to twenty-five. Two years later, in 1939, the number of academically qualified prehistorians had doubled. But the price for this support was collaboration or, at the very least, conformity—a legacy with which Härke feels German archaeologists are still grappling. Silberman (1995) goes so far as to suggest that "all archaeological stories—be they classical, biblical, nationalist, or evolutionary—can be read as narratives of the inevitability of certain lands to be conquered and the right of certain people to rule " (256). Chernykh (1995) points out that many of the nationalist movements unfolding throughout the old Soviet Union are actually being *led* by archaeologists, philologists, and historians.

Ancient history can be used to define a people as distinct and as the legitimate and primordial heirs to a range of territory. Archaeologists refer to this as the "essentialist" position: the belief that peoples and cultures have survived since time immemorial in recognizable form. Nelson (1995) has examined this in the Korean context, as has Kaiser (1995) in Soviet archaeology. Japanese archaeology has been subject to similar influences (Trigger 1995, 274). Indeed, "the emotional power of archaeology in Israel, Saudi Arabia, Syria, Cyprus, Turkey, Greece and the regions of the former Yugoslavia, for example, is that they all link the present to a particular golden age" (Silberman 1995, 257). Nor are such critiques limited to archaeology. Gamkrelidze and Ivanov's Indo-European homeland, outlined previously, which these scholars arrive at on the basis of linguistics, makes the Armenians practically indigenous in their present location. This has provoked D'iakonov (1985) to comment: "This thesis will receive—and has already received—cheers from dilettantes. Dilettantes desperately need one thing: the proof that the population of the Armenian Plateau spoke Armenian ever since the Palaeolithic period, if possible" (156–157). Anthony (1995b) notes that "Indo-European linguistics and archaeology have been exploited to support openly ideological agendas for so long that a brief history of the issue quickly becomes entangled with the intellectual history of Europe" (82).[1]

This is not a study of Hindu nationalism. However, many historians and social scientists tend to limit their focus and concerns on the most troubling motives underpinning certain individuals active in this debate, such as "to pander to a false sense of national pride" (Thapar 1996, 12) and "to prove that all those such as Muslims who came to India in historical times are foreigners" (Sharma 1998, 91). Challenges to the Aryan invasion theory are often generically construed as a priori and necessarily indicative of the nationalist mentality, which then spills over into the communal one. The whole enterprise of Indigenous Aryanism, in the perception of many historians, is exclusively a calculated strategy adopted to further sociopolitical changes that benefit those who propagate such discourses. There is an obvious basis for such critiques, which reflect genuine concerns and are imperative on the academic community given the present and past volatile situation in the subcontinent. But attention must also be given to the possibility that, in addition to the Indigenist discourses of the nationalists, there might be many other scholars who sincerely believe that the Aryan invasion theory is a seriously flawed historical construct produced by biased imperial powers with overt agendas of their own—in other words, that it was, and is, perceived as "bad history." Consideration must also be given to the perception of many Indian scholars that Europeans might have constructed the idea of an external home of the Aryans to "pander to a false sense of national pride" of their own.

No doubt voices challenging the theory of Aryan invasions were, and are, often co-opted and even, in certain cases, initiated and sponsored by nationalist and communal elements, but a wide range of motives have inspired Indian scholars to challenge the idea of Aryan invasions or migrations. Not *all* historical "revisionism," by which I intend the literal meaning of the word in the sense of "reexamination," is necessarily nationalist nor, most certainly, communal a priori. Perhaps the use of the term *rerevisionism* would illustrate the point: let us not forget that it was Europeans who originally "revised" India's Brahmanical notions of history and then imposed their version of events on their subjects. While I do not intend to minimize or gloss over the importance of this issue to Hindu nationalism, my reading of the Indigenous Aryan school is that its concerns are also to a great extent anti-imperial and anticolonial: it is determined to review the revision. Not all who share this concern are necessarily also impelled to find reason to consider themselves the original inhabitants of India so as to enhance their social legitimacy vis-à-vis other communities on the subcontinent.

The Aryans in *Hindutva* Ideology

But let us begin with *Hindutva*, since this is the element of most pressing concern to scholars who have some sense of the prevalence of Indigenous Aryanism in India. Savarkar's *Hindutva*, literally 'Hinduness', or the essential quality of being a Hindu, which he wrote in jail in 1923, has been a very influential expression of Hindu self-identity. It was hailed by prominent Hindu leaders such as Lala Lajpatrai and Madan Mohan Malaviya and eventually was adopted by the Hindu Mahāsabhā as its authoritative definition of *Hindutva* (Savarkar 1989, vii). It is still considered a seminal text by Hindu nationalist groups such as the Rāṣṭīya Svayaṁsevak Samāj (RSS). Savarkar's concern in this book is not explicitly the creation of a nation-state but the definition of a Hindu. Those who envision a nation-state based on notions of a Hindu identity of the majority have taken his writing very seriously.

In his book, Savarkar adopted a process-of-elimination method similar to that Hobsbawn was to use in *Nations and Nationalism since 1780*. Hobsbawn examines various features that might be considered causal factors in the formation of nationalistic consciousness—language, ethnicity, religion, patriotism, protohistorical consciousness, and so on, all traits featured in various discourses on nationalism at certain historical moments—only to discard them as occasional, partial, by no means universal, and certainly not inherent constituents of that "illusion," the nation-state. Other theoretical endeavors by leading Western historians attempting to formulate a minimally satisfactory definition of the elusive and intangible notion of "nationhood" have highlighted the lack of any inherent, universal, or exclusive determining factors in the concept and offer us glosses in terms that are more psychological than empirical: "I propose the following definition of the nation: it is an imagined political community" (Anderson 1983, 6); "the apparent universal ideological domination of nationalism today is a sort of optical illusion" (Hobsbawn 1990, 78); "Nationalism . . . invents nations where they do not exist" (Gellner 1983, 55). *Imagination*, *illusion*, *invention*, *nonexistence*, and the more frequently encountered *construction* are descriptive terms that, interestingly, echo many expressions of Vedantic or Buddhistic definitions of our social universe. In any event, Savarkar undertook a similar process of elimination but arrived at a very different conclusion.

At the time of writing his book, Savarkar had not "pinned [his] faith to any theory about the original home of the Aryans" (Savarkar 1989, 8) but proceeded according to the generally accepted theory that they were, indeed, intruders into India.[2] Striving to capture *Hindutva*, this essence of being a Hindu, Savarkar first considers whether geography might be an adequate factor to account for the concept. A Hindu, after all, "claims the land as his motherland" (82). Although geography is an ingredient, Savarkar soon dismisses it as a determinant, for "we would be straining the usage of words too much—we fear to the point of breaking—if we call a Mohammedan a Hindu because of his being a resident of India" (83).

Finding such a conclusion untenable, Savarkar proceeds with other possibilities. Common blood presents itself as another candidate, but here, too, Savarkar balks, since "the majority of Mohammedans may . . . come to love their fatherland . . . and inherit Hindu blood in their veins. But can we . . . recognize these Mohammedans as Hindus?" (91). Likewise, common civilization also contains a pitfall despite the fact that Hindus, Savarkar feels, are bound by a common Sanskritic culture, a common mother tongue (Sanskrit), common laws and rites, and common feasts and festivals:

> Take the case of a patriotic Bohra or a Khoja countryman of ours. He loves our land of Hindustan as his fatherland which indisputably is the land of his forefathers. He possesses pure Hindu blood, . . . loves our history, . . . worships as heroes our great ten avatars *only adding Mohammad as the eleventh*. He is, so far as the three essentials of nation, race and civilization are concerned, a Hindu. . . . why should he not be recognized as a Hindu? (101; my italics)

A single ingredient is missing. Prolonging his climax, Savarkar continues to dismiss other possible defining factors of *Hindutva* such as the allegiance to Hinduism,[3] Vedic Dharma, or Sanātana Dharma. The adoption of these rubrics would exclude and alienate heterodox and minority groups such as the Jains, Buddhists, and Sikhs who are valuable allies in the agenda of this type of Hinduism.[4] Finally, Savarkar reveals his ultimate determinant of *Hindutva*, the essential, indispensable ingredient:

> We have found that the first important essential qualification of a Hindu is that . . . the system or set of religions which we call Hindu dharma—Vaidic and Non-Vaidic—*is as truly the offspring of this soil as the men whose thoughts they are or who "saw" the Truth revealed to them*. . . . it was in this land that the Founders of our faith . . . from Vaidic seers to Dayananda, from Jina to Mahavir, from Buddha to Nagasen, from Nanak to Govind, from Banda to Basava, from Chakradhar to Chaitanya, from Ramdas to Rammohan, our Gurus and Godmen were born and bred. (110–112; my italics)

This is the crux of *Hindutva*. To be considered a real Hindu, *a person's religious faith must have an indigenous origin*.

What, then, of other Indians—those whose religious beliefs blossomed in other lands—where do they fit into such a scheme of things?

> That is why in the case of some of our Mohammedan or Christian country men who had originally been forcibly converted to a non-Hindu religion and who consequently have inherited, along with the Hindus, a common fatherland and a greater part of the wealth

> of a common culture—language, law, customs, folklore and history—are not and cannot be recognized as Hindus. For though Hindusthan to them is Fatherland as to any other Hindu yet it is not to them a Holyland too. Their holyland is far off in Arabia or Palestine. Their mythology and Godmen, ideas and heroes are not the children of this soil. . . . they must, to a man, set their holyland above their Fatherland in their love and allegiance. . . . We have tried to determine the essentials of *Hindutva* and in so doing we have discovered that the Bohras and such other Mohammedan or Christian communities possess all the essential qualifications but one and that is that they do not look upon India as their Holyland. (113)

Returning to the Aryan theme, it should be evident how the basis of Savarkar's *Hindutva* is undermined if the Vedic Aryans came from central Asia. If that were the case, then the followers of the Vedic religion (with its Indo-European elements) would have to be disqualified from being Hindus, since the original "founders of [their] faith" were not "born and bred" in Bharat. More catastrophically, since the Vedic truths are the matrix deferred to by the founders and followers of most later strands within Hinduism, the resulting elimination rate from eligibility to *Hindutva* would be truly enormous.

Acceptance of the Aryan invasion theory according to Savarkar's logic, then, necessitates that in the essential determining condition of *Hindutva*, that of holy land (defined, as outlined above, as the geographic locale of revelation), as well as in other nonessential but contributing aspects, such as motherland, and language, the forefathers of the Vedic Aryans are indubitable foreigners and their followers essentially no different from those revering other "foreigners" such as Muhammad or Christ. Not only that, but Savarkar envisions the Aryans as Sindhis who, upon arriving in India, disseminated their blood throughout the land by intermarriage with the real natives of the land, thereby creating a common blood link. Adopting this logic (which involves the old model equating language and race), if the Aryans came from somewhere near the Caspian Sea area, adjacent to Persia, they would actually share close blood links (and Indo-European linguistic and protohistoric religious ties) with the proto-Iranians who remained nearer the ancestral home and therefore diluted their blood less. This would therefore make the Vedic Aryans much closer relatives in language, protoreligion, and blood with the Muslims who came to India from these areas (as descendants of the proto-Iranians) than with the original non-Aryans of India whose blood needed to be transfused by mixed marriages. It is puzzling that Savarkar, who must have been aware that some of his contemporaries and predecessors had challenged the Aryan invasion theory, did not aggressively oppose it. Taken to its logical conclusion, his acceptance of the Aryan invasion theory seems incompatible with his stated objectives in formulating the concept of *Hindutva*.

Unlike Savarkar, M. S. Golwalkar, who inherited the leadership of the RSS from its founder, K. B. Hedgewar, was more lucid about the political pitfalls and embarrassing consequences for Hindu nationalism involved in the acceptance of the Aryan invasion paradigm:

> It was the wily foreigner, the Britisher, who, to achieve his ulterior imperialistic motives, set afloat all such mischievous notions among our people so that the sense of patriotism and duty towards the integrated personality of our motherland was corroded. He carried on the insidious propaganda that we were never one nation, that we were never the children of the soil *but mere upstarts having no better claims than the foreign hordes of Muslim* or the British over this country. (Golwalkar [1966] 1988, 109; my italics)

Here Golwalkar has elucidated what Savarkar has overlooked. The Aryan invasion theory would make the arrival of the Vedic people analogous with that of the Mughals and other invaders and undermine any indigenous formulations for *Hindutva*. In short, this brand of Hindu nationalism, which seems determined to alienate the Muslim community on the grounds of its lack of autochthonous religious pedigree, is obliged to refute the Aryan invasion theory or risk logical absurdity. Golwalkar, accordingly, rejects the theory but attempts to reconcile this position with Tilak's North Pole homeland. Unwilling to contradict the prestigious Tilak, who had accepted an external origin of the Aryans in the Arctic Circle, Golwalkar (1947) states that modern scientific research has shown the North Pole not to be stationary, and that "quite long ago it was in that part of the world . . . [which] is called Bihar and Orissa at the present" (13).

There is no doubt that defending extreme Indocentric viewpoints results in the most absurd types of explanatory gymnastics (which have their counterparts in nationalist discourse from Tamil Nadu).[5] Self-styled historian and ardent Hindu P. N. Oak,[6] for example, has his own unique way of resolving the *Hindutva* problem as it relates to the Muslims. According to Oak (1984):

> Allah is a Hindu God and the Kaba a Hindu temple. Evidence is also available indicating that prophet Mohammed Himself was born a Hindu and that when He chose to break away from the family's Hindu tradition and heritage and declare himself a prophet, the joint Hindu family broke up in an internecine feud and Hazrat Mohammad's own uncle had to lay down his life fighting to save Hinduism. . . . That means that like Buddha, Mahavira, Jaina and the ten Sikh Gurus, Hazrat Mohommad was yet another prophet which Hinduism gave to the world. Like the other reformers, Mohammad reiterated some of the basic values of Hinduism. (310–313)

Pursuing Oak's logic, then, the Muslims would qualify as stalwart members of *Hindutva*, since their prophet was born a Hindu, in contrast to the excluded followers of the Vedic religion whose Aryan founders came from outside India. Absurdity aside, I have made it a point to include this vignette to underline, once again, the fact that the Indigenous Aryan school is not a homogeneous group. There is a tendency, as will be discussed later, to select peripheral individuals such as Oak and highlight them as representative of everyone open to historical reevaluation in general. As, I hope, the arguments in the preceding chapters have demonstrated, there are many serious and sober scholars who sincerely feel that the Aryan migration theory is not supported by the available data. Their input on this issue should not be stereotyped or cursorily dismissed by associating it with positions, often encountered in India, such as that of Oak.

Shrikant Talageri (1993) adds a more serious and carefully constructed nuance to the issue in his resolution of Savarkar's dilemma.[7] Although he argues forcibly and, in places, quite coherently against the idea of Aryan immigration, he does not concede that the essential definition of *Hindutva* would be tarnished even if the external origin of the Aryans were to be hypothetically considered:[8]

> Hindu nationalism has nothing to do with any childish, petty and ridiculous idea of dividing Indians into "outsiders" and "insiders" on the basis of whether or not their ancestors, actually or supposedly, came from outside. Hindu Nationalism believes only in identifying the de-Indianising elements, as opposed to the Indianising ones. . . . Even if it is assumed

> that a group of people, called "Aryans," invaded, or immigrated into, India, . . . they have left no trace, if ever there was any, of any link, much less the consciousness of any link, much less any loyalties associated with such a link, to any place outside India. (47)

Where Savarkar specifies the physical importance of India as the geographic land of religious revelation in his criteria for *Hindutva*, Talageri considers the psychological bond to be more significant. He argues that while Indian culture absorbs and assimilates newcomers, Islam and Christianity do not: "Hinduism Indianises foreigners, Islam and Christianity foreignise or de-Indianise Indians" (47). In these latter two religions, the leaders, founders, saints, sacred languages, scripts, holy places, symbols, music, architecture, traditional attire, and other symbols all owe allegiance to cultures outside India. Of course, if the Aryans had, indeed, come from outside, they too would have introduced many foreign features such as the proto-Vedic language and gods, as well as many Indo-European cultural features, into the subcontinent.[9] The difference, from Talageri's perspective, is that the practitioners of these other religions actively cultivate allegiances with countries and cultures outside the subcontinent, whereas Hindus, even if their culture is accepted as being an amalgamation of indigenous and extraneous ingredients, maintain no such external loyalties but consider themselves exclusively members of a community centered in India.

Talageri's book, despite containing some quite well argued sections dealing with the historical evidence relevant to Indo-Aryan origins, is bound to alienate scholars who do not subscribe to Hindu nationalistic ideology. The first section of his book, which is explicitly nationalistic, is downright bigoted in places, containing such asides as "the religious music of Islam (if the wailing of the *muazzin* may be called that)" (30). He takes no pains whatsoever to disguise his hostilities: "Any event in any Muslim country gives Indian Muslims the right to take to the streets and start vicious riots, all over the country, in an orgy of loot, arson and vandalism (especially vandalism of Hindu temples, shops and houses situated near Muslim areas)" (23). There is no mention of any Hindu rioting, arson, or vandalism in Talageri's version of events.[10]

If Hindus are to be promoted, by whatever process of justification, as having more rights than other communities because they participate in a culture that is seen as being indigenous to India (or, at least, that has severed any hypothetical foreign connections), then what is to be the fate of the communities that do not subscribe to this culture? Talageri offers no proposal in this regard. Savarkar also completely avoids this consideration: for him, the Muslims and Christians can never participate in the benefits (whatever they might be) of *Hindutva* because their prophet was born on the wrong side of the Arabian Sea. Golwalkar, however, presents his version of an anecdote to describe the ideal Muslim acceptable to his brand of *Hindutva*. Upon being asked why he, a Muslim, was teaching Rāmāyaṇa to his children, an Indonesian replied: "Because Shri Ramachandra is our national hero par excellence. We very much desire that our children should emulate his lofty ideal. No doubt we belong to the Islamic faith. But that does not mean that we should give up our precious national heritage and values of life" (Golwalkar 1947, 209).[11] Golwalkar comments: "What an excellent lesson for our Muslim friends here" (209). In essence, he is requiring that the Muslims, if not completely convert to Hinduism, at least actively participate in its culture, symbols, and value systems.[12] He is expecting them to accept Hindu representations, concepts, and beliefs that might completely jar with their own religious sensibilities and which might, more seriously, run contrary to Qur'anic injunctions: "The non-Hindu people in Hindusthan must either adopt the Hindu culture and language, must learn to respect and hold in reverence the Hindu religion, must entertain no idea but those of glorification of the Hindu race and culture . . . or may stay in the country, wholly subordinated to the Hindu nation, claiming nothing, deserving no privileges, . . . not even citizen's rights" (55–56).

Stereotypes and Counterstereotypes

There can be no doubt that *Hindutva* is easily pressed into service in alienating and targeting the Muslim minority in communally volatile, modern-day India. For those observing such a situation, the Aryan/Semitic (i.e., in the Indian context, Hindu/Muslim) dichotomy being created by such constructions triggers nightmarish associations with the ideological co-optation of scholarship resurrecting itself from a very recent grave in Nazi Germany. One result of such associations is that some scholars, who might otherwise even be intrigued by the Indo-Aryan issue, are extremely reluctant to support, encourage, or even consider a historical version of events that is explicitly or implicitly threatening to the physical or mental security of major communities of non-Hindu Indians. Thus Hock states:

> Scholars now are running into the problem that the issue has become politically surcharged. . . . The problem . . . [is] the quest of present-day nationalist groups to establish their "authenticity" as the original inhabitants of India. . . . [G]iven the unfortunate consequences in my native country, Germany, of a nationalism that sought authenticity in non-scholarly interpretations of history and pre-history, I am extremely uncomfortable with . . . modern Indian nationalism. (1999b, 148)

Irfan Habib (1997) echoes similar concerns in a newspaper interview:

> I would like to cite the example of the Nazis, of how a particular perception of history held by a respectable section of the German intelligentsia. . . . This perception was not racist at least outwardly and certainly was not anti-Jewish. But how easily was this perception utilised by the Nazis? . . . So, here you have an example of how a historical theory is created by someone who had no idea of what use it can be put to. . . . Before 1947 the idea that the Aryans went out of India was hardly espoused by any serious historian. . . . But now, while some people deny that they espouse the Nazi race theory, they have in fact espoused it. (12)

And again: "The striking parallels between the Nazi campaign and the majoritarian project in India are not restricted to the revanchist campaigns being carried out by the RSS. The more important commonality of the two can be seen in the construction of the myth about the Aryans being a superior race" (Ananth 1998).

These concerns are certainly not without basis, and I fully support them when they are applied *according to the appropriate context and not in an indiscriminate and generic fashion*. Anthony (1985b) rightly admonishes us that, postmodernity notwithstanding, it is incumbent upon us to assess different interpretations of disputed evidence: "If we cannot agree among ourselves on how to distinguish the adequate from the inadequate, are we not responsible for encouraging the kinds of popular social abuses represented by the myth of the Aryan super-race?" (85). The South Asian context is a volatile one, and there are very real reasons to be concerned about the vulnerability of non-Hindu groups in the shadows of the sometimes violent assertions of a growing Hindu nationalism.

But, at the same time, a caveat is in order. One must be cautious about contributing to a sort of Indological McCarthyism whereby anyone reconsidering or challenging long-held assumptions pertaining to the Indo-Aryans is instantly dubbed a fundamentalist or nationalist or, more drastically, is accused of contributing to Nazi agendas.[13] There is a tendency in Western, and in elements of Indian, academic circles to a priori stereotype *everyone* reconsidering this aspect of Indian history in such ways: "Nationalistic bias makes it difficult for some North Indians to admit even the possibility of the Indus Civilization being pre-Aryan" (Parpola 1994, 58);[14] "Political motivation (usually associated with Hindu revivalism . . .) renders this opposition [to the Aryan invasion] devoid of scholarly value. Assertion of the indigenous origin of Indo-Aryan languages and an insistence on a long chronology for Vedic and even Epic literature are only a few of the most prominent tenets of this emerging lunatic fringe" (Erdosy 1995b, x); "The view [that the Aryans are indigenous to India] is forcefully propagated in India in some chauvinistic quarters" (R. S. Sharma 1993b).

Blanket stereotypification of the Aryan debate with Hindu nationalism was a source of great annoyance among numerous scholars I interviewed who were questioning the theory of external Aryan origins. Scholars such as Renfrew and Gamkrelidze and Ivanov can radically challenge established Indo-European homeland theories in the West, but the academic culture in India has developed to the point that *anyone* attempting to even question established paradigms in early South Asian history is in danger of being dubbed a Nazi. Such a culture has been created as much by remarks made in a *generic* fashion by some of the opponents of the Indigenous Aryan school as by the bigoted statements of certain Hindu nationalist "Indigenists." It is obviously unconducive to the pursuit of impartial scholarly research that is making at least some effort to be objective.

The RSS, which is the group that generally springs to mind when the topic of historical "revisionism" is raised, is the only body which I encountered at the time of my research that has attempted any sort of organized activity in this debate, but it is by no means widely representative. In 1994, the RSS had a center called the Deendayal Research Institute housed in a building on Rani Jhansi Road in New Delhi, which offers research facilities for the "social, economic, political, cultural and moral reconstruction of the nation."[15] The center for ancient historical research, however, called the Bhāratīya Itihāsa Saṅkalana Samiti, is across the road in the RSS Delhi headquarters ashram. The elderly and almost blind head of the center described to me an elaborate national network of branches and subbranches under the Samiti auspices for gathering material pertaining to the study of ancient Indian history. In reality, however, the Samiti's Delhi national headquarters is just a small, bare room in the RSS ashram, which doubles as an office and living quarters, with a metal closet half full of cheaply produced books and tracts in one corner. The dust billowing forth from the pile as I attempted to extract some copies suggested that there was clearly not a major rush on these books. I visited two other principal "branches" in 1995: the Varanasi "branch" turned out to be someone's living room in a small house down a gully with a steel almirah half full of (equally dusty) books out in the corridor, and the Hyderabad "branch," which consisted of a small metal desk in someone's ashram room in the RSS center there.

The quarterly journal of the Deendayal Research Institute, *Manthan*, brought out two volumes on the Aryan problem—one focused primarily on contextualizing the European origins of the theory, the other more data-oriented.[16] At least two RSS members have published books on the subject—one through the Samiti, the other through a publishing company called Voice of India.[17] This publishing house, which is privately owned, was specifically established for scholars reconsidering and rewriting aspects of ancient Indian history. Several books produced by this publishing house are considered unambiguously pro-Hindu in tone and content.[18] Any writers who are unconcerned about having their research connected with such associations would likely have no problem getting their work published by this company.

The Bhāratīya Itihāsa Saṅkalana Samiti cosponsored a conference on the Aryan problem in Poona, in 1994, which resulted in a publication (see Deo and Kamath 1993). The conference was well attended, but by no means all the participants that I met were RSS or BJP (Bharatiya Janata Party) supporters. Indeed, several of the papers presented at the conference supported the theory of Aryan invasions. In 1993, the Samiti (its identity unbeknownst to at least one of its invitees) also organized a small function in honor of several new books that had been published by Indigenous Aryanists. After arriving at the function in good faith, but then subsequently becoming aware of the affiliation of the organizers, one of the authors made it a point to publicly declare that he had absolutely no connection with the political viewpoints of the organizers. Here, again, the point is underscored that whitewashing all Indigenous Aryanists as right-wing Hindu fundamentalists is not just erroneous, but unscholarly, dogmatic, and offensive.

Mine is not a statistical study correlating opinions on the Indo-Aryans with political orientations, but these anecdotes illustrate the fact that by no means all members of the group I studied are RSS sympathizers or BJP supporters. Although I, too, arrived in India with my preconceived set of expectations about right-wing Hindu "revisionism," it soon became clear to me that themes resonating with *Hindutva*, that is, the prioritizing of Hindu culture as the indigenous, and therefore legitimate, heir to hegemonic power in India (with its anti-Muslim subtext), while blatantly and distastefully present in a number of publications, does not pervade the views of all the members of the Indigenous Aryan school. I often encountered scholars who were very open to reconsidering the whole idea of external origins of the Aryans but who made it a point to stress their support of Congress-I and their disapproval of communal elements in politics. Of course, there are well-known archaeologists reputed to have RSS backgrounds, and BJP supporters (including those who, while sympathizing with aspects of the BJP agenda, pointed out much of which they disapproved), but this political orientation was by no means representative. Some scholars refused to even discuss politics with me, finding it inappropriate that an interview that had been solicited to discuss the historical evidence of the Indo-Aryans should introduce issues connected with a scholar's personal political orientations. A few scholars were apolitical and did not participate in the democratic process, while one prominent Indigenous Aryanist turned out to be an atheistic and very irreverent Marxist.

An inevitable corollary of stereotyping is that it results in counterstereotypification. In India, some Indigenous Aryanists, being branded communal, then label their detractors either "colonial stooges" or "secular Marxists" who are motivated by their own particular political agendas. Chakrabarti (1997) has nothing but scorn for the Indian intellectual elites who "fail to see the need of going beyond the dimensions of colonial Indology, because these dimensions suit them fine and keep them in power" (213). In his view, "as the Indian historians became increasingly concerned with the large number of grants, scholarships, fellowships and even occasional jobs to be won in Western universities, there was a scramble for new respectability to be gained by toeing the Western line of thinking about India and Indian history" (2). The result is that "institutions on the national level have to be 'captured' and filled up with stooges of various kinds," and "making the right kind of political noises is important for historians" (212). Accordingly, "after independence, when the Indian ruling class modeled itself on its departed counterpart, any emphasis on the 'glories of ancient India' came to be viewed as an act of Hindu fundamentalism" (2).[19] I should note, however, that while Chakrabarti holds that the colonial framework is still in place and imbibed by a majority of Indian intellectuals, particularly "the 'mainstream' establishment historian," things have changed; my research in 1994 indicated that suspicion of colonial narratives and willingness to reconsider the Aryan Invasion theory are, by and large, representative of the feelings of a growing number of professional scholars—archaeologists and historians—whom I interviewed in over twenty-five university campuses in India, and not simply those outside the "charmed circle" of the establishment.

The tables seem to have recently been turned even more dramatically and, to some, sinisterly. Unfortunately, due to its recency at the time of completing this writing, I have not been able to properly research the latest furor surrounding the nomination of members to the Indian Council for Historical Research (ICHR). But from the few newspaper articles that have come my way, it is clear that there is a bitter struggle over control of this council. This body is the dominant voice in what kind of information is presented in school history books for the nation and what account of Indo-Aryan origins will be imbibed by young students. An editorial in the June 12, 1998, edition of the *Hindu* noted that the BJP government had reconstituted the ICHR and shown the door to all eighteen of the previously nominated members. The article voices "concern that most of those who have been nominated were identified with the Sangh Parivar's partisan appropriation and distorted representation of historical facts." The article quotes the new government's mandate that the ICHR "will give a 'national direction' to 'an objective and national presentation and interpretation of history.'" The author of the article sees in this "an intention on the part of the BJP-led government to re-write history." Another article in the same newspaper a few months later states:

> The BJP has introduced sweeping purges in all centrally-funded research institutes: Indian Council of Historical Research, Indian Council of Social Science Research, Indian Council of Philosophical Research and Indian Institute of Advanced Studies. Breaking most institutional norms and rules, these bodies have been cleansed of subject experts and packed with men distinguished by RSS sympathies. Change in personnel goes hand in hand with a methodological doctoring of facts in school textbooks designed for the BJP. . . . What are these changes in aid of? . . . The RSS professes the notion of Hindu Rashtra [nation]—that India belongs to Hindus alone. That notion depends upon a relentless hatred against all those who think otherwise. It has led to many bloody pogroms against all those who think otherwise. (Sarkar 1998)

The editorial goes on to describe five-year-olds in RSS infant training camps "clenching their fists in fury and swearing vengeance" after indoctrination sessions dedicated to anti-Muslin oratory (allegedly proudly told by the headmaster of one such camp to the author of the article). A few days later, another voice in a *Times of India* article expressed concern that "introducing a Hindutva element into the curriculum will further push back minority education: 'By default Muslim children will go to the Madrasa [traditional Islamic school]'" (Quraishi 1998).

From the other side, in the September 30 edition of the *Times of India,* Sandhya Jain states, as if in response, that "having spewed venom and cast aspersions on the intellectual credentials of historians recently nominated to the Indian Council of Historical Research, the once dominant Left-liberal school of historiography finds itself repenting at leisure as its own performance comes under public scrutiny." As far as she is concerned, "it has taken five decades for our secular apostles to admit that the basic premise of their study of ancient history was false." The data offered by this author to account for this change of premise are "incontrovertible evidence from Harappan sites excavated by Indian and foreign scholars [which] has established the indigenous evolution of the civilisation, while scientific examination of the bones found at Mohenjo-daro has unequivocally ruled out invasion or massacre as the cause of the city's decline." This is a typical example of how academic findings are selectively appropriated and propogated on a popular level.

Arun Shourie (1998) has written a book replete with furious invectives against what he perceives as the biased Marxist influences, as well as corruption of the "leftist" school of historians throughout the years when they controlled the ICHR. As far as he is concerned:

> They have made India out to have been an empty-land, filled by successive invaders. They have made present-day India, and Hinduism even more so, out to be a zoo—an agglomeration of assorted, disparate specimens. No such thing as "India," just a geographical expression, just a construct of the British; no such thing as Hinduism, just a word used by the Arabs to describe the assortment they encountered, just an invention of the communals to impose a uniformity—that has been their stance. For this they have blackened the Hindu period of our history, and, as we shall see, strained to whitewash the Islamic period. . . . These intellectuals and their patrons have worked a diabolic inversion: the inclusive religion, the pluralist spiritual search of our people and land, they have projected as intolerant, narrow-minded, obscurantist; and the exclusivist, totalitarian, revelatory religions and ideologies—Islam, Christianity, Marxism-Leninism—they have made out to be the epitomes of tolerance, open-mindedness, democracy and secularism. (xi)

They have been able to work all this mischief "because of the control they have come to acquire over institutions." The solution is to "enable a multitude of other institutions to come up" as well as "loosen their hold over existing institutions" (xii). Needless to say, it is control over the means of propogating ideologies that is at stake here. The book primarily claims to be a documentation of the bias and fraud extant in the leftist school. Shourie lists, to the rupee, the considerable resources that have been pocketed by the "leftist" historians during their tenure in the ICHR, ostensibly for contributions toward such enterprises as the multivolume *Towards Freedom Project*, almost none of which have seen the light of day despite the lapse of years. He also attempts to outline the Marxist parameters from within which his target group of historians represents the history and culture of the subcontinent to the invariable detriment of Hindu beliefs and practices. The message is clear–the 'Marxist ' historians are professionally incompitent, corrupt and ideologically blinkered, and it is time for a thorough change of guard.

The "Left-liberal" or "secular Marxist" stereotype is subject to an amount of disgust equal to that of the colonial stooge in Indigenist discourse. Rajaram (1995) states that "in the hands of politically driven historians of post-colonial India, these nineteenth century-creations [viz., arguments supporting the Aryan invasion theory] have become handy tools to be used in support of their vested interest in Marxist ideology and the version of history that goes with it" (xiv).[20] Secular Marxists are accused of maintaining a defunct theory in order to insist that the arrival of the Aryans is analogous to the arrival of the Muslims, Christians, and numerous other groups of newcomers to the subcontinent. In such an amalgamation of immigrants, no one has more claim to indigenous pedigree or cultural hegemony than anyone else. A secular state, from this perspective, is the only political system that can protect the equal rights of all citizens to define themselves as being Indian with cultural credentials that are as good as anybody else's.

Thus, anti–Aryan invasionist scholarship, in its turn, is stereotyped as being subservient to secular, Marxist ideology. The most maligned figureheads are precisely those who have most publicly opposed the Indigenous Aryan position, particularly R. S. Sharma, "a 'Marxist' historian of Indian variety who became a pillar of the historical establishment in his country," and Romila Thapar, "another 'mainstream' historian who harangued us on the importance of looking at ancient Indian history and archaeology through the prism of anthropological and sociological ideas, without telling us if such exercises by themselves would lead to a better historical understanding of ancient India" (Chakrabarti 1997, 164). Shourie's book outlines the entire cast of those assigned to the camp of Marxist historians.[21] A few examples of these back-and-forth and often acrimonious exchanges between the two camps will suffice to illustrate the point. Romila Thapar (1997), who holds that "indigenism . . . is intellectually and historiographically barren with no nuances or subtleties of thought and interpretation" (58), is the particular target of such counterstereotypification. In an article on the "perennial Aryans," she remarks:

> The theory of the Aryans being a people has been seen as fundamental to the understanding of the identity of modern Indians and the question of identity is central to the change in Indian society from caste to class. The upholding of a false theory is dangerous. The next step can be to move from the indigenous origin of "the Aryans" to propagating the notion of an "Aryan nation." (Thapar 1992, 23–24)

Rajaram and Frawley respond to her comments:

> This observation is puzzling, to say the least, and it is not at all clear what any of it has to do with ancient history. The first part about class and caste is standard Marxist fare. But Thapar's foray into futurology, the prediction that an "Aryan nation" could emerge from the discovery that the "Aryans" are native to India, is irrelevant to the history of India. It is relevant, however, to modern politics. The dreaded "Aryan nation" . . . was a European invention. Are we to discard evidence and cling to the Aryan-invasion theory because of a perceived political threat . . . ? (Rajaram and Frawley 1995, 15)

Thapar's comments are portrayed as "vintage Marxist rhetoric," which has "gratuitously drag[ed] in the bogey of the 'Aryan nation' . . . [as] a blatant attempt aimed at diverting attention away from the real issue" (Rajaram 1993, 33). Thapar (1996) finds Rajaram's writings "read rather like nineteenth century tracts but peppered with references to using the computer so as to suggest scientific objectivity since they claim that it is value-free! Those that question their theories are dismissed as Marxists" (88). From another perspective on the other side of the debate, and in interesting contrast to Thapar's concern about a single "Aryan nation," Talageri (1993) raises the alarm about multiple Marxist mininations: "The first principle of Leftist propaganda is that India is not a nation but a conglomerate of nations. . . . the rationale behind this is that if India breaks up into small "nations," these would be easier for the Leftists to gobble up one by one" (9).

Both sides of the debate sometimes refuse to even acknowledge that there is a legitimate controversy. Rajaram's book are replete with sweeping statements as to how scientists now recognize that archaeological and other scientific data convincingly show the Aryan invasion theory to be completely baseless. One prominent anti-Aryan invasionist archaeologist I met in Delhi, on the other hand (who is also associated by her detractors with the "Marxist Left"), was incensed that the course book of ancient Indian history of the Indira Gandhi National Open University in Delhi had dared to include a section entitled "The Aryan Invasion: A Myth or a Reality?" (personal interview, name withheld).

As his main conclusion to this book, Rajaram (1995) asserts: "The chronology of ancient India found in history books—beginning with the *Rigveda*—is too late by several thousand years. Archaeology points to a continuous evolution going back to 7000 BC. Astronomical references in the *Rigveda* itself go back to 4500 BC. . . . the Harappan civilization of the Indus Valley came at the end of the Vedic Age and was part of it" (228). It would be fair to say that some of these proposals are generally representative and fairly typical of Indigenous Aryanist positions. Many do highlight the evidence supporting an uninterrupted cultural continuum, primarily indigenous in origin, going back to the eighth and seventh millennia B.C.E, a certain period of which is expressed in the hymns of the Vedas.[22] Most also connect the Indus Valley with the Indo-Aryans and generally are open to considering a greater antiquity for the Vedas or, if they believe that the culture expressed in the Vedas is posterior to the Indus civilization, still view it as an indigenous and organic cultural evolute. This stress on the continuity of things, coupled with the generic use of the term *Vedic culture*, with its monolithic overtones and troublesome implications for minority cultures, is the feature of all this that is most troubling to those who fear the ideological corollaries inherent in such interpretations: "If the matter in these books were a result of a simple misunderstanding, it would call for our patience. But there is a nasty subscript, namely, that the true divide is not Aryan vs. Dravidian but that the Muslim is the true enemy. . . . For the *n*th time it is being said that Hindus are the sons of the soil. Thereby the Muslim Other, the invader, is created" (Ratnagar 1996b, 80).

Rajaram's publications triggered another response and counterresponse that are worth quoting because they capture some of the intense, present-day emotions and associations involved in the Aryan invasion debate. Robert Zydenbos, who in his colophon is described as a "European Indological scholar" from Mysore, published a response in the *Indian Express* to Rajaram's article. He concludes by making the same set of associations we have discussed above: "Why should it be so important that the Aryans . . . have been in the subcontinent since all eternity? That would come close to the Blut and Boden ideology of Nazism, with its Aryan rhetoric. Why the xenophobia? Does he really not see the parallel between Nazi attacks on synagogues in the 1930's and what happened in Ayodhya on December 6th?" (Zydenbos 1993). Elst (1996) responds:

> We would not have believed it, but it is really printed there, black on white: an academic tries to score against a fellow academic by arbitrarily linking him with an event which had not yet taken place when the latter's paper was published, and with which he had strictly nothing to do, viz. the demolition of the Babri mosque. Add to this that he accuses Prof. Rajaram of something "close to" Nazi ideology, and we wonder: how would he fare if he accused a western colleague in the same vein in a western paper? (23)

The preceding series of exchanges captures the essence of some of the primary concerns underpinning this debate. Clearly, the academic value of many statements—on all sides—has been singed by the emotional temperature such issues ignite. They reveal how an entire fascinating field of study has become inextricably linked with ideology and the politics of representation to the point where it is almost impossible to have a calm, objective and detached conversation on the matter in India.

That the emotional involvement in the process of historical reconstruction among professional scholars can reach astonishingly unprofessional levels is easily illustrated. The entire proceedings at the plenary session of the prestigious 1994 World Archaeological Congress in Delhi came to a complete (and ridiculous) standstill for more than thirty minutes as "leftist" and "rightist" historians actually clambered onto the dais, physically wrestled each other in attempts to snatch up the microphone, and hurled abuse into the air in front of over two hundred flabbergasted foreign delegates.[23] This breakdown in order was ostensibly triggered by a resolution condemning destruction of historical structures, but the Aryan invasion problem was also part of the agenda at the conference.

In addition to being stereotyped in an overly hasty fashion, the reconsideration of the Aryan invasion theory is often associated with the rewriting of other periods in Indian history and lumped under one generic label categorized under the convenient rubric of "revisionism." Indigenous Aryanism, the construction of a golden age of Chandragupta, biased accounts of the Mogul period, and material relating to the Ram temple in Ayodhya and the "evil Babur" are all juxtaposed as if emanating from a generic, undifferentiated, communal mentality. There are undoubtedly grounds for this in certain genres of literature, but such juxtapositions cannot be applied indiscriminately. Not only are such disparate historical periods and issues lumped together in this fashion, but radically different standards of scholarship are placed side by side as if all were the product of the same infantile genre of fundamentalism. Some of the material involved in the Aryan invasion debate (which, as has hopefully been demonstrated in the preceding chapters, can be well argued and provocative) is made to share equal time and credibility with arguments from the likes of P. N. Oak as if they all belong to one ubiquitous (and very poor) standard of professionalism and critical methodology (with the Oaks sometimes highlighted as representative in this regard).

Detractors of the Indigenist school can be just as selective in the views they extract for critique, as the Indigenists they ridicule. Habib (1997) caricatures all the Indigenous Aryanists as believing that the Dravidian language family is not distinct from the Indo-Aryan one—a view held by only a very few individuals and not at all representative of the Indigenous position. Misra (forthcoming) himself voices a similar complaint against a point made by Hock (forthcoming) in his review of Misra's book:

> Hock has himself invented . . . the Sanskrit-origin hypothesis, with which he has associated me . . . but my work shows no hint for such an assumption. I have never claimed that Sanskrit was the original language, nor have I said that Sanskrit was identical with proto Indo-European. I have only presented additional evidence . . . that Sanskrit presents the oldest literary evidence in the form of the Rigveda. . . . I do not understand why Hock has paid less attention to the Uralic evidence, which covers many pages of the book (Misra 1992, p. 16–34) and which is more significant for the dates of Rigveda, from a linguistic point of view. . . . On the other hand he has chosen a much less significant part of the book viz. the peacock evidence . . . quoted by me as complementary to my linguistic evidence."

As an aside, Misra, whom I have known for many years, has nothing to do with Hindu right-wing attitudes and actually happens to be very concerned that his views not be co-opted by nationalist or agenda-driven discourses. While it is important for scholars to draw attention to potentially communal rhetoric, we must exert caution not to lump everyone reconsidering ancient Indian history into the same convenient categories. By simply referring to extreme or not fully representative points of view, the more plausible points of contention in this debate are bypassed and frustrations get further aggravated.

Detractors of the Indigenous school also typically state that the latter promote all the Indo-Europeans as coming from India (Habib 1997; Thapar 1997, 57–58). As has been discussed, some do, indeed, promote this idea, and plenty of books with titles such as *The Indian Asuras Colonized Europe* abound in India. And, expectedly, whatever aspects of this whole issue trickle down to the popular level take on a life of their own. The appeal of an Indian homeland is perhaps amply represented in the Penguin novel *Return of the Aryans* by Bhagavan Gidwani (1994). Situated in the dawn of mankind in 8000 B.C.E., this epic novel (interwoven with poets, seers, kings, Gods, romance, and battles) traces the departure of the Aryans from their native land in India, through their adventures and conquests in western lands, to their eventual triumphant return:

> The historians do not pinpoint any single region as the homeland of the Aryans. At the last count, they must have mentioned twenty-two regions in the west and the north from which the Aryans could possibly have come. . . . none of the twenty-two showed even the slightest link with the high civilization and classical art and literature of India. . . . Is it not possible that these western languages were enriched by the Aryans moving out of India to those regions? . . . This novel will give a mosaic of a long-forgotten past . . . and will explain the origins of the names . . . Afghanistan, Iran, Egypt, Tibet, Hindu Kush mountains, Himalaya, Saraswati, Danube and Volga rivers and scores of other names, here and in Europe, West Asia and the Far East, given by or under the inspiration of the pre-ancient Hindu and Arya of Bharat Varsha. (Gidwani 1994, xiv)

Clearly, tales of Hindus being the initiators of world culture and civilization can be seen as cathargic for psches still recovering from the wounds of the colonial period. But this idea is by no means representative; many scholars simply claim the the available evidence is insufficient to conclude this issue. This a much more sober position that deserves attention, and one that it is disingenuous to confound with the more outlandish views.

As further illustration of all this, an unnamed contributor to the journal *Seminar*, after having dismissively described the fact that the Indigenous Aryan position had been outlined in a history textbook entitled *High School Itihas*, presents his readers with "some idea of what the thoroughly revised text books might be like." To accomplish this, this contributor selects a quote from a textbook used in the Saraswati Shishu Mandirs run by the Sangh Parivar,[24] which states: "Hundreds of villainous demons have looked towards our country with greedy eyes. . . . some came boasting of being world conquerors but they were seen fleeing away. . . . we went on winning one battle after another. . . . they all suffered humiliating defeat."[25] The impression created by such methods is that anyone reconsidering any aspect of Indian history is communal, has a puerile level of scholarship comparable to that exhibited in the Shishu Mandir textbooks, and is quite likely to be found destroying mosques in his or her spare time.[26]

This might be the place to note that additions were indeed made to the *High School Itihas* textbook for secondary schools in 1993, but a more accurate representation of the facts (and one that nonetheless did not hesitate to draw attention to the perceived underlying agenda of the changes) was reported by the National Steering Committee on Textbook Evaluation. It noted the following additions to the *High School Itihas* textbooks for secondary schools:

> P. 43: The following sentence has been added at the end of the chapter on the Harappan civilization: "With the finds of bones of horses, their toys and *yajna* altars, scholars are beginning to believe that the people of the Harappa and the Vedic civilization were the same."
>
> P. 48: The following section has been added at the end of the section on the original home of the Aryans: "But about the Aryans who were the builders of Bharatiya Sanskriti in Bharat and creators of the Vedas, this view is gaining strength among scholars in the country and abroad that India itself was the original home of the Aryans." (New Delhi: NCERT p. 2)[27]

The committee comments that "these changes have been made to establish that whatever is not indigenous is not desirable and that the Aryans were the sole creators of Indian culture" (2).

Intransigent, cavalier, and often grossly inaccurate generalizations of opposing views are evident on both sides of the issue; Indigenous Aryanists are by no means exempt from aggressively and sometimes unfairly stereotyping those who disagree with them. The stereotyped portrayals of Indigenist views are paralleled on the other side by many Indigenous Aryanists who typically relish gloating over outdated or peripheral tenets of the Aryan invasion theory—such as Wheelerian accounts of the sacking of the Indus cities by hordes of Aryans—in order to ridicule them as hopelessly inadequate. One is also relentlessly subjected, in Indigenous discourse, to harangues about the excesses of nineteenth century colonial bias. There may undoubtedly be plenty of justification for this, but not when it is at the expense of subsequently seriously engaging the real issues at stake in the present-day context. Lamberg-Karlovsky (1997) takes Chakrabarti to task for his polemics in *Colonial Indology: The Sociopolitics of the Ancient Indian Past*, a book wherein "there is little room for disagreement" (2). He points to the author's "hostility to the belief of an Aryan invasion [as] a constant theme throughout the book" (7). Chakrabarti is especially criticized for his intransigence in his belief that all aspects of Indian culture are indigenous and not due to foreign influences from any external source. Lamberg-Karlovsky (1997) does not mince his words in critiquing this attitude, which is by no means untypical of much Indigenist thinking:

> If one brings diffusion into play, one is not being sufficiently nationalist, that is to say, one is subordinating native Indian ingenuity in calling upon diffusion and foreign agency to inspire Indian development. . . . Diffusion *within* the territorial boundaries of India is permitted but diffusion from outside those boundaries into India is verboten! . . . Chakrabarti advocates a primordial model: that is to say that everyone and everything that ever was found on the land of what constitutes the India of today (which of course includes Pakistan) was always in the past and ever shall be Indian. . . . If you are a foreigner and Chakrabarti disagrees with you, you represent "neocolonial, and racist ideas" while, if you are an Indian and disagree with his views, you are among "a large body of cringing historians and archaeologists wanting to be counted not as one of the land [an Indian] but as one of 'them'". . . . Such paranoia naturally concludes with a "we" vs. "them" attitude. . . . Such thinking is considered "racist" if perpetuated in the West, in the Third World it is merely nationalist. (9–12)

D. K. Chakrabarti's book is a no-holds-barred settling of old scores, which is likely to be only one of the forerunners of an increasing number of publications from fully trained intellectuals and professional historians open to reconsidering the entire infrastructure of ancient Indian history: I met several scholars who were planning to write publications contesting the Aryan migration theory alone. Chakrabarti (1997) is not at all reticent in stating:

> It is the interplay of race, language and culture which has provided the most strong plank of the understanding of ancient India by the Westerns and the Indians alike. This plank was laid down at the height of Western political hegemony over India, and the fact that this still has been left in its place speaks a volume for the post-1947 pattern of the retention of Western dominance in various forms. . . . We believe that unless this major plank of colonial Indology is dismantled and taken out, it is unlikely that there will be a non-sectarian and multi-lineal perspective of the ancient Indian past which will try to understand the history of the subcontinent in its own terms. (53)

While R. Rocher (1998), in her review of Chakrabarti's book, objects that "proofs for the validity of an 'Indian' position take a back seat to scorn heaped on alternative interpretations"—a charge that can be accurately levied against much Indigenous Aryanism—there is nonetheless much that is representative in many of Chakrabarti's assertions even if they are articulated in a "sustained vituperative tone" that rearticulates "much that is well known" (308). Chakrabarti (1997) is forcefully pronouncing in print what many Indian intellectuals will reveal in private conversations:

> We have no hesitation in asserting that the "Nigger Question" is in various forms still very much a part of the Indological scene. Right from patronizing comments on "Babu English" to wry remarks on Indian nationalism for refusing to accept the idea of Greek and other extraneous origins of some of the crucial traits of Indian culture, the Western Indological literature has been consistent in viewing the general Indian scholarship in the matter as an inferior product. . . . Some Indians' refusal to acknowledge the veracity

of Aryan invasion of India is interpreted by Western Indologists as misdirected symptoms of "north Indian nationalism." (114)

Nonetheless, some Western scholars are beginning to find such colonial and neocolonial tar and feathering annoying and passé. Jamison refers to the "hostility toward the supposedly 'Western imperialist/colonialist' notions of an Indo-European language family and of the 'Aryan invasions,'" as well as "the determination to claim an exclusively subcontinental origin for the Indo-Aryan languages" as "emotional" and "unscientific."[28] Rocher (1998) finds Chakrabarti's book "a polemical survey of scholarship on ancient India" and a "rehashing [of] the 'racist' assumptions of Western Indology" (307). As anyone following the Indo-Aryan migration debates on the Indology nets and other conferences in the West can attest, the discussions almost invariably become exasperating and all too often degenerate into emotional name-calling as accusations of "neocolonial chauvinism" from one side and assertions of "Hindu nationalistic dogma" from the other inevitably start to be bandied about while the scholarly value of the discussions rapidly evaporates. As a consequence, the topic has long been banned by the moderator of the principal Indology List on the internet.

On the other hand, not all dissident or "revisionist" voices are articulated in a polemical and nationalistic tenor, and one must be cautious not to lump them all in one category. There are all-too-often a priori dismissive attitudes displayed in Western academic circles on the few occasions when dissonant views from India are cursorily referred to. Mallory (1997), for example, who is otherwise noteworthy for his thorough and fair approach to all points of view, characterizes S. S. Misra's entire position by a sole tongue-in-cheek comment that he sees fit to extract from Misra's book: "India has not been rejected as a potential homeland of the Indo-Europeans (*pace* Misra 1992: 41) only because 'it is a nice place to live and people would not move outside it'!" (104). Misra has dedicated a lifetime to writing dozens of specialized books on Indo-European languages, and, while one may not agree with some of his arguments in his book on the Aryan problem (such as the primacy of Sanskrit *-a* as detailed in chapter 4), his observations regarding the Finno-Ugric loans, at least, do merit a less flippant characterization and a more solid response. In his earlier works, Mallory himself, acknowledged that theories pertaining to an Asian homeland had long fallen out of repute, "but one wonders if this is not just partly due to the ridicule heaped upon them by their opponents rather than reasoned dismissal" (54).[29] As Chakrabarti (1997) comments:

> Rumblings against some of the premises of Western Indology have been heard from time to time, but such rumblings have generally emerged in uninfluential quarters, and in the context of Indian historical studies this would mean people without control of the major national historical organizations, i.e., people who can easily be fobbed off as "fundamentalists" of some kind, mere *dhotiwalas* of no intellectual consequence. (3)

Discourses of Suspicion

In the next few pages, I will draw attention to a few expressions from Indigenist literature that is to be found on the popular mass market, rather than the academic one. Much of this type of literature would be considered worthless from the perspective of critical scholarship (I provide some bio-data in footnotes). It ranges from the more overt advocates of Hindu nationalism (Waradpande 1989; Sathe 1991), to Hindu Puranic-based parallels of Christian Genesis-based literalism (Kulkarni 1988); to sincere, nonpolemical publications that have genuinely attempted to address at least some of the evidence available to the author (Sethna 1992). Here we find popular appropriations and renditions of, and reactions to, some of the material published by professionals.

These voices are useful since they afford an opportunity of comprehending *why* so many Indians are suspicious of the Aryan Invasion theory. It is precisely in these types of publications, with their more spontaneous (and often polemical) tone, that motives and sentiments can be more easily perceived. Moreover, this type of literature is more available to members of the urban literate middle-class than the less accessible, and often far more costly, publications of professional scholars. Therefore, it is very relevant in terms of informing and influencing popular understandings of Indian history and as such of interest to the historiographer.

As Chakrabarti has vociferously exemplified, the reconsideration of the Aryan invasion theory is, to a great extent, predicated on suspicion of the motives of nineteenth-century European scholars, and thus belongs to the more general sphere of postcolonial discourse. Whatever might be the polemical tone of such discourse, it is not without some basis and degree of justification, as I attempted to outline in chapter 1. A few examples from a cross section of these popular Indigenist publications should suffice to illustrate such suspicions. The Aryan invasion theory, from this perspective, is "the fabrication of a version of ancient history and tradition that was highly advantageous to missionary and colonial interests" (Rajaram 1995, 1); "Scholars, administrators and missionaries were working hand in hand to achieve the common goal of manipulating history" (Devendraswarup 1993, 39);[30] "There is evidence in the published utterances of Western scholars themselves that the Aryan-invasion theory was not put forward as a serious scientific theory, but as a politico-religious ploy" (Waradpande 1989, 203); "The West, a colonial West, created the myth . . . of the Aryans for their colonial expansion and commercial exploits (Choudhury 1995, 9);[31] "it was the colonialists who initiated history-writing and taught to Indians what history was. Their paramount interest was in acquiring a perfect grip over their Raj" (Singh 1995, B, 2).

Another principal motive behind the colonial commitment to the Aryan theory from Indigenist perspectives is the desire of colonial administrators to stress the Indo-European, or Aryan, kinship of the British and the Indian elite in order to strengthen the British colonization of the subcontinent: "The British wished to show that their invasion of India was the second great event, the first great event being its invasion by the Indo-Aryans" (Rathore 1994, 176). Since the Vedic Aryans were looked up to with great respect and adulation by most Hindu Indians, their colonial counterparts, the British, should likewise be respected and appreciated. Just as the first wave of Aryans had brought a new language and superior civilization to India, the British are seen as portraying themselves as the second wave of Aryans who, in resonance with their earlier kinsmen, were also bringing a new language and superior civilization to the subcontinent. As has been outlined in chapter 1, there are adequate grounds from nineteenth-century Western scholarship to validate such suspicions of the possible motives underlying the promotion of the Aryan invasion theory.

A further motive ascribed to the colonial investment in promoting the Aryan invasion theory, and one that causes the most concern to the Indigenous Aryan school (and is mentioned in many popular publications), is the desire "to sow dissentions among different sections of the Hindu society. . . . This gave rise to the Dravidisthan movement. . . . [This] propaganda succeeded in driving a wedge between the North and South Indians" (Waradpande 1989, 208); "Indian history has been misinterpreted to divide the Indians into Aryans and Dravidians, tribals and non-tribals etc., to initiate mainly a process of disintegration" (Choudhury 1993, 7); "the Britishers came to India as empire builders. . . . They drummed into our ears that we are a fragmented people" (Kulkarni 1988, 17);[32] "According to the corollaries of the theory, all Indians were divided into Aryan, Dravidian and Austro-Asiatic races. . . . A large number of Indian teachers and students do not know . . . the severe damage done . . . by this very theory" (Sathe 1991, 8);[33] "The Aryan Invasion Theory has been a cause of creating adversarial social relations in India. On the basis of this theory, the Dravidians are supposed to have a just cause of detesting the Aryans, since the latter displaced them from their original homeland . . . and often kept them at the lower end of the society."[34] The by now familiar charge of British divide-and-rule tactics are depicted as being a primary calculated motive behind the creation of the Aryan invasion theory.

Herein lies another motive for the reconsideration of the Aryan invasion theory. This discourse attempts to counteract forces of national divisiveness and promote unity—at least, that is, between Dravidians and northerners:

> An unhealthy movement has arisen in Tamil lands . . . which tends to make for a touchy and suspicious relationship between the two parts of our subcontinent. . . . the fact that the extra-origins of Aryanism has been a pernicious force amongst us and that its demolition would lead to greater harmony and cooperative creativity in India must not prejudice us as historians. We have to be calm and clear in our approach to the problem even while realizing that we cannot afford to be lax about a matter that keenly affects our collective future. (Sethna 1992, 1)[35]

Sethna's work is refreshingly void of anti-Muslim, nationalistic, or even anticolonial bias; he, too, is a good example of an Indigenous Aryanist who has little appreciation for the communalization of historical debates or of politics in general. But he is concerned about the divisive implications of the Aryan invasion theory. Present-day religious leaders reiterate the same objections: "The Indologists and Orientalists . . . introduced the till then unheard of concept of Aryans and Dravidians, which created mutual hatred" (Shankaracharya, Chandrasekharendra Saraswati 1988, 16). It must be noted, however, that this concern for Aryan-Dravidian unity is based on the common Sanskritic/Hindu culture shared by the majority populations of the two language groups. Even if anti-Muslim sentiments are not explicitly expressed in such discourses, the Muslims are invariably not specified as partaking of this interlingual, transcultural fraternity.

I should note that while I have come across many references supporting Indigenist suspicions regarding colonial and missionary biases and strategies using the Aryan connection in the variety of different ways that I attempted to outline in chapter 1, I have yet to come across any indication that the British consciously exploited the Aryan theory to create a divide-and-rule situation between the North and the South. However, whatever may have been the motives of colonial scholars or missionaries, the Aryan-Dravidian dichotomy was most certainly put to political use by separatist voices in the South of India. Tamil Nadu has a history of leaders of the Dravidian movement in South India who reject much that has come to be known as "Hinduism," portraying it as an invasive Aryan imposition on an indigenous Dravidian populace, as noted in chapter 2.

A missionary version of this divide-and-rule policy is also considered contributory to the propagation of the Aryan invasion theory. According to Devendraswarup (1993), as early as the 1840s, missionaries were propagating the idea that the "Brahmins had entered India from across the Indus river, had brought the Sanskrit language with them, and had foisted them on the aboriginal people of India" (32). Elst (1996) proposes that their idea was to portray these Aryans as immigrants who had "colonized India and chased the aboriginals to the most inaccessible places . . . until at long last the Christian missionaries came to give them back their dignity" (165).[36] By targeting the Aryans as invaders and oppressors, the missionaries are portrayed as discouraging the tribes and lower-ranking castes from identifying with Brahman-dominated Hinduism, gaining their sympathy, and offering them a new set of loyalties in the form of Christianity. Such views, as noted in chapter 1, can certainly be substantiated.

In any critique of Christian bias, the name of Max Müller invariably arises, as does his often-quoted statement: "This edition of mine . . . the Veda . . . will hereafter tell to a great extent on the fate of India. . . . it is the root of their religion, and to show them what that root is, is the only way of uprooting all that has sprung up from it during the last 3000 years."[37] Monier Williams is another target of indignation: "When the walls of the mighty fortress of Brahmanism are encircled, undermined, and finally stormed by the soldiers of the cross, the victory of Christianity must be signal and complete."[38] Resentment of such attitudes still resonates in Hindu religious discourse today. The Kanchi Kamakoti Peetham Sankaracharya echoes the same suspicions of pro-Christian Western hermeneutics: "Their conclusions would permit them to regard the ancient ṛiṣis as primitive men inferior to the moderns. . . . their analysis of our religious texts was motivated by the desire to show Christianity as a better religion" (Chandrasekharendra Saraswati 1988, 16)

From this perspective, it not only was important to depict the Aryans as immigrants but also was essential to depict the Vedic texts as the product of lusty marauding nomads whose highest philosophical aspiration in life was to enlist the support of the gods in stealing cattle and defeating enemies. This was in stark contrast to the traditional image of the *Veda* as being the product of enlightened, gentle *ṛṣis*. As noted in chapter 2, such portrayals have aggravated some Hindu writers ever since Western scholarship started to circulate in India: "It is one of the cruel ironies of fate that a people who have done so much for the spiritual and material welfare of humanity should . . . have been described as fierce nomads, reckless vandals and barbarous despoilers of superior cultures by distinguished historians" (Kalyanaraman 1969, vi); "Certain Western scholars always tried to show that the Aryans in India were not really advanced, that they were barbarous and that their achievements, if any, pertained to later dates after they had studied the Greek ideas" (Kulkarni 1988, 8); "English translations of the *Rigveda* . . . represent a massive misinterpretation built on the preconception that the Vedas are the primitive poetry of nomadic barbarians. Nothing could be further from the truth" (Rajaram 1995, xvi).

In addition to motives articulated in terms of *Hindutva*, anti-imperialism, missionary bias, and/or potential Dravidian separatism, there is another tension underlying much of the reaction of the Indigenous Aryan school to the invasion/migration theory. This dimension is much harder to document in a critical fashion, and to some extent I base my somewhat tentative presentation of this on years of living in India, as well as on many personal conversations with Indian scholars and intellectuals. The tension is an epistemological one. As a cross-cultural phenomenon, it can be situated in the universal encounter between tradition and modernity—between scriptural authority and critical scholarship. Of course, such tension between belief and academic discourse is not unique to India (Noll's *Between Faith and Criticism* is one in a long list of publications tracing the interaction between evangelism and biblical scholarship in America).

Although it is not framed as such by the participants involved, I perceive roughly corresponding elements to the age-old Indian dialectic between *pratyakṣa*, *anumāna*, and *śabda pramāṇa* ('empirical, inferential, and scriptural proof') being played out in the Indigenous Aryan debate. The Ṛgveda makes no mention of an external origin of the Aryans. The Ṛgveda is *Śabda pramāṇa* 'verbal proof'. Historically, within Brahmanical circles, it has been considered to be absolute and supreme among the three (or more) types of proof because its source is *apauruṣeya* 'not coming from mankind (and therefore divine)'. *Anumāna* 'inferential proof' and *pratyakṣa* 'empirical' knowledge have always been considered inferior by those accepting the authority of the Veda, since they are subject to the faults of human interpretation.[39]

If we filter the Aryan invasion debate through these traditional categories, we can perhaps—very roughly, in a heuristic rather than precise fashion—find correspondences between linguistics and *anumāna* 'inferential proof', and archaeology and *pratyakṣa* 'empirical' knowledge (which is, of course, interpreted by *anumāna*). Both these *pramāṇas*, and the disciplines I have associated with them, are subject to the defects of faulty human interpretation. The Vedas (and, perhaps equally of relevance to some, the Purāṇas),[40] which are *Śabda* (or *Śruti*) *pramāṅa* make no mention of an external homeland. Archaeology and linguistics, on the other hand, have been utilized to support such a theory. This results in the rejection or minimization of the authority of linguistics and archaeology among a few scholars and intellectuals, and in some form of cognitive dissonance for some others who attempt to reconcile, and make sense of, all three forms of *pramāṇas*.

I do not wish to make too much of all this or imply that such tension applies to all Indigenists, but to illustrate my basic point, we can recall the reactions to the Aryan invasion theory, mentioned in chapter 2, by some of India's early religious authorities in the modern period: "No *Sanskrit* book or history records that the Aryas came here from Iran. . . . How then can the writings of foreigners be worth believing in the teeth of this testimony?" (Dayananda, Sarasvati 1988 220); "The indications in the Veda on which this theory of a recent Aryan invasion is built are very scanty in quantity and uncertain in significance. There is no actual mention of any such invasion" (Aurobindo 1971, 24); "And what your European pundits say about the Aryans swooping down from some foreign land . . . this I say to you—to our pundits— . . . 'You are learned men, hunt up your old books and scriptures, please, and draw your own conclusions'" (Vivekananda 1970–73, 534–535). Many Hindus are much more likely to defer to the verdict of the Vedas, and of its religious representatives, than to that of Russian archaeologists laboriously digging up horse bones and excavating Kurgan graves in the Volga Valley. *Śabda pramāṇa*, for many, remains authoritative, even if ninety thousand horse bones have been dug up in Botai in the Ural Mountains (Ratnagar 1996b, 78), and not a single undisputed find has yet turned up in almost a million square miles of the Indus Valley.

Among professional scholars who do adopt and accept critical methods of scholarship and the empirico-rational approach, there is often a sense of satisfaction when archaeology and linguistics verify the validity of *Śabda pramāṇa*. The contradictory need for transcendence to be substantiated empirically is a common feature in the encounter of tradition and modernity. In India, this can occasionally be sensed in the examples noted previously regarding the discovery of the Sarasvatī: "At last we found true what was recorded in oral traditions" (Gupta 1989, x);[41] "Some authors believe that it [Sarasvatī] is a myth. There can hardly be a damage equal to such interpretations . . . which discredit the authenticity of the Veda" (Murthy 1980, 191).[42] In other cases, scholars like Sethna, being outside mainstream academic circles and therefore not threatened by ridicule or job insecurity, are not reluctant to acknowledge religious personalities as authority figures. Sethna constantly refers to, and to some extent elaborates on, the work of Śri Aurobindo (who took some pains to debunk the Aryan invasion theory):[43]

In any event, there are plenty of scholars who, while not concerned with whether the Vedic corpus is divine, still hold that *śāstra* is a form of *pramāṇa*, handed down by generations of forefathers through the millennia, and that there is no reason to minimize its authority even if this sometimes conflicts with other sources of knowledge. To put it another way: *śāstra* is innocent until proven guilty. The single most common argument that repeatedly appears in Indigenous Aryan publications is that the Vedic texts make no mention of an external origin of the Aryans. On this basis, all other forms of *pramāṇa*, while by no means rejected, do become at least suspect in this regard. This is not to say that all the scholars who have questioned the status quo regarding Aryan origins believe in an eternal Veda that is *apauruṣeya*: as I have repeatedly stressed, there are many different voices in the Indigenous Aryan school. Some, although accepting the textual tradition as an important source of information, are hard-core empiricists who consider even linguistics to be a pseudoscience.[44] When all is said and done, the various scholars in the Indigenous Aryan school, while sharing a common opinion that Indian history has been erroneously constructed, seem to reveal very different concerns in their scholarship. Ultimately, the motives underlying this issue are genuinely complex, and it becomes very difficult to categorize people into easily definable molds.

To complicate the picture even further, not all the scholars dealt with in this book are residents of India, nor, indeed, even Indian. There exists what has come to be known as the nonresident Indian (NRI) camp.[45] Intellectuals such as Rajaram and Subhash Kak are highly educated and articulate mathematicians and computer experts teaching in American universities who bring high-tech methods to bear on their research.[46] Other contributors to this debate, such as Frawley and Elst, are Westerners with a deep passion for Indian culture.[47] Elst, whose latest book on this topic (1999) does address a good deal of the relevant data, has nonetheless acquired a reputation for promoting pro-Hindu views in previous works. Frawley's work, also unambiguously pro-Hindu, has been much more successful in the popular, rather than the academic, market and is clearly directed and articulated at such. Nonetheless, his impact on the Indian community both in the diaspora and in India is by no means insignificant. He has written or coauthored three books on the origin of the Indo-Aryans. I was informed by the owner of the well-known Delhi publisher and distributor Munshiram Manoharlal that Frawley's book *The Myth of the Aryan Invasion of India* (which had just been released) sold out in eighteen days. A Western scholar debunking the Aryan Invasion theory has obvious appeal in India.[48] As an aside, when Indigenists refer to the theory of Aryan invasions having been disproved or rejected "even by Western scholars," they are likely referring to Frawley, Elst, and/or Shaffer.

Categorization is a tricky business. Where do American archaeologists such as Shaffer and Kenoyer (who are neither typical Indigenous Aryanists nor, certainly, Aryan Migrationists; who have no emotional, spiritual, cultural, or ideological bone of contention to pick with any of this; but who have also departed from previous assumptions that have hitherto been used to interpret the archaeological record) fit into the scheme of things?[49] This all goes to show that ideological analysis, while indispensable in a historiographical study such as this, must refrain from straitjacketing individuals into convenient and easily identified stereotypes or groupings. Indeed, many other publications from India, of varying worth, can be situated in the Indigenous Aryan camp but reveal no obvious motive whatsoever. There is no *Hindutva* undertone, no mention of colonial or missionary bias, no reference to Dravidian separatism, no apparent epistemological tension. They are not acrimonious, biased, angry, or ideological; nor, indeed, do they reveal any pressing concerns whatsoever. They appear, for all intents and purposes, simply to be interested in examining the evidence utilized in the construction of ancient Indian history and offering interpretations that differ with those that are generally promoted in the textbooks. How are these to be categorized?

Finally, this book has focused mostly on scholars who have actively argued for the indigenous origin of the Aryans. What about other South Asian historians—those who have written general histories of ancient India and have therefore had to deal with the question of Aryan origins but have not actively contributed to the debate? "How have they dealt with the Indigenous Aryan school? Examining a sample from this category further highlights how widespread suspicion of the standard version of Indo-Aryan origins is, and has always been, in India. Anyone can gain a sense of this by browsing through the shelves of a library with a good Indology section for books by Indian scholars with such titles as *Ancient History of India* or *Life and Culture in Ancient India* that are published in India and clearly intended for a local market. Such a sampling, when compared with publications by Western scholars on the topic of the Indo-Aryans, further underlines the major divide, and obvious lack of communication, and often interest, between many Indian and Western scholars on this subject. In Erdosy's recent *Indo-Aryans of South Asia*, for example, the only reference to the Indigenous Aryan school (apart from one article by A. Sharma) is a reference to it in a footnote of the preface as a "lunatic fringe."

In sharp contrast, most publications by Indian scholars who have undertaken to write histories of South Asia have very different perspectives and sensitivities on the matter. As I mentioned in the introduction, because of the already massive scope of this enterprise, I have restricted my research to English-language sources, but obviously it would be interesting to see how these issues translate into local vernaculars (my cursory glance at Hindi and Bengali publications suggested that the more scholarly and detailed work had been written in English). The treatment of the issue in English-language sources seems to fall into several categories, which I will attempt to illustrate with one or two examples from each. The first consists of scholars who outline the various homeland theories and the various objections raised against India being the homeland and orient themselves around the Indigenous Aryan position: "The Indians never knew for thousands of years that there was an Aryan invasion; their sacred literature is silent about it. About the middle of the last century . . . an invasion was suggested by the Western scholars. First it was an inference, then it became a presumption, and now it has become an article of faith (Pillai 1959, 67); "Hence the theory that the Aryans came to India from Central Asia *via* Persia requires rethinking. For a long time Indian scholars silently followed the European line of arguments. With the expansion of Indology to higher levels Indian scholars began to doubt the wisdom of European scholarship and were compelled by reason to think of an indigenous theory of the origins of the Aryans" (Pillai 1988, 78); "There is a growing volume of opinion among Indian scholars that Harappan culture was in fact Vedic" (Mazumdar 1979, 73).

The second category consists of scholars who outline the arguments in favor of the external origin of the Aryans, as well as the arguments that oppose it, but leave the issue unresolved—in other words, the Indigenous Aryan position is treated on equal terms with the standard version of events: "European scholars have been trying to prove that the Aryans came to India from outside and their guesses have extended to all sorts of places like Scandinavia, Austria, Czechoslovakia, Russia, Turkey, Central Asia and Armenia. But any of these places cannot yet be said to really be the homeland of the Aryans. We are still in the realm of speculation and are likely to remain so" (Vidyarthi 1970, 32); "Who were the progenitors [of Vedic culture], and wherefrom do they emerge in our historical view? Questions like these have been a bewildering source of controversy. . . . Some Indian scholars . . . strongly maintain that the Aryans were autochthons of the land" (Tripathi 1967, 26); "However it might be . . . [regarding the original homeland], both those who advocate the theory that the Āryans came from outside India . . . and those who dispute the foreign theory and believe the Āryans to be autochthons are of the same opinion [that Punjab was the abode of the Ṛgveda]" (Sastri and Srinivasat Chari 1971, 2; sequence reversed). In a similar vein, while not personally stating an opinion, R. C. Majumdar dedicates an appendix to the Indigenous Aryan position in the first volume of his famous *History and Culture of the Indian People* (see also Mahajan 1968).

A third category of writers gives the Indigenous Aryan school equal and respectful time but passes a verdict against them: "Many scholars have advocated the theory that India has been the original home of the Aryans. The main features of the indigenous origin of the Aryans are as follows . . . [the author lists a few of the main arguments I have presented here]; various scholars have been advocating their own views about the original home of the Aryans, . . . but the Central Asian theory is the most plausible" (Luniya 1978, 72) This particular statement is interesting because Luniya presents the Indigenous Aryan case in a very favorable manner—even chipping in a few objections against its detractors—so much so that this concluding statement comes as quite a surprise. A fourth category of historians simply represent the standard version of Aryan invasions without referring to the debate or the Indigenous Aryan school: "Two main Aryan waves started from Central Asia in the second millennium. . . . both affected

India" (Kosambi 1965, 77). A final category—more ideologically sensitive and, as as has been exemplified earlier, usually stereotyped as the Marxist camp—actively opposes the Indigenous Aryan school.

These groupings definitely correspond to the types of responses I found in my interviews with professional scholars, with the addendum that the first category—composed of those supportive or favorably inclined toward the Indigenous Aryan camp—was far larger than the other categories. All in all, the Indigenous Aryan school is undoubtedly taken much more seriously in India than in the West, to the point where it now seems to represent the opinion of, or is at least accepted as a possibility by, the majority of historians whom I interviewed in the 25 or so major campuses I visited all over the subcontinent. A last anecdote might help illustrate this tendency. In one of my interviews, the head of the ancient history department of a major university in South India told me that she had always been suspicious of the Aryan invasion theory but had felt compelled to teach it for many years because of her fear of stepping out of line with the status quo. As a result of these recent trends in the field, however, most of her colleagues in India were now expressing their doubts about or opposition to the theory. She vividly and poignantly described her sense of intellectual liberation when she, too, was able to begin voicing her doubts in public. This type of sentiment was by no means unique to her. Obviously, professional scholars are, or at least have in the past been, much more reserved and discrete in their academic publications, which, accordingly, lend themselves less easily to analysis such as this. But such scholars are beginning to speak out much more forcefully in the articulation of their suspicions and were certainly happy to voice their doubts in interviews (although, because such overtness seems to be a recent phenomenon, detractors immediately connect it with the rise of Hindu nationalism).

There are growing signs that the recognition of a difference of views (as opposed to an a priori, and oftentimes disparaging, dismissal of it) is surfacing in Western academic circles. Flood's *Introduction to Hinduism* (1996), although generally siding with the Parpola school, gives a fair and sensitive summary of some of the issues and adopts a note of inconclusiveness: "Wherever the Aryans originated, whether their culture was a development of indigenous cultures or whether they migrated from elsewhere . . . " Klostermaier's *Survey of Hinduism* (1994) comes out in full support of the main tenets of the Indigenous Aryanist position:

> The dating of the Vedic age as well as the theory of an Āryan invasion of India has been shaken. We are required to completely reconsider not only certain aspects of Vedic India, but the entire relationship between Indus civilization and Vedic culture. . . . One of the most intriguing pieces of evidence is afforded by the dating of the disappearance of the River Saraswatī. . . . Also, no evidence has been found of any large scale violent conflicts. . . . Astronomical evidence allow[s] us to set precise dates to certain passages in the Ṛgveda. . . . The certainty seems to be growing that the Indus civilization was carried out by the Vedic Indians. (34–38)

I myself am coediting a volume on this whole issue in which some of the Western authorities on this theme are prepared to dialogue, debate, and share space with some of the more sober members of the Indigenous Aryan school (Bryant and Patton, forthcoming). When I first embarked on this research in 1989, no Western scholar had any awareness that the theory of Aryan migrations was under contestation at all. It has since exploded into full view in all South Asian Internet conferences, whether historical, religious, or Indological, usually to the point of over-saturation and exasperation for all as a result of the often limited scholarly content of the opinions stated and the emotional fervor that the issue ignites on all sides.

Conclusion

Pollock (1993) has shown how the study of Sanskrit was adopted by various quite distinct agendas by multiple Orientalisms—the British for external colonial purposes, the Germans for internal, European colonization, and the Brahmans for the maintenance of their own elite dominance in traditional India. Similarly, Indigenous Aryanism is also multifaceted. It is adopted by some as a means of opposing European Orientalism—the scholarship of the colonial period. It is simultaneously promoted by others to serve an internal Orientalism (in the sense of the production of unflattering knowledge about the "Other," albeit not an Oriental one, for political domination), connected to the discourse of legitimacy in Hindu notions of nationhood.

Ancient Indian pre- and protohistory is an extremely rich and fascinating area of study, but, unfortunately, the origin of the Indo-Aryans has become inextricably enmeshed with the politics of representation. There is every reason to be concerned that if the Vedic Indo-Aryans are interpreted as being indigenous to India, then the Vedic "civilization" and all that developed from it will be construed as "truly Indian" and all subsequent cultural groups known to have immigrated into India could explicitly or implicitly be depicted as "Others." Indigenous Aryanism, as a result of such concerns, is generically portrayed as a discourse promoting communal tension. However, in such generalizations, distinctions are often not made between communal revisionism and postcolonial reconsideration, and a kind of uncritical McCarthyism has developed in some quarters toward those who favor the Indigenous Aryan point of view, despite the fact that this view is on the ascendancy in India (or, perhaps, as a consequence of it) irrespective of the motives and backgrounds of those interested in this issue. Such generalizations have been fueled by the appalling quality of much Indigenist literature. Aggressively promoting a point of view on the basis of a very meager and biased understanding of the actual data involved naturally indicates the existence of preconceived ideas that are nonnegotiable. Such ideas are generally ideological. Such publications contribute to the association of Indigenous Aryanism with Hindu nationalism.

However, in terms of some of the better Indigenist publications that nonetheless also have nationalistic undertones, even if writings are deeply disturbing because of their blatant political or other agendas that might disturb particular sensitivities, does that deprive them of all value whatsoever in those particular sections where they engage the historical data? The method employed in this book, as stated in the introduction, has been to present discussion of the evidence and discussion of ideologies in separate chapters. Talageri the linguist has been treated as a linguist in the chapter on linguistics and critiqued accordingly, while Talageri the nationalist has been dealt with as a nationalist in this chapter. Nationalistic bias does not a priori deprive his linguistic analysis of value, however troubling his nationalistic attitude vis-à-vis Muslims might be to those of us who do not share his attitudes. In this regard, Chakrabarti (1995), reviewing

Parpola's book, reacts to a remark made by the author: "To be a nationalist is not a crime in itself. . . . the author . . . would find many good examples of historical research inspired by nationalism in his own country" (429). He has a point, albeit one that is not always easy to confront: the whole history of Indo-European studies is steeped in Western nationalism, as we have seen, but in many instances this did produce tremendous advances in the field. Lamberg-Karlovsky (1997) warns scholars not to "make the mistake of diminishing the contributions of archaeology and/or archaeologists because of the political ideology under which they willingly, or unwillingly, worked" (40). He points our that the Soviet exerperience, at least, suggests that considerable advances can be made in a discipline despite its nightmarish context.

However exasperating and polemical some Indigenist anticolonialist harangues tend to be, there is nonetheless some very good reasons for Indian scholars to be highly suspicious of the fact that the ancient history of their country was constructed by an imperial power, as was outlined in chapter 1. This does not justify replacing one perceived myth with another. There are still *data* that have to be addressed in order to form a comprehensive picture of an ancient period. Simply ignoring major aspects of the evidence and focusing on features that are amenable to a specific alternative view with troubling ideological underpinnings is to duplicate the errors and excesses of the much maligned nineteenth century European historical enterprise. History cannot be written by decibel. While it is certainly legitimate to revisit the narrative of ancient Indian history that has been inherited from the pre-independence period, it remains very much incumbent on the academic community to draw attention to, and react against, alternative readings of the evidence that are likely to promote further divisiveness and violence between ethnic communities. Two wrongs do not make a right. European racism and elitism cannot be replaced by Hindu chauvinism. As I have stated repeatedly, it is the *Hindutva* agenda that has prevented many Western and Indian scholars from paying attention to the Indigenous Aryan school because they are justly troubled by the potential for alienation, hate, and aggression that such discourses have provoked. Kohl makes no bones about this: "Nationalist crazies . . . little fascists eager to distort their pasts to further their own, often violent, political ends are capable of sprouting up like weeds everywhere, and one must recognize them for what they are and not excuse them away on the basis of some slippery relativist standard" (quoted in Lamberg-Karlovsky 1997, 42–43).

From the other side, those most actively defending the theory of Aryan migrations, at least in India, are characterized as having ideological predispositions of their own. These are usually associated with secular Marxist agendas in some Indian contexts and neocolonialist ones in others. Despite its recent ascendancy, the Indigenist position has met vigorous opposition on the subcontinent. But the Indigenist position cannot be opposed by historians of the ancient period simply *because* of the political corollaries that might be latent in some of the discourses of its members, even though these must continue to be clearly and explicitly highlighted. Ultimately, the historian's task is to present the most comprehensive and coherent picture of a particular period on the grounds of *all* the available evidence, even while drawing attention to the sociological context of any act of interpretation. Indigenists have made some significant challenges to the established version of events regarding Indo-Aryan origins, and these need to be addressed in detail. I find the lack of awareness and attention to the linguistic data that essentially undergirds this whole question to be just as glaring on the Migrationist side of this debate in India as on the Indigenist side. There is sometimes a sense that the primary task is to oppose the Indigenists at all cost, and a secondary one is to produce some historical (almost invariably archaeological) grounds for doing so. This is understandable, given the alarming chain of events on the subcontinent during the last decade of this millennium, but it is ideological nonetheless. The result is an almost complete lack of communication between two mutually antagonistic and angry camps. The bitterness, antipathy, and sarcasm seeping from the pens of participants in this debate (from both sides of the fence) when referring (increasingly by name) to those holding opposing views is apparent for all to see.

In a progressive academic context, differences of opinions, however radical, challenge scholars to constantly reexamine their views, assumptions, and methods. This is the lifeline of healthy scholarship. But in the present academic climate in the subcontinent, it has become increasingly difficult, particularly for Indian scholars, to discuss the prehistory of the subcontinent in a rational, objective way without becoming associated with the ideologies that are immediately correlated with pro- or contra- stances for or against the Indigenous Aryan issue. This works to the obvious detriment of expanding and developing a nuanced understanding of the early history of the subcontinent. In our postmodern age, we can no longer take recourse to the myth of "objectivity," but it is incumbent on all of us, especially in the academic community, to attempt to confront our own predispositions and allow our perspectives to be modified and influenced by open-minded and genteel exchanges with those holding differing or opposing points of view. Casting off the legacies of colonialism opens up exciting new possibilities for the understanding of Indian protohistory, provided the constraints of the colonial period are not replaced with an equally constraining insistence on a different ideologically driven reading of the historical evidence, whatever that ideology might be.

Conclusion

So where has all this led? The Indigenous Aryan critique forces us to consider, a number of things and on several different levels. On the most immediate level of historical truth claims, what should we put in the textbooks? Did the Indo-Aryan languages originate outside the northwest of the subcontinent or didn't they? Let me briefly again summarize the most salient and plausible features of these two points of view. First, a Migrationist scenario.

Leaving aside the problems connected with the location of the original homeland, any Migrationist view will have the Indo-Aryans entering India through its northwestern passes from an external point of origin. From wherever might have been the original matrix, the Indo-Aryans spent a period to the north of the Caspian Sea, adjacent to the Finno-Ugric speakers (either as a distinct group or while still part of the undivided Indo-Iranians). Before the Indo-Aryans proceeded on their way, the Finno-Ugrics borrowed a number of words from them. There is no consistent archaeological evidence that can be traced across Asia and into India because the Indo-Aryans were primarily an itinerant, pastoralist people, unlikely to leave substanial remains; moreover, they may have absorbed aspects of the local cultures encountered during their trajectory. Their material culture, often associated with that of the Andronovo tribes of the steppes, accordingly could have adapted somewhat as it approached southeast central Asia (the BMAC perhaps being one source of influence). They did leave a trail of linguistic evidence, however, particularly in the form of hydronyms across central Asia. Archaeological evidence of their presence has also been revealed, on occasion, as in the chariot found in the Sintashta cemetery somewhat earlier than the sixteenth century B.C.E.

Around this time, a group of Indo-Aryan speakers, who had peeled off from the main body proceeding toward India, surfaced in the Mitanni kingdom of the Near East, where they had engineered their way into elite positions of dominance. Also around this time, or perhaps two or three centuries earlier, the main group of Indo-Aryans had reached the subcontinent proper. The date of the Mitanni kingdom helps secure the date of the composition of the Ṛgveda in India to around the middle of the second millennium B.C.E., a date that is further solidified by the references to iron in slightly later Vedic texts. The Indus Valley Civilization had reached a significant state of decline, facilitating the establishment of this new language group and culture. While continuities survived, this was also a period of transformation. The Ṛgveda, compiled some time after the arrival of the Indo-Aryans (but long enough to be several generations removed from any memories of their migrations), shows little awareness of the flourishing urban cities of the Mature Harappan period. It does, however, show clear linguistic traces of non-Indo-Aryan language speakers that preceded the Indo-Aryans on the subcontinent. These pre-Indo-Aryan speakers eventually became co-opted into the Aryan fold—but not without introducing syntactical, phonemic, and lexical innovations into the intruding language.

The Indo-Aryans introduced the horse, *Equus caballus*, into the subcontinent, and it is around this time that unambiguous evidence of this animal surfaces in the archaeological record. Their dominance of the Northwest of the subcontinent was so extensive that they even coined new names for almost all the rivers and other topographical features in that area, despite the generally conservative linguistic nature of such terms. Other words, however, such as those for unfamiliar local fauna and flora, were borrowed from the indigenes. Their spread across the rest of the subcontinent was less pervasive, since non-Indo-Aryan hydronomy and topography are still preserved in the eastern and central parts of India, while in the South, the Indo-Aryan language failed to displace the Dravidian languages. The southern cultures were heavily influenced nonetheless, both culturally and lexically. This spread across the subcontinent can be perceived in the chronologically later Sanskrit texts, which reveal the geographic boundaries of the Indo-Aryans as they progressed farther east and south. By the middle of the first millennium B.C.E., the Indo-Aryan dominance over the entire north of the subcontinent was secure.

This is a simplified summary of a typical Migrationist scenario. It still has much to recommend itself. However, the thrust of this work has been to explore how, if one were so inclined, one could reinterpret or reconfigure these arguments in some kind of a critical fashion to suggest that the Indo-Aryans could have been indigenous to the subcontinent for as long as can be determined from the available evidence—the Indigenist scenario. From this perspective, the fact that there is no consistent archaeological evidence of the Indo-Aryans across central Asia and into India indicates that the archaeological record, in its own terms, does not point to the trans-Asiatic trajectory of a linguistic or an ethnic group into the subcontinent in the second millennium B.C.E. It is linguistics that impels complicated and constrained readings of the archaeological record such as the convenient suggestion that the Indo-Aryans transformed their material culture as they journeyed eastward.

The Indo-Aryans whose names are recorded in the Mitanni treatises could have peeled off from the greater group of Indo-Aryans on their way into the subcontinent, as most scholars assume, or could have been Indo-Aryan speakers on their way out, as Indigenous Aryanists propose, as could the bearers of the river terms such as Haravaiti/Sarasvatī, and the other hydronomic terms across central Asia, with little in the data itself that favors either of these possibilities. If Misra is right, The one-way borrowings of Indo-Aryan (or Indo-Iranian) loans into the Finno-Ugric languages might enhance the possibility that it was the Indo-Aryans that were migrating out of the Northwest of the subcontinent toward such regions, and not emigrating away from them toward the subcontinent, as might an adjusted version of Nichols's somewhat relocated or enlargened Eastern homeland.

Within the subcontinent, the geographic boundaries of the historical Vedic texts need have no bearing on prehistoric geographic origins; the Indo-Aryans may certainly have spread east and south across the subcontinent, but it may not be a warranted move to then assume that they entered into the northwest itself, especially since there is no solid evidence of this in these texts. The existence of non-Indo-European linguistic features in Sanskrit texts could quite convincingly be evidence of a pre-Indo-Aryan substratum, but the possibility of these being the result of adstratum, as opposed to substratum, influences, and/or the result of internal developments and/or the result of Dravidian and Munda intrusions into an Indo-Aryan-speaking area and not vice-versa has yet to be discounted. All of these alternative arguments have been made at some point or another by scholars in the West, not just in India. In addition, the fact that the river names and place-names in the Northwest show no unambiguous evidence of a foreign pre-Aryan linguistic presence minimizes the conclusiveness of the substratum theory.

From the other readings of the data that commonly surface, the philological "evidence" extrapolated from the texts to create images of invading Aryans subjugating racially distinct natives is all subject to perfectly legitimate alternative interpretations. Apart from the horse evidence, linguistic paleontology has not provided much uncontroversial data to exclude an eastern homeland that cannot be reversed to support the same; neither has the evidence of loanwords, nor dialect geography, nor arguments based on homogeneity versus heterogeneity. Philology and linguistics can actually offer surprisingly little to compel disenchanted Indian scholars to modify their suspicions of the ability of these disciplines to make authoritative pronouncements on the origins of the Indo-Aryan-speaking peoples in prehistory.

Archaeologically (although the last word has yet to be spoken), a growing number of South Asian scholars in the field seem prepared to allow the Indo-Aryans a distinct presence in the Indus Valley. Even if it is accepted that the ethos of the Ṛgveda is predominantly a nomadic one, as has generally been accepted, we have yet to see whether archaeology might be revealing that this is not because of a lack of large settlements (and even towns like Pirac) in the post-Harappan period, when and where few would deny that the Aryans were present. In any event, nomads and urban dwellers have coexisted in India for millennia. The Ṛgveda could reflect the ethos of a nomadic community that nonetheless could have been contemporaneous with an urban Harappan one. The oft-cited horse evidence, admitedly remains a perennial obstacle to the Indigenist case, although to conclude that the place of its domestication is the place of the original IE homeland may be an unwarranted leap. The horse has always been a rarity and an import into India, which may explain the dearth of horse bones, but this need have nothing to do with the immigration of the Indo-Aryans themselves (although the burden of proof does rest with anyone suggesting that horse importation accured in India throughout the third millennuim BCE which an Indigenist case would require). And if the horse is absent from the archaeological record, so are the Aryans; there is general consensus among South Asian archaeologists that, as far as the archaeological record is concerned, clear, unambiguous evidence of invading or immigrating Aryans themselves is nowhere to be found either in central Asia or in the Indian subcontinent.

The possibility of the Vedic texts being pre-Harappan has to confront chronological issues. Some of the astronomical proposals—particularly that of the *kṛttikā*, as well as the specific information of the chronologically later Jyotiṣavedāṅga—do not detract from the possibility of the Ṛgveda existing at a time far earlier than the figure given in textbooks, although, as I have discussed, arguments have been levied against this position that cannot be arbitrarily discounted. In my opinion, here is the crux of the matter. If the texts are accepted as being older than the date presently assigned to them, or if the Indo-Aryan language at least is accepted as being older, then much of the evidence supporting Aryan migrations can be brought into question. Here, again, the decipherment of the script will prove decisive. Since the recent discovery suggests that the script could go back to 3500 B.C.E. (and providing that it encapsulates the same language throughout), an Indo-Aryan decipherment will radically alter the entire Indo-European homeland-locating landscape, not just the protohistory of the subcontinent. If it turns out to be a non-Indo-European language, then the Indigenous Aryan critique simply becomes another curious but closed chapter in the history of the Indo-European homeland problem.

Until the script is deciphered, those who are prepared to consider a greater antiquity for the Vedic texts, or who are unconvinced by the rationale underpinning the assignment of their present dates, are more likely to consider the case made in support of an Indigenous Aryan position. Those who feel that the arguments supporting a greater date for the Vedic texts are flimsy and unconvincing are unlikely to be interested in the Indigenous Aryan case except from the perspective of historiography. They need waste no further time weighing the pros and cons of the various interpretations of the historical evidence. They will only need to review their position if the Indus script does turn out to be Indo-Aryan. If that ever happens, they will need to revise their view rather thoroughly. It is premature to exclude Indo-Aryan as a possibility. Ventris, we can recall, who performed the exceptional feat of deciphering Linear B, was expecting a pre-Greek non-Indo-European language to emerge, and was surprised to find Greek encoded in the script. On the other hand, if the Indus script turns out to be a language other than an Indo-European one, then the Indigenist position need no longer detain the consideration of Indologists or serious scholars of ancient history. In my opinion, this eventuality will be the only development that will convince a large number of Indian scholars that the Aryans were, indeed, immigrants into India. The answer, after all is said and done, is written on the seals.

This, at least, leaves us with something positive and something very empirical. It is all well and good simply to deconstruct the scenarios suggested by linguists or to point out the discordant readings of the archaeological record by different archaeologists, but the script, if deciphered—as I have great hopes will happen one day, despite all the difficulties involved—leaves us with something solid and irrefutable. If it is Indo-Aryan, *everything* will need to be reconsidered—Indo-Aryans, Indo-Iranians, and Indo-Europeans. If it is not, then the Migrationist scenario outlined here will likely remain an excellent rendition of events that can always be updated and improved as new evidence surfaces.

In the meantime, the Indigenous Aryan position, although it can by no means carry the day, at least merits a serious response. Of course, the idea of an Aryan immigration into India remains a plausible and in places even convincing way of accounting for some of the presently available evidence. By Occam's razor, it requires less strain in accounting for at least some of the data; an Indigenous position requires more work accounting for all the data. This is partly because of the sheer bulk of the material involved—anyone upholding this point of view has to reevaluate a century and a half of prolific scholarship in multiple disciplines that has all been predicated on the assumption that the Indo-Aryans did invade India. But it is also partly because the corollary of the Indigenous position is that all the Indo-Europeans must have come from Northwest India and its borderlands. And this position has so far provided very little *positive* evidence with which to recommend itself.

Critiquing Migrationist scenarios is one thing, but offering a positive and convincing case for South Asia as an Indo-European homeland is entirely another. And archaeologists are not about to overlook the oft-cited lacuna of the horse in the Harappan period, not to speak of in a period in South Asia corresponding to that of the undivided Indo-Europeans, where the burden of proof does rest with the Indigenists, if they are to argue for a possible awareness of this beast in India during these periods, as their case requires that they must. (Although, as I have already noted, if unambiguous evidence of the horse does surface in an early Harappan context, one can anticipate an uproar in India, and Migrationist scenarios will likely be the object of ever greater scorn they have been so far.)

However, the fact that some sort of an Indigenous case (if not a South Asian homeland case) can be made at all, in my opinion, requires that, at the level of historical truth claims, the more sober voices from the Indigenous Aryan school cannot be denied representation in discussions concerning Indian protohistory. Indo-Europeanists will likely consider it a very myopic view, since it restricts itself solely to the history of one member of this huge language family, with almost no concern for how the other members got to be where they are. It limits its concerns primarily to deconstructing the opinions of others rather than offering anything innovative that can account for the entirety of the Indo-European problem. But this myopia itself, while unlikely to fully convince anyone that northwest South Asia and adjacent regions to its west were factually the homeland, can nonetheless be seen as a contribution to the field if it provokes scholars to reevaluate some of their assumptions, especially since this side of the family has historically received much less attention from Western scholars.

And as far as the textbooks are concerned, in my opinion all we factually know is that the Indo-Aryan dialects were spoken in at least the northwest of the subcontinent in protohistoric times. How these languages got to be related to the other members of the Indo-European language family in terms of their locus of origin can be no more decisively determined today, in my opinion, than in the time of Sir William Jones. There are just too many problems to be found with all the Indo-European homeland proposals offered so far, not least a South Asian one. And obviously no language has ever been indigenous anywhere for all eternity. The original Indo-European homeland simply means the last geographic area where all the Proto-Indo-European speakers remained together before splitting up into speakers of different dialects and journeying to the different historical Indo-European-speaking regions. Where the original Proto-Indo-European speakers came from before they arrived at that "original" area (i.e., any hypothetical Nostratic or other primordial homeland) is a problem that we do not have the resources, in my opinion, to even consider (given that we cannot even locate the Proto-Indo-European point of origin).

I hope the reader will forgive me for concluding my own research on such an agnostic note (although I do hold high hopes for the script). My project has not been to pass a final judgment on this debate—I leave that to each individual reader—but to outline in an accessible fashion the relevant historical material involved, as well as to try to give some sense as to *why* there might be a debate at all. In my view, any attempt to present a comprehensive account of the prehistoric period in South Asia—if it is to be an objective account—should give a fair and adequate representation of the differences of opinion on this matter, as well as of the criticisms that can be levied against any point of view. And attention must always be paid to the *context* of interpretation—from all sides, as well as the actual range of interpretations.

That two such diametrically opposed viewpoints can both claim interpretative jurisdiction over the data demonstrates the extreme malleability of the "evidence" involved. This leads to another level of analysis on a more theoretical level: What prompts scholars to favor a particular line of interpretation when there is so little that is unambiguous or compelling in the data themselves? What persuades one scholar that *a-nāsa* is an appropriate etymological breakdown of a word, and another that *an-āsa* better fits the context? What underlies the logic whereby the absence of the beech tree in India disqualifies it as a potential homeland in one explanatory model but favors it as such in another? Why does one scholar choose to read a 'fish' sign in an unknown script as an Indo-Aryan *ś* sound (based on the Sanskrit word for 'fish'), while another finds reason to propose that the same sign represents a non-Indo-Aryan astral divinity (based on the Dravidian word for 'fish')? Why is the horse "the most sought after animal in Indian archaeology," on one side, while every report claiming archaeological evidence of the animal in the Indus Valley Civilization is challenged, on the other?

Chapters 1 and 13 touched upon some of the forces that have influenced the scholarship involved with the incredibly resilient Aryan problem. It is structurally and chronologically appropriate that these two chapters—the first one on the European context, and the last one on the Indian one—sandwich the intervening chapters, which deal with the interpretation of the historical "evidence"; there is an intriguing symbiosis between the two. It was the testimony of the Bible that originally led scholars to propose the existence of a linguistically unified group of people living somewhere near the Caspian Sea, a subset of whom emanated forth and entered India. And it is the testimony of the Ṛgveda that is used to deny that any such people ever entered from any such place. The Bible laid the groundwork for the construction of the Aryan invasion theory, and the Ṛgveda has been the principal foundation for attempts at its deconstruction.

Although European scholars have long since forgotten the biblical roots of the Aryan problem, Old Testament narrative was certainly an initial factor causing European scholars to interpret the data in selective ways. One must bear in mind that European notions of human history had been based on Genesis for the better part of a millennium and a half. This formative influence was strengthened and then superseded by research intimately connected with the specific political exigencies extant in nineteenth-century Europe. This combination of factors contributed to the development of various assumptions concerning Indo-Aryan (and Indo-European) origins, some of which have remained by and large unquestioned, outside of India, to this very day. In parallel fashion, Vedic testimony has caused many Indian scholars to be a priori suspicious of the interpretations given by Europeans to the data. This starting premise has also been fueled by research partly motivated by various political orientations and developments in twentieth-century India. This combination of factors has resulted in the reconsideration and challenging of the very assumptions produced by the initial European religio-political combine.

There are other parallels between the European and (primarily) Hindu dialectic on this matter that are both comical and sinister. Both versions of Indo-Aryan history have produced their ludicrous contributions: their Dugald Stewarts, who propose that Sanskrit *was* Greek borrowed from Alexander by the wily Brahmanas so that their communication would not be understood by the masses, and their P. N. Oaks, who consider England to be derived from Sanskrit Angulisthan, which was so named by ancient Hindu explorers surging forth from an Indian homeland, due to it being the land (*sthan*) shaped like a finger (*anguli*). Under different circumstances, such outbursts might provide comical examples of the extent to which entrenched and self-centered notions of identity can influence the writing of history. But there is a frightening subtext that causes real concern. Both Europeans and Hindus have allowed elements from within their intelligentsia to utilize academic debate in support of ideological agendas, specifically in the discourse of Aryan/Semitic in its respective manifestations of German/Jew and Hindu/Muslim. The Aryan race ideologues, while by no means a thing of the past in the streets and politics of Europe and America, are not as immediate an issue of national or international concern in those countries as they are on the subcontinent. India's situation is much more immediately volatile. With the fruits of Europe's own Aryan ideology still a vivid memory, many concerned scholars and friends of India are very wary of the potential of the Aryan discourses in the Indian subcontinent.[1]

This point cannot be overstressed. It is the *Hindutva* element in the Indigenous Aryan group that has inhibited many Western scholars, at least, from analyzing and engaging with these alternative points of views or has caused them to be a priori hostile to them. However, the interpretation of evidence being presented by the Indigenous Aryan group cannot be opposed *because* of the *Hindutva* element: that would equally be allowing ideological beliefs to manipulate historical interpretation. Critical scholarship is mandated to attempt to detach debate on this topic from political orientations concerning personal visions for a modern Indian nation-state.

Having said that, an attempt was made to make a distinction between *Hindutva* revisionism and scholarly historical reconsideration motivated by a desire to reexamine the way Indian history was assembled by the colonial power. Unfortunately, these two ingredients are not always easily distinguishable, nor detachable. Nonetheless, this anti-imperialistic, postcolonial dimension to the Aryan invasion debate is an inherent ingredient. Most scholars in this group are concerned with reclaiming control over the reconstruction of the ancient history of their country. After all, it was Europeans who introduced archaeology, linguistics, philology, etc. into the subcontinent and presented their Indian subjects with a new, and in places unfamiliar, version of ancient events authorized by these seemingly formidable disciplines. Many members of the Indigenous Aryan school are quite understandably uncomfortable about inheriting an account of their ancient history that was assembled for them by their erstwhile colonial masters.

This point might be emphasized more poignantly if a clumsy analogy is considered. How would most Americans react if the reconstructed history of their country had continually been (and to a great extent were still being) written by their onetime governing authorities, the British (or even the Russians, Japanese, Iraqis, or any foreign group of scholars)? How would the British feel if the major contours of British history were determined by the French? How would they then feel if, upon objecting to what they considered to be inaccurate reconstructions, they were dismissed as patriots, ideologues, or even Nazis? This is not to say that only "Indian" scholars have a right to interpret the history of the subcontinent as some would have it. Surely, if it is objective and not partisan knowledge that we are after, any point of view that can be made with reason and argument will be welcome if it can throw light on the history of any country, irrespective of the ethnic origin of the contributor. Nonetheless, a principal motive of many Indian scholars in this debate is the desire to reexamine the infrastructure of ancient history that is the legacy of the colonial period and test how secure it actually is by adopting the very tools and disciplines that had been used to construct it in the first place. The Aryan invasion theory is a major foundation stone of ancient Indian history, the "big bang," and has therefore attracted the initial attention of many Indian scholars.

European intellectual hegemony is by no means a thing of the past. Indo-European studies, in particular, are still almost exclusively a Western undertaking, primarily because of lack of facilities and interest in India; and still retains control, in the view of many scholars, over the fate of the Indo-Aryans. And if truth be told, one still not infrequently encounters dismissive attitudes in the Western academy toward certain types of scholarship from India. There are justifiable reasons for this when it comes to the Indo-Aryan debate, given the appalling quality (particularly with regard to the linguistic issues) and polemical tone of some Indigenist literature. But frustrating as it might sometimes be, Western scholars must address the suspicions of the Indigenists—at least of those that are open to dialogue and exchange—given the neccessity of examining our own attitudes and biases made incumbent on us by the Orientalist critique. The postcolonial climate is a sensitive one, and it should be obvious why there might be very good reasons for Indian scholars to want to reevaluate the version of Indian history that was constructed during the colonial period. One cannot ignore or dismiss the sentiments and opinions of significant numbers of scholars about the history of their own country. And it is never a bad exercise to have one's own assumptions challenged, or to step out of one's own time-worn paradigms momentarily so as to consider things from other perspectives.

From the other side, it seems fair to state that while pointing out colonial biases is of fundamental importance—cleansing Indology from the ghosts of the past is a process that has only just begun—there is still solid empirical data that need to be confronted and addressed if one chooses to tackle a problem like that of the Indo-Aryans. Suspicion of colonial motives does not justify a priori jettisoning such theories nor make such data disappear. Besides, major advances have been made in the relevant diciplines since the nineteenth century, both in data accumulation and in theories and methods of interpretation. Moreover, not all nineteenth-century Western scholars themselves can be tarred and feathered with the same brush. There were, and still are, very good reasons to believe in Aryan migrations, and this evidence needs to be addressed. Many

Indigenous Aryanists have made sweeping proclamations about the fallacies of the theory and the biases of colonialism, often with not so much as a passing reference to the linguistic infrastructure of the problem except to dismiss it as nineteenth-century speculation and concoction. This understandably results in such scholarship being viewed as indicative of predetermined attitudes as opposed to serious research. It can only hope to appeal to those predisposed to a certain conclusion. A scholarly and more neutral disposition will at least take the time and energy to become familiar with all the relevant data before pronouncing an opinion.

This is no longer the colonial period; it is still a postmodern one where alternative, suppressed, and subaltern views are, if anything, glamorized. Established paradigms have been subverted left, right, and center throughout humanities departments all over Western academia. Why on earth would present-day Western Indologists still be invested in an Aryan invasion theory anyway? Surely an Indian Indo-European homeland would add prestige to our discipline of Indology at the very least, and possibly even academic resources? Why would Indologists resist such a boon? The fact is that most present-day Indologists have been generally unconvinced by the limited exposure they have had with Indigenist viewpoints because of the poor and selective quality of the arguments they encounter, not because they somehow have some mysterious investment in insisting on an external origin for this language group. Most Indologists are perfectly willing to change their views if appealed to with *informed* reason and arguments that address *all* the evidence.

In actual fact, no informed Western scholar speaks of "invasions" anymore anyway; more subtle models of language change and more nuanced forms of migrations are currently in vogue. Bashing nineteenth-century colonial scholarship, while perhaps cathartic, is hardly likely to affect the course of current scholarship. A major part of the problem is that most universities in India do not have the resources to keep up with current scholarship—there is very little funding from the Union Grants Commission (UGC), the government agency that funds universities. So, with the partial exception of scholars in places like Delhi, Madras, and Poona, most Indian scholars have no access to recent Western books or journals in subjects such as those pertaining to the Indo-Aryans. In contrast, while one would be lucky to find a book by Max Müller even in the antique book markets of London, one can find a plethora of recent-edition publications of his and other nineteenth-century scholars' works in just about any bookstore in India (some of these on their tenth or twelfth edition). Practically speaking, it is small Delhi publishers that are keeping the more crude versions of the Aryan invasion theory alive by their nineteenth-century reprints! These are some of the main sources on the subject available to most Indian readers.

It is imperative, from the Indian side, that the powers that be in Indian universities must recognize the need for historical Indo-European linguistics in their humanities departments if they are to make significant contributions to the protohistory of their subcontinent. Indo-European studies should, if anything, be an Indian forté, not exclusively a European one; many Indian scholars have a distinct head start due to their advanced knowledge of Sanskrit, which still plays a fundamental and extensive role in this field. In particular, it is simply unacceptable that research into substratum influence in Sanskrit texts has primarily been the preserve of a dozen or so Western scholars, however qualified. Vedic, Dravidian, and Munda are Indian languages; this should be a field dominated by Indian linguists. That their input has been so negligible in the one area that could determine much about the whole protohistory of the subcontinent is lamentable. One cannot simply ignore the linguistic evidence. If nothing else, I hope my work has underscored the need for facility to be directed into this field. Much of the literature from the Indigenous Aryan side, and also from the Indian Migrationist side, is hopelessly inadequate from the perspective of linguistics. This has understandably caused the Indigenist point of view to be neglected in toto, to the detriment of the more scholarly, sober, and cogent voices espousing this version of events.

Neglected viewpoints do not disappear. They reappear with more aggression due to frustration at being ignored. The Indigenous Aryan viewpoint has been around for over a century. It has been stereotyped and, on the whole, summarily dismissed and excluded from academic dialogue. It has hovered, until recently, on the periphery or outside of mainstream academic circles. Since, over the course of the last decade, it has become representative of many scholars *within* the Indian academy, it is now clamoring for attention more than ever before. It deserves a response articulated in a rigorously critical but fair and respectful fashion. If the claims of the Indigenous Aryanists cannot be decisively disproved, then they cannot be denied a legitimate place in discussions of Indo-Aryan origins. The opinions of significant numbers of Indian intellectuals about the history of their own country cannot simply be ignored by those engaged in research on South Asian history or be relegated to areas outside the boundaries of what is considered worthy of serious academic attention.

Unless attitudes to this issue change from all sides, I foresee two widening divides as the Indigenous Aryan position becomes more vociferous: one between individuals in Western academic circles, Indo-Europeanists as well as Indologists, and the more vocal scholars in the Indigenous camp, and the other between "leftists" and "rightists" in the subcontinent itself. Unfortunately, the views of the many scholars who are less politically or ideologically motivated in their interest in ancient history will likely be branded one way or the other depending on the views they are open to considering. More unfortunate still, if this happens, is that the entire field will suffer due to loss of communication between differing opinions and points of view—the lifeblood of a progressive field of study.

This raises another dimension that the Indigenous Aryan critique forces us to confront: What constitutes authority in areas of knowledge, particularly where the evidence is sometimes as malleable, scanty, and inconclusive as much of that concerning the Indo-Aryans? Max Müller's dating of the Veda illustrates the arbitrariness involved in the production of theories that are then propagated as "facts" in generations of schoolbooks. Müller, as I have noted, was fully aware of the arbitrary nature of his calculations (which, as Goldstucker pointed out, were based on a "ghost story" written in the twelfth century C.E.): "I . . . have repeatedly dwelt on the hypothetical character of the dates" (1892, xiv). As Whitney noted, however: "We have already more than once seen it stated that 'Müller has ascertained the date of the Vedas to be 1200–1000 B.C.'" ([1874] 1987, 78). Winternitz also objected that "it became a habit . . . to say that Max Müller had proved 1200–1000 B.C. as the date of the Rg Veda. . . . Strange to say it has been quite forgotten on what a precarious footing [this opinion] stood" ([1907] 1962, 256).

This is a sobering illustration, which is not completely unrepresentative of some of the theorizing that has gone into the reconstruction of Indo-Aryan history. A scholar with international status makes a tentative speculation, which is challenged and rejected by his intellectual peers (and, in this case, even retracted by the original scholar), but, because of the intellectual prestige of the individual, this opinion is taken as authoritative and promoted as an established fact outside of academic circles. In a very short time, the tentativeness of the initial speculation is completely forgotten, and further theories and assumptions are grafted onto the "established fact," producing a whole new generation of "established facts," with reproductive capacities of their own.

On the other hand, in the name of paradigm shifts or post-modernity, can anyone with a smattering of Sanskrit challenge the opinions of trained specialists in, say, Vedic, who have spent decades pouring over Sanskrit texts? Kuhn proposes that paradigm shifts do frequently occur at the margins of fields of knowledge, initated by individuals who have little or no stake in perpetuating the status quo (and are also less vulnerable to peer pressure). But does this require us to allot equal credibility to any dilettante that might decide to dabble with Vedic texts for a couple of months?

Having said that, there have been some quite persuasive arguments raised by Indigenists (who are not all, by any means, dilettantes). Yet, until extremely recently few in the West had even been aware that there exists an alternative view. Yet much of the logic and many of the assumptions underlying the theory of external Aryan origins have been challenged, primarily by Indians, for decades. This suggests that the extent of European intellectual hegemony in Indology is not entirely a thing of the past. The more cogent voices expressed in this work have never surfaced in mainstream Western academic circles, although some of them express critiques that are remarkably penetrating, perfectly in line with accepted standards of critical scholarship (sometimes well in advance of their Western peers), and even, on occasion, quite brilliant. While some of the more extreme, ill-informed, ideological or uncritically dogmatic publications of the Indigenous Aryan group do not exactly help the case along, even the more ludicrous outbursts from India are sometimes no more absurd than theories emanating from some of the most renowned Western scholars. That the early inhabitants of India are still being construed as non-Aryan, snub-nosed *dāsas* on the grounds of the solitary word *anāsa* is astounding, and yet such theories have only very recently been questioned in the West, after a life span of a century and a half. When theories become sufficiently long-lived and commonplace, they cease to strike one as theoretical and can often become the facts and building blocks of subsequent realities.

My goal here has been to stir up some of the assumptions that have remained dormant for well over a century and to remove jurisdiction over the Indo-Aryan problem from the exclusive control of specialists by laying out some of the basic contested issues in nontechnical terms for the benefit of the general scholar or student interested in Indian protohistory. I hope I have been successful in helping scholars to determine for themselves what overall position on Indo-Aryan origins best fits the presently available data. I trust I may be forgiven for not coming to a clear conclusion myself. Until the script is deciphered, the presently available data are not sufficient to resolve the issue in my mind. The Indo-European languages came from somewhere between the Caspian Sea area (and the Balkans) and northwest South Asia. I do not feel impelled to favor any particular area in this vast expanse: all homeland proposals (not least of all South Asian ones) have significant problems, as I have attempted to outline throughout this work. The Indigenous Aryan critique has certainly influenced my own agnosticism. I hope that scholars do not ignore the arguments being made by the Indigenous Aryan school because it contains a vociferous, element that is blatantly inimical and insensitive to non-Hindu interests. That element should be isolated and exposed, to be sure, but the whole debate cannot be rejected because of this, or stereotyped as being exclusively a nationalistic discourse. I have cautioned against the tendency of contributing to what I have termed an Indological McCarthyism in this regard.

Of most concern to me is that my analysis of the problem, which has, on the whole, been sympathetic to many of the arguments of the Indigenous Aryan position, will be understood in the proper spirit—as an attempt to contribute to scholarly debate—and not as a source of authority to be exploited by, or viewed as contributing to, the politics of authenticity. I especially hope that it will not be co-opted to bolster the often encountered quote that "even Western scholars have disproved the theory of Aryan invasions." The thought of this work being brandished about in support of preconceived agendas is personally very troubling to me. Let us be very clear: the essential, that is, pruned, elements of an Aryan migration theory have *not* by any means been disproved. That they are open to different interpretations does not at all mean that the Indigenist position can carry the day. But, to my mind, it does mean that an Indigenous position merits a place at the table.

I also hope and choose to believe that the many scholars of ancient Indian history whom I have had the privilege of meeting over the years will realize the potential for ideological misuse of historical revisionism and will, accordingly, without compromising their position on issues of critical scholarship, actively oppose communal agendas that attempt to appropriate academic debate. From the hodgepodge of characters who have been represented here, those, at least, who have sincerely adopted critical methods of scholarship in order to present their point of view should be responded to in kind, not stereotyped as communalists. They deserve a fair hearing. As for those who are not interested in academic dialogue, there is nothing academia can do for them (or they for academia), except be aware of their existence and expose them to public attention if they become ideologically menacing.

In conclusion, the Indigenous Aryan position is by now far too widespread to be ignored—most teachers and scholars of South Asian religion or cultural history will have been confronted with it by some of their second-generation South Asian students, in discussions with colleagues or friends in India, on the Indology lists on the internet, or in some other context. I hope this analysis will assist them in drawing a clearer picture of the logic and perspectives of this point of view. It is, of course, only one point of view—the Aryan invasion model, when trimmed of its excesses, still has much of its own internally consistent logic and perspectives, and it remains a reasonable way of accounting for a good deal of the available evidence. Trautmann, commenting on the longevity of the Aryan racial theory of Indian civilization discussed earlier, wonders: "Is it not time we did away with it?" (1997 215). I will stop well short of suggesting that we do away with the whole Indo-Aryan migration theory. But we do, at the very least, need to reappraise it all again very carefully and make a clear distinction between the data and their interpretations. The implications of the Indigenous Aryan critique for the entire area study of South Asia are far too immense to be ignored or taken lightly: from goddess worship in Kerala to tantra in Bengal; from bhakti in South India to Shaivism in Kashmir; from the caste system in Brahmanical culture to the daily *pūjā* performed in the temples and religious households across the subcontinent; from the separatist voices in Tamil Nadu to the social aspirations of Ravi Das's followers in the North; in Indian languages, music, medicine, art, and philosophy; in short, in almost everything South Asian, there is little that has not been predicated on the assumption that Indian culture, history, and religion are the amalgamation of external Aryan and indigenous non-Aryan characteristics.

Notes

Introduction

1. I will give relevant personal information about some of the individuals in the Indigenous Aryanist group in chapter 13, which focuses on the context and social history of the debate. Elsewhere in this book, which examines the interpretation of the data, I will simply refer to their arguments at face value. I should also note that chapters 3 to 12, which deal with the actual interpretation of data, will examine the more convincing material produced by Indigenous Aryanists. Some of the more outlandish positions, of which there is no shortage, will be touched upon in chapter 13.

2. Because of the already sufficiently massive cross-disciplinary scope of this enterprise, I have restricted my researches to European language sources. However, the limited ferreting that I undertook in Hindi and Bengali publications led me to believe that while there is material in Indian languages addressing this issue, most scholars engaging the conclusions of Western scholarship with any serious degree of depth have penned their dissent in English. Their exposure to Western views, after all, has almost invariably been through the English medium. Tracing this debate in modern Indian vernaculars would, nonetheless, provide material for an interesting study.

Chapter 1

1. For a useful collection of the first Indian source material relayed back to Europe by British scholars, see Marshall 1970.

2. Jones's disclosure was not the only factor that contributed to the birth of historical linguistics. A publication sponsored by Catherine II entitled *The Comparative Vocabularies of the Languages of the Whole World*, the first large-scale comparative treatise, was published in the same year Jones made his landmark address. The following year, his work was critiqued by C. J. Kraus, who noted that it was not vocabularies that determined language families but morphology, thus providing a more precise methodology for the new discipline.

3. Scholars connected the various people with the three sons of Noah in a variety of ways—the Europeans were often considered descendants of Japhet, the Asians, or sometimes the Arabs, as those of Shem, and the Africans, or sometimes the Tartars, as those of Ham. For Jones, the Indians are the sons of Ham, the Arabs of Shem, and the Tartars of Japhet. Trautmann (1997) notes that some aspects of Jones's instantiation of Mosaic sources may have been prefigured in Muslim sources wherein the Indians were considered to be sons of Ham (53).

4. Monboddo believed that ultimately civilization originated in Egypt.

5. Elsewhere, Müller opted for Pamir, along with a majority of scholars in the second half of the nineteenth century.

6. Elsewhere, Hunter was not even sure "whether anything that can properly be described as an Aryan race ever existed" or whether the term was "anything more than a philological expression." Quoted in Maw 1990, 36.

7. Although the French also made significant contributions to the disciplines.

8. As Justus Schottel, a prominent grammarian, of the period had declared (Poliakov 1971, p. 93).

9. The ethnologist Brinton (1890) rejected Latham's primacy in this regard quite forcefully: "For a score of years before he introduced it to the English public, this view had been repeatedly and ably defended by the eminent Belgian naturalist d'Omalius d'Halloy" (146).

10. In terms of presently known substrata in the Indo-European-speaking part of Europe, France preserves a non-Indo-European language—Basque—that is still spoken today. Similarly, Italy had Etruscan, Spain Iberian, and Scotland has maintained inscriptional evidence of non-Indo-European elements in Pictish. See Polomé (1990a) for research on substratum in Germanic.

11. The Finno-Ugric language group spoken in Finland is a language family distinct from the Indo-European one.

12. Scholars such as Otto Schrader (1890) cautioned that if a word was to be found in only one side of the language family, it could have been an innovation after the common Indo-European period shared by only that side of the family after it had already left the common homeland. In order to be eligible for a place in the original lexicon, therefore, an item of material culture must have cognates in both the eastern and western members of the family.

13. The Kurgan material includes such features as distinct dwellings, nomadic settlement patterns, pastoral economy, agnatic hierarchy, solar symbolism, and, especially, a distinct burial system (Gimbutas 1977, 278).

14. Mallory's publications, though primarily focused on the western Indo-Europeans, are particularly useful as outlines of the history of the Indo-European homeland quest, and as sober and comprehensive expositions of most of the factors involved in this problem to date. His most outstanding work, in my opinion, is his 1975 Ph.D. dissertation, which unfortunately has never been published in toto, although it has obviously provided much material toward his other publications.

15. Renfrew is especially concerned about the "why" of linguistic spread (and presents a theory that provides a very distinct explanation in this regard). This can be contrasted with Robb (1991), who undermines the traditional view of the Indo-European phenomenon being inaugurated by "why" or a single historic cause. Robb presents a "simulation of language diffusion" by creating a computer-generated model where smaller, numerous, and random interactions between a myriad of languages (including Indo-European) covering limited areas, can eventually result in the emergence of a dominant language like IE covering a vast area. In his model "the social groups responsible were small and segmentary in organization, and possibly lacked any one consistent factor, be it social, cultural, political, economic or technological, which could add cohesion or direction to movement beyond the purely local scale" (287).

16. Krell argues that squirrels, badgers, and donkeys are fauna evidenced in the Kurgan culture that cannot be reconstructed in Proto-Indo-European since terms for these animals have

no reflexes in any Indo-European language. On the other hand, comparative linguistics can reconstruct terms for duck, goose, salmon, eel/snake, crane, eagle, and bee, which have not been found in Kurgan sites. In terms of flora, the Kurgan culture evidences aspens, willows, cherries, elders, melons, and firs, none of which according to Krell are reconstructible to Proto-Indo-European. On the other hand, ash trees, barley, broad beans, flax, and maple trees are reconstructible linguistically but have not been retrieved archaeologically from Gimbutas's homeland. One would, however, need to ensure that Krell"s lists do refer to Proto-Indo-European terms, and not to regional terms that surfaced in later Indo-European languages after their break-up. Moreover, one would also need to ensure that the full representation of the material culture has been represented, and not just that outlined by Gimbutas in the material under criticisms.

17. Among other scholars who critiqued Renfrew, D'iakonoff (1988) while agreeing that the spread of Indo-European languages was connected with the spread of agriculture, prefers to relegate these languages to pre-Proto-Indo-European stage somewhere between Proto-Indo-European and Nostratic. Haarmann (1998), however, argues that the genetic picture of diffusion, or extension of the area of settlement, between western Asia and Europe does not correspond to the spread of agriculture (nor to the spread of Indo-European languages).

18. For recent overviews of homeland theories and methods, see Mallory 1992, 1997, 1998.

19. Similar studies could, of course, be conducted on the reaction of other countries such as Iran, Pakistan, and so on.

Chapter 2

1. In 1800, Marquess Wellesley, governor-general of India, proclaimed the establishment of a college at Fort William that was intended to transform untrained novices arriving fresh from Great Britain into experienced civil servants of the Crown, well groomed in the local languages and cultures. A further agenda for the college and its related bodies was the dissemination of European knowledge to the Bengali intelligentsia. For the mostly Bengali literati who were well steeped in traditional learning but deprived of conventional forms of support—which previously would have been provided by the indigenous ruling elite preceding the British, such as the maharajas and nawabs—the college provided a source of patronage. Employment was available for teachers, prose stylists, philologists, linguists, compositors, printers, publishers, and librarians (Kopf 1969, 109). Fort William College was the first institutional environment where Bengalis were exposed to Western knowledge and science. Within a year of its inauguration, the college opened the first institutional library in India to the local public. The demand for books was so great that, initially, the library had to impose legislation to attempt (unsuccessfully) to stem the massive theft of library books that eventually reappeared on the commercial market (119). With college support, presses were soon printing in local languages: the Serampore Mission Press in 1801; the Hindoostanee Press, which won the contract to publish the Asiatick Researches, in 1802; and the Sanskrit Press, which was managed by Bengalis, in 1807. The first vernacular newspaper appeared in 1818, the same year that the Calcutta School Book Society published its first series of textbooks (115). It was through the Calcutta School Book Society's publications that Indian students first became exposed to Western science and learning. Sometime between 1814 and 1816, Indian entrepreneurs first began to explore what turned out to be a very receptive book-dealing market. In 1816, the Hindu College was established by the Calcutta nouveau riche, who, despite being conservative upper-caste Hindus, declared in the very first section of their charter that "the primary object of the institution is, the tuition of the sons of respectable Hindoos, in the English and Indian languages and in the literature and science of Europe and Asia" (182) By 1829, the first members of the Bengali intelligentsia were admitted to membership in the Royal Asiatic Society, which had been founded by Warren Hastings in 1784. For the most part, until the Utilitarians started to undermine and belittle their tradition, the Bengali

elite, in the early part of the nineteenth century, proved to be enthusiastic recipients of the knowledge and ideas that were surging forth through these various outlets from the West.

2. Vivekananda could exhibit a level of romanticism as colorful as that displayed by any Orientalist discourse. He evokes a beatific Upanishadic scenario when reminiscing about his meeting with the great Western Aryan Max Müller: "That nice little house in its setting of a beautiful garden, the silver-headed sage, with a face calm and benign . . . speaking of a deep-seated mine of spirituality somewhere behind . . . creating a respect for the thoughts of the sages of ancient India—the trees, the flowers, the calmness, and the clear sky—all these sent me back in imagination to the glorious days of Ancient India, the days of our Brahmarshis and Rajarshis. . . .It was neither the philologist nor the scholar that I saw, but a soul that is every day realizing its oneness with the Brahman. . . .his heartbeats have caught the rhythm of the Upanisads. . . .And what love he bears towards India! I wish I had a hundredth part of that love for my own motherland!" (Vivekananda 1970–73, 4:281–281).

3. Ramaswami's lifework, crystallized politically first in the Self-Respect movement in 1925, then in the Justice Party, and finally in the Dravida Kazhagam in 1944 (which was the direct progenitor of both the Dravida Munnetra Kazhagam which came to power in Tamil Nadu in 1967 and the later ADMK; Diehl 1978).

4. Some of the information presented here is based on an unpublished paper written by Shukavak Das; the rest is from his article listed in the bibliography.

Chapter 3

1. The term is used herein in the sense of the study of a civilization based on oral and written texts, in contradistinction to such subjects as linguistics.

2. Iyengar (1914) gives the verse numbers to all these references, which I have not included so as not to overburden the quote.

3. The political construction of a white Aryan identity supposedly supported by Sanskrit textual sources is by no means a thing of the past in the West. David Duke supersedes the philological excesses of even nineteenth-century European philology. Surpassing Ripley's "frequent references" to the Dāsa nose (which was at least based on a possible translation albeit of a solitary reference), Duke, in a posting on his Web page entitled "My Indian Odyssey," makes the completely unfounded statement that "a great deal of Sanskrit literature describes many of the Aryan leaders as having light eyes and light hair." These Aryans, in Duke's narrative, belonged to the superior race of "Aryans, or Indo-European Caucasians [who] created the great Indian, or Hindu civilization." Their superiority, in this narrative, was short-lived, since "over dozens of generations a gradual change in the generation composition had occurred, almost imperceptible in a single generation, but dramatic after a millennium." The result of this racial miscegenation, over the ages, was the abysmal squalor and appalling poverty that Duke encountered during a trip to India in 1971. Needless to say, Duke's "light-haired" and "light-eyed" Aryans are hardly to be found in the Sanskrit texts.

4. However, Deshpande accepts the fair-dark dichotomy of the Aryas and Dāsas and notes a verse from Patañjali stating that no one looking at a dark person will recognize him as Brahmana (1993, 216).

5. Muir is here quoting Weber's *Indische Studien* (1849), 1:165.

6. This passage mentions that Agni traversed the earth, burning towards the east, but did not burn the Sadānīrā River. The text states that the Brahmanas had not formerly crossed this river, because it had not been burned by Agni, but that it had now become habitable for the Brahmanas after they had caused it to be tasted by sacrifices (i.e., had started making sacrifices on the other side of the river).

7. This evidence is seen as significant even by scholars who otherwise give little credibility to other pro-migration arguments. Thus Aklujkar (1996) notes that "it is generally held that the Aryans entered northwestern India in the distant past. . . .It is only the evidence pointing to a movement of the Sanskrit-speaking people(s) to the eastern and southern parts of the Indian subcontinent during the historical period that I find adequately strong" (61–62). Possehl (1996) refers to this as one of only two pieces of evidence that are decisive in this regard.

8. Talageri's work has yet to receive a response from Vedic scholars, and I have been unable to examine it thoroughly due to its recency at the time of preparing this manuscript for press.

Chapter 4

1. Even well after India itself had been rejected as a candidate for the homeland, its language was long considered the most faithful preserver of Proto-Indo-European words and forms. For an overview of linguistic science in the nineteenth century, see Sayce (1880) Jespersen 1922; Pedersen 1931; and Davis (1998). For a more thorough overview of the dethronement of Sanskrit, see Mayrhofer (1983).

2. A stop is basically a sound that "stops" or is obstructed in the mouth, such as *p*, *b*, *m*, *t*, *d*, and *n*. An aspirated stop, prominent in the Indic languages, is a consonant accompanied by a subtle expulsion of air and denoted by an *h* (i.e., the stops *dh*, *bh*, etc., are aspirated counterparts of the stops *d*, *b*, etc.).

3. The Italian Graziadio Ascoli; the Danes Vilhelm Thomsen and Karl Verner; the Swiss Ferdinand de Saussure; the Germans Karl Brugmann, Hermann Collitz, and Johannes Schmidt; and the Swede Esaias Tegner all helped alleviate the confusion that had thitherto surrounded consonant and vowel correspondences (Pedersen 1931, 278–280).

4. Cf. Skt. *ásti, sánti* with Doric Gk. *estí, *hentí* ('he is', 'they are'); Skt *bharāmaḥ* 'we bear' with Doric Gk. *phéromes* 'we bear'.

5. Palatals are produced from the hard palate at the front of the vocal tract, and the *e* is pronounced with the tongue raised toward the front: both sounds are articulated from the same part of the mouth. Velars, in contrast, are produced from the soft palate farther back in the vocal tract, which is where the tongue is placed to pronounce the *a* vowel. It is easier to combine consonants with vowels that are articulated from the same part of the vocal tract. Brugmann then determined that Proto-Indo-European *o* became Sanskrit *ā* in open syllables before resonants, thereby explaining the third person singular *cakāra* from what would today be reconstructed as Proto-Indo-European **kʷekora*.

6. Resonants are phonemes, such as *i*, *u*, *n*, *m*, *r* and *l*, that can function as either vowels or consonants.

7. The basic Indo-European ablaut pattern, as evidenced in the daughter Indo-European languages, consists of *e*, *o*, and *ø* (zero grade). These are known as *normal vowel grades*. In addition to these grades, there is a further triad of vowels, *ē*, *ō* and *ā*, which are known as *lengthened vowel grades*. Saussure perceived a parallel between these two sets of vowel grades. He postulated that Indo-European originally only had one vowel *e*, which, when combined with one of the two resonants, A and O, resulted in the lengthened vowel grades. These *coefficients sonantiques* themselves developed into the normal vowels *a* and *o*. Benveniste later further developed the laryngeal theory by proposing that all Indo-European root forms originally consisted of a CVC (consonant, vowel, consonant) structure. Most Sanskrit roots, for example, maintain this structure, but some common roots (*sthā* 'be situated', *dhā* 'place', and *as* 'to be') are CV or VC only. Benveniste proposed that the laryngeals initially provided the missing consonants in these cases (so *dhā* [from Proto-Indo-European **dhē-*] would originally have been **dheA-*). For a critical survey of various contributions to the laryngeal theory, see Jonsson 1978.

8. Another example demonstrating the efficacy of historical linguistics was found in Vulgar Latin. Certain reconstructed Latin words remained conjectural, unattested in the Latin preserved in written form which is mostly classical and "high." However, graffiti discovered in Pompeii and Herculaneum, revealed precisely these conjectured words.

9. His Ph.D. thesis, entitled "The Laryngeal Theory: a Critical Evaluation," was awarded a medal for the best thesis in literature for the year 1968 by Calcutta University; it was published in 1977.

10. Misra has more recently argued for a fifth millennium B.C.E. date for the Ṛgveda on linguistic grounds, as well as for an Indian homeland for the Indo-European language family (1992).

11. This group in the second Millennium B.C.E. consists of Hittite, Luwian, and Palaic.

12. Actually, Misra is not completely isolated in challenging the Laryngeal theory; there also have been a few skeptics in the West. Jonsson (1978), for example, in his comprehensive survey of all major opinions on Proto-Indo-European laryngeals, rejects the full theory and is only prepared to consider a very reduced version of it to be a "possibliity but no more" since the Hittite phoneme could have been a borrowing from another language family such as Caucasian. (For a list of words borrowed by the Anatolian languages from among the vast majority of linguists who do accept laryngeals, there has never been a consensus on specifics.)

13. Inspired by the existence of the laryngeals and various morphological features of Hittite, especially those it seems to share with Germanic, an Indo-Hittite school developed which argued that some of the features of Hittite such as the absence of masculine and feminine genders better reflect the original protolanguage, which this group accordingly called *Indo-Hittite* instead of *Indo-European*. From this perspective, it is the languages such as Sanskrit that have innovated. For a critique of this school by an Indigenous Aryanist, see Misra 1994. It should also be noted that Hittite borrowed a significant amount of non-Indo-European material from substrate languages such as Hurrian (and eventually became extinct), to the extent that scholars initially did not even recognize it as an Indo-European language.

14. See Lehmann and Zgusta 1979 for chronologically updated versions of the same fable and the collection in Sen (1994) of the collective efforts of a few well-known Indo-Europeanists to reconstruct a Folkloric text. Pulgram (1959), ever the skeptic, remarks that "to write an Aesopian fable. . .in reconstructed Proto-Indo-European is innocent enough as a pastime, but the text has no doubt little if any resemblance to any speech ever heard on earth. In other words, reconstructed Proto-Indo-European is not a language at all, at least not according to any defensible definition of the term language" (423).

15. Gypsy *kher* < Sanskrit *khara* 'donkey'; Gypsy *sosoi* < Sanskrit *śaśa* 'hare'. Dhar (1930) also remarks, in this regard, that Sanskrit *a* can be seen to develop into *e* and *o* allophones in the Prakrits. He concedes, however, that the palatalization of a velar is much more phonologically likely than the reverse but remarks that it remains possibe that foreign substrata influences on the Indo-European languages outside of India induced a reverse change from palatals to velars, and a corresponding allophonic distribution of Proto-Indo-European *a* to *e*, *o*, and *a*. Misra (1992) argues that *ṣ* can become a velar, as in *dvekṣi* from *dviṣ*, and wonders whether there might not have been a proto sound somewhere between *ś* and *k*. A publication by Nair, (1974) called *Sanskrit Family* (1974) also attempts to show in twenty-eight pages how the main linguistic features postulated for Proto-Indo-European are correlatable with post-Vedic changes visible in the Prakrits. According to this account, which attempts to equate Proto-Indo-European with Vedic, rather than being pre-Vedic, such Proto-Indo-European features are post-Vedic and, therefore "with certainty we can proclaim that the present popular comparative philology of Indo-European is myth rather than science" (13). This publication shows almost no awareness of any material in the field over the last 100 years.

16. Misra bolsters his case by producing other parallel linguistic developments where Sanskrit is accepted as having preserved Proto-Indo-European linguistic features that other Indo-European languages, including Gypsy, have lost. For example, Indo-European voiced aspirates are maintained only in Sanskrit but are deaspirated in other Indo-European languages and Gypsy. The general thrust of Misra's work is that Sanskrit should be reinstated to its original position of being the oldest and closest language to Proto-Indo-European. However Hock (forthcoming) points out that Misra neglects to draw sufficient attention to the areas where Sanskrit has innovated and other languages have preserved more archaic linguistic forms.

17. Misra, as head of the historical linguistics department of Benares Hindu University, and unlike many Indigenous Aryanists who tend to be linguistic dilettantes, is a fully qualified historical linguist who has dedicated half a century to teaching, researching, and publishing a considerable amount of material on comparative Indo-European linguistics. Unfortunately, Misra's work does not surface in mainstream academic journals where it can be critiqued by knowledgeable colleagues. This means that he is mainly working in isolation, deprived of the essential feedback and challenges that such controversial views require both to influence other academic perspectives on this material and to be influenced by them. For the most part, in contrast, the level of scholarship found in some of the publications of the Indigenous Aryan school, when it comes to challenging the reconstruction of the proto-language, are hopelessly inadequate. One does not have to look far to encounter such statements as: "The Sanskrit-speaking race, the Aryans, originally belonged to India. They emigrated to other parts of the globe to colonize alien lands and this gave birth to the whole bulk of other Indo-European languages" (Arya 1993, 57). This authoritative conclusion is predicated on a couple of pages of linguistic analysis that refers exclusively to the Iranian material and only reveals an awareness of linguists, such as Bopp and Grimm, from over a century ago. Such a firm conviction, based on such scanty grounds, is the type of scholarship that understandably results in the Indigenous Aryan school being stereotyped as having preconceived ideas promoted through a very poor level of scholarship.

18. The Śaṅkarācārya of Kañci Kāmakoṭi Pitham, in this regard, comments: "The wear and tear of words in use in literature as well as the spoken language does not apply to Vedic words. . . .The reason why the Vedic sounds have been maintained in their pristine purity is because, only by the correct intonation of words, would the mantras attain their power. Lest any mistake should creep in, a separate dedicated section of the community had made it its business to hand it down safely from one generation to the next, unsullied and in its original form" (Chandrasekharendra Saraswati 1988, 20).

19. It should be noted that few linguists nowadays perceive the protolanguage as a monolithic entity, recognizing that there were always various dialectical strata within the undivided Indo-European language group.

20. However, Zimmer (1990b) recently argued that Proto-Indo-European was a creolization of various languages including Indo-European, Semitic, and Caucasian, a position similar to that previously argued by N. Trubetzkoy.

21. Japanese scholars have also contributed to the field.

22. There is also a price factor: a recent Indo-European publication at the time of writing this book (Gamkrelidze & Ivanov 1995) is a tome of almost 900 pages, has a separate 250-page volume simly for its bibliography and index, and costs $600 (over three months pay for an average professor in Calcutta University in 1994). However, Beeks (1995) and Szmerenyi (1996) are more affordable and accessible.

23. In 1994–95, Calcutta and Varanasi were the only two universities in the subcontinent offering courses in Indo-European historical linguistics. Poona's course offerings were on hold, since there was a reserved vacancy for an appropriate faculty member, and Annamalai had closed its department.

24. There was some talk under way among some Indigenous Aryanists when I was in India about creating a facility for the advanced study of historical linguistics to explore the linguistic dimension of historical issues such as the Aryan problem.

Chapter 5

1. Ellis's work was brought to my attention by T. Trautmann.
2. Some scholars preferred to postulate a Munda substratum, and/or of other unknown language(s).
3. A linguistic area is one in which members of different but (usually) contiguous language families share linguistic traits with each other which they do not share with the other members of their respective language families.
4. Old Indo-Aryan *r* generally appears as *l* in the eastern inscriptions of Aśoka. Among a variety of arguments, Southworth asserts that the western languages—Marathi, Gujarati, and Panjabi—agree with Dravidian in the relative frequencies of retroflexes and dentals, while the eastern languages, characterized by classifier systems and absence of dental/retroflex distinctions, are linked to the Tibeto-Burmese group. Bloch had postulated a triple division: east-central, southwest, and northwest.
5. In 1956, Emeneau, in addition to retroflex consonants and gerundives (absolutives), drew particular attention to nominalized verb forms, echo words, and quantifiers (7–11) as Indo-Aryan innovations shared by Dravidian. In 1969, he added onomatopoeic words with common etyma to the items he considered had been diffused from Dravidian to Sanskrit. Returning again to the issue in 1974, he highlighted the five uses of *api* as being identical with the uses of Dravidian *um*. Kuiper, in 1967, added *iti* as another feature Sanskrit seemed to have borrowed from Dravidian (146). More features (causative verbs, conjunctive particles, explicator compound verbs, and the dative construction) have been discussed by Masica (1976). Most recently, Kuiper (1991) has presented the culmination of perhaps half a century of research extracting phonetic, morphological, and syntactical innovative elements in Indo-Aryan that he holds are the product of linguistic substrata. Southworth (1974) added a few more items.
6. (1) Inflection of nouns with particles postfixed to the oblique; (2) inflection of the plural by suffixing these identical particles to the invariable plural form; (3) two first person plural pronouns; (4) the use of postpositions instead of prepositions; (5) participial verbal formations; (6) relative clauses preceding the indicative clause; and (7) governing word following the governed word.
7. A proposal made by Rev. Dr. Stevenson in the *Journal of the Asiatic Society of Bombay* (1849).
8. Bloch (1924, 8–9) questioned how Dravidian could have been the origin of the cerebrals, since they can occur in the initial position in Sanskrit where they are not tolerated in Dravidian, which, conversely, allows nasal and liquid cerebrals in final position where they are never found in Sanskrit. Moreover, he noted that nominal verbal forms, which Sanskrit is supposed to have borrowed from Dravidian, also occur in Iranian, which suggests a tendency inherent in Indo-European itself rather than as a result of Dravidian influence.
9. "Structural differences [between Sanskrit and Dravidian gerunds], and the improbability of Dravidian having been spoken in the most remote and inaccessible areas through which the Aryans entered, force us to count with the possibility of some non-Dravidian sub- or adstratum as having provided the original model for the early syntactico-semantic. . .development of the Indo-Aryan gerund" (Tikkanen 1987, 322).
10. However, the Brahui claim that they came from Aleppo in Syria, thus weakening the value of their testimony, Hock speculates that this account could have been a later Islamicization of an existing tradition (1996b, 32).

11. This possibility has recently made its way into Indigenous Aryan discourse: "The whole issue hinges on the question: how exactly did this borrowing take place? Did the Sanskrit-speaking people borrow the words concerned from some people whom they overran, as has been made out by assuming that incoming hordes of the Indo-Aryans overran the Harappans? Or did the Sanskrit-speaking people borrow the Dravidian and Munda words from their neighbors with whom they had occasion to come in contact? The second hypothesis has a lot to recommend itself" (Lal 1997, 282).

12. Caldwell ([1856] 1875) considered a word to be a Dravidian loan when (1) it is isolated in Sanskrit without a root or derivatives but has related or derivative words in the Dravidian languages; (2) Sanskrit possesses synonyms of the word while Dravidian has only the word in question; (3) the word has no cognates in any other Indo-European language but is found in every Dravidian dialect; (4) Sanskrit lexicographers provide a fanciful etymology for the word, compared with a solid etymology derived from a verbal root proposed by Dravidian lexicographers; (5) the significance of the word is based on its root in Dravidian, while in Sanskrit its meaning is metaphoric; and (6) native southern scholars, despite privileging Sanskrit as being the language of the gods and the mother of all literature, claim the word to be purely Dravidian (453–454).

13. For example, if an alleged loanword occurs only late in Sanskrit sources but is to be found in the earliest Tamil sources when, Burrow supposed, Aryan influence would have been slight, the scales are tipped in favor of its Dravidian origin. Burrow also included phonetics as a further consideration: if assuming Sanskrit as the origin of a contested word results in an unlikely sound change occurring in the Dravidian equivalent, whereas, in contrast, holding the Dravidian form as the original allows for a natural sound change when forming the Sanskrit equivalent, then Dravidian emerges as the most convincing candidate. Likewise, if the Sanskrit word has suffered from assimilation or loss of consonants but its Dravidian counterpart has not, then the latter should be considered the more likely progenitor.

14. Southworth (1979), in this connection, is at least prepared to consider that "it is conceivable, but unlikely, that there was continuous contact between Indo-Aryans and Dravidians from the Indo-Iranian period" (203). This is based on the possibility that Dravidian was a fairly recent arrival in the subcontinent. Also, there are forms such as Old-Indo-Aryan *tanū*, 'body', which is shared by Dravidian and Iranian.

15. For example, the Dravidian loans into Sanskrit of *nīra* or *toya* 'water', *mīna* 'fish,' and *heramba* 'buffalo' are not found in Pali and are represented in Hindi by their Sanskrit synonyms *pānī*, *machlī*, and *bhaiṅs*, respectively.

16. Masica (1979) echoes Bloch's comments regarding the possibly provincial nature of many words in Sanskrit by remarking that "the differential survival of Sanskrit lexical items raises the question of whether they were used with the same frequency in all parts of India" (138–139).

17. For example, Thieme notes that the Ṛgvedic word *uru*khala* 'mortar', which Burrow assumed was a Dravidian loan on the basis of Tamil *ulakkai*, Malayalam *ulakka*, Kannada *olake* 'pestle', and Telegu *rokali* 'a large wooden pestle', occurs several times in 1.28.6, a hymn recited not in official sacrifices but in domestic functions in the household. Thieme (1955) proposes that the word was probably taken from the vernacular of the women in the kitchen, who would be using the mortar for their daily chores. *Khala*, in Sanskrit, is the special ground where the sacrificial implements were stored when not in use. *Urukhara*, then, could well be the vernacular rendition of the broad (*uru*) *khala/khara*, or threshing ground (439).

18. Ironically, Burrow himself is accused of being "caught up in the aura of sanctity that surrounds the Vedic oral tradition" (Sjoberg 1992, 513).

19. His earlier figure of "at least five percent" was amended in the *Indo-Iranian Journal* (Kuiper 1995, 261). Burrow (1968, 311) had pointed to only twenty-five loans in the Ṛigveda.

20. Mayrhofer, however, has provided an Indo-European etymology for about a third of these. Many names and words can be understood as Indo-European or Indo-Aryan if they have a known Indo-European or Indo-Aryan root, perhaps with known Indo-European and Indo-Aryan suffixes or prefixes.

21. Although he notes that the distribution changes in the older books: most of the foreign names are in the later books of the Ṛgveda (33).

22. This is based on his observation that the gerund in Indo-Aryan, which is a South Asian areal typological feature and therefore not evidenced in other Indo-European languages, increases in frequency chronologically through the later books of the Ṛgveda, yet contains an archaic ablaut vowel that stems from a remote period of pre-Indo-Aryan: "This would seem to allow but one conclusion, viz. that they had arisen among lower social circles of bilinguals, who were in a steady contact with speakers of Dravidian and other non-Aryan languages" (Kuiper 1991, 21).

23. Anyone who has ever spent time in places like Vrindavan can readily attest that the cry of a peacock sounds like a greatly amplified cat's meow.

24. These were taken from the publications of H. Gundert, R. Caldwell, F. Kittel, J. Bloch, T. Burrow, A. Master, M. B. Emeneau, and S. K. Chatterji (Acharya 1971, 11–13).

25. These were from the works of J. Przyluski, S. Levi, P. G. Bagchi, S. K. Chatterji, F. B. J. Kuiper, and T. Burrow (Acharya 1971, 159–166).

26. There is another language still extant in the Northwest of the subcontinent called Burushaski. I am not aware of any extensive studies attempting to attribute the non-Indo-European loans and syntactical features to this language.

27. For a list of such plant terms, see Southworth 1979.

28. Southworth (1990) uses such methods to suggest a Dravidian affiliation of the Harappan civilization. He takes Fairservis's identification of three basic pre-Harappan groups existing in west India. These are hunter-gatherers in Gujarat and Rajasthan; village farming groups along the Indus and Ghaggar Rivers; and village farming groups in the Baluchi and Afghani hill country. He considers the hunter-gatherers to have been tribals who provided the mysterious terms for the local flora and fauna—the "language x." He considers the Indus/Ghaggar group to have been the pre-Harappans, and the Baluchi/Afghani group the proto-Dravidians. During the Harappan period, the language of one of the groups, Dravidian, becomes dominant in the area of the Indus and the Ghaggar, becoming the language of the Harappan civilization. His grounds for this seem to be the similarity in the term for sesame between Dravidian and Elamite in Mesopotamia. Since sesame is known in the Indus Valley, he considers that there is a strong likelihood that Mesopotamia first obtained sesame from the Indus Valley through trade. Also, the word for 'date' is reconstructable for proto-Dravidian **kintū*, and dates were known in the Indus Valley. He further speculates that the term *Indus* itself (< *sindhu*) could have been derived from proto-Dravidian.

29. *phala* 'fruit', *puṣpa* 'flower', *puṣkara* 'lotus', *aṭavi* 'forest', *kapi* 'monkey', *sāya* 'evening', *rātri* 'night', *bīja* 'seed', *śava* 'corpse' (202). In a footnote, Talageri provides the appropriate page numbers of the etymologies of these words from Buck's *a Dictionary of Selected Synonyms in the Principle Indo-European Languages.*

30. I.e., *khaḍga* 'rhinoceros' from *khaṅḍ* 'to break'; *markaṭa* 'monkey' from *mark* 'to move swiftly'; *taṇḍula* from *taṇḍ* 'to beat' (Talageri 1993, 209).

31. See, in addition to Southworth, Singh and Singh (1983) and Singh and Vyas (1983).

32. At the time I submitted my manuscript for publication, Southworth was still preparing his book for publication. I was however fortunate to read the draft of one chapter of this manuscript called "Palaeobotanical and Etymological Evidence for the Prehistory of South Asian Crop Plants."

33. The homeland, we can recall, simply refers to the last place inhabited by the undivided Indo-European speakers.

34. Krahe determined that the words were only western Indo-European, since the hydronomy is shared by several, but not all, Indo-European languages.

35. An Indo-European etymology has been proposed for the Kubhā and the Sindhu. For the Kubhā, namely, *kubja* 'bent' and *kubhra* 'humped bull' are possibilities (Etymologisches Wörterbuch des Altindischen). Sindhu is generally accepted as derived from *sidh* 'to divide'. The Śatrudrī is from Indo-Aryan *Śata-dru* 'running in a hundred courses'. Witzel (1999, 51) believes that this is a popular etymology of a local non-Indo-Aryan name because there are several other forms for this word, which he feels point to different realizations of the original foreign term. Witzel further notes that in Kashmir, there is only one river name, the Ledarī (evidenced from a much later Puranic text), that is not Sanskritic. Kashmir is not mentioned in Vedic texts and is first referred to by Patañjali (150 B.C.E.).

36. Thus Karnaul can be derived from Karnapur, and Karauli from Kalyanpur, and so on (Growse 1883, 84).

37. See Ramachandran (1987) for a description and bibliography of all work done on place-names in India.

38. S. K. Chatterji (1993) did some preliminary analysis of the place-names in Bengal and concluded that "an investigation of the place names of Beṅgāl as in other parts of Aryan India, is sure to reveal the presence of non-Aryan speaking, mostly Dravīḍian all over the land before the establishment of the Aryan tongue (67).

39. Paper presented at the Arya and non-Arya in South Asia conference at the University of Wisconsin, Madison, 1996.

40. These evidences include non-Indo-Aryan or Dravidian suffixes and prefixes, and the fact that early words with retroflexes in Indo-Aryan are not Dravidian, and so on.

41. He specifies that there were also other more peripheral languages in South Asia such as Proto-Burushaski, and so on (Witzel 1999).

42. See Zvelebil (1990) for an overview and bibliography of attempts at establishing language connections with Dravidian.

43. Zvelebil (1990, 50) considers the Dravidians to have been a mountain folk primarily on the basis of the frequent occurrence of the elements **ko-/kō-* or **ku-/ kū-* 'mountain'. He notes, however, that the root could just as plausibly denote 'speak/speech'.

44. Tuite (1998) argues in favor of an original historical link between the Proto-Burushos and the Caucasus region.

45. Thomason and Kaufman (1988, 350) state that knowledge of both or all languages involved in a substrate setting is necessary before structural influence can be determined.

Chapter 6

1. Pictet's pioneering work *Les Origines Indo-Européennes* was severely criticized because he paid no attention to the diachronic occurrence of words in Sanskrit. Pictet correctly accepted words as cognates only if they appeared both in Sanskrit and in other Indo-European languages, but he was willing to take the Sanskrit words from Vedic as well as much later Sanskrit texts. His critics pointed out that words occurring in later texts may have been later innovations and therefore not present in the protoperiod. The same caveat, of course, applies to extracting words from the western languages, many of which are attested only at a much later stage of history.

2. Friedrich (1970) enumerates the various limitations involved: trees produce enormously varied quantities of pollen, making some trees much more difficult to locate than others. The hazel, for example, yields twenty times as much pollen as the linden. Different kinds of pollen vary greatly in their ability to survive, and therefore be located, in pollen form. Moreover, the pollen of various trees is identified with differing degrees of ease and accuracy: the exact species

of a tree genus is always difficult, and sometimes impossible, to identify. In addition, paleobotanical analyses are usually done in particular ecological niches, thereby failing to represent the actual varied conditions of a given environment.

3. These trees are known variously in the different Indo-European languages (some having more than one name), resulting in thirty different terms for these eighteen basic arboreal categories. L. Campbell (1990) has shown that some of these items have comparable forms with the Finno-Ugric languages, which might suggest shared boundaries.

4. After the Slavic languages, the Baltic and Italic stocks have the next highest number of reflexes for these trees, followed closely, in turn, by Germanic. Greek is relatively strong in reflexes but is noteworthy insofar as sixteen of the reflexes preserved in Greek have shifted their denotation, usually to another tree (e.g., the term for beech is transferred onto the oak). Albanian, although preserving fewer arboreal terms, shares up to ten of these innovations with Greek (which would represent the arboreal analogue of a linguistic isogloss uniting these two languages). These facts need to be accounted for in Nichols's model of language speakers, which will be discussed later.

5. The terms *linguistics* and *philology* were synonymous in the nineteenth century. Nowadays, philology generally refers to the study of the culture and civilization of an ancient historical period through textual analysis, and linguistics refers to an analysis of the actual mophological, phonemic, and other ingredients of languages.

6. Some of these tribes, continuing their wandering, might have again transferred these new terms onto further, unfamiliar, but similar items elsewhere, explaining the shift in meaning in Greek and Albanian.

7. Similar objections were raised by Palmer against arguments attempting to determine the substrata in northwestern Europe based on words shared by Celtic, Italic, Balto-Slavic, and Germanic but absent in Greek.

8. Renfrew (1987) also points out the same shortcomings in this method: "If we look at the modern boundaries for a particular species of tree. . .it will not surprise us that the various languages within the boundary have terms designating that tree, and presumably the languages which lie entirely outside the boundary will not have a name for a tree they do not know exists. . . .if we imagine that there was an original homeland *outside* the boundary, and that the territories within it came to speak Indo-European languages, . . .then they would need to develop an appropriate vocabulary after their arrival. They might well draw upon pre-existing terms in their own vocabulary which had previously held a rather different meaning (like the immigrants to the New World with their 'robin'), or entirely new words might be developed and be adopted" (81–82).

9. Thieme elaborates on this salmon argument in his *Heimat der Indogermanischen Gemeinsprache* (1953).

10. Diebold (1985) has contested the claim that the specific referent of the word is Thieme's Atlantic salmon, which he argues is a later semantic transfer, and has determined that it refers to a Proto-Indo-European "salmon trout; large andronomous salmonid" (48). His case for an eastern Pontic to western Kirghiz steppes homeland is developed on the grounds that the other salmonids, such as the huchen, char, grayling, and salmon, do not have Proto-Indo-European etymologies and were, therefore, encountered after the Proto-Indo-Europeans left the original homeland. He chooses his homeland on the grounds that it must contain the andronomous salmon trout and its variant, a smaller nonandronomous brooktrout, to the exclusion of all other salmonids (50).

11. However, Mallory (1997) states that the Proto-Indo-European word is not connected with *lakṣa* 'hundred thousand'.

12. An alternative argument offered by Elst (1996), using the etymological sense of 'red', is that the Indo-Europeans left India, saw an unfamiliar red fish on their travels, and called it **lakh*. However, since, in Tocharian, the word means 'fish', and in Iranian Ossetic 'trout', this type of argument would have to further postulate that the Iranians and Tocharians first mi-

grated to salmon-breeding areas, where they coined the word for the unfamiliar fish based on its color (or picked up the word from other Indo-European tribes already settled there), and then moved on to their own historic territories, where, due to the absence of salmon, the word was transferred to other fish or to fish in general. By Occam's razor, this would be a more complicated series of postulates.

13. D'iakonov (1985, 111–112) disapproves of this reasoning.

14. See Algeo (1990) for various examples of semantic change, such as transfer—the use of an old word for a new referent.

15. It is interesting to note here that, as early as 1887, Müller had rejected a European homeland (and particularly a Scandinavian one), since: "There is no name for the sea shared by the North-Western and South-Eastern branches [and] we look in vain in the ancient Aryan dictionary, not only for any special fishes, but even for a general word for fish. . . . In the Vedic hymns there is no mention of fishes being eaten" 1985, 117).

16. Gamkrelidze and Ivanov (1995), note in defense of their Anatolian homeland theory: "As the speakers of Indo-European dialect groups migrated into new ecological environments, new words arose to refer to previously unknown animals found in the new territories" (454).

17. Since some of these animals (such as monkeys and elephants) are inhabitants of more southern climes, Gamkrelidze and Ivanov (1995) eliminate central Europe as a possible homeland.

18. Since the word is also reconstructed in proto-Semitic, there is some disagreement regarding its origin; however, as D'iakonov (1985) points out, "Monkeys did not flourish in Asia Minor and the Near East" (131). They did, however, flourish in India. Accordingly, D'iakonov notes that the word may have been borrowed from Dravidian rather than Semitic.

19. Not all scholars fully accept that this word is inherited, since it may have been a later loanword from another language. D'iakonov notes that it does have cognates in Greek, Gothic, and Slavic, but that in addition to meaning elephant, it can mean an 'enormous animal' or even a camel (111). According to George Thompson (personal communication) in the Ṛgveda the word *íbha* occurs four times, twice probably meaning elephant but twice denoting not elephant but rather something along the lines of domestic servant. According to Geldner, Ṛgveda 1.84.17 and 4.4.1 do indicate elephant, a probability compounded by the fact that the word is collocated with *hastin*. Most scholars have accepted this etyma (although Kosambi and Renou are inclined to consider that the word refers to a low-caste or tribal people). Mayrhofer feels that it is unlikely that the term meant elephant in the Ṛgveda, although it did in the later language.

20. While agreeing that the homeland cannot be located in central and eastern Europe, D'iakonov (1985, 110) feels that Gamkrelidze and Ivanov have overinterpreted evidence, leading them to postulate the hot nature of the homeland based on a protoform for warmth. He notes that even languages such as Eskimo contain terms for heat.

21. Dolgopolsky (1989, 1990–93) also makes a distinction between what he calls proto-West-IE (PWIE), which includes all the Indo-European languages except Hittite, and Proto-Indo-European, which includes Hittite as well. He claims that much of the reconstructed landscape for the protoperiod, including the terms for horse and chariot, represents the chronologically later PWIE period. Hittite has no cognates for such terms, indicating that the protohomeland did not necessarily know the horse and chariot, and that its inhabitants were not necessarily pastoralists.

22. I have encountered such arguments in my interviews with Indigenous Aryanists.

23. However, Watkins (1995) suggests that Indo-European terms for 'ruler,' etc., may be related to the technical term for the chariot driver's means of guilding and controlling his horses, viz, the reins: "The designation of the reins rests squarely on a metaphor: the reins are the 'rulers'" (8).

24. Lehman notes that reconstructing the original form would provide substantial difficulties for strict application of the comparative method. Specifically, the initial *h* and the double

consonant in Greek *hippos* has caused controversy. He further comments that "whatever designation was applied earlier to the wild horse may not have been maintained, or it may have been an etymon of the widely adopted **ekuo*" (1993, 247).

25. The report on the External Land Trade of the Province of Sind and of Baluchistan for the Year 1900–1901 mentions horses, ponies, and mules as items of import from Seistan, Herat, and Kandahar (Chakrabarti 1977b, 29). Some British seemed to have success with breeding in the subcontinent, however. Captain Henry Shakespear noted in 1860, "I have bred horses for many years in the Deccan. . . .I am quite convinced that no foreign horse that is imported into India. . .can work in the sun, and in all weathers, like the horse bred in the Deccan" (224). The Deccan horse, however, was originally bred from imported Arab breeds. Arab traders who settled on the Kerala Coast sold horses brought by sea. Overall, access to horses has been a major concern of Indian Rulers throughout its history.

26. Nor does the absence of a common term prove its absence in the protoworld. Dhar (1930) points out that "from the absence of a common Aryan name for milk, no one can infer that milk was unknown to the primitive Aryas" (30). Here, again, we find Western scholars voicing the same objections.

27. Fraser's caricature was overstated, however. When Renfrew (1987) utilized it to disparage linguistic paleontology, his critics pointed out that Fraser's reconstruction from the Romance languages can only reconstruct the vulgar Latin of the early Middle Ages (when emperors and kings did exist), not the classical language. Also, linguists can determine that words like *tabac*, *bière,* and café are loans (D'iakonov 1988, 82–83; Dolgopolsky 1990–93 232–233).

28. Pulgram was aware that Fraser's reconstruction represents the vulgar Latin of the late Middle Ages and not that of proto-Romanic, yet he refused to assign much accuracy to the whole process of reconstruction. Referring, on another occasion, to the task of reconstructing proto-Romance, were Latin not known, he comments, "I am certain that many of the resulting asterisked forms would correspond to no kind of known Latin, and that many other lexical items of this uniform reconstructed proto-Romanic, looked at from the Latinist's point of view, would belong to different local and social dialects of different eras. Let us not forget that no amount of reconstruction would deliver, for example, more than two cases for the noun and four for the pronoun. This means that this proto-Romanic would, at best, correspond in this regard to some unknown and unattested koine of a late date and not at all to the predivisional proto-language of the proto-Romance Urheimat" (1959, 423).

29. It has been noted in this regard that the *-o* in **ekwos* indicates that it is a thematic stem of late Proto-Indo-European formation. It is also not a simplex noun but a derivative, further suggesting to some scholars that it is a late addition to the Proto-Indo-European lexicon (Hamp 1973, 1990a). However, if the word was introduced after the breakup of Proto-Indo-European, it would have had to have been introduced before satemization of *-k* > *-ś* occurred (**ekwos* > *aśva).* From an Indigenous Aryan position, this would still entail knowledge of the beast in the proto-Indo-Iranian period and would not, therefore, minimize the problem of the lack of horse bone evidence in the subcontinent which will be discussed later.

30. For a defense of linguistic paleontology, see Thieme 1957.

31. Rocher (1973), for example, comments that "the distribution of similar archaeological sites on the map does not conform to linguistic distribution. We submit that there is no reason why it should" (617).

Chapter 7

1. These Semitic loans had been noted in 1964 by Illic-Svityc, who also located the Proto Indo-Europeans in Asia Minor (Sheveroskin 1987, 227). Other proposed loans are identified from Elamite, Sumerian, Hurrian, and Urartian. Harris (1990) argues that although there are

limited phonological correspondences, the parallels noted by Gamkrelidze and Ivanov between Indo-European and Kartvelian are not structural; such parallels could have developed independently and not necessarily be indicative of immediate contact (1988). Nichols (1997) as will be discussed later, envisions an intermediary entity lying between Proto-Indo-European and Kartvelian. D'iakonov (1985) suggests any structural and lexical similarities may be the result of genetic inheritance from a protolanguage of both protolanguages.

2. He rather envisioned a triangle with Proto-Indo-European on the northwest corner in southeast Anatolia, Kartvelian on the northeast (but with some territory separating it from Proto-Indo-European) and Semitic in the south (southeast from Proto-Indo-European and southwest from Kartvelian).

3. Nichols (1997) notes that if a loanword is attested in all the branches of a language family, it can be assumed to have entered into the vicinity of the locus of the family (while dialectal attestation indicates entry at the periphery of the family range). Nichols's further assumption, which would seem to be in accordance with the opinions of most of the respective authorities, is that in the fourth millennium B.C.E., from the five language families considered in her study, the ancestors of Semitic and Sumerian were in or near southern Mesopotamia, West Caucasian (Abkhaz-Circassian) was situated along the Black Sea coast, East Caucasian (Nakh-Daghestanian) was spread over the eastern Caucasian foothills and the Caspian coastal plain, while South Caucasian's (Kartvelian's) protohistoric location is unknown (although its later attested location is in the South Caucasus). Nichols's study suggests that the largest number of word resemblances among these languages are between Indo-European and South Caucasian. Both of these languages share an equal number of loanword with Semitic, including numerals (which are not shared by the other members of this group), and two of these loanwords are common to all three languages. Neither Indo-European nor South Caucasian shares any loans with West Caucasian (which was not on a loanword trajectory because it shows no evidence of loans even with East Caucasian).

4. Of course, here a double assumption is involved: first that loans between Indo-European and Semitic indicate geographic proximity between these two languages and, second, that absence of Semitic loans in West Caucasian indicates that Indo-European was not geographically intermediate between these two. Clearly, even allowing the first condition (which is challenged by, e.g., D'iakonov 1985), one can still legitimately hold that a loan passed onto Indo-European from Semitic might not have been passed onto a further neighbor of Indo-European for reasons other than those suggested by Nichols. As noted, west caucasian had no loanwords and therefore, according to Nichols, no direct or indirect contact with any of these languages.

5. Dolgopolsky (1989, 17) points out that East Caucasian may have moved to its present location *after* the breakup of Proto-Indo-European. Accordingly, if Proto-Indo-European has no East Caucasian loanwords, this may be due to the fact that the latter had not yet situated itself in its historical location..

6. All these deductions also apply to South Caucasian. However, the Semitic loans in Indo-European and South Caucasian, respectively, are not obviously derived from each other, indicating that neither of these languages was the intermediary language separating the other from Mesopotamia.

7. She places South Caucasian somewhat, but not immediately, adjacent, to the southeast of Proto-Indo-European from where it moved westward to its attested situation.

8. Shevoroskin (1987) also finds reason to distance Proto-Indo-European from direct contact with the Caucasian languages, which he resolves by moving it farther west on the Anatolian plateau.

9. Haarmann (1994, 277) notes that the original homeland of the Uralic people—situated geographically in a region near the middle Volga around the basin of the Kama and Vyatka—is not under dispute, although there is some disagreement over how far west it extended.

10. Burrow (1973b, 373–374) does wonder whether one or two words, such as the word for 'bee,' might have been borrowed by Indo-Iranian from Finno-Ugric.

11. Koivulehto (1991) finds reason to propose that there was early borrowing into the Finno-Ugric languages from Indo-European in the form of words with laryngeals (although other linguists assign similarities between these language families to a greater proto-family).

12. That they are not Proto-Indo-European can be deduced from phonemic changes in the loans that are are post-Proto-Indo-European and characteristic of Indo-Iranian. These include assibilation of palatal stops *k*, *g*, *gh*; change of *s* > *ṣ* after *k*, etc.; and the changes of *l* > *r* and *m̥* > *a* (Dolgopolsky 1989, 24).

13. Also of relevance is the fact that Harmatta identifies *ek'* 'horse' in Udi (a Caucasian language) as the earliest loanword from the Indo-Iranian period (< **ekwa*). The antiquity of the loan is determined by the velar *k*, which is distinct from the later palatal *ś* in Sanskrit (*aśva*). This indicates that the word was borrowed before palatalization occurred in what (after palatalization) came to be known as the *satem* group. However, a problem arises here. If the loans were prior to the formation of the *satem* group, then Balto-Slavic Albanian and Armenian (the other members of this group) would have been in very close proximity with Indo-Iranian; but Finno-Ugric shows no evidence of having borrowed any loans from Balto-Slavic and Armenian.

14. Harmatta's (1981) earlier date is predicated on the argument, noted earlier, that the eastern languages have a different agricultural terminology than the western group, and that therefore the breakup of the Indo-European family must have occurred when agriculture began to develop in eastern Europe, which was at the very beginning of the Neolithic, in the early sixth millennium B.C.E. He also argues, on the basis of the nature of the loanwords, that "the migrations of the Proto-Indo-Iranians may have taken place in at least three successive periods. . . .the first type of migration was represented by the slow infiltration of small cattle breeding groups, . . .the second type was the movement of greater groups, clans or tribes, headed by a well-organized army of charioteers and warriors, . . .the third type may be characterized by the massive movements of equestrian nomads" (Harmatta 1992, 368).

15. Misra (1992) submits that construing these words as forms of Indo-Iranian, which is an unattested language, when the forms can be accounted for in an attested language—Indo-Aryan—is uneconomical and, therefore, less satisfactory.

16. These three chronological stages correspond to the following Linguistic changes: (1) Early borrowings preserving affricative *'c* (< **'k*), which had not yet become *ś*, and to some extent *e* and *o*, were passed from early Indo-Iranian to the East Caucasian languages in the steppe areas north of the Caucasus; (2) later borrowings, wherein affricative *c* becomes sibilant *ś* but *e* and *o* are still preserved, from Middle Indo-Iranian to the Uralic languages which Shevoroshkin seems to place around the lower Volga close to the Caspian; (3) latest stage of borrowings, just before the breakup of Indo-Iranian, where *a* is found instead of the *e* and *o* of earlier periods, to languages in Middle Asia.

17. See Collinder (1977) and Rédei (1991) for comprehensive lists of loans from Indo-Aryan and Iranian into Finno-Ugric. These lists have no category for Indo-Iranian but group the loans separately under Indo-Aryan and Iranian.

18. See Gamkrelidze and Ivanov (1995, 811) for references to scholars who have compiled lists of these words. (1995, 811).

19. For example, Zarathustra, while not rejecting the *haoma* (Vedic *soma*) sacrifice, seems to have condemned a form of animal sacrifice in which the sacrificial flesh was given to the laity to consume and the sacrificial meat was sprinkled with the sacred *haoma* fluid and then roasted (Kanga 1988, iii).

20. Although in the early parts of the Ṛgveda, the *asuras* also refer to benevolent gods.

21. Kanga (1988, xxi) notes that it is predominantly in syntax that Avestan shows marked individuality.

22. See Kanga (1988), who prepared an Avestan reader with footnotes containing the Sanskrit equivalents of forms that differed from Vedic.

23. Boyce calculates that the Achaemenian family were Zarathustrans at least from the time of Cyrus the Great in the mid–sixth century B.C.E. They acquired the faith from the Median magi whom Boyce (1992) figures must have adopted the religion no later than 700 B.C.E. Genealogical relationships within the texts cause her to add another 100 to 150 years (at 30 years per generation) to account for the minimum period needed to cover the internal narrative of the text. She proposes that a further 150 to 200 years are required to accommodate the time that must have passed after Zarathustra in order for the religion to have spread enough for one of his followers, Saena, to have been able to amass the hundred disciples for which he is famed (Boyce 1992, 29; Gnoli 1980, 161).

24. Humbach (1991) derives *Vaejah* from cognates of the Vedic root *vij* "'to move with a quick darting motion, speed, heave of waves' [suggesting] that it denotes the bed, or the course, or a cataract of a fast-flowing river, and its adjacent regions" (33).

25. "Ten are there the winter months, two the summer months, and even then [in summer] the waters are freezing, the earth is freezing, the plants are freezing, there is the center of winter, there is the heart of winter, there winter rushes around, there (occur) most damages caused by storm" (Humbach 1991, 35). Humbach, attempting to reconcile the paradisiacal aspect of *airiianəm vaējō* with this severe description, notes that in a Pahlavi translation of this verse, the following line is inserted: "'and thereafter (it is said): seven are the months of summer, five those of winter'"—which, he remarks, would be a climatic norm. Humbach suggests this inserted passage might represent a fragment from a lost text (36).

26. Gnoli (1980, 110) considers the lower Oxus region, south of the Aral Sea, to be an outlying area in the Avestan world because it is mentioned only once, when it is considered as being the very farthest horizon reached by Mithra's gaze.

27. Boyce (1992, 3) considers this to be the Arachosia of the Greeks.

28. For example, Boyce (1992, 32) finds references in the Yast section of the Avesta to "Whitely" and "Whitish Forests" existing in the *airiianəm vaējō*, which she finds characteristic of the white-stemmed birches of the Inner Asian steppes but, clearly, such references could just as well denote the snow-clad slopes of the Hindu Kush, where Gnoli would situate the homeland, or else could simply have symbolic value.

29. *Artasumara*, king of the Mitanni (< Skt. *Ṛtasmara*), *Urudīti*, king of Hurri, early sixteenth century (<*Urudīti*), *Subandu*, prince of southern Palestine (<*Subandhu*); *Sutarna* (<*Sutarṇa)*; *Parsasatar* (<*Praśāstár* 'ruler'); *Saussata* (<**Saukṣatra* 'son of *Sukśatra*); *Artadāma* (<*Ṛtadhāman*); *Artasumara* (<*Ṛtasmara* 'mindful of truth'); *Tusratha*; *Matiwaza* (<* *Mativāja* 'victorious through prayer') (Burrow 1973b, 27). Private documents from the area written in Assyrian reveal a number of proper names of local elite that are also Indo-Aryan: *Artamna* (<*Ṛtamna* 'mindful of the law'); *Bardasva* (<*Vārddhāśva* 'son of *Vṛddhāśva*'); *Biryasura* (<*Viryaśūra*, 'valorous hero'); *Puruṣa* (<*Puruṣa* 'man'); *Saimasura* (<*Kṣemaśura* 'hero of peace'); *Satawaza* (<*Sātavāja* 'one who has won prizes') (27). These Aryan names extend as far as Syria and Palestine: *Suvardata* (<* *Svardāta* 'given by heaven'); *Satuara* (<*Satvdāra* 'victorious; a warrior'); *Artamanya* (<*Ṛtamanya* 'thinking of the law'); *Biridasva* (<*Vṛddhāśva* 'possessing large horses'); *Biryawāza* (<*Vīryavāja* 'having the prize of valor'), *Indrota* (*Indrotá* 'helped by Indra,); and others.

30. The names are presently accepted as Indo-Aryan by specialists in this area such as Mayrhofer (1983; also, compare Burrow 1956, with the same, 1978). However, D'iakonov (1990) considers them to be specifically Kafiri, a third subbranch of Indo-Iranian.

31. Burrow (1973a) dismisses this, since "a theory involving such complication can be safely ignored" (125). This is, of course, complicated if the Ṛgveda is dated as more or less synchronis-

tic with the Mitanni documents, since the Indo-Aryans would have had to make an about-face, race back, and take over the Mitanni kingdom in no time at all. Of course, as with Konow's position, if the commonly accepted dating of the Veda in India is rejected as an arbitrary one, this complication is eliminated, since many generations could have elapsed between the earlier Veda as known in India, and the later Vedic traces found in the Near East. The dating of the Veda is discussed in chapter 12.

32. A little hammer from Susa, in Elam, with the date inscribed upon it, has two bird heads joined to a tail with "peacock eyes" that resemble the feathers of a peacock.

33. Akhtar (1978–79, 66) comments that the Anatolian and Semitic documents have been altogether ignored by Indian scholars, possibly because of the lack of opportunity in India to study cuneiform and the Akkaddian, Hurrian, Kassite, and Hittite languages.

34. Misra lists the following features (the Sanskrit form is given first, followed by the Near Eastern Indo-Aryan equivalent): (1) assimilation of dissimilar plosives ie. *sapta.* > *satta.* (2) semivowels and liquids not assimilated in conjunction with plosives, semi-vowels or liquids ie. *vartana*> *wartana*; *vīrya* > *Birya*; (3) nasals also not assimilated to plosives ie. *ṛtamna* > *artamna*; (4) frequent anaptyxis *ie. Indra* > *Indara*; *smara* > *sumara*. (5) initial *v* > *b ie. virya* > *birya*; *vṛdhāśva* > *bardasjva*. (6)¸*ṛ* > *ar* ie. *ṛta* > *arta*; *vṛdh* > *bard*.

35. Norman (1995) noticed three features: (1) *pt* > *tt* (as in example 1 above); (2) labialization of *a* > *u* after *v* e.g. *aśvasani* > *assussanni*; and (3) assimilation of *śv* > *ss* after labialisation of *a* > *u* (as in example no. 2).

36. However, see Hock (forthcoming), who, although accepting that the term is Indo-Aryan, raises possible counterarguments (which are rejected by Misra, forthcoming). Hock also holds that *satta* could have been a borrowing from the non-Indo-European language Hurrian, which has *sinta/sitta* for seven, rather than a prakritism. Misra rejects this on the grounds that the other numerals are Indo-Aryan.

37. Several Puranas record this movement. Pargiter ([1922] 1979, 108) lists the following references: Bhāgavata, IX.23.15–16; Viṣṇu, IV. 17.5; Vāyu 99.11–12; Brahmāṇḍa, III.74.11–12; Matsya, 48.9.

38. Talageri (1993) notes that a few Purāṇas mention one other king, Sucetas, as a successor of Pracetas.

Chapter 8

1. Renfrew's (1987) receptivity to this idea provided an additional reason for him to be subject to the criticisms of linguists.

2. Resonating with some of the comments articulated by Western scholars in the first chapter, (1994) Kak comments: "The question of the location of the homeland is in many ways an inappropriate question to ask with the current state of knowledge. The choice of the homeland. . .is strongly correlated with the nationality of the proponent" (189).

3. See Mallory 1975 for criticisms of the various problems involved in drawing "facile inferences from such a superficial and questionable methodology" (93). Diebold also objects that the migratory routes many languages pursue are little affected by such principles (1987, 46). Dolgopolsky (1987) points out that this line of reasoning completely conflicts with other evidence such as that of loanwords.

4. For pre-Indo-European substrata in North Europe with further references, see Polomé 1990a, b; Hamp 1990b; Salmons 1992; and Harmann 1996. For Greece, see *Acta of the Second International Colloquium on Aegean Prehistory 1972*.

5. A further feature that Dhar (1930) finds problematic is accounting "for the fact that India which is supposed to be the last home of the Aryan race produces the first or the most ancient record of the Aryas [viz., the Vedas], the like of which is not produced by them in their homes in Europe

or in Asia outside India" (55). He discounts the possibility that there might once have been older Indo-European texts in Europe that had become lost, since "the instinct of preservation is as strong among the Aryas outside India as in India, for we have Homer and the *Avesta* preserved to this day" (57). His solution is that "the greater the distance from the primitive Indian home of the Aryas, quite naturally the later in date was the birth of a new Aryan language and literature" (59). Again, similar arguments are invoked by Gamkrelidze and Ivanov (1995): "It is important that these dialects [Anatolian], which are the least removed from the Near Eastern homeland, are the earliest Indo-European dialects to be recorded in written documents" (791). The date for the written documents in Hittite and other Anatolian documents is from ca. 1700 B.C.E. Indigenous Aryanists unanimously consider the Veda to be much older than this, as will be discussed later. Needless to say, as D'iakonov (1985) points out in his review of Gamkrelidze and Ivanov, the fact that written languages as old as Hittite and Vedic have not been found does not mean that languages equally as archaic did not exist.

6. See also Feist (1932, 246), who notes that the Lithuanians were not always resident in their present location. For a long list of scholars who have used this line of reasoning, see Mallory (1975, 155). As a point of information, while Lithuanian has been remarkably stable in the nominal system, it has greatly remodeled the verbal system of Proto-Indo-European.

7. A conservative language is one that is *systemically* closer to the protoform, while an archaic one may preserve *individual* archaic features but not be conservative in general.

8. See Mallory (1975, chap. 5) for similar arguments offered by Western scholars over the decades involving identifying substrata interference as disqualifications and linguistic conservatism as qualifications among contenders for the homeland.

9. Elst's book at the time of this writing, is in the hands of his publisher in Delhi.

10. Velars are guttural sounds produced in the back of the throat like k. Palatals are sounds produced by the tongue in contact with the palate of the mouth like č. The *k* in *kentum* in the Germanic languages became a fricative velar, which eventually evolved into *h* (and the *t* became voiced to *d*), resulting in English *hund*red.

11. The language (which actually turned out to be two distinct languages called Tocharian A and B) was mostly preserved in texts of translated Sanskrit Buddhist documents from the second half of the first millennium B.C.E.

12. Although rejected by Beekes (1995, 20), at the time of this writing, Zoller's findings are still being debated.

13. Isoglosses, however, do not necessarily fall into neat bundles—different dialects, languages, and even language families may share common linguistic isoglosses, as is the case, for example, with Indo-Aryan, Dravidian, and Munda.

14. The model has been slightly amended by Palmaitis (1988).

15. The Stammbaum model, developed by August Schleicher, a linguist trained in biology, visualizes languages branching off from the main trunk of a language family tree and then further dividing into subbranches, and so on. Although this model is very useful conceptually, its shortcoming is that it does not allow mutual influences and interaction of the various branches once they have separated from each other. The wave model, developed by Schmidt in 1872, attempted to compensate for this by postulating that languages that are situated side by side over a given area are influenced by sound changes that spread like ripples extending out from a stone thrown in a lake. The ripple will reach a certain area and no more; the ripples from another stone thrown elsewhere in the lake will cover a different area. Ripples, or sound changes, initiating from one area may partly coincide with the ripples from sound changes elsewhere. As with stones of different sizes, the areal extension of the ripple may vary. Each linguistic ripple is called an isogloss. The problem with these models is that they are subject to being overly subjective: linguists disagree about what the significant isoglosses are that might be shared by different groups.

16. For a history of scholarship analyzing the grammatical and lexical relationships of dialects within late and post-Proto-Indo-European, see Polomé (1994).

17. This, of course, implies complete harmonization of all isoglosses—which is the same as no distinct isoglosses at all—but obviously there was no "pure" Ur-language. There would always have been some variety of isoglosses, and therefore dialectal distribution, even within Proto-Indo-European. The theory of Proto-Indo-European, in turn, being a daughter language in the Nostratic language family, as proposed by some linguists, is beyond the scope of this book (and, in the opinion of many linguists, beyond the scope of realistic speculation).

18. It should be noted that Gamkrelidze and Ivanov (1995) do not recognize the *kentum-satem* divide as a bona fide isogloss separating dialects, since they are "typologically natural and in principle can arise independently in different linguistic systems" (356).

19. There are, however, isoglosses breaching this conceptual divide, such as forms in * *-l*, which were shared by Anatolian and Tocharian from A, and Armenian and Slavic from B. The information on isoglosses in the following notes is from Gramkrelidze and Ivanov (1995).

20. These include the development of feminine gender, the masculine instrumental plural in **-ōis*, and the independent demonstrative pronoun, **-so*.

21. These consist of the o-stem instrumental masculine singular (**-oḥ*), which Indo-Iranian shared with Germanic and Baltic, and the locative plural (**-su*, Gk *-*si*), shared with Balto-Slavic and Greek.

22. The isoglosses joining the latter are the existence of the athematic and thematic aorist, and a genitive singular in **-(o)syo* (this is also found in italic).

23. These isoglosses consist of the genitive locative dual in **-os*, and first person singular pronoun forms in **-em*.

24. This isogloss is the comparative and superlative adjective forms in **-tero* and **-ist(h)o-*, respectively (which Greek also shares).

25. For one of the first attempts at a quantitative classification of the Indo-European languages, see Kroeber and Chrétien (1937), whose method consists of selecting a number of linguistic traits and then determining which of the various Indo-European languages share these traits. Graphs are then produced showing the relative similarity of the languages. For more recent mathematical models, see Raman and Patrick (1997) and Embleton (1991). For a lexicostatistical approach, see Dyen, Kruskal, and Black (1992).

26. It is Iranian, more than Indo-Aryan, that shares closer features with both Armenian and Greek, on one side, and Balto-Slavic, on the other. Elst (1996, 228) believes that these isoglosses form a serious objection against the south Russian (and any non-Indian) *Urheimat* theory. His argument is that Gamkrelidze and Ivanov's theory requires that Greek and Armenian split off west and south from a still united Indo-Iranian, which was moving east. Why, then, were the isoglosses common to Iranian, Greek, and Armenian not shared with Indo-Aryan as well? The same question could be posed for the Iranian and Balto-Slavic isoglosses.

27. Satemization is comfortably accommodated in this model as an isogloss spreading partially along each trajectory from the locus.

28. Nichols does not discuss the issue of Iranian (or Indo-Iranian or Indo-Aryan) loans into Finno-Ugric in this article, but this would need to be accounted for both chronologically and geographically.

29. One might also wonder that if Iranian obliterated other predecessor Indo-European dialects or languages in its western spread, these should presumably be evidenced as substrates: one would expect to find ancient Indo-European loans from other I-E languages in Iranian in such a model. Gamkrelidze and Ivanov (1983b, 77) note a number of words the eastern Iranian languages have in common with the ancient European dialects.

30. Hock's dialectal map (forthcoming) shows an isogloss (merger of velars and palatals) shared by Germanic, Celtic, Italic, Greek, and Hittite that could have occurred at the western point of contact of the two trajectories.

31. D'iakonov (1985) outlines the attraction of a similar linguistic spread from a Balkan

homeland: "From our point of view there was no migration as such. . . .There was a gradual spread from one center in all directions. In the course of such a spread the groups of dialects and specific isoglosses that had developed were maintained. . . .The biological situation among the speakers of modern Indo-European languages can only be explained through a transfer of languages like a baton, as it were, in a relay race, but not by several thousand miles' migration of the tribes themselves" (152–153).

32. It is relevant to note here that shared isoglosses, or "peripheral" isoglosses, between noncontiguous areas might be explained by the fact that these areas had once been contiguous, but that a later language (such as Iranian) had spread over part of this territory, thereby separating other parts of the area. In other words, one might find "relics in marginal areas of terms eliminated by recent innovations in other regions in-between" (Polomé 1994, 297).

33. As noted, there are isoglosses common to Iranian and other Indo-European languages that did not effect Indo-Aryan, e.g. PIE *bh, dh, gh* > *b, d, g,* which Iranian shared with Baltic, Slavic, Daco-Mysian, Germanic, Illyrian, Macedonian, and Celtic.

34. For analysis and further bibliography on the Hittites and the Indo-Europeans, see Steiner (1981, 1990; Drews 1997; Singer 1981; and Mellaart 1981).

35. These include the merger of *a* and *o*. There is also a dividing line of gen/abl merger between Germanic and Old Prussian, and Lithuanian and Latvian and Slavic on this continuum (Hock forthcoming). It is of relevance here, too, that Gamkrelidze and Ivanov (1983b 72) have produced loans from the ancient European dialects in the Yeniseian languages, which, according to toponymic data, occupied considerable portions of central Asia up to the end of the first millennium B.C.E.

36. The Gamkrelidze and Ivanov model has had problems accounting for the fact that Armenian, which had to barely move from the protohomeland, shows Hurrian-Urartaean substratum for local topography and flora (D'iakonov 1985, 146, 117).

37. In Phrygian, for example, satemization occurs only before the sonants *l*, *m*, *r*, and *n* (D'iakonov 1985, 166).

38. This isogloss did not completely affect the Kafir languages in the Hindu Kush, who preserved a *c*, which is still intermediate between the **k* and *ś*.

39. A further isogloss of *tt* > *tst* > *st* was shared by the western perimeter of the core area, namely, Iranian, with the dialects of Armenian, Greek, and Balto-Slavic adjacent to it on both sides. While the first part of this sound change, *tt* > *tst*, seems also to have affected Indo-Aryan in this central area, *tt* was eventually reintroduced (due to the loss of *-s-* from this cluster).

40. For example, Proto-Indo-European *ṅ*—*ṁ* > *a* in an area comprising Indo-Iranian, Daco-Mysian, Baltic, Germanic, and Albanian; Proto-Indo-European *o* > *a* in Indo-Iranian, Baltic, and Daco-Mysian; the deaspiration of unvoiced labials, dentals, and velars in Iranian (but not in Indo-Aryan), Balto-Slavic, Daco-Mysian, Germanic, Illyrian, Macedonian and Celtic; Proto-Indo-European *a* > *o* in the Indo-Aryan, Iranian, Baltic (but not Slavic), and Daco-Mysianian. Similar isoglosses can be traced in vocabulary such as that uniting Iranian and Slavic (Harmatta 1992, 360–361).

41. An immediate issue that comes to mind is determining whether the chronological sequence of these isoglosses (wheresoever they can be determined) can coexist in such a model.

Chapter 9

1. Sir Arthur Cunningham was the first to archaeologically examine (although not the first to visit) Harappa in 1853 and 1856. Finding some Kushana coins at the site, he attributed the city to the Kushana period (Imam 1966, 114). It is shocking to note that about one hundred

miles of the Lahore-Multan Railway was ballasted by bricks retrieved from the ruins at Harappa by rapacious railroad contractors: "No invader of India had ever so ruthlessly and wantonly destroyed her ancient remains as did the railway contractors in the civilized nineteenth century" (Iman 1966, 226–227).

2. Srivastava (1984, 442) points out that Wheeler was a brigadier in the British army during World War II and began his career as an archaeologist excavating Roman fortifications and other forts and castles in Britain. His interpretation of the Mohenjo-Daro evidence is best viewed with this military background in mind.

3. A glance at the school texts and popular books written on ancient Indian history prior to the seventies shows how widespread Wheeler's scenario was: "It is probable that the fall of this great civilization [the Indus Valley] was an episode in the movement of charioteering peoples which altered the face of the whole civilized world in the 2nd millennium B.C." (Basham 1959, 28).

4. Sir John Marshall was the first to speculate concerning the cause for this, which he suggested might have been decreased rainfall, a theory later revived by G. Singh (1971). Agarwal and Sood (1982, 225) proposed increasing aridity. Raikes (1964), supported by Dales (1966), argued that flooding, resulting from the damming of the Indus due to geological tectonic disturbances, prompted the gradual abandonment of various sites. S. R. Rao (1991) finds widespread evidence of debris and damage caused by flooding, especially in Harappa, Mohenjo-Daro and Lothal. According to Rao, Wheeler's so-called anti-Aryan fortification walls are actually antiflood dikes, which were continually raised and renewed in a struggle against Mother Nature. The shifting of riverbeds, which will be discussed later, supports his view and is a widely accepted cause (Lambrick 1967; Thapar 1975; Kenoyer 1987; Shaffer 1993). Another proposed theory identifies the depletion and overexploitation of natural resources as a principal circumstance in the gradual demise and abandonment of the valley (Fairservis 1961; Possehl 1967; Thapar 1975). Socioeconomic and cultural upheavals are further causes that have been considered (Gupta, 1993b). Nowadays, most scholars consider a combination of these natural calamities to be responsible factors (Agarwal and Sood 1982, 229; Allchin 1993, 389; Shaffer 1993). See Possehl (1999a) for a discussion of theories.

5. S. R. Rao (1979) describes how some of the houses had circular and rectangular pits cut into the floor, while in others the pits were built on mud-brick altars. The pits all contained ash, and "the absence of any opening for fuel and their unusual size and shape suggest that they could not have served as ovens" (216).

6. *Nadītame* (R.V. ii.41.16–18). All references to the Sarasvatī are from Reusch, who submitted a comprehensive exposition on the Sarasvatī, both textually and archaeologically, as a master's thesis at the University of Wisconsin, 1995. See also Bharadwaj 1987.

7. *Yatī giribhya ā samudrāt* (R.V. vii.95.1–2). Griffith translates *samudra* as 'ocean', a translation accepted by Macdonell and Keith ([1912] 1967, 432), who also note references to treasures of the ocean and to the story of Bhujyu, which suggests marine navigation. According to Madhav Deshpande, the word *samudra*, which means 'ocean' in later Sanskrit texts, usually means 'river' in the Ṛgveda (personal communication). The item literally mean 'with waves'.

8. *Pañca jātā vardhayantī* (R.V.6.61.12). Macdonell and Keith note that these five tribes are known under a variety of names in Vedic literature: *pañcamānuṣaḥ*, *pañcamānāvaḥ*, *pañcakṛṣṭayaḥ*, *pañcakṣitayaḥ*, and *pañcacarṣaṇyaḥ*. The *Aitareya Brāhmaṇa* explains the five to be gods, men, Gandhārvas and Apsaras, snakes, and the Fathers. Sāyaṇa considers them to have been the four castes and the Niṣādas. Zimmer (466–467) considers them to have been the Aryans, an interpretation favored by Indigenous Aryanists, which is the meaning assigned to them in later texts.

9. Sarasvatī is also invoked in the form of a deity and as *vāc* 'speech'.

10. Griffith 1973, 323. This position has been defended as late as 1986 by Chaṭṭopādhyāya.

11. See Keith and Macdonell ([1912] 1967, ii, 434–436) for a summary of opinions in this regard. The Triveṇī is the pilgrimage place where the three rivers are supposed to meet in Allahabad. Presently, two of these rivers, the Gangā and Yamunā, join at this confluence.

12. Prior to Sir Aurel, an Italian Indologist by the name of L. P. Tessatori visited some of the sites along the riverbed. He left some handwritten notes and photographs of his observations, which eventually came into the possession of Sir Aurel (Gupta 1989, 10–11). For a bibliographic list of the various scholars who have surveyed the Ghaggar/Hakra riverbed, see Mughal 1993.

13. The results of his survey were only recently published from a photocopy of a microfilm of his typed manuscript (Gupta 1989, viii). Sir Aurel had traversed Chinese central Asia, Baluchistan, and Iran, the Indian deserts of Bikaner, Sind, and Thar, and the various valleys and plains of the Indian subcontinent (Gupta 1989, vii). He died on his first trip to Afghanistan while working in the reserve collection of the Kabul museum.

14. Pal et al. (1984, 493) suggest that this could have been due to either tectonic uplift, or the capture of the Sutlej by a tributary of the Beas, or the existence of a fault in the former (493).

15. Ninety-nine of these sites were dated to the fourth millennium B.C.E., 214 to the third millennium B.C.E., and 50 before the end of the second millennium B.C.E. Ghosh's explorations in a small area of the riverbed to the north of Bikaner resulted in over 100 more sites being mapped (Ghosh 1989b, 101).

16. See, for example, Gupta 1993, 163. The logic here is that the Indus part of the title should be maintained because the largest and best excavated site of Mohenjo-Daro is on the banks of the Indus River, and also because this title has been in use for seventy years; Sarasvatī, however, should be conjoined with this title to reflect its actual significance in the valley. An international conference held in Atlanta on October 4, 1996, sponsored by the Hindu University of America and other organizations, was entitled "Revisiting Indus-Sarasvati Age and Ancient India." Obviously, the assignment of such nomenclature can be construed as an attempt to Vedicize the Indus Valley.

17. If the sites of the historic period, which were established on the bed after the river had gone dry, are excluded, that is, if only the sites situated on the riverbank itself are taken into account, the percentage of third and fourth millennium B.C.E. sites would be higher still.

18. Without mentioning the reference, R. S. Sharma (1995, 15) refers to a verse where a thousand horses are prayed for.

19. The authors give no reference for this claim, which, if accurate, would approach the dates for the origins of the domesticated horse in the Russian steppes.

20. Lal (1997, 162) notes that these came from section scraping and not from a stratified dig.

21. The authors note that this is a different species of horse, distinct from the type found in Afghanistan and the central Asian steppes.

22. See also Sethna 1992, 216–220, for reference to his personal correspondence with the veterinary doctor who identified the bones, insisting that they were definitely of the true horse, and not the domestic ass.

23. This identification was based on the finding of the right lower jaw containing the premolar and molar teeth, along with a second fragment containing the same teeth on the left side. These were found to be of identical dimensions as a skull of *Equus caballus* from the Indian museum (Marshall 1931, II, 653–654). This identification was accepted by B. Prasad, director of the Zoological Survey of India in 1936 (Prasad 1936, 4).

24. B. Prasad (1936, 4) recorded the remains of the domestic ass in Harappa and noted that, unlike at Mohenjo-Daro, there was no trace of the horse in the remains he examined. A. K. Sharma (1992–93) states that these bones were reexamined by J. C. George from M. S. University, Baroda, and quotes his comment that "the metacarpals recorded by Prasad are defi-

nitely not of the domestic ass and it is, therefore, possible to conclude that the smaller size of horse did exist in Harappa" (31). Sharma makes no mention of any published or unpublished paper or report produced by George in this regard.

25. Some of the Kalibangan bones were identified as horse bones by A. K. Sharma (1992–93) himself as far back as 1965.

26. The evidence from Lothal consists of a terra-cotta figurine and a molar horse tooth (Rao 1979; tooth measurement, p. 442, photo, plate CCXCVII). These findings occur from the mature level of the site, which Rao assigns to 2200 B.C.E.. Evidence of rice has also been found in Lothal and Rangpur. The apparent absence of rice in the Indus Valley had also previously been viewed as significant proof of the absence of rice-eating Aryans (Rao 1979, 219).

27. This is a late Harappan site the unpublished report of which was coauthored by Sharma, Joshi, and F. R. Allchin (Sharma 1992–93, 32).

28. This includes bones and horsemen figurines. The site is dated between 2000 and 1300 B.C.E. (458).

29. The information from Kuntasi was obtained by R. S. Sharma from personal information from the excavator (Sharma 1995 27 n. 49). The dates from this site range between 2200 and 1900 B.C.E.

30. Along identical lines, scholars emphasizing the importance of the fire altars of Kalibangan will usually mention that they have been accepted as such by the Allchins (e.g., Rao 1993, 173).

31. Due to the passions aroused by the horse issue in India, it seems useful to note an observation by the editor of this publication about "the manner in which the amicable and positive discussion between two distinguished authorities is set out" in reference to the exchanges between Meadow and Bökönyi.

32. The Rana Ghundai finds were accepted by Piggott (1952), who, as an Aryan Invasionist, was forced to conclude that "one cannot, therefore, hold that the Aryans were the first people to domesticate the horse in India or on its western border lands" (267).

33. I. Mahadevan, who is one of the principal scholars attempting to decipher the Indus script as a Dravidian language, considers this total absence of horse motifs on the thousands of extant Harappan seals the single most damning factor against the Indigenous Aryan school and one that alone refutes its whole premise, even irrespective of any other data (personal communication).

34. Parpola and Mahadeva have countered, in this regard, that the animals depicted on the seals are all male, hence the bull but not the cow (Sethna 1992, 179). From this perspective, the male horse should have been represented had it been an animal in the Indus Valley Civilization. A. K. Sharma's response to this, in turn, is that neither the male camel nor the ass is represented on the seals, although their bones have been reported from various sites (1992–93, 33). However Meadow (1996, 405) also casts doubt on whether the camel was known to the Mature Harappans, since the context of the evidence of this beast is either Late Harappan or uncertain.

35. Anyone visiting an Indian museum will be quite likely to find bags of bones, pottery, or other items lying neglected here and there.

36. Gurumurthy's (1994) attempt to read Indus graffiti on Tamil pottery has not received the attention of his colleagues.

37. The earliest iconographic representation of wheeled vehicles occurs in Uruk, a site of Mesopotamia, dated to the later part of the fourth millennium B.C.E. (Littauer and Crouwel 1979, 13). The number of representations of such vehicles increases in Mesopotamia, in the third millennium, with depictions of four-wheeled battle wagons and some two-wheeled vehicles, both drawn by cattle (Littauer and Crouwel 1979, chaps. 5, 6). Up to this date, the wheels depicted are solid.

38. Piggott (1977) considers the geographic location of the Indo-Iranians, whom he associates with the Andronov culture, to be suitable in accounting for the introduction of the chariot into Mesopotamia in the early part of the second millennium, as well as into Shang China in the later part of the same.

39. Littauer and Crouwel (1979, 71) note that the Kikkuli manual was written four or five centuries after the first attested representation of the spoked-wheel chariot.

40. Sethna (1992, 48–51) has tried, somewhat unconvincingly, to make the case that the symbol of a circle with six radials found on some Indus seals and bits of pottery is a representation of a spoked wheel.

41. Mackay's workmen were bringing in pieces of toy carts almost on a daily basis (Mackay 1943, 162).

42. *Newsweek*, May 6, 1999; *New York Times*, April 6, 1999. See also http://www.harappa.com./indus2/124.html. Meadow has confirmed the reports.

43. However, the Mayan hieroglyphs, which represent a language that can be adequately reconstructed from the twenty-five Mayan languages still spoken, are still only partially deciphered.

44. No known syllabic script has more than two hundred signs.

45. Rao is particularly renowned for his excavations at Bet Dvārkā, which he correlates with Śri Kṛṣṇa's renowned capital city described in the Purāṇas. His decipherment efforts have also been greeted with interest by some Western scholars (Maurer 1985).

46. The earliest representation of Brahmī known to date is the Piprahwa casket inscription of 450 B.C.E. The Aśokan inscriptions, with which most of Rao's comparisons are made, are from the third century B.C.E.

47. Moreover, Rao's (1991) decipherment does not reveal any indication of gender (268) Rao considers the Indus script to have developed just after the split between the Indo-Aryans and the Iranians. However, if the post-Hittite Indo-Europeans, and in particular the Indo-Iranians who preceded the Indus speakers, had number and gender, and the Vedic and later Sanskrit language forms had number and gender, how could the intervening Indus script have temporarily lost them? Further criticisms of Rao's work have been made by Mahadevan (1981–82; 1989).

48. This Indo-European genitive case marker is still preserved in English by *'s* in such words as John's.

49. Like all decipherers, Kak has his critics. Mahadevan has criticized Kak's efforts, claiming that some of his comparisons are far-fetched and that he has omitted some of the ten most frequent Indus signs and included others that are much less frequent (Mahadevan 1988, 619). Kak (1989) counters this by saying that his analysis was based on the data given in Mahadevan's own concordance.

50. Such efforts have resulted in the construction of a positional grid for the signs, which can be divided into three basic segments. The grid suggests that certain signs occur almost only in the first segment, while others are found at the end of the second segment. Some signs, in certain situations, tend to occur in pairs, others are mutually exclusive, still others almost always ocur at the end of words, and so forth.

51. Fairservis's (1992) method consists of identifying the signs according to their likely iconographic representation and other criteria; finding an equivalent lexeme in Dravidian that is widely represented in various Dravidian languages; likely to be an ancient word; is suitable by its syllabic, substantive, or homophonic potential; and is a lexeme that is appropriate to varying contexts where the sign occurs.

52. Mahadevan (1995) summarizes his rejection of Parpola's Dravidian decipherment on the grounds of "implausible identification of pictorial signs; arbitrary assignment of values to non-pictorial signs and diacritic marks; doubtful classification of basic, composite and variant

signs; and uncertainty in fixing the context of occurrence to provide clues to likely meanings and linguistic problems in the handling of Proto-Dravidian reconstructions and choice of homophones" (10).

53. For further criticisms of Rao and Parpola, see Lal 1997.

54. This occurs in *Jaiminīyabrāhmaṇa* which states that a three-headed *gandharva* is said to reside in a boat *nagara* (Rao 1976, 51).

55. Factually, the lists are far too extensive. Singh would have made a much more convincing argument by being much more limited and discrete in his semanticizing.

56. "The artificial barrier we have created between the Vedic and Harappan social systems collapses once we have a look at the list of professions. . .mentioned by name: . . .Rudra denotes a physician or therapist, the Aśvins, surgeons" (Singh 1995, 161–162).

57. Elizarenkova (1992) notes that the lexicon for house and dwelling is much less elaborate in the Ṛgveda than that for the cart and chariot. She notes several words for house: *dám*, *dāma*, *gṛhá*, *dúrya/dúria*, *duroṇá*, and *harmyá/harmiá*. The latter refers to a stationary palace or mansion in later texts.

58. Spoken in caricature of Parpola's reconstruction of events.

Chapter 10

1. Kennedy's article (1995) provides another useful summary of the history of racial science and the quest for the Aryans.

2. Asimov (1981) outlines some of the principal Russian contributions in this regard. He himself supports an Andronov route for the Indo-Iranians.

3. According to Kuzmina (1985), the Andronovo tribes are associated with "1) the establishment of the mixed farming-pastoral economy and the gradual transition from settled household cattle rearing to mobile stock breeding; . . .2) the flourishing of copper and tin extraction which made possible the export of bronze goods; . . .3) the development of transport: oxen to be harnessed to heavy four-wheeled carts, Bactrian camels and heavy-draught horses and the breeding of special types of light horses, which made possible chariot battle tactics in the 17th century B.C; . . .4) the evolvement of the types of a long-term dwelling and a light dwelling; . . .5). . . the Iranians or Indo-Iranians" (23–24).

4. The following characteristics of these graves are singled out: "1) types of grave structures; 2) types of burial pits and ceilings; 3) orientation; 4) cremation or inhumation rite and position; 5) other ritual features; 6) grave goods; 7) animal sacrifices; 8) funerary offerings" (Kuzmina 1985, 25).

5. This is in contradistinction to his earlier position in 1972, when he was prepared to consider the Indo-Iranian nature of the Andronovo culture.

6. He specifies the Pit and Ochre Burial Culture of the Lower Volga as the Indo-Iranian point of origin. See also Novgorodova 1981.

7. Other prominent sites include Tureng Tepe III C1, Mundigak IV, Shahr-i Sokhta IV, Altyn, and Namazga V.

8. Since there was no noticeable change in climate over the last five thousand years, this scholar holds that the reason for the abandonment of the sites "can be sought in the social sphere."

9. Trumpets were used to train and control horses in Egypt, as can be seen in bas-reliefs.

10. This level IV of Namazga also shows the replacement of female figurines typical of previous levels by female figurines in a different style.

11. For an adequate exposure to the wide variety of views from primarily Russian scholars on the origins of the Indo-Iranians, see the edited volume *Ethnic Problems of the History of Cen-*

tral Asia in the Early Period (1981) Summaries of some of these papers have been published in volume 1 of the *Journal of Central Asia* (1978).

12. This assumption, of course, can be challenged.

13. That women were making the pottery can be determined from the finger indentations on the pottery made during the molding.

14. However, Piankova (1994, 363), in evaluating this proposal, notes that there is minimal influence between the tribes from Iran in the west and the BMAC in terms of ceramics.

15. Hiebert and Lamberg-Karlovsky (1992, 1) give a bracket of 2100–1750 B.C.E.

16. This group included the Kāfir, Dad, and Pasha dialects.

17. The Aryans, he notes, never speak of their own forts because they were recently arrived invaders in the subcontinent (Parpola 1988, 110).

18. His victory over the ten kings took place on the river Parusṇī, which Yāska (nirukta 9, 26) identifies with the Irāvatī, the modern-day Ravi in the Punjab (Parpola 1994, 114).

19. An important element in Parpola's scenario involves correlating Śambara with Samvara, an enemy of Indra in the Mahābhārata. This deity surfaces as the later tantric Cakra Samvara in east India and Tibet. Parpola connects the Vedic protoform of this deity with Varuṇa, the chief deity of the Dāsas. He also connects the circular fort at Dashly-3 with the later maṇḍalas, which are the abodes of the deity, featured in the tantric religions prevalent in the eastern and northern areas of the subcontinent. The "autumnal" forts of the Dāsas, discussed previously, are connected with the goddess Durgā, who is called Śāradā 'the Autumn One' in Kashmir, since her festival falls at that time of the year and is always celebrated in *durgas*, 'forts' in Kashmir and Nepal. Parpola believes the origin of the goddess is the Inanna-Ishtar from the Near East, who is also connected with forts. All these features suggest to Parpola that the tantric religions of the East and North of the subcontinent belonged to the earlier wave of Indo-Aryans, the Dāsas, a hypothesis he reinforces by noting the reference in the Śatapatha to the *mlecchas* speaking a *māgadhī*-like Indo-Aryan Prakritic language to the east of the Vedic people.

20. Parpola quotes the following translation from Rau (1976, 25f.): "They drew that fortification (*pur*) around it. . . .Three times he draws a line. . .a threefold fort he thus makes for him; and hence that threefold fort is the highest form of forts. Each following (circular) line he makes wider."

21. Sethna examines a passage from the Aitareya Brāhmaṇa, which Parpola also quotes to support his case, and finds a cosmic drama recorded where the gods and the Āsuras are competing for the three worlds: the Āsuras make the earth into a copper fort, the air into a silver fort, and the sky into one of gold; the gods counteract these three forts by constructing three different types of sacrificial sheds connected with the Vedic *yajña* to counteract the respective three forts of the Āsuras. As far as he is concerned "neither the forts of the Asuras nor the 'counter-forts' of the gods in this account can by any stretch of the imagination be visualized as concentric" (Sethna 1992, 298)

22. While accepting that a few statements concerning Dāsas do refer to human beings, Sethna (1992) interprets most of the references to them as "vast forces recurrently taking particular forms which get dissolved by various divine powers at various periods" (335). He, too, opposes the idea of interpreting Ṛgvedic mythological narrative as factual history.

Chapter 11

1. The term for this culture is considered ill defined by other archaeologists working in this area (e.g., Tusa, 1977; Stacul 1975).

2. The graves are either pits covered with stones and sometimes lined with stones, or pits with walls made of monolithic stones. The burials consist of either cremated ashes deposited in

urns, or complete or fractional skeletons. It is relevant to note that although inhumation was carried out throughout all the periods of the graves, cremation peters out in the later periods. In Vedic literature, however, the reverse seems to be the case. Inhumation is referred to in the earlier periods but gives way to cremation in the later periods.

3. Stacul (1966, 68) notes that this grayware has been matched with the Jhangar culture of Sind, and a distinctive form of it found in Harappa.

4. Stacul (1969) finds the typological correlations between the pottery of Swāt on the one hand and that of western Iran on the other, in a span of time from about 1300 to 400 B.C., to be significant. He holds that these connections probably took place along several routes "which brought to the north-west regions of the Indo-Pakistan subcontinent the black gray burnished ware, distinctive of Tepe Hissar IIB-IIIC, in association with other elements of probably northern derivation" (86–87).

5. The Quetta hoard, for example, was accidentally stumbled across during the construction of a hotel on these premises.

6. However, a footnote on this page acknowledges awareness of Kenoyer's arguments against foreign conquest, which were published after Allchin's publication.

7. Kenoyer attributes this disruption to the shifting of river courses, resulting in a fatal disruption of agriculture.

8. He argued that the Malwa culture does not synchronize with the Aryan presence in that area; the Cemetery H culture is too limited in distribution; the similarities of the Banas culture with other Indo-European artifacts is too meager to build a case; the Copper Hoard culture has not been found in the Northwest, the Punjab, or the Sarasvatī valley, which are the principal locales of the Ṛgveda, and so on (Lal 1978).

9. Such as vague comparisons between ageless and universal terra-cotta types or figurines; misleading for example, the Sialk "teapots" associated with Navdatoli channel spouts; or drawn from separated assemblages, such as Catal Huyuk VI-A of the sixth millennium B.C.E. and Sialk Necropole B of the first millennium. All from Chakrabarti 1977b, 33.

Chapter 12

1. On written signs in Uruk in the Near East, on representations on a pot in Poland and a tomb in Züschen, in three-dimensional models in graves in Hungary, and in actual vehicle burials in Yamna graves in the steppes of Russia.

2. Since the first archaeological attestation of a solid wheel seems to be a representation on a Funnel Beaker pot from South Poland whose calibrated dates are 3500–3200 B.C.E., Anthony and Wailes (1988) are comfortable stating that "this indicates that European wheeled-vehicle technology (*a*) was acquired in eastern Europe, probably the Pontic Steppes; (*b*) was acquired there by ca. 3300 B.C." (443).

3. The date for Chandragupta Maurya was determined by correlating him with the Sandrocottus mentioned in Greek sources. There is a view, which has also been active for a century or so, that considers this identification of Sandrocottus with Chandragupta Maurya to be erroneous. According to this argument, the Chandragupta intended by the Greeks was the Chandragupta of the much later Gupta dynasty.

4. Müller ([1859] 1968, 213) connects this sutra-composing Kātyāyana with the Kātyāyana Vararuci of Somadeva because the former was the author of the Sarvānukramaṇī, which is also known as the Sarvānukramaṇī of Vararuci,

5. Thieme (1958) and Mehendale (1978–79) have argued that reference to iron is made even in the Ṛgveda, on the basis of the term *así* 'knife' (Latin *ensis* 'iron sword'; Greek *ásis* 'mud' < **ṇsi* 'black'). This involves reconstructing a Sanskrit terms for 'black' **asi* along with the existing synonym *asita* (paralleling the pattern *hári/hárita* 'yellow'; *róhi/róhita* 'red').

6. Some archaeologists are now dating this prior to 2600 B.C.E.

7. One would expect to find references to the Harappan cities in the later literature, so Southworth (1990) feels that this proposal does not help.

8. Misra's observation that the loans in Finno-Ugric are all Indo-Aryan is also relevant to this discussion. Harmatta had taken the commonly accepted opinion noted previously that Proto-Indo-European had broken up before the development of agriculture (on the grounds that the eastern and western branches had different terms for agricultural referents, suggesting they coined or borrowed these after their respective separation from the common stock). This suggests to him that the Indo-Iranians were a separate entity in the sixth millennium B.C.E. Harmatta therefore assigned the earliest loans into Finno-Ugric to the fifth millennium B.C.E. He considers the earliest loans (4500–3500 B.C.E.) to be Indo-Iranian and the later ones Iranian. Misra considers them all to be Indo-Aryan, as discussed previously, and argues that, if Harmatta's schema is accurate, Vedic Sanskrit should be dated to the fifth millennium B.C.E.

One might add that even if the Indo-Aryan nature of the loans is challenged, that is, allowing, with Harmatta, that after 3500 B.C.E. they are Iranian forms, this would still indicate that Indo-Aryan was a separate entity from Iranian at this early date. In his dating attempts, Misra is assuming that the earliest existence of Indo-Aryan as a separate entity is contemporaneous with the date of the Ṛgveda. If this, in turn, is questioned, and a 1500 B.C.E. date for the Vedas insisted upon, Harmatta's dates (with which many linguists would agree) would nonetheless indicate that Indo-Aryan remained more or less unchanged for about two millennia (3500–1500 B.C.E). Of course, as with everything else connected with the Indo-European problem, Harmatta's dates can be challenged.

9. Previously, the date of the Avesta was considered established at 500 B.C.E., as was discussed in chapter 6, so the date of the Veda was assumed, due to its linguistic similarity, to have been in close chronological proximity a few centuries earlier.

10. He compares words: (a) common to the two and identical in form; (b) nearly identical but with slight phonetic change; (c) equivalent but more changed, such as *figlio* and *hijo*; (d) different words that can be replaced by equivalents that are (i) nearly identical and (ii) much changed; (e) different words that cannot be so replaced, such as *fratre* and *hermano*.

11. Woolner dates the upper limit for these psalms to about 1400 C.E. and the lower one to about 1550 C.E.

12. Woolner (1986) bases his calculations on a 500 B.C.E. date for the Avesta, which was previously accepted by scholars, resulting in a 2200 B.C.E. date for the joint Indo-Iranian period by his method.

13. See also Wilford (1799) and Bentley (1799, 1808) for similar concerns.

14. There have been numerous books and articles written in India over the last century, examining the astronomical references in Epic and Purāṇic texts with a view to determining events such as the beginning of the Kali Yuga and of the Mahābhārata war. An analysis of such claims will be undertaken in the sequel to this book, called *In Quest of the Historical Kṛṣṇa* (New York: Oxford University Press, forthcoming.

15. Kim Plofker informs me (personal communication) that Bailly's hope was that the Indian astronomical texts preserved genuine information based on observation and could thus be used to test *modern* astronomical theories, which otherwise would require (and have required) centuries of further observation to corroborate or refute. The possibility of five-thousand-year-old astronomical data was a potential gift from heaven, enabling the testing of modern theories to be stretched into the records of the past rather than have to wait on a future that no living astronomer could hope to see for their confirmation.

16. Tilak was not the first Indian in this regard; much of his work was an elaboration of certain observations made by Krishna Shastri Godgole, who was interested in defending the traditional date of the *Kali Yuga*.

17. Tilak's Arctic homeland is based on a variety of references in Sanskrit texts, which he believed corresponded to prehistoric recollections of the Arctic Circle preserved by the Aryans in their sacred texts after they arrived in India. Statements such as that one day of the devas equals six human months indicated to him mythologized memories of the Arctic Circle, where there is more or less continuous light from the sun for six months of the year. Interestingly, much more recently, Bongard-Levin ([1974] 1980) has expanded on the same theme, not to argue that the Aryans themselves resided in the Arctic, but that they originally neighbored people who did: "Arctic details were merely a part of the 'northern cycle' of ancient Aryan mythology. . . . Accordingly, there are grounds to assert that, for the ancestors of the Indo-Iranian peoples, the whole circle of 'northern' notions examined by us could only be formed if there were direct contacts with those tribes of the North who lived near the Arctic regions" (121). He narrows down the best area for such contacts as "only the regions of South-East Europe—from the Dnieper to the Urals" (123).

18. In the West, too, although on the periphery of professional scholarly circles, books such as Frawley (1991) and Feuerstein, Kak, and Frawley (1995, 105–107), still promote the astronomical proposals of Jacobi and Tilak, as do more mainstream academic publications such as Kramrisch (1981), Deppert (1977), and Klostermaier (1994).

19. In point of fact, Thibaut did considerable work on astronomy, publishing the Pañcasiddhāntikā of Varāhamihira. Jacobi did his doctoral dissertation on the astrological term *horā*, and Tilak, contrary to Whitney's dismissive comment about his qualifications in this regard (Whitney 1895, 365), was a professional almanac maker. In fact, he created considerable controversy among traditional pundits due to updating the traditional almanac, which had become inconsistent because of the changes incurred by the precession of the equinoxes.

20. From an observer on the earth's plane, the winter solstice occurs when the sun's course across the sky reaches its lowest arc in relation to the horizon, and the day is the shortest of the year (around December 22). From that point, the sun's course creeps daily higher up the sky, and the days lengthen, until the sun reaches its highest arc in the celestial sphere, and the day is the longest in the year—the summer solstice (around June 22). The vernal equinox occurs exactly halfway on the sun's course from the winter solstice to the summer solstice, when the day and night are of equal length (around March 21); this has its counterpart, the autumnal equinox, when the sun's course has passed the summer solstice and is exactly halfway back down toward the winter solstice (around September 23).

21. The celestial Equator is the imaginary projection of the earthly equator into the celestial sphere (i.e., into the constellations).

22. In this discussion, following Pingree's use of the term (1970, 534), Vedic astronomy will refer to any astronomical data from texts that are generally considered to be older than about 500 B.C.E. (the Babylonian period).

23. A lunar year consists of twelve lunar months. Each lunar month consists of 30 *tithis* (each *tithi* representing each successive phase of the moon); hence, a lunar year consists of 360 *tithis*. It takes almost 29.5 days for the moon to complete a full circuit of the earth in relationship to the sun (i.e., 30 *tithis*, or from one full moon to the next). Twelve such months (called *synodic months*) comprise 354 solar days (which, in turn, equal 360 *tithis*). Because 354 lunar days are about twelve days short of a sidereal year of the approximately 366 solar days (calculated as the time it takes the sun to make a complete circle in the sky relative to the fixed stars), the lunar year is 12 days shorter than the solar year. The *Śatapatha Brāhmaṇa* mentions a thirteenth month, which was the intercalary month periodically inserted to compensate for this shortfall. According to the Vedaṅgajyotiṣa, the intercalary month is to be inserted after every thirty months, and again after every five years (ii, 2, 1, 27).

24. Other information contained in the early texts includes the description of various yugas or cycles consisting of two, three, four, five, or six years—the five-year cycle being the most fre-

quent. The Ṛgveda mentions three *ṛtus*, or 'seasons': *vasant* 'spring'; *grīṣma* 'summer'; and *śarad* 'autumn'. In most other Vedic texts, however, the seasons are either five—*vārṣā* 'rains' and *hemantaśiśira* 'winter' being added to the three seasons mentioned in the Ṛgveda—or six if, as per the Śatapatha Brāhmaṇa (II, 1, 6, 3), *hemanta* and *śiśira* are separated.

25. The first factor that Jacobi set out to determine is when the Indo-Aryans began their yearly calendar. Jacobi is convinced that Ṛgveda vii. 103, 9—the "frog hymn"—preserves an ancient record of the New Year. Jacobi (1909) translates the verse as: "They observe the sacred order, never forget the proper time of the twelfth (month) these men as soon as the raintime has come, the hot glow of the sun finds its end" (721). The crucial word in this hymn is *dvādaśasya*, the time of the year when the frogs croak because the rain has arrived. Jacobi construes this as an ordinal—'the twelfth' (i.e., month). If his translation represents the intention of the author of the hymn, then he has located the beginning of the year, since the month after the twelfth month would obviously be the first month, or the beginning of the year. The verse states that this twelfth month occurs at the commencement of the rainy season, which more or less corresponds with the summer solstice, so Jacobi has grounds to assign the beginning of the year to the summer solstice. Since, however, as his critics point out, *dvādaśasya* can also denote the simple numeral 'twelve', his hypothesis loses its persuasiveness. With this latter meaning, the word would simply be referring to the year itself—that is, that which has twelve (months)—and the frogs would simply be croaking at the time of the year when the rains arrive, without indicating when this year might have begun.

The next step in Jacobi's logic involves connecting this solstitial beginning of the year with the sun's position relative to the *nakṣatras* at that time. To do this, Jacobi (1909) produces verse 85.13 from the Ṛgveda and its variant 1.13 from the Atharvaveda. Jacobi's translation for the Atharvaveda verse is: "In Maghâ the kine are killed, in Phalgunî the marriage or precession—is held" (721). To this day in India, the marriage ceremony is performed at the bride's house, after which the bride is taken in a procession to the groom's house. Jacobi concludes, "without further argument, that when the marriage of the sun, or its procession into its new house, is spoken of, this point of time can be referred only to the beginning of a new revolution of the sun" (722). This conclusion, coupled with his interpretation of the frog hymn, which begins the year at the summer solstice, now permits Jacobi to state that at the time these verses in the Ṛgveda were compiled, a new year had begun with the sun in the *nakṣatra* of *Phalgunī* at the summer solstice. He calculates this event as occurring sometime in the period between 4500 and 2500 B.C.E.

Jacobi then seeks further confirmation for his thesis. He quotes the Sāṅkhāyana Gṛhyasūtra 4. 5, which fixes the commencement of the period for the study of the Veda, the *upākaraṇa*, at the beginning of the rainy season, which he has equated with the summer solstice. He then finds a verse in the Gobhila Gṛhyasūtra that fixes this *upākaraṇa* for the full moon of *Bhadrapadā*. From the perspective of an observer on the earth's plane, a full moon is situated in the constellation 180 degrees opposite the constellation where the sun is situated at the time (since a full moon occurs when the earth is interposed on the straight line between the sun and the moon). Therefore, the full moon in *Bhadrapadā* occurs when the sun is situated fourteen *nakṣatras* away, namely, in *Phalgunī*—where, according to Jacobi's previous calculations, the sun was situated at the summer solstice. Here is Jacobi's second confirmation supporting his ancient date for the Veda: according to the Gobhila Gṛhyasūtra, the full moon in *Bhādrapadā* also coincides with the rainy season and, hence, the summer solstice with the sun situated in *Phalgunī*.

26. For the history of this debate, see Sen and Shukla (1985, chap. 3). For an early defense of the indigenous origin of the system at the time of this debate, see Aiyar (1919).

27. The only explicit reference to the length of the year in the early Vedic texts is one of 360 lunar days, or 356 solar days, with no information specified regarding how the remaining days were to be intercalated. We might bear in mind, however, that the Vedas are books of hymns,

not astronomical manuals, so they should not be held to represent the complete extent of Indo-Aryan astronomical knowledge. The earliest actual manual, the Vedaṇgajyotiṣa, assigns 366 days to the year, which is 3/4 day in default (which is still not approximately correct for astronomical purposes).

28. The celestial equator is an imaginary circle extending out from the actual equator into the heavens, whose plane is at right angles to the celestial poles. Any stars aligned with this celestial equator are considered to have zero declination and will be perceived as being due east of the observer at rising. These stars will be visible at sunrise on the vernal equinox.

29. This idea was also expressed by Max Müller (1892, li) in defense of the indigenous origin of the *nakṣatra* system.

30. Tilak also attempted to argue that the Taittirīya Saṁhitā (vii.4, 8) preserved a reference to the full moon of *Maghā* occurring at the winter solstice (which would have been the case when the sun was in *Maghā* at the summer solstice.

31. The celestial pole is a theoretical extension of the earth's axis joining the North and the South Poles which is projected in a straight line into the constellations.

32. Jacobi (1909) comments that the present polar star was known in medieval Europe as the North Star, and not as the polestar, since at that time, due to the precession of the equinoxes, it was still about five degrees from the pole and was perceived to revolve around the North Pole like all the other stars.

33. Bühler allows a period from 3100 to 2500 B.C.E.

34. Tilak does not provide a reference for this quote.

35. To use Whitney's own words (1895) in one of his onslaughts against Jacobi, "What possible grounds has Prof. Jacobi for regarding it . . . as so certain that the opposing view has no claim even to be referred to?" (364) Here Whitney is reproaching Jacobi for not mentioning the possibility that the *nakṣatra* system might be of foreign origin and thus not acknowledging a debate that was raging at the time.

36. The formula is: the length of daytime = (12 + 2/61n) *muhūrtas*, where *n* is the number of days after or before the winter solstice.

37. An objection could be raised in this connection, which was kindly pointed out to me by Kim Ploffer. The Arthaśāstra utilizes the 3:2 daylight ratio, which is completely inappropriate for Ujjain, where it was composed. This text undoubtedly borrowed this information. If the knowledge of this ratio had been indigenous to the Northwest, why did an understanding of the mechanics behind this formula not accompany the ratio itself to Ujjain? From an Indigenous Aryan perspective, the response to this would have to be to question, in turn, why the mechanics behind the formula were not solicited from the Babylonians either, if they had been the source of this knowledge? The Northwest, as has been argued by archaeologists, shared closer economic, political, and cultural ties with southeast central Asia, Afghanistan and eastern Iran than with the rest of India. This area might have appeared as foreign to the people of Ujjain as Mesopotamia, despite the lingua franca.

38. Page numbers for Achar's article were not available to me, since the copy he kindly provided had yet to be published in the *Indian Journal for the History of Science*.

39. Achar also takes objections to the fact that Pingree considers it likely that the Indians borrowed the *tithi* (a lunar day, or one thirtieth of a synodic month) from Mesopotamia. As far as he is concerned, the Mesopotamians had no names for their *tithis*, unlike the Indians, who did. He finds references to *tithis*, *adhikamāsas* 'intercalary months', *yuga* 'five-year periods', the zigzag function, and water clocks (another item Pingree holds to have been borrowed) in Vedic texts that were older than the Mesopotamian ones.

40. The same holds true for mathematics. Indian mathematicians often object to the tendency to assign common knowledge between India and Babylonia as indicating borrowing by the former from the latter: "Neugebauer has shown that these values [of irrational numbers in

the Śulvasūtras] are identical with those found in certain Babylonian cuneiform texts. . . .He tried to imply that the Indian value after all represented the Babylonian one. . . .As we have shown, there is certainly no proof of such an assertion and the Indian value is certainly derivable from the methods contained in the śulbasūtras themselves" (Sen and Bag 1983, 11).

41. "The cord stretched in the diagonal of an oblong produces both [areas] which the cords forming the longer and shorter sides of an oblong produce separately" (Baudhāyana *sūtra* 1.48; Āpastambd *sūtra* 1.4; Kātyāyana *sūtra* 2.11). References from Seidenberg 1983, 98.

42. Seidenberg features prominently in the work of Indigenous Aryanists such as Kak (1994) and Rajaram (1995).

43. This sentiment was also directed to the controversy surrounding the origin of the *nakṣatras.*

44. The mechanics of this system have still not been unanimously agreed upon even with the help of the Vedaṅgajyotiṣa. But, as Apurba Chakravarty remarks, "the system actually existed and the correspondences between months and seasons were permanently maintained for hundreds of years. So some method of extracalation must have existed to prevent any derangement of seasons and to fit the lunar year into a solar one" (8).

Chapter 13

1. These agendas are not all necessarily sinister or exploitative. Anthony (1995b) dismisses Gimbutas's reconstructions of pre-Aryan Old Europe as "an interpretation that would have been largely ignored. . .except for the fact that it was discovered by eco-feminism," resulting in the construction of an elaborate gynocentric, egalitarian mythology (93).

2. His purpose, in so doing, appears to be to salvage the indigenousness of the name *Hindu*, by proposing that it may well have been a term current among the pre-Aryan people native to the Northwest, which was then Sanskritized into *Sindhu* by the incoming Aryans. Of course, there is no philological basis for this: *Hindu* is the term used by those outside the subcontinent to refer to those living on the other side of the Sindhu River.

3. Which he defines as the religion subscribing to the Śruti, Śmṛti, and Purāṇas.

4. Savarkar is especially keen on accommodating the Sikhs into the Hindu fold: "Really, if any community in India is Hindu beyond cavil or criticism it is our Sikh brotherhood in the Punjab, being almost autochthonous dwellers of the Saptasindhu land and the direct descendants of the Sindhu [Aryan] or Hindu people" (123).

5. There are southern Tamil-centric myths of origin that are just as creative as some of the Aryan-centered ones from the North. Thus, Purnalingam Pillai (1963) describes the original land of Tamilaham, which included the lost continent of Le Muria, the "cradle of civilization." This was submerged after a deluge, rending asunder Australia, China, and Africa (all supposedly proven by geological science). The survivors fled in crafts or on foot to North India, Europe, the Middle East, East Asia, and other regions. Accordingly, "in its widest sense, Tamilaham at present lies all the world over, wherever the enterprising Tamils have found their home" (5). Pillai finds evidence of this everywhere. According to him, there are liṅgas in Saint Paul's Cathedral; indeed, due to the "many semblences and traces of Saivism. . .in every nook and corner of England, it is impossible to think of England as anything else except a Saivite country." As for the Tamils, they "were the sons of Tamilaham itself. They were indigenous" (18–19). In fact, "history finds the Tamils in their present abode long before the Romans conquered Egypt or Christ was born in Bethlehem, before Porus met the Greek or Darius lost his crown; before Plato wrote his Dialogues and Solomon made his songs" (33).

6. Oak is best known, perhaps, for his continued efforts to prove that the Taj Mahal was originally a Śiva temple. Oak's books attempt to argue that everything of value in the world originally came from India or was part of a greater India. His etymologizing and general level of scholarship are astounding, even in the context of this genre of literature; for example,

England was originally pronounced as *Angulisthan*, since "ancient Hindu explorers and administrators who fanned over a virgin Europe looked across the English channel and called the British isles 'Anguli' ('sthan' or 'desh') i.e. a finger-size, finger-length land. If one imagines Europe to be a palm-size, palm-shaped continent Great Britain appears to be 'Anguli' namely the (extended) finger" (Oak 1984, 842). I was informed by a professor of history at Jawarhal Lal Nehru University that even the RSS, which previously had cultivated Oak, has since completely distanced itself from his views. Oak's insistence that all other cultures from all over the world in all historical epochs ultimately originated in Vedic India, however, does parallel some of the scholarship of the late eighteenth and early nineteenth century in Europe. Attempts were made to accommodate the newly discovered eastern traditions within a biblical narrative by suggesting etymologies such as Brahman being the Sanskrit for Abraham and Sarasvatī for Sarah.

7. At the time of my research, Shrikant Talageri was a bank clerk in Bombay actively involved with Hindu nationalist groups. The first part of his book *Aryan Invasion and Indian Nationalism* (1993) , explicitly promotes Hindu nationalistic themes (which he considers to be synonymous with Indian nationalism). The remainder of the book reveals a very keen mind examining the basis of the whole Aryan invasion theory (this part of the book is at its most vulnerable, I should note, when he attempts to promote Maharashtra as the homeland).

8. Talageri does not use the term *Hindutva*, but it seems evident that his perspectives on Hindu identity are negotiating with those of Savarkar's.

9. Talageri makes a point of noting that the majority of scholars hold that most of the elements that constitute Hinduism come from the pre-Aryan, indigenous culture.

10. I should note that he has seen fit not to include this first section in the second edition of his book.

11. The Indonesians, for Golwalkar, are noteworthy role models. His depiction of how the Muslims from that country relate to Hinduism informs his readers of his expectations concerning the Muslims in India: although Indonesians might profess Islam, they maintain Sarasvatī and Gaṇeśa as the presiding deities of their education and learning; children start their education from pictorial Rāmāyaṇas; the image of Garuḍa adorns the national airlines; and people maintain their Hindu names, as was exemplified by the previous president, Sukarno.

12. Savarkar, as is evidenced by his exclusion of the highly syncretic Bohra community from membership in Hindutva, would not be satisfied with even this. For Savarkar, the Muslims would have to renounce any recognition of Muhammad whatsoever.

13. Arvind Sharma (1995) comments in this regard: "It is often thought that a strong nationalist sentiment supports the tracing of the Aryans to India. Yet it is not entirely clear to me why the claim of an Indian homeland of the Aryans should be considered nationalistic. . . .A vigorous and aggressive nationalism would trace the original homeland outside India *as far as possible. . .thus* opening up the entire area. . .as territory India could potentially lay claim to depending on how strong it was militarily" (181). This, of course, may apply to the *external* aims of an aggressive nationalist state but is not relevant to the de facto concerns in South Asian politics. It is the *internal* politics of authenticity that are the present cause of alarm in Hindu nationalist politics.

14. Mahadevan (1995) responds to this comment with: "I agree with Parpola about the existence of 'nationalistic bias' but would like to remind him that S. R. Rao and Krishna Rao, leading proponents of the Indo-Aryan theory, can hardly be called 'North Indian' [Rao is a typical South Indian name]!" (5).

15. *Towards a New Horizon*, brochure for the Deendayal Research Institute, p. 52.

16. Vol. 15 nos. 2–3 (April–September 1994); vol. 15, no. 4 (October 1994); vol. 16, no. 1 (March 1995).

17. To my present knowledge, of the authors that will be quoted in the following pages, Devendraswarup and Shriram Sathe are both officially members of the Bharatiya Itihasa Sankalana Samiti. Talageri and Waradpande are also definitely on this side of the political spectrum.

18. The owner of this publishing house, Sita Ram Goel, an extreme and vociferous anti-Marxist, has published a number of his own books, whose titles speak for themselves: *Hindu Temples: What Happened to Them* (1990); *Defence of Hindu Society* (1994); "*Stalinist Historians" Spread the Big Lie* (1993); and *How I Became a Hindu* (1982). In the latter book, Goel, who was once a Marxist himself, explains how he became disenchanted with his previous beliefs.

19. As Lamberg-Karlovsky (1997) points out, however, "*nowhere* in the book does it indicate Chakrabarti's academic affiliation. While Chakrabarti admires those Indian students that did not sellout for a 'free drink' and steered clear of foreign institutions and learning, he has situated himself in the center of the enemy camp, one of the central institutions of Western Indology, the Faculty of Oriental Studies at Cambridge University" (4).

20. Rajaram's biographical data describe him as a mathematician and computer scientist living in Houston and Bangalore, with over twenty years' teaching experience in universities in the United States. Since 1984, he has also been an adviser to NASA, for which he was the first to develop and apply artificial intelligence methods. He has written at least two books on the Aryan debate, *The Politics of History* (New Delhi: Voice of India, 1995) and *Aryan Invasion of India: The Myth and the Truth* (New Delhi: Voice of India, 1993), and is writing several more on such topics as "Old World Mathematics" and "Ancient India in the Light of New Science." He is one of the members of the Indigenous Aryan school who advocates the application of hard science to the reconstruction of history. Rajaram is vociferously active in this debate in India. Both of his books, as well as at least one of his articles, sparked off a heated exchange, some of which I have reproduced here, since it reveals much about the intense political emotions enveloping this debate in India.

21. Romila Thapar is a well-known and well-published historian of ancient India who for many years was a professor at JNU. She and other professors affiliated with Jawarhal Lal Nehru University (JNU) (and also Delhi University), such as S. Ratnagar and R. S. Sharma, are particularly targeted and demonized as the "secular Marxist" ideologues and are the targets of much invective from some members of the Indigenous Aryan camp. From my interviews with some of these "leftist" professors, it was clear that the feeling of antipathy is rather mutual.

22. This is not to say that *all* foreign cultural influences are denied.

23. *Indian Express*, December 12, 1994, 1.

24. The Sangh Parivar, simply put, consists of a political wing, the Bharatiya Janata Party (BJP), which is heading the coalition government of India at the time of writing; the Vishva Hindu Parishad (VHP), the cultural organization that interfaces with Hindu religious representatives and organizes a variety of religious functions including childrens' camps, and so on; and the Rashtriya Svayamsevak Sangh, which trains members, particularly youth, in a physical as well as ideological form of militaristic Hinduism. Many prominent members of the BJP and VHP come from an RSS matrix.

25. Seminarist, "State Sponsored Communalization" *Seminar,* December 1992, 25–29.

26. This is an important point. Some Indigenous Aryanists are professional scholars and publish their research in professional publications in a professional manner. Quite commonly, however, their conclusions are seized upon with great enthusiasm, taken out of context, and rearticulated—sometimes in ways that are quite comical from the perspective of critical scholarship—by nonprofessional people in publications that it would be quite appropriate to label communalist (some blatantly so). Such publications abound in India. It is essential for scholars to point out and condemn such abuses of scholarship. But caution must be exercised not to ignore the distinction between the genres and not to automatically conclude that the original research

and the point of view it represents are of the same ilk as the publications that appropriate them. For a summary of the textbook controversy, see Rudolph and Rudolph 1984.

27. Recommendations of the National Steering Committee on Textbook Evaluation. Jan 30–31 1993. National Council of Educational Reasearch and Training Campus, New Delhi.

28. Excerpted from the UCLA Indo-European newsletter in a review on "Recent Work in Vedic Studies."

29. He notes, too, in this regard, that "all too often has one discredited line of argument been used to ridicule another theory which came to the same conclusion" (Mallory 1975, 56).

30. Devendraswarup, whose specialization is in the colonial period, is the principal scholar-historian of the Bharatiya Itihasa Sankalana.

31. Choudhury has written a two-volume publication entitled *Indian Origin of the Chinese Nation* (Calcutta: Dasgupta, 1990). One need comment no further than to note that, as is obvious from the title, this book claims that the Chinese people, language, religion, literature, and science all emanated from India. Another of this author's publications, *The Aryans: A Modern Myth* (New Delhi: Eastern, 1993), contains major portions that are unabashedly blatant word-for-word paraphrases of Poliakov, to whom the author gives no credit.

32. Kulkarni is the general editor of a thirteen-volume series called *The Study of Indian History and Culture* (1988), which has rewritten Hindu history in line with traditional Purāṇic chronology. The volumes with which I am familiar rearticulate common arguments such as the Sandrocottus/Chandragupta Gupta correlation mentioned earlier. Despite the word *Indian* in the title, the books are definitely promoting an exclusively Hindu view of history.

33. Shriram Sathe, who was living in the RSS ashram in Hyderabad when I interviewed him, has published various books defending a literal view of Purāṇic chronology with such titles as *Dates of the Buddha* (Hyderabad: Bharatiya, 1987) and *Search for the Year of the Bharata War* (Hyderabad: Navabharati, 1983). The books are not of high quality.

34. Ashok Chowgule, "Aryan Invasion Theory and Social Issues in India Today." E-mail circular. May 11, 1999.

35. K. D. Sethna, a charming and very well read gentleman, has been a resident of the Aurobindo Ashram in Pondicherri for half a century. In addition to his book *The Problem of Aryan Origins from an Indian Point of View* (New Delhi: Aditya Prakashan, 1980). Sethna has also published another book entitled *Ancient India in a New Light* (Delhi, Aditya Prakashan, 1989). This book claims that the Sandrocottus known to the Greeks was not Chandragupta of the Mauryan dynasty but Chandragupta of the Gupta dynasty. As I noted, this is another bone of contention that surfaces periodically. Whatever one may make of Sethna's conclusions, his books are seriously researched works, unlike some other publications of this genre, and are written in a scholarly and objective fashion and tone.

36. Elst has recently completed his Ph.D. in Holland, submitting a thesis on linguistics and the Aryan debate. While this recent work is a serious and critical piece of scholarship, it is likely to be associated with his pro-Hindu stance in such previous publications as *Ayodhya and After: Issues before Hindu Society* (New Delhi: Voice of India, 1991).

37. *The Life and Letters of Max Müller*, vol. 1, London edition, 328, quoted by Bharti (1992, 63–64). Some Indian scholars seem to have a love-hate relationship with Max Müller. He is sometimes vilified and sometimes venerated by the same author.

38. Monier Williams, *Modern India and the Indians* pp. 261–262, quoted by Kulkarni 1988, 6.

39. These faults are sometimes enumerated as the imperfect nature of human sensory perception, the propensity of humans to exploit each other (politically or otherwise), the tendency to be subject to illusion, and the tendency to commit mistakes.

40. "If the forefathers of the Aryans had really come from a foreign land some reference to this must surely be found in our ancient texts, especially in the *Purāṇas*" (Siddhantashastree 1978, 8); "These Orientalists from Europe have been persistently dinning into the ears of

their credulous disciples that for the purpose of reconstructing the history of ancient India, our Puranic literature is altogether useless and unreliable" (Venkatachelam 1953, 5). In the 1950s, Venkatachelam was one of the first traditional Hindu scholars to defend Puranic chronology. With the exception of Sethna, many subsequent writers on this theme, such as Siddhantashastree and Sathe, seem to more or less rearticulate his arguments.

41. S. P. Gupta is an archaeologist working for the Archaeological Survey of India. His book *The Indus Sarasvati Civilization* (Delhi: Pratibha Prakashan, 1996), contains an entire section supporting the Indigenous Aryan position. Gupta has been very active in this debate.

42. S. R. N. Murthy is the former director of the Geological Survey of India, who has published books such as *Ancient Indian Theories of the Earth* (Poona: Centre of Advanced Study, 1992); and *Geological Foundations of Indology* (Bangalore: Kalpataru, 1994), which opposes the Aryan invasion/migration theory.

43. "The conclusion at which we have arrived is exactly that of Shri Aurobindo" (Sethna 1992, 18).

44. Rajaram, who, as noted, repeatedly promotes hard science (such as archaeology and the mathematics of the *Śulbaśastras*) and the scientific method as indispensable in ancient historical reconstruction, is cavalier in his dismissal of linguistics.

45. The arch-detractors of these individuals such as Romila Thapar opine: "That Indian scientists in America should take it upon themselves the task of proving the Harappan to be Vedic. . .and to proving that the Aryans proceeded on a civilising mission issuing out of India and going westwards can only suggest that the 'Indo-American' school is in the midst of an identity crisis in its new environment. It is anxious to demarcate itself from other immigrants and to proclaim that the Indian identity is superior to others who have also fallen into the 'great melting-pot'" (1996, 88; see also Ratnagar 1996b).

46. Kak is a professor at Louisiana State University. In addition to his work on the Indus script cited previously, Kak has recently written *The Astronomical Code of the Rgveda* (New Delhi: Aditya Prakashan, 1994), which proposes that an astronomical code is encoded in the hymns of the Ṛgveda. Kak, Frawley, and Feuerstein have co-authored a book, *In Search of the Cradle of Civilization* (Wheaton: Quest, 1995), which has had some success on the popular market. Kak is a well-read and articulate spokesman for the Indigenous Aryan position, as well as for other issues related to ancient Indian science and culture, and is particularly respected by the Hindu diaspora.

47. Frawley (1991), who is described in his books as "one of the few westerners ever recognized in India as a Vedacharya or teacher of the ancient wisdom," is committed to channeling a symbolic-spiritual paradigm through a critical empirico-rational one: "A new era of Vedic studies is dawning which allies. . .spiritual studies with new archaeological work in India" (18). Among numerous publications on astrology, Ayurveda, and Vedic mysticism, Frawley has also published another book on the Aryan debate entitled *Gods Sages and Kings* (Salt Lake City: Passage, 1991), in addition to the one noted in this chapter, and has coauthored a third on the same topic (Feuerstein and others). He is very active in, and well received by, the Indian community, both in the West and in India. Frawley runs the Institute of Vedic Studies in Santa Fe, New Mexico.

48. See, for example, "Sarasvati's Child: An American's Route to a New Indian Yesterday," *India Today International*, February 22, 1999, 41.

49. Shaffer teaches at Case Western Reserve University, and Kenoyer at the University of Wisconsin.

Conclusion

1. It should be noted, however, that the Aryan discourses in India are articulated in terms of culture, rarely of race (see Jaffrelot 1995).

Works Cited

Achar, Narahari. Forthcoming. "On the Vedic Origin of the Ancient Mathematical Astronomy of India." *Indian Journal of the History of Science.*

Acharya, A. S. 1971. "Non-Indo-Aryan Elements in Sanskrit Vocabulary." Ph.D. diss., Deccan College.

Acta of the Second International Colloquium on Aegean Prehistory. 1972. Athens: Ministry of Culture and Science.

Agarwal, D. P., and R. K. Sood. 1982. "Ecological Factors and the Harappan Civilization." *In Harappan Civilization: A Contemporary Perspective* (223–231). Ed. Gregory L. Possehl. New Delhi: Oxford.

Agrawal, Dinesh. 1996. "Aryan Invasion Theory." *Hinduism Today,* July, 3.

Aiyar, B. V. Kamesvara. 1919. "The Lunar Zodiac in the Brahmanas." *Indian Antiquary* 48: 95–97.

——. 1922. "The Age of the Brahmanas." *Quarterly Journal of the Mythic Society* 12:171–193, 223–246, 357–366.

Akhtar, Jamna Das. 1978–79. "Indo-Aryan Rulers of Ancient Western Asia and Their Documents." *Puratattva* 10:66–69.

Aklujkar, Ashok. 1996 "The Early History of Sanskrit as Supreme Language." In *Ideology and Status of Sanskrit: Contributions to the History of the Sanskrit Language* (59–88). Ed. Jan E. M. Houben. Leiden: Brill.

Algeo, John. 1990 "Semantic Change." In *Research Guide on Language Change* (399–408). Ed. Edgar C. Polomé. Berlin: Mouton de Gruyter.

Allchin, Bridget. 1977. "Hunters, Pastoralists and Early Agriculturalists in South Asia."In *Hunters, Gatherers and First Farmers beyond Europe* (127–144). Ed. J. V. S. Megaw. Leicester: Leicester University Press.

——. 1997. "Editor's Note." *South Asian Archaeology* 13:316.

Allchin, Bridget, and Raymond Allchin. 1982. *The Rise of Civilization in India and Pakistan.* Cambridge: Cambridge University Press.

Allchin, F. R. 1993. "The Legacy of the Indus Civilization." In *Harappan Civilization* (385–393). Ed. Gregory Possehl. New Delhi: Oxford University Press.

——. 1995. *The Archaeology of Early Historic South Asia: The Emergence of Cities and States.* Cambridge: Cambridge University Press.

Alur, K. R. 1971. "Animal Remains." In *Protohistoric Cultures of the Tugabhadra Valley* (107–125). Ed. M. S. Nagaraja Rao. Dharwar: Rao.

——. "Aryan Invasion of India, Indo-Gangetic Valley Cultures." In *New Trends in Indian Art and Archaeology* (561–566). Ed. B. U. Nayak and N. C. Ghosh. New Delhi: Aditya Prakashan.

Ambedkar, B. R. 1946. *Who Were the Śudras?* Bombay: Thacker.

Ananth, Krishna V. 1997. "Distortion of History." *The Hindu,* January 8.

——. 1998. "The Aryan and Dravidian Myths." *The Hindu,* November 11.

Anderson, Benedict. 1983. *Imagined Communities.* London: Verso.

Andronov, M. 1964. "On the Typological Similarity of New Indo-Aryan and Dravidian." *India Linguistics: Journal of the Linguistic Society of India.* 25:119–126.

——. 1968. *Two Lectures on the Historicity of Language Families.* Annamalainagar: Annamalai University.

Anthony, David W. 1986. "The 'Kurgan Culture,' Indo-European Origins, and the Domestication of the Horse: A Reconsideration." *Current Anthropology* 27:291–313.

——. 1990. "Migration in Archaeology: The Baby and the Bathwater." *American Anthropologist* 92:895–914.

Anthony, David W. 1994. "The Earliest Horseback Riders and Indo-European Origins: New Evidence from the Steppes." *Die Indogermanen und das Pferd* (185–195). Ed. B. Hänsel and S. Zimmer. Budapest: Bernfried Schlerath.

——. 1995a. "Birth of the Chariot." *Archaeology* 48, no. 2:36–41.

——. 1995b. "Nazi and Eco-Feminist Prehistories: Ideology and Empiricism in Indo- European Archaeology." In *Nationalism, Politics and the Practice of Archaeology* (82–96). Ed. P. Kohl and C. Fawcett. Cambridge: Cambridge University Press.

——. 1997. "Prehistoric Migration as Social Process." In *Migrations and Invasions in Archaeological Explanation* (21–31). Ed. John Chapman and Helena Hamerow. BAR International Series 664. Oxford: Archaeopress.

——. 1998. "The Opening of the Eurasian Steppe at 2000 BCE." In *The Bronze Age and Early Iron Age Peoples of Eastern and Central Asia*" (1:94–113). Ed. Mair Institute for the Study of Man. Oxford: Archaeopress.

Anthony, David, Dimitri Y. Telegin, and Dorcas Brown. 1991. "The Origin of Horseback Riding." *Scientific American,* December, 94–100.

Anthony, David, and Bernard Wailes. 1988. Book review of *Archaeology and Language* by Colin Renfrew. *Current Anthropology* 29:441–445.

Antonini, Chiara S. 1963. "Preliminary Notes on the Excavation of the Necropolises Found in Western Pakistan." *East and West* 14:13–26.

——. 1969. "Swāt and Central Asia." *East and West* 9:100–115.

——. 1973. "More About Swāt and Central Asia." *East and West* 23:235–244.

Arya, R. P. 1993. "The Aryan Problem: A Linguistic Approach." In *The Aryan Problem* (51–57). Ed. S. B. Deo and Suryanath Kamath. Pune: Mythic Society.

Asimov, M. S. 1981. "Ethnic History of Central Asia in the 2nd Millennium B.C.: Soviet Studies." In *Ethnic Problems of the History of Central Asia in the Early Period* (44–52). Ed. Editorial Committee M.S. Asimov. Moscow: Nauka.

Aurobindo, Shri. 1956. *On the Veda.* Pondicherry: Shri Aurobindo Ashram.

——. 1971. *The Secret of the Veda.* Pondicherry: Shri Aurobindo Ashram.

Babayev, A. 1989. "West Pamir Cemeteries of Late Bronze Age and Their Connection with the Religions of Local Tribes." *International Association for the Study of the Cultures of Central Asia* 15:85–102.

Bailly, Jean-Sylvain. 1977. *Lettres sur l'origine des sciences et sur celle des peuples de l'Asie*. Paris: Frêres Debure.

——. 1805. *Histoire de l'astronomie ancienne et moderne*. Paris: L'Ecole Polytechnique.

Baldi, P. 1988. Review of *Archaeology and Language* by Colin Renfrew. *Current Anthropology* 29:445–447.

Banerjee, N. R. 1981. "The Use of Iron in the 2nd Millennium B.C. and Its Bearing on the Aryan Problem." In *Ethnic Problems of the History of Central Asia in the Early Period* (311–320). Moscow: Hayka.

Basham, A. L. 1959. *The Wonder That Was India*. New York: Grove Press.

——. 1989. *Classical Hinduism*. New York: Oxford University Press.

Beekes, Robert S. P. 1995. *Comparative Indo-European Linguistics: An Introduction*. Amsterdam: John Benjamins.

Bender, Harold H. 1922. *The Home of the Indo-Europeans*. Princeton, N.J.: Princeton University Press.

Bentley, J. 1799. "Remarks on the Principal Aeras and Dates of the Ancient Hindus." *Asiatic Researches* 5:315–343.

——. 1808. "On the Hindu Systems of Astronomy and Their Connection with History in Ancient and Modern Times." *Asiatic Researches* 8:195– 244.

——. [1825] 1981. *A Historical View of the Hindu Astronomy*. New Delhi: Cosmo Publications.

Bharadwaj, O. P. 1987. "The Vedic Sarasvatī." *Journal of Indological Studies* 2, nos. 1–2: 38–58.

Bharti, Brahm Datt. 1992. *Max Müller: A Lifelong Masquerade*. New Delhi: Erabooks.

——. 1961. "Animals of Prehistoric India and Their Affinities with those of the Western Asiatic Countries." *Records of the Indian Museum* 59:337–367.

——. 1963. "Advances in the Study of Prehistoric and Ancient Animal Remains in India: A Review." *Records of the Zoological Survey of India* 61:1–13.

Bisht, R. S. Forthcoming. "Harappans and the Ṛgveda: Points of Convergence." In *Dawn of Civilization*.

Blackwell. 1856. "The Arian Race." *Calcutta Review* LlI: 476–548.

Blavatsky, H. P. 1975. *From the Caves and Jungles of Hindostan*. Wheaton: Theosophical Publishing House. 1st ed 1892.

——. n.d. In *Ancient Survivals and Modern Errors*. Los Angeles: Theosophy.

Bloch, J. 1924. "Sanskrit et Dravidien." *Bulletin de la Societe de Linguistique de Paris* 76:1–21.

——. 1928–30. "Some Problems of Indo-Aryan Philology." *Bulletin of the School of Oriental Studies* 5:719–756.

——. "Brahui et Tsigne." *Journal of the Royal Asiatic Society* 199–201. Vol 12.

Bloomfield, Leonard. 1929. *Language* 267–276.

Blust, Robert. 1991. "Sound Change and Migration Distance." In *Currents in Pacific Linguistics* (27–43). Ed. Robert Blust. Australian National University.

Bökönyi, Sandor. 1997. "Horse Remains from the Prehistoric Site of Surkotada, Kutch, Late 3rd Millennium B.C." *South Asian Archaeology* 13:297–307.

Bond, George Clement, and Angela Gilliam, eds. 1994 *Social Construction of the Past*. London: Routledge.

Bongard-Levin, G. M. [1974] 1980. *The Origin of the Aryans*. Delhi: Arnold.

Bopp, F. n.d. "Analytical Comparison of the Sanskrit, Greek, Latin, and Teutonic Languages." *Annals of Oriental Literature* 5, no. 1:1–65.

Bosch-Gimpera, P. 1973. "The Migration Route of the Indo-Aryans." *Journal of Indo- European Studies* 1:513–517.

Boyce, Mary. 1992. *Zoroastrianism: Its Antiquity and Constant Vigour*. Costa Mesa, Calif.: Mazda.

Boyer, Carl B. 1989 *A History of Mathematics*. New York: Wiley.

Braarvig, Jens. 1997. "Horses and Ships in Vedic and Old Greek Material." *Journal of Indo-European Studies* 25:345–351.

Brentjes, B. 1981. "The Mitannians and the Peacock." In *Ethnic Problems of the History of Central Asia in the Early Period* (145–148). Moscow: Soviet Committee on the Study of Civilizations of Central Asia.

Brinton, Daniel G. 1890. *Races and Peoples.* New York: Hodges.

Bryant, E., and Patton, L. Forthcoming. *The Indo-Aryan Controversy: Evidence and Inference in Indian History.* Richmond: Curzon.

Buck, Carl Darling. 1949. *A Dictionary of the Selected Synonyms in the Principal Indo-European Languages.* Chicago: University of Chicago Press.

Bühler, G. 1894. "Note on Professor Jacobi's Age of the Veda and on Professor Tilak's Orion." *Indian Antiquary* 23:238–249.

Bunsen, Christian. 1854. *Philosophy of Universal History.* London: Longman.

Burrow, T. 1945. "Some Dravidian Words in Sanskrit." *Transactions of the Philological Society* 77–120.

——. 1946. "Loan Words in Sanskrit." *Transactions of the Philological Society* 1–30.

——. 1947–48. "Dravidian Studies VII: Further Dravidian Words in Sanskrit." *Bulletin of the School of Oriental and African Studies* 12:365–396.

——. "Sanskrit and the Pre-Aryan Tribes and Languages." Reprinted in *The Bulletin of the Ramakrishna Mission Institute of Culture* (Vol 8, 1956): 319–340.

——. 1963. "On the Significance of the Term *arma-, armaka-* in Early Sanskrit Literature." *Journal of Indian History* 41:159–166.

Burrow, T. 1968a. "Some Dravidian Loans in Sanskrit." *Collected Papers on Dravidian Linguistics* (236–284). Annamalai: Annamalai University.

——. 1968b. "Further Dravidian Loans in Sanskrit." *Collected Papers on Dravidian Linguistics* (178–235). Annamalai: Annamalai University.

——. 1968c. "Sanskrit and the Pre-Aryan Tribes and Languages." *Collected Papers on Dravidian Linguistics* (319–340). Annamalai: Annamalai University.

——. 1973a. "The Proto-Indo-Aryans." *Journal of the Royal Asiatic Society* 1:123–140.

——. 1973b *The Sanskrit Language.* 3rd ed. London: Faber and Faber.

——. 1976–77. Review of *The Meaning of* Pur *in Vedic Literature* by Wilhelm Rau. *Kratylos* 21:72–76.

——. 1983. "Notes on Some Dravidian Words in Sanskrit." *International Journal of Dravidian Linguistics* 12:8–14.

Caldwell, R. [1856] 1875. *Comparative Grammar of Dravidian or South Indian Languages.* London: Trübner.

Campbell, A. D. [1849] 1991. *A Grammar of the Teloogoo Language.* Madras: Asian Educational Services.

Campbell, Lyle. 1990. "Indo-European and Uralic Tree Names." *Diachronica* 7:149–180.

Chakrabarti, D. K. 1968. "The Aryan Hypothesis in Indian Archaeology." *Indian Studies Past and Present* 9:343–358.

——. 1976. "India and the Druids." *Antiquity* 197:66–67.

——. 1977a. " Distribution of Iron Ores and the Archaeological Evidence of Early Iron in India." *Journal of the Economic and Social History of the Orient* 20:166–184.

——. 1977b. "India and West Asia: An Alternative Approach." *Man and Environment* 1:25–38.

——. 1984a. "Archaeology and the Literary Tradition: An Examination of the Indian Context." *Archaeological Review from Cambridge* 3, no. 2:29–35.

——. 1984b "Origin of the Indus Civilization: Theories and Problems." In *Frontiers of the Indus Civilization* (43–50). Ed. B. B. Lal and S. P. Gupta. New Delhi: Books and Books.

——. 1986. "Further Notes on the Aryan Hypothesis in Indian Archaeology." In *Ṛtambharā Studies in Indology* (74–75). Ed. K. C. Varma et al. Kavinagar: Society for Indic Studies.

——. 1993–94. "The Iron Age in India: The Beginning and Consequences." *Puratattva* 24:12–25.

——. 1995. Review of "Deciphering the Indus Script," by Asko Parpola. *Journal of the Royal Asiatic Society*, 3d ser., 5, no. 3:428–430.

——. 1997 *Colonial Indology: The Sociopolitics of the Ancient Indian Past.* New Delhi: Munshiram Manoharlal.

Chakravarty, Apurba. 1975 *Origin and Development of Indian Calendrical Science.* Calcutta: Indian Studies.

Champion, T. C. 1990. "Migration Revived." *Journal of Danish Archaeology* 9:214–218.

Chandra, A. N. 1980. *The Rig-Vedic Culture and the Indus Civilisation.* Calcutta: Ratna Prakashan.

Chandra, Bipan. 1984. *Communalism in Modern India.* New Delhi: Vikas.

Chapman, John. 1997."The Impact of Modern Invasion and Migrations on Archaeological Explanation." In *Migrations and Invasions in Archaeological Explanation*" (11–20). Ed. John Chapman and Helena Hamerow. BAR International Series 664. Oxford: Archaeopress.

Chapman, John, and Helena Hamerow, eds. 1977. *Migrations and Invasions in Archaeological Explanation.* BAR International Series 664. Oxford: Archaeopress.

Chatterji, S. K. [1926] 1993. *The Origin and Development of the Bengali Language.* Calcutta: Rupa.

Chattopadhyaya, Aghorechandra. 1901. *The Original Abode of the Indo-European Races.* Calcutta: Sanyal.

Chaṭṭopādhyāya, Kshetres Chandra. 1986. *Ṛgvedic Sarasvatī.* New Delhi: Northern.

Chernykh, E. N. 1995. "Postscript: Russian Archaeology after the Collapse of the USSR: Infrastructural Crisis and the Resurgence of Old and New Nationalisms." In *Nationalism, Politics and the Practice of Archaeology* (120–138). Ed. P. Kohl and C. Fawcett. Cambridge: Cambridge University Press.

Childe, Gordon V. 1926. *The Aryans.* London: Paul.

Choudhury, Paramesh. 1993. *The Aryans: A Modern Myth.* New Delhi: S. Chakraborty.

——. 1995. *The Aryan Hoax.* Calcutta: Choudhury.

Cleuziou, Serge. 1986. "Tureng Tepe and Burnished Grey Ware: A Question of 'Frontier'?" *Oriens Antiquus* 25:221–256.

Colebrooke, H. T. 1803."On the Religious Views of the Hindus." *Asiatic Review* 7:232–312.

Coleman, Robert. 1988. Book review of *Archaeology and Language* by Colin Renfrew. *Current Anthropology* 29:449–453.

Collinder, Björn. 1977. *Fenno-Ugric Vocabulary: An Etymological Dictionary of the Uralic Languages.* Hamburg: Bjorn.

Crossland, Ronald. 1971. "Immigrants from the North." In *The Cambridge Ancient History* (vol I, pt 2, 824–876, 989–993). Ed. I. E. S. Edwards et al. Cambridge: Cambridge University Press.

——. 1972. "Recent Reappraisal of Evidence for the Chronology of the Differentiation of Indo-European." In *Acta of the 2nd International Colloquium on Aegean Prehistory* (46–55). Athens: Ministry of Culture and Science.

——. 1988. "Review in: *Book Review: Archaeology and Language. Current Anthropology* 29:437–468.

——. 1992. "When Specialists Collide: Archaeology and Indo-European Linguistics." *Antiquity* 66:251–260.

Curzon, A. 1855. "On the Original Extension of the Sanskrit Language over Certain Portions of Asia and Europe." *Journal of the Royal Asiatic Society* 16:172–201.

Dales, George F. 1964. "The Mythical Massacre at Mohenjo-Dara." *Expedition* 6, no. 3: 36–43.

——. 1966. "The Decline of the Harappans." *Scientific American*, 241 (July-Dec) 92–99.

Dani, A. H. 1968. *Timargarha and Gandhara Grave Culture*. Ancient Pakistan. no. 3. Peshawar, Pakistan: Department of Archaeology, University of Peshawar.

——. 1978. "Gandhara Grave Culture and the Aryan Problem." *Journal of Central Asia* 1:42–55.

——. 1992. "Pastoral-Agricultural Tribes of Pakistan in the Post-Indus Period."In *History of the Civilizations of Central Asia* (395–419). Ed. A. H. Dani and V. M. Masson Paris: UNESCO.

Das, Abhinas Chandra. [1920] 1980. *Rgvedic India*. New Delhi: Cosmo Publications.

Das, R. P. 1995. "The Hunt for Foreign Words in the Ṛgveda." *Indo-Iranian Journal* 38:207–238.

Das, Satyanarayan, and Sunanda Das. 1987. *Dravidian in North Indian Topography*. Varanasi: All India.

Das, Shukavak. 1996–97. "Bhaktivinode and the Problem of Modernity." *Journal of Vaishnava Studies* 5:127–150.

Dasgupta, Probal. 1982. "On Conceiving of South Asia as a Linguistic Area." *Indian Linguistics: Journal of the Linguistic Society of India* 43, nos.3–4:37–48.

Datta, Bhupendra Nath. 1936–37. "Vedic Funeral Customs and Indus Valley." Parts 1 and 2. *Man in India* 16:223–307; 17:1–68.

Davies, Anna Morpurgo. 1998. "Nineteenth-Century Lingusitics." In *History of Linguistics*, Vol. 4. Ed. G. Lepschy. London: Longman.

Day, John V. 1994. "The Concept of the Aryan Race in Nineteenth-Century Scholarship." *Orpheus* 4:15–48.

Décsy, Gyula. 1991. *The Indo-European Protolanguage*. Bloomington: Eurolingua.

Deendayal Research Institute. n.d. *Towards a New Horizon*. [Delhi]: n.p.

Demoule, Jean-Paul.1980. "Les Indo-Européens: Ont-ils existé?" *L'Histoire* 28:108–120.

Deo, S. B., and Suryanath Kamath, eds. 1993. *The Aryan Problem*. Pune: Bharatiya Itihasa Sankalana Samiti.

Deppert, Joachim. 1977. *Rudras Geburt*. Wiesbaden: Steiner.

Deshayes, Jean. 1969. "New Evidence for the Indo-Europeans from Tureng Tepe, Iran." *Archaeology* 22:10–17.

Deshmukh, P. R. 1982. *Indus Civilization, Rigveda and Hindu Culture*. Nagpur: Saroj Prakashan.

Deshpande, Madhav M. 1979. "Genesis of Ṛgvedic Retroflexion: A Historical and Sociolinguistic Investigation." In *Aryan and Non-Aryan in India* (235–315). Ed. M. Deshpande and P. Hook. Ann Arbor: University of Michigan Press.

——. "Aryan, Non-Aryans, and Brāhmaṇas: Processes of Indigenization." *Journal of Indo-European Studies* 21:215–236.

Devendraswarup. 1993. "Genesis of the Aryan Race Theory and Its Application to Indian History." In *The Aryan Problem* (30–39). Ed. S. B. Deo and Kamath Suryanath. Pune: Bharatiya Itihasa Sankalana Samiti.

Dhar, Lachhmi. 1930. *The Home of the Aryas*. Delhi: Delhi University Publications.

Dhavalikar, M. K. 1995. "Fire Altars or Fire Pits?" In *Śrī Nāgābhinandanam*. Ed. V. Shivananda and M. V. Visweswara. Bangalore: Nagaraja Rao.

D'iakonov, I. M. 1985. "On the Original Home of the Speakers of Indo-European." *Journal of Indo-European Studies* 13, nos. 1–2:92–174.

——. 1988. Review of *Annual of Armenian Linguistics* by Colin Renfrew. *Current Anthropology* 9:79–87.

——. 1990. "Language Contacts in the Caucasus and the Near East." In *When Worlds Collide* (53–65). Ed. T. L. Markey and J. Greppin. Ann Arbor: Karoma.

——. 1997. External Connections of the Sumerian Language." *Mother Tongue* 3:54–62.

Diebold, Richard A., Jr. 1985. "The Evolution of Indo-European Nomenclature for Salmonid Fish: The Case of 'Huchen.'" *Journal of Indo-European Studies* 5:1–65.

——. 1987. "Linguistic Ways to Prehistory." In *Proto-Indo-European: The Archaeology of a Linguistic Problem* (19–71). Ed. Susan Skomal and Edgar Polomé. Washington, D.C.: Institute for the Study of Man.

——. 1991. *The Indo-European Protolanguage*. Bloomington, Ind.: Eurolingua.

——. 1992. "The Traditional View of the Indo-European Palaeoeconomy: Contradictory Evidence from Anthropology and Linguistics." *In Reconstructing Languages and Cultures* (317–367). Ed. Edgar C. Polomé and Werner Winters. Berlin: Mouton de Gruyter.

Diehl, Anita. 1978. *Periyar E. V. Ramaswami*. New Delhi: B. I. Publications.

Dikshit, K. N. 1985. "The Antiquity of Iron in India." *International Association for the Study of the Cultures of Central Asia Information Bulletin* 8:51–60.

Dikshit, Sankar B. 1985. "The Age of the Satapatha Brahmana." *Indian Antiquary* 24:245–246.

Dixon, R. M. W. 1997. *The Rise and Fall of Languages*. Cambridge: Cambridge University Press.

Dogra, S. D. 1973–74. "Horse in Ancient India." *Journal of the Oriental Institute* 23:54–58.

Dolgopolsky, Aron. 1987. "The Indo-European Homeland and Lexical Contacts of Proto-Indo-European with Other Languages." *Mediterranean Language Review* 3:7–31.

——. 1989. "Cultural Contacts of Proto-Indo-European and Proto-Indo-Iranian with Neighbouring Languages." *Folia Linguistica Historica* 8, nos. 1–2:3– 36.

——. 1990–93. "More about the Indo-European Homeland Problem." *Mediterranean Language Review* 6–7:230–248.

Drews, Robert. 1997. "PIE Speakers and PA Speakers." *Journal of Indo-European Studies* 25:153–177.

Duff, Rev. Alexander. 1840. *Missions: The Chief End of the Christian Church*. Edinburgh: Johnstone.

Dumont, P. E. 1948. *Aram Naharaim*. Analecta Orientalia 26. Calcutta: A. K. Bose.

Dyen, I. 1956. "Language Distribution and Migration Theory." *Language* 32:611–627.

——. 1965. "A Lexicostatistical Classification of the Austronesian Languages." *International Journal of American Linguistics* (suppl.) 31:1–64.

Dyen, Isidore, Joseph B. Kruskal, and Paul Black. 1992. "An Indoeuropean Classification: A Lexicostatistical Experiment." *Transactions of the American Philosophical Society* 82:1–132.

Dyson, Robert H., Jr. 1968. "The Archaeological Evidence of the Second Millennium B.C. on the Persian Plateau." In *The Cambridge Ancient History* (2:3–36). Ed. I. Edwards et al. Cambridge: Cambridge University Press.

——. 1993. "Paradigm Changes in the Study of the Indus Civilization." In *Harappan Civilization* (571–581). Ed. Gregory L. Possehl. 2d ed. New Delhi: Oxford University Press.

Ehret, Christopher. 1988. "Language Change and the Material Correlates of Language and Ethnic Shift." *Antiquity* 62:564–574.

Eichhoff, E. W. 1845. *Vergleichung der Sprachen von Europa und Indien*. Leipzig: Schrey.

Elfenbein, Josef. 1987. "A Periplus of the 'Brahui Problem.'" *Studia Iranica* 6:215–233.

Elizarenkova, T. Y. 1989. "About Traces of a Prakrit Dialectal Basis in the Language of the Ṛgveda." In *Dialects dans les Littérateurs Indo-Aryennes* (1–17). Ed. Colette Caillat. Paris: Institut de Civilisation Indienne.

——. 1992."Wörter und Sachen." In *Ritual, State and History in South Asia* (128–141). Ed. A. vanden Hoek, D. Kolff, and M. Dort. Leiden: Brill.

——. 1996–97. "The Concept of Water and the Names for It in the Ṛgveda." *Orientalia Suecana* 45–46:21–29.

Ellis, Francis Whyte. 1816. Note to the introduction. In A. D. Campbell, 1816. 1–20.

Elphinstone, Mountstuart. 1841. *History of India*. London: Murray.

Elst, Koenraad. 1993. *Indigenous Aryans*. New Delhi: Voice of India.

——. 1996. *Linguistics and the Aryan and Non-Aryan Invasion Theory*. Privately published: Leuven.

Embleton, Sheila. 1991. "Mathematical Methods of Genetic Classification." In *Sprung from Some Common Source* (365–387). Ed. Sydney M. Lamb and E. Douglas Mitchell. Stanford, Calif.: Stanford University Press.

Emeneau, M. 1954. "Linguistic Prehistory of India." *Proceedings of the Amercican Philosophical Society* 98:282–292.

——. 1956. "India as a Linguistic Area." *Language* 32:3–16.

——. 1962a. "Bilingualism and Structural Borrowing." *Proceedings of the American Philological Society* 106:430–442.

——. 1962b. *Brahui and Dravidian Comparative Grammar.* Berkeley: University of California Press.

——. 1966. "The Dialects of Old Indo-Aryan." In *Ancient Indo-European Dialects* (123–138). Ed. Henrik Birnbaum and Jaan Puhvel. Berkeley: University of California Press.

——. 1969. "Onomatopoetics in the Indian Linguistic Area." *Language* 45:274– 299.

——. 1971. "Dravidian and Indo-Aryan: The Indian Linguistic Area." In *Symposium on Dravidian Civilization* (33–68). Ed. Andrée F. Sjoberg. Austin, Tex.: Jenkins.

——. 1973. *Historical Linguistics: An Introduction.* New York: Holt.

——. 1974. "The Indian Linguistic Area Revisited." *International Journal of Dravidian Linguistics* 3:92–134.

——. 1980. *Language and Linguistic Area.* Stanford, Calif.: Stanford University Press.

Erdosy, George. 1989. "Ethnicity in the Rigveda and Its Bearing on the Question of Indo-European Origins." *South Asian Studies* 5:35–47.

——. 1995a. "Language, Material Culture and Ethnicity: Theoretical Perspectives." In *The Indo-Aryans of Ancient South Asia* (1–31). Ed. George Erdosy. Berlin: Mouton de Gruyter.

——. 1995b. Preface to *The Indo-Aryans of Ancient South Asia* (x–xvii). Ed. George Erdosy. Berlin: Mouton de Gruyter.

Evolution of Early Indian Society. 1990. Vol 3. Delhi: Indira Gandhi National Open University.

Fairservis, Walter A., Jr. 1961. "The Harappan Civilization: New Evidence and More Theory." *Novitates* 2055:1–35.

——. 1992. *The Harappan Civilization and Its Writing.* New Delhi: Oxford University Press.

——. 1995. "Central Asia and the Ṛgveda: The Archaeological Evidence." In *The Indo- Aryans of Ancient South Asia* (206–212). Ed. George Erdosy. Berlin: Mouton de Gruyter.

——. 1997. "The Harappan Civilization and the Ṛgveda." In *Inside the Texts beyond the Texts.* (61–68). Harvard Oriental Series. Opera Minora (2:61–68). Ed. M. Witzel. Cambridge: Department of Sanskrit and Indian Studies, Harvard University.

Farrer, Rev. Frederic. 1870. *Families of Speech: Four Lectures.* London: Longmans.

Febvre, Lucien. 1946. *Michelet.* Paris: Traits.

Feist, Sigmund. 1932. "The Origin of the Germanic Languages and the Indo-Europeanising of North Europe." *Language* 8:245–254.

Feuerstein, George, Subhash Kak, and David Frawley. 1995. *In Search of the Cradle of Civilization.* Wheaton, Ill.: Quest.

Figueira, Dorothy. 1994. *The Exotic: A Decadent Quest.* Albany: State University of New York Press.

Filliozat, Jean. 1969. "Notes on Ancient Iranian and Indian Astronomy." *Journal of the K. R. Cama Oriental Research Institute* 42:100–135.

Flood, Gavin. 1996. *An Introduction to Hinduism.* Cambridge: Cambridge University Press.

Francfort, Henri-Paul. 1985. "The Indo-French Archaeological Project in Haryana and Rajasthan." In *South Asian Archaeology* (260–264). Ed. K. Frifelt and P. Sørenson.

——. 1989. *Fouilles de Shortughaï. Recherches sur l'asie Centrale Protohistorique.* Paris: Diffusion.

——. 1992. "Evidence for Harappan Irrigation System in Haryana and Rajasthan." *Eastern Anthropologist* 45:87–103.

Fraser, J. 1926. "Linguistic Evidence and Archaeological and Ethnological Facts." *Proceedings of the British Academy* 12:257–272.

Frawley, D. 1991. *Gods, Sages and Kings.* Salt Lake City, Utah: Passage Press.

——. 1995. *The Myth of the Aryan Invasion of India.* New Delhi: Voice of India.

Friedrich, Paul. 1970. *Proto-Indo-European Trees.* Chicago: University of Chicago Press.

Gamkrelidze, Thomas V., and Vjaceslav V. Ivanov. 1983a. "The Ancient Near East and the Indo-European Problem: Temporal and Territorial Characteristics of Proto-Indo-European Based on Linguistic and Historico-Cultural Data." *Soviet Studies in History* 22:7–52.

——. 1983b. "The Migration of Tribes Speaking the Indo-European Dialects from Their Original Homeland in the Near East to Their Habitations in Eurasia." *Soviet Studies in History* 22: 53–95.

——. 1985a. "The Problem of the Original Homeland of the Speakers of Indo-European Languages." *Journal of Indo-European Studies* 13:174–184.

——. 1985b. "Response to I. M. Diakonoff (1982)." *Journal of Indo-European Studies* 13:175–202.

——. 1990a. "The Early History of Indo-European Languages." *Scientific American*, March, 110–116.

——. 1990b. "On the Problem of an Asiatic Original Homeland of the Proto-Indo-Europeans." In *When Worlds Collide.* Ed. T. Markey and J. Greppin. Ann Arbor: Karoma.

——. 1995. *The Indo-European and the Indo-Europeans.* Trends in Linguistics Studies and Monographs 80. Berlin: Mouton and Gruyter.

Gaur, R. C. 1980–81. "The Aryans: A Fresh Appraisal." *Puratattva* 12:133–135.

——. 1993. *Excavations at Atranjīkherā.* Delhi: Motilal.

Gathercole, P., and D. Lowenthal. 1990. *The Politics of the Past.* London: Unwin Hyman.

Geiger, L. 1878. *Zur Enwicklungsgeschichte der Menschheit.* Stuttgart: Berlag.

Gellner, Ernest. 1983. *Nations and Nationalism.* Oxford: Oxford University Press.

Gening, V. F. 1979. "The Cemetery at Sintashta and the Early Indo-Iranian Peoples." *Journal of Indo-European Studies* 7:1–29.

Ghirshman, R. 1977. *L'Iran et la migration des Indo-Aryens et des Iraniens.* Leiden: Brill.

Ghose, Bimal, et al., 1979. "The Lost Courses of the Saraswati River in the Great Indian Desert: New Evidence from Landsat Imagery." *Geographical Journal* 145:446–451.

Ghosh, A. 1989a. *An Encyclopaedia of Indian Archaeology.* Vol 1. New Delhi: Munshiram Manoharlal.

——. 1989b."The Rajputana Desert: Its Archaeological Aspect." In *An Archaeological Tour along the Ghaggar-Hakra River* (98–106). Ed. S. P.Gupta. Meerut: Kusumanjali Prakashan.

Gidwani, Bhagavan S. 1994. *Return of the Aryans.* Delhi: Penguin.

Giles, P. 1922. "The Aryans." In *Cambridge History of India* (1:65–76). Ed. E. J. Rapson. Cambridge: Cambridge University Press.

Gimbutas, M. 1966. "Proto-Indo-Europan Culture: The Kurgan Culture during the Fifth, Fourth, and Third Millennia B.C." In *Indo-European and Indo-Europeans* (155–197). Ed. George Cordona, Henry Hoenigswald, and Alfred Senn. Philadelphia: University of Pennsylvania Press.

——. 1974. "An Archaeologist's View of PIE in 1975." *Journal of Indo-European Studies* 2:289–307.

——. 1977. "The First Wave of Eurasian Steppe Pastoralists into Copper Age Europe." *Journal of Indo-European Studies* 5:277–338.

——. 1985. "Primary and Secondary Homeland of the Indo-Europeans." *Journal of Indo-European Studies* 13:185–202.

——. 1997. *The Kurgan Culture and the Indo-Europeanization of Europe.* Ed. Miriam Dexter and Karlene Jones-Bley. Washington, D.C.: Institute for the Study of Man.

Gnoli, G. 1980. *Zoroaster's Time and Homeland.* Naples: Istituto Universitario Orientale.

Godgole, Krishna Shastri. 1881. "Antiquity of the Veda." *The Theosophist*, October, 22–24, 34–35, 72–74, 125–127.

Gokhale, Gopal Krishna. 1920. *Speeches*. Madras: Natesan.

Goldstücker, Theodore. [1860] 1965. *Pāṇini*. Varanasi: Chowkhamba Sanskrit Series Office.

Golwalkar, M. S. 1947. *We, or Our Nation Defined*. Nagpur.

——. [1966] 1988. *Bunch of Thoughts*. Bangalore: Jagarana Prakashana.

Gonda, Jan. 1975. *Vedic Literature*. Vol. 1 of *A History of Indian Literature*. Ed. Jan Gonda. Wiesbaden: Otto Harrassowitz.

Goodenough, Ward H. 1966. "The Evolution of Pastoralism and Indo-European Origins." In *Indo-European and Indo-Europeans* (253–265). Ed. G. Cardona, H. Hoenigswald, and A. Senn. Philadelphia: University of Pennsylvania Press.

Grant, Charles. [1790] 1970. "Observations on the State of Society among the Asiatic subjects of Great Britain, particularly 'with respect to morals; and on the means of improving it, written chiefly in the year 1792.' Report on the Select Committee on the Affairs of the East India Company 1831–32." Reprinted as *Irish University Press Series of British Parliamentary Papers Colonies: East India*. Vol. 5. Shannon: Irish University Press.

Grantovsky, E. A. 1981. "'Grey Ware,' 'Painted Ware' and the Indo-Iranians." In *Ethnic Problems of the History of Central Asia in the Early Period* (245–276). Ed. M. S. Asimov. Moscow.

Grassmann, Hermann. 1963. "Über die Aspiraten und ihr gleichzeitiges Vorhandensein im An- und Auslaute der Wurzeln." *Zeitschrift für Vergleichende Sprachforschung* 12:81–138.

Graves-Brown, Paul, et al., eds. 1996. *Cultural Identity and Archaeology*. London: Routledge.

Grierson, George. 1903. *The Languages of India*. Calcutta: Office of the Superintendent.

Griffith, T. H. 1973. *The Hymns of the Rgveda*. Delhi: Motilal.

Growse, F. S. 1883. *Mathura: A District Memoir*. N.p.

Guha, B. S., and B. K.Chatterjee. 1946. "Report on the Skeleton Remains." Part 2 of "A Chalcolithic Site in Northern Baluchistan" by E. J. Ross. *Journal of Near Eastern Studies* 5:315–316.

Gundert, H. 1869. "On the Dravidian Element in Sanskrit." *Journal of the German Oriental Society* 23:17–28.

Gupta, S. P. 1979. *Archaeology of Soviet Central Asia and the Indian Borderlands*. 2 vols. Delhi: D. K. Publishers.

——. 1993a. "The Late Harappan: A Study in Cultural Dynamics." In *Harappan Civilization* (51–58). Ed. Gregory L. Possehl. Delhi: American Institute of Indian Studies: Oxford: I.B.H. Publishing.

——. 1993b. "Palaeo-Anthropolgy and Archaeology of the Vedic Aryans." In *The Aryan Problem* (153–165). Ed. S. P. Gupta and Suryanath Kamath. Pune: Bharatiya Itihasa Sankalana Samiti.

——. 1996. *The Indus Sarasvati Civilization*. Delhi: Pratibha Prakashan.

——, ed. 1989. *An Archaeological Tour along the Ghaggar Hakra River*. Meerut: Kusumanjali Prakashan.

Gurumurthy, S. 1994. *Graffiti on the Ancient Indian Pottery and the Decipherment of the Indus Script*. Tract. Madras: Department of Ancient History and Archaeology.

Haarmann, Harold. 1994. "Contact Linguistics: Archaeology and Ethnogenetics: An Interdisciplinary Approach to the Indo-European Homeland Problem." *Journal of Indo-European Studies* 22:265–289.

——. 1996. "Aspects of Early Indo-European Contacts with Neighboring Cultures." *Indogermanische Forschungen* 101:1–14.

——. 1998. "On the Problem of Primary and Secondary Diffusion of Indo-Europeans and Their Languages." *Journal of Indo-European Studies* 26:391–419.

Habib, Irfan. 1997. "Distortion of History." *The Hindu*, August 1, 12.

Hainsworth, J. B. 1972. "Some Observations on the Indo-European Place Names of Greece."

Acta of the 2nd International Colloquium on Aegean Prehistory (39–45). Athens: Ministry of Culture and Science

Halle, Morris. 1977. "Towards a Reconstruction of the Indo-European Accent."Ed. L. Hyman. *Studies in Stress and Accent* (209–239). Southern California Occasional Papers in Linguistics 4. Los Angeles: Department of Linguistics, University of Southern California.

Hamp, Eric P. 1973. "Language and Prehistory." *Science* 179:1279–1280.

——. 1990a. "The Indo-European Horse." In *When Worlds Collide* (211–226). Ed. T. L. Markey and John Greppin. Ann Arbor: Karoma.

——. 1990b. "The Pre-Indo-European Language of Northern (Central) Europe." In *When Worlds Collide* (291–309). Ed. T. L. Markey and John Greppin. Ann Arbor: Karoma.

——. 1996. "On the Indo-European Origins of the Retroflexes in Sanskrit." *Journal of the American Oriental Society* 116:719–723.

Hankins, Frank H. 1948. "Aryans." In *Encyclopaedia of the Social Sciences.*

Härke, Heinrich. 1991. "All Quiet on the Western Front? Paradigms, Methods and Approaches in West German Archaeology." In *Archaeological Theory in Europe* (187–222). Ed. Ian Hodder. London: Routledge.

Harmatta, J. 1981. "Proto-Iranians and Proto-Indians in Central Asia in the 2nd Millennium BC (Linguistic Evidence)." In *Ethnic Problems of the History of Central Asia in the Early Period* Ed. M. S. Asimov (75–82). Moscow: Nauka.

——. 1992. "The Emergence of the Indo-Iranians: The Indo-Iranian Languages." In *History of Civilizations of Central Asia* (1:357–378). Ed. A. H. Dani and V. M. Masson. UNESCO.

Harris, Alice C. 1990. "Kartvelian Contacts with Indo-European." In *When Worlds Collide.* Ann Arbor: Karoma.

Hastie, W. 1882. *Hindu Idolatry and English Enlightenment.* Calcutta: Thacker.

Havell, E. B. 1918. *The History of Aryan Rule in India.* London.

Heine-Geldern, Robert. 1936. "Archaeological Traces of the Vedic Aryans." *Journal of the Indian Society of Oriental Art* 4, no. 2:23–113.

Hemphill, Brian E., et al. 1991. "Biological Adaptions and Affinities of Bronze Age Harappans." In *Harappan Excavations, 1986–1990* (137–182). Ed. Richard H. Meadow. Madison, Wis.: Prehistory Press.

Herder, J. G. 1803. *Outlines of a Philosophy of Man.* Trans. T. Churchill. London.

Hicks, Harry H., and Robert N. Anderson. 1990. "Analysis of an Indo-European Vedic Aryan Head: 4th Millennium B.C." *Journal of Indo-European Studies* 18:425–446.

Hiebert, Fredrik T. 1995. "South Asia from a Central Asian Perspective." In *The Indo-Aryans of Ancient South Asia* (192–205). Ed. George Erdosy. New York: Walter de Gruyter.

——. 1998. "Central Asians on the Iranian Plateau: A Model for Indo-Iranian Expansion." In *The Bronze Age and Early Iron Age Peoples of Eastern and Central Asia* 1:148–161. Ed. Mair. Washington D. C.: Institute for the Study of Man.

Hiebert, Fredrik T., and C. C. Lamberg-Karlovsky. 1992. "Central Asia and the Indo-Iranian Borderlands." *Iran* 30:1–15.

High School Itihas. 1993. Delhi: National Council for Educational Research and Training.

Hillebrandt, Albert. 1913. *Lieder des Ṛgveda.* Göttingen: Vandenhoeck.

Hiltebeital, Alf. 1978. "The Indus Valley 'Proto-Śiva,' Reexamined through Reflections on the Goddess, the Buffalo, and the Symbolism of *Vāhanas.*" *Anthropos* 73:767–797.

Hlopina, L. I. 1972. "Southern Turkmenia in the Late Bronze Age." *East and West* 22:199–213.

Hobsbawn, E. J. 1990. *Nations and Nationalism since 1780.* Cambridge: Cambridge University Press.

Hobsbawn Eric, and Terence Ranger, eds. 1993. *The Invention of Tradition.* Cambridge: Cambridge University Press, 1993.

Hock, Hans Henrich. 1975. "Substratum Influence on (Rig-Vedic) Sanskrit?" *Studies in the Linguistic Sciences* 5, no. 2:76–125.

——. 1979. "Retroflexion Rules in Sanskrit." *South Asian Languages Analysis* 1:47–62.

——. 1982a. "Aux-Clitization as a Motivation for Word Order Change." *Studies in the Linguistic Sciences* 12, no. 1:91–101.

——. 1982b. "The Sanskrit Quotative: A Historical and Comparative Study." *Studies in the Linguistic Sciences* 12, no. 2:39–85.

——. 1984a. "(Pre-)Rigvedic Convergence of Indo-Aryan with Dravidian? Another Look at the Evidence." *Studies in the Linguistic Sciences* 14, no. 1:89–107.

——. 1984b. *Principles of Historical Linguistics*. Berlin: Mouton de Gruyter.

——. 1993. "Subversion or Convergence? The Issue of Pre-Vedic Retroflexion Reexamined." *Studies in the Linguistic Sciences* 23, no. 2:73–115.

——. 1996. "Pre-Ṛgvedic Convergence between Indo-Aryan and Dravidian? A Survey of the Issues and Controversies." In *Ideology and Status of Sanskrit* (17–58). Ed. Jan E. M. Houben. Leiden: Brill.

——. 1999a. "Out of India? The Linguistic Evidence." In *Aryan and Non-Aryan in South Asia* (1–18). Harvard Oriental Series Opera Minora 3. Ed. J. Bronkhorst and M. Deshpande. Cambridge: Department of Sanskrit and Indian Studies, Harvard University.

——. 1999b. "Through a Glass Darkly: Modern "Racial" Interpretations vs. Textual and General Prehistoric Evidence on Ārya and Dāsa/Dasyu in Vedic Indo-Aryan Society." In *Aryan and Non-Aryan in South Asia* (145–174). Harvard Oriental Series Opera Minora 3. Ed. J. Bronkhorst and M. Deshpande. Cambridge: Department of Sanskrit and Indian Studies, Harvard University.

Hodge, Carleton T. 1981. "Indo-Europeans in the Near East." *Anthropological Linguistics* 23:227–244.

Hodgson, B. H. 1848. "The Aborigines of Central India." *Journal of the Asiatic Society of Bengal* 17:550–558.

Hoernle, A. F. R. 1880. *A Comparative Grammar of the Gaudian Languages*. London: Trübner.

Humbach, H. 1991. *The Gāthās of Zarathustra*. Heidelberg: Carl Winter.

Hunter, W. W. 1897. *Annals of Rural Bengal*. London.

Imam, Abu. 1966. *Sir Alexander Cunningham and the Beginnings of Indian Archaeology*. Dacca: Asiatic Society of Pakistan.

Imperial Gazatteer of India: The Indian Empire. 1909. Vol. 1. Oxford: Clarendon Press.

Irschick, Eugene F. 1971. "Dravidianism in South Indian Politics." In *Symposium on Dravidian Civilization* (148–169). Ed. A. Sjoberg. Austin: Jenkins.

Ivanov, Vyacheslav. 1999. "Comparative Notes on Hurro-Urartian, Northern Caucasian and Indo-European." *UCLA Indo-European Studies* 1:147–264.

Iyengar, S. 1914. "Did the Dravidians of India Obtain Their Culture from Aryan Immigrant [*sic*]." *Anthropos* 1–15.

Jacobi, H. 1894. "Beitrage zur Kenntnis der Vedischen Chronologie." *Nachrichten von der Königl. Gesellschaft der Wissenschaften* 105–115.

——. 1895. "Der Vedische Kalender und das Alter des Veda." *Zeitschrift der Deutschen Morgenländischen Gesellschaft* 218–230.

——. 1909. "On the Antiquity of Vedic Culture." *Journal of the Royal Asiatic Society* 721–726.

——. 1910. "The Antiquity of Vedic Culture." *Journal of the Royal Asiatic Society* 456–467.

Jacobi, Hermann. 1984. "The Gaina Sutras." in *Sacred Books of the East*, Vol 22. Oxford: Clarendon Press.

Jaffrelot, Christophe. 1995. "The Ideas of the Hindu Race in the Writings of Hindu Nationalist Ideologues in the 1920s and 1930s: A Concept between Two Cultures." In *The Concept of Race in South Asia*. Ed. Peter Robb. Delhi: Oxford University Press.

Jamison, S. 1989. Review of *The Sanskrit Gerund: A Synchronic, Diachronic and Typological Analysis*, by B. Tikkanen. *Journal of the American Oriental Society* 109, no. 3:459–461.
Jarrige, Jean Françoise. 1973. "La Fin de la Civilisation Harappeenne." *Paleorient* 1:2.
——. 1985. "Continuity and Change in the North Kachi Plain at the Beginning of the Second Millennium BC." In *South Asian Archaeology* (35–68). Ed. Janine Schotsmans and Maurizio Taddei. Naples: Istituto Universitario Orientale.
——. 1989. "Excavations at Nausharo 1987–88." *Pakistan Archaeology* 24:21–67.
Jarrige, Jean-Francoise. 1994 "The Final Phase of the Indus Occupation at Nausharo and Its Connection with the Following Cultural Complex of Mehrgarh VIII." *South Asian Archaeology* (295–313). Ed. A. Parpola & P. Koskikallio. Helsinki: Suomalainen Tiedeakatemia.
Jarrige, Jean Francois, and Usman Hassan. (1989) "Funerary Complexes in Baluchistan at the End of the Third Millennium in the Light of Recent Discoveries at Mehrgarh and Quetta." *South Asian Archaeology* (150–166). Ed. Karen Frifelt and Per Sorensen. Naples: Instituto Universitario Orientale.
Jarrige, Jean Fançois, and Richard H. Meadows. 1980. "The Antecedents of Civilization in the Indus Valley." *Scientific American*, August, 122–133.
Jarrige, J. F., et al. In press. "Excavations at Mehrgarh-Nausharo, 16th to 20th Seasons."
Jespersen, Otto. 1922. *Language: Its Nature, Development and Origin*. London: Allen.
Jettmar, K. 1981."Fortified 'Ceremonial Centres' of the Indo-Iranians." In *Ethnic Problems of the History of Central Asia in the Early Period* (75–82). Ed. M. S. Asimov. Moscow: Nauka.
Jha, Ganganatha. 1940. "'Aryan Invasion of India': Is It a Myth?" In *D. R. Bhandarkar*, Vol. 1–2. Ed. Bimala Churn Law. Calcutta: Indian Research Institute.
Joki, Aulis J. 1973. *Uralier und Indogermanen*. Helsinki: Suomalis.
Jones, W. 1788. "On the Gods of Greece, Italy, and India." *Asiatic Researches* 1:221–275.
——. 1790a. "On the Chronology of the Hindu." *Asiatic Researches* 2:111–147.
——. 1790b. "A Supplement to the Essay on Indian Chronology." *Asiatic Researches* 2:391–403.
——. 1792. "On the Origin and Families of Nations." *Asiatic Researches* 3. Reprinted in *The Collected Works of Sir William Jones* (185–204). New York: New York University Press, 1993.
Jonsson, Hans. 1978. *The Laryngeal Theory*. Lund: Skrifter Utgivna.
Kaiser, Timothy. 1995. "Archaeology and Ideology in Southeast Europe. In *Nationalism, Politics and the Practice of Archaeology* (99–119). Ed. Philip Kohl and Clare Fawcett. Cambridge: Cambridge University Press.
Kak, Subhash C. 1987a. "On the Decipherment of the Indus Script: A Preliminary Study of Its Connection with Brahmi." *Indian Journal of History of Science* 22:51–62.
——. 1987b. "The Study of the Indus Script." *Cryptologia* 11:182–191.
——. 1988. "A Frequency Analysis of the Indus Script." *Cryptologia* 12:129–143.
——. 1989. "Indus Writing." *Mankind Quarterly* 30:113–118.
——. 1990. "Indus and Brahmi: Further Connections." *Cryptologia* 14:169–183.
——. 1992. "The Indus Tradition and the Indo-Aryans." *Mankind Quarterly* 32:195–213.
——. 1994a. "On the Classification of Indic Languages." *Annals of the Bhandarkar Oriental Research Institute* 75:185–195.
——. 1994b. *The Astronomical Code in the Rgveda*. Delhi: Aditya Prakashan.
Kalyanaraman, A. 1969. *Aryatarangini: The Saga of the Indo-Aryans*. Bombay: Asia Publishing House.
Kanga, M. F. 1988. *Avesta Reader*. Pune: Dharmadhikari.
Kanga, M. F., and N. S. Sontakke, eds. 1962. *Avestā*. Poona: Vaidika Saṁśodhana Maṇḍala.
Kar, Amal, and Bimal Ghose. 1984. "The Drishadvati River System of India: An Assessment and New Findings." *Geographical Journal* 150:221–229.
Karamshoyev, D. 1981. "The Importance of Pamiri Language Data for the Study of the Ancient

Iranians' Ethnic Origins." In *Ethnic Problems of the History of Central Asia in the Early Period* (230–238). Ed. M. S. Asimov. Moscow: Nauka.

Kay, G. R. [1924] 1981. *Hindu Astronomy.* New Delhi: Cosmo Publications.

Keislar, Allan. n.d. "Deciphering the Indus Script." Unpublished paper, University of California at Berkeley.

——. 1909. "On the Antiquity of Vedic Culture." *Journal of the Royal Asiatic Society* 1100–1106.

Keith, A. B. 1933. "The Home of the Indo-Europeans." In *Oriental Studies in Honour of Cursetji Erachji Pavry* (188–199). Ed. J. D. Pavry. London: Oxford University Press.

Keith, A. B., and A. A. Macdonell. [1912] 1967. *Vedic Index of Names and Subjects.* 2 vols. Delhi: Motilal Banarsidass.

——. 1933. "The Home of the Indo-Europeans." In *Oriental Studies in Honour of Cursetji Erachji Pavry* (189–199). Ed. Jal Dastur Cursetji Pavry. London: Oxford University Press.

Kennedy, Kenneth. 1982. "Skulls, Aryans and Flowing Drains: The Interface of Archaeology and Skeletal Biology in the Study of the Harappan Civilization." In *Harappan Civilization* (289–295). Ed. Gregory L. Possehl. New Delhi: Oxford University Press.

——. 1984. "A Reassessment of the Theories of Racial Origins of the People of the Indus Valley Civilization from Recent Anthropological Data." In *Studies in the Archaeology and Palaeoanthropology of South Asia* (99–107). Ed. K. Kennedy and G. Possehl. Oxford: American Institute of Indian Studies.

——.1994. "Identification of Sacrificial and Massacre Victims in Archaeological Sites: The Skeletal Evidence." *Man and Environment* 19:247–251.

——. 1995. "Have Aryans Been Identified in the Prehistoric Skeletal Record from South Asia?" In *The Indo-Aryans of Ancient South Asia* (32–66). Ed. George Erdosy. Berlin: Walter de Gruyter.

Kennedy, Vans. 1828. *Researches into the Origin and Affinity of the Principal Languages of Asia and Europe.* London: Longman.

Kenoyer, J. M. 1987. "The Indus Civilization." *Wisconsin Academy Review.* March 22–26.

——. 1991a. "The Indus Valley Tradition of Pakistan and Western India." *Journal of World Prehistory* 5:331–385.

——. 1991b. "Urban Process in the Indus Tradition: A Preliminary Model from Harappa." In *Harappa Excavations 1986–1990* (29–60). Ed. Richard H. Meadow. Madison, Wis.: Prehistory.

——. 1995. "Interaction Systems, Specialized Crafts and Culture Change: The Indus Valley Tradition and the Indo-Gangetic Tradition in South Asia." In *The Indo-Aryans of Ancient South Asia* (213–257). Ed. George Erdosy. Berlin: Walter de Gruyter.

——. 1997. Paper presented at a panel on the Indo-Aryans at the Madison South Asian Conference.

Kesarwani, Arun. 1982. "History and Archaeology of Ethnic Movement during the Second Millennium B.C. from the Caspian Sea to the Indus Basin." Ph.D. diss., Banaras Hindu University.

Khlopin, I. 1989. "Origins of the Bronze Age Cultures in South Central Asia." *International Association for the Study of the Cultures of Central Asia Information Bulletin* 15:74–84.

Kiparsky, Paul. 1977. "Towards a Reconstruction of the Indo-European." In *Studies in Stress and Accent* (209–239). Southern California Occasional Papers in Linguistics 4. Los Angeles: Department of Linguistics, University of Southern California.

Kittel, F. 1894. *Kannada English Dictionary.* Mangalore.

Klaus, Konrad. 1989. "*Samudrá* im Veda." In *Zeitschrift der Deutschen. Morgenländischen Gesellschaft* (364–371). Stuttgart: Franz Steiner.

Klejn, L. 1984. "The Coming of the Aryans: Who and Whence?" *Bulletin of the Deccan College Research Institute* 43:57–72.

Klostermaier, Klaus, K. 1994. *A Survey of Hinduism.* Albany: State University of New York Press.

Kohl, Philip. 1981. *The Bronze Age Civilization of Central Asia: Recent Soviet Discoveries.* New York: Sharpe.

——. 1984. *Central Asia: Palaeolithic Beginnings to the Iron Age.* Paris: Recherche sur les Civilisations.

Kohl, Philip, and Clare Fawcett. 1995a. "Archaeology in the Service of the State." In *Nationalism, Politics and the Practice of Archaeology* (120–138). Ed. P. Kohl and C. Fawcett. Cambridge: Cambridge University Press.

——. 1995b. "Nationalism, Politics, and the Practice of Archaeology in the Caucasus." In *Nationalism, Politics and the Practice of Archaeology* (149–174). Ed. P. Kohl and C. Fawcett. Cambridge: Cambridge University Press.

——. eds. 1995c. *Nationalism, Politics and the Practice of Archaeology.* Cambridge: Cambridge University Press.

Koivulehto, Jorma. 1991. *Uralische Evidenz für die Laryngaltheorie.* Vienna: Österreichischen Akademie der Wissenschaft.

Konow, Sten. 1921. "The Aryan Gods of the Mitanni People." *Kritiania* 3:3–39.

Kopf, D. 1969. *British Orientalism and the Bengal Renaissance.* Berkeley and Los Angeles: University of California Press.

Kortlandt, Frederik. 1990. "The Spread of the Indo-Europeans." *Journal of Indo- European Studies* 18:131–140.

Kosambi, K. K. 1965. *Ancient India.* New York: Random House.

Koshelenko, G. 1986. "Central Asian Foreign Contacts in the Early Iron Age." *International Association for the Study of the Cultures of Central Asia Information Bulletin* 11:69–75.

Kossina, G. 1902. "Die indogermanische Frage archaologisch Beantwortet." *Zeitschrift für Ethnologie* 34:161–222.

——. 1925a. *Die Deutsche Vorgeschichte.* Leipzig: Kabitzich.

——. 1925b. *Ursprung und Verbreitung der Germanen in vor- und Frühgeschichtlicher Zeit.* Leipzig: Kabitzich.

Krahe, H. 1964. *Unsere Altesten Flussnamen.* Wiesbaden: Otto Harrassowitz.

Kramrisch, Stella. 1981. *The Presence of Śiva.* Princeton, N. J.: Princeton University Press.

Krell, Kathrin, S. 1998. "Gimbutas' Kurgan-PIE Homeland Hypothesis: A Linguistic Critique." In *Archaeology and Language* (2:267–289). Ed. Roger Blench and Matthew Spriggs. London: Routledge.

Krishna, Rao, M. V. N. 1982. *Indus Script Deciphered.* Delhi: Agam Kala Prakashan.

Krishnamurti, Bh. 1985. "An Overview of Comparative Dravidian Studies since *Current Trends* 5 (1969)." In *For Gordon H. Fairbanks.* Ed. V. Acson and R. Leed. Honolulu: University of Hawaii Press.

Kristiansen, Kristian. 1996. "European Origins: 'Civilisation' and 'Barbarism.'" In *Cultural Identity and Archaeology* (138–144). Ed. Graves-Brown et al. London: Routledge.

Kroeber, A. L., and C. D. Chrétien. 1937. "Quantitative Classification of Indo-European Languages." *Journal of the Linguistic Society of America* 13:83–103.

——. 1939. "The Statistical Technique and Hittite." *Journal of the Linguistic Society of America* 15:69–71.

Kuhn, Thomas S. 1962. *The Structure of Scientific Revolutions.* Chicago: Chicago University Press.

Kuiper, F. B. J. 1955. "Rigvedic Loan Words." *Studia Indologica* (Bonn) 137–185.

——. [1967] 1974. "The Genesis of a Linguistic Area." *Indo-Iranian Journal* 10:81–102. Reprinted in *International Journal of Dravidian Linguistics* 3:133–153.

——. 1991. *Aryans in the Rigveda.* Leiden Studies in Indo-European 1. Atlanta: Rodopi.

——. 1995. "On a Hunt for Possible Objections." *Indo-Iranian Journal* 38:239–247.

Kulkarni, S. D. 1988. *Beginnings of Life, Culture and History*. Vol. 1 of *Bhishma's Study of Indian History and Culture*. Bombay: Bhisma.

Kumar, G. D. 1973. "The Ethnic Components of the Builders of the Indus Valley Civilization and the Advent of the Aryans." *Journal of Indo-European Studies* 1:66–80.

Kuzmina, Y. Y. 1976. "The 'Bactrian Mirage' and the Archaeological Reality on the Problem of the Formation of North Bactrian Culture." *East and West* 26:111–131.

——. 1981. "The Origins of the Indo-Iranians in the Light of Recent Archaeological Discoveries." In *Ethnic Problems of the History of Central Asia in the Early Period* (101–125). Ed. M. S. Asimov. Moscow: Nauka.

——. 1983. "The Pottery of the Vedic Aryans and Its Origins." *International Association for the Study of the Cultures of Central Asia Information Bulletin* 4:21–30.

——. 1985. "Classification and Periodisation of Andronovo Cultural Community Sites." *International Association for the Study of the Cultures of Central Asia Information Bulletin* 9:23–46.

——. 1994. "Horses, Chariots, and the Indo-Iranians: An Archaeological Spark in the Dark." In *South Asian Archaeology 1993* (403–412). Ed. Asko Parpola and Petteri Koskikallio. Helsinki: Suomalainen.

Lahovary, N. 1963. *Dravidian Origins and the West*. Calcutta: Orient Longmans.

Lal, B. B. 1966. "The Direction of the Writing on the Indus Script." *Antiquity* 50:52–55.

——. 1978. "The Indo-Aryan Hypothesis vis-à-vis Indian Archaeology." *Journal of Central Asia* 1:21–41.

——. 1984. "Some Reflections on the Structural Remains at Kalibangan." In *Frontiers of the Indus Civilization* (55–62). Ed. B. B. Lal and S. P. Gupta. New Delhi: Books and Books.

——. 1997. *The Earliest Civilization of South Asia*. Eryan Books.

Lal, B. B. forthcoming. "Aryan Invasion of India: Perpetuation of a Myth." In *Evidence and Evocation in Indian History*. Ed. E. Bryant, and L. Patton. London: Curzon.

Lamberg-Karlovsky, C. 1988. "Indo-Europeans: A Near Eastern Perspective." *Quarterly Review of Archaeology* 9(1):1–10.

——. 1993. "Reflections on the Central Asian Bronze." *International Association for the Study of the Cultures of Central Asia Information Bulletin* 19:29–40.

——. 1997. "Colonialism, Nationalism, Ethnicity, and Archaeology." Parts 1 and 2. *Review of Archaeology* 18, no. 2:1–14 and 35–47.

——. Forthcoming. "The Indus Civilization: The Case for Caste Formation."

Lambrick, H.T. 1967. "The Indus Flood-Plain and the 'Indus' Civilization." *Geographical Journal* 133:483–495.

Lassen, Christian. [1851] 1867. *Indische Alterthumskunde*. London: Williams and Norton.

Latham, R. G. 1851. *The Germania of Tacitus with Ethnological Dissertations and Notes*. London: Taylor.

——. 1862. *Elements of Comparative Philology*. London: Walton and Maberly.

Law, N. N. 1965. *Age of the Rgveda*. Calcutta: Firma K. L. Mukhopadhyay.

Lazzeroni, Romano. 1984. "Indoeuropeo e Indoeuropa: Un Problema di Metodo." *Incontri Linguistici* 9:89–100.

Leach, Edmund. 1990. "Aryan Invasions over Four Millennia." In *Culture through Time* (227–245). Ed. Emiko Ohnuki-Tiernev. Stanford, Calif.: Stanford University Press.

Legge, F. 1902. "The Home of the Aryans." *Academy* 63:710–711.

Lehmann, Winfred P. 1993. *Theoretical Bases of Indo-European Linguistics*. London: Routledge.

Lehmann, Winfred P., and L. Zgusta. 1979. "Schleicher's Tale after a Century." In *Studies in Diachronic, Synchronic, and Typological Linguistics: Festschrift for Oswald Szemerényi* (455–466). Ed. Bela Brogyanyi. Amsterdam: Benjamins.

Leibniz, G. 1981. *New Essays on Human Understanding*. Trans. P. Remnant and J. Bennett. Cambridge: Cambridge University Press.

Leopold, Joan. 1970. "The Aryan Theory of Race." *Indian Economic and Social History Review* 7:271–297.

Levitt, Stephan. 1989. "What Does 'Noseless' Mean in the *Rgveda?*" *Annals of the Bhandarkar Oriental Research Institute* 70:47–63.

Littauer, M. A, and J. H. Crouwel. 1979. *Wheeled Vehicles and Ridden Animals in the Ancient Near East.* Cologne: Brill.

Litvinsky, B. A., and P'yankova L.T. 1992."Pastoral Tribes of the Bronze Age in the Oxus Valley (Bactria)." *History of Civilizations of Central Asia* (1:379–394). Ed. A. H. Dani and V. M. Masson. Paris: UNESCO.

Lubotsky, Alexander. forthcoming. "Indo-Iranian Substratum." *Proceedings of the Tvarminne Conference.*

Luniya, B. N. 1978. *Life and Culture in Ancient India.* Agra: Lakshminarain Agarwal.

Lyonnet, Bertille. 1993. "Relations between Central Asia and the Indian World—From the Palaeolithic Period to the Islamic Conquest: New Interpretations in the Light of a Comprehensive Study of Ceramics." *Man and Environment* 29:75–86.

——. 1994. "Central Asia, the Indo-Aryans and the Iranians: Some Reassessments from Recent Archaeological Data." *South Asian Archaeology* (1:425–434). Ed. Asko Parpola and Petteri Koskikallio. Helsinki: Suomalainen Tiedeakatemia.

Mackay, Ernest J. H. 1943. *Chanhu-Daro Excavations.* American Oriental Series 20. New Haven, Conn.: American Oriental Society.

Mahadevan, Iravatham. 1981–82. "S. R. Rao's Decipherment of the Indus Script." *Indian Historical Journal* 8 (1–2):58–73.

——. 1988. "What Do We Know about the Indus Script: Neti Neti." *Proceedings of the India History Congress,* Forty-ninth Session (599–628). Dharwad, Karnatak University.

——. "An Encyclopaedia of the Indus Script." *The Book Review* [New Delhi], June, 1–13.

Mahajan, V. D. 1968. *Ancient India.* Delhi: Chand.

Mahdi, Waruno. 1998. "Linguistic Data on Transmission of Southeast Asian Cultigens to India and Sri Lanka." In *Archaeology and Language* (2:390–415). Ed. R. Blench and M. Spriggs. London: Routledge.

Mahendale, Y. S. 1947. "Wadi Names of the Retnagiri State." *Bulletin of the Deccan College Research Institute* 8–9:398–421.

Mahulkar, D. D. 1992. *Some Misconceptions in Linguistic Studies Past and Present.* New Delhi: Manohar Publications.

Maine, Sir Henry Sumner. 1875. *Lectures on the Early History of Institutions.* New York: Henry Holt.

Majumdar, A. K. 1977. *Concise History of Ancient India.* Vol. 1. Delhi: Munshiram Manoharlal.

Majumdar, M. A. [1934] 1981. *Explorations in Sind.* Memoirs of the Archaeological Survey of India 48. Karachi: Indus.

Majumdar, R. C. [1946] 1970. *An Advanced History of India.* Delhi: Macmillan.

——. 1951. *The History and Culture of the Indian People: The Vedic Age.* London: Allen and Unwin.

——. 1959. "Ṛgvedic Civilization in the Light of Archaeology." *Annals of the Bhandarkar Oriental Research Institute* 40:1–15.

Makkay, János. 1988. "Cultural Groups of SE-Europe in the Neolithic: The PIE Homeland Problem and the Origins of the Greeks." *AION* 10:117–137.

Mallory, J. P. 1973. "A History of the Indo-European Problem." *Journal of Indo-European Studies* 1:21–66.

——. 1975. "The Indo-European Homeland Problem: The Logic of Its Inquiry." Ph, D. diss., University of California.

——. 1976. "Time Perspective and Proto-Indo-European Culture." *World Archaeology* 8:44–56.

——. 1989. *In Search of the Indo-Europeans.* London: Thames and Hudson.
——. 1992. "Human Populations and the Indo-European Problem." *Mankind Quarterly* 33:131–154.
——. 1997. "The Homelands of the Indo-Europeans." In *Archaeology and Language* (93–121). Ed. R. Blench and M. Spriggs. London: Routledge.
——. 1998. "A European Perspective on Indo-Europeans in Asia." In *The Bronze Age and Early Iron Age Peoples of Eastern and Central Asia* (1:175–201). Ed. Mair. Washington D.C.: Institute for the Study of Man.
——. 1999. "Some Aspects of Indo-European Agriculture." In *Studies in Honor of Jaan Puhvel.* Part I. *Ancient Languages and Philology* (221–240). Monograph no. 20. Ed. D. Disterheft, M. Huld, and F. Greppin. Washington, D.C.: Institute for the Study of Man.
Mallory, J. P., and D. Q. Adams, eds. 1997. *Encyclopedia of Indo-European Culture.* London: Fitzroy.
Manczak, Witold. 1990. "Critique des Opinions de Gamkrelidze et Ivanov." *Historische Sprachforschung* 103:178–192.
Marcucci, Ettore. 1855. *Lettere di Filippo Sassetti.* Florence: Felice le Monnier.
Marshall, Sir John. 1931. *Mohenjo-Daro and the Indus Civilization.* Vol. 1 and 2. London: Arthur Probsthain.
Marshall, P. J. 1970. *The British Discovery of Hinduism in the Eighteenth Century.* Cambridge: Cambridge University Press.
Masica, C. 1976. *Defining a Linguistic Area.* Chicago: University of Chicago Press.
——. 1979. "Aryan and Non-Aryan Elements in North Indian Agriculture." In *Aryan and Non-Aryan in India* (55–151). Ed. M. Deshpande and P. Hook. Ann Arbor: University of Michigan Press.
——. 1991. *The Indo-Aryan Languages.* Cambridge: Cambridge University Press.
Masson, V. M. 1992. "The Decline of the Bronze Age Civilization and Movements of the Tribes." In *History of Civilization of Central Asia* (337–356). Ed. A. H. Dani and V. M. Masson. Paris: UNESCO.
Maurer, Walter Harding. 1985. "Review of 'The Decipherment of the Indus Script' by S. R. Rao." *Journal of the American Oriental Society* 105:374–378.
Maurice, Thomas. [1812] 1984. *Indian Antiquities.* New Delhi: Naurang Rai.
Maw, Martin. 1990. *Visions of India.* Frankfurt: Verlag Peter Lang.
Mayrhofer, Manfred. 1974. "Die Arier im Vorderen Orient: Ein Mythos?" *Sitzungsberichte. Osterreichische Akademie der Wissenschaften* 294, no. 3:1–93.
——. 1983. "The Earliest Linguistic Traces of Aryans Outside India and Iran." *Journal of the K. R. Cama Oriental Institute* 50:87–95.
——. "Sanskrit und die Sprachen Alteuropas." *Nachrichten der Akademie der Wissenschaften in Göttingen* 5:1–33.
——. 1986. *Etymologisches Worterbuch des Altindoarischen.* Heidelberg: Winter.
Mazumdar, Akshoy Kumar. 1979. *The Hindu History.* Allahabad: R. S. Publishing House.
McAlpin, David W. 1974. "Toward Proto-Elamo-Dravidian." *Language* 50:89–101.
McCully, Bruce Tiebout. 1966. *English Education and the Origins of Indian Nationalism.* Gloucester: Peter Smith.
McDonnell, Arthur Anthony, and Arthur Berriedale Keith. [1912] 1967. *Vedic Index of Names and Subjects.* 2 vols. Delhi: Motilal Banarsidass.
Meadow, Richard. 1987. "Faunal Exploitation Patterns in Eastern Iran and Baluchistan: A Review of Recent Investigations." *Orientalia Iosephi Tucci Memoriae Dicata* (881–916). Ed. G. Gnoli and L. Lanciotti.
——. 1996. "The Origin and Spread of Agriculture and Pastoralism in Northwestern South

Asia." In *The Origins and Spread of Agriculture and Pastoralism in Eurasia.* Ed. David Harris. London: UCL Press.
——. 1997. "A Comment on 'Horse Remains from Surkotada' by Sandor Bokonyi." *South Asian Archaeology* 13:308–315.
Megaw, J., and M. Megaw 1992. "The Celts: The First Europeans?" *Antiquity* 66:254–260.
Mehendale, M. A. 1978–79. "Prof. Thieme's Etymology of Skt. *asî* and Its Bearing on the Iron-Age in India." *Puratattva* 10:79–80.
——. 1993. "The Indo-Aryans, Indo-Iranians and the Indo-Europeans." In *The Aryan Problem* (43–50). Ed. S. B. Deo and Suryanath Kamath. Pune: Mythic Society.
Melchert, H. Craig. 1987. "PIE Velars in Luvian." *Studies in Memory of Warren Cowgill* (182–204). Ed. Calvert Watkins. Berlin: Walter de Gruyter.
——. 1994. "The Feminine Gender in Anatolian." *Früh-, Mittel- und Spätindogermanisch* (231–244). Wiesbaden: Verlag.
Mellaart, James. 1981. "Anatolia and the Indo-Europeans." *Journal of Indo-European Studies* 9:135–149.
Metcalf, G. J. 1974. "The Indo-European Hypothesis in the 16th and 17th Centuries." In *Studies in the History of Linguistics: Traditions and Paradigms* (233–257). Ed. D. Hymes. Bloomington: Indiana University Press.
Michelet, J. 1864. *Bible de l'humanité.* Paris: Chamerot.
Mill, James. [1820] 1975. *The History of British India.* Chicago: University of Chicago Press.
Misra, Satya Swarup. 1977. *The Laryngeal Theory: A Critical Evaluation.* Varanasi: Chaukhambha Orientalia.
——. 1992. *The Aryan Problem: A Linguistic Approach.* New Delhi: Munshiram Manoharlal.
——. 1994. *New Lights on Indo-European Comparative Grammar.* Sharada: Delhi.
——. Forthcoming. "Date of Rigveda and Original Home of the Indo-Europeans: A Linguistic Assessment."
Misra, V. N. 1989. "Climate, a Factor in the Rise and Fall of the Indus Civilization: Evidence from Rajasthan and Beyond." In *An Archaeological Tour along the Ghaggar-Hakra River* (125–171). Ed. S. P. Gupta. Meerut: Kusumanjali Prakashan.
——. "Indus Civilization and the Ṛgvedic Sarasvatī." In *South Asian Archaeology* (510–525). Ed. Aske Parpola and P. Koskikallio. Helsinki: Suomalainen.
Monboddo, Lord James Burnet. 1774. *Of the Origin and Progress of Language.* Edinburgh: Balfour.
Monier Williams, Monier. 1891. *Brāhmanism and Hinduism.* New York: Macmillan.
Moorey, P. R. S. 1986. "The Emergence of the Light, Horse-Drawn Chariot in the Near-East c. 2000–1500." *World Archaeology* 18:196–215.
Mughal, Rafique M. 1988. "The Decline of the Indus Civilization and the Late Harappan Period in the Indus Valley." *Lahore Museum Bulletin* 1, no. 1:1–17.
——. 1993. "Recent Archaeological Research in the Cholistan Desert." In *Harappan Civilization* (85–94). Ed. Gregory L. Possehl. New Delhi: Oxford.
Muir, J. [1860] 1874. *Original Sanskrit Texts.* London: Trüber.
Müller, F. Max. 1847. "On the Relation of the Bengali to the Arian and Aboriginal Languages of India." *Report of the British Association for the Advancement of Science* 319–350.
——. 1854a. *The Languages of the Seat of War in the East.* London: Longmans.
——. 1854b. "The Last Results of the Researches Respecting the Non-Iranian and Non-Semitic Languages of Asia and Europe, or the Turanian Family of Languages." In *Outlines of the Philosophy of Universal History, Applied to Language and Religion.* Ed. Christian Bunsen. 2 vols. London: Longmans.

——. [1859] 1968. *A History of Ancient Sanskrit Literature.* Varanasi: Chowkhamba Sanskrit Series Office.
——. 1875. *The Science of Language.* New York: Scribner.
——. [1881] 1981. "On the Results of Comparative Philology." Inaugural Lecture, Strassburg, 23 May 1872. In F. Max Müller, *Selected Essays on Language Mythology and Religion* (2:174–225). London: Longmans, Green.
——. 1883. *India: What Can It Teach Us?* London: Longmans.
——. 1884. *Biographical Essays.* Oxford.
——. [1887] 1985. *Biographies of Words and the Home of the Aryas.* New Delhi: Gayatri.
——. 1891. *Physical Religion: The Gifford Lectures.* London: Longmans.
——. 1892. *Rig-Veda Samhita.* Vol. 4. London: Oxford University Press.
——. 1899. *Auld Lang Syne.* New York: Scribner.
——. 1902. *The Life and Letters of the Right Honourable Friedrich Max Müller.* Edited by his wife. Vol. 1. London: Longmans.
Murthy, S. R. N. 1980. "The Vedic Saraswatī a Myth or Fact: A Geological Approach." *Indian Journal of the History of Science* 15:189–192.
Nair, M. Ramakrishnan. 1974. *Sanskrit Family.* Cochin: Nair.
Nath, Bhola. 1959. "Remains of the Horse and Indian Elephant from the Protohistoric Site of Harappa (West Pakistan)." *Proceedings of First All India Congress of Zoologists* 2:1–14.
Nelson, Sarah M. 1995. "The Politics of Ethnicity in Prehistoric Korea." In *Nationalism, Politics and the Practice of Archaeology* (218–232). Ed. P. Kohl and C. Fawcett. Cambridge: Cambridge University Press.
Neugebauer, Otto. 1975. *A History of Ancient Mathematical Astronomy.* Berlin: Springer-Verlag.
Newman, Henry Stanley. n.d. *Days of Grace in India.* London: Partridge.
Nichols, Johanna. 1997. "The Epicentre of the Indo-European Linguistic Spread." In *Archaeology and Language I* (122–148). Ed. Roger Blench and Matthew Spriggs. London: Routledge.
——. "The Eurasian Spread Zone and the Indo-European Dispersal." In *Archaeology and Language II.* Ed. Roger Blench and Matthew Spriggs. London: Routledge.
Norman, Kenneth R. 1995. "Dialectical Variation in Old and Middle Indo-Aryan." In *The Indo-Aryans of Ancient South Asia.* Ed. George Erdosy. Berlin: Walter de Gruyter.
Novgorodova, E. A. 1981. "Early Stage in the Ethnic History of Central Asia in the 2nd Millennium B.C." In *Ethnic Problems of the History of Central Asia in the Early Period* (207–215). Ed M. S. Asimov. Moscow: Nauka.
Nyberg, Hari. 1995. "The Problem of the Aryans and the Soma: The Botanical Evidence." In *The Indo-Aryans of Ancient South Asia* (382–406). Ed. G. Erdosy. Berlin: Walter de Gruyter.
Oak, P. N. 1969. *Tajmahal–the True Story: The Tale of a Temple Vandalized.* Houston: Gosh.
——. 1984. *World Vedic Heritage.* New Delhi: Oak.
Ohashi, Yukio. 1997. "The Legends of Vásiṣṭha: A Note on Vedaṅga Astronomy." Paper presented at the Twenty-third General Assembly of the International Astronomical Union, August 25.
Olcott, Henry Steel. 1881. "A Glance at India, Past, Present and Future: The Past." *The Theosophist* 2:123–128.
Oldenberg, H. 1894. "Der Vedische Kalender und das Alter des Veda." *Zeitschrift der Deutschen Morgenländischen Gesellschaft* 629–648.
Oldham, C. F. 1893. "The Saraswati and the Lost River of the Indian Desert." *Journal of the Royal Asiatic Society* 49–76.
Olinder, Maurice. 1992. *The Languages of Paradise.* Cambridge, Mass.: Harvard University Press.
Oswalt, Robert L. 1991. "A Method for Assessing Distant Linguistic Relationships." In *Sprung from Some Common Source* (388–404). Ed. Sydney M. Lamb and E. Douglas Mitchell. Stanford, Calif.: Stanford University Press.

Pal, Yash, et al. 1984."Remote Sensing of the 'Lost' Sarasvati River." In *Frontiers of the Indus Civilization* (491–497). Ed. B. B. Lal and S. P. Gupta. New Delhi: Books and Books.

Palmaitis, L. 1988. Review of Gamkrelidze and Ivanov. *Indogermanische Forschungen* 93:280–292.

Pargiter, F. E. [1922] 1979. *Ancient Indian Traditions.* New Delhi: Cosmo.

Parpola, Asko. 1988."The Coming of the Aryans to Iran and India and the Cultural and Ethnic Identity of the Dāsas." *International Journal of Dravidian Linguistics* 17:85–228.

——. 1993. "Margiana and the Aryan Problem." *International Association for the Study of the Cultures of Central Asia Information Bulletin* 19:41–62.

——. 1994. *Deciphering the Indus Script.* Cambridge: Cambridge University Press.

——. 1995. "The Problem of the Aryans and Soma: Textual-Linguistic and Archaeological Evidence." In *The Indo-Aryans of Ancient South Asia* (353–381). Ed. George Erdosy. Berlin: Mouton de Gruyter.

——. 1997. "The Dāsas and the Coming of the Aryans." In *Inside the Texts Beyond the Texts.* Harvard Oriental Series. Opera Minora 2. 193–202.

——. 1998. "Aryan Languages, Archaeological Cultures, and Sinkiang: Where Did Proto-Iranian Come into Being, and How Did It Spread?" In *The Bronze Age and Early Iron Age Peoples of Eastern and Central Asia* (1:114–147). Ed. Mair. Washington D. C. Institute for the Study of Man.

Parsons, J. 1767. *The Remains of Japhet.* London: Davis.

Pathak, Suniti. 1974. "Sanskrit and Central Asia." *Acharya Dr. Vishva Bandhu Commemoration Volume* 12:246–259.

Patil, P. G. transl. 1991 *Collected Works of Mahatma Jyotirao Phule.* Bombay: Education Department, Government of Maharashtra.

Pedersen, H. 1931. *Linguistic Science in the Nineteenth Century.* Cambridge, Mass.: Harvard University Press.

Pejros, Ilia. 1997. "Are Correlations between Archaeological and Linguistic Reconstructions Possible?" In *Archaeology and Language* (1:149–157). Ed. Roger Blench and Matthew Spriggs. London: Routledge.

Pejros, Ilia. 1999. "Family Evolution, Language History and Genetic Classification." In *Historical Linguistics and Lexicostatistics* (259–306). Ed. V. Shevoroshkin and P. Sidwell. Melbourne: Association for the History of Language.

Pejros, Ilia, and Viktor, Shnirelman. 1989. "Towards an Understanding of Proto-Dravidian Prehistory." In *Reconstructing Languages and Cultures* (70–71). Ed. Vitaly Shevoroshkin. Bochum: Studienverlag.

Penka, K. 1883. *Origines Ariacae.* Vienna: Taschen.

Piankova [P'yankova], L. 1982. "South Western Tajikistan in the Bronze Age." *International Association for the Study of the Cultures of Central Asia Information Bulletin* 1:35–46.

——. 1994. Central Asia in the Bronze Age: Sedentary and Nomadic Cultures." *Antiquity* 68:355–372.

Pictet, A. [1859] 1877. *Les Origines Indo-Européennes.* Paris: Sandoz et Fischbacher.

Pierce, William. 1976. *History of India.* London: William Collins.

Piggott, Stuart. 1952. *Prehistoric India.* Middlesex: Penguin.

——. 1970. "Copper Vehicle-Models in the Indus Civilization." *Journal of the Royal Asiatic Society* 200–202.

——. 1977. "Chinese Chariotry: An Outsider's View." In *Arts of the Eurasian Steppelands* (32–52). Ed. Philip Denwood. Colloquies on Art and Archaeology 7. London: SOAS.

——. 1983. *The Earliest Wheeled Transport.* London: Thames and Hudson.

Pillai, C. 1940. *A Short History of the Faulty Study Conducted in the Indo-European Field.* Palamcottah: Palamcottah.

Pillai, Govinda Krishna. 1959. *Vedic History.* Allahabad: Kitabistan.

Pillai, M. Arjunan. 1988. *Ancient Indian History.* New Delhi: Ashish Publishing House.

Pillai, Purnalingam. 1963. *Tamil India.* Madras: South India Saiva Siddhanta Works.

Pingree, David. 1970. "History of Mathematical Astronomy in India." *Dictionary of Scientific Biography* 15:533–633.

——. 1973. "The Mesopotamian Origin of Early Indian Mathematical Astronomy." *Journal for the History of Astronomy* 4:1–12.

——. 1987. "Babylonian Planetary Theory in Sanskrit Omen Texts." In *From Ancient Omens to Statistical Mechanics.* Acta Historica Scientiarum Naturalium et Medicinalium 39 (91–99). Ed. J. Berggren and B. Goldstein.

——. 1989. "MUL.APIN and Vedic Astronomy." *DUMU-E-DUB-BA-A* (439–445). Ed. H. Behrens, D. Loding, and M. Roth. Philadelphia: Occasional Publications of the Samuel Noah Kramer Fund.

——. 1992. "Mesopotamian Omens in Sanskrit." In *La Circulation des biens, des personnes et des idées dans le Proche-Orient ancien* (375–379). Ed. D. Charpin and F. Joannes. Paris: Editions Recherche sur les Civilisations.

Pissani, Vittore. 1949. *Glottologia Indoeuropea.* Turin: Rosenberg and Sellier.

Poesche, T. 1878. *Die Arier.* Jena: Hermann Costenoble.

Poliakov, L. 1971. *The Aryan Myth.* London: Sussex University Press.

Pollock, S. 1993. "Deep Orientalism." In *Orientalism and the Postcolonial Predicament* (76–133). Ed. Carol A. Breckenridge and Peter van der Veer. Philadelphia: University of Pennsylvania Press.

Polomé, Edgar C. 1979. "Creolization Theory and Linguistic Prehistory." In *Studies in Diachronic, Synchronic, and Typological Linguistics* (679–690). Ed. Bela Brogyanyi. Amsterdam: Benjamins.

——. 1985. "How Archaic Is Old Indic?" In *Studia Linguistica Diachronica et Synchronica* (670–683). Ed. Werner Winter. Berlin: Mouton de Gruyter.

——. 1990a. "The Indo-Europeanization of Northern Europe: The Linguistic Evidence." *Journal of Indo-European Studies* 18:331–338.

——. 1990b. "Types of Linguistic Evidence for Early Contact: Indo-Europeans and Non-Indo-Europeans." In *When Worlds Collide* (267–289). Ed. T. L. Markey and John A. Greppin. Ann Arbor: Karoma.

——. 1992. "Comparative Linguistics and the Reconstruction of Indo-European Culture." In *Reconstructing Languages and Cultures* (369–390). Ed. Edgar C. Polomé and Werner Winter. Berlin: Mouton de Gruyter.

——. 1994. "Isoglosses and the Reconstruction of the IE Dialectical Split." *Journal of Indo-European Studies* 22:289–305.

Possehl, Gregory L. 1967. "The Mohenjo-Daro Floods: A Reply." *American Anthropologist* 69:32–40.

——. 1979. "Pastoral Nomadism in the Indus Civilization: An Hypothesis." In *South Asian Archaeology* (537–551). Ed. M. Taddei. Naples: Istituto Universitario Orientale.

——. 1996. *Indus Age: The Writing System.* Philadelphia: University of Pennsylvania Press.

——, ed. 1993. *Harappan Civilization.* New Delhi: Oxford University Press.

Possehl, Gregory L. 1999a. "The Transformation of the Indus Civilization." *Man and Environment* 24(2):1–33.

——. 1999b. "The Early Iron Age in South Asia." In *The Archaeometallurgy of the Asian World* (153–175). Ed. V. Pigott. University Museum Monograph 89, MASCA Research Papers on Science and Archaeology Volume 16. Philadelphia: University of Pennsylvania.

Prakash, Buddha. 1966. *Rgveda and the Indus Valley Civilization.* Hoshiapur: Vishveshvarananda Institute.

Prasad, B. 1936. *Animal Remains from Harappa.* Memoires of the Archaeological Survey of India 51. Delhi: Manager of Publications.

Prasad, Gorakh. 1935. "Astronomical Evidence on the Age of the Vedas." *Bihar and Orissa Research Society* 21:121–136.

Pulgram, E. 1958. *The Tongues of Italy.* Cambridge, Mass.: Harvard University Press.

——. 1959. "Proto-Indo-European Reality and Reconstruction." *Language* 35:421–426.

Pusalkar, A. D. 1950. "Some Problems of Ancient Indian History." *Bhāratīya Vidya* 11:110–123.

Quraishi, Humra. 1998. "Hindu Education Will Create More Madarsas." *Times of India,* December 12.

Ragozin, Zénaïde A. 1895. *Vedic India.* New York: Unwin.

Rai, Lajpat. 1917. *England's Debt to India.* New York: Huebsch.

Raikes, Robert L. 1964. "The End of the Ancient Cities of the Indus." *American Anthropologist* 66:284–299.

——. 1965. "The Mohenjo-Daro Floods." *Antiquity* 155:196–203.

Rajaram, N. 1993. "The Politics of History." *Indian Express,* November 14.

——. 1995. *The Politics of History.* New Delhi: Voice of India.

Rajaram, N., and David Frawley. 1995. *Vedic "Aryans" and the Origins of Civilization.* Quebec: W. H. Press.

Ramachandran, Puthusseri. 1987. *Perspectives in Place Names Studies.* Trivandrum: Place Name Society.

Raman, Anand, and Jon Patrick. 1997. "Linguistic Similarity Measures Using the Minimum Message Length Principle." In *Archaeology and Language I* (262–279). Ed. Roger Blench and Matthew Spriggs. London: Routledge.

Ramaswami, E. V. 1981 "Ramayana, a True Reading." In *Collected Works of Thanthai Periyar.* E. V. Ramasami. Madras: Periyar.

Ramaswamy, Sumathi. 1997. *Passions of the Tongue.* Berkeley: University of California Press.

Ranade, Justice M. G. [1915] 1992. *The Miscellaneous Writings.* Delhi: Sahitya Akademi.

Randhawa, M. S. 1980. *A History of Agriculture in India.* New Delhi: Council of Agricultural Research.

Rangacharya, V. 1937. *Vedic India.* In *History of Pre-Musalman India.* Madras: Indian Publishing House.

Rao, Ramchandra. 1880. "Puzzles for the Philologists." *Theosophist* 1:305–308.

Rao, S. R. 1979. *Lothal.* 2 vols. New Delhi: Archaeological Survey of India.

——. 1991. *Dawn and Devolution of the Indus Civilization.* New Delhi: Aditya Prakashan.

——. 1993. "The Aryans in Indus Civilization." In *The Aryan Problem* (173–180). Ed. S. B. Deo and Suryanath Kamath. Pune: Bharatiya Itihasa.

Rathore, Nisha. 1994. "On Colours and Classes: The Invasion Myth." *Genesis of the Aryan Myth. Journal of the Deendayal Research Institute* 15:175–186.

Ratnagar, Shereen. 1996a. "Does Archaeology Hold the Answers?" Paper presented at the International Conference on Aryan and Non-Aryan in India, University of Michigan.

——. 1996b. "Revisionist at Work." *Frontline,* Febuary 9, 74–80.

Rau, Wilhelm. 1974. "Vedic Texts on the Manufacture of Pottery." *Journal of the Oriental Institute* 23:137–142.

——. 1976. *The Meaning of* Pur *in Vedic Literature.* Munich: Wilhelm Fink Verlag.

——. 1977. "The Earliest Literary Evidence for Permanent Vedic Settlements." In *Inside the Texts Beyond the Texts* (203–206). Harvard Oriental Series. Opera Minora 2.

Raychaudhuri, Tapan. 1988. *Europe Reconsidered.* Delhi: Oxford University Press.

Rédei, Károly. 1991. *Uralisches Etymologisches Wörterbuch.* Wiesbaden: Otto Harrassowitz.

Renfrew, C. 1987. *Archaeology and Language.* New York: Cambridge University Press.

——. 1988. "Author's Précis" and "Reply." *Book Review: Archaeology and Language. Current Anthropology* 29:437–441, 463–466.

——. 1990. "Archaeology and Linguistics: Some Preliminary Issues." In *When Worlds Collide* (15–24). Ed. T. L. Markey and John Greppin. Ann Arbor: Karoma.

——. 1998. "The Tarim Basin, and Indo-European Origins: A View from the West." In *The Bronze Age and Early Iron Age Peoples of Eastern and Central Asia* (1:202–211). Ed. Mair. Washington D. C.: Institute for the Study of Man.

——. 1999. "Time Depth, Convergence Theory, and Innovation in Proto-Indo-European: 'Old Europe' as a PIE Linguistic Area." *Journal of Indo-European Studies* 27(3–4):258–293.

Reṇu, L. N. 1994. *Indian Ancestors of Vedic Aryans.* Bombay: Bharatiya Vidya Bhava.

Reusch, Beatrice. 1995. "The Sarasvatī River." M.A. thesis, University of Wisconsin- Madison.

Richter-Ushanas, Egbert 1997. *The Indus Script and the Ṛgveda.* Delhi: Motilal.

Ringe, Don, et al. 1998. "Computational Cladistics and the Position of Tocharian." In *The Bronze Age and Early Iron Age Peoples of Eastern Central Asia* (1:391–413). Washington D.C.: Institute for the Study of Man.

Ripley, William Z. 1899. *The Races of Europe.* London: Kegan Paul.

Risley, H. H. 1891. "The Study of Ethnology in India." *Journal of the Anthropological Institute of Great Britain and Ireland* 20:235–263.

——. N.d. *The Races of Europe.* London: Kegan Paul, Trench, Trubner.

Robb, John. 1991. "Random Causes with Directed Effects: The Indo-European Language Spread and the Stochastic Loss of Lineages." *Antiquity* 65:287–291.

Rocher, Ludo. 1986. *The Puranas.* History of Indian Literature. 2. Wiesbaden: Harrassowitz.

Rocher, Rosane. 1973. Review of *Indo-European and the Indo-Europeans,* edited by G. Cordona, Henry Hoenigswald, and Alfred Senn. *Journal of the American Oriental Society* 93:616–617.

——. 1998. Review of *Colonial Indology: The Sociopolitics of the Ancient Indian Past,* by D. Chakrabarti. *American Oriental Society* 118:307–308.

Ross, M. D. 1991. "How Conservative Are Sedentary Languages? Evidence from Western Melanasia." In *Currents in Pacific Linguistics* (443–451). Ed. Robert Blust. Canberra: Australian National University.

Rudolph, Lloyd I., and Susanne Hoeber Rudolph. 1984. "Rethinking Secularism: Genesis and Implications of the Textbook Controversy, 1977–79." In *Cultural Policy in India* (13–41). Ed. Lloyd I. Rudolph. Delhi: Chakya Publication.

Saint-Hilaire, Barthelemy. 1861. *Journal des Savants.*

Salmons, Joe. 1992. "Northwest Indo-European Vocabulary and Substrate Phonology." *Perspectives on Indo-European Language, Culture and Religion* (2:265–279). Monograph Number 9. McLean, Va: Institute for the Study of Man.

Sankalia, H. D. 1974. *Prehistory and Protohistory of India and Pakistan.* Poona: Deccan College.

Sankarananda, Swami 1967. *The Rigvedic Culture of the Pre-Historic Indus* Calcutta: Abhedananda.

Santoni, M. 1988. "Aspects matériels des cultures de Sibri et de Mehrgarh VIII." In *L'Asie Centrale et ses rapports avec les civilizations orientales, des origines a l'age du fer* (135–141). Paris: Diffusion de Boccard.

Saraswati, Chandrasekharendra. 1988. *The Vedas.* Bombay: Bharatiya Vidya Bhavan.

Saraswati, Swami Dayananda. 1994. *Light of Truth.* 4th ed. New Delhi: Sarvadeshik Arya Pratinidhi Sabha. 1st ed. Allahabad: Bhalla, 1915.

Sarda, Har Bilas. 1946. *Life of Dayanand Saraswati.* Ajmer: Bhagavan.

Sarianidi, V. 1977. "New Finds in Bactria and the Indo-Iranian Connections." In *South Asian Archaeology* (643–659). Ed. Maurizio Taddei. Naples: Istituto Universitatio Orientale.

——. 1987. "South-West Asia: Migrations, the Aryans and Zoroastrians." *International Association for the Study of the Cultures of Central Asia Information Bulletin* 13:44–56.

——. 1990. "Togolok 21, an Indo-Iranian Temple in the Karakum." *Bulletin of the Asia Institute* 4:150–156.

——. 1993b. "Margiana in the Ancient Orient." *International Association for the Study of the Cultures of Central Asia Information Bulletin* 19:5–28.

——. 1993c. "Recent Archaeological Discoveries and the Aryan Problem." In *South Asian Archaeology 1991* (251– 264). Ed. Adalbert Gail and Gerd Mevissen. Stuttgart: F. Steiner.

——. 1994 "Margiana and the Indo-Iranian World." In *South Asian Archaeology* (667–680). Ed. A. Parpola and P. Koskikallio. Helsinki: Suomalainen Tiedeakatemia.

Sarianidi, V. 1999. "Near Eastern Aryans in Central Asia." *Journal of Indo-European Studies* 27(3–4):295–326.

Sarianiidi, V., and V. M. Masson. 1972. *Central Asia before the Achaemenids.* New York: Praeger.

Sarkar, Tanika. 1998. "Hindu Rashtra or Secular State?" *The Hindu*, November 24.

Sastri, Nilakanta. 1967. *Cultural Contacts between Aryans and Dravidians.* Bombay: Manaktalas.

Sastri, Nilakanta, and G. Srinivasachari. 1971. *Advanced History of India.* Bombay: Allied Pub.

Sathe, Shriram. 1991. *Aryans: Who Were They?* Mysore: Bharatiya Itihas Sankalana Samiti.

Savarkar, V. D. 1989. *Hindutva.* 6th ed. New Delhi: Bharti Sahitya Sadan.

Sayce, A. H. 1875. *The Principles of Comparative Philology.* London: Trübner.

——. 1880. *Introduction to the Science of Language.* London: Paul.

——. 1883. "The Origin of the Aryans." *The Academy* 24:384–385.

——. 1887. "The Original Home of the Aryans." *The Academy* 31:52–53.

Scheteliсh, Maria. 1990. "The Problem of the 'Dark Skin' (Kṛṣṇa Tvac) in the Rgveda." *Visva Bharati Annals* 3:244–249.

Schlegel, A. W. von. 1842. *Essais littéraires et historiques.* Bonn.

Schlegel, Friedrich von. 1977. *Über die Sprache und die Weisheit der Indier.* Amsterdam Studies in the Theory and History of Linguistic Science. Amsterdam: Benjamins.

Schleicher, A. 1871. *Compendium der Vergleichenden Grammatik der Indogermanische Sprache.* Weimar: Böhlau.

Schmid, Wolfgang P. 1987. "'Indo-European'—'Old European' (On the Reexamination of Two Linguistic Terms)." In *Proto-Indo-European: The Archaeology of a Linguistic Problem* (322–338). Ed. S. Skomal and E. Polome. Washington, D. C.: Institute for the Study of Man.

Schmitt, Rüdiger. 1974. "Proto-Indo-European Culture and Archaeology: Some Critical Remarks." *Journal of Indo-European Studies* 2:279–287.

Schrader, Otto. 1890. *Prehistoric Antiquities of the Aryan Peoples.* New York: Scribner and Welford.

Schwab, R. 1984. *The Oriental Renaissance.* Trans. Gene Paterson-Black and Victor Reinking. New York: Columbia University Press.

Seidenberg, A. 1960. "The Ritual Origin of Geometry." *Archive for History of Exact Science* 1:488–527.

——. 1978. "The Origin of Mathematics." *Archive for History of Exact Sciences* 18:301–342.

——. 1983. "The Geometry of the Vedic Rituals." In *The Vedic Ritual of the Fire Altar* (2:95–126). Ed. Frits Staal. Berkeley: Asian Humanities Press.

Sen, Keshub Chandra. 1954. *Lectures in India.* Calcutta: Navavidhan. 1st ed. London: Cassell, 1901–1904.

Sen, Subhadra Kumar. 1994. "Proto-Indo-European: A Multiangular View." *Journal of Indo-European Studies* 22(1–2):67–90.

Sen, S. N., and A. K. Bag. 1983. *The Śulbasūtras.* New Delhi: Indian National Science Academy.

Sen, S. N., and K. S. Shukla, eds. 1985. *History of Astronomy in India.* New Delhi: Indian National Science Academy.

Sen, Umapada. 1974. *The Rig Vedic Era.* Calcutta: Sumitra Sen.

Sergent, Bernard. 1997. *Genese de l'Inde.* Paris: Editions Payot & Rivages.

Sethna, K. D. 1980. *The Problem of Aryan Origins.* Calcutta: S & S.
——. 1981. Karpāsa in *Prehistoric India.* New Delhi: Biblia Impex.
——. 1992. *The Problem of Aryan Origins: From an Indian Point of View.* New Delhi: Aditya Prakashan.
Shaffer, Jim G. 1984a. "Bronze Age Iron from Afghanistan: Its Implications for South Asian Protohistory." In *Studies in the Archaeology and Palaeoanthropology of South Asia* (41–75). New Delhi: Oxford University Press.
——. 1984b. "The Indo-Aryan Invasions: Cultural Myth and Archaeological Reality." In *The People of South Asia* (77–90). Ed. John Lukacs. New York: Plenum Press.
——. 1986. "Cultural Development in the Eastern Punjab." In *Studies in the Archaeology of India and Pakistan* (195–235). Ed. Jerome Jacobson. New Delhi: Oxford University Press.
——. 1992. "The Indus Valley, Baluchistan, and the Helmand Traditions: Neolithic through Bronze Age." In *Chronologies in Old World Archaeology* (441–446). Ed. Robert Echrich. Chicago: University of Chicago Press.
——. 1993. "Urban Form and Meaning in South Asia: The Shaping of Cities from Prehistoric to Precolonial Times." *Studies in the History of Art* 31:53–67.
——. 1995. "The Cultural Tradition and Palaeoethnicity in South Asian Archaeology." In *Language, Material Culture and Ethnicity: The Indo-Aryans in Ancient South Asia* (1–43). Ed. George Erdosy. Berlin: Walter de Gruyter.
Shaffer, Jim G., and Diane Lichtenstein. 1989. "Ethnicity and Change in the Indus Valley Cultural Tradition." In *Old Problems and New Perspectives in the Archaeology of South Asia* (117–126). Ed. Jonathen Mark Kenoyer. Madison: University of Wisconsin.
Shakespear, Henry. 1860. *The Wild Sports of India.* Boston: Ticknor.
Sharma, A. K. 1974. "Evidence of Horse from the Harappan Settlement at Surkotada." *Purātattva* 7:75–76.
——. 1992–93. "The Harappan Horse Was Buried under the Dunes of . . . " *Purātattva* 23:30–34.
Sharma, Arvind. 1995. "The Aryan Question: Some General Considerations." In *The Indo-Aryans of Ancient South Asia* (177–191). Ed. George Erdosy. Berlin: Walter de Gruyter.
Sharma, B. R. 1949. "The Vedic Sarasvatī." *Calcutta Review* 112:53–62.
Sharma, G. R., et al. 1980. *Beginnings of Agriculture.* Allahabad: Abinash Prakashan.
Sharma, R. S. 1993a. "The Aryan Problem and the Horse." *Social Scientist* 21, nos. 7–8:3–16.
——. 1993b. "Who Were the Aryans?" *Sunday Statesman Review.* Miscellany December 19.
——. 1995. *Looking for the Aryans.* Madras: Orient Longman.
——. 1998. "The Indus and the Sarasvatī." *Frontline,* May 4.
Sherratt, Andrew. 1988. Review of *Archaeology and Language,* by Colin Renfrew. *Current Anthropology* 29:458–463.
Sheveroskin, Vitaly. 1987. "Indo-European Homeland and Migrations." *Folio Linguistica Historica* 7:227–250.
Shnirelman, Victor A. 1995. "Soviet Archaeology in the 1930's and 1940's." In *Nationalism, Politics and the Practice of Archaeology* (120–138). Ed. P. Kohl and C. Fawcett. Cambridge: Cambridge University Press.
Shourie, Arun. 1998. *Eminent Historians.* New Delhi: Asa.
Siddhantashastree, R. 1978. *History of the Pre-Kaliyuga India.* Delhi: Inter-India Publications.
Sidharth, B. G. 1993. "Calendaric Astronomy, Astronomical Dating and Archaeology: A New View of Antiquity and Its Science." Paper presented at the B. M. Birla Science Centre, Hyderabad, July.
Silberman, Neil Asher. 1995. "Promised Lands and Chosen Peoples: The Politics and Poetics of Archaeological Narrative." In *Nationalism, Politics and the Practice of Archaeology* (249–262). Ed. P. Kohl and C. Fawcett. Cambridge: Cambridge University Press.
Singer, Itmar. 1981. "Hittites and Hattians in Anatolia at the Beginning of the Second Millennium B.C." *Journal of Indo-European Studies* 9:119–134.

Singh, A. N., and R. S. Singh. 1983. "On the Identity of and Indo-Greek Relation Reflected in the Plant Names and Uses Evidenced Thereof in the *Kauṭilīya Arthaśāstra* with Particular Reference to '*Kiratatikta*' of 'Kaṭuvarga.'" *Indian Journal of History of Science* 18:172–175.

Singh, Bhagavan. 1995. *The Vedic Harappans*. New Delhi: Aditya Prakashan.

Singh, Gurdip. 1971. "The Indus Valley Culture." *Archaeology and Physical Anthropology in Oceania* 4:177–189.

Singh, R. S., and V. D. Vyas. 1983. "The Identity and Critical Appraisal of the Basis of Nomenclature and Ancient Socio-Cultural and Geographical-Historical Reflections Evinced with the Pāṇinia Perfume Plant." *Indian Journal of History of Science* 18:166–171.

Singh, S. P. 1988–89. "Ṛgvedic Base of the Paśupati Seal of Mohenjo-Daro." *Puratattva* 19:19–26.

Sinor, Denis. 1990. *The Cambridge History of Early Inner Asia*. Cambridge: Cambridge University Press.

Sjoberg, Andrée F. 1971. "Who Are the Dravidians? The Present State of Knowledge." *Symposium on Dravidian Civilization* (2–31). Ed. A. Sjoberg. Austin, Tex.: Jenkins.

——. 1992. "The Impact of Dravidian on Indo-Aryan: An Overview." In *Reconstructing Languages and Cultures* (507–529). Ed. Edgar C. Polomé. Berlin: Mouton de Gruyter.

Skjaervo, Oktor, P. 1995. "The Avesta as Source for the Early History of the Iranians." In *The Indo-Aryans of Ancient South Asia* (155–173). Berlin: de Gruyter.

Smith, George. n.d. *The Conversion of India*. New York: Young People's.

Smith, V. A. 1933. *The Oxford Student's History of India*. London: Oxford University Press. Original, 1920.

Sonnerat, Pierre de. 1782. *Voyages aux Indes Orientales et la Chine*. 2 vols. Paris.

Southworth, Franklin C. 1974. "Linguistic Stratigraphy of North India." *International Journal of Dravidan* 3:201–223.

——. 1979. "Lexical Evidence for Early Contacts between Indo-Aryan and Dravidian." In *Aryan and Non-Aryan in India* (191–233). Ed. Madhav Deshpande and Peter Cook. Ann Arbor: University of Michigan Press.

——. 1982. "Dravidian and Indo-European." *International Journal of Dravidian Linguistics* 11:1–21.

——. 1988. "Ancient Economic Plants of South Asia: Linguistic Archaeology and Early Agriculture." In *Languages and Cultures* (649–668). Ed. M. Jazayery and W. Winter. Berlin: Mouton.

——. 1990. "The Reconstruction of Prehistoric South Asian Language Contact."In *The Uses of Linguistics* (207–234). Ed. Edward Bendix. New York: New York Academy of Sciences.

——. 1993. "Linguistics and Archaeology: Prehistoric Implications of Some South Asian Plant Names." In *South Asian Archaeology Studies* (81–85). Ed. G. Possehl. New York: International Science.

——. 1995. "Reconstructing Social Context from Language: Indo-Aryan and Dravidian Prehistory." In *The Indo-Aryans of Ancient South Asia* (258–277). Ed. George Erdosy. Berlin: Mouton de Gruyter.

——. Forthcoming. *Linguistic Archaeology of the South Asian Subcontinent*.

Srivastava, K. M. 1984. "The Myth of Aryan Invasion of Harappan Towns." In *Frontiers of the Indus Civilization* (437–443). Ed. B. B. Lal and S. P. Gupta. New Delhi: Books and Books.

Stacul, Giorgio. 1966. "Preliminary Report on the Pre-Buddhist Necropolises in Swat (West Pakistan)." *East and West* 16:67–79.

——. 1969. "Excavation Near Ghālīgai (1968) and Chronological Sequence of Proto-historical Cultures in the Swāt Valley." *East and West* 19:44–91.

——. 1973. "Inhumation and Cremation in North-West Pakistan at the End of the Second Millennium B.C." In *South Asian Archaeology* (197–201). Ed. Norman Hammond. Duckworth.

——. 1975. "The Fractional Burial Custom in the Swāt Valley and Some Connected Problems." *East and West* 25:323–332.

——. 1993. "Further Evidence for 'the Inner Asia Complex' from Swat." *South Asian Archaeology Studies* 111–121.

Starke, Frank. 1995. *Ausbildung und Training von Streitwagenpferden.* Weisbaden: Verlag.

Starostin, Sergei. 1999. "Historical Linguistics and Lexicostatistics." In *Historical Linguistics and Lexicostatistics* (3–50). Ed. V. Shevoroshkin and P. Sidwell. Melbourne: Association for the History of Language.

"State Sponsored Communalism." 1992. *Seminar* 400:25–29.

Steblin-Kamensky, I. M. 1981. "Pamiri Language Data on the Mythology of the Ancient Iranians." In *Ethnic Problems of the History of Central Asia in the Early Period* (238–242). Ed. M. S. Asimov. Moscow: Hayka.

Steiner, Gerd. 1981. "The Role of the Hittites in Ancient Anatolia." *Journal of Indo-European Studies* 9:150–173.

——. 1990. "The Immigration of the First Indo-Europeans into Anatolia Reconsidered." *Journal of Indo-European Studies* 18:185–214.

Stevenson, Rev. 1844. "An Essay on the Language of the Aboriginal Hindus." *Journal of the Bombay Branch of the Royal Asiatic Society* 1:103–126.

——. 1851. "Observations on the Grammatical Structure of the Vernacular Languages of India." *Journal of the Bombay Branch of the Royal Asiatic Society* 3:71–77.

Sullivan, Herbert P. 1964. "A Re-examination of the Religion of the Indus Civilization." *History of Religion* 4:115–125.

Swadesh, M. 1972. *The Origin and Diversification of Language.* London: Routledge.

Szemerényi, Oswald J. L. 1996. *Introduction to Indo-European Linguistics.* Oxford: Clarendon Press.

Talageri, S. G. 1993. *Aryan Invasion and Indian Nationalism.* New Delhi: Voice of India.

Talageri, Shrikant. 2000. *The Rigveda: A Historical Analysis.* Delhi: Aditya.

Tatya, Tukaram. 1887. *A Guide to Theosophy.* Bombay.

Taylor, I. [1892] 1988. *The Origin of the Aryans.* Delhi: Caxto.

——. 1990. "Iranian Hydronyms and Archaeological Cultures in the Eastern Ukraine." *Journal of Indo-European Studies* 18:109–129.

Taylor, Timothy. 1992. "The Gundestrup Cauldron." *Scientific American,* March, 84–89.

Thapar, B. K. 1970. "The Aryans: A Reappraisal of the Problem." *India's Contribution to World Thought and Culture* (147–164). Ed. L. Chandra et al. Madras: Vivekananda Rock Memorial Committee.

——. 1975. "Kalibangan: A Harappan Metropolis beyond the Indus Valley." *Expedition* 17, no. 2:19–33.

Thapar, B. K., and Abdul Rahman. 1996. "The Post-Indus Cultures." In *History of Humanity* (1:266–279). Ed. A. H. Dani and J. P. Mohen. Paris: Routledge.

Thapar, Romila. 1992. "The Perennial Aryans." *Seminar* 400:21–24.

——. 1996. "The Theory of Aryan Race and India: History and Politics." *Social Scientist* 2, nos. 1–3:3–29.

——. 1997. "A Paradigm Shift." *Frontline,* August 22, 55–58.

Thibaut, G. 1875. "On the Śulvasutras." *Journal of the Royal Asiatic Society of Bengal* 44:227–275.

——. 1895. "On Some Recent Attempts to Determine the Antiquity of Vedic Civilization." *Indian Antiquary* 24:85–100.

Thieme, P. 1953. *Die Heimat der Indogermanischen Gemeinsprache.* Wiesbaden: Academie der Wissenschaften.

——. 1955. "Review of *The Sanskrit Language,* by T. Burrow. *Language* 31:428–457.

——. 1957. "Review of Indo-European Languages and Archaeology, by Hugh Hencken. *Language* 33:183–190.
——. 1958. "Review of "Dictionnaire étymologique du proto-indo-européen," by Albert Carnoy. *Language* 34:510–515.
——. 1960. "The 'Aryan' Gods of the Mitanni Treaties." *Journal of the American Oriental Society* 80:301–317.
——. 1964. "The Comparative Method for Reconstruction in Linguistics." In *Language in Culture and Society* (585–598). Ed. Dell Hymes. London: Harper.
——. 1994. "On M. Mayrhofer's "*Etymologisches Wörterbuch des Altindoarischen.*" *Bulletin of the School of Oriental and African Studies* 57:321–328.
Thomas, Homer L. 1982. "Archaeological Evidence for the Migrations of the Indo-Europeans." In *The Indo-Europeans in the Fourth and Third Millennia* (61–85). Ed. E. Polomé. Ann Arbor, Mich: Karoma.
——. 1992. "The Indo-European Problem: Complexities of the Archaeological Evidence." *Journal of Indo-European Studies* 20:1–29.
Thomas P. K., and P. P. Joglekar 1994. "Holocene Faunal Studies in India." *Man and Environment* 19:179–203.
Thomason, Sarah Grey, and Terrence Kaufman. 1988. *Language Contact, Creolization, and Genetic Linguistics.* Berkeley: University of California Press.
Tikkanen, B. 1987. *The Sanskrit Gerund: A Synchronic, Diachronic and Typological Analysis.* Helsinki: Studia Orientalia.
Tilak, Lokamanya. 1925. *Vedic Chronology and Vedanga Jyotisha.* Poona: Messrs Tilak Bros.
——. N.d.a. *The Arctic Home in the Vedas.* Poona: Messrs Tilak Bros.
——. N.d.b. *The Orion.* Poona: Messrs Tilak Bros.
Tosi, Maurizio. 1988. "The Origins of Early Bactrian Civilization." In *Bactria: An Ancient Oasis Civilization from the Sands of Afghanistan* (41–66). Ed. Giancarlo Ligabue and Sandro Salvatori. Rome: Erizzo.
Tosi, M., S. Malek Shahmirzadi, and M. A. Joyenda. 1992. "The Bronze Age in Iran and Afghanistan." In *History of Civilizations of Central Asia* (1:191–223). Ed. A. H. Dani and V. M. Masson. Paris: UNESCO.
Trautmann, Thomas R. 1982. "Elephants and the Mauryas." In *India History and Thought* (245–281). Ed. S. Muckerjee. Calcutta: Subarnarekha.
——. 1997. *Aryans and British India.* Berkeley: University of California Press.
Tripathi, R. S. 1967. *History of Ancient India.* Delhi: Motilal Banarsidass.
Trigger, Bruce. 1981. "Anglo-American Archaeology." *World Archaeology* 13 no. 12:138–155.
——. 1995. "Romanticism, Nationalism, and Archaeology." In *Nationalism, Politics and the Practice of Archaeology* (263–279). Ed. P. Kohl and C. Fawcett. Cambridge: Cambridge University Press.
Trubetzkoy, N. S. 1939. "Gedanken über das Indogermanenproblem." *Acta Linguistica* 1:81–89.
Tucci, Giuseppe. 1958. "Preliminary Report on an Archaeological Survey in Swat." *East and West* 9:279–328.
Tuite, Kevin. 1998. "Evidence for Prehistoric Links between the Caucasus and Central Asia: The Case of the Burushos." In *The Bronze Age and Early Iron Age Peoples of Eastern and Central Asia* (1:448–475). Ed. Mair. Washington D.C.: Institute for the Study of Man.
Turner, R. L. 1966. *A Comparative Dictionary of the Indo-Aryan Languages.* London: Oxford University Press.
Tusa, Sebastiano. 1977. "The Swat Valley in the 2nd and 1st Millennia BC: A Question of Marginality." *South Asian Archaeology* 6:675–695.

Tyler, S. 1968. "Dravidian and Uralian: The Lexical Evidence." *Language* 44:798–812.

Vacek, J. 1987. "Towards the Question of Comparing Dravidian and Altaic." *Information Bulletin.* International Association for the Study of the Cultures of Central Asia 13:5–16.

Van der Veer, Peter. 1994. *Religious Nationalism.* Berkeley: University of California Press.

Varma, Kailash Chandra. 1984. *The Āryans, the Veda and the Kaliyuga Era of 3102* B.C. Varanasi: Banaras Hindu University.

Varma, Radha Kant. 1994. *Art and Archaeology of the Vindhyan Regions and Aryans: A Myth or Reality.* Rewa: Department of Ancient Indian History and Culture.

Vasasisy, K. L. Jain. 1990. *The Indian Asuras Colonised Europe.* Delhi: Itihas Vidya Prakashana.

Venkatachelam, Pandit Kota. 1953. *The Plot in Indian Chronology.* Vijayawada: n.p.

Vennemann, Theo. 1994. "Linguistic Reconstruction in the Context of European Prehistory." *Transactions of the Philolological Society* 92:215–284.

Vidyarthi, M. L. 1970. *India's Culture through the Ages.* Meerut: Meenakshi Prakashan.

Vine, Brent. 1990. "Vedic *kūḷáyati* and 'Spontaneous Cerebralization' in Sanskrit." In *Proceedings of the Fourteenth International Congress of Linguists* (2528–2532). Ed. Werner Bahner et al. Berlin: Akademie Verlag.

Vinodgradova, N. 1993. "Interrelation between Farming and 'Steppe' Tribes in the Bronze Age South Tadjikistan." *In South Asian Archaeology 1991* (289–301). Ed. Adalbert Gail and Gerd Mevissen. Stuttgart: F. Steiner

Virchow, R. 1886. "Gesammtbericht über die von der deutschen anthropologischen Gesellschaft veranlassten Erhebungen über die Farbe der Haut, der Haare und der Augen der Schulkinder in Deutschland." *Archiv fur Anthropologie* 16:275–477.

Vivekananda, Swami. 1970–73. *The Complete Works of Swami Vivekananda.* 5 vols. Calcutta: Advaita Ashram.

Waradpande, N. R. 1989. *Aryan Invasion:. A Myth.* Nagpur: Baba Saheb Smarak Samiti.

Watkins, Calvert. 1995 *How to Kill a Dragon.* New York: Oxford University Press.

Weber, A. 1857. *Modern Investigations on Ancient India.* Trans. Fanny Metcalfe. London: Leipzig.

Wheeler, Sir Mortimer. 1947. "Harappā 1946: The Defenses and Cemetery R 37." In *Ancient India* (59–128). Bulletin of the Archaeological Survey of India No. 3. Delhi: Manager of Publications.

——. 1953. *The Cambridge History of India. Supplementary Volume: The Indus Civilization.* Cambridge: Cambridge University Press.

——. 1966. *Civilizations of the Indus Valley and Beyond.* London: Thames and Hudson.

——. 1968. *The Indus Civilization.* Cambridge: Cambridge University Press.

Whitney, W. D. [1874] 1987. *Oriental and Linguistic Studies.* Delhi: Satguru Publications.

——. 1895. "On a Recent Attempt by Jacobi and Tilak to Determine on Astronomical Evidence the Date of the Earliest Vedic Period as 4000 BC." *Indian Antiquary* 24:361–369.

Widney, Joseph P. 1907. *Race Life of the Aryan Peoples.* London: Funk.

Wilford, Francis, 1799. "Chronology of the Hindus." *Asiatic Researches* 5:241–301.

Wilson, H. H. 1860. "Max Müller's Ancient Sanskrit Literature." *Edinburgh Review* 112:361–385.

Winternitz, M. A. [1907] 1962. *History of Indian Literature.* Calcutta: University of Calcutta.

Witzel, Michael. 1989. "Tracing the Vedic Dialects." In *Dialectes dans les littérateurs Indo-Aryennes* (97–265). Ed. C. Caillat. Paris: Institut de Civilisation Indienne.

——. 1995a. "Early Indian History: Linguistic and Textual Parametres." In *The Indo-Aryans of South Asia.* (85–125). Ed. George Erdosy. Berlin: Walter de Gruyter.

——. 1995b. "Ṛgvedic History: Poets, Chieftains and Polities." In *The Indo-Aryans of South Asia* (307–352). Ed. George Erdosy. Berlin: Walter de Gruyter.

——. 1993. "Nepalese Hydronomy: Towards a History of Settlement in the Himalayas." *Nepal Past and Present* (217–266). New Delhi: Sterling.

——. 1999. "Aryan and Non-Aryan Names in Vedic India: Data for the Linguisitic Situation, c. 1900–1500 B.C." *Aryan and Non-Aryan in South Asia* (337–404). Harvard Oriental Series vol. 3. Ed. J. Bronkhorst and M. Deshpande. Cambridge: Dept of Sanskrit and Indian Studies.

Witzel, Michael. *forthcoming* a. "The Home of the Aryans." In *Beihefte Münchener Studien zur Sprachwissenschaft.* Ed. A. Hintze and E. Tichy.

——. *forthcoming* b. "The Languages of Harappa."

Wojtilla, Gy. 1986. "Notes on Indo-Aryan Terms for 'Ploughing' and the 'Plough.' *Journal of Indo-European Studies* 14:27–37.

Woolner, A. C. 1986. "The Philological Argument for an Upper Limit to the Date of the Ṛgveda."In *Ṛtambharā Studies in Indology.* Ed. Varma et al. Kavinagar: Society for Indic Studies.

Yule, Paul. 1983. "On the Function of the Prehistoric Copper Hoards of the Indian Subcontinent." *South Asian Archaeology* 23:495–508.

Zeuner, Frederick E. 1963. *A History of Domesticated Animals.* New York: Harper and Row.

Zide, Arlene, R. K. 1973. "How to Decipher a Script (and How Not To)." In *Radiocarbon and Indian Archaeology* (347–358). Ed. D. P. Agrawal and A. Ghosh. Bombay: Tata Institute of Fundamental Research.

——. 1979. "A Brief Survey of Work to Date on the Indus Script." In *Ancient Cities of the Indus* (256–260). Ed. G. Possehl. Durham: Carolina Academic Press.

Zide, Norman H. 1969. "Munda and Non-Munda Austroasiatic Languages." *Current Trends in Linguistics.* Vol. 5: *Linguistics in South Asia.* Ed. T. Sebeok. The Hague: Moulton.

Zimmer, Stefan. 1988. "On Dating Indo-European: A Call for Honesty." *Journal of Indo-European Studies* 16:371–375.

——. 1990a. "The Investigation of Proto-Indo-European History: Methods, Problems, Limitations." In *When Worlds Collide* (311–344). Ann Arbor: Karoma.

——. 1990b. On Indo-Europeanization." *Journal of Indo-European Studies* 18:140–155.

Zvelebil, Kamil V. 1972. "The Descent of the Dravidians." *International Journal of Dravidian Linguistics* 1(2):57–63.

——. 1990. "*Dravidian Linguistics: An Introduction.* Pondicherry: Pondicherry Institute of Linguistics and Culture.

Zydenbos, Robert, J. 1993. "An Obscurantist Argument." *Indian Express,* December 12.

Index

Achar, N., 261
Acharya, A. S., 88–89
Adstratum, 83, 93, 102, 106, 300
  definition of, 81
  and Indo-Aryan and Iranian loans, 135
Aika, 137–138
Aiyar, B. V. K., 257
Ambedkar, B. R., 50–51, 62–63
Anāsa, 60, 67
Anatolian, 153–154
  date of, 266
  and language subgroupings, 147–149
  See also Hittite language
Andronovo, 137, 205–207, 211–212, 218, 238
Anthony, D., 39, 199, 240
Archaeology and language, 34, 44, 221–222, 231–236
arma/armaka, 187
Ārya
  as distinct from *Dāsas* in Vedas, 60–62, 67
  in textbooks, 158
Aryans
  and aboriginals, 50
  and anthropology, 33
  and colonial exigencies, 26–29
  and early Hindu nationalism, 47–49
  in missionary discourse, 21–23, 27–28
  and race science, 22, 24–26, 157
  in the skeletal record, 230–231
  and Tamil separatism, 49–50
  in traditional narrative, 51
  See also Indian homeland; Indo-Aryans; Indo-European homeland; and Indo-Iranians
Aryan migrations, 63–65, 106–107, 235, 298–300. *See also* Indo-Aryans; Indo-European homeland
Aurobindo, 52–53
  and the Aryan invasion, 55
  and philology, 57
  and the racial evidence, 60
Avestha, 130–135, 151, 200, 250

Bactria Margiana Archaeological Complex (BMAC), 175, 207
  and fire altars, 212–213
  and horse, 214
  and Iranian Plateau, 215–216
  as state, 213
Balbūtha, 87, 96
Bangani, 147, 150
Beech tree, 109–110
Bhadrapadā, 254, 255
Bhaktivinode, 53–54
Bhāratas, 66
Bhāratīya Itihāsa Saṅkalana Samiti, 276–277
Bible, 303
  and genesis of human race, 14–16
  and origin of the human race, 17–18
Bilingualism, in ancient India, 78
Bisht, 189, 193
BJP (Bharatiya Janata Party), 277, 278
Blavatsky, H. P., 55
Bloch, J., 80, 83, 84, 85, 97

Bökönyi, 172
Bopp, F., 19–20, 22, 34, 69
Brentjes, B., 137
Burrow, T., 83, 90, 187
and Indo-Aryans in the Near East, 130
and loans, 86
Bühler, G., 244–245, 252, 254
Brāhmī, script, 82, 180–182
Brahui, 77, 80, 83, 102

Caldwell, R., 77, 79, 80, 84
Caspian Sea, 36, 39, 149, 152, 201–202, 204, 298, 308
Caucasian languages, 125–126
Center of Origin Method, 142
Chakrabarti, D., 3, 21, 27, 221, 280, 287
the Aryans and archaeology, 233
and colonial Indology, 278, 284–286
the Ṛgveda and agriculture, 191, 248
Chariot, 175–177, 191, 194
Coeurdoux, P., 16
Coleman, R., 117
Communalism, 8, 283, 295
Convergence of South Asian languages, 81
Curzon, A., 18, 65

Das, R. P., 88
Dāsa, 61, 219, 308
and noses, 60
and Parpola's theory, 218
in textbooks, 158
and race science, 25, 67
Dashly-3, 219
Dayananda, Sarasvati, 55, 290
Deendayal Research Institute, 276–277
Devendraswarup, 30, 287, 289
Dhar, L., 113, 115, 120
and the beech tree, 110
and Indo-Aryan homogeneity, 143–144
Dhruva, 258, 264
D'iakanov, I., 137, 145, 242, 269
Diebold, R., 111, 116
Dikshit, S., 256–257, 260
Dixon, R., 242–243
Dolgopolsky, A., 39, 111, 113, 116, 127–129, 242
Dravidian language
as adstratum, 102
agricultural terms and, 91
arguments against substratum of, 80
discovery of, 77
and the Indus script, 183–184
and the Indus Valley, 175, 196
loans in Sanskrit, 84–98
map of, 79
migrations, 85
number of loans in Ṛgveda, 87
origins of, 102–105
problems of comparison with, 82–83, 88
Druhyus, 138
Duff, A, 23
Dyen, I., 142, 152

Elephant, 112, 114
Elphinstone, Mountstuart, 21
Elst, Koenraad, 289, 291
and the horse, 119
and an Indian homeland, 146, 149–150, 154
and linguistic palaeontology, 114
and Zydenbos, 282
Emeneau, M., 76, 78, 83, 87, 89
Ephedra, 212–213
Erdosy, G., 234, 292
Equus caballus Linn, 115–119, 170–173, 176. *See also* Horse

Fairservis, W., 184
Filliozat, J, 260
Finno-Ugric languages, 36, 154, 298, 300
and Sanskrit loans, 126–129
Fire altars, 160–161, 207, 212–213
Fish seal, 183–184
Flora, terms for, 299
agricultural nature of, 90
as intrusive, 93
in the Northwest, 94–95
Flood, G., 294
Fraser, J., 121–122
Frawley, D., 280, 291

Gamkrelidze, T., and Ivanov, V., 110, 123, 124, 198
and Armenian nationalism, 269
and Finno-Ugric loans, 128
and the horse, 115
and Indo-European homeland, 42
and linguistic paleontology, 113–114
and model of dialectical relationships, 145–150

German Aryanism
and blond hair and blue eyes, 32–33
and indigenous origins, 30–31
and the second renaissance, 30
Gerunds, 79–80, 82
Ghirshman, R, 209–210
Gidwani, B., 283
Gimbutas, M., 39–40, 123
Glottochronology, 239–240
Gnomon, 260
Gobineau, 33
Golwalkar, M., 272–273, 274
Gorgan Plain, 208–210, 216
Grant, C., 23
Grayware, 209–210
Greek astronomy, 255, 256
Gupta, S. P., 169, 291

Habib, I, 275
Hakra/Ghaggar, 166–169. *See also* Sarasvatī
Halhed, 14, 16
Harappa. *See* Indus Valley
Harmatta, J., 128
High school Itihas, 284
Hindu nationalism, 7–9, 275
Hindutva, 267, 292, 296, 304
definition of, 270–271
Hittite language, 239
and the laryngeals, 71–72
Hock, H. H., 139, 151, 283
Hindu nationalism, 275
and Indian homeland, 145–146
and indigenous linguistic developments, 80
and language convergence, 81
and loans, 86, 87
and the racial evidence, 62
Hoernle, A., 217
Horse, 194, 300, 303
and archaeology, 169–175
and Beshkent and Vakhsh culture, 207
and BMAC, 214
as import, 228
and linguistic palaeontology, 115–120
and Pirac, 227
in Ṛgveda, 170
Hydronomy, of India, 98–100

Indian Council of Historical Research, 278–280
Indian homeland
and archaeology, 197, 199–200
defense of by Curzon, 65
and devil's advocacy, 141
and dialectical geography, 146–156
and Finno-Ugric loans, 126–127
and linguistic conservatism, 142–145
and linguistic palaeontology, 110–115, 119
necessary corollary of Indigenous position, 6, 74
19th-century arguments against, 20–21
and Romantics, 18–19
and Talageri, 65–66
and theosophists, 55
Indigenous Aryanism
and anti-colonialism, 269–270
and archaeology, 235, 237
and dating of the Ṛgveda, 238–239
definition of, 4, 8
and detractors, 283–284
and Indus Valley, 193, 195
and linguistic evidence 74, 82, 107, 296–297
and local publications, 292–294
and motivations, 287–291
multifaceted, 295
and Muslim community, 271–275, 281, 304
and Nazism, 275
and stereotypes, 275–276
and substratum data, 107
Indo-Aryan language
and Central Asian loans, 133–134
and conservatism, 142–145
and dialect geography, 147–150, 153–154
and Finno-Ugric, 129–130
and homogeneity, 150–151
in the Mitanni documents, 135–138
and spontaneous evolution, 83–84
See also Ṛgveda; Sanskrit; Vedas
Indo-Aryans, 218–219
in the archaeological record, 192, 200, 222, 231–235
and astronomical knowledge of, 253, 264
as nomads, 91
and pastoralism, 191
and pottery, 205, 211
and urban centers, 175, 233
See also Aryans; Ṛgveda; Vedas

Indo-European homeland, 3, 302, 308
and beech tree, 109–111
disillusionment with, 37, 45
Gamkrelidze and Ivanov on, 42
Gimbutas and kurgan theory on, 38–40
history of various theories on, 35–37
and the horse, 115–120
and the Indus script, 194
and linguistic heterogeneity, 142
location of, 11–12
Nichols on, 152–153
and nomadism, 43, 91
present-day differences among scholars about, 43–44
and the proto-language, 73
Renfrew on, 40–42
and the salmon, 112
and Semitic loans, 124–126
See also Indian homeland
Indo-European language, proto-
and comparative linguistics, 68–69
date of, 201–203, 239–243
definition of, 20
and desanskritization of, 72–73
discovery of, 15–16
and discovery of new languages, 71
family tree, 17
and plant terms, 96
and relevance to homeland quest, 73–74
Indo-European linguistics
accuracy of, 68
facility in India for study of, 74–75
Indian participation in, 69, 74–75
ignored by Indigenists, 74–75, 82
the role of Sanskrit in, 68–69
Indo-Europeans. *See* Indo-European homeland
Indo-Germanic language, 20. *See also* Indo-European language
Indo-Iranian language, 124, 134, 205, 242
and dating, 250
and dialectical subgroupings, 148
and Finno-Ugric, 126–129
and homogeneity, 142, 150–154
Indo-Iranians, 191, 206, 207, 216–217, 223, 239
and Central Asia, 205–208, 209–212
Indological McCarthyism, 7, 276, 295, 309
Indophobia, 23–24
Indra, 186, 218
and the *purs*, 159
stands accused, 157–159
Indus seals, 173
Indus script, 102, 177–184, 194, 301
Indus Valley, 157
and caste organization, 164–165
and Cemetery H, 229
and Central Asia, 215
and chariot, 175–177
and fire altars, 160–161
and horse bones, 170–175
and iron, 185
and military conquest, 159
and proto-Śiva, 162–163
and the Ṛgveda, 184–191
and rivers, 165–168
and script, 177–184
and seals, 173
and the skeletal record, 230–231
Iron, 185, 246–248
Iti, 79–80

Jacobi, H.
and the date of the Veda, 252, 254–256, 258–259
and the Mitanni treaties, 136–137
and the polestar, 258–259
and the transmission of the Veda, 245
Jar seal, 182
Jarrige, J. F., 192, 216, 227, 228
Jones, Sir William, 12, 302
and astronomy, 251
researching Hindu chronology, 14–15
Royal Asiatic Society, address, 15

Kak, S., 291, 292
and the Indo-European homeland, 141
and the Indus script, 181–182
Kalibangan, 160
Keith, A. B., 117, 122, 257, 259
Kennedy, K., 160, 200, 230–231
Kenoyer, J., 190, 192, 233, 292
Klostermeier, K., 294
Krell, K., 40, 122–123
Kṛttikā, 253, 264, 265
as mouth of the year, 255–257
Kṛṣṇa ayas, 246–248, 265

Kuiper, F., 78, 79, 80–81, 82, 83
and foreign words in the Ṛgveda, 87–88, 90, 97
Kurgan culture, 38–40, 203–204, 290
Kuzmina, Y., 205, 206, 211

Lal, B. B., 161, 175, 179, 190, 229–230, 233
Lamberg-Karlovsky, C., 164, 231, 284–285, 296
Language and archaeology, 43–44, 198–199
Language 'x,' 78, 81, 92, 105, 194
Laryngeals, 71
Latham, R., 31–32, 142
Law, N. N., 252
Leach, Edmund, 159, 222
Leopald, J., 47, 48
Linguistic area, 78
Linguistic convergence, 81, 84
Linguistic palaeontology, 34
and beech tree, 109–110
criticisms of, 120–123
and geography, 111–113
origin of, 108
and salmon, 112
Loan words
into Indo-Aryan and Iranian, 133–135
increase in later texts, 89–90
non-Indo-European nature of, 95–96
in Sanskrit, 84–98
See also Bloch; Hock; Kuiper; Masica; Southworth; Witzel
Lubotsky, A., 133–135
Lyonnet, B., 198, 200, 206, 220

Marshall, Sir John, 158, 162, 169–170, 185
Mallory, J., 286
and agriculture, 191
and Eastern homeland, 154–155
and Gimbutas, 39
and history of homeland quest, 35–37
and Indo-Iranians, 216–217
and migrations, 235–236
Marxism, 277, 279
and stereotypes, 280–281
Masica, C., 91–92, 96
Maw, M., 26, 30
Meadow, R., 171, 192
Mehrgarh, 191, 215
Method, of book, 9–10
Mesopotamia, 125–126, 259
and astronomy, 261
and mathematics, 263
Mill, James, 23, 24
Misra, S. S., 138, 139, 146, 283, 286
and Asian languages, 130
and Finno-Ugric languages, 126–129
and laryngeals, 72
Mitanni treaties, 135–138, 206, 209, 210, 249, 266
Mohenjo-Daro. *See* Indus Valley
Mṛgaśīrā, 254
Mukham, in astronomy, 255
Müller, Max, 21, 289, 306, 307
and the date of the Veda, 243–246, 249
and Genesis, 16–17
and Indophobia, 22–23
and language and race, 22, 24–25, 33
and racial references in Vedas, 60
Munda, 76, 78, 95, 105, 106
as adstratum, 102
agricultural terms and, 90–92
and the early Ṛgvedic strata, 101–102
and Indus script, 102
loans in Ṛgveda, 88
problems of comparison with, 83
and topography, 99
See also Kuiper; Witzel

Nakṣatra, 255–257, 259, 261, 264
Namazga, 207
Nationalism and archaeology, 268–269
Nazis, 7, 269, 275, 276, 304
Nichols, J., 197
and Indo-European language spread, 151–154
and Semitic loans, 124–126
Nomads, Indo-Aryans as, 90–91, 93
Nostratic, 104, 302
NRI (nonresident Indian) camp, 291

Oak, P. N., 273, 282, 304
Occam's razor, 146, 155, 302
Oriental Renaissance, 30

Palatals, law of, 69–71
Pānini, 70, 77

Parpola, A., 169, 276
  and the Indus script, 183–184
  and two waves, 218–220
PGW (Painted Gray Ware), 168, 229–330
Phule, 50
Piggott, Stuart, 159, 171, 176
Pingree, D., 252, 260–261
Pirac, 190, 227–228
Pitṛyāṇa, 255
Place names, 100
Poliakov, L., 18–19, 26, 33
Polomé, E., 72–73, 107, 113
Possehl, G., 179, 181, 184, 185, 247
Postcolonial reconsideration, 7–9, 304
Postmodernism, 198, 306
Prasad, G., 264
Precession of equinoxes, 253, 255
Pulgram, E., 121–122
Pur, 186–187
Pythagoras' Theorem, 262–263

Race science, 60
Rajaram, N., 82, 280, 281, 287, 291, 292
Ramaswami, E., 49, 50
Rao, S. R., 161, 179–181
Ratnagar, S., 141, 191, 281, 290
Rau, W., 186–187, 193, 211, 218
Renfrew, C., 122
  and dates for Indo-European, 241–242
  and Indo-European homeland, 40–42
Retroflexes, 79–82
Ṛgveda, 130
  date of, 138–139
  and horse, 170
  implications of date of, 238–239
  and iron, 247
  and Müller's dating, 243–246
  and Munda, 101
  and pastoralism, 169, 195–196
  and Sarasvatī, 165–168
  and urbanity, 184–191, 196, 233
  See also Aryans; Indo-Aryans; Vedas
Roy, Ram Mohan, 47
RSS, 276–277, 278–279

Sakharam, Vishnu, 51
Salmon, 111–112
Sambara, 66, 219
Sangh Parivar, 284
Sanskrit language
  as conservative, 143
  as a daughter language, 19–20
  and Indo-European vowel system, 69–70
  and Indus script, 179–182, 194–96
  and law of palatals, 69–71
  as most recent Indo-European language, 72, 145
  as original language, 19
  See also Indo-Aryan language
Sarasvatī
  and the Avestha, 133
  and dating, 168–169
  and landsat imagery, 166–167
  Vedic references of, 165
Saraswati, Dayananda, 49, 55
Sarianidi, V., 207, 212–213, 223
Sassetti, F., 16
Śatapathabrāhmaṇa, 219
  and agriculture, 248
  and astronomy, 256–257
  and iron, 246
Satem languages, 146–7
Saussure, F. de, 71
Savarkar, V., 270–272, 274
Schwab, R., 30
Scrader, O., 108
Seidenberg, A., 262–263
Sethna, K., 248, 287
  and Dravidian separatism, 288
  and Indo-European homeland, 140
  and Parpola's theory, 219–220
  and seals, 173
Shaffer, J., 185, 192, 232–233, 292
Sharma, A. K., 171–172, 174
Sharma, R. S., 237, 269, 276
Shourie, A., 279–280
Singh, B., 187–188, 193, 234
Sintashta, 176, 205
Śiva, proto-, 162–164
Southworth, F., 78, 83, 87, 92, 248
  linguistic geography, 93–94
Stewart, D., 24, 304
Substratum, linguistic, 306
  based on consistent pattern, 87
  definition of, 76
  early detection of in Indian texts, 77
  relevance of in homeland quest, 76
  See also Bloch; Dravidian; Kuiper; Munda; Southworth; Witzel

Sūdas, 66, 218–219
Śulvasūtras, 262–264
Superstratum, 81, 135
Surkotada, 171–171
Swat, 225–226

Tacitus, 30
Talageri, S., 138, 281, 295
  and the definition of Hindu, 274
  and geography of Vedic texts, 65–66
  and loan words, 92, 96
  and method, 10
Taylor, I., 25–26
Tepe Hissar, 208, 209
Thapar, R., 269, 280
Thieme, P., 86, 89, 90, 120
Tilak, B. G., 259, 260
  and date of the Vedas, 252, 255–256
  and Mitanni treaties, 136
Theosophists, 48, 55
Thibaut, G., 252, 255–256, 262
Tocharian, 71, 147, 153–154
Togolok-21, 212
Trautman, T., 17, 24, 25–26, 62, 309
Tripura, 189, 219
Trubetzkoy, N., 140

Vasiṣṭha's head, 164, 266
Vedāṅgajyotiṣa, 260, 264, 265
  astronomical knowledge of, 253
  date of, 259
Vedas
  and burial rites, 202–203
  and diet, 91
  geographical parameters of, 63–67
  and horse, 170
  modern views on racial references in, 62
  and reference to Aryan invasions, 55–56, 59, 64
  in traditional understanding, 53
  See also Indo-Aryans; Ṛgveda
Vedic accent, 143
Vedic fire-altars, 161
Vedic language and Avestan, 130, 151
Vedic philology and early Indian scholars, 57–58. *See also* Ṛgveda
Vedic scholarship and archaeology, 193
Virchow, R., 32–33
Vivekananda, Swami, 290
  and Aryan invasions, 55–56
  and Hindu spiritual superiority, 47–48
Voice of India, 277

Wheeler, Sir Mortimer, 159
Whitney, W. D., 252, 256, 259
Wheel, 175–176, 240–241
Williams, Monier, 289
Winternitz, M., 243, 245–246, 257
Witzel, M., 176, 190
  and the Beas, 168
  and geography of Vedic texts, 64, 66–67
  and the Indus script, 184
  and linguistic palaeontology, 112
  and place names, 101
  and river names, 99–100
  and tribal names in the Ṛgveda, 87, 97
Woolner, A., 249–250
World Archaeological Congress, 282

Zarathustra, 130–131
Zigzag function, 261
Zoller, 142